Léon Blum

HUMANIST IN POLITICS

Léon Blum

HUMANIST IN POLITICS

JOEL COLTON

The MIT Press
Cambridge, Massachusetts, and London, England

FOR SHIRLEY

and

FOR VALERIE

and

KENNETH

First Published in 1966 by Alfred A. Knopf, Inc., New York
Copyright © 1966 by Joel Colton

First M.I.T. Press paperback edition, April 1974

Library of Congress Cataloging in Publication Data

Colton, Joel G.   1918–
  Léon Blum: humanist in politics.

  Reprint of the ed. published by Knopf, New York.
  Bibliography: p.
    1. Blum, Léon, 1872–1950. I. Title.
DC373.B5C6 1974   944.081'5'0924 [B] 73-21892
ISBN 0-262-53027-9

L'homme n'a pas deux âmes différentes, l'une pour chanter et pour chercher, l'autre pour agir; l'une pour sentir la beauté et comprendre la vérité, l'autre pour sentir la fraternité et comprendre la justice. Quiconque envisage cette perspective se sent animé d'un invincible espoir.

LÉON BLUM, *À l'échelle humaine, 1941*

Preface

In the long and crowded years of Léon Blum's lifetime, from 1872 to 1950, the French Socialist leader and republican statesman led a richly varied life. When he first entered the Chamber of Deputies in 1919 at the age of forty-seven, he already had behind him two distinguished careers outside politics. He had reached high rank as a jurist in the Conseil d'État, France's supreme jurisdiction in administrative law, and had won a permanent place in French jurisprudence for his trial briefs and recommendations. Even more, he had been a shining figure in the *fin de siècle* French world of letters as a literary critic, drama critic, and essayist. In his youth—he was nineteen when his first poem appeared—he had published poetry and literary fragments. He was a friend of André Gide and Marcel Proust, of Tristan Bernard, Georges de Porto-Riche, and Jules Renard, of Thadée and Alexandre Natanson, and of a whole galaxy of young literary stars who were on the threshold of fame in the opening years of the twentieth century. If he had not been diverted to politics, he would be remembered as a man of letters and, some would say, as one of the foremost drama and literary critics of his day.

I have myself treated these literary years before 1914, as well as his legal contributions, only as a prologue to his career in politics. With a political biography as my objective, I have focused my major attention on Blum as a statesman who assumed a major role in national and international affairs at several critical moments. Essentially, the book is a study in leadership, for Blum, as successor to Jean Jaurès, headed one of the great European Socialist parties of the years between the two world wars; his record as a Socialist will, I hope, throw some light on the theory and practice (and frustrations) of democratic socialism in twentieth-century Europe. As a national leader, he was three times Premier of France—the first Socialist and the first Jewish Premier of his country. He is best known for his Popular Front cabinet of 1936–7, the "French New Deal," with all its high promise, accomplishments, and weaknesses, mirroring the challenges and dilemmas of the 1930's and the tragic events of the period that followed. The heart of the book is devoted to these "years of responsibility" and "years of anguish."

Although Blum's shortcomings as a political leader—his self-conscious introspection, his lack of political flexibility, his desire to conciliate rather than to impose his views—have not been neglected in these pages, one emerges with a profound respect for this man of high moral integrity, deep idealistic convictions, and steadfast personal courage who, beginning life as a humanist, literary critic, and jurist, threw himself into the maelstrom of French politics. For his service to his ideals he suffered the most severe abuse and calumny from the extreme Right in France, wartime imprisonment and trial by the Vichy government, and deportation to German concentration camps, from which he was miraculously rescued at the end of the war to return to France and serve out his last years as elder statesman of his party and the republic. In the deepest moments of adversity he never abandoned his inveterate optimism. "When a man grows troubled and discouraged," he wrote from his Vichy prison cell, "he has only to think of humanity." And he never abandoned his belief that the creative talents of the human race, which had produced the great artistic and scientific accomplishments of all ages, must also be employed to create a better world for all mankind. "The human race has created knowledge, science, and art; why should it be powerless to create justice, fraternity, and peace?" was his constant query.

There were few private papers left after Blum's return from Germany after the war, no diaries or journals, no cache of unpublished memoirs. With some exceptions, the materials for his career have had to be reconstructed on the basis of his speeches, his writings, his public acts, and the memoirs of his contemporaries. Yet rarely did any man explain himself so fully in public utterance. He was constantly revealing his thoughts, examining his innermost feelings, leaving a written record of his reactions to the events of the day in his daily newspaper column in *Le Populaire* and in his speeches before Parliament, party congresses, and elsewhere. There is no dearth of public sources for the political biography of Léon Blum.

For hospitality and assistance in France, when as a Guggenheim Fellow I sought out additional fugitive materials (and insights), I must express my gratitude to the family, friends, and former political

Preface

associates of the French political leader: to his widow, Mme Jeanne-Léon Blum; to his son and daughter-in-law, Robert and Renée Blum; to his former law associate and *chef de cabinet*, André Blumel; to his editorial assistant on the staff of *Le Populaire*, the late Oreste Rosenfeld; to Mme Cletta Mayer and Maximilien Rubel of the Société des Amis de Léon Blum; to Mme Suzanne Blum; and to many others.

I am indebted to the Guggenheim Foundation for the fellowship that enabled me to conduct my research in France; to the Rockefeller Foundation for subsidizing a leave that helped me to write, and rewrite, my manuscript; to my colleagues and to the authorities at Duke University for making it possible for me to accept the Foundation fellowships and for generously adding sums for research expenses.

To many American, British, and continental European scholars, historians and others, who have known of my labors and patiently encouraged me, I am also grateful. And finally I cannot describe adequately my gratitude to my wife, who not only endured with me all the trials and tribulations of this undertaking from beginning to end but actively and critically contributed to the editing and preparation of the manuscript in all its successive drafts.

JOEL COLTON

Duke University
Durham, North Carolina
March 1965

Contents

——— ⚜ ———

FROM THE YEARS OF PREPARATION
TO THE YEARS OF LEADERSHIP

——— ⚜ ———

THE YEARS OF RESPONSIBILITY

Contents

---❧---

THE YEARS OF ANGUISH

---❧---

EPILOGUE: THE RETURN

Illustrations

---❖---

From the Years of Preparation to the Years of Leadership

THE EARLY YEARS

1872–1914

"Nevertheless," said Goethe, "life is not a great highway; it is not a matter of putting one's head down and marching squarely forward."[1]

ÉON-ANDRÉ BLUM—the André was soon dropped—was born April 9, 1872, in the Rue Saint-Denis in Paris, a street of crowded shops and tenements not far from Les Halles, the central markets. In the spring of 1872 France was still nursing its wounds from its "terrible year"—defeat in the Franco-German War of 1870–1 and the bloody episode of civil war and popular insurrection, the Paris Commune. Léon was the second of five sons born to Abraham and Marie Blum, both of Alsatian Jewish background. His father, later known as Auguste Blum, had come to Paris as a young boy shortly before 1848; his mother, née Adèle-Marie-Alice Picart, was born in Paris. They were married in 1869. A few years before Léon's birth, his father had become head of the wholesale silk and ribbon shop in which he had first worked as an employee. The firm was a prosperous enterprise and

---

[1] *Les Nouvelles Conversations de Goethe avec Eckermann* (1901), *L'Oeuvre de Léon Blum* (Paris: Éditions Albin Michel; 1954–), I, 261. References to Blum's works, wherever possible, are to this multi-volume collection (hereafter cited as *Oeuvre*), which conveniently reproduces his major writings and a large but selected portion of all his other writings and speeches; for details see Bibliography. Translations from the French throughout the present work are, in all instances, my own.

Note: The Blum family has always pronounced its name in a way that indicates its Alsatian origin. The pronunciation of Blum (blōōm) resembles the English "plume," not "plum."

the family lived in comfortable circumstances, but not, as legend later had it, in luxury. For a time the growing family made its home in the second story of the building on the Rue Saint-Denis in which the shop was located. Three of the five sons, Lucien, Marcel, and Georges, eventually entered the business, which came to be known as Blum Frères and moved to much more impressive quarters on the Rue du Quatre-Septembre; René, the youngest son, like Léon, followed other inclinations and achieved international renown as director of the Ballets Russes de Monte Carlo.[2]

The writer and critic Thadée Natanson, who knew Léon's father, described him as "a shrewd, upright, Jewish merchant," completely wrapped up in his business life but magnanimous and philanthropic.[3] Blum always retained a quiet respect for his father, who died in 1921, but the earliest influences on him as a child appear to have stemmed from his mother and, even to a greater extent, from his grandmother. Widowed at an early age, his maternal grandmother, Henriette Picart, supported her family by operating a bookstore near the law courts of the Palais de Justice for a clientele of lawyers and law students. Blum recalled her as a vibrant, energetic woman with radical leanings, actively interested in politics, an ardent champion of the insurrectionaries of June 1848 and the Communards of 1871. The more "bourgeois" members of the family dubbed her the Communarde. Through her, the young Léon seems first to have been exposed to egalitarian, republican, and revolutionary ideas. It was she who taught him to recite endless verses of her beloved Victor Hugo.

Although Blum's mother did not share her own mother's interest in politics, and lacked her buoyant personality, she was possessed of a strong sense of fairness and a passion for justice, which she inculcated in her children at an early age. Blum once described her as "the most just human being" he had ever known, as one who pushed her scrupulous

---

[2] For Blum's early life there is a useful autobiographical statement in an interview in 1931 published by a Socialist journalist and friend, Louis Lévy, *Comment ils sont devenus socialistes* (Paris, 1932), pp. 17–23. Otherwise Blum spoke and wrote very rarely of himself. The best sources for his family background and early life are Marc Vichniac: *Léon Blum* (Paris, 1937), and Geoffrey Fraser and Thadée Natanson: *Léon Blum: Man and Statesman* (London and New York, 1938). Neither is a critical study. Vichniac did a conscientious job of reconstructing Blum's early life by careful interviewing of family and friends. The value of the Fraser-Natanson book derives principally from Natanson's intimate acquaintance with Blum during these early years. For a discussion of these and other biographical studies, see Bibliography.

[3] In Fraser and Natanson: *Blum*, p. 24.

fair-mindedness "to the point of morbidity." "I was raised with a brother a little older than myself," he related. "When my mother gave us apples . . . she would cut two apples in halves and give to each child a half of each fruit. Thus only did the division seem fair to her."[4] Blum always maintained that he had learned distributive justice at his mother's knee.

His mother was pious: she observed the Orthodox ritual and dietary laws in the household and lit candles and said prayers on the Sabbath. Her husband, although somewhat less pious, observed the high holy days and arranged for his sons to receive some religious training. Léon himself was not deeply affected either by his mother's piety or by his religious training. He received the elementary and rather perfunctory religious instruction that enabled him to say his prayers in Hebrew and, at thirteen, to be confirmed in the traditional services.[5] His religious instruction did not involve close study of the Bible. It disturbed André Gide, who as a good Protestant read the Old Testament avidly and found creative inspiration in it, to find that French Jewish intellectuals, in their eagerness to achieve assimilation, sometimes vaunted their ignorance of the Bible. He meant to ask his friend Léon Blum about that phenomenon, he recorded in his diary.[6]

Although Blum always retained a respect for the faith of his fathers, he took the path of many other assimilated French Jews. At an early age he considered himself "emancipated," heir to the rationalism and anticlericalism of the Enlightenment. In the 1890's he was writing: "Among ordinary people, religion is only a collection of family superstitions, to be obeyed without conviction and only out of respect toward one's ancestors who have conformed to them for twenty centuries; for enlightened people, it no longer means anything." In 1900 he referred to "religious beliefs of which I do not retain the slightest trace."[7]

Blum's indifference to the Jewish faith in which he was reared did not mean that he rejected "being Jewish." He always remained a Jew in the face of antisemitism, which he despised in all its forms. And no one ever let him forget that he was a Jew, either in his early literary career or later during his political life. In 1914 Gide petulantly raised

---

[4] Blum in Lévy: *Comment . . . socialistes*, pp. 17–18.

[5] Vichniac: *Blum*, p. 10; Fraser and Natanson: *Blum*, p. 29; cf. André Blumel, *Léon Blum: juif et sioniste* (Paris, 1951), p. 4.

[6] *Journal, 1889–1939* (Paris: Gallimard; 1948), entry for end of February 1902, p. 132. Gide had just completed his *Saül*.

[7] *Nouvelles Conversations*, *Oeuvre*, I, 266; *Au théâtre: réflexions critiques*, I (Paris, 1906), *Oeuvre*, II, 208.

the suspicion that Blum as a literary and drama critic showed partiality to Jewish writers and vaguely accused him of philosemitism. Many years later Gide apologized; Blum had always been, he said, a superb example of "semitism and humanism."[8] Once involved in national political life, Blum was subjected to constant calumny by Right extremists. Though he never went out of his way to identify himself as Jewish, he nonetheless responded with vigor to public attacks. To an antisemitic outburst in Parliament in 1923, he replied from the rostrum: "I am a Jew indeed. . . . One does not in any way insult me by recalling the race in which I was born, a race which I have never denied and towards which I retain only feelings of gratitude and pride."[9] On the other hand, he disdainfully ignored the many broadsides, pamphlets, and scurrilous private notes of an antisemitic nature that singled him out as a target.[1]

In Blum's mind, a special importance derived from being a French Jew. One could be proud of the role played by the Enlightenment and the French Revolution in the political and civic emancipation of European Jewry. He belonged, he said in 1936, "to a race which owed to the French Revolution human liberty and equality, something that could never be forgotten."[2] Jewish emancipation was one link in the chain that bound him all his life to the traditions of the French Revolution and republicanism.

There was a link also between his Jewish heritage and his socialism. As a religion which did not accept "personal immortality," Judaism, as he saw it, stressed salvation on this earth; it held out the "optimistic dream" of a "harmonious and just society" in this world. "The race from which Judith springs," he wrote in reviewing a play by Maurice Donnay in 1903, "having limited our existence to *this* life, wishes to establish justice on *this* earth."[3] Here was a "rational" and "secular" faith that he could accept. In one of his early writings, his fictionalized dialogues between Goethe and Eckermann, written when he was already a socialist, he has Goethe, the philosopher-poet of the Enlightenment say:

[8] *Journal, 1889–1939*, entry for January 24, 1914, pp. 396–7; *Journal, 1939–1949* (Paris: Gallimard; 1954), entry for January 8–9, 1948, pp. 319–20. See also Gide: "Léon Blum," *Vendredi*, June 5, 1936.

[9] *Chambre des Députés, Débats Parlementaires*, January 11, 1923; hereafter cited as *Chambre, Débats*.

[1] His widow, Jeanne-Léon Blum, makes this point: *Léon Blum, 9 avril 1872–30 mars 1950* (Paris, 1951; originally published anonymously), pp. 45–6.

[2] Speech, May 15, 1936, *L'Exercice du pouvoir: discours prononcés de mai 1936 à janvier 1937* (Paris, 1937), p. 128.

[3] *Au théâtre*, I (Paris, 1906), 113. His comment on the published play (*Retour de Jérusalem*) but not his original review is reproduced in *Oeuvre*, II, 205–9.

The Jew has the religion of Justice . . . in the same way that the positivists have had the religion of "facts" or Renan the religion of science. Only the idea of inevitable justice has sustained and united the Jews in their long tribulations. Their Messiah is nothing but the symbol of eternal justice which can undoubtedly abandon the world for centuries but which cannot fail to reign there one day. It is not at all, as in the case of the Christians, from another life that they await reparation and equity. The ancient Jews did not believe in the immortality of the soul. It is this world . . . which must rearrange itself someday according to the rule of Reason, make the rule of Reason apply to all, and render to each his due. Is that not the spirit of socialism? It is the ancient spirit of the race. If Christ preached charity, Jehovah desired justice. The Old Testament says a just man when the New says a saint.[4]

And one of his characters "smilingly but gravely" remarks: "It was not by an inadvertency of Providence that a Marx and a Lassalle were Jews."[5] The idea of justice (and social justice) haunted Blum all his life. A complete secularist, he found a rationalization of his beliefs in the faith of his fathers.

Blum received his first schooling in the public schools of the Paris neighborhood in which he grew up. From the beginning he showed himself extraordinarily precocious; he had learned to read in the circle of the family at a tender age—according to family legend, at the age of three. In school he was invariably at the head of his class. At thirteen he was one of the children chosen for the guard of honor to accompany the funeral procession of Victor Hugo, who always remained one of his idols. After completing elementary school, he attended the Lycée Charlemagne, where he remained for five years, from 1884 to 1889. Here a spirit of rebelliousness manifested itself. Chafing at what he considered to be unjust discipline, he ran away from the *pension* in which he was boarding. Whether the flight was occasioned by a "revolt against injustice," as he later claimed,[6] or by his extreme sensitivity cannot be determined. There is no doubt that he was a sensitive child. In one of his essays he recalled that the young Mozart,

[4] *Nouvelles Conversations, Oeuvre*, I, 267.
[5] Ibid.
[6] In Lévy: *Comment . . . socialistes*, p. 18.

famous at the age of ten, would ask everyone before he would play a concert: "*M'aimez-vous?*" "We have all passed," he wrote, "through this state of sensitivity and for some more tender spirits it persists. When I was an adolescent, I very often had the desire to ask also *M'aimez-vous?* of everyone whose life I felt penetrating mine in some way."[7] Blum's desire to be esteemed by all with whom he came into contact never quite disappeared; it was not the sternest equipment for a socialist leader or statesman.

In 1889 Blum went on to the Lycée Henri IV, a school which always attracted the brightest students. His classmates there included André Gide and Pierre Louÿs; that year, when Blum was only seventeen and Gide twenty, they founded the little poetry magazine *La Conque*, in which Blum's first poems appeared. All this time Blum was devouring books of all kinds—literature, history, philosophy. He drank deep of the French classical writers, Corneille, Racine, Pascal, La Bruyère, and Saint-Simon, and remained a lifelong admirer of the clarity and conciseness of the classical style. Endowed with a prodigious memory, an invaluable asset throughout his life, he assimilated everything with equal ease—except foreign languages, in which he never acquired facility. In 1889 he won a philosophy prize with his baccalaureate essay; one of his teachers remarked: "If a youngster of seventeen wrote that, he is a monster."[8]

His teachers at the Lycée, and his parents, who hoped that he would pursue a teaching career, encouraged him next to take the entrance examinations for the École Normale Supérieure. He was admitted at eighteen, with the entering class of 1890. No "normal school" in the American sense, the institution on the Rue d'Ulm has, ever since the Revolution, prepared future teachers and professors for the lycées, colleges, and universities of the country. What made the École Normale so important an institution in French national life was that many of its graduates became leaders not only in academic but in political life as well. The complaint was frequently heard that the training school for professors was actually a breeding ground for Left politicians. Nevertheless, to be a *normalien* marked one as belonging to an elite; it was a lifetime distinction for Blum to have entered with the *promotion* of 1890. His intellectual restlessness, sensitivity, and independence, however, led

[7] *Nouvelles Conversations, Oeuvre*, I, 203; cf. "Declamatio Suasoria," *La Revue Blanche*, III (1892), 134–45.

[8] The essay was in later years published in *Le Monde*, June 23, 1954; the incident is reported by Vichniac: *Blum*, p. 15, and Fraser and Natanson: *Blum*, p. 58.

him into irreconcilable difficulties. The regimen was austere: a three-year course of concentrated study, preparation of research papers, written and oral examinations, almost monastic regulations and severe discipline. In the first two years students were not even permitted to sit in on courses and lectures given at the Sorbonne, or the Collège de France, only a stone's throw away. And there was little time for the cafés of the Boulevard Saint-Michel and the student life of the Latin Quarter.

Apparently the distractions were too many and the discipline too severe for the independent young *littérateur*. Having ceased to live at home, he had thrown himself into the student life of the Latin Quarter while still at the Lycée, rejecting the somewhat puritanical home atmosphere in which he had been reared. An accomplished dancer and fencer, he earned a reputation also as an organizer of student dances and parties. He found time for serious pursuits, too, but only those of his own choosing. While at the École Normale, he continued to read widely, joined in the discussions of Henri Bergson, who was then the rage, and continued to write. He was introduced to Marxist ideas by fellow students, although, as yet, Marxist philosophy made no deep impression on him. His random reading and writing, and other distractions, coupled with his resistance to the stern discipline of the school, caused him to neglect his studies and, despite his natural abilities, to fail his first-year examinations. Deep within him, one suspects, he did not wish to prepare himself for a teaching career, certainly not for some obscure post in the provinces far from the excitement of Paris. Light-heartedly, he accepted the "recommendation" of the authorities that he withdraw. Satirizing the director's letter cataloguing his faults and shortcomings, he drew up a mock "funeral oration" for himself. He was nineteen at the time.[9]

Still uncertain as to a career, Blum next enrolled simultaneously in the Faculty of Law and the Faculty of Letters at the Sorbonne. While he studied law, he immersed himself in lectures and readings in history, political thought, pure philosophy, and classical and contemporary literature. André Gide commented in his diary in January 1890: "Léon Blum does not know; he is seeking; he is groping; [he] has too much intelligence and not enough individuality (*personnalité*)."[1] Gide did not approve of his friend's dilettantism.

---

[9] For the document (in translation), Fraser and Natanson: *Blum*, pp. 48–50. His brother René believed he had no desire to teach in the provinces, "Mon frère Léon," *Vu*, June 10, 1936, p. 661.

[1] *Journal, 1889–1939*, entry for January 1890, p. 15.

Not much later Blum himself wrote to Pierre Louÿs: "I do not know whether I shall ever be capable of shaping a work—or my life—according to a clearly established method and with a really sustained will. It seems to me that there will always be in me, insofar as I can know myself, something of the undecided, of the uncompleted." But in the same breath, with pride and self-confidence, he added: "Note that I am proud of this. Because I like free-flowing lines, personalities that are not sharply defined do not displease me. And, on the other hand, to please oneself is a goal too easily attained."[2]

There is some evidence that, in the midst of his preoccupation with literature and philosophy, politics, too, was already within his consciousness. The poet Fernand Gregh recalls an incident, sometime about 1892, when he was walking with Blum one June morning in the countryside, "engaged in one of those conversations of young people in which one passes the universe in review. Blum had asked me what I wished in life. 'A few fine verses,' I said to him. 'And you?' 'Politics.' " The answer startled Gregh, for he had believed that his companion, like himself, was committed to the world of letters.[3] But the young Blum was still "groping."

All the while the carefree life continued. Thadée Natanson reports that Blum danced, smiled, and charmed his way into various circles of Parisian society. Elegant, personable, and witty, he was the center of attention of many a fashionable salon. He was slender and graceful, even to the point of effeminacy. "Graceful as Antigone . . . ," his friend Jules Renard (later to become famous as the author of *Poil de Carotte*) described him in his journal, "a beardless young man who in a girlish voice can recite for two hours by the clock Pascal, La Bruyère, Saint-Evremond, etc." Another entry in the journal likened him to "the nymph Egeria."[4] There was, even in later years, a feminine delicacy and sensitivity about Blum, but it belied the masculine strength beneath; like a willowy pine, he could withstand hurricane winds better than many a sturdier oak.

He began his career as a writer during these student years, making his literary debut with poetry; his first sonnet appeared in March 1891 in *La Conque*. Nine of the eleven issues that appeared contained poems

[3] *Souvenirs*, II: *L'Âge d'airain: souvenirs, 1905–1925* (Paris, 1951), 86.

[2] The letter, dated November 6, 1891, which was sold at auction in the 1930's, was published in *Le Temps*, December 14, 1936.

[4] *Oeuvres complètes de Jules Renard: Journal inédit* (5 vols., Paris, 1925–7): entries for November 1, 1895, I, 348; May 20, 1899, II, 640; April 19, 1904, IV, 1095.

of his. He was in distinguished company, for several of the leading symbolists published in it—Henri de Régnier, Leconte de Lisle, Swinburne, Paul Valéry. At the same time he contributed poetry and prose "fragments" to another "little" magazine of the day, *Le Banquet*, founded by Fernand Gregh, to which Proust contributed. In July 1892 he began writing for *La Revue Blanche*, the newly founded magazine edited by Thadée and Alexandre Natanson, which played an influential role in the intellectual life of *fin de siècle* France, introducing Ibsen and Tolstoy to the French public and serving as a vehicle for such regular contributors as Gide, Proust, Mallarmé, Verlaine, Barrès, Anatole France, and others. Associated with the magazine for many years, Blum came to know intimately the men who dominated French letters for over a generation. Despite his youth, his critical judgment won him the respect of the editors and contributors. Thadée Natanson recalls Anatole France saying on more than one occasion: "That is my feeling about it, but let us hear what Blum has to say."[5] And the young Blum was never at a loss for an opinion.

Although one of his early articles was on a political theme, his contributions to *La Revue Blanche* were principally on literary and philosophical subjects. He wrote "fragments"—dialogues, essays, and sketches on such themes as "friendship," "fame," "prayer"; in his literary criticism he ranged widely over the leading nineteenth-century writers. He also took responsibility for a column that reviewed other magazines. In collaboration with Tristan Bernard, he began a sports column in 1894; they covered the horse races at Auteuil and Longchamps, the bicycle races, and other athletic contests; it was one of the most literary and philosophical sports columns ever conducted. Blum made his own epigrammatic contribution to Darwinism: sports, he commented, reflected not the "struggle for existence" but "existence for struggle."[6]

In 1896 he took over the book-review column, which he continued to write for seven years until Gide succeeded him. He began also to publish anonymously the series of philosophical, literary, and political essays cast in dialogue form which he called *Les Nouvelles Conversations de Goethe avec Eckermann*. Rewritten and expanded, the dialogues appeared in book form, still anonymously, in 1901, and then with

[5] Fraser and Natanson: *Blum*, p. 56.

[6] *Nouvelles Conversations*, *Oeuvre*, I, 206. Examples of his earliest writings, including his poetry, appear in this first volume of his collected works, pp. 1–75, 547–77; a valuable bibliographical index of his literary writings for the years 1891–1914, compiled by Louis Faucon, appears in the second volume, pp. 601–39.

the author's name on the cover in 1909. Blum chose a resurrected Goethe, as symbol of the European Enlightenment, to discourse with Olympian omniscience on all manner of subjects, including the political events of the 1890's. Eckermann, the learned librarian of Weimar, records the conversations in a journal that pretends to run from July 1897 to September 1900. The book is filled with Blum's observations and judgments on literature, philosophy, politics; some of them were to find their way, almost unchanged, into his thought and writing many years later.

Blum's association with *La Revue Blanche* helped develop the young man-about-town into an increasingly serious-minded man of letters. In his early twenties, even before he had finished his formal studies, he was making a name for himself in literary criticism and belles-lettres. Yet the question of a career was still to be settled. In 1894 he passed his examinations at the Sorbonne and received his *licence* both in law and in literature. It was understood and freely accepted, even with a sense of pride, by the family that, unlike his brothers, he would not enter the family business. Undoubtedly Blum would have liked to live as a writer, but as that was an uncertain profession, he turned to law and government service. Had not Stendhal, one of his literary heroes, been a member of the Conseil d'État and even recommended the *Code Civil* as a model to all stylists? At once he prepared to take the difficult civil service examinations for the Conseil d'État, the important French tribunal which serves, among other functions, as the highest court of administrative law in France and hears all cases in which citizens are involved in litigation with the government. Failing in his first effort, he passed on the second try with ease. In 1895 he was appointed an *auditeur;* subsequently he was promoted to *maître des requêtes* and, after 1910, served as *commissaire du gouvernement*, in which capacity he prepared and proposed recommendations to the court, acting not as an attorney for the state, as the title might imply, but as a jurist summarizing existing jurisprudence and weighing the merits of each specific case for the benefit of the court. He remained with the Conseil d'État for a quarter of a century; in 1919, upon entering Parliament, he resigned, retiring with a Legion of Honor rosette and the right to a lifetime pension.

His career as a *commissaire du gouvernement* was distinguished; the briefs he drew up and his recommendations as a trial examiner were models of legal excellence. In later years Georges Bonnet recalled the early months of 1914 when he himself had just entered the Conseil d'État: "Léon Blum was then a brilliant *commissaire du gouvernement* there. The young *auditeurs* would go to hear his 'conclusions,' which were admired as much for the elegance of their form as for the subtle and penetrating strength of his reasoning."[7] His recommendations became part of the permanent administrative jurisprudence of the country and are still cited in the French legal manuals and studied by French law students. There was nothing in his post to wrench the conscience of a Socialist. He was pleased to share in the court's function of protecting the citizenry from injustice at the hands of the state.

The year after his appointment to the Conseil d'État, when he was twenty-four, he married Lise Bloch, whom he had met at one of the fashionable salons that he frequented. She belonged to a Jewish family of considerable standing: one of her brothers held an important legal post at the Cour des Comptes; others were army officers. In June 1902, their son, Robert, was born; there were no other children. In later years, Robert, a graduate of the École Polytechnique, became a successful engineer and industrial executive. A Socialist, but not actively engaged in politics during his father's lifetime, he often served as his literary assistant and editor.

Blum's married life was untroubled and happy, a point he took special pains to emphasize when he wrote *Du mariage* in 1907, his provocative tract on sex and marriage. The book was semi-fictional in nature, making its point through anecdotes and "case studies." His theme was the need for varied sexual experience for both partners before marriage as the only solid basis for a truly happy and stable relationship. This was already the practice for young men, he noted; the novelty of his book lay in a similar prescription for young women. The volume was not meant merely to shock the respectable middle classes but to call attention to the instability of conventional marriage and to raise the question of women's equal rights under a "double standard" of morality. It was half tongue-in-cheek, half Nietzschean, a protest

---

[7] *Défense de la paix*, I: *De Washington au Quai d'Orsay* (Geneva, 1946), 70. On Blum's legal career, see Pierre Juvigny: "Un Grand Commissaire du gouvernement: Léon Blum," in *Le Conseil d'État: livre jubilaire* (Paris, 1952), pp. 337–40; and Charles E. Freedeman: *The Conseil d'État in Modern France* (New York, 1961), pp. 68–9, 148–9. Blum's "conclusions" in one of his most famous trial hearings, the Lemonnier case, are reproduced in *Oeuvre*, II, 593–9. See also, for Blum's various technical contributions to French legal jurisprudence, Gilbert Ziebura: *Léon Blum: Theorie und Praxis einer sozialistischen Politik*, I: *1872 bis 1934* (Berlin, 1963), 158–60; on this and other aspects of Blum's career this detailed work by a German political scientist, projected in two volumes, is excellent.

against bourgeois institutions, bourgeois morality, and bourgeois inequality. Dedicating the book to his wife, the author stated in the preface that it was written "by a happy man"; and there is every reason to believe that this was so. He had no thought, he made clear, that any of his advanced views would be adopted in the imminent future.[8]

Many years later, in December 1931, after thirty-five years of marriage, Blum's first wife died. He subsequently was married twice again: in 1932 to Thérèse Pereyra, an old family friend and Socialist comrade-in-arms, who died in February 1938; and during the Second World War, in 1943, to Jeanne Levilliers Humbert, who survived him.

———

But we must return to the early years of Blum's political development and his evolution as a socialist. Blum often reflected on the ways in which men who "differed in origin, milieu, culture, [and] previous opinions were transformed into socialists."[9] He recalled that the English Socialist H. M. Hyndman once proposed to some friends, as a kind of parlor game, that they describe the first experience, emotional or intellectual, that had oriented them toward socialism. For some, it was a sudden awareness of poverty or social injustice; for others, an evocative phrase of a writer or poet, or of a religious text; for still others, the persuasive influence of a powerful individual. For some, it emerged in a sudden revelation; for others, from an idea planted on soil already carefully prepared.[1] This kind of intellectual analysis satisfied Blum. He felt no need to probe the unconscious or the hidden springs of behavior. He never thought in terms of complexes, frustration, alienation, and psychological compensation; nor would he have understood the acceptance of socialism as a means of satisfying an emotional craving for companionship and security. For all his interest in human behavior, Blum never paid attention to Freud or twentieth-century psychology, and he remained an undiluted intellectualist.

As for himself, he reports that it was "by a slow incubation" that he came to socialism.[2] At the very beginning, at the age of fourteen, he recalled, he experienced a sudden awakening of his social conscience.

[8] *Oeuvre*, II, 1–181. Gide remarks that it was much discussed: *Journal, 1889–1939*, entry for June 16, 1907, p. 248; and see his own critical comments, ibid., entry for June 22, 1907, p. 250. See the extended comments in Paul Abram: *L'Évolution du mariage* (Paris, 1908), with a preface by Blum.

[9] Blum, in preface to Lévy: *Comment . . . socialistes*, p. 17.

[1] Blum: "L'Idéal socialiste," *La Revue de Paris*, May 1924, p. 92.

[2] In Lévy: *Comment . . . socialistes*, p. 17.

Seated one afternoon in the library of the Lycée Charlemagne, he was reading a book selected at random, *Les Effrontés* by Émile Augier, when all at once the dialogue in the third act struck him "like a bolt of lightning." One of the characters, Giboyer, speaks of the need to re- construct the existing order of society because the pre-1789 feudal aris- tocracy had merely been replaced by a new aristocracy of inherited wealth. It was necessary, he said, to create a truly democratic society based on "the very principle of democracy—on personal merit." Al- though conceding that family wealth was originally the product of hard work and intelligence and other laudable qualities, Giboyer in- sisted that inherited riches or inherited social position ought not to involve an advantage over those born with nothing but their native in- telligence. The social conscience of the fourteen-year-old boy was stirred. To these words, he later claimed, he owed his first troubled thoughts about the organization and laws of existing society—the "an- tinomy posed by Giboyer between the individual character of merit and the hereditary character of property." "Even today," he wrote in 1924, forty years after the episode, "my intelligence as a man, though better trained, still finds no reply to it."[3] The link between democracy and socialism remained a reality to him all his life. In the *Nouvelles Conversations*, and, repeating himself almost word for word, in the 1940's, he described the rightly ordered society: "The son of a black- smith ought to be able to become prime minister, but a prime minister's son, if he has no talent, should not expect to be more than a black- smith."[4] The ultimate goal was a society affording opportunity for the fulfillment of individual abilities with no advantage accorded to in- herited wealth or social position. This he called "the simplest, most clearly understandable definition of the 'socialist ideal.' "[5]

Shielded by his middle-class background from any direct experi- ence of poverty and social degradation, it was his reading that con- tinued to arouse his social conscience. He was already familiar with the eighteenth-century *philosophes;* he turned next to the nineteenth- century French utopians and read Saint-Simon, Fourier, and Proudhon. In 1890 André Gide gave Blum the book that his uncle, the economist Charles Gide, had just written on Fourier.[6] He seems to have read and discussed, in a desultory way, the ideas of Marx with fellow students,

[3] "L'Idéal socialiste," pp. 92–4.

[4] *Oeuvre*, I, 256; and cf. *À l'échelle humaine, Oeuvre*, V, 472.

[5] "L'Idéal socialiste," p. 94.

[6] Jean Delay: *La Jeunesse d'André Gide* (Paris, 1956), I, 426.

and was exposed also to the ideas of Benoît Malon and his humanitarian, universalist "integral socialism."[7]

But before he turned to socialism, Blum found himself sympathetic to philosophical anarchism. His first political article, published in *La Revue Blanche* in July 1892, made this clear. Entitled "Les [*sic*] Progrès de l'a-politique [non-politics] en France," and dedicated to Maurice Barrès (the Barrès of the *culte du moi* and Blum's literary idol before the Dreyfus Affair), it was a paean to philosophical anarchism and was filled with scorn for political reform movements.[8] "The future in France at least," he asserted, "belongs not to different varieties of socialism but to anarchism." Socialism, he insisted, would always face the impossible task of forcing individual thought and will into a "common mold." The ruggedly individualistic Clemenceau of *La Justice* and Barrès (as well as Nietzsche) were then his idols. Years later he apologetically recalled his short-lived flirtation with anarchism. "One must appreciate how seductive individualist doctrines are for very young men."[9]

Thus, by the age of twenty, he had begun to take a critical view of existing society and to reject its class basis; but, as yet, nothing positive had appeared to fill the void. He compared himself to someone who, because his feet hurt, decided to take off his shoes without worrying about what he would put on later.[1] There still existed only a "latent and diffuse disposition of mind to which some years later the two men who were my masters, Lucien Herr and Jean Jaurès, were to furnish a precise form."[2]

The "determining factor," he believed, in bringing him to socialism was his resumption of contact in 1893 with Lucien Herr, the scholarly librarian of the École Normale. Blum had not known Herr well at the École and had not seen him since leaving the school. By mere chance they met one day on the Place de la Concorde. "We walked for two hours on the Champs-Élysées. The renewed acquaintance blossomed into a lasting and intimate friendship."[3] The chance encounter with Herr, who was a dedicated Socialist, changed Blum's life. Herr had

[7] Fraser and Natanson: *Blum*, pp. 65–6; on Malon's influence, Ziebura: *Blum*, I, 66–8.

[8] *La Revue Blanche*, III (1892), 10–21; not reproduced in the collected works, the article was republished by Robert Blum in *Preuves*, February 1956, pp. 38–44.

[9] Blum, in Lévy: *Comment . . . socialistes*, pp. 20–21.

[1] Ibid., p. 22.

[2] "L'Idéal socialiste," p. 92.

[3] Blum, in Lévy: *Comment . . . socialistes*, p. 21.

read widely in political philosophy, both French and German; he knew the French utopians and Proudhon, as well as Fichte, Marx, and Engels. He had begun research for what was to be an authoritative book on Hegel, which he never completed. Along with his colleague at the École Normale, the philosopher Charles Andler, he had already joined the Socialist group founded by Jean Allemane, one of the many small competing Socialist organizations that had emerged in France in the 1880's.[4]

As director of the library at the École Normale from 1888 to 1926, Herr not only served as inspiration and scholarly mentor to many generations of young scholars but exerted an enormous influence in converting many of these young intellectuals to socialism. (When some of his converts moved into influential positions in French academic and political life, in some quarters he was regarded as the *éminence grise* of the Third Republic.) It was Herr who converted Jaurès to socialism, convincing him that socialism was the logical extension of the republicanism to which he was devoted. Édouard Herriot was a fish that got away. Admired for his erudition, Herr also possessed a powerful and dominating personality, to which Blum years later, in writing his memoirs of the Dreyfus Affair, bore witness. "For another thirty years," Blum wrote, "he would remain father-confessor, proselytizer, and guide to the best minds of the universities; and for countless men high in public life he would remain the confidant and director of their conscience and thought."[5] "The churches of bygone days," Charles Andler wrote, "would better understand the great role of a man like Herr."[6]

It was Herr, Blum claimed, who "crystallized all the diffuse tendencies" in him and was responsible for the "profound reorientation" of his individualist and anarchist outlook toward socialism.[7] Not only did Herr exert a strong personal influence on his friends and protégés, he also helped them to form a "little library of the social sciences" of

[4] For biographical details on Herr, Charles Andler: *Vie de Lucien Herr* (Paris, 1932); cf., for a less sympathetic view, Édouard Herriot: *Jadis*, I: *Avant la première guerre mondiale* (Paris, 1948), 63–4. For a harsh view of the École Normale, with many acid observations on Blum and others, Hubert Bourgin: *De Jaurès à Léon Blum: L'École Normale et la politique* (Paris, 1938).

[5] *Souvenirs sur l'Affaire* (Paris, 1935), pp. 28–30. Georges Lefranc exaggerates Blum's continued dependence on Herr; *Le Mouvement socialiste sous la Troisième République* (Paris, 1963), pp. 223, 326, 328.

[6] *Herr*, p. 303.

[7] In Lévy: *Comment . . . socialistes*, p. 21.

their own and closely guided their political reading.[8] A few years after their encounter in 1893, Herr won Blum over to an active role in the Dreyfusard struggle and introduced him to Jaurès.

Jean Jaurès was the other great influence on Blum's development as a Socialist. Blum came to know Jaurès at the end of 1897. Their association grew into a close political and personal friendship, abruptly terminated by the tragic death of Jaurès at the hands of an assassin on July 31, 1914. Robust, expansive, a son of the Midi, careless in his appearance and dress, he was in marked contrast to the delicate, refined Blum and his Parisian elegance, yet the strongest ties existed between the two men. A filial, and almost religious, devotion bound Blum to Jaurès. Blum prided himself on being the "witness of his life, the disciple of his thought."[9]

At first Blum shared in the general prejudice of the time that Jaurès was only a sophist and a florid orator "intoxicated with the music of his own eloquence." But as he came to know him, he found him to be a man who combined the "gift of vision" with "the most active, most precise, most penetrating intelligence."[1] A brilliant stylist and orator, Jaurès was at home also in the most intricate technical details of political, fiscal, tariff, legal, and military matters. For a time he was the dominating figure in the entire Chamber.

Jaurès, like Blum, had not turned to socialism because of a proletarian background or personal experience with poverty or injustice.[2] After graduation from the École Normale in 1881, he had taught philosophy for a few years and then entered the Chamber, not as a Socialist at first, but as a progressive republican. Defeated for re-election in 1889, he returned to teaching and to academic research, among other activities, and completed his two doctoral theses, one in metaphysics and one on the origins of German socialism. In 1893, re-elected to the Chamber, he assumed leadership of the parliamentary Socialist group.

[8] Andler: *Herr*, p. 91.

[9] Blum, testimony at the trial of Raoul Villain, Jaurès's assassin, March 25, 1919; *Le Procès de l'assassin de Jaurès* (Paris, 1919), p. 75.

[1] Ibid., pp. 73–4. Among Blum's many speeches acknowledging his debt to Jaurès, see especially that of July 31, 1917, reprinted in *La Revue Socialiste*, May 1950, pp. 385–406; and his *Jean Jaurès*, a lecture delivered on February 16, 1933, at the Théâtre des Ambassadeurs (Paris, 1933, 1944).

[2] For details on Jaurès, see Harvey Goldberg's excellent *Life of Jean Jaurès* (Madison, Wis., 1962), and Marcelle Auclair: *La Vie de Jean Jaurès* (Paris, 1954), a more personal account. On Jaurès's socialism, see also Marcel Prélot: *L'Évolution politique du socialisme français*, 1789–1934 (Paris, 1939), pp. 177–204, and Lefranc: *Mouvement socialiste*, pp. 134–40, 160–95.

Defeated in 1898 again, he wrote two remarkable volumes for the collaborative *Histoire socialiste de la Révolution Française* and threw himself into the Dreyfus Affair; after 1902 he served without interruption in the Chamber until his assassination on the eve of the war.

For Jaurès, socialism—and this was the burden of his bequest to Blum—was the logical outgrowth and extension of the republic created by the French Revolution. The bourgeoisie had founded a republic based on civic and political equality; the next step was its revolutionary transformation into a higher form of social and economic justice—a socialist republic. From Marx, Jaurès derived the notion that class struggle was the motivating force in all historical change and that in the contemporary state of economic development the proletariat was the revolutionary class that had as its historic mission the transformation of existing property relations and the emancipation of all humanity. Otherwise he rejected much of Marx's metaphysics and economic doctrine, as did Blum.[3] Indeed both men added an ethical element derived more from Kant than from Marx and Hegel, namely, that the socialist revolution would come not because of the inexorable dialectic of history but because it was in conformity with the aspirations and social conscience of reasonable men, proletarians and non-proletarians alike. Because political democracy was one of the instruments for achieving economic and social democracy, Jaurès believed it to be the sacred duty of socialists to cherish and protect the democratic republic. He belonged, Blum later remarked, "to what Michelet once called the great republican church."[4]

Not only was socialism the sequel to the great revolutionary tradition of France, but it represented for Jaurès, in Blum's phrase, "the climax . . . of all the civilizations that humanity has engendered since the beginning of time."[5] Had not Jaurès himself acknowledged his debt to "the rigorous logic of Aristotle, the skepticism of Montaigne, the humanism of Rabelais, the cry for justice in the Bible and in Rousseau"?[6] To carry forward the great tradition was the mission of social-

[3] In 1900 Blum was writing: *"Nul n'ignore, parmi les socialistes réfléchis, que la métaphysique de Marx est médiocre . . . que sa doctrine économique rompt une de ses mailles chaque jour."* La Revue Blanche, January 1900, p. 41. On the debt of Jaurès (and Blum) to Marx, see James Joll: *Intellectuals in Politics: Three Biographical Essays* [Blum, Rathenau, Marinetti] (London, 1960), pp. 12–13. On this and other matters Joll's long essay on Blum is excellent.

[4] Testimony, *Procès de l'assassin de Jaurès,* p. 76.

[5] Speech on Jaurès, 1917, *La Revue Socialiste,* May 1950, pp. 404–5; see also his 1933 lecture, *Jaurès,* pp. 40–41.

[6] Goldberg: *Jaurès,* p. 78.

ism. Blum liked to quote Jaurès's famous words: "It is by descending toward the sea that the river remains faithful to its source." The sense of continuity with the Western humanist tradition, the idea of socialism as an extension of the republican idea born of the French Revolution, the synthesis of democracy and class action—all formed the cornerstone of Jaurès's political philosophy, as of Blum's. In later years Blum would say: "In difficult moments it was always from his memory and his teachings that I have sought the guide to my actions. I did not ask myself: 'What would he have done in my place?'—I never had the presumption to substitute myself for him even in my thought—but I asked myself: 'What would he have wanted me to do, I such as I am?' "[7]

If Jaurès believed in democratic social reform, he was also "an uncompromising Socialist who strove for the total transformation of his society."[8] He refused to exclude the possibility of a violent revolution; violence always remained the "last resort of history at bay." Yet he believed firmly that the existence of political democracy in France could make possible the achievement of socialism without upheaval; he called universal suffrage "the revolutionary instrument of the modern period." Jaurès's attempted synthesis of revolution and evolution was another part of his legacy to Blum.[9]

Blum, too, prided himself on being no mere reformist Socialist and all his life retained a verbal allegiance to the idea of revolution. On the other hand, he always insisted that "revolutions do not gain time over regular evolution." The great revolution of 1789, necessary though it was, did not accomplish, even after many years, all its objectives, and all of France's unhappy political oscillations since 1789 were the result. *Natura non facit saltus* was a maxim as valid for political change as for natural science; nature's leap came only after the proper preparation.[1] Revolution and evolution were both necessary, bearing in mind that revolution, the transformation of society, in the modern age would not be "bloody and cruel"; the old style of revolution with Paris in flames and insurgents on the barricades was gone forever.[2] The syn-

---

[7] Blum: *Jaurès*, 1933, p. 9.

[8] Goldberg: *Jaurès*, pp. 152, 474.

[9] See, e. g., *Nouvelles Conversations, Oeuvre*, I, 252.

[1] Cf. his remarks in later years, speech in commemoration of the Revolution of 1848, *Oeuvre*, VI, 427.

[2] *Nouvelles Conversations, Oeuvre*, I, 289–90; cf. *À l'échelle humaine, Oeuvre*, V, 428.

thesis inherited from Jaurès would remain a delicately balanced one. And it was Blum's destiny to carry forward Jaurès's ideas on socialism, revolution, and democracy into the age of the Bolshevik Revolution.

_____ *unfortunately !*

The Dreyfus Affair, in which Blum worked closely with Herr and Jaurès, catapulted Blum into active political life. The stormy episode not only intensified Blum's zeal for humanitarianism and justice but wedded him irrevocably to socialism, for it linked in his mind the cause of socialism with the defense of republican institutions. In 1899, in the midst of the Affair, Blum joined his first Socialist organization—the Socialist Unity group, which met in the Librairie Bellais, a cooperative publishing house and bookstore and a headquarters for the Dreyfusard Left Bank intellectuals. This is not the place to explore the many ramifications of the Affair which rocked a generation and deepened existing chasms within the French nation. The memoirs Blum wrote some thirty-five years later on that turbulent era, *Souvenirs sur l'Affaire*, are among the most sensitive evocations of the tragedy. As a British scholar has recently noted, an objective study of the case, shielded from the blinding passions of both sides, reveals a picture "not of virtue at grips with villainy, but of fallible human beings pulled this way and that by their beliefs, their loyalties, their prejudices, their ambitions and their ignorance."[3] To Blum and his contemporaries, caught up in the Affair, the picture was simpler; a grave injustice had been done to a human being, and no such excuse as "reason of state" or "honor of the Army" could be permitted to perpetuate the injustice.

Yet Blum, like many others, had little interest at first in the case of Captain Dreyfus, who had been arrested in October 1894, found guilty of treason by a court-martial, and deported to Devil's Island. In the next few years the episode was all but forgotten. Almost everyone, outside the circle of Dreyfus's immediate family, was convinced of his guilt. His conviction had been based on a memorandum, apparently in his own handwriting, listing the documents transmitted by him to the German military attaché; there was no reason to suppose anything irregular in his trial and condemnation. The public had been informed that although he had vehemently protested his innocence at the scene of his public military degradation, he had confessed to the crime in his

[3] Guy Chapman: *The Dreyfus Case: A Reassessment* (London, 1955), p. 360.

prison cell. The only nagging thought was the absence of a plausible motive: Dreyfus was happily married, had an independent financial income, and had enjoyed rapid professional advancement, the first Jewish officer to be appointed to the General Staff.

French Jewish circles in particular were eager to forget the episode and they viewed with apprehension the beginnings of the campaign in 1896 to reopen the case. Even when evidence of Dreyfus's innocence mounted, they were reluctant to provide possible ammunition for anti-semites like Édouard Drumont, who charged that the defense of Dreyfus was based on a sense of "race" and group solidarity. "Assimilated" Jews of Dreyfus's age who, like him, had made their way in the private professions or in government service, were filled with despair that passions aroused by the case might blight their own irreproachable careers. Blum, who knew these circles well, described this attitude in scathing terms; yet he confessed that to some extent he at first shared in it.[4]

Only a few men kept the case alive. It had been learned, on good authority, that there never had been any confession in prison; second, that the memorandum, which the official experts had hastily attributed to Dreyfus, had been interpreted differently by other experts. The handwriting was recognized as that of Major Walsin-Esterhazy, a dissolute officer overwhelmed with gambling debts. When one of Dreyfus's early champions, the literary critic Bernard Lazare, tried to impart this information to Blum, he listened with incredulity and indifference. He had "no more inclination than the next person to be received into the Dreyfusard faith."[5]

The apostle who converted him was Lucien Herr. One afternoon in September 1897, Herr bicycled out to the Seine countryside where Blum was vacationing to enlist him in the Dreyfusard campaign. Herr had already won over Jaurès, who had at first been skeptical. With fervor and characteristic forcefulness, he summarized for Blum the mounting evidence that pointed to the innocence of Dreyfus. Convinced by Herr, Blum threw himself into the crusade to reopen the case. It was then that he met and found himself working with Jaurès, who made a powerful impression on him with his incisive mind and his humanitarian zeal. Unlike some Socialists who believed that the defense of a bourgeois army officer was not the concern of the proletariat and would serve only as a diversion from the true class struggle, Jaurès,

[4] *Souvenirs*, pp. 25–7.
[5] Ibid., pp. 19–22, 27.

once he took up the cudgels for Dreyfus, linked the socialist cause with the Rights of Man; it was a lesson that Blum never forgot.[6]

The campaign to reopen the court-martial verdict of 1894 had to be launched immediately. The Dreyfusards had neither the time nor the right to wait. "For indeed there was not only the Dreyfus trial, or the Dreyfus case," Blum later wrote. "The judicial error had flesh and bones. Over there, thousands of kilometers away, an innocent man in torment was close to succumbing beneath an almost indescribable burden of suffering. . . . It was necessary to free that unfortunate man and at the same time to avenge the truth. The truth could have waited if necessary, but not the man."[7] The twin motivating forces of Blum's life—humanity and justice—found early expression in the Dreyfus Affair.

For two hectic years, from the launching of the campaign for a new trial in the fall of 1897 to the presidential pardon of September 1899, all energies, Blum tells us, were consumed in the case. All relationships hinged on a single question: was a man a Dreyfusard or was he not? Blum confessed to having broken off with old friends who did not share his views and to have warmly embraced men from whom he had once been estranged. The saddest individual disappointment came when Maurice Barrès, whom Blum had long admired and whom he had personally volunteered to enlist in the campaign, refused to join; since the evidence was inconclusive, Barrès maintained, he would throw in his lot with the honor of the Army.[8] "The present attitude of Barrès," Jules Renard, in his diary entry of May 1899, quotes Blum as saying, "makes one afraid to reread what he has done. Impossible for it to be as good as one believed, one must have been mistaken."[9] (The remark was undoubtedly made with sarcasm, but it has an Orwellian ring!) But Barrès was an exception. For the most part, Blum's old friends of *La Revue Blanche* and other literary circles were on the Dreyfusard side.

To Blum, looking back upon these events in the 1930's, the Affair was "a crisis of humanity," to be compared in some ways with the French Revolution or the First World War. It possessed the common element of all such crises—a disregard for human life. "Neither for

[6] For the impact of the Dreyfus Affair on French socialism, Aaron Noland: *The Founding of the French Socialist Party, 1893–1905* (Cambridge, Mass., 1956), pp. 61–85, and Goldberg: *Jaurès*, pp. 208–69.

[7] *Souvenirs*, pp. 32–3.

[8] Ibid., pp. 84–9.

[9] *Journal de Jules Renard*, entry for May 20, 1899, II, 640.

my friends, nor for myself, did life count. We would have sacrificed ourselves without the slightest hesitation and without the slightest effort for what we held to be the cause of truth and justice. And undoubtedly, although with somewhat more difficulty, we would have sacrificed the men who barred the way to justice and to truth."[1] His strong words mirrored the intensity of the Affair. By latter-day standards there was not much overt violence, but passions and emotions seethed in a cold civil war.

It was Émile Zola who brought matters to a head. His letter "J'Accuse," published in *L'Aurore* in the summer of 1898, dramatically indicted the General Staff for concealing evidence and sanctioning illegal procedures. Zola and his friends knew that this act of open defiance and provocation would lead to prosecution and trial, but such a trial, they hoped, would bring the facts to light and reveal the evidence that had been suppressed earlier in the Esterhazy court-martial. Blum now played a modest but active legal role in the preparation for Zola's trial. By his own characterization, he was at the time "a lawyer of some passing ability" (*un juriste passible*).[2] Placing himself at the disposal of Fernand Labori, Zola's defense counsel, he assisted in the preparation of the defense briefs and was present at all of the sessions. That Zola was found guilty was unimportant. The evidence produced seemed to make inevitable a retrial for Dreyfus. In a masterful analysis of the proceedings, which he published anonymously in *La Revue Blanche* of March 15, 1898, Blum pointed out that the trial had yielded "more light and more truth than anyone had dared to hope for."[3]

Six months later, in July 1898, Blum fell into despair again. Minister of War Cavaignac, whose integrity and republican sympathies were beyond question, announced to the Chamber of Deputies that after a fresh investigation of the case which he had personally conducted, he was convinced that Dreyfus was guilty and that no new trial would be held. Virtually the entire Chamber acclaimed his speech. The cause of the nationalists seemed vindicated. It was Jaurès who dispelled his friends' gloom by triumphantly assuring them that the document on which Cavaignac had based his conclusions was false. In a series of

---

[1] *Souvenirs*, pp. 14–15.

[2] Ibid., p. 137.

[3] "Un Juriste": "Le procès," *Le Revue Blanche*, March 15, 1898, *Oeuvre*, I, 343.

newspaper articles, he demonstrated the inconsistencies of the entire case against Dreyfus and proved that the secret document most recently revealed was a forgery fabricated inside the General Staff.

With dramatic suddenness, Jaurès's charges were substantiated. The false document was traced to a General Staff officer, Colonel Henry, who confessed the crime to Cavaignac and then committed suicide. Esterhazy fled to England. The news of these developments reached Blum while he was vacationing in Switzerland. "I am not sure," he later wrote, "that in my entire life I have experienced a stronger emotional upheaval."[4]

Yet new battles and disappointments faced the Dreyfusards even after Henry's suicide. The case entered an intensely political phase in the summer of 1898. The anti-Dreyfusards made a hero of Henry— the victim of the "Jewish syndicate." The government delayed reopening the case. Emotion mounted and violence broke out. Bands roamed the streets shouting *"Vive l'armée!"* and *"Mort aux Juifs!"* In February 1899, on the occasion of President Félix Faure's funeral, Paul Déroulède and his nationalist Ligue des Patriotes attempted a *coup d'état* against the republic. Six months later, in June 1899, the new president, Émile Loubet, was physically assaulted at the Auteuil race track. The Dreyfusards responded with a mass republican and socialist demonstration at Longchamps—in defense of the republic. Blum marched alongside Herr, Jaurès, Charles Péguy.[5] The events of June 1899 foreshadowed the assault on the republic on February 6, 1934, and the emergence of the Popular Front. It was a dramatic prologue to Blum's career in politics.

Here now was the real Dreyfus Affair—"the other Affair," Blum called it—a political war that created and left deep cleavages in France. The anti-Dreyfusards sought to coordinate the confused public reactions into a nationalist, antirepublican movement. The Action Française and the Camelots du Roi made their appearance; the Ligue des Patriotes had shock troops in the streets. At the other end of the spectrum, the political-minded Dreyfusards sought to transform the Dreyfusard coalition of republicans and socialists into "a permanent army in the service of Human Rights and Justice." The Dreyfusards directed their attack against the military, which in a spurious, misguided desire to preserve the honor of the Army had perpetuated the outrage,

[4] *Souvenirs*, p. 163.
[5] Andler: *Herr*, pp. 142–6.

and against all those who had allied themselves with the military establishment: the antisemites, the former Boulangists, the monarchists, the clerical Right.

After the attempted *coup d'état* and the assault on President Loubet, a "cabinet of republican defense" under Waldeck-Rousseau was formed; the defense of the republic was added to Dreyfusism. The country was divided into two clearly delineated camps. The struggle now, in Blum's words, was "for or against the Republic, for or against 'militarism,' for or against the secular state."[6] A "democratic counteroffensive" was launched by the vitriolic, anticlerical Émile Combes, Waldeck-Rousseau's successor. The "Dreyfusard Revolution," instead of healing the nation's wounds, set out to purge and punish. Former Dreyfusards like Charles Péguy were disillusioned because the sacred cause of human justice had become tarnished by sordid political calculations and vindictiveness. *Tout commence en mystique et finit en politique* was his famous lament.[7]

Blum, too, shared in the disenchantment. The Dreyfusards did not accomplish any profound renovation. Soon the republican and socialist coalition fell apart and parliamentary life reverted to its old weaknesses —personal rivalries, unprincipled wrangling, amorphous groupings and regroupings. Years later, the France in which Blum attempted to exercise political leadership was still a house divided. The anti-Dreyfusards nursed their grievances and bided their time. Vichy, in some ways, would be the revenge of the anti-Dreyfusards, and Blum one of Vichy's victims.

Meanwhile, the disillusionment with the merely superficial political changes of the post-Dreyfusard years reinforced Blum's belief that a more profound social transformation was necessary. If the Dreyfus Affair reinforced his allegiance to the republic and its institutions, it reaffirmed his socialist convictions as well.[8]

Intellectually, Blum was "already a Socialist" before the Dreyfus Affair, converted by his awakening social consciousness and by Lucien Herr's successful proselytizing. But the Dreyfusard campaign—the identification of the Socialists with the defense of the republic and with the cause

[6] Blum: *Souvenirs*, pp. 171–3.

[7] *Notre Jeunesse* (Paris, 1910), in *Cahiers de la Quinzaine*, 2nd ser., LXVII, No. 12, 27.

[8] *Souvenirs*, pp. 175–80.

of human justice—and his contacts with Jaurés solidified his convictions and oriented them in the direction of Jaurès's democratic socialism. The first Socialist organization that Blum joined, in 1899, the group of intellectuals associated with the cooperative bookstore Librairie Bellais, called itself significantly Socialist Unity.[9] They were dedicated to the unification of the various organizations which under different names and separate leaders called themselves socialist yet agreed on little except the goal of a future collectivist society. Although by the 1890's the ideology of the French Socialist movement was predominantly Marxian, conflicting ideological interpretations and the clash of strong personalities led to endless disputes over the nature of the future Socialist party—its role in the French parliamentary republic, its relations with the syndicalist trade union movement, its attitude toward reform legislation, toward national defense, and other issues. Interpretations ranged from those of the orthodox hard-shell Marxist Jules Guesde, who rejected the notion that the "revolution" could come through legal methods alone, to frankly reformist Socialists like Alexandre Millerand, who repudiated the class struggle as anachronistic and saw a gradual, progressive movement toward socialization through universal suffrage, parliamentary action, and reform legislation. Between the two extremes were finely calibrated differences. Jaurès lent his special talents to creating a synthesis of the conflicting views. Although insisting that the parliamentary republic was the institutional framework within which socialists must work to achieve their goal, he never abjured the idea of revolution and class struggle.[1]

Blum himself, observing the growth of reformist socialism, saw the need for an "intermediate group" between revolutionists and reformists. Socialists, he said, must try to secure "all progress compatible with existing forms of property," but at the same time must "prepare" men's minds for further revolutionary changes, the transition to a collective society.[2] The "preparatory" mission always remained a cherished idea with Blum. It opened him later to the criticism that it had taken the place of revolution itself.[3]

In 1899 the "Millerand affair" threatened to disrupt and shatter

[9] Lévy: *Comment . . . socialistes*, p. 22; Andler: *Herr*, p. 162.

[1] On earlier socialism, Prélot: *L'Évolution politique*, pp. 113–204, and Noland: *The Founding of the French Socialist Party*, pp. 1–86.

[2] *Nouvelles Conversations, Oeuvre*, I, 290–1.

[3] See Joll: *Intellectuals in Politics*, p. 11; and cf. Colette Audry: *Léon Blum ou la politique du Juste: essai* (Paris, 1955), pp. 46–52, 194. See comment on Audry's book in Bibliography.

the tenuous Socialist unity that had hesitantly been forming since the Dreyfus Affair. When Alexandre Millerand, without consulting his Socialist colleagues in Parliament, accepted from Premier Waldeck-Rousseau a post in the cabinet formed in 1899, discord and recriminations ran through Socialist ranks.[4] To some Socialists, like Jaurès, the acceptance of a cabinet post in a bourgeois ministry might be admissible under certain circumstances. Others, with Guesde in the lead, denounced any identification with the "bourgeois" state: "The Socialist party, a class party," they proclaimed, "cannot, without risking suicide, be or become a ministerial party." Only the deepest disillusionment of the working class could result; a lone Socialist minister would be a voice crying in the capitalist wilderness.

At a congress of the various Socialist organizations, held in the Salle Japy in Paris in December 1899, where the issue was debated, Guesde, who had the backing of the German-dominated Second International, persuaded the Socialists to condemn Millerand's act. As a concession to Jaurès, the Socialists agreed that they could "under exceptional circumstances" examine the question of participation in a cabinet; for the present, however, they would seek only elective offices. Blum, like Jaurès, conceded that Millerand had been wrong to proceed without the approval of his colleagues and that Socialist cabinet participation was "in principle not desirable." At the same time he expanded on the "exceptional circumstances" argument. He could visualize situations in which it might be not only permissible but even necessary for the party to authorize participation in a cabinet. Such a step would not be "in contradiction to the revolutionary notion of the class struggle" but, on the contrary, "an example, a model, a form of revolutionary act," which he defined as "any act which seems to advance perceptibly the regular course of political evolution." "Millerand," he predicted, "has furnished a prototype, opened up a series which, without any doubt, history in the near future will see continued."[5] Blum's prophecy was accurate, although no French Socialist would enter a cabinet, save

[4] On the Millerand affair, Noland: *The Founding of the French Socialist Party*, pp. 86–114; Prélot: *L'Évolution politique*, pp. 130–54; Andler: *Herr*, pp. 148–50; Goldberg: *Jaurès*, pp. 249–77, 307–42; and cf. Leslie Derfler: " 'Le Cas Millerand': une nouvelle interprétation," *Revue d'Histoire Moderne et Contemporaine*, X (1963), 81–104. In addition, see Blum's contemporary account in *Les Congrès ouvriers et socialistes français* (Paris, 1901), *Oeuvre*, I, 480–2, and comments in *Nouvelles Conversations*, ibid., pp. 286–92.

[5] *Nouvelles Conversations*, ibid., pp. 289–90.

for the wartime "sacred union" cabinets of the First World War, until Blum himself became Premier in June 1936. The problem of Socialist participation in office became one of Blum's continuing preoccupations.

The prewar debate reached a climax when Guesde, bent on stemming the tide against reformism, enlisted the active backing of the German Social Democrats in the International. At its congress in Amsterdam in August 1904, the International condemned "ministerialism" but at the same time appealed for the creation of a unified Socialist party in each country. The resolution against "ministerialism" passed over the protests of Jaurès. On the other hand, the mystique of unity meant so much to him that he subordinated everything to it, including his own personal convictions. He accepted the pact of unity. Shortly thereafter, Blum made his first speech at the congress of the Socialist group to which he belonged, and also urged acceptance of the pact.[6] Unification was achieved in April 1905 at a historic session in the Salle du Globe in Paris.[7] The modern French Socialist party was born; technically, it was known as the French Section of the Labor International, the Section Française de l'Internationale Ouvrière, or S.F.I.O. Its unity lasted only until 1920, when in the wake of the Russian Revolution a deep schism occurred and a French Communist party emerged; in that chapter of its history Blum would be intimately involved.

Although formal unity was achieved, many differences persisted within the party. In the years from 1905 to 1914 the differences focused primarily on questions of national defense and internationalism. Once again Jaurès sought to serve as synthesizer and harmonizer, attempting to reconcile socialist antimilitarism and patriotism. It took all of Jaurès's genius for compromise to keep the party together. Selflessly and magnanimously, he accepted the dogmatic prohibition against holding ministerial office although it ran counter to his convictions. The party's official position and his premature death prevented him from ever attaining the high office and national leadership for which his abilities and talents admirably equipped him. It remained for Blum to fulfill the frustrated national ambitions of Jaurès.

[6] At Rouen, *Parti socialiste français*, March 26–28, 1905; Lévy: *Comment . . . socialistes*, p. 22. For the debate, Noland: *The Founding of the French Socialist Party*, pp. 181–4.

[7] Blum intervened briefly at the unification congress: *Parti socialiste, Section française de l'internationale ouvrière, 1er congrès national, Paris, 23–25 avril 1905*, p. 20.

There is a passage in Blum's fictionalized dialogues between Goethe and Eckermann in which one glimpses Blum's insight into the evolving socialism of these early years. All of his later preoccupation with problems of freedom and social justice, of power and responsibility, and of the pitfalls of politics are contained in it. His Goethe speculates on the problem of human freedom and happiness. At one time freedom meant freedom from political constraint, but the progress of science and technology had transformed the problem into one of social justice. Two questions trouble him: Why do some men lack bread when enough is produced for all? And why do others eat bread which they have not earned by their labor? Blum's Goethe decides to re-create Faust and launch him on a new task: "to impose justice on humanity." He will send Faust into modern industrial society as "a socialist leader" accompanied by a disguised Mephistopheles, unrecognized by Faust as his old antagonist, the ironic demon and incarnation of evil.

In a heated discussion Faust maintains against Mephistopheles that it is possible to preach an evangelical gospel of social justice and induce the privileged members of society voluntarily to renounce their unjust privileges. For Faust has a "horror of bloodshed, he wants the revolution to be peaceful and fraternal." But in one episode after another Faust meets with failure. He arouses the government—"a trembling Parliament"—to pass reform legislation, but in the reaction that follows, the socialist leader and his companion are thrown into prison. In another episode an inventor creates a labor-saving loom, and despite the efforts of Faust to curb the "violent instincts" of the people, Mephistopheles incites the workers to smash the new machinery. In a third episode Faust enters Parliament with a number of friends and tries in vain to create a united, disciplined party. Overwhelmed with work, he finds that he must master all kinds of technical detail and do everything himself. Mephistopheles mocks him: "You have become a bourgeois businessman." Faust has met only bitterness and disappointment. The conclusion is clear. Mephistopheles is the stronger and will remain so for a long time. On the other hand, every unsuccessful act of Faust has served to "produce fruitful results for the future." "Faust understands it," Blum has Goethe conclude, "and despite his suffering he will never despair of his task. He would not even exchange his suffering for something else that would bring happiness."

All of Blum's lifelong optimism and his determination to persevere in the crusade for social justice are contained in the passage. The

Faustian symbol of Western man's striving for knowledge and wisdom becomes a Faust striving for the application of knowledge and wisdom to the reorganization of society. "Will Faust succeed?" Blum asks. "I am fully convinced of it."[8]

The movement of the various socialist organizations toward unification came under Blum's close scrutiny when in 1901 he wrote a history of the labor and socialist congresses held in France from 1876 to 1900, *Les Congrès ouvriers et socialistes.* More a chronicle and summary of proceedings than a history, and based principally on the formal minutes, it is nonetheless a clear, objective, and detailed account of the vicissitudes of the socialist and syndicalist movements as they groped their way toward unity.[9] The two small volumes comprised Blum's contribution to the *Bibliothèque Socialiste* series, published under the auspices of the cooperative publishing house and bookstore, the Société Nouvelle de Librairie et d'Édition, directed by Herr; it was the successor to Péguy's enterprise, the Librairie Bellais, which had run into financial difficulties. Blum served also as a member of the five-man administrative board and assisted Herr in the technical and financial aspects of the establishment, which published not only socialist studies but a number of important scholarly works as well.[1] An unfriendly critic and former colleague of Blum's on the board described Blum's self-assured, limpid elucidation of various technical matters. His intellectual colleagues, he noted, preferred Blum's "certainty to the discomfort of ambiguity."[2]

In the decade before 1914 Blum not only pursued his dual career in literature and law but also followed political affairs closely and deepened his ties with socialism. His diverse talents and brimming energies

[8] *Nouvelles Conversations, Oeuvre,* I, 240–5.

[9] 2 vols., Paris, 1901, reproduced in *Oeuvre,* I, 391–491. Noland, writing in 1956, called it "an extremely useful survey": *The Founding of the French Socialist Party,* p. 214.

[1] On the publishing house and Blum's activities, Andler: *Herr,* pp. 151–67. Péguy, who had been ousted from control of the organization, nursed a grievance against all his former colleagues and especially against Blum. There is an extensive polemical literature on Péguy's quarrels with his fellow socialists; see, e.g., Pierre Dournes: "Le Socialisme de Péguy face au parti socialiste," *La Nef,* V (June–July 1950), 79–87.

[2] Bourgin: *De Jaurès à Léon Blum,* p. 497.

were such that he could cultivate all of his interests with ease. Continuing his close association with Jaurès, he assisted him in 1904 in launching the new Socialist newspaper, *L'Humanité*, and he and Lucien Lévy-Bruhl helped to finance it by raising funds among their well-to-do friends. Once it was under way Blum wrote the literary column and contributed occasional political articles.[3] Through Jaurès he had a direct link with activities in the Chamber, Jaurès often discussing with him the outlines of speeches he was preparing and consulting him on technical matters.[4] Blum kept himself informed in detail on parliamentary affairs. "Blum knows the Deputies by their vote," Jules Renard noted in his diary. He added the telling remark that his friend held no high opinion of the Deputies: "I believe it would be easy to equal most of those men," Blum told him.[5] Yet when Jaurès twice pressed him to stand as a candidate for the Chamber, in 1902 and again in 1906, each time he declined.[6] Interested as he was in politics, he still held himself aloof from active involvement. Ironically, another friend, André Gide, disappointed in Blum because of his intensive interest in politics, complained: "Oh, if politics did not dominate all his thoughts, what a fine critic he would be! . . . One cannot imagine reviews more accurate or of greater clarity, elegance, and felicity than those that Léon Blum writes immediately after an event, a book, or a play." He attested also to his remarkable intellectual abilities. "His is an intelligence marvelously organized, sharp, organizing and classifying everything; ten years later it can find each idea exactly in place, the way one finds an object in a closet."[7]

Despite Gide's complaint of Blum's obsession with politics, Blum spent the eight years from 1906 to 1914 busied essentially with literary, and not political, activities. His duties at the Conseil d'État allowed him sufficient time to review books and plays on a regular basis and to write literary criticism. He had abandoned the thought of writing fiction or drama of his own and had even set aside a novel and a play that he had begun. He recognized his literary talents as those of a critic and essayist. In 1906 *En lisant*, a collection of his book reviews written from 1903 to 1905, appeared, and in 1907, as we have

[3] Blum in Lévy: *Comment . . . socialistes*, p. 23; Andler: *Herr*, pp. 169–82; Goldberg: *Jaurès*, pp. 319–20.

[4] See, e.g., *Journal de Jules Renard*, entry for February 28, 1908, V, 1421.

[5] Ibid., entries for May 1, 1902, III, 906, and February 6, 1903, IV, 982.

[6] Lévy: *Comment . . . socialistes*, p. 23.

[7] *Journal, 1889–1939*, entries for January 5, 1907, p. 228, and January 24, 1914, p. 396. Cf. entry for April 27, 1906, p. 209.

seen, his semi-sociological, semi-fictional *Du mariage*, which Octave Mirbeau considered worthy of the Prix Goncourt.[8] In 1914 he completed his most ambitious effort at literary criticism, a study of one of his literary favorites, *Stendhal et le beylisme*, a book still read and admired by *beylistes*. In the years 1906 to 1911 he published four volumes of his collected drama criticism, the product of his reviewing for *Comoedia*, *La Grande Revue*, *Gil Blas*, and *Le Matin*; included were public lectures he had delivered on Shakespeare, Corneille, and Ibsen.[9] One of his critical reviews, in the lusty literary world of those days, led in October 1912 to a challenge and duel with the playwright Pierre Véber; neither was hurt and the honor of each was upheld.[1] As a literary and drama critic, Blum earned a distinguished reputation. Although devoted to classical standards and style, he was receptive to new forms of expression and was among the first to recognize the genius of many then unknown novelists, playwrights, and poets. His evaluations of Gide, Proust, D'Annunzio, for example, were remarkably discerning at a time when academic critics were largely ignoring these authors. The poet Fernand Gregh recalled that Blum alone, of all his critics, had the perception to see the twin influences of Hugo and Verlaine on his poetry. In later years François Mauriac looked back upon Blum as "the most lucid critic . . . of his time."[2]

They were pleasant and agreeable years. He counted among his friends, and entertained in his book-lined home, the most eminent men and women in the world of arts, letters, science, music, and politics. Georges de Porto-Riche, the dramatist, remained his closest literary friend.[3] Mme Simone, the actress and novelist, recalled him in that era: "He explained to me his resolution to organize each of his days as if it were to be his last, making sure that it included even if only in tiny measure a little of what he called his 'treasures': love,

---

[8] *Journal de Jules Renard*, December 6, 1907, V, 1394.

[9] For his literary and drama criticism, *Oeuvre*, II, and the bibliographical index, ibid., pp. 601–39.

[1] Fraser and Natanson: *Blum*, pp. 105–6. See recollections of the duel by Joseph Renaud, *Le Matin*, August 17, 1931.

[2] Gregh: *Souvenirs*, III: *L'Âge de fer: souvenirs, 1925–1955* (Paris, 1956), 32, and cf. *Souvenirs*, II, 52; Mauriac: "Bloc-Note," *L'Express*, June 12, 1954. There is no serious full-length study of Blum as a literary critic; Marcel Thiébaut: *En lisant M. Léon Blum* (Paris, 1937), is polemical and hostile. Various discussions by Jacques Carat and others are listed in the Bibliography of the present work.

[3] Thadée Natanson catalogues the impressive list: Fraser and Natanson: *Blum*, pp. 100–5.

friendship, reading, thought, music, and, not least, the duties of his job and his profession."[4]

They were in a sense ivory-tower years, far removed from militant socialism or the storm centers of politics—a strange preparation for leadership of a proletarian party. Yet he never considered himself in retreat from the world of reality. He saw himself as fulfilling a role that he had carefully described a few years earlier, the high calling of the critic-philosopher. In his dialogues between Goethe and Eckermann, he argued that the scientist and the creative artist were no longer able, because of the specialization of their work, to grasp universal truth—"that total contemplation of the universe which ennobles human thought, recalls to man his true place in creation, inscribes in one's heart the meaning of life." It was the critic-philosopher —the "race of Herder" he has Goethe say—who alone could penetrate all knowledge and make it meaningful to the universe.

The "critics" of today, Blum asserted, would be the "men of politics" of tomorrow: "For tomorrow the just constitution of the City will once again become, as in the time of Aristotle and Plato, the supreme task, the culmination of human effort." The "critics" alone would be able to frame the laws of the future society, which would be no "chance find" but the synthesis of all knowledge and wisdom. It was for the philosopher-critics to preach the new secular faith: "The idea of man, of happiness, of human justice will embrace and will explain everything as did the Christian idea for the thinkers and the painters of the Middle Ages." They must preach it "with a prophetic fervor and point the way for us to a world dominated for the first time, no longer by Force or by Miracle, but by Justice and Reason."[5]

Here was Blum's justification for withdrawing from involvement in politics—the high calling of the philosopher-critic preparing the way for the philosopher-king, dreaming of a new Heavenly City, supremely confident of the triumph of reason and social justice. From the great poets of all ages—he names Homer, Shakespeare, Hugo—in whom human creativity reached its zenith, men must absorb their confidence in the human destiny: "Men do not have two souls," he insisted, "one to sing, the other to act." Since the poets had been able to fulfill their task, the scholars, the philosophers, and the statesmen must fulfill

---

[4] Simone (Pauline Porché): "Souvenirs sur Léon Blum," *Les Nouvelles Littéraires*, April 6, 1950.

[5] *Nouvelles Conversations, Oeuvre*, I, 334–5.

theirs too.[6] Blum was the last of the eighteenth-century *philosophes*.

The First World War and the assassination of Jaurès shattered his tranquillity and thrust him into the maelstrom of politics. In the tempestuous years ahead, he often recalled the phrase from Tolstoy's *War and Peace* which had impressed itself indelibly on his mind as a young man: "Everything was so strange, so different from what he had hoped."[7] Yet his optimism never deserted him.

[6] Ibid., pp. 253–4.
[7] *Souvenirs*, p. 129.

II

"TO GUARD THE OLD HOUSE"
War Socialism and Party Schism
1914–1920

. . . while you pursue your adventures, someone must remain to guard the old house.[1]

THE ILLUSION that the proletariat would be able to prevent the outbreak of war was cruelly dispelled in the summer of 1914; the dream of an international European Socialist movement perished when each of the major Socialist parties rallied to its country's flag and national loyalties proved stronger than class loyalties. In France socialism suffered an irreparable blow when Jaurès, the very symbol of the party, was assassinated on the eve of the war by a demented nationalist fanatic. Jaurès, whose socialism was infused with the highest patriotism, was the victim of a man who branded him an internationalist and a traitor.

When mobilization began, there was no need for the French government to put into effect its careful preparations to cope with mass resistance and subversion. The French workers and their leaders, determined to defend France against the "German autocracy," responded patriotically and without protest.[2] On August 4, the Socialist Deputies in the Chamber joined in the unanimous vote for war credits. At the funeral of Jaurès that same day, Premier René Viviani delivered a

---

[1] Blum: *Parti socialiste (S.F.I.O.), 18ᵉ congrès national*, Tours, December 25–30, 1920, *compte-rendu sténographique* (Paris, 1921), p. 274.

[2] For French Socialist reactions to the war, see the relevant pages in the general histories of French socialism by Georges Lefranc, Daniel Ligou, Paul Louis, Marcel Prélot, and Alexandre Zévaès, listed in the Bibliography of the present work.

[36]

eulogy; Socialist and labor leaders made patriotic speeches. Three weeks later, all initial hesitation swept aside by the advances of the German army toward the Marne, the Socialist party accepted Viviani's invitation to join the coalition government; the party named two of its leaders to serve the "cause of national defense in a cabinet of sacred union." Jules Guesde became Minister of State without portfolio; Marcel Sembat became Minister of Public Works. The cabinet had a third Socialist minister when Albert Thomas became undersecretary of state for armaments production in May 1915.

It was as Marcel Sembat's *chef de cabinet*—the minister's personal administrative assistant—that Blum, at the age of forty-two, made his debut in government circles. Sembat, one of the leading figures in the party before 1914, a Deputy, lawyer, and distinguished art critic as well, had come to know Blum through Jaurès and was aware of Jaurès's high regard for Blum's abilities. He knew also that Blum, from his years of service in the Conseil d'État, possessed invaluable legal and administrative experience.

Blum accepted Sembat's invitation with alacrity. Exempted from military service because of his nearsightedness, he was eager to serve in the war effort and to satisfy his own ardent patriotism. His conception of the republic as inextricably linked to the cause of socialism overcame all other scruples about the war. He was convinced also that had Jaurès lived he would have unhesitatingly collaborated in national defense and accepted the highest posts of national leadership in the struggle.[3]

Blum performed his wartime duties with zeal, energy, and skill. For two and a half years, from August 1914 until December 1916, when Sembat left the cabinet, he remained Sembat's inseparable and intimate collaborator. He met with committees concerned with problems of transportation and food and fuel supply; he dealt with top-level military and civilian authorities and with industrial leaders; he attended inter-ministerial and Allied conferences in Paris and London.

Blum's post proved to be an invaluable introduction to the inner circles of politics. Working closely not only with Sembat but also with other members of the cabinet, the permanent civil service officials, and the appropriate parliamentary committees, he was "involved in-

---

[3] Speech on the third anniversary of Jaurès's assassination, July 31, 1917, *La Revue Socialiste*, May 1950, pp. 386–406. His opinion on what Jaurès might have done is not shared by everyone; see, e.g., Lefranc: *Mouvement socialiste*, pp. 193–5, Daniel Ligou: *Histoire du socialisme en France, 1871–1961* (Paris, 1962), pp. 261, 271, and Goldberg: *Jaurès*, pp. 473–4, 567, n. 39.

directly," he later wrote, "in the intimate debates of the government" and was a "confidant and frequent adviser to the ministers."[4] He followed closely the discussions of wartime policy in the Chamber and frequented the corridors of Parliament.

He began also at this time to meet and consult with fellow Socialists when the first rifts and disagreements over the party's policy of collaboration in the war effort were beginning to appear. In 1915, a minority in the party, insisting that all governments had their share of responsibility for the outbreak of the war, was beginning to criticize the policy of "class collaboration" and "sacred union." With his patience, perseverance, and tact, Blum was increasingly able to exercise influence and to attempt measures of conciliation; quietly and unobtrusively he was building up a position of prestige and authority in various circles of the party, which had had no leader since the death of Jaurès.

Hubert Bourgin, in his highly colored and prejudiced memoirs, makes some curious observations on Blum during the years of the First World War.[5] A product of the École Normale, Bourgin was a former Socialist, Dreyfusard, and close associate of Blum at the turn of the century in the Librairie Bellais; in later years he became an extreme nationalist and Rightist. Although the memoirs are filled with violent strictures against his old political friends, both Socialist and Radical, they are, in their way, oddly perceptive. Himself an administrative assistant to one of the Socialist ministers, he saw a good deal of Blum during the war and he maintains that in these years Blum first felt the stirrings of political ambition "on the three levels of power—party, parliament, and government." He depicts Blum as entranced by the military and diplomatic intrigues of high politics and the war, all of which he viewed as an exciting game. Blum, "in the know," jubilantly revealed to him, for example, the news of Italy's entry into the war on the side of the Allies in the spring of 1915. He concludes that Blum's ambitions were spurred, above all, when he saw himself in the midst of mediocre men with little originality and without ideas or goals. One day, at the Chamber, he observed the future Socialist leader in one of the deserted corridors:

> He was there, nervous, feverish . . . His eyes shone with a
> prodigious gleam, a Dantesque flame, his face was pale, the
> muscles tense without moving; his mustache revealed a sensual

[4] *Mémoires* (1940), *Oeuvre*, V, 34–5, 73; see also Fraser and Natanson: *Blum*, pp. 136–8; Vichniac: *Blum*, p. 111.

[5] Bourgin: *De Jaurès à Léon Blum*, pp. 501–15.

mouth which seemed to be savoring the taste of a voluptuous prey. This living statue of political passion, this symbolic figure, deeply animated and agitated within, was perhaps terrifying but had in it also a kind of concentrated splendor. . . . It seemed to me that I was watching the opening up, the unfolding of this superior and strange person, this admixture of messianism and Jewish prophetism adapted to the modern age, of Oriental passion, of Asiatic frenzy, of an intelligence European, French, and Cartesian, of a refined estheticism. . . . Having seen that apparition rise one evening in the winter of 1916, I was in a position to understand Léon Blum and nothing could henceforth astonish me in his political fortunes.[6]

Even if Bourgin's overwrought imagination can be heavily discounted, an element of truth remains. Much had changed since the pre-1914 years. Jaurès was gone; someone had to pick up the fallen prophet's mantle. Blum's experience with *haute politique*, even in a role as minor administrator, his awareness of his superiority over lesser men in government and parliamentary circles, the trouble brewing in the party, the challenge of the war and the problems that the postwar world would bring—all stirred his ambitions and desires. He had written a few years earlier, half in earnest, half in jest: "Everyone laughs in speaking of the Academy, as of the Chamber, and everybody wishes to be a part of it." "The French," he had added, "make fun only of what they fear or envy."[7]

In December 1916, when Sembat left the cabinet during a ministerial crisis, Blum's association with the cabinet came to an end. Back at his post in the Conseil d'État, with leisure to write once again, Blum took up his pen and on the basis of his recent observations in the inner councils of government, wrote a long essay dissecting the weaknesses of the French parliamentary system and proposing various recommendations for reform. His observations first appeared as two unsigned articles, "Lettres sur la réforme gouvernementale," in *La Revue de Paris* in three consecutive issues in December 1917 and January 1918, and then in book form, though still anonymously, at the end of 1918, with a foreword.[8]

[6] Ibid., pp. 508–9.

[7] *Nouvelles Conversations, Oeuvre*, I, 202.

[8] Paris: Bernard Grasset; 1918. It was reissued in 1936, when Blum was Premier, with an introduction by Robert Blum. The 1936 edition included articles Blum had published in October 1934 criticizing Gaston Doumergue's constitutional proposals.

Devoted to the idea of parliamentary government in France, Blum nonetheless had no illusions about its effectiveness, and he feared for the future if its weaknesses were not remedied. Stressing the urgent need for a stronger executive so that the parliamentary system might operate more effectively and yet not harm the spirit of the democratic constitution, the essays ranged over a wide variety of topics: the need to strengthen the Premier in relation to the cabinet and Parliament, the choice of ministers, the organization of the cabinet, the excessive role of the permanent civil officials, the contribution that could be made by well-organized, disciplined political parties, the problem of the Senate, the working methods of the Chamber, and a score of other subjects. Many of his observations and suggestions were directly inspired by the English system, of which he always remained an admirer; he especially envied the relationship of the British Prime Minister to the cabinet and to Parliament. Parliamentary institutions would also profit, he believed, from the leadership, organization, and efficiency that he saw in modern industrial enterprise. None of these observations were socialist ideas; they demonstrated rather his devotion to the parliamentary institutions of the republic, which, like Jaurès, he cherished but wished to strengthen. When he became Premier in 1936, not only was his book reissued but he was able to put some of his suggested cabinet reforms into effect. On the other hand, some of the very defects in French political life which he had underscored would prove his own undoing.

Toward the end of the war Blum found himself plunged deeply into the internal affairs of the party. By the summer of 1915, as we have seen, the unanimity with which the party had agreed to share in the defense of the nation and to participate in the "sacred union" cabinets had disappeared. A growing minority led by Jean Longuet and Paul Faure, reviving older Socialist traditions of pacifism, antimilitarism, and internationalism, and reflecting the profound warweariness in the party and the nation, openly attacked the zeal with which the party majority leadership was supporting the war. It called for the withdrawal of Socialists from the cabinet, the resumption of international Socialist ties, and a speedy end to the war itself. At the same time a more revolutionary type of opposition also appeared. At two international Socialist conferences in Switzerland, in which Russian exiles played a major role, at Zimmerwald in September 1915 and Kienthal in April 1916, delegates denounced the military struggle as a "capitalist" and "imperialist" war and attacked the Socialists in each camp who were cooperating in the war effort as "class collaborationists" and "social patriots"; they demanded a return to the purer Marxian doctrines of class struggle, revolution, and international proletarian action. Only a few French Socialists and syndicalists participated in the conferences, and only on an unofficial basis, yet these delegates reflected the rising tension within the French party. The seizure of power by the Bolsheviks in November 1917 and the subsequent withdrawal of Russia from the war strengthened the minority in the party. By July 1918 the "national defense" majority Socialists led by Pierre Renaudel and Albert Thomas had all but lost control of the party to the opposition.

Blum himself never faltered in his support of the war effort and the "sacred union" policy.[9] In 1917 he welcomed America's entry into the war and Wilson's pronouncements on the peace as decisive proof that the war was being fought for the defense of democratic and republican ideals and a new international order. "Our victory will be the emancipation and reconciliation of men through Liberty and Justice," he wrote when America entered the war.[1] Calling for "war as long as necessary for the triumph of Wilson's peace," he at the same time insisted that it was not a "victory" of one side over the other that they sought, but only a peace based on Wilson's principles.[2] In the summer of 1918, when the final German offensive was threatening Paris, he issued resounding calls for a Jacobin defense of the capital and a mobilization of all resources for a supreme effort.[3]

Blum rejected the criticisms leveled at the party's majority leadership. Rightly or wrongly, he was convinced that in supporting the war the party was keeping faith with the legacy bequeathed by Jaurès —a devotion both to the nation and to internationalism—for from an Allied victory in the war he saw emerging the international order of brotherhood dreamed of over the centuries. "We have been completely faithful to our national duty without renouncing our international

[9] According to Andler, Blum and Lucien Herr favored acceptance of Clemenceau's invitation to join his cabinet so that the party might better "watch over" him. Although many Socialists viewed Clemenceau's highhandedness with misgivings, they prized the energetic determination with which he was pursuing the war. *Herr*, pp. 245–6.

[1] "Vers la république," *L'Humanité*, April 8, 1917.

[2] "La Victoire et la paix," *L'Humanité*, July 9, 1918, and "Et Paris," ibid., June 8, 1918.

[3] *L'Humanité*, June 8, 27, and July 4, 1918.

duty or, as I would prefer to say, our human duty," he wrote in July 1918.[4]

At the same time Blum did not wish to identify himself with the Renaudel–Albert Thomas right wing, which, in reaction to the Bolshevik Revolution, was assuming an increasingly reformist position. He himself was extremely critical of the new Bolshevik dictatorship, its "intransigent fanaticism," its cruelty and violence, its "mystical belief in the sole immediate virtue of revolution in itself, no matter what the conditions, the circumstances, the means employed." Yet he would not, on the other hand, accept a simple reformism and reject the idea of revolution itself. "We profess in our doctrine and our action that socialism is a daily work of education, of reform, of progress. But we profess equally that the vital element, the motivating force of this daily effort, is a revolutionary faith." To the dilemma posed by Albert Thomas and the right wing in the party that Socialists had to choose "between Wilson and Lenin, between democracy and Bolshevik fanaticism," his reply was: "I choose neither Wilson nor Lenin. I choose Jaurès. . . . We remain revolutionary socialists without being tainted in the least by the world of Bolshevism."[5]

Developing his delicately balanced ideas with finesse and subtlety, Blum logically emerged in the summer of 1918 as the leader of a small "centrist" group in the party whose primary concern was to preserve unity. He tried desperately to reconcile the opposing groups with the argument that they were all faithful to the cause of patriotism *and* internationalism. They were all "at the same time republicans and socialists, socialists and French patriots, French patriots and champions of working-class internationalism." He accepted with pride the "centrist" mission "to serve as conciliator in order to maintain and consolidate the unity of the party."[6]

Although he had little organizational support for his centrist position,[7] he filled an important need in the bitterly divided party. As the disciple and friend of Jaurès, he alone was trying to carry on the

[4] *L'Humanité*, July 31, 1918.

[5] The quotations are from "Il faut s'entendre," *L'Humanité*, November 15, 1918.

[6] "Pour l'unité," *L'Humanité*, August 19, 1918.

[7] At the party congress of October 1918, the Longuet "hard line" group received 1,528 votes as against 1,212 for the Renaudel "national defense" group. The "centrist" resolution introduced by Blum and Sembat received only 181 votes. The permanent administrative committee, under the rules of the party laid down in 1905, reflected this distribution on a proportional basis: 12 for the Longuet group, 10 for the Renaudel group, 1 for the center; Ligou: *Socialisme*, p. 301.

great tribune's role of harmonizer, conciliator, and synthesizer. As he had been dissociated from party politics since the Dreyfusard years, he could plausibly maintain also that he was entering the political arena only to carry on the work of Jaurès and to preserve the unity of the party. "I entered the active affairs of the party when the unity of the party was being created," he later wrote. "I again took up the militant life when unity was threatened."[8]

Blum's centrist position, his personal prestige, and the role which he steadfastly assumed as conciliator and as apostle of Jaurès thrust him to the forefront of the party's activities at the end of 1918. Although deeply divided in its political orientation, the party had to think of the first postwar elections. Agreeing at its October 1918 congress on the need to prepare a new "program of action," it entrusted the drafting of the document to a commission of fifty-two party leaders representing all tendencies.

As chairman of the commission, Blum drew up the compromise program and served as its spokesman at the congress of April 1919. The program and his speech represented a heroic effort to reconcile the opposing factions of the party. In his long and effective speech, he insisted that all groups in the party believed in "revolutionary" socialism, in a radical transformation of society and of the existing structure of property relations, but he warned that a revolution signified more than just a seizure of political power; a true social revolution could occur only when conditions were ripe for it. No one knew when or how the social revolution would occur in their country, whether by legal or by extralegal means, or by a combination of both. Their immediate duty as Socialists, therefore, was to work for the education of the masses and at the same time for the orientation of capitalist society along collectivist lines. In that way, they would "prepare for the revolution in the most effective and most complete manner." For the immediate future, he asked them to rally the country behind a program of political, economic, and social innovation that would repair the ravages of the war, renovate and modernize the nation's productive facilities, of which they were the "heirs apparent," and advance the lot of the workers.

The party had its eye on two fixed poles, he told them, existing society and future society. Without an attachment to the realities of the present, their socialism would be "merely a religious dogma, a

[8] Statement in Lévy: *Comment . . . socialistes*, p. 23; and cf. his statement at the congress held at Tours, p. 273.

metaphysical philosophy"; without an attachment to their vision of the future, the party would be "merely a party of democratic reform." Unity must represent "an equilibrium between divergent movements . . . a kind of resultant of opposing forces."[9] His speech drew a prolonged and enthusiastic ovation. For the moment the congress of April 1919 seemed to have restored unity. Marcel Sembat hailed with enthusiasm the "program of which Léon Blum was the lucid and convincing spokesman. . . . The congress, marvelously served by the tremendous and precise work of Léon Blum, succeeded completely in the difficult task of reaching unanimous agreement."[1] Actually the congress merely glossed over the profound differences within the party and postponed an open rift.

With national elections scheduled for November 1919, the maintenance of unity, even if only superficially, was a practical necessity for the party. Thanks to Blum, to all external appearances the party entered the election united, with Blum's "program of action" as its campaign platform. Blum himself campaigned vigorously in the Seine department. As a demonstration of its "hard line" orientation, the party had resolved not to form an electoral coalition with the major "bourgeois" party of the Left, the Radicals, but to run its own lists and to campaign independently on its own program even though the election system of 1919 afforded a substantial advantage to parties combined in a voting bloc. For the moment ideological considerations were more important than practical ones.

The absence of a Left electoral coalition and the strong patriotic atmosphere of the time resulted in a setback for both parties of the Left and an easy parliamentary victory for the Right and Center coalition (the *bloc national*). Although the Socialist popular vote rose by 300,000 votes (from 1,398,000 to 1,700,000), its representation in the Chamber declined from the 103 seats it had held in 1914 to 68. Among the prominent party leaders defeated were Jean Longuet, L. O. Frossard, Paul Faure, and Renaudel.[2] The Socialist leaders consoled themselves that the party had made a correct choice between merely

---

[9] *Commentaires sur le programme d'action du parti socialiste*, speech to special party congress, April 21, 1919 (Paris, 1919).

[1] *La Victoire en déroute* (Paris, 1925), pp. 101, 105. The book was published posthumously with a preface by Blum. An English translation appeared as *Defeated Victory* (London, 1925).

[2] Prélot: *L'Évolution politique*, p. 220 and n. 2; Ligou: *Socialisme*, pp. 308–9.

seeking electoral gains on the one hand and maintaining its Socialist integrity and independence on the other.[3]

Despite the Socialist electoral setback, Blum won one of the ten seats in the Seine department to which the party's vote entitled it. At the age of forty-seven, Blum entered the Chamber for the first time; a new life opened up before him. He launched his parliamentary career on December 30 with *éclat*, delivering a brilliant maiden speech, lasting four hours, in a complex technical debate on the railroads, involving questions of subsidies, deficits, and rates. Although his speech was conducted on a proper technical level, he also made it clear that he spoke as a Socialist: "We are the joint managers—with the same title to be such as all of you—of the nation's general interests; one day we hold the hope of being its sole managers."[4] As became his practice, he used only brief notes and spoke mainly from memory. Shortly after his parliamentary debut, he was chosen secretary of the Socialist parliamentary group and later president; in the years to come he would annually present its report at the party congresses. With his immense capacity for concentrated work, his ability to sustain and develop subtle and complex arguments, his dedication to his mission as a Socialist Deputy, he rapidly emerged as the recognized spokesman for the parliamentary group. "No leader," wrote Charles Andler, "had any full authority before the appearance of Léon Blum, whose shining talent revealed itself after the election of 1919."[5]

Blum's maiden speech and the innumerable speeches he delivered over the years from the parliamentary rostrum all had the same qualities of lucidity and logic that distinguished his writing. He did not have a naturally strong voice or the tricks of the born orator. Nor did his sentences roll forth sonorously, with the eloquence of the Midi, as did Jaurès's. In Parliament, as in the party, he compelled attention with his rigorous clarity and reasoning. His speeches were more the construction of an architect than the composition of a painter, an anonymous writer in the London *Times* once noted;[6] another British observer said of his speeches that they were "as sinless in form as the music of Mozart."[7] They were characterized chiefly by dialectical ingenuity rather than

[3] Blum: "La Victoire," *L'Humanité*, November 22, 1919.

[4] *Chambre, Débats*, December 30, 1919.

[5] *Herr*, p. 246. Andler, dissatisfied with the Leftist currents in the party, withdrew in 1919.

[6] "Léon Blum: The 'Aristocrate' of the Left: An Appreciation by a Friend," London *Times*, June 13, 1936.

[7] W. L. Middleton: "Léon Blum," *Contemporary Review*, May 1950, p. 262.

passion or fire. Jacques Chastenet, editor of *Le Temps* and a far from sympathetic historian, recalled Blum's early career in the Chamber: ". . . his vast culture, his intellectual agility, his eloquence, and the charm of his personality quickly earned for him a rare prestige."[8]

Only on infrequent occasions was he provoked by the opposition into an outburst of impatience. In February 1925, when he rose to speak during a stormy debate over the closing down of the French embassy at the Vatican, a fury of abuse was unleashed from the Right, in part antisemitic in nature, and so violent that he could not continue. "I hate you! (*Je vous hais!*)," he exploded. From that day on the extremists of the Right referred to him as *Je-vous-hais-Blum* and made him out to be a man of implacable Marxian class hatred.[9] The episode was without doubt an explosion of impatience at the intolerance of the Right and not an expression of class hatred. Actually, Marxist or not, Blum was incapable of class or other hatreds.

After his election to the Chamber, Blum faced a personal financial problem, for a Deputy's stipend was small and he could no longer retain his post at the Conseil d'État. Following the custom of many Deputies with legal background, he entered private practice. Here he met with considerable success.[1] Ironically, his private law practice in the world of bourgeois business made possible his career as a Socialist leader in Parliament and in the party. He was financially comfortable all during the 1920's and 1930's. The press carried exaggerated reports of his wealth and the luxury of his Paris apartment, and even created the legend of a fabulous silver collection (which, the story went, an official in all innocence once sought to borrow for a national exhibition). Only when hostile journalists spoke of his "castles on the Riviera" or "in Switzerland" was he moved to reply.[2]

By 1919 the humanist critic was deep in politics. It was a time of great crisis for the party and for the country. As his life now entered its new political phase, he told one of his friends with some self-consciousness that it was the "test that would teach him whether to *act*

---

[8] *Déclin de la Troisième, 1931–1938* (Paris, 1962), Vol. VI of his *Histoire de la Troisième République*, p. 151.

[9] The episode does not appear in the official record: see *Chambre, Débats*, session of February 2, 1925. Many years later, Blum confessed to having uttered the word "hate" from the rostrum; see *Le Populaire*, August 11–12, 1946, *Oeuvre*, VI, 262.

[1] Fraser and Natanson: *Blum*, pp. 166–8. André Blumel became his law partner.

[2] See *Le Populaire*, March 31, April 12, 1927, and October 9, 1938.

lay within his abilities as much as to *understand* and to *know*."[3] It was a challenge that every intellectual entering politics has had to face; in Blum's case, even as the years went by, he could not quite shake off his introspection and self-doubt.

———

Unity in the elections of November 1919 temporarily obscured the crisis that was brewing within the French Socialist party and the world of international socialism ever since the Bolshevik Revolution. There was widespread criticism of the "sacred union" policy followed during the war and resentment because the settlement at Versailles had failed to fulfill the promise of the Wilsonian "peace without victory." Blum himself called the peace settlement "a denial, a betrayal."[4] When the war ended, social and economic unrest was rife. Great strikes broke out in 1919 and 1920, and the Socialist party, because of its internal dissension, was unable to exercise any leadership. The new recruits flocking to the party and to the trade unions were young, impetuous, more radical than the older members, and filled with excited admiration for the revolution in Russia. (In December 1920 the S.F.I.O. membership reached a high of 180,000, over half of whom had joined since the end of the war.[5]) The momentous question before the party was its attitude toward the old Second International and the new dynamic Third International in Moscow, the home of the first successful "proletarian revolution."

By the last months of the war, as we have seen, the left wing had wrested control of the party from the wartime majority, the Renaudel–Albert Thomas wing. Step by step, the new leadership took the party down the path of affiliation with the Third International.[6] At the party congress in April 1919, the majority voted to help "reconstruct" the old Second International along revolutionary lines, a policy that Blum also favored. But by the end of 1919 most members began to favor abandoning the organization altogether, as a number of European parties had already done. At the Strasbourg congress of February 1920, the party voted overwhelmingly to leave the Second International and to try to form a new international organization of all

[3] Bracke (A. M. Desrousseaux): introductory essay, *Oeuvre*, I, 342.
[4] *L'Humanité*, July 19, 1919.
[5] Ligou: *Socialisme*, p. 321.
[6] In addition to the relevant pages in Lefranc and in Ligou, see Paul Louis: *La Crise du socialisme mondial* (Paris, 1921), and Annie Kriegel: *Aux origines du communisme français, 1914–1920*, 2 vols. (Paris, 1964).

Socialist parties that were reconstructing themselves along revolutionary lines.

Unwilling to defend the old Second International, Blum and his center group supported the majority proposal at Strasbourg. He intervened at the congress only to protest what he considered an unwarranted attack on the party's wartime leadership and to defend the party's participation in the government under the extraordinary circumstances of the war, though he agreed that under ordinary peacetime circumstances it must not take part in bourgeois governments.[7] Unswervingly faithful to the wartime sacred union policy, he nonetheless rejected simple reformism for the future and hence did not isolate himself completely from the majority of the party.

At Strasbourg the proponents of immediate affiliation with the Third International had shown considerable strength, but their resolution was defeated by a vote of 3,031 to 1,621. However, the congress did agree to dispatch delegates to Moscow to explore with the Russian leaders the possibility of a unified reconstructed international organization of which the Russians would form a part. In the summer of 1920 support for affiliation with the Third International grew stronger. All Socialists, Blum among them, sympathized with the embattled Bolsheviks in the civil war against the Whites and the foreign armies of intervention.[8] The arrest by the French government of several Socialist and syndicalist leaders, and the repression that followed the strike movement of the spring, also helped to inflame revolutionary tempers.

That summer Marcel Cachin and L. O. Frossard left for Moscow as delegates of the party on an "informational" mission. As official observers, they attended the second congress of the Third International, which formally adopted the famous "twenty-one conditions" for affiliation. The conditions were rigid. Any party seeking affiliation had to subscribe, without reservation, to the code of orthodoxy. A rigorously disciplined and centralized Communist party, bearing that name and no other, was to be set up in each country. The leadership of each party, organized into a powerful central committee, would exercise absolute control over the activities of the party in every sphere—propaganda, the press, Parliament, and the trade unions. All "reformist" and "semi-reformist" elements in the party were to be eliminated. Strong super-

---

[7] *Parti socialiste (S.F.I.O.), 17ᵉ congrès national*, Strasbourg, February 25–29, 1920 (Paris, 1920), *compte-rendu*, pp. 539–40.

[8] See his editorial, "Le Document secret," *L'Humanité*, June 18, 1920.

visory powers were to be vested in the Executive Committee of the International in Moscow.

Despite these conditions, Cachin and Frossard, swept away by the enthusiasm they found in Russia, and convincing themselves that they could interpret the rigid conditions in an elastic way, sent home messages urging immediate affiliation. The dispatches caused great excitement in party circles. It was a measure of the revolutionary, antireformist temper of the French Socialists, of their disaffection with the war and the postwar settlement, and of their complete intoxication with the Bolsheviks' success, that Cachin and Frossard's messages could arouse such great enthusiasm. Large numbers in the party were willing to accept the twenty-one commandments handed down from on high. "With our party what it is," said one Socialist, "they would have the right to impose on us not twenty-one but twenty-one thousand conditions."[9] Many, of course, believed that they were not accepting subordination to Moscow but were returning to the pristine purity of prewar Marxian socialism, unsullied by class collaboration, wartime chauvinism, and reformism.

In the autumn of 1920 the Executive Committee of the Third International made clear that it had no interest in compromising on any of the conditions for affiliation. In an open letter to "all French Socialists and proletarians," it denounced in scathing terms the wartime and postwar policies of the French Socialist party and of the trade unions, and declared that it would be impossible to welcome the French Socialist party as a whole into the bosom of the Third International. The party must accept its "twenty-one conditions," reorganize itself along centralized lines, end the traditional separation of political and trade union organizations in France, purge its ranks of all reformists and semireformists—and accept the guidance of the Third International in all these tasks.[1]

The severity with which the Third International laid down its conditions did not daunt the affiliationists in France. The Bolsheviks had "made" the revolution that the French had talked about for years, ran the argument; they had every right to dictate the terms of enlistment in the combat army of revolution. Frossard and Cachin, after their return

---

[9] Cited by Alexandre Zévaès: *Le Socialisme en France depuis 1904* (Paris, 1923 ed.), p. 206.
[1] For the letter, Gérard Walter: *Histoire du parti communiste français* (Paris, 1948), pp. 25–30.

from Russia, where they had "seen" the Revolution, whipped up support in a series of enthusiastic popular rallies all through the autumn of 1920. "It is the most formidable event of the century. . . . They have seized the flame," said Frossard. "We are left with the ashes." "Instead of attacking the Revolution," Cachin told critics, "it would be preferable to study it and then, above all, to imitate it."[2] One after another the party's departmental federations registered support for affiliation without reservation.

Blum labored to stem the tide. There was no longer any question of unity in his mind. He undertook to defend the traditions of French socialism against what he considered to be a form of Marxism suited for backward Russia and not for the more advanced countries of Western Europe, certainly not for the French republic. He recognized that one could not join the Third International with reservations, that it was all or nothing. He had already warned against the messages of Cachin and Frossard, which, he said, were attempting to stampede the party into joining the International even without a decision by a party congress.[3] Now, in the autumn of 1920, in a series of articles in *L'Humanité*, Blum came forward as spokesman for a small group that was vigorously resisting affiliation and opposing the Bolshevization of the French party —a "Committee of Resistance." He condemned the Moscow conditions as "unacceptable . . . contrary to the entire theoretical and historical tradition of socialism." Hoping also to win back some of the ardent admirers of Bolshevism, he wrote: "A Socialist can feel in himself the greatest love for the Russian Revolution, be resolved to protect it by all means, without agreeing . . . that Russian revolutionary methods are applicable to French socialism."[4] It was a remarkable series of editorials, contrasting, in a profoundly prophetic way, the spirit and structure of democratic socialism and communism. His words, however, fell on deaf ears.

There were three resolutions before the congress that convened at Tours in December 1920 after the departmental federations had met and instructed their delegates. The resolution with the strongest support pledged to it, sponsored by Cachin and Frossard, favored immediate affiliation with the Third International and implied that all differences could easily be surmounted; the second, sponsored by Jean Longuet and

2 Cited by Walter: ibid., pp. 30–2.
3 *L'Humanité*, July 23, 1920. He was interim editor during Cachin's absence.
4 See his series of editorials: "À Moscou?" in *L'Humanité*, October 19, 24, 27, and November 19, 1920.

Paul Faure, equally favored affiliation but requested reservations and amendments that would prevent wholesale exclusions and purges, permit greater autonomy and democratic representation within the party, and safeguard the traditional separation of Socialist and trade union organizations in France. The third resolution, of which Blum was a sponsor (along with Sembat, Bracke, and Renaudel), repudiated the Moscow conditions and opposed affiliation; it could count on very little support either in advance of the congress or at it. Thus, the two strongest groups were not even disputing the question of affiliation but only whether it should be unconditional or conditional. The whole debate, Blum noted on the eve of the congress, had been "thrown out of focus."[5]

Blum was fully aware of the mood that had spread through the congress like a contagion. "We were right," Marcel Sembat would later say, "but it is a terrible thing to be right against youth."[6] Even those who might have been their allies, the Longuet-Faure group, were willing to entreat with the Third International as suppliants. Blum, at Tours, was like the fictional Faust he had created years before, combating "evil," conscious of the obstacles ahead before right could prevail but impelled to engage in the struggle. At the congress he had to plead to be heard above the din. Those speakers whose position ran counter to the majority were frequently heckled and interrupted. "I have a naturally weak voice," he told the congress when he rose to speak on the third day, December 27.[7] "Moreover, I am very tired, as all of you are, and it would be physically impossible for me to overcome by the strength of my voice and lungs this tumult and these violent interruptions." He spoke of the "disagreeable task" imposed on him by his group, to speak to an "assembly whose decision was already determined." His intervention could not change the outcome, yet he delivered one of the major speeches of the congress and one of the most memorable speeches of his career, in many ways a summary of his political creed. Like the articles he had written the month before, it was a devastating dissection of the differences between democratic socialism and communism.

The basis of his opposition to the Moscow theses was his own definition of "revolutionary socialism" and of a Socialist party, which

[5] *L'Humanité*, October 27, 1920.

[6] *La Victoire en déroute*, p. 136.

[7] For his speech, Tours congress, 1920, pp. 243–75; later published in pamphlet form, *Pour la vieille maison* (Paris, 1921, 1934).

contrasted sharply with that of Lenin and the Bolsheviks. In abandoning democratic socialism for the dictatorship of a central committee, the party would cast out its most cherished traditions of internal freedom and democratic control. He reiterated that he himself was no "reformist" or "revisionist" who believed that the simple accumulation of reforms would lead to a revolutionary transformation of society. He accepted the idea of revolution, even the idea of a temporary and provisional dictatorship, for it was understandable that in a revolution there would have to be the "suppression of all previous constitutional forms." But a revolution, to be meaningful, could come only at the proper stage of capitalist development and when the masses were properly prepared. A seizure of political power would be meaningful only if it were to permit the transformation of society itself.

The Leninist view, as he saw it, was to equate the seizure of political power with social revolution. The conditions for the revolutionary transformation of society, he pointed out, had not been realized in Russia either in economic development or in the education and organization of the masses. Disregarding the country's state of development, the Bolsheviks believed in insurrection in the Blanquist tradition, a revolutionary vanguard leading the masses. From this misconception, everything else flowed: "Moscow does not believe in the least," he said, "that the conditions for a total revolutionary transformation have been realized in Russia. It counts on the dictatorship of the proletariat to lead to a kind of forced maturation regardless of the country's previous state of economic evolution." The dictatorship of the proletariat was not, therefore, conceived of as a necessary, temporary expedient, but as one that would have to last indefinitely. "For the first time in all Socialist history," he said, "you conceive of terror not as a measure of last resort only . . . but as a means of government."

The gravest danger was that the Bolsheviks were seeking to impose on international socialism arguments derived from local and particular Russian conditions. The twenty-one conditions on the nature, organization, and conduct of the Communist parties were diametrically opposed to the principles of the Socialist and Social-Democratic parties that had long existed in France and other countries in Western Europe. On all points there was "a formal opposition and contradiction between what has hitherto been socialism and what will tomorrow be communism." Socialists had believed in a broadly based party that had a place for liberty of expression and tolerance of all nuances of opinion, in which divergent points of view were represented on the governing bodies;

they would have instead a narrowly based elite party organized on a hierarchical military basis with a secret central committee, all under the close supervision of the Executive Committee of the Communist International. "The most serious decisions of the party," he warned, "will be decided upon by men whom you do not know."

He objected also to the silence of the International on the question of national defense. As much as anyone, he held to the belief that only the establishment of international socialism could prevent future wars. Yet for him there were circumstances in which Socialists had to obey the call of national defense: "We affirm that even in a capitalist system international duty and national duty can coexist in a Socialist conscience." He told the congress (which heckled and hooted at him at this point) that the new party had nothing to substitute for the fusion of nationalism and internationalism in which he fervently believed.

In a moving peroration, he went beyond his repeated pleas for unity. His conscience dictated something more precious and even more fundamental than unity—the very survival of the socialist ideal.

> . . . the cry of conscience within us [is] strong enough to choke off the concern for unity that has always guided us. We are deeply convinced that while you pursue your adventures, someone must remain to guard the old house. . . . There is a more urgent question than whether socialism will be united or not. It is the question whether socialism will survive or not.[8]

His final plea was that they not separate as enemies. "Let us know how to abstain from words that wound and lacerate, actions that injure, everything that would be a fratricidal division. . . . In spite of all, let us remain brothers, brothers separated by a quarrel which is cruel but which is a family quarrel, and whom a common hearth will some day reunite." That appeal remained unheeded in the years to come, and the harshest Communist invective was reserved for Blum himself.

Blum spoke in a lost cause. The vote for affiliation was a foregone conclusion, and there was every indication that the Longuet-Faure center group would go along with the verdict. But before the vote was taken, Moscow itself intervened in an unexpected dénouement. A telegram, signed by Zinoviev and other members of the Executive Committee in Moscow, congratulated the congress on its deliberations but in no uncertain terms ordered the exclusion from the new party of the Longuet-Faure group, which had insisted on amendments to the

[8] Tours congress, 1920, p. 274.

twenty-one conditions. In addition, the German Communist leader Clara Zetkin made a dramatic personal appearance as a representative of the Third International to demand the purge of all "reformers." The vote for affiliation *without* conditions was 3,208; the Longuet-Faure resolution, affiliation *with* reservations, received 1,022 votes; Blum's group withdrew its resolution in advance, so weak was the support pledged to it.[9]

After "Zinoviev's pistol shot," the Longuet-Faure minority could not join the majority even if they wished to. They left the meeting hall along with Blum's group. Their exclusion providentially provided Blum with recruits to help "guard the old house" but made the problem of leadership of the new Socialist party even more difficult. The French Communist party, joining the Third International, took with it the majority of the party membership and even Jaurès's old newspaper, *L'Humanité*. "The congress of Tours," Sembat commented, "was the second assassination of Jaurès."[1] Jaurès's old party, to which Blum would now fall heir, had little left but its name and the dedication of a small band of followers.

[9] For Blum's resolution, ibid., pp. 586–91.
[1] *La Victoire en déroute*, p. 117.

III

PARTY LEADER:
Theory and Tactics
1921–1933

. . . the currents always present within the
party and within each Socialist.[1]

IN THE YEARS following the Communist secession of December
1920, Blum emerged as spokesman for the Socialist party on the
national scene. In those same years he sought to reconcile and
synthesize conflicting revolutionist and reformist currents within the
party. The challenge would have taxed all the resourcefulness and
harmonizing abilities of a Jaurès, for the unresolved contradiction in
the nature of the party inherited from the past was now intensified by
the emergence of communism as a powerful and dynamic rival. Although the S.F.I.O. was committed, as it had been since the prewar
years, to participation in the political and parliamentary life of the republic, the party would not renounce its Socialist mission and its dedication to Marxian principles of class struggle and proletarian revolution.
Sensitive to its own traditions and alarmed by the competition from the
Communists, it refused to accept the role of a mere democratic reform
party. The dilemma of the S.F.I.O. in the years after 1920 centered on
the extent to which it could accept full political responsibilities in the
parliamentary republic and at the same time honor its revolutionary
credo. Could it in good conscience enter into firm parliamentary cartels
with middle-class Radicals? Or accept cabinet posts in Radical-formed
ministries? It was Blum who employed his dialectical talents and conciliatory abilities to work out a compromise to the party's dilemma.
Like most compromises, it failed to satisfy everyone.

[1] Blum: *Le Populaire*, April 21, 1927.

The party faced an uphill fight in the 1920's. The schism of December 1920 had carried over to the Third International three fourths of the old S.F.I.O. membership (including some of its most ardent spirits), its treasury, and its newspaper. On the positive side, fifty-five of the sixty-eight Deputies elected in 1919, almost all of the Socialist mayors and municipal councillors, and most party leaders at the federation level remained faithful to the S.F.I.O. Otherwise, the party could count on few resources save the devotion and organizing abilities of those who had remained loyal. Thus it was remarkable that the Socialists rapidly and steadily regained their strength while the Communists, beset by factionalism, sectarianism, expulsion and withdrawals, lost their initial advantage. Within a year of the schism the S.F.I.O. was winning back members and electoral support. In 1921 the Communists could count on a membership of 131,000 and the Socialists 35,000; a dozen years later the proportion was almost exactly reversed; and in 1932 the Socialists received 1,964,000 votes and elected 131 Deputies in the Chamber whereas the Communists received 797,-000 votes and elected only 11 Deputies.[2]

Conscious of the revolutionary *élan* that had swept the French masses after the Bolshevik Revolution and had led to the Communist triumph at the congress of Tours in 1920, the S.F.I.O. embarked with determination on its own "hard" ideological line, asserting the true "revolutionary" nature of the party. At its very first meeting after Tours, a national council of the party reaffirmed its fidelity to traditional prewar orthodoxy, condemning such reformist practices as entering into parliamentary coalitions with other parties, participating in cabinets, or voting for the budgets of bourgeois governments. A resolution of February 1921 proclaimed: "In its goal, its ideal, its methods, the

[2] The most useful sources for this chapter and for many of the chapters that follow are the daily files of *Le Populaire* and the proceedings of the party congresses. For the vicissitudes of the French Socialist and Communist parties in the years 1921–33, including statistics on membership, voting strength, and parliamentary representation, see the general histories of French socialism by Lefranc, Ligou, Louis, Prélot, Zévaès, and (for the Communist party) Walter, all listed in the Bibliography. A number of specialized treatments are also listed there. François Goguel: *La Politique des partis sous la IIIe République* (Paris, 1958 ed.) is invaluable for French politics during this period: Ziebura: *Blum: Theorie und Praxis*, I, Chaps. 6–12, covers these years in great detail. I have myself treated some of the material in this chapter in different form in "Léon Blum and the French Socialists as a Government Party," *The Journal of Politics*, XV (1953), 517–43.

Socialist party, while seeking the fulfillment of immediate reforms demanded by the working class, is not a party of reform but a party of class struggle and revolution. . . . Neither Left blocs nor ministerialism, condemned both in theory and practice, will find in its ranks the slightest chance of success."[3] The party was, in effect, condemning the wartime collaboration in the sacred union cabinets which had produced widespread disenchantment and had made it possible for the Communist secessionists to attack the party as "class-collaborationist." The S.F.I.O. was bent on demonstrating that it merited the allegiance of all militant-minded proletarians and that the Communists were merely usurpers of the old Marxist heritage.

Paul Faure, who as secretary-general controlled the S.F.I.O. organizational machinery, took the lead in reorienting the party along the "hard," or "pure," revolutionary line. He resurrected the intransigent principles of his old master, Jules Guesde, the revolutionism of Édouard Vaillant, and the more revolutionary facets of the synthesis evolved by Jean Jaurès. Faure, along with Jean Longuet, it will be recalled, had led the ambivalent centrist group at the congress of Tours, which would have accepted affiliation with the Third International if only a greater degree of autonomy had been conceded. In the end, Moscow rejected the centrists, not the other way around. There had been little disagreement on the fundamentals of revolutionary doctrine or on the condemnation of "reformism."

Although the neo-Guesdist, anti-reformist line of Paul Faure was dominant in the party, there was also a strong current of reformist opinion, of which Pierre Renaudel, Albert Thomas, and Joseph Paul-Boncour were the chief exemplars. All had been closely identified with the wartime patriotism of the party and had remained firm in resisting the blandishments of the Third International. This current was powerful among the parliamentary Deputies, even if it was weakly represented on the party's executive committee (the *commission administrative permanente*), a body of some twenty to thirty members elected at each annual congress on a proportional basis to represent the different "tendencies" in the party. The reformists refused to apologize for the

SFIO not content

---

[3] *Parti socialiste, 19ᵉ congrès national*, 1921, Paris, *rapports*, p. 58. *Le Populaire*, November 27–December 26, 1929, reprinted all of the party's resolutions on tactics in a series of articles entitled "La Participation ministérielle: les textes socialistes depuis la guerre." A national council (*conseil national*) was smaller and could be convened more rapidly than a national congress; both consisted of delegates of the departmental federations with votes in proportion to the membership strength of the federations.

party's participation in the wartime cabinets and hoped, when the time was appropriate, to see the party resume the evolutionist, parliamentary direction of the pre-1914 years. Paul-Boncour, in particular, urged the party to integrate itself immediately into the political life of the nation, work closely with the middle-class Radicals, and make the broadest possible appeal to the middle classes of the country, both urban and rural.

The divergent trends within the party contributed to a crisis in leadership. Although Paul Faure was the administrative head of the party and in many ways, with his gifts as a speaker, writer, and organizer, largely responsible for the remarkable reconstruction of the S.F.I.O., his deep commitment to the anti-reformist line made it impossible for him to assume the mantle of party leadership. There was no one after Tours to step into the role played before 1914 by Jean Jaurès. A leader was needed who was uncompromised either by the reformist, national defense orientation of the party during the war or by too close an identification with the revolutionary wing that had all but gone over to the Communists.

Various logical candidates were thus eliminated. Like Paul Faure, Jean Longuet, an important party leader in the years before 1914 (and a son-in-law of Karl Marx), was too closely identified with the Leninist enthusiasm of the postwar period. On the other hand, Pierre Renaudel, Jaurès's successor as editor of *L'Humanité* in the war years and a man of unimpeachable integrity and ability, was an unreserved champion of the party's wartime patriotism. Another leader closely identified with the sacred union policy was Albert Thomas, who, many would agree, "undoubtedly best recalled the powerful personality of Jaurès"; he not only had been a cabinet minister during the war but soon became the first secretary-general of the International Labor Organization at Geneva, where he performed monumental services, though his energies and abilities were lost to the party. Two other prewar leaders and logical candidates for leadership, Jules Guesde (one of the giants of the prewar party but in declining health in his later years) and Marcel Sembat (Blum's wartime chief), both died in 1922. Joseph Paul-Boncour was too closely identified with parliamentary reformism and too widely suspected of ministerial ambitions to suit the rank and file.[4]

[4] On the candidates for leadership, Prélot: *L'Évolution politique*, pp. 232–7; the comparison of Albert Thomas with Jaurès is on p. 232; and see also Lefranc: *Mouvement Socialiste*, pp. 241–9. On the course the party might have taken under Thomas's leadership, B. W. Schaper: *Albert Thomas: trente ans de*

If Léon Blum possessed certain qualities in the early 1920's that suited him for the role of party leader, he had definite disadvantages as well. He was an intellectual, a man of letters, financially comfortable, respectably established in the bourgeois life of the republic, a brilliant career behind him as a jurist on the Conseil d'État, a successful private member of the bar, a Deputy in the Chamber, a Parisian, and a Jew. With his soft, high-pitched voice, he was scarcely a proletarian orator. His tall, slender appearance, the drooping mustaches, the rimless pince-nez, and his somewhat precious gestures made him an easy prey for cartoonists like Sennep. Dressed impeccably with gloves, gaiters, and an ever-present breast-pocket handkerchief—"the revolution in pearl-gray gloves," Léon Daudet once sarcastically called him[5]—he was hardly a figure to appeal to proletarians or to lead a revolutionary party. The party in the 1920's still had a heavily proletarian nucleus inherited from the prewar years; only gradually was its "new growth" drawn from the ranks of civil service workers, white-collar employees, teachers, and various other groups of the lower middle class.

Yet in some ways, in the circumstances of the 1920's, Blum was admirably suited to step into the vacant role. He was not associated with right-wing reformism, as Renaudel and Albert Thomas were. Nor, as we have seen, was he as tarnished by the party's wartime collaboration in the government; his service had been merely that of an administrative assistant to a Socialist minister. Above all, he was both politically and personally identified with Jaurès. The synthesis of reformism and revolutionism that Jaurès had evolved—and his martyrdom—made him a hero to all wings of the party (and to the Communists too). Everyone conceded that Blum had entered political life and accepted an active role in the party only because of the master's death. The very handicap of his bourgeois background also turned into an advantage. Blum had claim to special respect as one who was sacrificing a successful life of bourgeois comfort in order to serve socialism and the party. When Jean Longuet was later asked why a newcomer like Blum had risen to leadership, he replied simply: "Because Léon Blum stood out by virtue of his knowledge, his cultivation, and, above all, his intel-

---

réformisme social (Assen, 1959). Paul-Boncour's memoirs are invaluable for the frame of mind of French reformism in this period: *Entre deux guerres*, II: *Les Lendemains de la victoire* (Paris, 1945).

[5] *Au temps de Judas* (Paris, 1921), cited by Zévaès: "Léon Blum écrivain," *Les Nouvelles Littéraires*, June 6, 1936. The broad-brimmed black felt hat, familiar in bohemian circles, was his one sartorial concession to the Left, Paul Reynaud informs us: *Mémoires*, I: *Venu de ma montagne* (Paris, 1960), 141.

lectual honesty."[6] Blum also had a personal dignity and equanimity matched by few. He was always ready to forgive, to soothe ruffled feelings, to conciliate.

Better than anyone else, Blum could work at creating a compromise between the parliamentary reformism of Renaudel, Paul-Boncour, and Albert Thomas and the doctrinaire sectarianism of Paul Faure and the other neo-Guesdists on the party executive. Like Jaurès, he could work magic with words. If he lacked the fiery eloquence of the great tribune, he possessed the same ability to coin phrases and to draw up resolutions that would reconcile the irreconcilable; he could strike a consensus where none seemed possible; he could, like a mathematician or physicist, determine the "resultant" of opposing forces—his own figure of speech.[7] He could keep the party united by juggling political realities in one hand and the Socialist faith in the other. "If Jaurès was the soul of unity," a French scholar has said, "Blum was its brain."[8]

Blum's speeches were models of clarity and logic. He could build up the point of view of an opponent step by step; then, precisely when it became an imposing structure, proceed to demolish it. Clemenceau had sarcastically remarked of Jaurès in the years before 1914 that one could always recognize a speech by Jaurès because all the verbs were in the future tense.[9] In Blum's speeches the subordinate clauses all began with the word "but." He carried his audiences with him by his sympathetic insight into the position of his opponents and by the devastating counterlogic of his own syllogisms.

Moreover, in the hurly-burly of popular mass meetings of the 1920's, just as at Tours, he showed courage and skill in standing up to Communist heckling and even to threats of physical violence. Paul-Boncour has recalled vividly the hostile working-class audiences they both faced shortly after the Communist schism, the attacks that were directed especially against Blum, and Blum's success in winning over many of his listeners "solely by the superiority of his intelligence and the precision of his analysis."[1]

Blum made no conscious effort to assume the party leadership but gradually moved into the vacuum that existed. As we have seen, it was he, even before the Communist schism, who drafted and won approval

[6] Vichniac: interview with Longuet, *Blum*, p. 123.

[7] *Commentaires sur le programme d'action du parti socialiste*, p. 21.

[8] Prélot: *L'Évolution politique*, p. 248.

[9] Cited by Gordon Wright: *France in Modern Times* (Chicago, 1960), p. 334.

[1] *Entre deux guerres*, II, 68–72. The tribute is the more impressive because Paul-Boncour is critical of Blum in many ways.

for the party program of 1919. He consolidated his leadership by his intervention at Tours, his performances in the Chamber against the reactionary and chauvinistic *bloc national* majority, his role in party congresses from 1921 on, and his contributions on the international Socialist scene, where he served as one of the major spokesmen for the party beginning with the congress at Hamburg in 1923.[2]

No matter how preoccupied he was with practical politics as the years went by, Blum never abandoned the idealistic side of his socialism. He utilized his literary and humanistic talents, which had once found other outlets, in eloquent essays on the Socialist faith, even if he made no profound doctrinal contributions. There was a difference, he always believed, between a mission of "propaganda" and "an apostolate."[3] In one of his early brochures, *Pour être socialiste*, addressed to the younger generation, he rehearsed the old Socialist formulas in stately cadences:

> Men have worked, suffered, and thought on this earth for a long time now. Their efforts, accumulated over the centuries, have created little by little a universal morality and a common patrimony of feelings, which each of us carries within himself from birth . . . We are born with a sense of equality, with a sense of justice, with a sense of human solidarity. . . . From what is socialism born? From the revolt of all those feelings which are bruised by life, ignored by society. Socialism is born of the concern for human equality because the society in which we live is founded on privilege. It is born of the pity and anger that is aroused in every honest heart by the intolerable spectacles of poverty, unemployment, cold, hunger . . . it is born of the contrast, scandalous and heart-rending, between the luxury of some and the privation of others, between crushing toil and insolent idleness. It is not, as has been so many times charged, the product of envy, which is the lowest of human motives, but of justice and compassion, which are the noblest.[4]

The humanist—and the moralist—had not lost his touch. The strong sense of moral justice, not some inexorable dialectic of history, would turn men one day to the Socialist creed.

---

[2] See Maria Sokolova: *Les Congrès de l'internationale socialiste entre les deux guerres mondiales* (Paris, 1953), especially pp. 64–70; and Lefranc: *Mouvement socialiste*, pp. 259–61.

[3] *À l'échelle humaine, Oeuvre*, V, 462, 492.

[4] *Pour être socialiste* (Paris, 1919), pp. 3–4; cf. "L'Idéal socialiste," *La Revue de Paris*, May 1924, pp. 3–4, and speech of June 30, 1934, *La Jeunesse et le socialisme* (Paris, 1934).

The supreme vehicle for Blum's talents and one that contributed most to establishing his leadership in the party was the party's new daily newspaper, *Le Populaire*, which first made its appearance on April 8, 1921, edited jointly by Blum, Longuet, and Faure. In the beginning, the paper ran into serious financial problems; its subscriptions totaled far less than the 15,000 needed for survival. A loan from Belgian co-operatives and contributions from various individuals, including Blum, helped keep it alive. It limped along until June 1924, was forced to appear fortnightly from June 1924 to December 1925, and in 1926 had to suspend operations. It eventually reappeared on a stable basis on January 22, 1927, with Blum as its "political director."[5] Never rivaling the big dailies nor even other political newspapers in circulation, it grew, nevertheless, in volume of readers and public esteem. Unlike the British *Daily Herald*, it did not serve both the party and the labor unions; the French labor confederation, the Confédération Générale du Travail (C.G.T.), had its own press, *Le Peuple*. For a long time the party members regarded *Le Populaire* as an "extra" newspaper. "They bought it," a historian of the French press has written, "for the article by Léon Blum on the first page and for the announcements of group and section meetings on the last."[6] But it steadily extended its coverage. Blum wanted the paper to cover all facets of life and to provide features for all members of the family; it was to be "complete—neither over-serious nor frivolous."[7] Under his inspiration and with the aid of a number of able collaborators, it soon took on the form of a full modern newspaper and lost its character as merely a party organ. Among its most sensational articles was André Gide's exposé in 1927 of colonial exploitation in the Congo.[8]

Blum's own signed front-page articles, which appeared almost daily, covered not only party problems but all manner of domestic and international affairs. At times he pursued the same subject in a series of editorials for a week or longer; at other times he commented briefly on some one aspect of the previous day's developments. His editorials

[5] For the financial tribulations of *Le Populaire*, Ligou: *Socialisme*, pp. 281, 337–9; Vichniac: *Blum*, p. 142; Prélot: *L'Évolution politique*, p. 233; and also Blum's statements in *Le Populaire*, January 18, 1931, recalling the launching of the paper. In 1934 he remarked that he had contributed to *Le Populaire* a good part of his inheritance from his father's business; Toulouse party congress, May 1934, p. 78. Technically, the paper was known as *Le Populaire de Paris*.

[6] Raymond Manevy: *Histoire de la presse, 1914–1939* (Paris, 1945), p. 128.

[7] "Notre journal," *Le Populaire*, January 22, 1927.

[8] For Blum's comments on these articles, *Le Populaire*, July 5, 7, 11, 20, 25–27, 1927.

became a national institution in French journalism and were closely scanned by friend and foe alike to learn the party's probable line on some impending cabinet crisis or other problem of internal politics or on a diplomatic development. The editorials were always dignified, vigorous, and incisive, free from the invective found in political journalism of the Left and the Right. He insisted that Socialists attacked "the system, not men," and that the party "must guard against hatred."[9] So far as the party was concerned, he wanted the paper to be "a journal of education and a journal of combat."[1] As political editor of *Le Populaire*, Blum served as conscience and guide for the party and as its spokesman to the nation at large. It sealed his claim to moral and political leadership.

In Parliament, his concept of the proper role for the party was that of a "constructive opposition." He rejected the deliberate, systematic obstructionism of the Communists, the avowed resolve to do no more than carry the class struggle into the legislative halls.[2] On more than one occasion Raymond Poincaré paid tribute to Blum's qualities as an opponent and to the kind of "loyal opposition" that he embodied. Blum's ideal was the Leader of the Opposition, British-style. At the same time he saw no inconsistency between the constructive opposition of the party in Parliament and its revolutionary mission. It was "serving and preparing the revolution by demonstrating that Socialist theory and action could inspire the most useful and most just solutions for the problems of the day."[3]

Blum stressed the active legislative role of the party in advancing the cause of the workers. "Our mission is to throw ourselves with persistence and diligence into the tasks in Parliament, to defend . . . the rights and interests of the working class which are constantly threatened or under attack, to bar the way to all enterprises directed against it, to spare no effort to transform into positive legislation even the smallest token of justice and progress."[4] He always believed that the ultimate goal of the party must not interfere with the need to improve living conditions for the masses here and now.

The party energetically attempted to wrest reforms from the conservative Chamber elected in 1919 and to thwart reactionary measures.

[9] *Le Populaire*, January 22, 1927.
[1] Ibid.; see also *Le Populaire*, February 11, 1927.
[2] See his *Bolchevisme et socialisme* (Paris, 1927), esp. pp. 19–21.
[3] Ibid., p. 20.
[4] Blum, reporting for the parliamentary group: *20ᵉ congrès national*, Lille, February 1923, *rapports*, p. 66.

The parliamentary group practiced a highly developed technique of division of labor, the various members becoming specialists in different areas depending on their interests and their membership on the various parliamentary committees. Together with delegates of the party executive, they worked out their legislative proposals. Blum himself specialized in matters affecting the economy and international affairs, but, even more important, he coordinated the activities of the entire group. "Léon Blum watched over [the group] with touching concern and devotion," Paul-Boncour recalled, "lending his fine mind to the smallest details of procedure and method, giving all his time to the organization of the group; our work permitted us, even though small in number, to hold an honorable place in the Chamber and to speak up effectively in all of the important debates."[5] In vain the Socialists demanded a capital levy on fortunes accumulated during the war instead of the heavy consumer taxes being imposed. They proposed, also without success, the nationalization of the railroads and a number of constructive international arrangements to handle the thorny issue of German reparations.[6] In all the important debates Blum was in the forefront.

To formulate the political tactics that would best serve the party's combined parliamentary and revolutionary role was Blum's great challenge in the 1920's. In the political context of the legislature that sat from 1919 to 1924, the "blue horizon" Chamber with its strong conservative majority, the problem of parliamentary tactics was simple to resolve. Isolated and with only a small representation (68 initially in a Chamber of over 600, reduced to 55 after the Communist secession of 1920), the party could assume a role of opposition which suited its mood and temper and could satisfy the party rank and file as well. The parliamentary group actively opposed the conservative financial measures of the *bloc national* cabinets as well as their clerical tendencies, anti-Soviet orientation, and ultra-nationalist foreign policy toward Germany. In 1923, when Poincaré, against the advice of Great Britain and the United States, answered the German default on reparations by occupying the Ruhr, Blum took the lead in fighting against what he considered an affront to world democratic opinion and an unjustified

[5] *Entre deux guerres*, II, 39.

[6] Vincent Auriol: *Hier . . . demain* (Paris, 1945), I, 267–73; Ligou: *Socialisme*, pp. 345–50.

assault upon the Weimar Republic; he warned that German nationalism and fanaticism alone would profit. For his pains Rightist elements in the Chamber called him an "agent of the Boches" and hurled antisemitic taunts as well.[7]

In the first postwar election of 1919, as noted in the previous chapter, the Socialists, in their mood of revolutionary intransigence, insisted on running alone. In the second postwar election, in May 1924, the party decided to abandon its isolated position, despite the orthodox line it was continuing to follow, because the election system again favored party combinations and might have resulted in a new *bloc national* majority. The S.F.I.O. agreed to join with the other major party of the Left, the Radical Socialists, "bourgeois" party though it was, in presenting joint departmental lists throughout the country. It kept its "orthodox" conscience clear by stipulating that no post-election commitment was involved.

Even so, the decision was not easily made. Although the reformist group favored a common minimum program with the Radicals and the pledge, in the event of victory, of a firm parliamentary bloc and even a coalition government, a majority opposed such cooperation. Blum went along with Faure and Longuet in viewing the election alliance as simply a strategic expedient necessitated by the election law, "a bitter pill" that had to be swallowed.[8] Because the election coalition was generally honored and because there was widespread public reaction against the nationalist policies of the previous legislature, the result was a parliamentary victory for the Left combination, the *cartel des gauches*.

The party itself substantially increased its representation in the Chamber, from 55 to 104, Blum easily retaining his seat in the Seine department. Only a few years after the Communist schism had all but destroyed it, the S.F.I.O. had regained its prewar parliamentary strength and was now the second leading party in the Chamber and in the Left majority. Moreover, its membership had more than doubled. The victory of the Left cartel and the very strength of the party now posed new problems.

It was logical for Édouard Herriot, despite the Socialists' preelectoral resolutions, to count on Socialist support and to invite the party to enter the cabinet that he was forming. Shortly after the elec-

---

[7] *Chambre, Débats,* January 11, February 1, and December 14, 1923. The session of January 11, 1923, was the stormiest.

[8] *Le Populaire,* April 27, 1924. The decision to cooperate at the polls was reached at a special congress at Marseilles in January 1924.

tion, negotiations began. Herriot appealed personally to Blum for the "full cooperation" of his party. *"Mon cher Blum,"* he wrote on May 31 (the salutation itself thoroughly provoked the Right, which was already incensed by the prospect of the country's destinies in the hands of an anticlerical Radical and a Jewish Socialist), "the Socialists and Radicals have together campaigned against the coalition of high finance and slander. The evident will of the country is that this collaboration continue in the councils of government."[9] A delegation led by Blum, Paul-Boncour, Renaudel, Auriol, and Marius Moutet agreed to discuss portfolios with Herriot and the Radicals, but to no avail. Although Blum and the Socialists had the highest regard for Herriot, whose integrity, intellectual abilities, and republican sympathies were above question, the party was not ready to enter his cabinet. Instead of an outright refusal, the Socialist leaders raised many demands, insisting on a large number of portfolios, including the Finance Ministry for Vincent Auriol. (Camille Chautemps jested at the time that there might be only an undersecretaryship left for Herriot.) On the other hand, many of Herriot's Radical colleagues, far from eager to give a large share of the cabinet posts to the Socialists, wanted to grant them only token representation. "On both sides," Paul-Boncour recalled, "one offered what one knew would be refused."[1]

By a large majority, at the congress convened in June 1924, the party as a whole rejected the Radical overtures, fleeing from the offer of seats in the cabinet as from a threat of seduction. It pledged instead a policy of full parliamentary support for the new government. As a token of good faith, it even released its Deputies, at least for the coming legislature, from their traditional Socialist obligation to vote against the annual budget. In a letter to Herriot, Blum hailed the success of their joint election victory and voiced his hope that the popular enthusiasm aroused by the Left triumph would not be disappointed even if the offer of cabinet posts had to be rejected.[2] Herriot could do nothing but drop his invitation and hope for the parliamentary support of the Socialists.[3]

The refusal to join the cabinet was a symptom of the tensions within

---

[9] Cited by Michel Soulié: *La Vie politique d'Édouard Herriot* (Paris, 1962), p. 146.

[1] *Entre deux guerres,* II, 93.

[2] Herriot, *Jadis,* II, 135–6.

[3] Blum later commented that the Radicals had not insisted on their participation but there is no doubt that Herriot had opened the door wide; cf. Blum: *Radicalisme et socialisme* (Paris, 1927), pp. 4–6.

the party, reflecting the determination of Paul Faure and the neo-Guesdist majority to reaffirm the party's orthodoxy and to provide proof that the S.F.I.O. was not merely a party of reformists. Ironically, the French Socialists were the only ones busily whipping the dead horse of "ministerialism." All other Socialist parties in Europe had abandoned the old injunctions introduced at the beginning of the century in the wake of the Millerand affair; many were participating in cabinets formed by other parties or had formed cabinets of their own. The Second International, when reconstructed in 1923, had even ruled that its pre-1914 resolutions were no longer binding, and that only resolutions adopted since 1923 would apply. Each constituent party was free to decide the question of cabinet participation solely on grounds of practicality.[4]

Blum, who had never condemned ministerialism on doctrinal grounds in the years before 1914, acceded to the strong pressure within the party. "Rightly or wrongly," he wrote a few years later, summarizing the party's decision after the election of 1924, "we were convinced that . . . we would bring more real strength to the Radical ministry by supporting it from without, with the unanimity of our party, than by collaborating in the name of an uncertain and divided party."[5] Party considerations prevailed over the stabilization of the Left majority which Socialist participation in the cabinet might have provided. Many in the country who had voted for the *cartel* were disappointed at the Socialists' decision,[6] but in Blum's view the unity of the party would have been threatened by the premature adoption of an outright reformist position.

Following the line laid down at the congress of June 1924, Blum led the party in loyal support of the Herriot government. Despite the unwillingness of the Socialists to join the cabinet, there was a true *cartel* enthusiasm, the parties of the Left hoping to create the better postwar world that the conservative Chamber of 1919 had failed to bring about. The three leaders of the Left—Herriot, the *normalien*, Blum, the humanist-critic and jurist of the Conseil d'État, and Paul Painlevé, the distinguished mathematician who headed the Socialist Republicans—were widely portrayed as a triumvirate of intellectuals governing the country; the Third Republic had become a "republic of

---

[4] Prélot: *L'Évolution politique*, p. 238; Sokolova: *Les congrès de l'internationale socialiste*, p. 81.

[5] *Radicalisme et socialisme*, p. 7.

[6] See, e.g., Paul-Boncour: *Entre deux guerres*, II, 90–1.

professors." Herriot's pipe and portly figure, Blum's cigarette and tall, stooped silhouette, and Painlevé's notorious absentmindedness were the target of the cartoonists.

For a time the party's support was consistent and complete. At the very opening of the legislature Blum actively backed Herriot in forcing the resignation of Alexandre Millerand as President of the Republic for his partisan Rightist speeches during the election campaign. (Millerand had made a 180-degree turn in politics since his Socialist days.) The party also supported Herriot's anticlerical legislation. Above all, it lent enthusiastic backing to his stand on foreign affairs: his support for the League of Nations and his conciliatory German policy, which resulted in the signing of the Geneva protocol in 1924 and the Locarno treaty in 1925. The party approved also the preliminary plans for a general disarmament conference and the resumption of diplomatic relations with the U.S.S.R. The "Geneva policy," initiated by Herriot and continued by Aristide Briand, would continue to receive the endorsement of Blum and the Socialists for many years.[7]

The party supported Herriot also in his fight against the Bank of France and financial circles which refused to grant the government the loans it needed. On financial matters, however, disagreement manifested itself within the *cartel.* The Socialist program was considerably more advanced than that of the Radicals. Blum and Auriol continued to champion a special levy on capital and a forced consolidation of Treasury bonds in order to cope with the growing budgetary deficit and the declining franc. Herriot had named as Finance Minister the conservative-minded Étienne Clémentel, who had continued many of the policies of the *bloc national* and was adamantly opposed to the Socialist program. For months Herriot hesitated to override his Finance Minister even though Clémentel's orthodox policies were obviously not succeeding. On March 25, 1925, Blum privately wrote to Herriot urging him to act, to break with "all delays, vain hopes, half hopes, half measures." A levy on capital accumulations would "once and for all deliver the state, the Treasury, and the country itself from the embarrassment which oppresses it."[8] Herriot finally yielded and prepared to propose the capital levy and forced loan, but his Finance Minister dramatically resigned. On April 11, 1925, a conservative coalition in the Senate, attracting those Radicals opposed to the extraordinary

[7] Ibid., II, 113–14; Soulié: *Herriot,* pp. 148–51; Ligou: *Socialisme,* pp. 361–2.
[8] Cited by Soulié: *Herriot,* p. 230.

capital levy, brought down the cabinet.[9] The *cartel des gauches* never recovered. The episode revealed the deep divergency of views between the Socialists and the Radicals on financial matters and the ability of the Right to exploit those differences. The Socialists vented their wrath on the Senate and continued to press for their own financial program.[1]

In the next fifteen months, from April 1925 to July 1926, a succession of six Left and Left-Center cabinets attempted to cope with the falling franc but with little success. The support of the Socialists was no longer to be counted on. When economies involving a reduction in salaries for civil servants were proposed, the Socialists refused to back such measures and contributed to the downfall of the cabinets sponsoring them, even though they were headed by independent progressives like Painlevé and Briand. Herriot and the Radicals were deeply irritated. They charged the Socialists with nullifying the Left victory of 1924 and with aggravating government instability.[2]

The charge was soon echoed in the reformist wing of the party itself. Pierre Renaudel and many of the Socialist Deputies argued that only participation in the cabinet would insure the stability of governments faithful to the Left majority and frustrate the return of "reaction." Participation in the cabinet, they argued, was no more than the logical corollary to parliamentary support of a Left government. They urged acceptance of the invitations tendered by the Radicals and by progressives like Painlevé and Briand. The reformist wing, faithful to the *cartel* spirit, was strong, but the party stalwarts held fast, resolutely opposing participation as sheer reformism and harmful to the party's Socialist mission. The party would not "participate in power" but must await the revolutionary "conquest of power."[3]

Blum himself faced a dilemma. He wished to satisfy the revolutionary-minded rank and file, the *militants*, and to protect the party from the charge of class collaboration that would surely be hurled at it if it chose to join the cabinet. Yet at the same time he recognized the need

[9] Herriot: *Jadis*, II, 215–23.

[1] Blum's speech in the Chamber on the party's financial program, June 16, 1925, was also published in pamphlet form, *La Politique financière du parti socialiste* (Paris, 1925). For a detailed analysis of the party's economic and financial program in the 1920's, Ziebura: *Blum: Theorie und Praxis*, I, 246–87.

[2] Herriot: *Jadis*, II, 241, 248–9; Soulié: *Herriot*, pp. 256–7.

[3] The resolution to reject participation was adopted at the special congress in April 1925 by the narrow margin of 1,700 to 1,400; Ligou: *Socialisme*, p. 364.

to support the alliance with the Radicals and other progressives for the sake of strengthening the democratic forces in the country as a whole. At two special party congresses, in August 1925 and in January 1926, he helped evolve a compromise. He refused to go along with the Left elements in the party who opposed participation in principle, but, on the other hand, he gave many practical reasons why the party ought not to participate in cabinets.

The case in France was different from that of other countries, he argued. It was easier for Socialists to collaborate with Catholic parties in countries like Belgium and Germany, where doctrinal differences were distinct and alliances were formed obviously on grounds of expediency, than for the French Socialists to collaborate with the liberal and progressive Radical party, with whom they might be too readily confused by the electorate. He noted also the tremendous gap between theory and practice among the Radicals, who were loosely organized and heterogeneous in composition. Finally, he pointed out, the existence in France of an important Communist movement, which was eager to make capital of Socialist "reformism," also made the French case different from that of the Scandinavian countries, Britain, and Belgium, where Socialist parties had joined postwar cabinets. In essence Blum provided *tactical* arguments for the revolutionary-minded elements in the party who were opposed to participation on doctrinal grounds.[4] The special party congress held in the Salle Japy in Paris in August 1925, overriding the reformists, endorsed Blum's analysis. The party, without ruling out participation in principle, rejected participation in any cabinet that might be formed in the immediate future. For the time being at least, its "ministerial virginity" was to be preserved.[5]

Yet the issue was far from settled. At the end of 1925 Herriot once again invited the Socialists to join a cabinet he was attempting to form.[6] The executive committee of the party rejected the invitation by a narrow margin despite considerable pressure from the reformists. A second special congress had to be convened. Blum proceeded to the congress of January 1926 sensitive to the legitimate arguments of the reformist

[4] For Blum's analysis, see his speech to the special congress in the Salle Bellevilloise, January 10–11, 1926, reproduced along with Paul Faure's speech in pamphlet form: *Le Parti socialiste et la participation ministérielle* (Paris, 1926). Blum set forth many of these arguments also in "Les Textes français depuis la guerre," *Le Populaire*, November 27–December 26, 1929, and in two pamphlets based on articles that first appeared in *Le Populaire: Radicalisme et socialisme* (Paris, 1927) and *Bolchevisme et socialisme* (Paris, 1927).

[5] Ligou: *Socialisme*, p. 380; Prélot, *L'Évolution politique*, p. 342.

[6] Soulié: *Herriot*, pp. 255–8.

wing of the party, including most of his fellow Deputies, and still seeking a way out of the impasse. He personally did not believe that the party ought to wait for the revolution—the "conquest of power" —before it assumed office, yet he saw the disadvantages in joining Radical-directed cabinets. Eager as he was to integrate the party into the parliamentary republic, he recognized the need to keep faith with the rank-and-file membership and with the party's special "revolutionary" mission. His solution was a formula which he called the "exercise of power"—the willingness to form Socialist or Socialist-directed cabinets.[7]

Briefly, he first insisted that the party's true goal remained the "conquest of power," that is, an assumption of power with a mandate to transform the existing order. On the other hand, an "exercise of power" within the existing system was possible—and under certain circumstances even inevitable. The party could agree to form a cabinet on its own, either all-Socialist or a coalition; the essential condition was that the party exercise leadership and have the dominant voice. He still opposed participation in cabinets formed by other parties unless very special circumstances arose.

Blum conceded that there were dangers inherent in a Socialist "exercise of power," principally that the party's supporters and the working class as a whole might mistake it for the "conquest of power" and might consequently suffer deep disappointment if a revolutionary tranformation of society did not follow. Another danger lay in the acceptance of responsibility for a capitalist society and an economic system to which Socialists were resolutely opposed. "The exercise of power within capitalist institutions is and will always be a particularly painful and difficult experience for Socialist parties," he warned. Yet, despite all disadvantages, the exercise of power could not be avoided once Socialists accepted a parliamentary role. It was "the consequence of parliamentary action itself." Should the party possess a majority in Parliament (an unlikely prospect), or if it were the strongest group in the majority, or the strongest group in an opposition capable of rallying a majority, it would be "obliged" to accept the responsibilities of office. There would, of course, be compensations. The party would "accelerate the rhythm of reform" and demonstrate that it was not "a party like all others." A Socialist-directed government would act "with an energy, a resolution,

---

[7] In later years he described it as his most important contribution to Socialist doctrine; see his lecture, May 30, 1947, "Exercice et conquête du pouvoir," *La Revue Socialiste*, November 1947, pp. 383–95.

and a decisiveness that would not be halted by obstacles which other governments find insurmountable."

On the other hand, participation in a cabinet formed by another party involved all the disadvantages and dangers of the "exercise of power" without the same compensations. The party would be a minority in the cabinet, without control over policies, and yet its very presence would lead its supporters to expect vigorous Socialist action. Simple participation was thus ruled out. An exception, Blum noted, would be participation in a cabinet whose goal was "defensive," for in such cases the danger of confusing Socialist participation in the government with the revolutionary conquest of power would be minimal. He placed in that category the wartime sacred union cabinets. And in his 1926 speech he remarked prophetically: "We would tomorrow do the same if the dangers of fascism, or counter-revolution, suddenly became alarming."

Despite his willingness to accept the responsibilities of office, he took pains to emphasize that he was not a legalist or reformist where the party's revolutionary goal was concerned. The conquest of power under modern conditions need not necessarily involve bloody insurrection or street fighting, yet in a country like France, where all regimes since 1789 had been created by revolutionary acts, he recognized that a profound transformation could well be accompanied by extralegal measures. In a revolutionary situation, there might admittedly be need for a brief period of dictatorship—a "suspension of legality" (*vacances de légalité*). But that had nothing to do with the Socialist exercise of power, the willingness to form and head a cabinet under the existing system. Here he barred anything but complete legality:

> Although I am not a legalist insofar as the conquest of power is concerned, I declare categorically that I am insofar as the exercise of power is concerned. I believe that if, as a result of the operation of parliamentary practices, we were called upon to exercise power within the framework of existing institutions and within the framework of the present constitution, we would have to exercise it legally, loyally, without committing that kind of swindle (*cette espèce d'escroquerie*) that would consist in profiting from our presence within the government to transform the exercise of power into the conquest of power.[8]

[8] Speech at 1926 congress, *Participation ministérielle*, p. 5.

Blum was straining to satisfy both the revolutionists and the reformists within the party. Without abandoning the revolutionary credo of the party, he was at the same time reassuring the country at large that he and his party could be trusted in office when the proper moment presented itself.

Blum stressed that it was neither cowardice nor fear of assuming responsibility that restrained the Socialists from taking seats in cabinets formed by other parties. It was rather the delicacy of the party's double task: its obligations to serve from day to day as a democratic party within the parliamentary republic and its revolutionary mission to create a future socialist society. "The party in everyday politics, in parliamentary politics, is often forced to walk a tightrope."[9]

Blum's subtle formula satisfied neither the revolutionist wing nor Pierre Renaudel and the moderates. Paul Faure frankly admitted that he still believed in the "old-fashioned" doctrine that the party should abstain from office in all forms until the revolutionary conquest of power, yet he accepted Blum's compromise.[1] Renaudel and the moderates, on the other hand, regarded Blum's formula as entirely irrelevant under the circumstances, since no one was going to ask the Socialists to "form" or "direct" a cabinet; they suspected that it was simply an artful means of keeping the party from office. From their point of view, there seemed to be no logical grounds for accepting the "exercise of power" and rejecting participation in a cabinet formed by another party. Against their better judgment, however, they grudgingly accepted Blum's proposal as a compromise and as a means of preserving unity. The resolution with which Blum won over the special congress held in January 1926 in the Salle Bellevilloise proclaimed the party's willingness to *form* a government but not to participate in a cabinet formed by any other party.[2] Given the division between the militant-minded, orthodox neo-Guesdists, who controlled the machinery of the party, and the reformist wing, strong in the parliamentary group, Blum's formula was an ingenious compromise. Despite the impatience of the reformists, he was moving the party from its neo-Guesdist orientation, but only as quickly as he believed it possible without alienating the more militant-minded membership.

[9] Ibid., p. 23.
[1] Faure: speech at 1926 congress, *Participation ministérielle*, p. 31.
[2] *23e congrès national* (Paris, 1926), *rapports*, pp. 30–1, and "Les Textes socialistes depuis la guerre," *Le Populaire*, December 8, 1929.

For ten years the resolution of 1926 remained the law of the S.F.I.O. All invitations to join cabinets formed by other parties were rejected. But the proclamation of the party's willingness to form a cabinet on its own remained purely academic. The Socialists would not take cabinet office until the Popular Front election victory of May 1936, when, as the leading party of the majority in the Chamber, it could fulfill Blum's formula and attempt an "exercise of power" by forming a coalition cabinet on its own. That episode must await another chapter.

The third postwar general election in the spring of 1928 resulted in the return of a conservative majority in the Chamber. Despite some Socialist gains, the small-district system employed in this election (in contrast to the departmental lists and modified proportional representation used in 1919 and 1924) proved disastrous for Blum, who ran in Paris for the seat once held by Édouard Vaillant. In the second section of the 20th *arrondissement*, the Communists could muster greater strength than the Socialists; moreover, Jacques Duclos, under a prison sentence for political activities, won sympathy as a victim of capitalist injustice. Blum refused to heed the pleas of friends that he run elsewhere. On the first ballot no candidate received a majority, but Duclos was in the lead. On the second runoff ballot Blum fell victim to a combination of votes from all camps which gave victory to Duclos. The Socialists charged that reactionary elements were out to defeat Blum at all costs and, knowing that the total Communist representation would be small, had agreed to elect a Communist in preference to the leader of the Socialist party.[3] Yet the result was more indicative of the persistent strength of the Communists in Paris than of anything else. Blum did not have to remain on the sidelines very long, however. The following year, in May 1929, when a vacancy occurred at Narbonne, the logical candidate, Eugène Montel, the Socialist secretary of the Aude federation, stepped down in his favor. Blum won the by-election and returned to the Chamber amidst general congratulations, including those of Poincaré, against whose financial experiment from 1926 to 1928 Blum had conducted a moderate but never obstructionist campaign of opposition. It was symptomatic of the waning strength of the Socialists in Paris and in the industrial areas of France that

[3] For Blum's comments on the 1928 elections and his defeat, *Le Populaire*, March 23, April 30, and May 6, 10, 1928. For the voting statistics on his defeat, Lefranc: *Mouvement socialiste*, p. 276.

their party leader would be returned henceforth from a rural con-
stituency; that it should be someone as urbane as Blum heightened the
paradox.

The question of Socialist representation in the cabinet arose anew
after Poincaré's retirement in July 1929 and the opening of a new
period of cabinet instability. The latent conflict within the party between the Deputies and the party stalwarts grew sharper. The rank
and file of the party viewed with deep mistrust the Socialist representatives in Parliament, convinced that the Deputies lost their doctrinal
fervor and party loyalty once they entered Parliament. They suspected
them of seeking only the advancement of their own political careers
and of being attracted by cabinet portfolios.

Even if the suspicions of the party rank and file were exaggerated,
it remained a fact that the Deputies were a different breed. They were
often elected by votes which were only in part Socialist, their support
coming from a heterogeneous electorate which voted now Radical, now
Socialist, and was more interested in a liberal reform program than
in Marxism. Closer to the Radical-minded, middle-class voters and to
their fellow Radical Deputies in Parliament, they were more preoccupied
with day-to-day compromises and working agreements than with the
mystique of ultimate revolution. Some, of course, were intensely ambitious personally. Moreover, the Deputies received strong electoral
support in areas of the country where the party membership itself was
relatively weak. The Socialist vote was strong in the less industrial,
less "dynamic" areas; the membership was stronger in the more proletarian areas. "The center of gravity of the mass of Socialist voters,"
the French scholar François Goguel has well observed, "was geo-
graphically and psychologically clearly distinct from that of the mass
of party *militants*."[4] In view of these differences, the Deputies resented
the fact that, although they represented some two million voters, they
were under the control of a party apparatus that represented no more
than 130,000 party members. (The proportion of Socialist party members to Socialist voters, one to fifteen, was far smaller in France than
in Belgium, the Scandinavian countries, Austria, and Weimar Germany, where the party membership and the party votes almost coincided.)[5]

[4] Goguel: *La Politique des partis*, p. 469, and discussion, pp. 469–70; see also
Prélot: *L'Évolution politique*, pp. 275–8, and Ziebura: *Blum: Theorie und Praxis*,
I, 214–45.
[5] Prélot: *L'Évolution politique*, p. 276.

In the conflict between the reformist Deputies and the orthodox rank and file, Blum, as we have seen, had attempted to steer a middle course. On some questions he sided with the *militants*, insisting on the distinct, autonomous nature of the party, opposing participation in cabinets formed by other parties, and favoring parliamentary action and the winning of labor reforms not as ends in themselves but as a means of strengthening the working class for the eventual revolution. Yet, as the president of the Socialist parliamentary group, no one was more attuned to the restlessness of the reformists within the party than Blum. Sincerely concerned with the political responsibilities of the party on the national scene, he was sensitive to the problems that faced the governments of the day and to the need for stable cabinets. Yet his loyalty to his Socialist ideal and to the party ran deep, and he recognized, as well, his own special role as political director of *Le Populaire*, the party organ. With his usual optimism, he believed that a compromise was possible. He hoped to reconcile the conflict between the parliamentary group and the rank and file, to demonstrate that the party's Deputies could, while fulfilling their political responsibilities in Parliament, remain faithful to their Socialist traditions and commitments. That he could not himself be charged with crass political ambition lent moral strength to his position.

In October 1929 the question of participation in the cabinet came to the fore. The Radical leader, Edouard Daladier, who had a reputation for favoring close cooperation with the Socialists, offered the party an equal number of seats in a government he was attempting to form. His invitation precipitated open conflict in the party. A majority of the parliamentary Socialist group voted to give a favorable reception to Daladier's proposal.

To Blum's despair, he found himself in the minority in the parliamentary group. He held fast in opposing participation in the cabinet even under the generous terms offered by Daladier—a "sharing of power." "There is something that one does not share," he wrote in *Le Populaire*, "and that is leadership."[6] He repeated his previous warnings about the disadvantages of participation in cabinets formed by other parties and once again urged delay until an exercise of power was possible. Meanwhile the executive committee of the party and a hastily convened national council, both dominated by Paul Faure and the rank-and-file *militants*, overruled the Deputies. But the vote in the national council was extremely close, 1,590 to 1,461, and the issue had

[6] "Exercise et partage du pouvoir," *Le Populaire*, December 14, 1929.

to be thrashed out further at a special party congress in January 1930.[7]

The participationists were ably led at the congress in January 1930 by Renaudel and Marcel Déat. Déat, a gifted *normalien* and professor of sociology, restless and eager to "modernize" the party's doctrine and tactics, did his best at the congress to demolish Blum's position, insisting that the difference between Blum's exercise of power and participation in cabinets was a difference of degree, not of kind. If you accept the whole, he inquired, why not the part? He dismissed Blum's proposed constitutional exercise of power as no more than a pledge to manage current business for the bourgeoisie. They who were theoretically on the Right in the party, he pointed out, did not hesitate to proclaim their determination to make political office a prelude to the establishment of socialism.

Despite Déat's impressive speech, Blum's point of view, supported by Paul Faure, carried the congress. The Center and the Left prevailed by a vote of 2,066 to 1,057. Reiterating the stand of 1926, the party announced its readiness to take office either alone or in a Socialist-directed coalition so that it would be assured of "the preponderant voice in arriving at solutions of decisiveness, energy, and will." The only concession made to the participationists was a clause stating that under "exceptional circumstances" the party, in the form of a national council, might vote an exception to the general rule and authorize participation.[8]

Thus, if the cabinets for the remainder of the 1928–32 legislature —that is, from 1930 to 1932—were conservative-oriented, that situation, in part, was of the Socialists' own making. The unwillingness of the party in 1929 and 1930 to accept the invitation of the Radicals to help form cabinets made it impossible to revive the *cartel* of the Left. Blum himself had chosen to conciliate the *militants* within the party and to oppose the participation increasingly demanded by his fellow Deputies.

The months following the fourth postwar general election of May 1932 brought the nagging conflict between the Deputies and the party leadership, and the dreary debate over cabinet participation, into its

[7] Ligou: *Socialisme*, pp. 380–1.

[8] For speeches at the 1930 congress, resolutions, and Blum's comments, *Le Populaire*, January 25–28, 1930; cf. Prélot: *L'Évolution politique*, pp. 251–3, and Ligou: *Socialisme*, pp. 381–2.

sharpest focus. As the world economic depression began belatedly to reach France, the country reacted in the election against the Right-oriented governments of the preceding legislature. In the new Chamber there was a potential Left majority of some strength. The Radicals, the big winners in the Chamber, were returned with 160 seats; the Socialist representation rose from 107 to 131, Blum himself winning an easy victory in Narbonne.

Unlike the campaign of 1924, there was no pre-electoral coalition between the Radicals and the Socialists. The Radicals, increasingly concerned over Socialist gains in the rural constituencies, campaigned on the first ballot against the Socialists as well as against the parties of the Center and Right. Nor did Herriot this time look to any close co-operation with the Socialists after the election; he even rejected in advance the possibility of Socialist participation in the cabinet. Yet there was a growing sentiment in both parties that the Radicals could form stable progressive governments only with the support of the Socialists and that the *cartel* needed to be revived and strengthened. In view of the new problems that had arisen—the economic depression, the growing strength of Nazism in Germany, popular dissatisfaction with the previous legislature—the Socialists themselves raised the question of participation.

Blum himself explained that exceptional circumstances—"the present state of France and Europe"—justified participation in the cabinet. But participation had to be on the party's terms. Taking the initiative, the S.F.I.O. announced its willingness to participate in a Radical government under Herriot if he would agree to a nine-point reform program drawn up by Blum and Auriol which included extensive nationalization and social insurance measures. From the hall in which the Socialist congress of June 1932 was held, the Salle Huyghens, the program came to be known as the *"cahier de Huyghens."*[9] (The Radicals would later say that the program, named for the Dutch astronomer, never did have its feet on the ground.) The new policy was a compromise designed to satisfy both the participationists and the anti-participationists in the party and, at the same time, to demonstrate the party's willingness to cooperate with the Radicals.

There is no doubt, however, that Blum made it difficult, if not impossible, for the Radicals to accept the party's proposition, for it

[9] See Blum's editorial following the May 1932 elections, "Les Conditions minima," *Le Populaire*, May 16, 1932; his speech at the party congress and the resolution adopted, *Le Populaire*, May 31 and June 1, 1932.

was an advanced program, close to that demanded by the Left-wing Socialists, and it was disingenuous of Blum to argue that it contained nothing not in the election program of the Radicals either past or present. Given the deteriorating financial situation of the country and Herriot's own earlier unhappy experience in coping with finances, the Radical leader could not have been expected to view the program with much sympathy. In a long, detailed response, Herriot rejected the proposal.[1] The short-lived negotiations came to an end. Herriot formed an all-Radical government and hoped for Socialist support in Parliament.

The party supported the Herriot government but only for a few months. When it deserted the government in July 1932 on its financial and military program, Herriot's political position became precarious. And in December 1932, Herriot, in insisting on payment of the war-debt installment due the United States, ran afoul of heavy opposition from all sides, including Blum and the Socialists, and fell from office. With a note of bitterness, Herriot remarked on his special "chagrin" in finding Blum aligned against him in a matter involving "moral as well as political principles."[2] Blum, on the other hand, insisted that moral responsibility must not be misplaced; it was his opinion that the American emphasis on the contractual obligation had distorted the moral spirit behind the loan. His principal public argument was that payment of the inter-Allied war debts would incite the French Right to reopen the question of German reparations. Privately, however, he told Paul Reynaud that he understood the justice in Herriot's position.[3] There is little doubt that the episode hurt Blum deeply. He left it to Auriol to present the party's statement of opposition in the Chamber, although he defended the refusal to pay in *Le Populaire* a few days later and in a special article written for *The New York Times*.[4]

The Socialists contributed not only to the fall of the Herriot government but also to that of its successor six weeks later, the Paul-Boncour government, when it proposed financial economies affecting government workers. It was "a decision," Blum said, "not taken with a

---

[1] Herriot: *Jadis*, II, 301; Herriot reproduces the Socialist party letter, his reply, and other documents on pp. 297–305. For Blum's reactions, *Le Populaire*, June 5–12, 1932, and *Les Radicaux et nous, 1932–1934* (Paris, 1934), pp. 9–17, 19–23.

[2] *Jadis*, II, 347; Soulié: *Herriot*, pp. 413–15; and cf. Chastenet: *Histoire*, V: *Les Années d'illusions, 1918–1931* (Paris, 1960), 44.

[3] Reynaud: *Mémoires*, I, 347–8.

[4] See his editorials in *Le Populaire*, December 15, 22, 1932; and article, *The New York Times*, December 17, 1932.

light heart."[5] The S.F.I.O. seemed again to be contributing to the fall of Left governments and paving the way for the return of governments of the Right. Renaudel and the reformist wing of the party were increasingly impatient. After Paul-Boncour's fall, at the end of January 1933, Daladier once again offered the Socialists a "share" in the cabinet he was forming. After heated discussion in the parliamentary group, in which Blum argued against acceptance except on the basis of the Huyghens reform program, the group voted to accept Daladier's invitation if Daladier promised to respect at least the spirit behind the Huyghens program. Daladier would make no such promises. On the very day that Adolf Hitler became Chancellor in Germany, the Socialists were rejecting Daladier's invitation to join his cabinet. Blum refused to concede that the terms of participation were unrealistic and insisted that the party had never refused to cooperate with a government willing to accept a program of democratic reform.[6] His inflexible position, and that of Paul Faure and the party executive, were beginning to provoke the Renaudel wing to an extreme step.

In 1933 the debate within the party went far beyond the question of Socialist relationships with the Radicals and reflected the growing crisis in France, Europe, and the world. The unrest within the party was tied to the world-wide economic depression, the emergence of Hitler in Germany, and the growing restiveness at home in the face of parliamentary weakness and the instability of cabinets. The same ferment had already sent millions flocking to the banner of the Nazis in search of new slogans and new goals. Blum was conscious of the mood. "More and more," he wrote at the end of 1932, "looking at the world, one has the impression of an audience which is somewhat bored, somewhat disappointed, somewhat impatient, waiting restlessly for the end of one act and at the same time listening to the stage hands behind the scenes arranging the scenery for the act that is to follow."[7] But neither he nor anyone else was prepared for the kind of drama that did unfold.

So far as the conflict within the party was concerned, Blum was still torn in many directions. Although he was president of the parlia-

---

[5] *Le Populaire*, January 28, 1933. Paul-Boncour had left the Socialist party in 1931, despite Blum's pleas, when the party congress that year confirmed its refusal to support military budgets; see *Entre deux guerres*, II, 265–9.

[6] *Le Populaire*, January 30–February 1, 1933; and Blum: *Les Radicaux et nous*, pp. 7–9.

[7] Speech, December 9, 1932, reproduced as *Le Socialisme devant la crise* (Paris, 1933), p. 36.

mentary group of Deputies and responsible to his colleagues in Parliament, he was also political director of *Le Populaire* and responsible to the party *militants* as a whole. He saw the validity of Renaudel's strictures that the party was helping to weaken the parliamentary republic by its reluctance to join with the Radicals, but he would not surrender the idea of the revolutionary nature of the party. Although conscious of the menace of Hitler, he refused to accept the view that the advent of Nazism made it necessary for the party to abandon its traditional antimilitarism. In the crisis that developed in 1933, Blum did not come forward to exercise strong leadership in moving the party in new directions but strove to preserve party unity. His special position in the party, he believed, required him to assume that mission. Conceiving his role as that of "arbiter, referee, and builder of syntheses," he sought, as he had been doing since the 1920's, to bridge the gap between the reformist and revolutionist elements and between the parliamentary group and the rank and file.[8]

By the early 1930's the party was divided into three wings. A Left wing of "pure" revolutionists, strong in the Seine federation, attacked all reformist tendencies within the party and insisted that salvation for the proletariat against the rising threat of fascism and war lay in organization, direct action, the general strike, and revolution. It pointed to the tragic example of the reformist German and Austrian Social Democrats, who were impotent in the face of the fascist onslaught. Denying the efficacy of parliamentary action, the Left wing opposed alliances with the bourgeois Radical party and, a fortiori, participation in bourgeois cabinets formed by Radicals. Some in this group, like Jean Zyromski, came to favor close cooperation with the Communists; others, like Marceau Pivert, were Bolshevik in spirit but anti-Stalinist and pro-Trotskyite.[9]

The large Center group, dominated by Faure (and with which Blum, insofar as he permitted himself to be associated with any group, identified himself), accepted the parliamentary role of the S.F.I.O.

---

[8] Speech at Narbonne, *Le Populaire*, June 11, 1933.

[9] On the state of the party in 1933 and the crisis that followed, John T. Marcus: *French Socialism in the Crisis Years, 1933–1936* (New York, 1958), pp. 3–45; Lefranc: *Mouvement socialiste*, pp. 283–301; Ligou: *Socialisme*, pp. 383–90; and Prélot: *L'Évolution politique*, pp. 274–89. Ligou notes that when Leon Trotsky urged his followers in 1934 to work within the S.F.I.O., they joined the Pivertistes. On the relationship of Trotsky and the Left Revolutionary wing of the French Socialists in the 1920's and 1930's, see the revealing memoirs of Daniel Guérin: *Front Populaire: révolution manquée* (Paris, 1963).

but insisted that its activities as a parliamentary party must not obscure its commitment to a revolutionary goal. As with the Left wing, the developments in Germany served to reinforce its antagonism to reformism and to promote an emphasis on a "hard" Marxian line. Strong among the party membership and in control of the party machinery, the Center group, like the Left, watched jealously lest the Socialist Deputies in Parliament seek ministerial portfolios or coalitions with the bourgeois Radicals, or forget any of their traditional obligations. Championing disarmament and internationalism, it exercised special vigilance lest the Deputies vote for national defense credits or support rearmament. The depression, too, reinforced the confidence of the Center and the Left in the Marxian analysis of the "contradictions of capitalism."[1]

The Right wing of the party, with which a majority of the party's parliamentary representatives identified themselves, scorned orthodox Marxism as outdated. There were really two groups in the Right wing. Pierre Renaudel had long been urging the party to work closely with the Radicals and even to participate in coalition cabinets; the alternative, to his mind, was continued instability and an invitation to reaction. When Hitler came to power, Renaudel insisted that close cooperation with the Radicals had become more imperative. He and many of his colleagues in Parliament were anxious to repudiate the old ritual of voting against the budget; because of the Nazi threat, moreover, they opposed the reduction of national defense expenditures. Differing from Renaudel but associated with him in opposing the official party line were the self-styled "neo-Socialists," led by Déat and Adrien Marquet, who modeled themselves in good measure on the Belgian Socialist Henri de Man; they demanded a complete revamping of Socialist theory and action in the face of the depression and the spread of rival ideologies. Invoking some of the spirit and even the phrases of fascism, they advocated rejuvenating socialism with a national and authoritarian spirit so that, like fascism, it too could rally the masses, who were eager for leadership and authority. Like Renaudel, they denounced the inertia of the official party and its "revolutionary verbalism," and favored cooperation with the Radicals and support for national defense.

In four successive crises—in February, April, May, and October 1933—the conflict between the Renaudel group and the party apparatus mounted to a climax. In February a majority of the Deputies, following Renaudel, voted for the Daladier government's budget and

[1] See Blum: *Le Socialisme devant la crise* (Paris, 1933).

the military credits it included, even though the vote violated the party statutes and traditions, and was not permissible without special authorization from the party's governing organs. Blum found himself in a minority in the parliamentary group. Some in the minority rebelliously refused to honor the ancient rule of collective discipline which required the party to cast a unanimous vote in the Chamber once a majority decision had been reached; they insisted that the vote for the budget and for national defense credits so egregiously violated the traditions and statutes of the party that they could not go along with it. Blum respected their motives but declined to carry the party dissension into the Chamber itself; he would not "diminish the public prestige of the [parliamentary] group" and he personally refused to break the rule on collective discipline.[2] On the other hand, his position as president of the parliamentary group was increasingly embarrassing. At the end of February he and Vincent Auriol regretfully submitted their resignations as president and secretary.[3]

The Left and Center groups in the party sharply condemned Renaudel and his supporters. At the party congresses in April and July, tempers flared. Speaking for the Left, J.-B. Séverac insisted that the party could not "remain in tow" behind the Radicals, confine themselves to supporting bourgeois cabinets, and vote war appropriations. Faure demanded a showdown. "It is time to choose between those who have been faithful to the law of the party and the decisions of the rank and file, and those who have not." It was the "mission" of the party's Deputies in Parliament, he added, to express and defend the will of the party. He told the reformist group that because of them the Radical government was so sure of Socialist support that it did not have to legislate reforms. "You are reformists without reforms," he charged. "And you," came the reply, "are revolutionists without revolution."[4]

Blum entered the debate on the side of Faure and the party leadership. He favored supporting progressive governments and doing everything possible to avoid instability in Parliament. "Let us avoid the massacre game that will end in discrediting parliamentary institutions," he pleaded. While he rejected "systematic opposition of the Bolshevik type," he reiterated the party's distinctive revolutionary mission. It

[2] Blum: "L'Unité de vote," *Le Populaire*, June 11, 1933.

[3] Letter of February 28, 1933, *Le Populaire*, March 2, 1933.

[4] For the congresses at Avignon and Paris, *Le Populaire*, April 17 and July 16–17, 1933. For a statement by Paul Faure of his position, *Le Populaire*, June 2, 1933. The clash referred to occurred at the Avignon congress; *Le Populaire*, July 16–17, 1933.

must not identify too closely with the Radicals by forming Left blocs or by joining their cabinets. "We are not the marching wing of one great democratic party nor the vanguard of a single party of reform," he reminded the delegates at the congress in April, "but a fighting organization distinct from all others." It was what most of the party wished to hear. He described the Socialist parliamentary group as "the political emanation" of a revolutionary party. The Deputies had to vote against military credits regardless of the government proposing them. Such a vote represented "a traditional and symbolic act of revolutionary affirmation."[5]

On the question of military credits, his defense of orthodoxy was more than a gesture of solidarity with the party faithful. Here his orthodoxy fused with his own deep-seated antimilitarism and internationalism. He was, to be sure, imbued with a patriotism which marked him off from the more extreme *militants* and which he never abjured. "Never will I recognize," he told the party congress in July 1933, "that the concept of national defense is inconceivable in a capitalist regime."[6] But his own formulas for peace were "peace and disarmament" (*la paix désarmée*) and "security through arbitration and disarmament." Believing in "the virtue of example," he saw no paradox in disarming even in a dangerous world.[7] Moreover, he insisted that the Versailles powers had had a legal and moral obligation to work toward disarmament ever since the peace settlement. Before and after the Disarmament Conference opened in February 1932, he maintained that the only way to prevent the rearming of Germany was for the former victors to accept progressive arms reduction; thus would one best satisfy the argument of the German delegates at the conference, "justified in principle," that Germany was entitled to equality of treatment.[8]

Even after Hitler came to power in January 1933, Blum continued

[5] Speech at Avignon congress, *Le Populaire*, April 17, 1933; also speech at Narbonne, *Le Populaire*, June 11, 1933.

[6] Speech at Paris congress, *Le Populaire*, July 16–17, 1933.

[7] See, e.g., his speech at special party congress in Paris, January 30–31, 1932, reprinted in pamphlet form as *Notre plate-forme* (Paris, 1932), p. 14; see also *Le Populaire*, January 13, 1931. For a sampling of his views on disarmament, see his editorials in *Le Populaire* in September and October 1927, March 1928, May 1930, and February 1931; about a dozen of the 1930–31 editorials were gathered together in book form as *Les problèmes de la paix* (Paris, 1931), English translation by A. Werth (London, 1932). On his differences with Herriot on the subject, Soulié: *Herriot*, pp. 376–91.

[8] *Le Populaire*, September 8, 1932; *Chambre, Débats*, October 19, 1932.

to preach disarmament and arms reduction; the Nazi triumph signified only that France must work even harder, with or without Germany, for disarmament agreements. If Germany refused to accept such agreements, then she would be branded by "public opinion." Appalled though he was by the Nazi atrocities, his principal concern was not the threat of German nationalism as such, but the fear that it would serve to reinforce French militarism and reaction and a general war atmosphere. Against Renaudel's argument that in view of the "spread of fascism in Europe" they could no longer afford the luxury of voting against military credits, he maintained that a reversal of the party's traditional position would lead to misinterpretation. "You will not be able to prevent European public opinion from attaching to this reversal a dangerous significance. . . . We would be aggravating the war psychosis."[9] At the various party congresses as well as in the Chamber and in his editorials in *Le Populaire*, he reiterated his thesis that the holocaust of war could be avoided only by progressive general disarmament; it was difficult for him even in the age of Hitler to change these views.[1]

Meanwhile, on the question of party tactics his efforts at compromise were best seen in the resolution he drew up for the congress that met in April 1933. Accepting the fact that the parliamentary group had a legitimate duty to preserve a stable Left majority in Parliament, he nonetheless maintained that it could not do so at the price of violating party statutes. "No concern over parliamentary majorities," the resolution read, "may prevail against the fundamental principles of the party on such matters as military appropriations, funds for colonial conquests, or the rejection of the budget as a whole." The resolution did not altogether ignore parliamentary political realities. It permitted the parliamentary group some flexibility and freedom of maneuver, subject to the close supervision of the party itself, lest strict adherence "materially aid the worst enemies of the regime."[2] Blum's resolution, adopted by a vote of 2,807 to 925, did not settle the conflict between the Renaudel group and the party leadership. In formal opposition to

[9] Speech at Paris congress, *Le Populaire*, July 16–17, 1933.

[1] For his views on disarmament after Hitler's coming to power, a subject to which we shall return, see his editorials in *Le Populaire*, February 9, 10, March 16, and April 24, 1933, and his speech in the Chamber, *Chambre, Débats*, April 6, 1933. For Blum's prediction that the Nazis would never come to power, *Le Populaire*, March 14, 15, November 8, 9, 1932, and January 18, 1933; cf. his editorial admitting his error in *Le Populaire*, February 9, 1933. In later years Blum noted Rauschning's disclosures of Hitler's own despair of achieving power in November 1932: *Le Populaire*, January 15, 18, 1940.

[2] *Le Populaire*, April 17 and July 18, 1933.

the decision of the party congress, the majority of the parliamentary group again voted for the Daladier government's budget, and the party executive committee was forced to censure the fractious Deputies.

The debate in the summer of 1933 transcended the question of tactics and seemed suddenly to vindicate Blum's opposition to the neo-Socialists. Déat, Marquet, and Barthélemy Montagnon insisted that the appeal of fascism arose from the introduction of a sense of order and authority into contemporary society and the nation. The Socialists must abandon their old-fashioned internationalism in an age of resurgent nationalism and autarchy and accept the "new reality of the nation." Strong governments committed to action were needed to discipline national energies.[3] When Blum heard Adrien Marquet at the congress of July 1933 proclaim: "Order and authority are the foundations of the action we must undertake to win the masses," he blurted out: "I confess that I am frightened." "There were moments," he said in his own speech the following day, "when I wondered if this was not the program of a 'national socialist' party that I heard. You tell us that we need slogans of order and authority and that we must pose as the defenders of authority and order before the country. I shall not even ask what that has to do with ministerial collaboration. . . . Socialist propaganda is not propaganda for order in the sense that you mean it but . . . propaganda for liberty and justice." "I must warn you against the dangers in Marquet's statement," he added, "the danger that in our opposition to fascism we come to adopt its methods and even its ideology."[4]

The congress of July 1933 ended with a solemn warning to the dissidents and the threat of disciplinary action in the event of any new violations of the party's rules. It forbade the Socialist Deputies to vote for the budget unless specifically authorized in advance by a national council. The neo-Socialist faction was undaunted; publicly proclaiming that they would continue to act as they had in the past, they repudiated the libelous charge of fascism. Marcel Déat directed

[3] The speeches of Montagnon, Marquet, and Déat at the July 1933 congress were published in book form as *Néo-socialisme? ordre, autorité, nation* (Paris, 1933). For an excellent statement by Déat, see his letter in the opinion column of *Le Populaire*, "Tribune du parti," June 9, 1933. See also the discussion of neo-Socialism in Lefranc: *Mouvement socialiste*, pp. 280–300; Ligou: *Socialisme*, pp. 383–95; Prélot: *L'Évolution politique*, pp. 287–93; Marcus: *French Socialism in the Crisis Years*, pp. 32–40; and Milorad M. Drachkovitch: *De Karl Marx à Léon Blum* (Geneva, 1954), pp. 127–37.

[4] *Le Populaire*, July 16–17, 1933; also his editorials in *Le Populaire*, July 19, 1933, and issues immediately following.

his attack at Blum personally: "Subtly, by your Byzantinism, you are leading us to fascism. I, who know you, see a completely Oriental passivity; action is precisely the opposite of what you stand for."[5] Blum replied that action divorced from reason was senseless and dangerous.[6] (The taste for action led both Déat and Marquet in the Second World War to collaboration with the German invaders and to outright fascism; Déat eventually ended his days as a refugee from republican justice in an Italian monastery.)

That summer in his editorials and speeches Blum had to concern himself also with the Left-wing Socialists who were advocating direct Socialist action to check fascism. Conceding that the working classes had everything to lose from a system which preserved capitalism but destroyed democracy, he still rejected the argument that the only way to check fascism was through direct Socialist action, that is, to take office and make use of "total power" to suppress fascism—"to kill the devil before he kills you." It was dangerous, he argued, to think of seizing power in a kind of defensive *coup d'état*. On the other hand, he accepted the need for political action against fascism, so long as it was free of false revolutionary illusions. "One can occupy office in a defensive and preventive capacity to bar the path to fascism, but without the illusion that this will lead to socialism."[7] While guarding against Left-wing adventurism, he accepted the party's responsibility for assuming office if such a step were to help thwart the success of fascism.

The last act in the neo-Socialist drama was played out at the end of October 1933, when the Daladier government, over the protests of the C.G.T., introduced a bill reducing salaries and pensions for civil servants. With the S.F.I.O. holding the balance of power, a negative Socialist vote would mean the fall of the government. Renaudel, insisting that the government's foreign policy ought to be the party's principal concern, especially since Germany had just left the Disarmament Conference and the League, repeated his warnings about the dangers of parliamentary instability. In the midst of the debate Renaudel openly separated himself and his followers from the party group. They refused to accept responsibility, he announced, for another government crisis, and voted for the cabinet. Blum, for his part, laid the onus on

[5] See Déat's letter to Blum, July 27, 1933, printed in *Le Populaire*, August 1, 1933.

[6] *Le Populaire*, August 13, 1933.

[7] *Le Populaire*, July 24–30, 1933; speech to international conference, ibid., August 24, 1933. Blum expanded on this theme two years later, speaking of a "holding of power" *(occupation du pouvoir)*; *Le Populaire*, July 1, 2, 4, 1935.

Daladier for presenting the Socialists with an unacceptable bill and deplored the "heart-rending choice" offered by the Radical leader.[8] With the Socialists voting against it, the Daladier cabinet fell.

A few days later a national council read the dissident Socialists out of the party.[9] Some twenty-eight Deputies and seven Senators, taking with them 20,000 party members, left the party to found a new organization. The neo-Socialists were, however, too heterogenous to flourish and soon fused with other independent Socialist groups. Déat and Marquet abandoned socialism entirely. Renaudel, dismayed at the outspoken fascism of some of his associates, died heartbroken in 1935. It cannot be denied that the inflexibility of Blum and the official party leadership, even in the face of the depression and the rise of Nazism, had been partly responsible for the dissidence in the party and the schism that resulted. Blum had not come forth with any new, revitalizing theories. He had been right in guarding against the irrational activism of the neo-Socialist extremists, but because of his desire to placate the orthodox in the party he had rejected Renaudel's insistent pleas also. Despite all their denials, Blum and the party had contributed to the instability of the parliamentary regime.

In the years from the Communist secession of December 1920 to the neo-Socialist schism of November 1933, Blum was guided by a double vision: to keep faith with his Socialist idealism and to act as the responsible leader of a national parliamentary party. To protect the party from being outstripped by the Communists on the left, he reaffirmed the party's allegiance to its classical Marxist tenets of class struggle, internationalism, and revolution, employing the same catchwords as Paul Faure and the neo-Guesdists, the phraseology that party *militants* were accustomed to hearing before 1914 and wished still to hear. He accepted the ancient ritual of voting against the budget and against national defense credits. To demonstrate the revolutionary distinctiveness of the party even further, he guarded it from too close an identification with the large, amorphous, middle-class, liberal party on its right, the Radicals, opposing firm parliamentary coalitions with them and participation in their cabinets. He refused to allow success at the polls to transform the S.F.I.O. into a mere reformist party.

[8] *Chambre*, *Débats*, October 23, 1933, and *Le Populaire*, October 25, 1933.
[9] *Le Populaire*, November 5, 1933.

At the same time, he led the party to accept its parliamentary role and to follow a policy of constructive opposition.

In the years between 1920 and 1933 Blum had become a national political figure; in the Chamber he was one of the "club." His newspaper "leaders" were widely read and discussed. The fate of cabinets frequently depended on what Blum, with his prestige as parliamentary leader of the Socialists, could induce his party to do. To remain faithful to a revolutionary idealism and at the same time to act as responsible head of a parliamentary party, one had to be precisely the kind of tightrope-walker which Blum had described in 1926. Despite his efforts to keep harmony between the rank-and-file *militants* of the party and the party's elected representatives in Parliament, there were times when one or the other had to prevail. In such cases, he made his choice in this period in favor of the party and its traditional doctrines. He could have led the party to accept a role in the government and to serve as an integral part of a parliamentary Left bloc; he could have helped to prevent the serious cabinet instability that threatened, as he well knew, to discredit parliamentary institutions altogether. But in these years, before the party was entrusted with responsibility for the government, his allegiance to party doctrine came first. He feared that in a minor role in the government the party would lose its pristine idealism and its revolutionary appeal: the more militant would desert to the Communists, the reform-minded to the Radicals.

Perhaps the reasons for his position are not difficult to perceive. We have seen how he rose to fill the vacuum in party leadership in the postwar years. He was, in a sense, an outsider, an intellectual, a bourgeois, a Jew. He had to prove his right to be the leader of a Socialist "movement" not just of a party. He had to be the apostle of a faith, not merely the leader of a political party or a politician in Parliament. "Socialism," he wrote, "is a morality—a religion almost—as much as a doctrine."[1] To demonstrate his fitness for leadership he had to demonstrate also that he was devoid of personal ambition. He would not follow the well-traveled path of a Millerand or a Laval—"one of those evolutions of which the parliamentary history of France offers a goodly number of examples. . . . I have very well sensed more than once that to gain the kind of stature that I lacked, to become a true 'statesman,' to receive even the supreme award of an academy, it would have required just a short time, the time of a betrayal toward those who had

[1] *Pour être socialiste*, p. 4.

always had confidence in me; no hard effort would have been needed."[2] To him *fidélité* was all-important. He commented in 1931 on the defection of Ramsay MacDonald: "The true victim is MacDonald. Fidelity is the first rule of political morality."[3]

Yet could he not have modified the old Marxian formulas and presented a new revisionism? Could he not have reconciled the reformist deeds of the party with its revolutionary words? The answer was that he could not bring himself to disavow the antiquated tenets because he could not face the charge of breaking faith. Years later he made a fatal admission: "The Socialist group in Parliament, by ritual fidelity to an old symbol, continued to refuse military credits whose fate it very well knew did not depend on its vote; and in that its gesture was not exempt from a certain amount of hypocrisy."[4] Paradoxically, his own idealism and morality drove him to this act of hypocrisy. In identifying himself with the orthodox leadership of the party, he failed to respond to the new challenges that had arisen in Europe. His devotion to socialism and to the mystique of unity within the party obscured from his vision the totalitarian challenge on the horizon.

Yet if he did not throw off the restraints of Marxism, he was gradually leading the party to accept its role in the republic against the purists who insisted that the party must not take office before the revolutionary "conquest of power." He patiently explained that there were no doctrinal objections to participation in the cabinet even though the dangers and disadvantages were so great that it must not be considered a normal or habitual practice. On the other hand, he wanted it understood that acceptance of only a few seats in cabinets formed by other parties was weighted with so many disadvantages that it ought to be rejected in favor of the "exercise of power," that is, Socialist-directed cabinets. And against Leftists in his own party, he insisted on a scrupulous regard for existing institutions if the party were to take office.

In retrospect, one can see the flaws in his reasoning. He was always concerned about *la déception révolutionnaire*, the danger that the masses would mistake the presence of Socialists in the government for the revolution itself. Yet it could be argued, in contradiction, that a Socialist-formed cabinet, an exercise of power, would one day raise the hopes

[2] Testimony at Riom trial, 1942, *Oeuvre*, V, 265; and statement, *Le Populaire*, July 2, 1935.

[3] *Le Populaire*, August 27, 1931.

[4] *À l'échelle humaine*, *Oeuvre*, V, 454.

and aspirations of the masses higher than any simple participation in a cabinet formed by another party. Who would have believed that the revolution had arrived if Blum had become Minister of Justice in Herriot's cabinet in 1924 or Renaudel taken the Foreign Affairs Ministry in Daladier's 1933 cabinet? But the hopes and aspirations raised when Blum became Premier of a Socialist-directed coalition cabinet a few years later were vibrant indeed—and the frustrations deeper when it did not accomplish all that was hoped for it. Moreover, when the experiment was tried, the Radicals were so strongly represented in the cabinet, and the Left majority in the Chamber so unstable, that Socialist leadership was all but nullified. It could be argued that by participating in Radical cabinets the party might have become inured to setbacks, better prepared for the possible failures in an exercise of power. And participation would have added stability to Radical cabinets, helping to prevent the crisis of parliamentary institutions which Blum himself sought to avoid.

Yet there was one great advantage in Blum's tactics. If his compromise had not saved the party from the secession of the neo-Socialists, he had preserved the party for the new trials that lay ahead. When it was necessary to counter the antiparliamentary threat that arose in the country in 1934, Blum and the Socialists were untarnished by the hapless experiences of the Radical governments. Around Blum there could gather many of the floating, unattached liberal elements seeking a symbol of democratic reform, republicanism, and humanism in a world increasingly threatened by barbarism.

IV

THE FORMATION
OF THE POPULAR FRONT:
From the "Sixth of February"
to the Elections of 1936

*Historians will one day regard these two
years as a decisive phase in the evolution
of Europe and it seems to me that we can
already anticipate their judgment.[1]*

A POLITICAL PHENOMENON like the Popular Front does not
spring up like a mushroom between the first ballot one Sunday
and the runoff ballot the next," Blum in later years correctly
pointed out.[2] More than two years went by between the riots of
February 6, 1934, and the Popular Front election victory in May 1936.
The "political phenomenon" known as the Popular Front had many
origins. The depression which was striking France with increasing
severity by 1934, the rise of Hitler and the rearmament of Germany,
the various financial scandals which reached into French public life,
cabinet instability under the legislature elected in 1932, the growth of
Rightist armed leagues which were reviving the old latent anti-
republicanism in France—all played their part. The immediate catalytic
agent was the antiparliamentary riots of February 6, 1934, which were
widely interpreted by the Left as an assault upon the republic and a
harbinger of a fascist triumph in France. It required many months,
however, before the Left could unite. At least six months went by before the two working-class political parties, the Socialist party and the

---

[1] Blum: *Le Populaire*, February 9, 1936.
[2] Testimony at Riom trial, *Oeuvre*, V, 232.

Communist party, were able to work out an agreement for concerted action, and many more months were needed to broaden the coalition to include the Radical Socialist party as well as other "antifascist" labor, intellectual, and civil liberties organizations.[3]

Blum once described the Popular Front as "no more than a reflex of instinctive defense . . . against the perils that threatened the republic . . . and against the prolongation of the economic crisis which was crushing the working classes, the farmers, the middle class of the country."[4] Yet it was more than defensive. It carried with it an electric atmosphere, charged with enthusiasm and hope for the future. Its program sounded a keynote of social and economic reform, civil rights, and peace. The most exciting political phenomenon of the interwar years in France, it captured the imagination of liberals and intellectuals the world over; its weaknesses, built-in limitations, and pitfalls were often hidden from view.

Blum himself emerged as one of the great symbols of the Popular Front. Although he moved gingerly in his relations with the Communists and the Radicals in the months after February 1934, he was among the first to sound the tocsin for a rally of popular forces against the threat of fascism; and in the tense atmosphere of 1934–6 he came close to being physically lynched. The Popular Front years tested his courage as well as his political leadership.

Whether there really was a "sixth of February"—an actual threat of a

[3] The stages in the formation of the Popular Front are discussed in the general histories of socialism by Ligou, Louis, Prélot, Walter, and Zévaès already cited, and in Goguel: *La Politique des partis.* Some important specialized accounts are Georges Dupeux: *Le Front Populaire et les élections de 1936* (Paris, 1959), Henry W. Ehrmann: *The French Labor Movement from Popular Front to Liberation* (New York, 1947), Marcus: *French Socialism in the Crisis Years,* already cited, and James Joll: "The Making of the Popular Front," a chapter in Joll (ed.): *The Decline of the Third Republic* (London, 1959). Alexander Werth's *France in Ferment* (London, 1934) and *Destiny of France* (London, 1937), both based on his dispatches to the *Manchester Guardian* at the time, are colorful and perceptive. Some of the flavor of the period is recaptured in Louis Bodin and Jean Touchard: *Front Populaire 1936* (Paris, 1961), which reproduces a number of contemporary documents and has a valuable bibliography. The most comprehensive (though not entirely satisfactory) treatment of the Popular Front period is now Georges Lefranc: *Histoire du Front Populaire, 1934–1938* (Paris, 1965), which was published after the manuscript of the present book was completed.

[4] Testimony at Riom trial, *Oeuvre,* V, 233, and also p. 322.

fascist overthrow of the republic on February 6, 1934—cannot be resolved here.[5] There seems to have been no premeditated or coordinated
plot to overthrow the regime, no recognized leadership, nor any
military support for such an endeavor. On the other hand, the participating organizations—veterans' groups and paramilitary leagues—
were nationalist and authoritarian in complexion, and not unlike fascist
groups elsewhere in Europe. The origins of the riots are well known.
At the end of January 1934 a Radical cabinet headed by Camille
Chautemps fell victim to the public unrest brought on by the
Stavisky financial scandals. Serge Stavisky, a financial adventurer, had
among other exploits helped float frandulent municipal bond issues.
Chautemps was accused of failing to investigate the affair thoroughly
enough and some Radical politicians even seemed to be implicated. The
riots of February 6 occurred when the new Radical Premier, Édouard
Daladier, dismissed a police official known to be friendly to the Rightist
organizations. The demonstrators rallied to march on the Palais
Bourbon, where Daladier sought a vote of confidence for his government
from the Chamber. Only action by the police and the *gardes mobiles*
that evening stopped them from storming the bridge at the Place de la
Concorde, but not before fourteen rioters and one police officer were
killed, over one thousand persons injured, and a government building
set on fire. What the demonstrators would have done had they succeeded in reaching the Chamber remains open to conjecture.

While the riots raged, panic and pandemonium spread in the
Chamber itself. The parties of the Right and the Communists on the
Left showed an implacable hostility to Daladier, who could hardly
read his ministerial declaration. Amidst persistent demands from the
Right and Center that the session be adjourned without a vote, and
with many Deputies quietly slipping away on their own, Blum stood
calm and steadfast. He and the Socialists were adamantly opposed to
an adjournment in the face of the street riots. Although his relations
with Daladier had been strained ever since he and the party had
brought down Daladier's cabinet in October 1933, he now took the
rostrum to present a declaration of Socialist support for Daladier's
government, which had pledged that it would enforce order and de-

[5] Two useful treatments are Max Beloff: "The Sixth of February," a chapter
in Joll (ed.): *The Decline of the Third Republic*, and Geoffrey Warner: "The
Stavisky Affair and the Riots of February 6, 1934," *History Today*, June 1958,
pp. 377–85. For the Right in France in historical perspective, René Rémond:
La Droite en France de 1815 à nos jours: continuité et diversité d'une tradition
(Paris, 1954).

fend the republic. Scarcely able to make himself heard above the din, he read the Socialist statement:

> The vote which [the Socialist group] is going to cast is not a vote of confidence, it is a vote of combat. . . . If the government wages the struggle with enough energy, with enough faith in the popular will, it can count on us. If it fails in its duty, it is we who will launch an appeal in the entire country to all republican forces and to the mass of workers and farmers. . . . In the battle that is engaged from this moment on, we seek our place in the first ranks. Fascist reaction shall not pass.[6]

He also demanded vigorous steps to relieve the profound causes of unrest in the country and a "purification" of the political atmosphere in the nation. With unconcern for his own personal safety he remained at his post when the angry mob might have invaded the Chamber at any moment and chosen him as one of its prime victims.

Blum, like others on the Left, interpreted the riots as an insurrection against the regime, as proof that the potential danger of fascism existed in France. "I do not believe myself to be among those who have an exaggerated idea of the fascist danger in France," he wrote a month after the episode, "but the events of February 6 have revealed the existence of this danger; they have revealed that the fascist organizations were strong enough, and skillfully enough led, to divert and exploit to their profit . . . a troubled and aroused public opinion."[7] Later on he objected strongly to the tendency to minimize the insurrectionary nature of the riots and to condemn the government for "unnecessary" bloodshed. Without the action of the police, he maintained, the Chamber would have been invaded and a provisional government proclaimed by the rioters.[8]

[6] *Chambre, Débats,* February 6, 1934; see also *Oeuvre,* IV, pt. 1, 8–10. For Herriot's description of the scene and his tribute to Blum, *Jadis,* II, 376.

[7] "L'Émeute fasciste du 6 février," *Le Populaire,* March 3, 1934; see also editiorial, March 29, 1934. Blum insisted that the Socialists neither championed the parliamentary regime as such nor equated the parliamentary system with democracy, but believed that in France attacks on Parliament were a certain prologue to dictatorship; see *Le Populaire,* February 16, 1934.

[8] Testimony to parliamentary commission, 1947. The postwar investigation of this commission, including reports, testimony, and documents, which will be frequently cited in this work, has been published as: Commission d'Enquête Parlementaire: *Les Événements survenus en France de 1933 à 1945: Rapport,* 2 vols., and *Témoignages et documents,* 9 vols. (Paris, 1947–54). Blum appeared before the commission on June 18, July 23, and July 30, 1947. His testimony on the 1934 episode is in *Témoignages et documents,* I, 123–4. The postwar

Although Daladier won his vote of confidence, and the demonstrations subsided late that night, the Radical leader did not believe that his government could maintain order if new demonstrations were to occur. At a moment when he was under great pressure to resign in favor of a new government that would have broader "national"—that is, Rightist —support, "Blum alone," Daladier later testified, advised him to remain in office and fight back.[9] On the morning after the riots, Blum assured Daladier that if he remained as Premier he could even count on the Socialists to take the unprecedented step of joining his cabinet. However, when Daladier explained that he could not control the situation in the streets without adjourning Parliament and declaring martial law by decree, Blum balked. Blum insisted that if martial law were imposed it had to be under parliamentary control. He stiffly lectured Daladier: "A republican cabinet fights against an uprising with the constant support of the nation's representative assembly and by giving a constant accounting to it of its acts. . . . You must request Parliament to declare martial law. You must not prorogue Parliament. Parliament must sit in permanent session."[1] Despite the crisis Blum could not shake off his legalistic scruples and his attachment to the prerogatives of Parliament. The fact is that if martial law were needed to cope with the dangerous situation, there was neither time nor reason for debating the matter in a divided Parliament or for keeping Parliament in permanent and undoubtedly turbulent session. Even if Blum had little confidence in the determination of the "bull of the Vaucluse" to stand firm, this course of action was not the way to stiffen his resolve. Daladier needed only an additional excuse to ease himself out of his difficult position and to resign. As a Socialist observer noted twenty years after the event, when the facts were known, neither Blum nor Daladier emerged from the episode with enhanced stature.[2]

---

parliamentary investigation will henceforth be referred to as *Événements* and, unless otherwise indicated, the volumes of testimony and documents *(Témoignages et documents)* will be meant.

[9] Daladier: testimony, 1947, *Événements*, I, 12–13.

[1] Blum: testimony, 1947, *Événements*, I, 124. Blum referred to these conversations in a news release in *Le Populaire*, February 9, 1934, and discussed them at the Toulouse party congress, May 1934, p. 113. See also his "Un Peu d'histoire," *Le Populaire*, August 28, 1934, reprinted in his pamphlet *Les Radicaux et nous*. Blum did not reveal until after the war that he had agreed to martial law.

[2] Fernand Robert: "Il était déjà trop tard: les travaux de la commission Jacquet sur les événements de 1933 à 1945 en France," *La Revue Socialiste*, June 1956, pp. 36–7.

The first effort to unite the two major parties of the Left in the face of the antirepublican threat thus foundered. Daladier resigned that very day, less than twenty-four hours after the riots began. Violence in the streets had brought down a legally constituted government even though it had a majority in the Chamber behind it.

The former President of the Republic, Gaston Doumergue, succeeded Daladier, forming a "national union" cabinet in which almost all parties were represented, the seventh cabinet to be formed in the twenty months since the legislative elections of 1932.[3] Herriot and the Radicals took seats alongside conservatives like André Tardieu, Marshal Pétain, and Louis Barthou. The only party that rejected the invitation to join the cabinet was the Socialist, which, moreover, entered into active opposition.[4]

Blum vigorously opposed the plans for constitutional reform which Doumergue outlined in a series of paternalistic broadcasts to the nation. Doumergue and Tardieu proposed to strengthen the powers of the executive by permitting the President of the Republic to dissolve the Chamber and hold new elections in the event of a no-confidence vote. Fearing the abuse of power in the hands of a Rightist cabinet, Blum denounced the proposals as an attack on republican liberties and as a prologue to fascism. British constitutional practice provided no analogy, he maintained, for in Britain a Prime Minister acted in the name of a large homogeneous political party. The closest analogy he saw was Marshal MacMahon's historic dissolution of the Chamber in 1877.[5] Although there had been support in the country, and even in Socialist circles, for a modification of the constitution that would provide some remedy for the nagging cabinet instability, Blum and the Socialists refused to accept such reforms from Doumergue or Tardieu. Blum's attacks on the Doumergue proposals attracted wide attention and aroused apprehension in Radical circles. The proposals were soon dropped. For over half a century, from 1877 on, the men of the Left

[3] For the eleven cabinets from the elections of May 1932 to those of May 1936, see Appendix II, p. 491. Blum's reactions to many of these cabinets appear in the selection of editorials and speeches reproduced in *Oeuvre*, IV, pt. 1, 19–98.

[4] See Blum's speech, *Chambre, Débats*, February 15, 1934; and speeches and editorials, *Oeuvre*, IV, pt. 1, 19–46.

[5] Blum's articles appeared in *Le Populaire*, October 19–24, 1934, and were reprinted in the new edition of his *La Réforme gouvernementale* (Paris, 1936), pp. 211–35. In the crisis of 1877 Marshal MacMahon's dissolution of the Chamber backfired. A republican majority was again returned in the new elections and he himself resigned as President of the Republic. The episode sealed the principle of legislative supremacy for the Third Republic.

had mistrusted the motives of those who sought to strengthen the powers of the executive and to bring stability to the parliamentary system; in the autumn of 1934, any such constitutional reform was inconceivable. The men of the Third Republic were not ready for the Fifth.

Although the effort to form a coalition of Socialists and Radicals on the parliamentary level failed, the riots of February 6 had important immediate repercussions outside the sphere of government and Parliament. Aroused by the threat to working-class liberties and to the republic, the Socialist party, the Communist party, and the two trade-union confederations (the independent but pro-Socialist C.G.T. and the Communist C.G.T.U.) girded their forces for a counter demonstration of popular "antifascist" strength.

For the Communists this step marked an about-face. On the eve of the February 6 demonstrations, they were not only attacking the Daladier cabinet, the Radical politicians, and the Socialists but denouncing the parliamentary regime itself for impotence and corruption. André Marty had singled out three targets when he summoned his party to join in the demonstrations of February 6: "the fascist bands, the government that protects them, and social democracy which divides the working class and makes every effort to weaken it."[6] Thus the Communists were out in the streets along with the Rightist groups on the evening of February 6, even if for different reasons. Their presence increased the general confusion, heightening the danger to the Daladier government and to the regime itself. Blum was right in charging that Communist "fraternization with the reactionaries" had "added to the disorder."[7]

Once the demonstrations had turned into bloody riots, however, and assumed a quasi-fascist complexion, the Communists quickly mobilized in protest and called for demonstrations on February 9. The C.G.T. had already called for a nationwide general strike on February 12. Despite a government ban on street demonstrations, the Communist party proceeded with its mobilization. A clash with the police resulted: six workers were killed and dozens wounded. In the eyes of many, the blood of the Communist martyrs washed away their fraternization with the fascist demonstrators on February 6.

With this added provocation, all branches of the labor movement

[6] *L'Humanité*, February 6, 1934, cited by Walter: *Parti communiste français*, p. 251.

[7] Speech to Toulouse party congress, May 1934, p. 125.

rallied to support the C.G.T. nationwide protest strike. Blum hailed the rallying of labor to the republic. "When the republic is threatened, the word 'republican' changes its meaning. It takes on its old historic and heroic significance."[8]

February 12 became one of the "great days" in the history of French labor. The general strike and the demonstrations were impressive not only in Paris but all over the country as well. In the capital, Socialists and Communists marched for hours, first separately and then joining forces at the Cours de Vincennes. Amidst cries of "Unity! Unity!" Blum and the Communist leaders appeared together for the first time in fourteen years. There was one common slogan: "Fascism shall not pass." "We are all united here to defend the republic," asserted Blum, "because we know that only under the republic can we march forward."[9] His words satisfied those who wished to defend the political liberties which the republic symbolized and also those who thought of the republic as a stage in the march toward a new society.

Yet the hope for working-class unity of action soon received a setback. To agree on the principle of unity of action proved to be more difficult and complex than to hold a few demonstrations or to speak from the same platform. Neither Socialists nor Communists could forget the long years of fratricidal war since the schism of Tours in 1920. The Communists, in particular, were not yet prepared to abandon the tactic they had long pursued of appealing directly to the Socialist rank and file over the heads of the S.F.I.O., a policy, in their own picturesque phrases, of "extending an open hand" to the rank and file while "brandishing a fist" to the leaders, and "plucking the feathers from the Socialist goose" (*plumer la volaille socialiste*). Neither the depression nor the emergence of Hitler had changed matters; nor for the moment did the events of February 6 and 12. The Communists continued to hurl invective and vituperation at the S.F.I.O. leaders. A month after the demonstration of unity in February 1934, the Communists reiterated their interest in joint action, but only "at the base,"

[8] *Le Populaire*, February 11, 1934. The Communists for a time insisted that they were defending "democratic liberties," not the republic.

[9] *Le Populaire*, February 13, 1934. What is to be thought of Blum's comment years later (in the political climate of June 1947) that he and his Socialist friends did not know, when the Communist paraders approached at Vincennes, whether it was to fight them or to join them? See *Le Populaire*, June 7, 1947, and *Populaire-Dimanche*, February 12, 1950, the latter reproduced in *Oeuvre*, IV, pt. 1, 13–17.

and announced their intention to win the Socialist workers away "from the paralyzing influence of their party."[1]

Blum accused the Communists of insincerity in calling for joint action and at the same time denouncing the Socialist party leadership. He singled out especially the "antifascist committees" proposed by the Communists, which were to be outside party control. Along with Paul Faure, he was apprehensive lest the highly disciplined Communists dominate the rank-and-file "antifascist committees" and use them to undermine the leadership and structure of the S.F.I.O. He cautioned his party in March 1934: "You must favor the current leading toward unity and even take the initiative in it, but without falling into the traps that are being set for you."[2]

Throughout the spring of 1934 the hard feelings between the two parties persisted. Yet in both groups a strong current of opinion among the rank and file was rising in favor of unity of action. Not only were the mistakes of the German working class still fresh in mind but the crushing of the Socialists by Dollfuss in Austria in February 1934 had intensified the fear of fascism. The Left wing of Blum's party, strong in the Paris area (the Federation of the Seine), wished to submerge all differences with the Communists and work toward unity of action, and even toward a reunification of the two parties ("organic unity"). On the very night of February 6–7 these Left Socialist leaders in the Seine had made direct overtures to the Communists but had been rebuffed. Disregarding the party's warnings, they continued their activities in the months that followed. At the same time, within the Communist party, Jacques Doriot, in defiance of the party line, was urging direct negotiations with the Socialist party leadership; for this and other breaches of discipline he was shortly to be expelled. Ironically, in the spring of 1934, Thorez and Duclos were working as hard to prevent Doriot from trying to override the Communist party leadership as Blum and Paul Faure were to prevent the Leftists of the Seine Federation from bypassing the leadership of *their* party. Unity of action was not in sight, although both parties paid lip service to it.[3] Two separate processions,

[1] See *L'Humanité*, March 4, 1934. For the Communist position toward the Socialists since 1932, Walter: *Parti communiste français*, pp. 232–64, and Dupeux: *Front Populaire*, pp. 69–75.

[2] Speech to the national council of the party, *Le Populaire*, March 12, 1934. Unless otherwise indicated, such speeches may be assumed to have been delivered the day before they appeared in *Le Populaire*.

[3] See Blum's statements to the Toulouse party congress, May 1934, p. 366, and resolutions adopted, pp. 393–9. For the Communists, Walter: *Parti communiste français*, pp. 258–73.

Socialist and Communist, marched in May 1934 in the annual ceremony honoring the Communards of 1871.

At the end of May, however, came a turning point in the Communist line. A *Pravda* article, reproduced in *L'Humanité* on May 31, 1934, reflected the growing anxiety in the U.S.S.R. over the consolidation of Nazi power and all that it presaged for the security of the Soviets. Acting on their interpretation of the new directives, the French Communists for the first time now appealed directly to the Socialist party leadership. They asked for joint demonstrations to "save Thälmann," the German Communist leader threatened with execution by the Nazis, as well as other action to combat fascism. In the last week of June the national congress of the Communist party called for negotiating a "unity of action pact" with the Socialists and even set forth the concessions they were prepared to make.[4] But Blum and the Socialist leaders were openly skeptical of the Communists' intentions, especially when Communist attacks on the party leadership did not altogether cease.[5] It was the Left-wing leaders of the Seine Federation who took matters into their own hands. On their own initiative, they arranged a joint demonstration with the Communists on July 2 at the Salle Bullier. Speakers from each party called for the freeing of Thälmann and other political prisoners, the dissolution of the fascist leagues in France, peace, and a struggle against the reactionary retrenchment decrees of the Doumergue government. Another joint demonstration quickly followed.[6] It became impossible for Blum and the party leaders to ignore the pressure now building up within the Left-wing rank and file of the party or to reject the Communist overtures.

Blum tried to clarify for the party his own reactions to the new Communist line. A series of editorials which he published in *Le Populaire* during the week of July 7–July 14 reflected the important new developments in the air but also his refusal to rush forward without careful meditation. The editorials were a compound of admonitions, words of caution, misgivings, and a search for ulterior motives, ending eventually in a reluctant acceptance of the Communist offer.[7] The Communists in recent months reminded him of "a shower that ran hot and

[4] For the Communist party congress at Ivry and related events, ibid., pp. 274–5.

[5] See especially Thorez in *Les Cahiers du Bolchevisme*, June 15, 1934, cited by Walter, p. 275. For the first breakdown in negotiations, *Le Populaire*, June 21, 1934.

[6] Walter: *Parti communiste français*, p. 276; Ligou: *Socialisme*, pp. 402–4.

[7] Blum's editorials in *Le Populaire*, July 7–14, 1934, variously entitled "Les Problèmes de l'unité," "L'Unité d'action," etc., are reproduced in *Oeuvre*, IV,

cold" (*une douche écossaise*), one day hurling insults, the next pleading for reconciliation. Were they now sincere, or was it a new maneuver? "*Que cache ce bloc enfariné?*" Was it a case of the wolf in sheep's clothing? Would the Socialists be launching their party on a "dangerous adventure?" Most troubling to him was the absence of a "completely satisfying intellectual explanation" for the change in the Communist position. He found the most likely motive in Communist concern for the security of the Soviet Union. The consolidation of Nazi power had placed the Russian Revolution in its gravest danger since 1919. The willingness of the Soviets to sign non-aggression pacts and to enter the once-maligned League of Nations reflected Soviet uneasiness over German nationalism and a search for allies (such as France). In this situation, the task of the French Communist party was undoubtedly to rally the French masses around the struggle against fascism and to insure French support for the Soviet Union.[8]

Despite his misgivings about the motives of the Communists, he recognized that he had to accept their appeal for joint action; the Socialist rank and file would not have it otherwise. He bluntly warned the Communists, however, against using the antifascist unity movement to promote their own ends. His party would not be a "dupe." Joint meetings were not to turn into public debates or occasions for mutual recrimination between the two parties; "action" or "antifascist" committees were not to act independently of the political parties. The traditional autonomy and independence of the French labor movement was to be respected. Finally, the joint action must not be diverted from a broader objective: "to draw to our sides all groups, all citizens who are resolved like us on the all-out effort and sacrifice needed for the defense . . . of democratic liberties."[9] (Blum failed to foresee that the Communists would transform *their* sectarianism into moderation, republicanism, and patriotism with far greater ease than the Socialists.) The result of Blum's caution and timidity, and his long list of reservations, understandable though they were, was to give the Socialist party the appearance of dragging its feet and of failing to assume the leadership of the antifascist movement that was sweeping the country.

At a meeting of the Socialist national council on July 15, many of the

---

pt. 1, 157–73. He also made an important speech to the national council; see *Le Populaire*, July 16, 1934. The quotations that follow are from both the editorials and the speech.

[8] On the link to Soviet foreign policy, see especially his editorial, *Le Populaire*, July 13, 1934.

[9] *Le Populaire*, July 10, 1934.

party leaders echoed Blum's suspicions even though the Communists were agreeing to all the concessions the party had requested. Compared with the misgivings of some of these men, Blum's were minor. Many could not forget Tours and the Communist insults and vituperation over the years. The principal argument for caution resembled Blum's, that the Communists were not masters of their own house but were under Moscow's dictation. Among the "peace" elements of the party there was apprehension also that unity of action would lead to support for a policy of militarism and war. "I am for unity," Marx Dormoy said, "but for an honest unity and not that desired by Moscow, which under the mask of Bolshevism pursues a tsarist policy." Would the antifascist policy of the Communists and the Soviets not conflict with the traditional pacifism and antimilitarism of the Socialists? Dormoy feared, too, that as the much larger party, they had a great deal to risk by unity of action and by exposure to Communist infiltration. Salomon Grumbach called for a delay of negotiations until the two Internationals could work out an agreement. Many were sarcastic about the change in the Communists' line and their new conciliatory attitude. "We are far from the twenty-one conditions of Tours," said Paul Faure. In the end, Blum's position of watchful cooperation, with the safeguards he had stipulated, was adopted by a large majority, and all motions to delay negotiations were defeated.[1]

Once begun, the negotiations quickly reached fruition. The unity of action pact, signed on July 27, 1934, stated that the two parties would work together in the struggle against "fascism" and against "war and preparations for war." It called for "the defense of democratic liberties," the dissolution of the armed leagues in France, and for the liberation of Ernst Thälmann and other political prisoners abroad. It urged opposition to the Doumergue government and its retrenchment decrees, and demanded new elections. Both parties pledged to abstain from attacks and criticisms of each other in their joint meetings and demonstrations. Outside the area of joint action, each party retained full independence to develop its own propaganda and recruitment. A coordinating committee representing both parties would supervise the enforcement of the pact.[2]

---

[1] For the national council, *Le Populaire*, July 16, 1934; the resolution adopted is reproduced in *Oeuvre*, IV, pt. 1, 220–21.

[2] For the pact, *Le Populaire*, July 28, 1934, and *Oeuvre*, IV, pt. 1, 222–3, and, in an English translation, Werth: *France in Ferment*, p. 285. A "platform of common action" was signed in September 1935; *Le Populaire*, September 23, 1935.

The unity of action pact was signed in time for a giant demonstration at the end of July commemorating the twentieth anniversary of the death of Jaurès and the outbreak of World War I. A few weeks later, in September, Blum, speaking at a joint meeting on the same platform with Marcel Cachin, described his satisfaction. For fourteen years he had cherished the notion that one day the Communists would return to the "old house." Was it possible that this too might come to pass? "I know very well what still separates socialism from communism, but the first steps at *rapprochement* have been taken." Whether or not they united, they would work together in the pressing tasks at hand.[3] Blum had moved slowly and cautiously toward unity of action; actually, strong pressure from below had imposed the policy.[4] Yet the Socialist leader sensed deeply the *élan* of the unity movement and could be counted on to be its enthusiastic champion.

One significant event for the future was the cooperation of the Socialist and Communist parties at the polls in the cantonal elections of October 1934. The Communists, profiting from their new moderate and republican orientation, made important gains. Meanwhile, in the controversy that developed over the Doumergue-Tardieu constitutional proposals, Herriot and the Radicals resigned from the Doumergue cabinet, and the cabinet itself fell in November 1934. Socialists and Communists could unite in opposing the Center-Right cabinets formed by Flandin and Laval in the months that followed. The Radicals, although represented in these governments, were growing restless and were looking to the Left.

Both Socialists and Communists recognized the need to broaden the united front (*front unique*) of the two proletarian parties into a larger popular coalition (*Rassemblement Populaire*). Both saw the need to enlarge their alliance to include the middle classes and especially the party of the petty bourgeoisie, the Radical Socialists. If any lesson had been learned from the experience of the Germans and the Italians, it was the urgent necessity to keep the lower middle classes from flocking to the banner of the fascists.

In a sense, Blum had been among the first to urge such an alliance. In his speech to the Chamber on February 6, he had called for a rally

[3] *Le Populaire*, September 21, 1934.

[4] For Blum's admission of this, ibid.; comment on correspondence received, *Le Populaire*, July 11, 1934; and speech to Mulhouse party congress, June 1935, p. 95.

of "all republican forces in the entire country." At the Toulouse party congress in May 1934, he had spoken of proletarian unity as a basis for a wider unity, a "union (*rassemblement*) between ourselves and the whole of the country."[5] In his articles in July he had warned that the working-class parties must not permit sectarianism and revolutionary extremism to alienate the middle classes. Finally, he had cautioned his own party against the slogan "socialism or fascism."[6]

Yet he did nothing concrete to take the initiative. After the unity of action pact of July 1934, it was the Communists who called for the broader front and who showed a far greater flexibility in making it possible. In October 1934, Thorez asked for the creation of a broad "common front" against fascism—a "Popular Front of work, liberty, and peace." At the same time, the Communist representatives on the unity of action coordinating committee proposed a program for such a coalition. Designed to attract wide antifascist support in the country, the Communist-sponsored program excluded all economic provisions that might antagonize the middle class. The program was limited to the defense of constitutional liberties, the dissolution of the fascist armed leagues, the protection of wages, salaries, and pensions, and a call for disarmament and peace. Moreover, Thorez packaged his appeal in an unprecedented patriotism. "We mean to work with all our strength to spare our country, which we love, the shame and unhappiness of fascist dictatorship."[7]

Still deeply suspicious of the Communists and fearing a new trap, Blum and the Socialists refused to abandon their own Socialist program. On the unity of action coordinating committee, he and the other Socialist delegates would not agree to limit the economic proposals to merely practical and immediate demands, but insisted on the need to incorporate more fundamental measures—"structural reforms" such as the nationalization of the credit banks and various key industries, all of which appeared in the Socialist party program and in the C.G.T. Plan drawn up that year. A Popular Front program, Blum insisted, had to include "the preliminary measures . . . that would make possible an eventual modification of the capitalist structure along socialist lines."[8] The reformist Socialists were now the sectarian Marxists; it was the

[5] Toulouse congress, May 1934, p. 366.

[6] *Le Populaire*, July 10, 1934; Toulouse congress, May 1934, p. 357.

[7] For the proposed program and the Communist statements, Walter: *Parti communiste français*, pp. 283–9.

[8] Speech to national council, *Le Populaire*, November 26, 1934; see also "Le Programme commun," *Le Populaire*, January 20, 1935.

Communists who were urging that the country adopt, in Thorez's phrase, "a program, precise and limited, for immediate action." By the end of January 1935, in the face of the obstacles presented by the Socialists, the coordinating committee was even ready to abandon its task of drawing up a Popular Front program designed to win the support of the middle classes.

The deep sense of insecurity vis-à-vis the Communists persisted. There were complaints at S.F.I.O. meetings that the Communists were making inroads in rural areas where they had never previously been active, that they were utilizing "unemployment committees" to further their own ends, that they were meddling in the affairs of the C.G.T., that they were continuing to attack the Socialist leaders. Paul Faure, increasingly the spokesman for the pacifist wing of the party, feared also that the Communists were furthering Moscow's plans to re-create the pre-1914 system of alliances, which, in his view, could lead only to war. Blum summed up the misgivings of the party at its national council in March 1935: "No one has asked that we break the unity of action pact, but no one has spoken of it without some reservations." He, too, complained that the party had allowed the Communists to capture the initiative in all their joint activities. "In practicing unity of action have we known how to say no? Have we not let them decorate the halls, put up the posters, prepare the agenda?" At the same time he defended the pact and reminded his audience that it had caused "something like a galvanizing current to pass through the population, creating an *élan* of confidence and enthusiasm . . . which had barred the way to fascism in France."[9] Blum was torn between the desire to promote unity of action against fascism and an unwillingness to allow the Communists to exploit such action for their own ends. The result was a kind of inertia and grudging acceptance of the pact, making it possible for the Communists to present themselves as the true champions of a dynamic antifascist policy.

Zyromski and the partisans of unity in the Federation of the Seine displayed marked impatience at the lack of enthusiasm in the party leadership. "There are those who inspire and push unity of action," said one of Zyromski's followers, "and those who barely tolerate it." With a pointed reference to Blum and his cautious editorials, the same

[9] Speech to national council, *Le Populaire*, March 4, 1935, and other speeches and resolutions at the same meeting; also Blum's editorials, "L'Unité d'action" and other titles, *Le Populaire*, February 25–March 1, 1935. See comments by Paul Faure and others, Mulhouse party congress, June 1935, pp. 60–97, esp. 76–7.

critic noted: "There is not always perfect harmony between the second floor where the executive committee of the party sits and the first floor where the newspaper is located."[1]

In the spring of 1935 the signing of the Franco-Soviet Pact placed an obligation on the Communists to work even more energetically to create the broadest possible coalition of proletarian and middle-class groups; a strong antifascist France was needed as the ally of the Soviet Union. Shortly after the signing of the pact and after Laval's visit to Moscow came the startling official Soviet communiqué of May 15: "Stalin understands and fully approves the policy of national defense being followed by France in order to maintain its armed strength at the level required for its security." The new *volte-face* left Blum astonished.[2] The Communists were rallying to the cause of national defense and rearmament. Only two months earlier, Thorez had stated in the Chamber that even an invasion of the country could not induce the Communists to support a war initiated by capitalist and imperialist governments.[3] After Stalin's announcement, it was Blum's turn to be more "revolutionary" than Thorez: "Without denying the duty to defend the national soil against invasion, we refuse to identify ourselves with the military planning and military organization of the bourgeoisie.[4]

Despite Blum's tones of righteous indignation in opposing rearmament and his bold words designed to make the Communists uncomfortable, the Communist acceptance, for the moment, of a national defense policy made cooperation between the two parties easier, not harder.[5] Within the Socialist party, however, Marceau Pivert, forming a new Left-wing faction opposed to Blum, the *Gauche Révolutionnaire* (Revolutionary Left), took up the theme (now confined to the Trotskyites) of "revolutionary defeatism" and opposed class collaboration and national defense under any circumstances.[6]

Meanwhile, in the spring of 1935, progress was made toward a coalition of the three Left parties even before a Popular Front program

---

[1] Mulhouse congress, June 1935, p. 69.

[2] *Le Populaire*, May 17, 1935.

[3] *Chambre, Débats*, March 15, 1935.

[4] See his two consecutive editorials, *Le Populaire*, May 17, 18, 1935.

[5] See Blum's comment, Mulhouse congress, June 1935, p. 219.

[6] See Blum's statements at the Mulhouse party congress, June 1935, pp. 214–21; and the discussion at the special party congress, *Le Populaire*, February 2, 1936. Pivert was also irritated because Blum in the course of a Chamber debate on December 6, 1935, had pledged dissolution of the Socialist "self-defense" groups if the Rightist leagues would disarm.

could be agreed upon. In the municipal elections of May, the Socialists and Communists cooperated on the runoff ballot to defeat Rightist candidates and won impressive victories. The most spectacular victory was the election in Paris of Professor Paul Rivet, a Socialist and one of the founders of the Vigilance Committee of Antifascist Intellectuals; all the Left parties—Socialist, Communist, and Radical—supported him on the runoff ballot. The lesson was obvious.

The Communists in the Chamber, accepting seriously their new republican and parliamentary role, made direct overtures to the Radicals for increased cooperation. The Radicals were in an uneasy position. Herriot and other party leaders had continued to hold posts in every cabinet since Doumergue's, even though these cabinets were Rightist-oriented. Whereas Herriot claimed that the presence of Radical ministers was needed to prevent cabinet instability, a large and growing group in the party opposed participation in these Center and Right cabinets. One group had even left the party in May 1934 in protest; others, the so-called "young Radicals," men like Jean Zay and Pierre Cot, were working within the party to orient it to the Left and to cooperate with the Socialists in a revived Left *cartel* (which would now include the Communists as well). The "young Radicals" received strong support from Herriot's rival for leadership, Edouard Daladier. Toward the end of May a Communist proposal to revive the old pre-1914 steering committee of the Left (the *délégation des gauches*) was accepted. The Communist, Socialist, and Radical parties began to meet to coordinate their action in Parliament and to devise a concerted opposition to the domestic and foreign policy of Flandin and Laval.

In June, after the fall of the Flandin government, the Communists pledged their support to any Radical government that would act in a positive way to relieve the sufferings of the depression and defend democratic liberties and peace. Blum noted that the Communists for the first time had acted "constructively" in a ministerial crisis.[7] The Socialists, meanwhile, launched their own bid for cooperation with the Radicals, calling for "a great popular movement to defend democratic liberties against the political, economic, and social effects of the capitalist crisis." Blum praised those Radicals who were helping to combat the retrenchment measures of the Laval government.[8]

[7] *Le Populaire*, June 10, 1935, and cf. statement at Mulhouse congress, June 1935, pp. 216–20.

[8] For the resolution adopted, Mulhouse congress, June 1935, p. 570; for Blum's statements, ibid., p. 223.

That same month, the younger Radical leaders took a major step toward facilitating the creation of the Popular Front by participating in an antifascist meeting on June 28 which was to be the prelude to a great popular demonstration of all Left organizations planned for Bastille Day. Next, overcoming Herriot's reluctance, the Radicals agreed to participate as a party in the 14th of July demonstration. When the Radical Socialist party's executive committee also refused to condemn "both fascism and communism" as equal threats to the republic,[9] a turning point was reached; the Popular Front was finally a distinct possibility. A generation of liberals in the 1930's refused to condemn both fascism and communism as equal threats and embraced the Communists as allies against fascism; it was the hallmark of the Popular Front years.

With the Radicals actively cooperating, a committee was set up to organize and direct the new antifascist Popular Front, the *Rassemblement Populaire;* the program would follow later. Nine major organizations named representatives to the committee, including the political parties of the Left (Socialist, Communist, Radical, and the Socialist Republican Union), the C.G.T. and the C.G.T.U., the League of the Rights of Man, the Vigilance Committee of Antifascist Intellectuals, and the Amsterdam-Pleyel Committee against War and Fascism.

The first fruit of cooperation was the tremendously successful demonstration held on the 14th of July 1935. Hundreds of thousands marched from the Place de la Bastille to the Place de la Nation. The red, white, and blue tricolor of the republic mingled with the traditional red flag of militant labor. Blum, Thorez, and Daladier marched side by side and returned a clenched-fist salute to the ovation of the feverish masses. The intellectuals were committed too. Writers, scientists, and Sorbonne professors marched; Henri Barbusse, Paul Langevin, and Paul Rivet were present at the head of the procession. At the Buffalo Stadium ten thousand delegates took the oath of the *Rassemblement Populaire*:

> In the name of the people of France assembled today over the whole expanse of our territory,
> We, delegates or members of the *Rassemblement Populaire* of July 14, 1935,
> Inspired by the unanimous determination to give bread to the workers, work to young people, and peace to the world,

[9] Cited by Dupeux: *Front Populaire*, p. 93. For developments in the Radical party during this period, ibid., pp. 87–93; for Herriot's "reserved" position, Soulié: *Herriot*, pp. 469–73.

Take the solemn oath to remain united, to disarm and dissolve the seditious leagues, to defend and develop democratic liberties, and to insure peace for humanity.[1]

The theme of Blum's editorial that day was *Vive la Nation et Vive la Révolution!* The republic, born in the revolution, was to be defended by a revolutionary mobilization of the whole nation. The "Marseillaise" could be sung with new meaning and impassioned feeling.[2]

The Popular Front had come into being. In the world of Hitler and Mussolini, of depression and unemployment, under the threat of internal dictatorship and of fascist aggression and war, it was a manifestation of the popular will to defend liberty and peace and to unite in a common cause liberals, progressives, intellectuals, organized labor, civil libertarians, Socialists, and Communists. It symbolized the determination that what had happened in Germany, Italy, and Austria could not happen in France. The enthusiasm that the Popular Front generated concealed the fact that there was more agreement on what it opposed than on what it signified in a positive way. Nor was it apparent to all who supported it how directly linked it was to the needs and purposes of the Communist movement. It was Thorez and the Communists who had sparked the movement, not Blum and the Socialists. Thorez went off to Moscow that summer to receive the plaudits of the International for giving "the international proletariat an example of the way in which fascism must be fought."[3] France, as in 1789, was to serve as a beacon light to Europe and the world. The Popular Front became the new line of the Comintern after its world congress of August 1935.

Despite the show of unanimity in the great popular demonstration of July 14, six months elapsed before a common program could be worked out by the Popular Front organizational committee. Blum and the Socialists were again the major obstacle. The Socialists continued to insist on broad structural reforms—the nationalization of key industries and monopolies. Although Blum never accepted the thesis that a Socialist society could be created by piecemeal nationalization measures, he believed that the nationalization of *de facto* monopolies represented a

[1] *Le Populaire*, July 14, 15, 1935. The oath is reproduced in Walter: *Parti communiste français*, p. 288.

[2] See his editorials, *Le Populaire*, July 14, 16, 1935.

[3] Statement by Dmitrov in report of August 2, 1935, cited by Walter: *Parti communiste français*, p. 288. See also Joll: "The Making of the Popular Front," *The Decline of the Third Republic*, pp. 55–6.

fulfillment of political democracy and popular sovereignty. Moreover, such measures were needed to cope with the depression. "Holding in its hand the nation's key industries and credit facilities as a rudder," he argued, "the national community will be able to govern the capitalist economy in such a way as to relieve misery, alleviate injustice, and establish in the midst of chaos a small retreat of order and clarity."[4] There was much truth in Blum's contention that more fundamental economic changes were needed for the ailing and technologically backward French economy than was being written into the Popular Front program, but the attitude of the Communists, who were unwilling to alienate the Radicals and the middle classes, made it difficult to insist on such a program. As a concession, the Communists cooperated with the Socialists in preparing a "platform of common action" incorporating these more sweeping proposals, but it was signed only by the two proletarian parties and kept quite separate from the program for the broader Popular Front.[5]

Finally, by the beginning of January 1936, after six months of difficult negotiations, the Popular Front program was ready.[6] The Socialists yielded on their economic demands but won out against the Communists on organizational principles, the second source of contention. The *Rassemblement Populaire* emerged only as a coordinating center for the affiliated political parties and organizations. Each party and each organization participated "without abdicating anything of its doctrine, its principles, and its special goals." Autonomous "action committees" on the local level were ruled out; on all levels, committees would consist exclusively of delegates authorized by the participating organizations. Blum and the Socialists could feel more secure about Communist inroads.

The program, described as "voluntarily limited to measures immediately applicable," raised specific political and economic demands. Under the heading of "defense of liberty," it called for a general amnesty for political offenses, the disarming and dissolution of the "fascist" leagues, controls over unwholesome influences on the press, equal access for all political organizations to government-owned radio facilities, enforcement of respect for the rights of trade unions, pro-

---

[4] *Le Populaire*, August 7, 1935; see also his series of editorials, July 10–12, August 2–7, 1935, reproduced in *Oeuvre*, IV, pt. 1, 203–19.

[5] *Le Populaire*, September 23, 1935; for the "platform," *Oeuvre*, IV, pt. 1, 223–5.

[6] The program, published in *Le Populaire*, January 11, 1936, is reproduced in *Oeuvre*, IV, pt. 1, 225–9.

tection against church interference in the school system, extension of the age at which young people were permitted to leave school. For France overseas, notably French North Africa and Indochina, a parliamentary investigation of political, economic, and social conditions was urged.

The plank on foreign policy, the "defense of peace," was deliberately ambiguous. The program sought to satisfy the widespread desire for peace and the determination to check fascist aggression. It called for "international collaboration for collective security within the framework of the League of Nations" and for "automatic and unanimous application of sanctions in case of aggression." What had occurred in Manchuria in 1931 and what was happening at the moment in Ethiopia was not to be repeated. On the other hand, another clause spelled out a reduction and limitation of armaments—an "unceasing effort to pass from an armed peace to a disarmed peace," a phrase recognizably Blum's. Nothing was said about the contradiction between the two propositions. As a step to insure control over armaments, private munitions plants were to be nationalized—the only nationalization in the program. It was the age of the Nye munitions investigation in the United States; the "devil theory of war" had wide currency among the parties of the Left.

The economic demands focused on "the restoration of purchasing power destroyed or reduced by the depression" as an answer to the retrenchment and deflationary policies of all governments since Doumergue's. The program demanded the repeal of Laval's economy decree-laws and immediate relief for those classes of the population most severely affected by them. To increase the purchasing power of workers, it asked for a reduction of the work week without a corresponding reduction in wages (the forty-hour week, part of the Socialist program and of the C.G.T. Plan, was not specified as such in the Popular Front program); adequate pensions for older workers so that their jobs might be available for young people; the establishment of a national unemployment insurance system; and extensive urban and rural public works. On the agricultural front, the goal was a restoration of farm prices and farm income; a national wheat office was proposed to prevent speculation by middlemen. The financial measures included protection against the "destruction of savings" by stricter regulation of the banks. A thorough organizational reform of the nation's largest credit bank, the privately held Bank of France, was demanded in order to remove credit and savings from domination by the "economic oligarchy" ("To

make the Bank of France, today a private bank, into France's Bank").
There were to be fiscal reforms as well as strict control over the "flight
of capital."

The promise of sweeping reform concealed the limitations of the
program. Compromises were necessary in order to reassure the Radicals
and the middle-class voters that no "structural reforms" or socialist
measures were intended. The phraseology of the program obscured the
inadequacy of public credit facilities for putting many of the reforms
into effect, the need for a devaluation of the overvalued franc, and the
possible need for exchange control to check the "flight of capital." In
international matters, the delicate question of rearmament and the
means of preventing fascist aggression were ignored. But, all in all, it
had the surface appearance of an impressive and exciting program to
combat the depression, to institute long-overdue reforms, and to save
the peace. The very existence of the program meant that, unlike 1924
and 1932, a Left *cartel*, if victorious at the polls, would have a ready-
made agenda for a parliamentary majority and for a Popular Front
government.

Blum hailed the Popular Front program as soon as it was announced,
greeting it as a "program for cooperation on the second runoff ballot, a
program for a parliamentary majority, a program for a cabinet."[7] With
some disingenuousness, however, he claimed the chief credit for his
party: "I can say that by our attitude . . . we launched and popularized
in France the two ideas from which emerged proletarian unity of action
on the one hand and the republican Popular Front on the other."[8] In
some ways, despite his boast, he and his party had been followers rather
than leaders. But once the Popular Front was in existence, it had no
more loyal champion than Blum. To him it represented "unity against a
possible assault by fascism, an effort to govern jointly, and to govern
immediately, as quickly as possible after the election victory, and to
govern in such a way as to relieve the miseries and injustices in which
fascism finds its breeding ground."[9]

It quickly became apparent that Blum's interpretation of the Popular
Front as essentially a *political* coalition differed from that of the Communists. As soon as the Popular Front program was signed, Blum
acted on the assumption that the conditions for a Left coalition were

[7] *Le Populaire*, January 11, 1936.

[8] Speech to Paris rally, *Le Populaire*, January 14, 1936, also reprinted as a
pamphlet, *Le Socialisme a vu clair* (Paris, 1936), where the statement is on p.
24.

[9] *Le Populaire*, January 26, 1936.

already in existence. When the Radical ministers withdrew from the Laval cabinet in January 1936—and thereby ended the anomaly by which their party had been both a government party and an opposition party—Blum announced that the Socialists were ready "to assume full governmental responsibility" and to help form "a Popular Front government."[1] But the Communists were not willing to equate the Popular Front with a Left coalition or to accept a narrow parliamentary interpretation of it. A Communist party resolution stated that the Popular Front consisted in the "organization and mobilization of the masses . . . and not in the offers of cabinet participation which we regret to see being repeatedly made by organizations claiming to represent the working class." Jacques Duclos even published a series of articles reviving the hoary issue of "Millerandism" and resurrecting Blum's old statements in support of Millerand at the turn of the century.[2]

Blum was visibly annoyed. As he interpreted it, the *Rassemblement Populaire* was an electoral alliance, the basis for a parliamentary and governmental coalition, an enlarged republican *cartel*, with a limited reform program to which he and his party must remain scrupulously loyal. As the Communists saw it, the *Front Populaire* (the more militant term which they preferred to use) was a mobilization of the masses of which government action formed only one arm; this conception was shared by the Left wing in Blum's own party, men like Zyromski and Pivert in the Federation of the Seine. The latent weakness and incoherence of the future Popular Front governments had already appeared.[3]

Only a few months before the elections, the two parties were raking over old coals of disagreement concerning the events of February 1934. *L'Humanité* chided Blum for having failed to mention the Communist-sponsored counterdemonstration of February 9 in his editorial commemorating the events of 1934. Blum retaliated by reprinting the charges in *L'Humanité* on February 8, 1934, that the Radicals and the Socialists were "preparing the bed for fascism."[4]

The discussions on reunification of the two parties, which had been

[1] *Le Populaire*, January 22, 1936.

[2] "Le Néo-millerandisme," *L'Humanité*, February 4, 5, 1936. The Communist party resolution adopted at the Villeurbanne congress is cited in *Le Populaire*, January 26, 1936.

[3] On the distinction between the two terms, Dupeux: *Front Populaire*, p. 95. For Blum's editorial, *Le Populaire*, January 26, 1936. In general usage, the term *Front Populaire* came to be used almost exclusively.

[4] *Le Populaire*, February 11, 1936.

under way intermittently since April 1935, quite naturally came to naught. The Communists had originally proposed a "charter of unity" which would have created a united party along strictly Bolshevik lines; the Socialists had proposed reunification on the basis of the old "pact of unity" of 1905, providing for a loose organization and a more democratic determination of policy. Some progress toward reconciling the two points of view seemed to have been made when, at the beginning of January 1936, *L'Humanité* suddenly republished without emendation its original "charter of unity." "This is not the charter of a unified party of the working class," expostulated Blum, "but the charter of a Communist party."[5] Any possibility of organic reunification was fading. On the other hand, the C.G.T. and the C.G.T.U. were accomplishing the successful reunification of the two labor confederations, which took effect in March 1936. The Communists had shown much greater willingness to make concessions to reunite the two labor confederations than they had to reunite the two proletarian political parties.[6] However, despite their disagreements, the two parties held joint celebrations to commemorate the second anniversary of the events of February 1934. A few days later, they had occasion for a new joint demonstration.

On February 13, 1936, Blum was physically assaulted by royalist student ruffians. While driving with his Socialist friend and parliamentary colleague Georges Monnet and Mme Monnet, their car, with Monnet at the wheel, was halted in the Boulevard Saint-Germain near the Rue de l'Université for the funeral procession of Jacques Bainville, the royalist historian. The Action Francaise and its youth organization, the Camelots du Roi, were lining the streets for the ceremonies when Blum was suddenly recognized. A group of young vigilantes smashed the windows of the car, dragged him from it, and beat him savagely. Someone struck him on the temple with a sharp object torn from the vehicle. He was bleeding profusely and might well have been very seriously injured if a group of construction workers, some passers-by, and two policemen had not helped him to find refuge in a nearby apartment building.[7] Bleeding badly from the wound in his head, he was

[5] *Le Populaire*, January 10, 1936. For Blum's account of the reunification negotiations, see his speech to the special party congress, *Le Populaire*, February 2, 1936.

[6] Ehrmann makes this point: *French Labor*, p. 31. For Blum's comments hailing the reunification of the labor confederations, *Le Populaire*, January 28, 29, 1936.

[7] For the details, *Le Populaire*, February 14, 1936, and issues immediately succeeding.

brought to a hospital, where several stitches were taken; fortunately, a vein and not an artery had been punctured.

That afternoon he was photographed swathed in head bandages. The antifascist Popular Front had a martyr. Jean Guéhenno, one of the Popular Front literary heroes, wrote a tribute to him in *Vendredi* that dramatically conveyed the admiration of the intellectuals for the humanist who had entered the stormy paths of politics and embraced the popular cause:

> These men hate in you what makes you in our eyes most esteemed —the respect of the people. . . . If the hatred of these men has singled you out, it is because there is allied in you an admirable culture and a sense of justice, because it is clear that for you the revolution is but the ultimate achievement of reason and wisdom. I personally am filled with admiration that the objects of your studies, before you turned to Marx and Engels, were Stendhal and Goethe—of Stendhal, who recommended that one must not spend one's life in hating and in fearing, of Goethe, who sought always more enlightenment. . . . That a man like you is with us is a sign of the greatness of our cause.[8]

On February 16, the largest demonstration to date was held to protest the assault. Messages of sympathy were publicly extended to Blum by spokesmen for the various parties in the Chamber. As a concrete step, the Sarraut cabinet took advantage of a law passed recently against the armed leagues to issue a decree dissolving the royalist organization. The very day of the assault on Blum, Charles Maurras, in his column in *L'Action Française*, had urged that "the knife" be used against the 140 Deputies who had voted for sanctions against Mussolini; he was subsequently indicted and sentenced to four months in prison for inciting to murder. The assault on Blum was the culmination of a long series of journalistic incitements to violence against the Socialist leader who had been singled out, in the words of one Rightist gutter journal, as "public enemy No. 1."[9]

The police were able to apprehend some of Blum's assailants thanks to pictures of the assault taken by a photographer who happened to be at the scene. Although the chief assailant escaped identification, two of the other ringleaders received prison terms. Blum himself, suffering

[8] Cited in *Le Populaire*, February 18, 1936.
[9] *La Solidarité Française*, January 28, 1935. A number of these vicious summons to action were gathered and published by *La Lumière*, February 22, 1936.

from shock and loss of blood, required a long rest. He left Paris to convalesce at the home of Vincent Auriol in southern France, where he remained all during the election campaign that spring.

Widespread public indignation and sympathy toward Blum helped the Popular Front election campaign. The assault on Blum was like a repetition of February 6. Blum became, for the moment, a personal symbol of the republic. The episode revealed also the continuing depths of political passion in France and the persistence of a fascist or quasi-fascist mentality. The country was more fiercely divided than at any time since the Dreyfus Affair—at a time when the international situation was steadily growing more critical.

During the early 1930's Blum's position on foreign affairs was ambivalent. Although he was morally repelled by the truculence and belligerence of the dictators and advocated a firm stand against fascist aggression, he remained the champion of disarmament. Even after Germany quit the Disarmament Conference and the League in October 1933, he persisted in his hope for an international disarmament plan, strongly criticizing Louis Barthou's note of April 17, 1934, which ended all disarmament talks and which categorically stated that France would have to look to its own resources for its security.[1] Denouncing the failure of the Disarmament Conference to reach an agreement, he put the blame for German rearmament squarely on the Versailles powers. "If the Conference had succeeded in time, Germany could not have rearmed."[2] He continued to believe that an arms control plan could be worked out—"with or without Germany"; "world conscience" and "universal reprobation" would force Hitler to comply.[3] "What Hitler fears above all," he wrote in January 1935, "is pressure that would oblige him to reintegrate himself into the framework of international law."[4] How Hitler was to be cajoled or pressured into re-entering the international framework—short of a "preventive war," which he naturally excluded[5]—he never made clear.

[1] *Le Populaire*, May 12, 1934.

[2] *Le Populaire*, June 4, 1934.

[3] See his speeches, *Chambre, Débats*, sessions of June 14, December 1, 1934, and December 28, 1935; also the selection of editorials written in 1935 reproduced in *Oeuvre*, IV, pt. 1, 105–32.

[4] *Le Populaire*, January 23, 1935.

[5] *Le Populaire*, November 24, 1935. For his later references to the possibility (and impossibility) of a "preventive war," see his testimony, 1947, *Événements*, I, 121–2 and *À l'échelle humaine, Oeuvre*, V, 424.

Blum's campaign for universal disarmament was accompanied by his insistence that France set an example in working toward disarmament and in resisting all pressure to rearm—"to disarm on its own as much as is necessary in order to encourage an international agreement."[6] In 1935 he and the party fought the law which extended military service from one to two years, a measure intended to compensate, during the coming "hollow" period, for the reduced number of men born during the First World War and then reaching military age.[7] During the debate in the Chamber on March 15, 1935, he maintained that "one played into the hands of Hitler" by stressing the "rearmament" of France and not the "disarmament" of Germany.[8]

Blum opposed rearmament not only because he believed that a fatal armaments race must result but because it would strengthen the cause of French "militarism" as well. Among the proposals he campaigned against in 1935 was Colonel Charles de Gaulle's plan for an elite corps of armored divisions then being sponsored in the Chamber by Paul Reynaud. Blum denounced the creation of a professional corps that might be used for antirepublican purposes—as a "praetorian guard"—adding that de Gaulle's divisions, capable of lightning offensives, would harm rather than preserve peace.[9]

To be sure, de Gaulle's words were not calculated to allay the apprehensions of a pacifist, antimilitarist intellectual. De Gaulle had noted in his book that the necessary spiritual renovation of the country had to begin with the army. "In the hard work that must rejuvenate France, its army will serve it as a source of vitality. For the sword is the axis of the world and greatness is not divisible."[1] The sword the axis of the world! Blum was not the only good republican, let it be said also, who was frightened by the term "professional army." It disturbed men like Daladier too.[2] Even the long faithful Reynaud, in later years, admitted de Gaulle's "imprudence" in using the phrase, especially as a title for

[6] *Le Populaire*, March 16, 1934.

[7] See resolution, Toulouse congress, May 1934, p. 393.

[8] Speech in Chamber, *Chambre, Débats*, March 15, 1935. This important speech is not reproduced in *Oeuvre*, Vol. IV.

[9] In addition to the Chamber speech just cited, see editorials in *Le Populaire*, November 28, 30, and December 1, 1934. The episode is discussed further in Chapter VII below.

[1] *Vers l'armée de métier*, quoted in his *Mémoires de guerre*, I: *L'Appel, 1940–1942* (Paris, 1954), p. 10.

[2] Testimony, 1947, *Événements*, I, 22.

his book.[3] Blum later explained that his opposition to de Gaulle's proposal was dictated by anxiety for the security of the republic.[4] With
the shadow of February 6, 1934, still over France, the old republican
mistrust of the army and the old Socialist antipathy to war were too
strong to permit Blum to rally at that moment to rearmament and national defense, and certainly not to de Gaulle's bold policy. We shall
have occasion in later pages to return to Blum's attitude toward de
Gaulle's armored divisions.

Although Blum opposed rearmament, he insisted that if French soil
were invaded all Frenchmen would rise to their country's defense. "I
am absolutely convinced," he announced during the debate in March
1935, "that in answer to a clear-cut aggression on the part of Hitler
Germany all the workers of this country would rise up with all other
Frenchmen."[5] A *levée en masse*—a popular mobilization as in 1792 and
a girding of the nation's entire population and resources—would be
France's protection, not a large peacetime army of professionals and
conscripts; such, he said (with only partial accuracy), had been the
lesson of 1914–18.

Unwilling to abandon his hope for a general disarmament plan,
Blum also continued to press for negotiations with the dictators. "When
the question of peace with Germany and Italy is involved, we are ready
to shake all hands, even hands stained with blood," he told the
Chamber in December 1934.[6] He returned to this theme again and
again. The horror and hatred that he felt for the dictatorial regimes
did not deter him from seeking all possible avenues that might save
the peace.

On the question of the *rapprochement* between France and the
U.S.S.R., Blum was at first of two minds. He wanted it clearly understood that Socialist policy in France was not to be dictated by Russian
foreign policy no matter what the Communists did. He knew also how
intensely Paul Faure and other anti-war elements in the party opposed
a revival of the Franco-Russian military and diplomatic alliance of

[3] *Mémoires*, I, 23, and II, 488–9. The conservative historian Jacques Chastenet
notes that in later years the French paratroopers, organized as an elite corps,
played a highly political role in 1958 and 1961 and that Blum's fears "were not
without some foundation"; *Histoire*, VI, 287, n. 8. See also, on the general
subject, my letter in the London *Times Literary Supplement*, May 18, 1962.

[4] *Mémoires* (1940), *Oeuvre*, V, 111–12.

[5] *Chambre, Débats*, March 15, 1935.

[6] Ibid., December 1, 1934.

1893 and the division of Europe into two armed camps; he himself shared that view.[7] Yet once the Franco-Soviet pact was in the negotiation stage, and after Hitler in March 1935 reintroduced universal military training, Blum spoke out in favor of the pact, whose purpose was "not to make [war] but to prevent it." The pact, along with other special arrangements, was acceptable so long as it was part of the broader League structure and "linked to continued efforts at general disarmament and international agreement."[8] There were still misgivings in the party, however; the old antipathy to armed alliances died hard. Although willing to accept the pact, Paul Faure, in the spring of 1936, expressed the determination of the party, "not to allow ourselves to be dragged into a game of military alliances and an armaments race as in the pre-1914 years; this is what the General Staffs and, even more so, the sinister international of munitions makers want."[9]

Blum, like many others in the party (and like their British Labour colleagues), was genuinely torn between the desire for disarmament and peace and the grim appraisal that only military and diplomatic strength, even at the risk of war, could check fascist rearmament and aggression.[1] The vague term "collective security" served only to gloss over the basic contradiction. Blum, as usual, sought to help his own party find some middle ground. Although he still clung to his hope for a general disarmament agreement, he pleaded for rejection of an oversimplified doctrinaire pacifism:

> This attitude of opposition, absolute, determined opposition to war . . . there are moments when it is not enough. It is not enough when war is a fact [as in 1914] . . . or when it assumes the appearance of something that seems to be drawing close, presenting a serious threat, casting a shadow over the world. At such moments it is no longer enough for a party, on every possible occasion, to say only, "Everything in the world to prevent war!"[2]

[7] See e.g., his speech to national council, *Le Populaire*, July 16, 1934; also *Le Populaire*, September 21, 1934.

[8] Editorials, *Le Populaire*, April 10, 11, 1935; series of editorials, April 11– May 5, 1935, and February 11, 1936; and see statements at Mulhouse congress, June 1935, p. 213.

[9] *Le Populaire*, February 6, 1936; for Blum's comments, ibid., February 11, 1936.

[1] See his revealing comments on the British Labour party debate in October 1935, *Le Populaire*, October 9, 1935. It was like a classical tragedy, he wrote, in which each speaker presented his case with irreproachable logic and nobility.

[2] Mulhouse congress, June 1935, p. 215.

The rearmament of Germany and the aggression of Mussolini, he added, presented them with such a "moment." The struggle for peace could demand the "eventual application of force"; terrible though war was, it was yet "better than a cowardly surrender to aggression."[3] He appealed also for an abandonment of "revolutionary defeatism," the thesis that the working classes had to work for the defeat of their own capitalist governments. That thesis no longer had validity once one introduced "degrees of responsibility between the powers," and once one believed that it was not "capitalism in itself" that was responsible for war.[4]

In the Ethiopian crisis in 1935, Blum demanded firmness in rejecting Mussolini's demands from the very beginning.[5] When the actual invasion by Italian troops got under way and sanctions were imposed, he rejoiced at the prospect of a resurrection of the League of Nations and a renewal of confidence and hope. He scorned the argument that sanctions would provoke Mussolini into widening the scope of war and thereby threaten the peace of Europe. The real danger, he maintained, was that Laval's policy of appeasing Mussolini would discourage and divide the democratic world and interfere with a union of forces against an even greater danger, Hitler's rearmed Germany.[6]

When news leaked out in December 1935 of the Hoare-Laval agreement to buy off Mussolini by conceding much of Ethiopia to him even before he had conquered it, Blum spared no words in denouncing Pierre Laval. His editorials in *Le Populaire* and his masterful interpellation in the Chamber contributed to the weakening of Laval's government and to its eventual fall. "You have proceeded in the great affairs of the world in the same way we have seen you proceed here," he assailed him in the Chamber. "You have tried to give and to hold back. . . . You have nullified your words by your deeds and your deeds by your words."[7]

The failure of the League to enforce even the limited sanctions that were invoked against Mussolini left Blum exasperated and crushed.[8]

---

[3] *Le Populaire*, October 9, 1935.

[4] *Mulhouse congress*, June 1935, p. 217

[5] *Le Populaire*, July 27, and August 20, 27, 29, 1935.

[6] *Le Populaire*, October 3, 4, November 24, and December 5, 12, 15, 23, 26, 1935.

[7] *Chambre, Débats*, December 27, 1935; and *Le Populaire*, December 15, 23, 1935. Blum was especially bitter because the party had supported the "Rome accords" without suspecting that Ethiopia had been discussed; Mulhouse party congress, June 1935, pp. 208–9.

[8] *Le Populaire*, April 22, 1936.

The Ethiopian episode was a turning point in many ways. Because of the Socialist support for sanctions against Mussolini, the Right charged that the Socialists—the former "bleating pacifists," as they liked to term them—had now turned into "warmongers." The same elements on the Right meanwhile opposed ratification of the Franco-Soviet pact as a step that would antagonize Hitler and lead to war. The accusation that the Socialists were bent on war was far from true, but there were signs that the traditional pacifism of the Left and the belligerence of the Right were being reversed.[9]

On the other hand, it cannot be said that in the Rhineland crisis the Socialists acted to strengthen the stand of the government. On March 7, 1936, when Hitler marched his troops into the Rhineland in flagrant violation of the Versailles agreement and the Locarno Pact, France would have been legally justified in taking stern measures. Indeed, Premier Sarraut's words were firm. But, refusing to act without some guarantee of British support, discouraged by the military, which insisted that only total, and not partial, mobilization would be effective, and with an eye to the general elections less than two months off, the Sarraut government in the end did nothing.[1] The Socialists condemned Hitler's act but appealed for "calm and *sang-froid*." The party warned against unilateral action and insisted that the whole matter be submitted to the League. Paul Faure considered it senseless to risk war in order to force Germany into accepting the demilitarization of its own territory "seventeen years after the peace treaty."[2] Blum himself was away from Paris recuperating from his injuries, but he associated himself fully with the party's position, and hailed it as proof of the Socialists' unshakable will for peace despite the charges of their political opponents that they had "deserted the great tradition of Jaurès . . ." "There comes this dramatic event, the occupation of the Rhineland. Who now, if not the Socialist party, has set the example for *sang-froid*, calmness, firmness, reason?"[3] As if compensating for the strong stand he had

[9] For the reversal of traditional positions on foreign affairs, Charles Micaud: *The French Right and Nazi Germany, 1933–1939* (Durham, N.C., 1943); on attitudes toward the Franco-Soviet pact, William Evans Scott: *Alliance Against Hitler: The Origins of the Franco-Soviet Pact* (Durham, N.C., 1962), esp. pp. 251–2.

[1] For the episode, W. F. Knapp, "The Rhineland Crisis of March 1936," in Joll (ed.): *The Decline of the Third Republic*.

[2] See comments by Oreste Rosenfeld and Paul Faure, and the statement drawn up by Vincent Auriol for the Socialist parliamentary group, *Le Populaire*, March 9, 10, 11, 1936.

[3] For Blum's letter of comment, *Le Populaire*, March 12, 1936.

urged against Mussolini, he was now eager to restore the image of the Socialists as a party of peace, which of course pleased many in his own party. Before long, he and others recognized the full implication of the failure to resist Hitler's move into the Rhineland. Accomplished with impunity, Hitler's act undermined the confidence of France's friends and allies everywhere. The diplomatic weakness of France was part of the heritage of Blum's own Popular Front government. In the months to come the same tension, the pull between the desire to check aggression and the desire to abstain from any positive action that might threaten peace, continued in Blum's party—and in Blum himself.

Foreign affairs were overshadowed in the spring of 1936 by the excitement of the coming elections. Each of the Popular Front parties campaigned on its own platform as well as on the program of the Popular Front—and on the slogan "Peace, Bread, and Liberty." Each asked the electorate to support its own candidates on the first ballot, but in the runoff election all would withdraw in favor of the leading Popular Front candidate.[4]

Blum set the tone for the Socialists in a radio speech on April 21, 1936, delivered from Narbonne.[5] (He was especially pleased that he had wrested from the government a pledge of equal broadcasting time for each party.) He summarized the threefold anxiety weighing upon the population: the troubled state of international affairs, the threat of internal fascism in France, and the social and economic ravages of the depression. Had the Socialist party been heeded in international affairs, a strong unbroken front against Mussolini would have prevented the conquest of Ethiopia and a general European disarmament program would also have been worked out—"with, without, or against Hitler." The preservation of peace in Europe, he reiterated, continued to lie in collective security through the League, regional mutual assistance pacts, and unremitting efforts toward general disarmament.

Referring to the threat of fascism in France, he boasted, in a thinly veiled reference both to the Communists and to the Radicals, that his party had never hesitated in its antifascism, nor compromised with reaction in any way since February 6, 1934. He recalled their fight against the "masked fascism" of Doumergue and Tardieu, their campaign

[4] For a summary of the party programs and election campaign speeches in 1936, Dupeux: *Front Populaire*, pp. 101–22.

[5] *Le Populaire*, April 22, 1936; the speech is reproduced in *Oeuvre*, IV, pt. 1, 234–44.

against Laval for his complicity with fascism within and without the country. Warning against a sense of false security, he predicted that the paramilitary leagues, which had not yet been dissolved, were merely biding their time.

He dwelt finally on the bitter ravages of the depression, insisting that any effective defense against fascism and war must be directed at the suffering caused by the depression. He attacked the deflationary and retrenchment policies pursued by the Rightist governments. It was necessary "not to restrict production but to increase general consumption. The authority of the state must be applied to all nerve centers of economic life in order to revive and stimulate activity." It was necessary "to breathe life again into the economic organism hurt by the depression and bled by deflation." He recalled the Socialist proposals that his own party still believed in, including the nationalization of the country's key industries, and injected a specific Socialist appeal. His party sought to "make all men of good faith understand that the cause of our common miseries resides in an evil social system . . . incapable of distributing among consumers the ever-increasing quantity of riches created by the continued progress of technology." Socialism alone had as its objective "to spread among all humanity the collective benefits of nature and of material progress."

As to the Popular Front coalition and its program, Blum pledged that he and his party would faithfully fulfill their obligations. He described the program as "incomplete and imperfect in comparison to our Socialist program—but at the very least it tends toward the preservation of peace in Europe, calls for energetic action against fascism, and, on the economic plane, insures relief for the most crying distress." It was an effective appeal, enhanced by Blum's tone of moderation, sincerity, and reasonableness and his air of serene self-confidence.

All the Left parties profited from the generalities of the Popular Front program, which denounced the "two hundred families" and the "merchants of death" and called for the dissolution of the fascist leagues, the repeal of the Laval economy decrees, protection for the rights of labor, a shorter work week, and other measures to help spread employment and increase the purchasing power of the people. In the election campaign no one had to deal concretely with the ways and means of coping with mounting budgetary deficits, the difficulties of the Treasury, the overvalued franc, the drying up of credit facilities, and other economic problems. Such troublesome matters could be postponed until after the elections.

The elections, on the two successive Sundays of April 26 and May 3, resulted in an impressive victory for the Popular Front coalition. Careful observers noted that it was more a victory in terms of a parliamentary majority than in popular vote. The rough division between Left and Right throughout the country had not altered very much from previous elections, the total of the Center and Right vote showing only a slight decline. Within the Left camp itself, the Radicals, with 1,955,000 votes, were the heavy losers, dropping almost 400,000 votes. The Communists, on the other hand, increased their voting strength by almost 700,000 (to 1,469,000). The Socialists showed a small decline of some 34,000 votes (largely because of the secession of the "neos") but, with 1,997,000 votes, had edged out the Radicals and were the leading Left party in terms of popular votes. Under the small-district, single-candidate method of voting, the coalition of Socialists, Communists, and Radicals held firm, rallying on the runoff ballot to the leading Popular front candidate. The second ballot was crucial, for only 174 Deputies (among them Blum) received a majority immediately; runoffs in 424 districts were necessary.

The parliamentary results were striking. First, the Socialists, with 146 seats, were returned as the leading party of the Chamber—and that despite the secession of the "neos," which had left them with only 97 seats at the end of the old legislature; second, the Radicals lost their former leading position, dropping from 159 to 116 seats; third, the Communists made a spectacular gain, increasing their seats from 10 to 72.[6] It was not noticed very much at the time that the Communist and Socialist successes on the first ballot caused sufficient alarm among some Popular Front voters to make them shift to anti-Popular Front parties on the second ballot.[7] The defection of these middle-class voters, torn between the fear of fascism and the prospects of social revolution, was an ill omen for the future stability of the new coalition. The momentary panic on the Bourse during the week of the election, reflecting anxiety in investment circles over the successes of the Left, was another disturbing note.

The new legislature divided between 378 supporters of the Popular Front coalition (the Socialist, Radical, and Communist parties, the

[6] For an exhaustive analysis of the election, Dupeux: *Front Populaire*, pp. 123–71, and maps and charts, and Georges Lachapelle: *Les Élections législatives des 26 avril et 3 mai 1936* (Paris, 1936). The popular vote was 5,628,921 for the Popular Front parties and 4,218,345 for their opponents.

[7] Dupeux: *Front Populaire*, p. 137.

Socialist Republican Union, and other independents of the Left) and some 220 opponents on the Center and Right.[8] The Left majority had not merely gained some 40 seats over its 1932 strength; the crucial difference lay in the existence of a coalition pledged to work together and to support a program drawn up in advance. Coalitions, to be sure, have a notorious habit of falling apart after victories. This coalition was a particularly uneasy one; its common program obscured profound differences and ignored others. Moreover, no coalition of political parties could anticipate the difficulties that were destined to arise in the life of a great nation in a troubled world. But no one had such gloomy thoughts in the spring of 1936. Blum, as Premier-designate, was on the threshold of the most important years of his entire political career.

[8] Ibid., pp. 138–9. These figures will vary somewhat, depending on whether press reports or the official statistics are used. On the first vote of confidence, the government received 384 affirmative votes to 210 opposed.

The Years of Responsibility

THE "GREAT FEAR"
OF JUNE 1936

*I remember what they were saying to me.
. . . Alors, quoi? the Revolution? What will
they leave us?*

*I played the role of a conciliator, a role for
which I would almost dare to say I was
destined.*[1]

N OT ONLY did the Popular Front coalition win an impressive
victory in the elections of April 26 and May 3—"of proportions and significance that almost no one dared hope for,"
in Blum's words[2]—but the Socialists for the first time in the country's
history were returned, with 146 seats, as the leading party in the
Chamber. "The Socialist party is ready," Blum announced immediately
after the election. "The Socialist party has become the strongest party
not only of the majority but of the entire Chamber. We wish to state,
without losing a moment, that we are ready to accept the role that has
fallen to us—to form and to assume direction of the Popular Front
government."[3]

The preconditions for the "exercise of power"—the formation of a
government by the party—which he had elaborated on in the 1920's,
had been fulfilled. The Socialists were the strongest party of the victorious coalition; the coalition had a substantial majority in Parliament;
and the Popular Front program provided a basis for common action.[4]

[1] Testimony at Riom trial, *Oeuvre*, V, 259, 326.
[2] *Le Populaire*, special edition, May 4, 1936.
[3] Ibid. Blum was also making sure that the President of the Republic would
not bypass the Socialists when the new government was formed.
[4] Blum's speech to national council, May 10, 1936, *Le Populaire*, May 11,
1936; also *Exercice du pouvoir*, pp. 29–48, esp. p. 30.

A party committed to democratic socialism seemed also to be the natural axis for a coalition that included Communists on the one hand and middle-class republicans on the other. Moreover, no one had better qualifications to lead such a coalition than Blum—a Socialist but a respected member of the Chamber for almost twenty years, leader of the opposition for many of those years, and a devoted servant of the parliamentary republic. The elections had shown, too, that within the country there was a widespread desire for action and innovation. A non-Socialist colleague of Blum in Parliament said to him: "Go to it. France is waiting for you. She awaits you nervously but only with the nervousness of a new bride!"[5]

No one denied the Socialists the right to form the cabinet. There was even a note of satisfaction in conservative circles. *Le Temps* commented that those who had been free with their advice would now have to "pay the piper." "M. Léon Blum," its editorial admonished on May 6, "will now have to take responsibility for the inviolability of the national frontiers, the prosperity of France, the integrity of our currency and foreign exchange, the state of the Treasury, the recovery of business, the absorption of unemployment, and many other things." *Le Temps* was correct. The Popular Front government was inheriting a long list of internal problems as well as a deteriorating international situation. (The elections, it will be remembered, took place only two months after Hitler had remilitarized the Rhineland and when Mussolini's conquest of Ethiopia was all but complete.) The French Socialists were taking on the responsibilities of government for the first time in their history at a bleak and unpropitious moment. "A new era is opening up for our party. Now our troubles really begin," noted Bracke, the respected elder statesman of the party.[6] Prepared as everyone was for difficulties, no one anticipated the avalanche that descended even before Blum took office.

Under constitutional procedure there was an interval of a month before the convening of the new legislature and the formation of the new government, the time generally being employed for the distribution of seats in the cabinet among the victorious parties. The month from May 4 to June 4, 1936, when Blum, in Paul Reynaud's phrase, was "*le dauphin couronné*" and when Premier Albert Sarraut presided over what was universally recognized as a caretaker—indeed a lame-duck—

[5] Related by Blum, ibid., pp. 47–8.
[6] Bracke (A. M. Desrousseaux), to national council, *Le Populaire*, May 11, 1936.

ministry, proved to be one of the stormiest in the history of the republic.

The first repercussions of the election results appeared in financial circles. Despite the election pledges of moderation and the presence of moderate and even conservative-minded Radicals in the victorious coalition, genuine uncertainty developed over the new government's economic plans. For some time private capital had been fleeing the country, and speculators had been converting their francs into foreign currency. After the elections, speculation became more active in anticipation of a possible devaluation of the franc. In the week following the elections, prices on the Bourse declined, the Bank of France lost 2.5 billion francs from its gold reserves as a result of private foreign exchange purchases, and the franc weakened.[7]

To avert the panic that was shaping up, Blum hastened to reassure business and financial circles that they had nothing to fear from the Popular Front government that was soon to assume office. His most cherished desire, he stated, was to win the confidence of all classes of the nation so that the economy could be revived and prosperity restored. It was ridiculous to think that he would act in any way to sow panic or throw the country "into the anguish of a currency crisis." He also reassured the country about the non-revolutionary character of the Popular Front, which sought only to increase purchasing power, restore the economy, and relieve suffering, not to revolutionize society or introduce reforms more advanced than those in the coalition's program.[8] His reassurances helped calm the financial unrest.

At the very time that Blum was trying to convince the business interests of his moderate intentions, impatience developed in Socialist circles. The Left wing of Blum's party demanded that he capitalize on the wave of popular enthusiasm and set aside all scruples about ordinary constitutional practices. It insisted that he take office immediately, act decisively against the "deserters of the franc," and launch a sweeping reform program boldly and rapidly. Marceau Pivert, spokesman for the Revolutionary Left group in the party (the *Gauche Révolutionnaire*), which was now close to the Trotskyites in its thinking, proposed his own timetable: "Within three days chase out the accomplices of fascism in the higher administrative echelons; within three weeks free all victims of the depression from its suffocating strangle-

[7] See, e.g., Marc Joubert: "Un Mois d'histoire de la Bourse," *Le Populaire*, May 25, 1936.

[8] Blum used his speech to the national council, May 10, 1936, to make these points; see *Exercice du pouvoir*, esp. pp. 36–45; see also editorials in *Le Populaire*, May 6, 8, 9, 1936.

hold; within three months carry out the entire Popular Front program; within three years insure such a recovery of the economy, such a rise in the standard of living of the workers, that the immense majority of the nation will be decisively won over to socialism." And he urged Blum to appeal to the country for revolutionary action if there should be any attempt to interfere with or overthrow his "Socialist cabinet."[9] Jean Zyromski and the *Bataille Socialiste* group, the pro-Communist faction within the party, also demanded a dynamic antifascist policy, a government closely tied to "the working classes and peasant masses," and the closest collaboration between the Socialists and the Communist party. He rejected the idea of "a government wishing simply to manage the interests of bourgeois society."[1]

Blum was a man walking a tightrope. He himself had once used this analogy to describe the dilemma of a Socialist in Parliament, and it was even more apt now that he was a Socialist heading a non-Socialist government. He had to define goals and methods that would inspire national confidence and at the same time produce results satisfactory to the Left wing of his own party. Yet this was precisely the kind of challenge at which he excelled. Determined to respect traditional constitutional practices, he turned a deaf ear on all suggestions that he assume office immediately, and proceeded instead with his cabinet negotiations. The Popular Front government under the first Socialist Premier in French history would take office "in the most normal, most legal way." He refused to aggravate existing anxieties by any other course of action. But he also reassured the party in bold words that nothing would thwart the will of the electorate and the desire for sweeping change: "We are not just a few isolated men entering into office as the result of a chance parliamentary maneuver. There are behind us the popular masses whose representatives and spokesmen we are, the popular masses to whom there would be no need to appeal twice if anyone acted against their will."[2] *L'Écho de Paris* sarcastically but pointedly remarked that Blum was trying to please both Pivert and Zyromski on the one hand and the country's investors on the other.[3]

---

[9] "La Parole est aux militants," in the "free opinion" column, "Tribune du Parti," *Le Populaire*, May 12, 1936; and speech to the national council, *Le Populaire*, May 11, 1936.

[1] "Pour un gouvernement du 12 février," in "Tribune du Parti," *Le Populaire*, May 9, 1936.

[2] Speech to national council, May 10, 1936, *Exercice du pouvoir*, pp. 37–8, 44–5.

[3] "Revue de la Presse," *Le Populaire*, May 12, 1936.

Blum appealed for the support and trust of all elements of the party at this critical moment. "In a battle like this, a leader is necessary; it is essential that command be exercised under your continuing control but with full powers vested in me. I have never used language like this with you before. You know that whatever standing I possess with the party I owe to a constant effort of conciliation and persuasion. Today something else is needed. In the face of new circumstances, a new man must emerge." Blum disparaged his own capabilities. "I do not know if I have the qualities of a leader for so difficult a battle; I cannot know it with any more exactness than any of you. You will put me to the test, and I shall put myself to the test as well."[4] This public soul-searching and self-abasement was typical of Blum and familiar to his audiences; for the moment the very sincerity and simplicity of his appeal quieted the Left wing.

In forming the cabinet, Blum's objective was to have all the Popular Front parties represented. As expected, the Radicals and the small Republican Socialist Union party accepted his invitation. Although the Communists had made clear before the elections that they would not participate in the cabinet, he urged them to "reconsider."[5] They declined, ostensibly on the ground that their presence in the cabinet would serve as a pretext for reactionaries in the country to raise the specter of revolution.[6] Actually, Thorez and the Communists were bent on retaining their independence; in that way they could dissociate themselves from policies of which they might not approve and exert pressure on the government from the outside—as a "ministry of the masses." In any event, they were giving Blum a dose of his own medicine. They were adopting the policy that he and his party had followed for many years with respect to the Radicals, pledging to support the cabinet without participating in it. There were advantages and disadvantages in not having the Communists in the cabinet, but Blum later had reason to regret, on balance, that the Communists were not in the cabinet sharing in its responsibilities and decisions and less free to criticize from the outside. Blum invited the C.G.T. into the cabinet as well, but Léon Jou-

[4] Speech to national council, May 10, 1936, *Exercice du pouvoir*, p. 46.

[5] See Blum: "Le Front Populaire et le pouvoir," *Le Populaire*, May 8, 1936; letter to the Communist party, *Le Populaire*, May 12, 1936; and Blum: speech to national council, May 10, 1936, *Exercice du pouvoir*, pp. 32–3.

[6] See letter, Communist party to S.F.I.O., *Le Populaire*, May 14, 1936. Thorez later claimed that he personally wanted his party to take seats in the cabinet but that he was overridden by the political bureau; *Fils du peuple* (1960 ed.), p. 121.

haux pleaded the traditional syndicalist avoidance of direct participation in political affairs. He promised, however, that the C.G.T. would support the cabinet in every possible way and even take an active part in technical government advisory organizations.[7] Blum, disappointed though he was, put the best face possible on the refusal of the Communists and the C.G.T. to join the cabinet.[8]

In the midst of the cabinet negotiations, before anyone realized what was happening, the greatest strike movement in the history of the Third Republic began. On May 14, less than two weeks after the Popular Front election victory, metalworkers of the Bloch factory in one of Paris's industrial suburbs struck to protest the management's refusal to consider their demands. It was a "sitdown strike." The workers stayed on the premises and even spent the night in the plant; their families and sympathetic municipal authorities brought them food. The next day the company yielded on all points, signing a contract and granting a wage increase, paid vacations, and compensation for time lost during the strike. A few days later short sitdown strikes in other industrial suburbs of the Seine produced similar results, and the technique attracted attention.[9] Meanwhile the labor groups impatiently awaited the investiture of the new government. At the traditional ceremonies at the end of May honoring the martyrs of the Paris Commune, Blum was received with acclamation but also with shouts exhorting him to action. "*Blum au pouvoir!* To work, Blum! There are things to be done!"[1] The next day the Communist party central committee called attention to the growing restlessness in the country.[2]

Blum's appeals for patience were not sufficient.[3] In the fourth week after the election, beginning on Tuesday, May 26, a second wave of sitdown strikes erupted, crowding everything else from the headlines.

---

[7] See letter of invitation and C.G.T. reply, *Le Populaire*, May 12, 14, 1936. For details on the C.G.T. in this period, Ehrmann: *French Labor*, esp. pp. 3–37.

[8] "Deux Réponses," *Le Populaire*, May 15, 1936.

[9] For the most detailed account of the 1936 labor crisis and for many other aspects of the Popular Front years, see Jacques Danos and Marcel Gibelin: *Juin 36* (Paris, 1952), preface by Édouard Dolléans. Although carefully documented, it is written from a militant Leftist viewpoint and must be used cautiously. There is a vivid narrative of the sitdown strikes, written at the time, in Werth: *Destiny of France*, pp. 292–313.

[1] News account in *Le Populaire*, May 25, 1936.

[2] *L'Humanité*, May 26, 1936, cited by Danos and Gibelin: *Juin 36*, p. 47.

[3] "Une Fois de plus," *Le Populaire*, May 27, 1936.

Sitdown strikes broke out among the metalworkers in the most important automobile and airplane factories in the Seine area. The 35,000 workers of the Renault plant went on strike (Louis Renault's reputation in labor relations was no better than Henry Ford's in the 1930's). The strike spread to other industries, even to the construction workers who were erecting the buildings for the International Exposition due to open the following spring.

Although the grievances raised by the strike committees differed on specific details, the demands invariably included collective-bargaining rights—contracts providing for guaranteed minimum wage rates, a forty-hour week with compensation for overtime, paid vacations, and the right to elect shop stewards. The demands for collective contracts were understandable; employers and employer associations in France had for a long time stubbornly resisted collective bargaining. After years of submissiveness, the workers were intoxicated and exhilarated by the Popular Front election triumph and were now testing their strength. Like the peasant masses in the "great fear" of 1789, they were determined not to wait for the slow processes of government.[4] Pressure from below might even guarantee that the Blum government would take bolder and quicker action than otherwise.

Everywhere the strikes took a common form. The workers remained in the plants day and night, posting security guards, solicitously caring for the machinery. Food and blankets were brought in by their families and sympathizers; entertainment was provided. There was little or no vandalism. Indeed the workers seemed to be treating the factories as if the plants already belonged to them, which was enough to frighten the bourgeoisie. *Le Temps* saw something sinister in the very order that reigned in the factories.[5]

Seizing upon the new situation, Pivert and the Revolutionary Left Socialists heralded the "revolution." "Everything is possible," Pivert announced in *Le Populaire*, and directed his words squarely at Blum: "Let no one come and sing lullabies to us; the entire people is now on the march with a sure step toward its magnificent destiny. . . . We are at an hour which will undoubtedly not soon reappear on the stage of history." He demanded "surgical operations" in every area of public life, the nationalization of the country's key industries, and severe penalties

---

[4] Blum used the analogy, from which the title of this chapter is derived, in his testimony at the Riom trial in 1942, *Oeuvre*, V, 327.

[5] *Le Temps*, May 31, 1936; cf. Blum's remarks in the portion of his Riom testimony just cited.

against "deserters of the franc." Nothing, he believed, could "delay the hour of France's social revolution."[6]

But Pivert was in a minority. Blum, the majority of his party, the C.G.T., and even the Communists regarded the labor upheaval not as an opportunity but as an obstacle, a danger to the immediate task at hand—the experiment of a Popular Front government based on combined working-class and middle-class support and seeking the broadest possible unity to combat the depression, defend the republic against internal fascist threats, and play a role on the international front against fascism. There were different shades of emphasis in the thought of Thorez, Jouhaux, and Blum at this moment, but all three saw in the labor upheaval an untimely challenge to their immediate objectives. Individually and together, they sought ways and means of ending it while expressing their sympathy with the strikers.

The Communists made their position clear. Although conceding that there was justification for the impatience of the masses, the central committee of the party defeated a "Leftist" resolution calling for a break with the projected Blum government.[7] The Communist leader Marcel Gitton replied to Pivert's "Everything is possible" with an editorial in *L'Humanité* crisply stating: "Everything is not possible." His language indicated that international considerations were the chief factor in the Communist restraint. "We consider impossible," Gitton wrote, "in the face of the Hitler threat, a policy that would risk placing the security of France in jeopardy."[8] Nothing would be permitted to weaken the military and diplomatic strength of the ally of the U.S.S.R. Revolution and internal upheaval were not the Communist line for France in May and June 1936. In this crisis Blum could count on the Communists for support, and on those Left Socialists in his own party, led by Zyromski, who advocated close ties with the Communists.

As to the organized labor movement, far from having initiated the strikes, Jouhaux and the C.G.T. seem to have been taken by surprise. The labor movement, disunited since the schism of 1921 and demoralized after the crushing of the postwar general strikes, had known lean and hollow years in the 1920's and early 1930's, in which the unions were weak and impoverished, collective bargaining was unknown, and the open shop reigned. With the coming of the depression, the rise of Hitler, and the internal threat to the republic, the C.G.T. had come

[6] "Tribune du Parti," *Le Populaire*, May 27, 1936.
[7] Walter: *Parti communiste français*, pp. 310–12.
[8] *L'Humanité*, June 3, 1936.

forward with its own program of reform to meet the depression and had also rallied to the Popular Front. The reunification of the non-Communist and Communist confederations in March 1936 had filled the rank and file with great confidence and exuberance, and the elections were greeted as a labor victory. Impatient and excited, the rank and file seemed to be acting on its own in the sitdown strikes.

The C.G.T. leadership, non-Communist and Communist, sought to check what was rapidly becoming a runaway movement. Jouhaux made every effort to calm the workers and induce them to return to work. He feared that labor's role in the political life of the country would be jeopardized if the middle classes were unduly antagonized. He was haunted also by the fate of organized labor under fascism and by the grim prospects in France if the Popular Front were to fail.[9] Concern grew as the strikes went beyond control. A member of the C.G.T. administrative committee later recalled the anxiety that prevailed in the national office.[1] Despite the tone of the C.G.T. newspaper, *Le Peuple*, and the communiqués of the labor federations celebrating the irresistible advance of the movement and recommending calm and discipline, everywhere the trade union leaders were finding it impossible to lead the strikes, to stop them from spreading, or to foresee the consequences.

After a brief lull at the end of May, the crisis broke out again and grew worse. Sarraut's caretaker government struggled along, eagerly looking forward to being relieved shortly of its responsibilities. *Le Temps* offered its commiseration: "What a fate for Léon Blum, who is offering to experiment with his ideas and show what he can do, to know in advance that he will not be able to move, act, or think except with a raised fist."[2]

When Blum spoke before the Socialist party congress on May 31, a few days before he took office, he dealt with the challenge presented by the strike movement. Explaining it as the natural consequence of their political victory, he pledged that the government would win the confidence of the workers "by rapid, energetic action." At the same time, recalling his classic distinction between "the exercise of power within the framework of capitalist society" and the "revolutionary conquest of power," he sharply warned against a misreading of the election results. The party had not received a mandate to change the existing

[9] See, e.g., his radio speech of June 5, *Le Populaire*, June 6, 1936.
[1] André Delmas: *A gauche de la barricade* (Paris, 1950), p. 93.
[2] *Le Temps*, May 29, 1936.

system; the elections had not returned a Socialist majority, nor even a majority for the working-class parties, but a majority based on a coalition of the laboring classes and the middle classes, Socialist and non-Socialist, organized around the Popular Front program. "Our mandate, our duty is to accomplish and carry out that program . . . We shall act within the present regime, the same regime whose contradictions and injustices we pointed out in the course of our election campaign. That is the object of our experiment, and the true problem that this experiment will pose is to learn if from this social system it is possible to extract the maximum of order, welfare, security, and justice for all who work and produce."

He did, however, try to convince the skeptical Left wing that the Popular Front experiment was not a matter simply of saving bourgeois society but of determining "whether within the framework of the present system we can prepare, in men's minds and in deeds, for the inevitable coming of the society which remains our goal." He even added that if it proved impossible to "amend present society from within," he would confess that failure and ask them to draw the consequences.

For the benefit of the country as a whole, Blum denounced rumors that the strike movement had been unleashed by the Communists or by the C.G.T. in order to embarrass him, to have him feel their power, or to dictate the policies of the new government, declaring that the Communists and the C.G.T. were as involved in the success of the coalition as his own party. "It is a common insinuation in the reactionary newspapers to speak of Kerenskys who prepare the bed for Lenins. . . . I certainly hope that the government which the Socialist party will form will not be a Kerensky government. But even if it were, you may be sure that in the France of today it is not a Lenin who would succeed."[3] Socialists, Communists, and the C.G.T. were all working together to prevent the advent of a fascism that would spell their common ruin.

There was enthusiastic acclaim for Blum's speech; no one paid much attention to Pivert's diatribes against "reformist illusions." "Several times in the course of it," wrote Alexander Werth, who was present as a correspondent for the *Manchester Guardian*, "the whole congress rose like one man and cheered frantically, and when the speech was over dozens of militants rushed to the tribune to shake his hand and to em-

[3] For the congress, *Parti socialiste* (S.F.I.O.), *33ᵉ congrès national*, Paris, May 30–June 1, 1936, *compte-rendu sténographique* (Paris, 1936); for Blum's speech, pp. 182–98, and also *Oeuvre*, IV, pt. 1, 258–70.

brace him. Many of the older men had tears in their eyes."[4] The party hailed Blum: "It reaffirms its affectionate confidence in Léon Blum and thanks him once more for placing in the service of the republic and of the proletariat the richness of his experience, the prestige of his culture, and the sum total of the rare qualities that make of him the statesman who is indispensable today for France and the world."[5]

Meanwhile the sitdown strikes picked up new momentum. By Thursday, June 4, the last day of Sarraut's government, they had spread to all major industries. Although Paris was still the center of the movement and the metal-trades industry the hardest hit, the agitation was becoming nationwide and threatened to paralyze the entire economy. In a number of cases management representatives were locked in their offices by the strikers and telephone communications were cut off. The C.G.T. and some of its constituent federations, appealing repeatedly for order and discipline, warned against excessive demands and urged redoubled efforts to end the strikes by negotiations, but their appeals went unheeded. The employers' associations called upon the government to assume responsibility, but we have Sarraut's testimony that they did not press the government to evacuate the plants by force, fearing, like everyone else, that bloodshed would aggravate the tension and add to the difficulty of winning back control of the plants.[6]

The true seriousness of the situation became apparent on the evening of June 4, when Blum formally presented his cabinet to President Lebrun. After the formalities, Lebrun communicated to him an urgent request from the Sarraut government. "They consider the situation so grave," the President told Blum, "that they ask you not to wait until tomorrow morning for the transfer of authority. They urgently beg that you take over the Ministry of the Interior and the Ministry of Labor from this moment on, as of nine o'clock, so that there will be no interruption in the direction of these services. They do not wish to remain invested a moment longer with only interim authority under present circumstances." Blum complied at once. Roger Salengro and Jean Lebas assumed their posts at the Interior and Labor ministries respectively that very evening.[7]

After the others had gone, Blum remained with Lebrun. The two

---

[4] Werth: *Destiny of France*, p. 287.

[5] *Le Populaire*, June 2, 1936; for a similar resolution by the parliamentary group, *Le Populaire*, June 7, 1936.

[6] *Sénat, Débats*, July 7, 1936; cf. Blum: *Chambre, Débats*, June 6, 1936.

[7] Blum: *Chambre, Débats*, June 12, 1936; and testimony at Riom trial, 1942, *Oeuvre*, V, 259; also *Le Populaire*, June 5, 1936.

men had no liking for one another. Lebrun was conservative, reluctant to see a Socialist assume the premiership. He was not favorably inclined toward the Popular Front, but he accepted it, recognizing that it had originated as a defense against the fascist-minded leagues and that it had received the endorsement of the electorate.[8] Despite a weakness and ineffectiveness that would be fatal in the dark days of June 1940, he was a loyal servant of the republic. Now genuinely alarmed, he described the desperate situation to Blum. When, he asked, would Blum and his cabinet be able to present themselves to Parliament? Blum replied that he could not do so before Saturday, since it would be physically impossible to convene the legislature for the next day; moreover, he needed time to prepare his ministerial declaration and to convoke a cabinet meeting to approve it. If Blum could not call Parliament together before Saturday, would he at least speak to the workers over the radio on Friday? There was urgency in Lebrun's plea. "Tell them that Parliament is going to meet, that as soon as it meets, you will request the immediate passage of the measures they are demanding, in addition to the wage increases they are seeking. They will believe you, they will have confidence in you, and this agitation may end."[9]

From a strictly constitutional point of view, as Blum pointed out to the President, he was not legally Premier before presenting himself and his cabinet to the legislature and receiving a vote of confidence, but he agreed to act. On Friday, June 5, at noon, he delivered an address over the radio; a recording was repeated during the day to reach the widest possible audience. The Popular Front government, he announced, was "resolved to act with decision and rapidity." He would appear before Parliament the very next day and request the immediate consideration and adoption of "the principal reforms demanded by the working class . . . the forty-hour week, collective bargaining, and vacations with pay." He appealed for the loyal cooperation and support of labor in the meantime. "The government asks the workers to look to the law for those of their demands that can be satisfied by legislation, to press all other demands with calm, dignity, and discipline."[1] With the workers listening carefully to his every word, it would have been easy to sound the note of a revolutionary offensive or to rail vindictively

---

[8] Lebrun states in his memoirs that he thought of resigning at the time of the formation of the Popular Front government: *Témoignage* (Paris, 1946), p. 243; see also his testimony, May 27, 1948, *Événements*, IV, 955.

[9] Blum: testimony at Riom trial, *Oeuvre*, V, 259–60.

[1] For the speech, *Le Populaire*, June 6, 1936; *Exercice du pouvoir*, pp. 75–6; and *Oeuvre*, IV, pt. 1, 271–2.

against labor's painful years of subjection; it might even have been his duty as leader of a proletarian party. But Blum was not the man for that. The tragedy was that the vested interests of the country would be no more grateful to him once the crisis was over.

Neither Blum's appeal nor that of Jouhaux the same day had much effect. A C.G.T. delegation calling on Blum the evening of June 5 found him "smiling but rather nervous."[2] The seriousness of the situation was brought home when Blum's administrative assistant, Jules Moch, and Henri Raynaud, a Communist trade union official, were jointly dispatched to obtain the strikers' consent to a delivery of fuel oil needed by the city's bakers; they returned in humiliation to confess that the workers "would not even open the door to them."[3] The workers were listening to no one and the strikes were spreading. Over half a million were on strike by June 6.

The cabinet which Blum presented to the President was unexpectedly large—twenty-one ministers and fourteen undersecretaries, of which eighteen were Socialists, thirteen Radicals, and four Republican-Socialist Unionists. Of the key posts, the Radicals received National Defense (Édouard Daladier), Foreign Affairs (Yvon Delbos), and Education (Jean Zay); the Socialists assumed the Interior (Roger Salengro), Finance (Vincent Auriol), National Economy (Charles Spinasse), Labor (Jean Lebas), Public Works (Albert Bedouce), Agriculture (Georges Monnet), and Colonies (Marius Moutet). Three ministers of state without portfolio were to assist in general coordination and to provide liaison with their respective parties: Camille Chautemps for the Radicals, Paul Faure for the Socialists, and Maurice Viollette for the Republican-Socialists. A precedent was shattered with the inclusion of three women as undersecretaries (at a time when women did not even have the vote): Irène Joliot-Curie for Scientific Research, Suzanne Lacore for Child Welfare, and Cécile-Léon Brunschvicg for Education. The comparative youth of several of the ministers was also something of a novelty. A new undersecretaryship for "Leisure and Sports" was created, to which Léo Lagrange (Socialist) was named; it soon became a favorite target for political attack.[4]

[2] Delmas: *À gauche de la barricade*, p. 93.

[3] Ibid., p. 96.

[4] A complete list of the cabinet is given in *Oeuvre*, IV, pt. 1, 250–1. Jules Moch gives some inside details in "Avec Léon Blum en juin 1936," *Le Populaire*, March 29, 1953; see also Jean Zay: *Souvenirs et solitude* (Paris, 1945), p. 282.

In forming his cabinet, Blum put into effect three innovations he had recommended in the book he had written almost twenty years earlier on the basis of his administrative experiences during the First World War.[5] The first was that the Premier must leave himself free for over-all supervision and policy guidance and not assume the direction of any specific ministry. The second was the establishment of a staff organization to assist the Premier in his coordinating task; this institution became a regular feature of French political life after the Second World War. The third change was a grouping of related ministries into major divisions so that greater coordination and liaison would be possible despite the size of the cabinet. Blum had hoped to appoint a minister as head of each ministerial group and undersecretaries to head the departments within each group, but politically this proved unfeasible. As a necessary compromise, he created the ministerial groups. The six groups (he had originally envisaged four in his book) were National Defense, Internal Administration, Foreign Relations, Finance, National Economy, and Social Welfare. For the most part, these groupings remained of theoretical value only, although the joining of the War, Navy, and Air departments into a National Defense Ministry was an important step toward the coordination of the military departments.

Except for these innovations, there was nothing very striking about the Socialist-directed Popular Front cabinet. The presence of a large number of Radicals and especially of such seasoned—and slightly tarnished—politicians as Chautemps and Daladier presaged a powerful voice for the Radicals, who would be able to check any overly bold projects. One labor leader later complained: "We expected a sort of Committee of Public Safety, a small group of men each with broad

---

For background on the cabinet members, Walter Kolarz: *Das Regime Blum* (Prague, 1937); also Werth: *Destiny of France*, pp. 289–96. A few cabinet changes were made later. After Roger Salengro's suicide in November 1936, he was succeeded as Minister of the Interior by Marx Dormoy. In September 1936, Professor Jean Perrin replaced Mme Joliot-Curie as undersecretary for scientific research. On Suzanne Lacore's appointment, Bodin and Touchard: *Front Populaire*, pp. 97–8. It is to be noted that despite his "revolutionism," Marceau Pivert accepted a minor post in the cabinet, charged with supervising questions relating to the press, radio, and motion pictures.

[5] Blum's *Lettres sur la réforme gouvernementale*, it will be recalled, appeared first as anonymous articles in *La Revue de Paris* in 1918, then in book form that same year; it was reissued with an additional chapter as *La Réforme gouvernementale* in 1936. For the specific recommendations put into effect, see (1936 ed.) pp. 59, 89–97, 101–4. Blum remarked on his cabinet innovations in his testimony at the Riom trial, *Oeuvre*, V, 250.

powers. . . . Instead, there appeared a cumbersome cabinet of thirty-five ministers—in theory, organized in groups. . . . And when one tried to guess why particular personalities had been chosen, one perceived with sadness that the need to balance the respective influences of groups, subgroups, and factions . . . had prevailed over the vital obligation to assemble men capable of thinking and acting without being restrained by outmoded theories or worthless practices."[6]

Yet the fate of the cabinet depended less on structure or personalities than on other major weaknesses. The representation of the Radicals in the cabinet and the reliance on Radical support in the Chamber limited Blum. Even a more resolute man would have found it difficult under the circumstances to exercise the strong executive leadership that he knew was necessary. Also the cabinet did not accurately reflect the parliamentary Popular Front majority, or the Popular Front *esprit* of the country as a whole, for the Communists, by their own decision, were not present. They could exercise pressure on the government in and outside Parliament without sharing responsibility for decisions. Finally—something that received little attention at the time—Popular Front support in the conservative Senate was much weaker than in the Chamber. The Radicals in the Senate were far more conservative on social and financial matters than those in the Chamber.

Blum's immediate personal assistants were devoted Socialist followers. André Blumel, an old friend with whom Blum had been associated in private law practice and one-time secretary of the Socialist parliamentary group, was his administrative assistant (*chef de cabinet*); Marx Dormoy was an undersecretary attached to the Premier's office; and Jules Moch, an energetic graduate of the Polytechnique, served as secretary-general of the newly organized staff services for the Premier's office. Blum also remained in close touch daily with Oreste Rosenfeld, who was managing editor of *Le Populaire*.

More through his own personal qualities than through the organization of his cabinet, Blum kept himself posted on every important detail of his government's activities. He believed firmly that the Premier had to work closely with each of his important ministers and he did exactly that. Jean Zay, his Education Minister, later recalled one episode. Zay had been wrestling with the draft of a complicated education bill. "After having spent some hard nights on it, I took my recommendations to the Matignon Palace. Léon Blum, who in the past few hours had been discussing the affairs of Spain with Delbos, the financial situation

---

[6] Delmas: *A gauche de la barricade*, pp. 85–6.

with Vincent Auriol, the 14-billion-franc rearmament program with Daladier, sat me down and without opening my dossier, without my speaking, gave me a complete and documented exposition on the question that brought me. No decree, no regulation issued on the subject in the last fifty years was unknown to him. That man knew everything."[7]

There was not the shadow of justification for charges that the cabinet was predominantly Jewish. Blumel and Moch were the only Jews associated with the top levels of the cabinet and they were assistants to Blum rather than ministers or undersecretaries. Jean Zay, Minister of Education, born of a Jewish father and Protestant mother, styled himself a Protestant.[8] A number of other Jews were associated with the cabinet but only as administrative assistants (*chefs de cabinet*) to the ministers or undersecretaries. The facts, however, did not deter the antisemites then or later. "There were at least five Jewish ministers or undersecretaries in the first Popular Front cabinet," the journalist-historian Raymond Recouly wrote in 1941 with complete inaccuracy. "Given the tiny proportion of Jews in our total population, was this not truly a violation of propriety and reasonableness?"[9]

The Jewish issue flared up at the opening session of the new Chamber when the Rightist Deputy Xavier Vallat, just defeated by Herriot for the presidency of the Chamber, announced: "Your arrival in office, *M. le Président du Conseil*, is incontestably a historic date. For the first time this old Gallic-Roman country will be governed by a Jew." Herriot interrupted at once and called him firmly to order, but Vallat went on: "I have the special duty here . . . of saying aloud what everyone is thinking to himself: that to govern this peasant nation of France it is better to have someone whose origins, no matter how modest, spring from our soil than to have a subtle Talmudist." The important decisions of the government, he warned, would henceforth be made by a "small Jewish coterie" consisting of Blum, Blumel, Moch, and Rosenfeld. Blum, livid with rage, wished to respond, but Herriot insisted on censuring the speaker himself and closing the episode.[1]

---

7 *Souvenirs et solitude*, p. 284.

8 Ibid., pp. 88–9.

9 *Les Causes de notre effondrement* (Paris, 1941), p. 12. Pertinax (André Géraud) speaks of Blum "surrounding himself with some ten, if not more, Jews in the Premier's office"; *Les Fossoyeurs* (New York, 1943), II, 79, n. 13.

1 *Chambre, Débats*, June 6, 1936. Herriot, who had declined to serve in the cabinet, had just defeated the Rightist Deputy for the presidency of the Chamber by a vote of 377 to 150.

"Antisemitism," one French historian could write of the Popular Front years, "attained a virulence forgotten since the Dreyfus affair."[2]

The reaction in Jewish circles to the fact that a Jew had become Premier for the first time was mixed. There was a swell of pride in these groups even if one dismisses Recouly's wild account of wealthy and fashionable Jewish circles so gratified at having a co-religionist elevated to high office that they toasted Blum in champagne and then sang the "Internationale"![3] On the other hand, in May 1936 one of the leading rabbis of Paris tried to dissuade Blum from taking office so that he would not expose his fellow Jews to criticism and attack. Blum listened politely and respectfully during the conversation, and closed the interview.[4] He was aware that he was the first French Jew ever elevated to the premiership, but shrugged it off as unimportant.[5] Primarily he was a Frenchman, and his religion was of no relevance.

In the midst of the labor crisis, the afternoon of Saturday, June 6, Blum and his cabinet appeared before the Chamber for the first time. Paul Reynaud recalled watching him on the ministerial bench, "moving slowly, elegant, a white splash of handkerchief sticking up out of his pocket, his eyes gleaming behind their spectacles, his hand on his long drooping mustache, tense, ready for the return thrust." Despite his disagreement with Blum's policies, Reynaud could only think to himself that "this aristocrat" (*ce racé*) was worthy of the high post he was filling after so many years of public life in the opposition.[6]

Blum had just passed his sixty-fourth birthday when he took office, although his youthful, agile appearance belied his years. When he mounted the rostrum, his tall, supple figure dominated it completely. Softly and solemnly, amidst attentive silence, Blum read his ministerial declaration, the Deputies straining to hear his every word. The government's majority was already established, he said. Its objectives were known: to defend democratic liberties, to seek new remedies for the depression, and to insure peace. To meet the great labor crisis,

[2] Chastenet: *Histoire*, VI, 168.

[3] *Les Causes*, p. 13.

[4] See Blumel: *Blum*, p. 9, and cf. Pierre Lazareff: *De Munich à Vichy* (New York, 1944), p. 88. For a discussion of the Jewish reaction, Pierre Aubery: *Milieux juifs de la France contemporaine* (Paris, 1957), pp. 180–3.

[5] See, e.g., speech before the American Club in Paris, May 15, 1936, *Exercice du pouvoir*, p. 128.

[6] Reynaud: *Mémoires*, II, 62–3.

which was their common concern, he would quickly introduce a series of bills which both houses would be asked to vote upon before they adjourned for the summer. The very first bills would institute three major labor reforms: a forty-hour week, collective bargaining, and paid vacations. In addition, measures would be introduced providing for a public works program, the nationalization of private munitions manufacture, a wheat office to raise and stabilize agricultural prices, extension of compulsory schooling, reform of the statutes governing the Bank of France, and repeal of the retrenchment decrees affecting civil service workers and veterans. A second series of measures was to follow later, including a broad revamping of the tax system. He urged Parliament to understand "with what impatience great accomplishments are expected, how dangerous it would be to disappoint the eager hope for relief of distress, for change, for renovation, which is not limited to a political majority or to a social class but is shared by the entire nation."[7]

Of the several hostile speeches of the opposition, Paul Reynaud's alone was constructive. His theme, which he had been belaboring for over two and a half years, was the need for immediate devaluation of the franc. Without this step, he prophesied, the Popular Front experiment was doomed to failure. The new labor reforms would only increase costs at a time when French prices were already too high to compete in the world market. In the United States, he reminded Blum, the New Deal had devalued the dollar before embarking on a social program. Blum rejected this advice. The Popular Front government, he affirmed, had no intention of devaluing the franc.[8]

The opposition (with some Radicals joining in) focused their attacks mainly on the sitdown strikes and on the government's plans for coping with them. Blum insisted that there were legitimate causes for the social explosion after the years of depression. He explained that the strikers had chosen the sitdown form of strike because of their concern lest their places be taken by the unemployed. But he admitted the seriousness of the strikes, their nationwide scope, and the fact that on occasion they had passed beyond the control of the responsible labor organizations. He admitted, too, that the occupation of the

[7] The ministerial declaration is reprinted in *Exercice du pouvoir*, pp. 66–71, and in *Oeuvre*, IV, pt. 1, 272–5.

[8] *Chambre, Débats*, June 6, 1936; see also Reynaud: *Au coeur de la mêlée* (Paris, 1951), pp. 193–5; and *Mémoires*, II, 64–7. Blum's reply to the interpellations is reproduced in *Oeuvre*, IV, pt. 1, 275–89.

factories was "not legal . . . not in conformity with the rules and principles of French civil law." Yet it was inconceivable that his government would use the police or the army to evacuate the plants. "If you expect that from the government, I can tell you that you will wait in vain." The factory owners themselves, he added, had not asked his predecessor or himself to use force.

He outlined the threefold course of action which his government was following. First, he was requesting the Chamber to act at once on the three most important labor reforms so that by the end of the following week they would be enacted into law by both houses. Secondly, the government was taking emergency measures to insure such vital public services as food and fuel deliveries. Finally, the government was offering its services as mediator and arbitrator to encourage negotiations and help settle differences wherever possible. At that very moment arrangements had just been completed for an unprecedented meeting in his office at the Matignon Palace between the top-echelon employers' and labor organizations, the C.G.P.F. (Confédération Générale de la Production Française) and the C.G.T. He received an overwhelming vote of confidence (384 to 210), proof that he had the weight of the Chamber behind him and that it could be expected to vote the reforms requested.[9] The support of the Senate would be given more grudgingly.

Blum could proceed to the epoch-making Matignon conference with a vote of support behind him. Although few were aware of it at the time of the sitdown strikes, the initiative for the Matignon meeting seems to have come from industry. On Friday, June 5, M. Lambert-Ribot, an official of the Comité des Forges and once a legal colleague of Blum at the Conseil d'État, asked Blum through mutual friends to exert every effort to arrange a meeting at once between the important employers' associations and the C.G.T. to cope with the sitdown strikes. The employers, he let it be known, were willing to discuss a general wage increase in exchange for the immediate evacuation of the occupied plants.[1] That the initial impulse came from the employers demonstrated their apprehension over the gravity of the situation. Only

[9] For the speech and interventions, *Chambre, Débats*, June 6, 1936; see also *Oeuvre*, IV, pt. 1, 275–89.

[1] Blum: testimony at Riom trial, *Oeuvre*, V, 260. He added: "Beyond any doubt I would have myself attempted what has been called the Matignon agreement." See also his series of editorials three years later, *Le Populaire*, June 21,

after the event did the legend grow that the strikes had not been serious and that a little show of force and authority might have ended them.

Blum responded readily to the overtures. After various preliminaries —including an initial conference in his own home, where he talked very frankly to the management representatives and warned them of the danger of "grave disturbances in the streets, bloodshed, not to speak of foreign complications"—the meeting was arranged.[2] Roger Salengro, the Minister of the Interior, visited the C.G.T. office to invite the labor leaders to the high-level conference; it was flattering to them to have a minister of the republic tender the invitation personally.[3]

That Sunday, June 7, at three in the afternoon, Blum gathered around the conference table at the Matignon Palace the four representatives who would speak for industry and the six men delegated by the C.G.T. to represent labor; for the government, Salengro, Marx Dormoy, and Jules Moch were also present. Everyone was aware of the historic nature of the occasion. It was the first meeting of its kind between the top management and labor organizations. To be sure, neither could pretend to be the spokesman for all of industry or for all of labor. The principal management organization, the C.G.P.F., was at the time a loosely organized confederation whose activities and interests had hitherto largely been confined to lobbying; it had left questions of wages and labor conditions to the separate employers' organizations in each industry; moreover, all management groups in the country were not affiliated with it, especially in small and medium-sized industry. On the labor side, the Catholic labor confederation, the C.F.T.C. (*Confédération Française des Travailleurs Chrétiens*), was not represented, but it was relatively weak. The later criticism that neither management nor labor was fully represented was valid, but, on the other hand, a large proportion of the productive forces of the country were clearly represented by the two national bodies.[4]

22, 26–29, 1939. Corroborative details for much of what follows are provided by the then head of the employers' confederation: René-P. Duchemin, "L'Accord Matignon: ce que j'ai vu et entendu," *La Revue de Paris*, XLIV (February 1937), 584–94. The conference is related in some detail in Danos and Gibelin: *Juin 36*, pp. 76–86.

[2] Duchemin: "L'Accord Matignon," p. 587.

[3] Delmas: *À gauche de la barricade*, pp. 99–100.

[4] See, e.g., *Chambre, Débats*, June 9, 12, 1936. On the employers' organizations, see Ehrmann: *Organized Business in France* (Princeton, 1957), pp. 3–57.

Blum had already made clear the objectives of the meeting: to arrive at an agreement on blanket wage increases for the entire country and to decide on the clauses to be incorporated into all collective contracts. Agreement on these matters, along with the legislation on the forty-hour week, vacations with pay, and legal protection for collective bargaining rights, they could all hope, would end the labor upheaval and restore order in the country.

The employers' representatives were genuinely apprehensive over the threat to private property and capitalism and fearful that the country was on the brink of revolution. Now that almost a million workers were participating in the sitdown strikes, the use of force to evacuate the plants could precipitate even greater danger; nor were the employers' delegates so naïve as to believe that the Popular Front government would use force against the workers. They saw, moreover, that the C.G.T. representatives, instead of acting the part of blustering bullying labor chiefs, were themselves shaken by a sense of uncertainty, fear, and anxiety. The result was that the employers agreed to concessions far greater than any they had ever made before. Such concessions, they hoped, might enable the C.G.T. leaders to regain control of the runaway situation. They knew too that if they refused to yield, the government might be pushed into an even more radical position. The Premier was a man whose political program they abhorred but whose word they could trust. For all his talk at the Socialist party congresses about revolutionizing society, Léon Blum believed in legality and order. At the same time, as a Socialist, he had the confidence of the working classes. In some ways, so far as they were concerned, it was an act of Providence that such a man was in office. Perhaps no one was better qualified to calm the labor agitation, avert chaos and bloodshed—and save capitalism. It behooved industry not to make difficulties for Blum at that moment.

The head of the C.G.P.F., René Duchemin, described the conference as a "polite, difficult, and painful" meeting in which no one raised his voice and all opinions were freely expressed.[5] After a brief discussion, agreement was reached on the clauses to be incorporated into all collective contracts. (The groundwork had already been laid for these clauses during the negotiations that had been under way in the metallurgical strikes.) Article 1 of the Matignon agreement established unequivocally industry's acceptance of the principle of collective bargaining: "The employers' delegation agrees to the immediate conclusion of collective

[5] "L'Accord Matignon," p. 591.

bargaining contracts."[6] All contracts, the remaining clauses stipulated, would guarantee the right of workers to join and belong to unions of their choice and would forbid dismissals or other reprisals because of union membership. In all plants employing more than ten workers, the workers were to have the right to elect shop stewards (*delégués ouvriers*), who would be authorized to present individual personnel grievances to the management.

The question of the general wage increase caused the most difficulty. What M. Duchemin had called "painful" was the evidence brought in by the C.G.T. delegates of the pathetically low wages in various parts of the country. The labor delegates demanded wage increases ranging from 10 to 15 per cent and the pledge of a more substantial adjustment for "abnormally low" wages. They cited instances of wage rates in the neighborhood of 2 francs (11 cents) per hour. But the employers' delegates, insisting that industry could not absorb the burden of a large wage increase along with the projected labor reforms, proposed wage increases ranging from 7 to 10 per cent and varying with the financial condition of each industry. The discussion became heated. Blum recalled the sharp exchange when M. Lambert-Ribot protested: "What! You are not satisfied with these figures? But when have the workers in France ever had a general wage increase of this size?" "And when," retorted one of the C.G.T. delegates, "have you seen in France a strike movement of this size and scope?"[7] Blum had warned at the outset that if they could not agree on the general wage increase he would have to arbitrate the matter himself. This became necessary, and a brief recess was declared. During that time Blum managed to put in an appearance at a Popular Front mass meeting. He alluded to the important negotiations under way, hinted that a great labor victory was in the offing, and added a good word for the representatives of industry, praising their "spirit of conciliation and understanding of the situation."[8]

Blum's award strongly favored the workers yet represented enough of a compromise to be acceptable to the employers. The scale of increases ranged from 15 per cent for the lowest wages to 7 per cent for the highest, with the maximum average increase in any individual

[6] For the text of the Matignon agreement, *Le Populaire*, June 8, 1936, and other daily newspapers; also reprinted in *Oeuvre*, IV, pt. 1, 291–2, and in an English translation in Ehrmann: *French Labor*, pp. 284–5.

[7] Blum: testimony at Riom trial, 1942, *Oeuvre*, V, 262.

[8] *Le Populaire*, June 8, 1936.

company not to exceed 12 per cent. In the case of "abnormally low" wages, an initial adjustment was to be made prior to the general increases. Affecting all the industrial workers of the country, it was one of the most sweeping arbitration awards in industrial history.

Under the Matignon agreement, the employers' organizations were accepting the principle of collective bargaining and the right of labor to organize. Politically, they acquiesced in the government's program of labor reforms. Even if they did not explicitly accept the government's entire reform program—the forty-hour week, for example—they recognized that the labor reforms were an essential part of the government's efforts to end the strikes. At 12:30 a.m., June 8, the document was signed by Blum and the delegates, and communicated to the press.

Popular Front spokesmen and the labor press hailed the Matignon agreement as a great triumph for labor. "In twenty years of effort," wrote *Le Populaire*, "the working class had never obtained, never hoped for anything like this. . . . They will support even more firmly the Popular Front government, the government of their class."[9] Jouhaux was jubilant: "The victory obtained Sunday night marks the beginning of a new era. . . . In one historic night, we caught up with and surpassed other countries that have been moving in this direction for fifty years." He stressed the "high moral value" of the agreement as a demonstration of what a democracy could accomplish. Since the average blanket wage increase was to be 12 per cent, the C.G.T. estimated that with the promised forty-hour week and the two weeks of paid vacations, labor was receiving the equivalent of a 35 per cent total increase.[1] *Le Temps* saw the other side of the coin—the costs to industry. "35%? One might think one was dreaming and yet the figure is exact."[2] The debate over wages and wage costs was only beginning.

Complaints from industry were heard at once. The day after the agreement was signed, M. Lambert-Ribot protested that the employers' representatives had signed only because they had no other choice. They had had "to accept the arbitration of the government but they had no illusions about the consequences of the experiment that has been imposed on them . . ." They had accepted the government's proposals, he stated, "with the most explicit reservations."[3] Paul Reynaud charged

---

[9] Ibid.
[1] See statements by Jouhaux in *Le Populaire*, June 9, 17, 1936.
[2] *Le Temps*, June 10, 1936.
[3] Statement to the press, *Le Populaire*, June 9, 1936.

in the Chamber that Blum had dealt with the big employers and that small business would not be able to absorb the added labor costs. One Deputy denounced the agreement as a *Diktat*.[4]

Blum, sweeping aside these charges in a speech before the Chamber, expressed his pride in the agreement but warned that the crisis was not yet over. The next step was for the legislature to do its part, to enact at once the promised reforms. "We are, gentlemen, as you well know, in circumstances where each hour counts."[5]

The circumstances were indeed still urgent. Before the situation improved, it grew worse. The Matignon agreement by no means ended the strikes or even restored control to the responsible labor organizations. There was a critical week after Matignon when the strikes grew and continued to be uncontrollable.[6] Leon Trotsky announced during this week: "The French Revolution has begun. . . . These are not just strikes, this is *the* strike, the union, as clear as can be, of the oppressed against their oppressors." All that was missing, he lamented, was revolutionary leadership for the great working-class movement.[7]

They were feverish days. The strike delegates of the Paris metal-workers refused to accept the terms proposed by the C.G.T. national leaders for returning to work. New strike calls affected additional thousands all over the country. In some cities public-utilities workers went on strike. Agriculture was hit too; thousands of farm workers struck and "occupied" the bigger farms. In Paris the strikes spread to the big department stores and to cafés, restaurants, and hotels. How, asked a provincial Deputy in Parliament, was he to live in Paris while on his official duties?[8] By June 11 most workers in all the major industries in Paris and the Seine area were on strike.

The strikes threatened to paralyze the economy. On June 11, at their peak, well over a million strikers could be counted; the official estimate of the figure was 1,165,000.[9] *Le Temps* commented: "It is apparent that the problem of authority has not been resolved, that it is becoming less and less so, and that there is a strong chance that it will shortly become incapable of solution."[1] Paul Reynaud described Paris

[4] *Chambre, Débats*, June, 12, 1936.

[5] *Chambre, Débats*, June 9, 1936.

[6] Danos and Gibelin: *Juin 36*, pp. 94–113.

[7] Cited in ibid., p. 191.

[8] *Chambre, Débats*, June 9, 1936.

[9] Salengro: *Chambre, Débats*, June 26, 1936; Danos and Gibelin set the figure at close to two million, *Juin 36*, p. 112.

[1] *Le Temps*, June 12, 1936.

as "a ship without a rudder."[2] The foreign press printed accounts of revolution, bloodshed, and turmoil.[3]

The government stepped up its mediation efforts. Urgent telegrams were dispatched to all prefects urging them to serve as mediators. The Socialist ministers and undersecretaries were especially active: Salengro, Auriol, Lebas, and others passed their nights and days in efforts to arrange negotiations and settle the disputes. "We are spending our lives at it," Blum told the Chamber.[4] Auriol succeeded in averting a bank employees' strike; the others were less successful.

Meanwhile, Blum obtained from Parliament the promised legislation. On June 11 the Chamber voted the laws on paid vacations and on collective bargaining, and revoked the pay cuts of government workers instituted by previous governments; on June 12 it voted the forty-hour law. On June 12 the bills were introduced in the Senate. All the bills, except the forty-hour bill, passed in the Chamber almost unanimously; the forty-hour bill was debated more heatedly but passed with a comfortable majority (408 to 100). In the Senate the bills met with greater resistance but on June 17 and 18 were adopted there too. As he had promised, Blum put through a body of the most important social legislation ever adopted in the country, and with unprecedented rapidity.

In addition to the mediation efforts and the legislative program, the government also adopted certain security measures. Troops and *gardes mobiles* were prepared to advance into the Paris area and into other trouble spots if necessary. The government seized the June 12 issue of the Trotskyite newspaper, *La Lutte Ouvrière*, because it called for the establishment of workers' armed militia groups.[5] Blum repeatedly assured both the Chamber and the Senate that he was determined to prevent any disorders in the streets, that his was not "a government of anarchy" but of "order."[6] At the government's request, the national committee of the *Rassemblement Populaire* even canceled the victory celebration planned in Paris for Sunday, June 14, in order to avoid possible disturbances.

For a time, however, it seemed that nothing could check the agita-

---

[2] *Chambre, Débats*, June 12, 1936; *Mémoires*, II, 69.

[3] See official communiqué protesting accounts in the English newspapers, *Le Populaire*, June 22, 1936; and cf. Werth: *Destiny of France*, p. 313.

[4] *Chambre, Débats*, June 12, 1936.

[5] For the various security measures, see statement by Roger Salengro: *Sénat, Débats*, July 7, 1936; and Danos and Gibelin: *Juin 36*, pp. 116–17, 142–3, 217–19.

[6] See, e.g., *Chambre, Débats*, June 12, 1936.

tion. Unable to control the movement, the government, the C.G.T., and the Popular Front leaders increasingly warned of outside agitators and provocateurs, which they variously described as either Croix de Feu "Rightists" or Trotskyite "Leftists," who were accused of fanning the flames of discontent for their own purposes, raising demagogic and extravagant demands, and deliberately seeking to prolong the unrest in order to embarrass the government.[7] In a cartoon in *Le Populaire*, a fascist "type" wearing a Croix de Feu beret was shown urging an industrialist in traditional silk top hat: "Do not give in!" At the same time, a shadowy character was saying to a group of workers who were holding a sign reading "We want Bread": "Louder! Louder! Ask for *pâté de foie gras!*"[8] Echoing earlier statements by Salengro, Blum told the Chamber on June 12: "It is quite true that since yesterday the face of things has taken on another appearance. . . . One senses the presence of groups that are suspect and foreign to the trade union movement."[9] The truth is that the rank and file had a will to action which their commanding officers had to restrain; the movement was still beyond anyone's control.

In the end it was not Blum but Thorez who was able to stem the tide. The turning point of the crisis came with Thorez's speech on June 11, which was directed at the metalworkers, who were then spearheading the strike movement. The Communist leader warned that they were running the risk of alienating large segments of the petty bourgeoisie and of dislocating the Popular Front alliance of middle class and workers. Compromises had to be accepted. Although it was important to know how to lead a strike movement, he said, "it is necessary also to know how to end it." He called upon them not to jeopardize the Popular Front by adding to the unrest. The time for the "revolution" had not come.[1]

Thorez's statements had an immediate effect. The very next day the metalworkers' strike delegates accepted the proposed agreement. On Saturday evening, June 13, amidst parades, music, and fanfare, the evacuation of the plants began. Workers in other industries followed suit. By the end of the following week the movement had subsided in the Seine area, the Nord, and elsewhere in the country. On June 26 Salengro told a relieved but irritated Parliament that the

[7] See, e.g., statements of Roger Salengro in *Le Populaire*, June 11, 13, 1936.
[8] *Le Populaire*, June 13, 1936.
[9] *Chambre, Débats*, June 12, 1936.
[1] For Thorez's speech, *L'Humanité*, June 12, 13, 1936.

number of workers on strike throughout the nation had declined from the peak figure of 1,165,000 to 165,000.[2] A few strikes lingered on but they too soon ended. The crisis of June 1936 was over.

Salengro expressed the feelings of satisfaction shared by Blum and the government when he told a victory celebration at Lille on Sunday, June 14: "We have known a peaceful revolution. Not a machine has been broken, not a drop of blood has been spilled." The country had seen an end to "the most formidable social upheaval that the republic has ever known."[3]

Bastille Day, July 14, was the occasion for a gigantic fete throughout the nation to celebrate the victories already won and the hopes for the future. In Paris, Blum joined the other Popular Front leaders to receive the salutes of the paraders and to hear endless choruses of the "Internationale," the "Carmagnole," and the "Marseillaise." Red flags mingled with the tricolor. It was a greater demonstration than the Bastille Day celebration of the preceding year. *Vive Blum! Vive le Front Populaire!* punctuated the air. Spokesmen for all the affiliated parties and organizations of the Popular Front held forth.

For Blum it was a moment of exultation and triumph. He had helped save the nation from civil war and had helped win enormous victories for labor. What could be more satisfying? On this 14th of July commemoration France was appropriately celebrating the unity of the middle classes and the proletariat. His government had afforded proof that the republic could provide social reform for the workers and a defense of republican liberty for all. The year 1936, he was convinced, would go down in history as one of the great years of republican triumph, like 1792, 1848, 1870. "The cause of the workers struggling for social justice and the cause of republicans struggling for civic and political liberties must be indissolubly linked." The labor reforms just achieved would strengthen the attachment and the loyalty of the workers to France. "Every effort, every advance toward social justice attaches the workers of France to the republic and to the country. The very object of the Popular Front is to furnish them with new

[2] *Chambre, Débats,* June 26, 1936. Shortly thereafter, in the Senate, Salengro was maneuvered into stating that the government would end any new sitdown strikes "by all appropriate means"; *Sénat, Débats,* July 7, 1936. The statement led to a storm of protest in labor circles.

[3] Speech at Lille, *Le Populaire,* June 15, 1936; *Chambre, Débats,* June 26, 1936; and cf. Blum: *Chambre, Débats,* August 7, 1936.

reasons to defend it."[4] One day he would have occasion to recall his words when he and the Popular Front were accused of undermining the strength and morale of the country. Meanwhile Blum pledged that the government would go forward with its program of reform and with its campaign to combat the depression; there would be no stagnation or retreat. Few realized at the time how profoundly the storm that had just ended would affect the entire course of the experiment.

Blum never in later years regretted his actions in the great crisis of June 1936. At his wartime trial by the Vichy government in 1942, one of the charges against him was his "weakness," "apathy," and "systematically passive attitude" in the face of the sitdown strikes. "The government," the prosecution charged, "while recognizing in principle the illegality of the occupations, refused—despite the pressing demands by the directors of the plants and the interpellations . . . of the two parliamentary assemblies—to order, or permit, the employment of force in order to cause these establishments to be evacuated."[5] Blum proudly accepted the accusation that he had not used force to end the sitdown strikes in June 1936. To have done so, he asserted, would have brought on bloodshed, a repetition of the bloody June days of 1848—and even civil war. "My principal concern was to prevent bloodshed. I am even now convinced that the use of brute force in the weeks that followed my assumption of office might have unleashed a veritable civil war which I wished at all costs to avert." Internal disorder, he added, would have constituted an open invitation to the fascist nations to step in. Hence he flung back the challenge. "I have had the time to reflect, I can assure you. No, I was not mistaken. My duty was clear, overriding. It was to spare France both civil war and foreign war . . ."[6] The loss in defense production during that month, greatly exaggerated by the prosecution and principally a loss in terms of outmoded planes and tanks, was as nothing compared to the grave consequences of civil convulsion and war, he emphasized.[7]

At the Riom trial, as during the crisis itself, he admitted the illegality of the sitdown strikes from a purely juridical point of view and conceded that his duty as Premier was to uphold the law and enforce respect for private property rights, but he told the court that every

[4] Speech of July 14, *Le Populaire*, July 15, 1936.
[5] For the bill of charges, prepared in 1941, *Oeuvre*, V, 192–3.
[6] Testimony at Riom trial, *Oeuvre*, V, 149, 209, 265, 313.
[7] Ibid., pp. 309–13.

statesman must search his own conscience for the resolution of duties that conflict with and contradict each other—"in this case to enforce respect for property rights on the one hand and to preserve public peace on the other."[8] No one, he added, could have persuaded him to use force. "My mind was made up. I would not have used force; I would not have called out the *garde mobile* and then the army." He knew how his opponents would have relished "a bloodbath carried out by a leader of the Socialist party." Rather than use force, he would have resigned. "If I had not been able, by persuasion and by conciliation of workers and employers, to restore what I have called civil order and republican order, I would have given up my office and perhaps my political life as well."[9] There is no reason to doubt his statement; it was no idle boast after the event.

Nor would he have practiced the "cruel deception" of promising the workers the social reforms they were demanding and then proceed to turn his back on these promises once the crisis was over. Working-class history was filled with such betrayals. To have done so would have undermined the faith of the workers in democratic leadership, in the parliamentary system, and in the republic itself. He had ended the crisis by refusing to use force, by playing the "role of a conciliator," by insuring that the reforms demanded by the workers were adopted. In that way he had preserved civil peace. He had kept faith with the duties of his office and with his republican and Socialist conscience.

Blum was fully aware that the industrialists had looked to his prestige and talents to cope with the upheaval. Again in his own words: "At that moment, among the bourgeoisie, and especially in employer circles, they considered me, looked to me, put their hope in me as a savior. Circumstances were so anguished and the country was so close to something that resembled civil war that one could only hope for a kind of Providential intervention: the arrival in office of a man to whom one attributed sufficient power of persuasion, sufficient influence over the working class, to make it listen to reason and persuade it not to use— or abuse—its strength."[1]

Did he ever see the other side of the coin—that the head of the Socialist party might have acted less the conciliator and more the proletarian leader, and that he might have unleashed the revolutionary

8 Ibid., p. 309.
9 Ibid., p. 313.
1 Ibid., p. 264.

potential of the aroused working classes? Did he not himself later classify the situation as "quasi-revolutionary?"[2] Although the movement never assumed the character or scope of a true revolution directed either against the capitalist owners of industry or against the government, the striking workers had certainly passed beyond control of their own trade unions, their own political parties, and the Popular Front government itself. It could have been fanned into revolution. The movement was, in fact, a great undeclared general strike throughout the nation, an impressive display of strength, unity, and determination. Arising spontaneously, spreading not by command but by contagion, it reflected a sense of working-class self-confidence, independent action, and power that could have been turned in any direction. It met the criteria for the "classical beginning of a revolution."[3]

Why did Blum not turn the movement into revolutionary channels? Of overriding importance to him and the other Popular Front leaders, like Thorez and Jouhaux, was the desire to avoid anything that might isolate the working class from the rural and urban middle classes, separate the proletarian parties from the Radical Socialists, and break the unity of the Popular Front. Secondly, neither the Communists nor the C.G.T. had revolution on their agenda; an attempt at encouraging revolution would have been foolhardy and adventurous. The result would have been not revolution but anarchy, bloodshed, and civil war —in a time of grave international tension. Despite later insinuations, it was not Blum and the Socialists alone who resisted any attempt to convert the great sitdown strikes of May–June 1936 into a social revolution.[4]

Finally, a personal element was involved. Blum had been elected to office on a limited reform program with the backing of middle-class Radicals and others who did not believe in socialism. His party had received no mandate to transform society. He was pledged to carry out his experiment within the framework of republican legality and the existing economic system. To have gone back on his pledge, to have encouraged revolution, was inconceivable. This was the first time that a Socialist-directed government had ever been formed in France. It was of deep consequence to Blum that the party demonstrate its

[2] Ibid., p. 261.

[3] The phrase is that of Danos and Gibelin, in *Juin 36*, p. 167; see also their discussion, pp. 162–7.

[4] This is the substance of Colette Audry's charge in *Léon Blum ou la politique du Juste*, pp. 101–16. Her retrospective point of view is essentially that of Pivert and the *Gauche Révolutionnaire* at the time.

fidelity to the republic, its sense of responsibility, and its capacity for governing. He could not have lived with his conscience if he had violated his promise to carry out his experiment within the framework of the existing political and economic order, or if he had permitted the unleashing of revolt, bloodshed, and war.

Nor could he have satisfied his conscience without the conviction that he had won substantial gains for labor. If the workers did not win a revolution in June 1936, he believed that he had won tremendous gains for them, that he had "transformed" their lives. Was he right? What did the Popular Front experiment over which he presided mean for labor—and for the nation?

VI

THE "EXERCISE OF POWER":
The Blum Experiment

> *. . . perhaps the most important progress ever made in a democracy in the realm of social legislation.*[1]

WITH THE ENDING of the sitdown strikes, the Blum experiment, properly speaking, could begin. Again and again, the Socialist Premier stated that he and his party had received no mandate to transform society but only to carry out the Popular Front program of January 1936 in faithful alliance with the other parties of the coalition. The experiment could not involve the nationalization of key industries—that is, structural reforms—for such measures had been excluded by both the Radicals and the Communists when the compromise Popular Front program had been hammered out. The objective would be to extract from the existing regime the "maximum

---

[1] Blum: speech to Senate, June 16, 1936, *Oeuvre*, IV, pt. 1, 299. A variety of works on the "Blum experiment" as a whole and on the specific reforms are listed in the Bibliography. Among the most useful specialized treatments are those by Albertini, Danos and Gibelin, Caunes, Ehrmann, Franck, Kalecki, Laufenburger, Lefranc, Marjolin, Mossé, Théry, Vaucher, and Weill-Raynal; also recommended are the relevant portions of the books by Bodin and Touchard, Dupeux, Goguel, Lorwin, Sturmthal, Werth, and Wolfe. For statistical information, see Statistique Générale, *Mouvement économique en France de 1929 à 1939* (Paris, 1941). I have myself examined one aspect of industrial relations under the Popular Front in *Compulsory Labor Arbitration in France, 1936–1939* (New York, 1951). I am grateful to M. Jean Touchard for having made available to me mimeographed copies of papers presented at a colloquium on the Blum government held in Paris, March 26–27, 1965. The papers, to be published under the auspices of the Fondation Nationale des Sciences Politiques, include valuable discussions by various scholars of many aspects of the Popular Front experiment. The manuscript of my own book was completed before this colloquium was held.

of order, well-being, security, and justice" that it was capable of providing.[2]

The one unifying economic theme behind the experiment was the need to combat the depression by increasing the purchasing power of the masses and restoring consumer demand. The retrenchment and deflationary policies of previous governments would be swept aside. Blum proposed to have his government employ "the authority of the state . . . not to restrict production but to increase consumption . . . not to destroy and prohibit, not to ration and limit, but to create and to stimulate . . . to breathe life again into an economic organism crushed by the depression and bled by deflation."[3] He never concealed the fact that he was inspired by the American New Deal and Roosevelt. "Seeing him act," Blum declared, "the French democracy has had the feeling that an example was traced for it, and it is this example that we wish to follow, adapting it to the conditions and resources of our country."[4] Not socialism, but a "French New Deal" was his objective, Roosevelt not Marx his guide.

If the experiment was limited in advance by the nature of the Popular Front coalition and its compromise program, it was conditioned in an entirely different way by the momentous strike movement that accompanied the government's entry into office. The timetable of reform had to be accelerated immediately and the emphasis placed all at once on the social legislation demanded by the sitdown strikers. Certainly

[2] Speech to national party congress, May 31, 1936, *Oeuvre*, IV, pt. 1, 262; and cf. speech to Senate, September 30, 1936, ibid., p. 442.

[3] Radio speech, April 21, 1936, ibid., p. 240.

[4] Speech to American Club, *Le Populaire*, February 23, 1937; cf. speech to Senate, June 16, 1936; to Chamber, September 29, 1936; and at Lyons, January 2, 1937; *Oeuvre*, IV, pt. 1, 303, 425, 476. Blum's admiration for Roosevelt continued through the President's years in office. An amusing incident is recounted by Ambassador Bullitt in a letter to Roosevelt on November 8, 1936, on the occasion of his first re-election: ". . . Blum came personally to express his congratulations. That is unheard of. If you could have seen the manner of his coming, it would have done you good. . . . He entered the front door, flung his broad-brimmed black hat to the butler, his coat to the footman, leaped the three steps to the point where I was standing, seized me and kissed me violently! I staggered slightly but having been kissed by Stalin, I am now immune to any form of osculation, and I listened without batting an eye to as genuine an outpouring of enthusiasm as I have ever heard. . . . Blum himself said to me that he felt his position had been greatly strengthened because he is attempting in his way to do what you have done in America. . . ." Bullitt to Roosevelt, November 8, 1936, "President's Secretary's File, France, B-5," Roosevelt Library, Hyde Park, New York. I am grateful to Professor Richard Lowitt for calling this item to my attention.

neither the opposition in the Chamber and Senate nor the nation's employers would have sanctioned these sweeping changes had it not been for the sense of panic and the acute need to restore industrial peace. As Blum later said, it was the "ransom that had to be paid to avoid civil war."[5]

Immediately thereafter, a whole series of additional reforms were introduced. Here too, speed was of the essence. Blum had warned Parliament of the impatience with which the reforms were awaited and of the danger of disappointing hopes that had been aroused.[6] With Blum holding the whip, Parliament in the summer of 1936 moved with unprecedented rapidity. It adopted a public works program providing for an expenditure of 20 billion francs over the next three years, revised the statutes governing the Bank of France, set up a Wheat Office to help restore agricultural prices and curb speculation, extended compulsory schooling to the age of fourteen, granted loans to small and medium-sized industries, took steps toward the nationalization of the armaments industry, and introduced measures against illicit price rises. A government decree dissolved the fascist-type leagues. In keeping with the promise that a "republican wind" would "sweep through" the top echelons of the civil service, a few administrative changes were made—a new governor for the Bank of France, a new director-general for the Paris police. Other reforms were promised for the autumn, when the two houses reconvened—national unemployment insurance, agricultural disaster insurance, a sweeping re-examination of the tax system.[7] (Another promised measure which a later generation would have appreciated, the Blum-Viollette bill, intended to be the first step in extending the suffrage to the Arab population in Algeria, was blocked by the representatives of the *colons* in the Chamber and Senate.[8])

When Blum read the decree adjourning the regular session of Parliament at 7:00 a.m. on August 14, 1936, after one of those all-night sittings which taxed the nerves and sensitivities of everyone, he boasted with justification: "There is not a single one of the pledges made by

[5] *À l'échelle humaine, Oeuvre*, V, 460.

[6] Ministerial declaration, June 6, 1936, *Oeuvre*, IV, pt. 1, 274.

[7] The measures are outlined in "Une Année d'action," *Le Populaire*, June 4, 1937; in the Socialist party pamphlet *Le Gouvernement à direction socialiste* (Paris, 1937); and in the editor's note, *Oeuvre*, IV, pt. 1, 251–2.

[8] The Blum-Viollette measure would have given the vote and other civil rights to about 40,000 Arabs as a preliminary step toward full rights; see Chastenet: *Histoire*, VI, 169, 254, and 291, n. 5.

the government in its ministerial declaration that has not been fulfilled. In ten weeks there has been adopted a body of legislation of which I do not believe the parliamentary history of this country offers many examples."[9] Paul Reynaud calculated that 133 laws had been passed in 73 days.[1] The country was ready to cope with the depression "by new means"; and more had been accomplished for labor than ever before in the entire history of the Third Republic. Moreover, Blum had reaffirmed at Geneva the country's will to stand by France's allies, work toward a strengthened League of Nations, and do everything possible to preserve peace.

That summer the immediate impact of the Popular Front reforms was electrifying and inspiring. With wage increases, paid vacations, collective contracts, shop representation, and the shortened work week, labor had a right to believe that a new era had been inaugurated and that the long-awaited social republic was dawning. At the same time the reforms were not designed to benefit labor alone; the middle classes, the farmers, and the country as a whole would benefit too. The nation could take new faith in itself and its destiny. The spirit behind the July 14 celebration of 1936 recaptured the hopes and aspirations of 1848.

The "conquests of June" were now put into effect. One of the least debatable of the reforms was the paid-vacations act. The law of June 20, 1936, providing for a two-week vacation with pay for all workers, was, in the words of a French observer, "one of the first and most grandiose demonstrations of the coming of the Popular Front to power."[2] For years the C.G.T. had pressed for such a law. As an indication of the snail's pace of French social legislation, a bill adopted by the Chamber as early as 1931 had grown dusty in the Senate files. Now, for the first time, it became a reality. The young, energetic Léo Lagrange, named by Blum as "undersecretary of state for leisure and sports," arranged for popularly priced trips, reduced prices in resort hotels in the Alps and on the Riviera, camping facilities, and various other types of recreational activities. For the first time, in August 1936, hundreds of thousands of workers left their factories and offices to enjoy the vacation spots and resort areas hitherto reserved for the

[9] *Chambre, Débats*, August 13–14, 1936, and *Oeuvre*, IV, pt. 1, 320.
[1] Reynaud: *Mémoires*, II, 77.
[2] Robert Mossé: *L'Expérience Blum: un an de Front Populaire* (Paris, 1937), p. 54.

upper and middle classes (to the consternation, to be sure, of the habitués of those resorts). It was one of the first visible manifestations of the "new era"; the Popular Front was demonstrating that a democratic society could provide recreational opportunities for its people no less than fascist societies could. "We want to make our youth healthy and happy," Lagrange told Alexander Werth. "Hitler has been very clever at that sort of thing and there is no reason why a democratic government should not do the same."[3] If the program was never so extensive as Mussolini's *Dopolavoro* or Hitler's *Kraft durch Freude*—who could dictate to Frenchmen ways of spending their leisure?—it nonetheless was responsible for a minor revolution in the French way of life. Blum's paid vacations remained a permanent feature of the post-1945 world as well, and in 1956 the two weeks with pay were extended to three. There was more than rhetoric in Blum's boast that his government "had brought a form of beauty and light into lives that were filled with harshness and gloom."[4]

Perhaps the most far-reaching of all the new labor reforms was the collective-bargaining act of June 24, 1936, which established on a firm legal basis the principles agreed to in the Matignon agreement of June 8. The agreement and the law, like Article 7A of the National Recovery Act and the Wagner Labor Relations Act in the United States, opened, in Jouhaux's widely quoted words, "a new era in industrial relations." Guaranteeing the rights of trade unions and their freedom to organize, the law encouraged collective bargaining by providing for active government intervention in promoting the negotiation of contracts. The law launched the unions also on an unprecedented organizing drive. "Just two typewritten sheets," Blum once said of the Matignon agreement, "yet a history-making document."[5] The new order of collective bargaining destroyed forever the old "divine right absolutism" of industry. Therein lay perhaps the greatest similarity between the American and the French New Deal.[6]

Before 1936, collective bargaining was almost nonexistent in France. In 1934, scarcely 4 per cent of all French workers were covered by

[3] Werth: *Destiny of France*, p. 327. Léo Lagrange was killed in action in June 1940; see Blum's moving postwar tribute, June 10, 1945, *Oeuvre*, VI, 446–7.

[4] Testimony at Riom trial, *Oeuvre*, V, 289. See Alfred Sauvy's judgment that it was the *only* lasting reform, in *L'Express*, April 28, 1960, and Reynaud's comment in *Mémoires*, II, 72.

[5] Speech to Socialist Federation of the Seine, *Le Populaire*, June 7, 1937.

[6] Rudolf von Albertini: "Zur Beurteilung der Volksfront in Frankreich (1934–1938)," *Vierteljahrshefte für Zeitgeschichte*, February 1959, p. 150, makes this point.

collective contracts; only 28 contracts were signed in 1935. Now, in June–September 1936 alone, over 700 contracts were signed; by December the total had risen to 2,336, and it continued to grow. By the end of the Popular Front government in June 1937, collective contracts with clauses on employment practices, minimum wage rates, and shop representation covered the major part of the working class and all branches of industry.[7] Concurrently, in 1936–7, union membership grew dramatically. "The C.G.T. experienced an increase in membership," one scholar has noted, "which in suddenness and extent had not been equalled by the union movement of any other country."[8] From about 1 million, membership soared to an estimated 5.3 million. As in the United States, the most impressive growth was in the mass-production industries and in skills previously unorganized.[9]

Although the introduction of collective bargaining was hailed as the harbinger of "a new era in industrial relations," and the night of Matignon compared with the night of August 4, 1789, it could be argued that France was merely catching up with a pattern already established in other industrial countries. Moreover, the changes did not inaugurate a permanent and sound basis for collective-bargaining relations. For one thing, both under the provisions of the law and in actual practice, the government played a more active role than in most democratic countries. Twice it extended the original contracts by legislative action in order to prevent the outbreak of industrial strife when the contracts were due to expire.[1] To avoid a recurrence of sit-down strikes and to provide for peaceful wage adjustments in a time of rising prices, the government also, with labor's consent, persuaded Parliament to adopt a compulsory conciliation and arbitration law. Blum's hope that the C.G.T. and the employers' confederation would collaborate to set up the machinery of the law was shattered when

[7] See, among others, Mossé: *L'Expérience Blum*, pp. 56–70; Ehrmann: *French Labor*, pp. 43–5; Val R. Lorwin: *The French Labor Movement* (Cambridge, Mass., 1954), pp. 76–7; Danos and Gibelin: *Juin 36*, pp. 205–8; and Pierre Laroque: *Les Rapports entre patrons et ouvriers* (Paris, 1938), in which he summarizes his own report of 1934 to the Conseil National Économique.

[8] Ehrmann, *French Labor*, p. 51.

[9] Unlike the growth of labor under the American New Deal, the expansion of the C.G.T. in the Popular Front years proved temporary; after November 1938 its membership declined precipitously. For labor and industrial relations in these years, see Ehrmann: *French Labor*, pp. 36–125, and Lorwin: *French Labor Movement*, pp. 74–84.

[1] Ehrmann: *French Labor*, p. 45; Colton: *Compulsory Labor Arbitration*, pp. 53–5.

after two months of negotiations the employers broke off talks in November 1936 and shifted responsibility to the government. The system, established on a temporary basis by the law of December 31, 1936, and, with some changes, on a permanent basis by the law of March 4, 1938, provided much-needed mediation machinery and helped settle peacefully a significant number of labor disputes. Although the law provided that all collective disputes had to be submitted to conciliation and arbitration procedures before strikes or lockouts were permitted, no real sanctions were provided at first against strikes and lockouts except the moral pressure of public opinion. The law, and the labor jurisprudence that developed in connection with it, was one of the solid achievements of the government even if both management and labor tended to shift the settlement of important disputes to the government-appointed arbitrators. The prosecution at Blum's wartime trial at Riom may have taken pains to avoid mention of the arbitration law because it provided evidence of Blum's efforts to smooth over class friction and encourage industrial peace.[2]

Industrial relations remained stymied, however, because many employers refused to accept in good grace the concessions they had agreed to in the near-panic days of June 1936. The one-time open-shop stalwarts in the United States reconciled themselves far more readily to the transformation of industrial relations than did their French counterparts. Reorganizing to win back their lost authority, the employers in the autumn of 1936 staged a "palace revolution" in the C.G.P.F. and installed a more aggressive leadership. "Employers, be employers!" exhorted a brochure written by its new president. Changing its organization and techniques, and even its name, the C.G.P.F. launched a belligerent counteroffensive against the Matignon *Diktat*, the forty-hour week, and all Popular Front reforms. The result was a vigorous reaction on the part of the unions and an embittering of industrial relations.[3]

[2] Colton: *Compulsory Labor Arbitration*, p. 155 and passim; Ehrmann: *French Labor*, p. 49; Lorwin: *French Labor Movement*, pp. 78–9; Blum: testimony at Riom trial, *Oeuvre*, V, 287, 321.

[3] For Blum's comments on the employers' counteroffensive, speech to Senate, December 27, 1936, *Oeuvre*, IV, pt. 1, 331–2, and testimony at Riom trial, *Oeuvre*, V, 284; cf. Ehrmann: *French Labor*, pp. 53–5, and *Organized Business in France*, pp. 32–53. The brochure referred to was C. J. Gignoux: *Patrons, soyez des patrons!* (Paris, 1937). To emphasize its new orientation the organization changed its name from Confédération Générale de la *Production* Française to Confédération Générale du *Patronat* Français.

Nor were the unions interested in creating an atmosphere of industrial peace. They never freed themselves from their traditional mistrust of management or their ideological opposition to capitalism. Even Blum himself complained of their pressure-group mentality and admitted that the key position occupied by labor in public life during the Popular Front did not lead to a deeper sense of responsibility.[4]

Even more controversial than the collective bargaining legislation was the forty-hour week. The shortened work week was later held responsible not only for interfering with economic recovery but also for causing a lag in armaments production and hence contributing to the military defeat of 1940. It loomed large in the prosecution's charges at Riom.[5] The favorite whipping boy of all opponents of the Popular Front, the forty-hour law came to assume, in the words of an American observer, "a symbolic importance which was completely out of proportion to its economic significance."[6] Yet its economic significance was not to be lightly dismissed.

The true origins of the law are to be found in the labor turmoil of May–June 1936, when the forty-hour week became one of the battle cries of the sitdown strikers. Although it was part of the C.G.T. Plan, and Blum was on record as having called for it as early as 1933,[7] no one in France before June 1936 regarded its adoption as an imminent possibility. It was generally thought that it would be achieved within the framework of an international agreement under the auspices of the International Labor Office at some distant date. The Popular Front program itself did not specifically mention the forty-hour week, but it did demand, as a measure to spread employment, a "reduction of the work week without reduction of weekly wages."

With the outbreak of the sitdown strikes, the forty-hour week became a slogan of the strikers and one of the measures pledged by Blum; it was accepted by the employers and enacted by Parliament. It must be said, however, that neither Blum nor his advisers carefully considered the implications of the reform. An economist friendly to the Popular Front later remarked: "Let us say only that in June 1936 the forty-hour week was part of the *mystique* and that it was not

[4] *À l'échelle humaine, Oeuvre*, V, 462–4.

[5] Indictment of Blum at Riom trial (*réquisitoire*), October 16, 1941, *Oeuvre*, V, 188–9.

[6] Ehrmann: *French Labor*, p. 50.

[7] See *Le Populaire*, January 5, 1933, and comment by Reynaud in *Mémoires*, II, 102.

possible to examine the problem with all the objectivity desirable."[8] Blum, too, without disowning personal responsibility, described the law as "imposed on me by the circumstances in which I took over the government."[9]

It is now a matter of record that various miscalculations were made in connection with the law. First, the relative rapidity with which it was applied created difficulty. The law merely established the principle of a forty-hour week with no reduction in wages, authorizing the executive branch, after stipulated consultations, to issue administrative decrees announcing the time and method of applying it to each industry. (The practice of requesting a brief general enactment by the legislature and leaving the details of application to the executive was followed at Blum's suggestion for much of the Popular Front legislation in order to prevent excessive parliamentary wrangling.[1])

Once the law was on the statute books, Blum had to face pressure from the unions, which wanted the shortened work week applied quickly, and resistance from industry, which tried to defer its application. Consultations were begun, but Blum and Charles Spinasse, his Minister of National Economy, waited until after the devaluation of the franc before promulgating any decrees.[2] The first ones, issued in October and November 1936, applied the law to the metallurgical, textile, and building industries; by the spring of 1937 the law had been applied throughout the economy. In June 1937 the Minister of Labor reported that over 90 per cent of all workers in the major industries of the country were covered.[3]

Blum later stated that he would have preferred to apply the law more slowly, over a period of years. He insisted, however, that in the autumn of 1936 wholesale and retail prices were rising rapidly and that many industries were already incorporating into their wholesale prices the

---

[8] Mossé: *L'Expérience Blum*, p. 47; cf. Paul Vaucher: "Social Experiments in France," *Politica*, III (1938), 103.

[9] Testimony at Riom trial, *Oeuvre*, V, 254; cf. speech to Chamber, September 28, 1936, *Oeuvre*, IV, pt. 1, 426.

[1] Blum: speech to Chamber, June 6, 1936, *Oeuvre*, IV, pt. 1, 275; testimony at Riom trial, *Oeuvre*, V, 247; and Jules Moch "Avec Léon Blum en juin 1936," *Le Populaire*, March 29, 1953.

[2] See statement in June 1936 to U.S. Secretary of the Treasury Morgenthau by Blum's financial emissary, Emmanuel Monick: John Morton Blum (ed.): *From the Morgenthau Diaries* (Boston, 1959), p. 158.

[3] *Le Temps*, June 13, 1937; Vaucher: "Social Experiments," p. 104; Robert Marjolin: "Reflections on the Blum Experiment," *Economica*, V (May 1938), 183–4; cf. Reynaud: *Mémoires*, II, 172–3.

anticipated additional labor costs. The government had to apply the law quickly, he claimed, in order to avert a situation in which an industry would raise prices a first time in anticipation of the decree and a second time upon its promulgation. In addition, he acted, he said, to avoid the disillusioning experience of the eight-hour-day reform of 1919, which, introduced piecemeal, had led to inordinate delay.[4] He did not mention that labor pressure was undoubtedly the important factor. The unions in the Popular Front years would not have permitted the forty-hour law to remain a dead letter. Blum probably could not have attempted a slower application of the reform even if he had wished to.

Surprisingly enough, the length of the existing work week proved to be another of the miscalculations in connection with the law. Neither Blum nor his advisers were aware of the average work week in force in the major plants of the country. Blum seems to have believed that workers in these plants were not working forty hours a week.[5] Actually, at the time of the law's adoption, workers in major plants—that is, those employing over 100 workers—were working an average week of 44.5 hours. (About 87 per cent of these workers were working more than 40 hours, and 67 per cent were working 48 hours.) Statistics were not kept for smaller plants.[6] To be sure, workers in the major plants comprised only 40 per cent of the total labor force, but these were the very plants on which the country's basic production depended. Accurate information was important. If, as Blum believed, workers were already employed fewer than forty hours, the law was merely a symbolic gesture without a foreseeable effect on production. On the other hand, if major plants were working over forty hours, as was the case, all kinds of difficulties might have been predicted. Lack of statistical information and the pressure of circumstances made it impossible to think clearly about labor's demand for a shortened work week. Alfred Sauvy, one of France's leading statisticians, has said retrospectively of the forty-hour law: "A capital decision was taken in darkness, and the Popular Front, which in December 1936 [that is, after devaluation] held economic victory in its hand, lost it through ignorance."[7]

[4] Testimony at Riom trial, *Oeuvre*, V, 248.

[5] Ibid., p. 268; cf. Daladier's testimony, in Maurice Ribet: *Le Procès de Riom* (Paris, 1945), p. 121.

[6] The inquiry of June 1, 1936, involved 8,488 establishments employing a total of 2,217,384 workers; Fernand Maurette: "A Year of Experiment in France," *International Labour Review*, XXXVI (1937), 8.

[7] Sauvy: "Information, clef de la démocratie," *Revue Française de Science*

Inspired by the example of Roosevelt's wage-and-hour reform, the Popular Front leaders did not, however, understand that the American example was misleading for France. In contrast to the situation in France, the average work week in the United States *had* fallen well below forty hours, from 46.2 hours in 1929 to 33.8 in 1933, so that American industry, unlike its French counterpart, did not have to cut down on working hours when the law was applied. Moreover, no blanket wage increase on the order of the Matignon agreement was ever applied in the United States to add to labor costs.[8]

The emphasis given to absorbing the unemployed as part of the Popular Front program, understandable though it was from a political and social point of view, was based on a misunderstanding of the economic problem. France never had an unemployment problem as serious as that of Great Britain, the United States, or Germany. The maximum estimate of totally unemployed in France in February 1936, approximately 825,000, represented only about 8 per cent of the total working population, compared with a figure of over 15 per cent in England in 1932 and similarly higher figures elsewhere. Even if part-time unemployment is taken into account, it was not as serious a problem as elsewhere.[9] Shortening the work week in order to absorb the unemployed—without increasing production—was not the road to economic recovery.

What everyone failed to anticipate also was the lack of flexible overtime provisions. Although there was exaggeration in the prosecution's charge at the Riom trial that the government, in administering the law, had rendered "recourse to overtime work practically impossible," the difficulty of securing authorization for overtime and the bureaucratic red tape involved was significant. The law and the accompanying decrees clearly provided for overtime when justified by technical or economic reasons (or defense needs); in practice, it was charged, authorizations were doled out only "parsimoniously" and "at

---

Politique, 1951, p. 30; and cf. his *Le Pouvoir et l'opinion* (Paris, 1949), pp. 100–10; his criticism is answered, but not convincingly, by the Socialist Étienne Weill-Raynal: "Les Obstacles économiques à l'expérience Léon Blum," *La Revue Socialiste*, June 1956, pp. 52–3. Cf. also Reynaud: *Mémoires*, II, 103.

[8] These points are made effectively by Henri Laufenburger: "Experience Roosevelt et expérience Blum," *Revue Économique Internationale*, XXIX (June 1937), 442–4, 448–50.

[9] Marjolin: "Reflections on the Blum Experiment," p. 185; Ehrmann: *French Labor*, p. 16. The official statistics on "unemployed workers receiving assistance" were 420,000 in June 1936; most authorities agree that these figures need to be doubled for a more accurate picture.

nearly prohibitive rates." Blum in replying to these accusations, conceded that the regulations had been drawn up strictly, but only in order to prevent the kind of wholesale evasions that had occurred under the eight-hour-day law of 1919. The provision for a time-and-a-quarter overtime rate, he freely admitted, was intended to penalize overtime work in order to induce industry to hire additional workers. Finally, he acknowledged that some officials in the Inspectorate of Labor, eager to curry favor with the government, might have been overpunctilious and stubborn in considering exemptions.[1] Here, too, on the authorization of overtime, the contrast to the American example is again striking. A French economist observed that under the United States wage-and-hour law there was no legal limitation on the number of hours worked so long as overtime rates (set at time and a half) were paid; no special authorization was required. The American law, unlike the French, was a "norm for wages rather than a limitation on work."[2]

All observers agree that both industry and labor were uncooperative and intransigent in the administration of the law. The unions generally refused to accept overtime work unless it could be clearly demonstrated that there were no unemployed workers in the area in question; at other times they blamed the need for overtime on management's faulty work schedules or on inadequate equipment. In his wartime memoirs Blum conceded that labor had "quibbled over and refused" overtime hours on important projects, including defense contracts and construction work for the Exposition of 1937.[3] Employers, for their part, refused to add overtime rates to their wage and production costs, which, they complained, were already too high.[4]

Above all, the most serious interference with production was the unanticipated form taken by the law. The decrees prepared by Minister of Labor Jean Lebas under Blum's close supervision made it possible to apply the law in a variety of ways: a five-day eight-hour-a-day week (with Sunday and either Saturday or Monday as the two rest days), or some form of distributing the working hours over a six or five-and-a-half-day week. But almost everywhere the five-day week, or "week of

---

[1] Testimony at Riom trial, *Oeuvre*, V, 277–80.

[2] Laufenburger: "Expérience Roosevelt et expérience Blum," p. 448.

[3] *À l'échelle humaine*, *Oeuvre*, V, 463–4.

[4] The increase in the cost of the work hour between June 1936 and October 1937 has been estimated at 72 per cent for industrial workers; the increase in production costs at 27 to 30 per cent; see Ehrmann: "The Blum Experiment and the Downfall of France," *Foreign Affairs*, XX (1941–2), 155–6; and Danos and Gibelin: *Juin 36*, pp. 221–2.

two Sundays," became the pattern. (The old "English weekend" was giving way to the new "French weekend," remarked Jules Moch.[5] It was not planned that way or written into the law. The trade unions, the employers, and the government all shared responsibility. The unions regarded the five-day week as the most satisfactory form for labor and also the best means of enforcing the law. As there were only 172 labor inspectors for the entire country, the insecurity and suspicion of the unions may have been well grounded,[6] but the attractiveness of the two-day weekend rather than concern over enforcement seemed to be the paramount consideration. As early as October 1936, the labor column in *Le Populaire* stated: "We believe that the five-day week, with an eight-hour day and two consecutive days of rest, constitutes the most attractive form and it would be wise to institute it wherever possible."[7] Jules Moch admitted that the five-day week as requested by the unions "seduced us too."[8] In November, Blum publicly noted that the forty-hour law was becoming in reality a five-day week everywhere and raised no objections.[9] In April 1937 he said regretfully: "The five-day week has become established in France by a phenomenon that was in large part spontaneous; for my part, it is not the form that I would have preferred, for it has only made it easier for employers not to hire additional workers."[1]

Had new plant schedules incorporating multiple shifts been worked out, the five-day week need not have harmed production. But the forty-hour *work* week soon became the forty-hour *plant* week. Machinery as well as men worked only forty hours and the factories shut down completely for two days. Here again a serious miscalculation lay behind the law. The scarcity of highly skilled and specialized labor in the country made it impossible to set up multiple shifts. Even though the scarcity of skilled labor was sometimes exaggerated, and even though industry showed no willingess to seek out skilled workers more systematically,[2] such a scarcity nevertheless existed. The depression had reduced the number of apprenticeship and training programs, and

[5] Royan party congress, June 1938, p. 312.
[6] Ehrmann: *French Labor*, p. 90.
[7] *Le Populaire*, October 16, 1936.
[8] Royan party congress, June 1938, p. 312.
[9] Speech to national council, *Le Populaire*, November 9, 1936.
[1] Speech to Federation of the Seine, April 9, 1937, *Le Populaire*, April 14, 1937.
[2] Ehrmann has carefully explored this in *French Labor*, pp. 89–92, and "The Blum Experiment," pp. 159–60; see also the official Inquiry into Production, initiated by Premier Chautemps in August 1937, *Journal Officiel Annexes Administratives*, December 18, 1937–January 14, 1938, pp. 13738–44.

the backwardness of French technology made industry more dependent on skilled labor than employers in other industrial countries. To look for skilled workers in the ranks of the unemployed was fruitless, for the unemployed consisted mainly of unskilled workers. Charles Spinasse, Blum's Minister of National Economy, later conceded the harm done by the application of the law "in a country like ours where skilled workers are scarce and where the unemployed are almost all, by definition, unskilled laborers."[3] Because multiple shifts were impossible, the very objective of the law, to absorb the unemployed, could not be fulfilled.

There was no spectacular absorption of the unemployed, certainly nothing approaching what had been predicted. The number of workers on relief (*chômeurs secourus*) declined during the Blum government, but not very significantly, from 420,000 in June 1936 to 330,000 in June 1937; and the figure had risen again by February 1938 to 412,000. In the two years between the winter of 1936, when the forty-hour week was first applied, and September 1938, when the unemployment figure had reached its lowest point, the number of assisted unemployed declined by only 70,000. Part-time workers and workers not on relief were absorbed to some extent.[4] Of course, the forty-hour week was far from being the only factor involved in the failure to stimulate employment. Employers were reluctant to hire new workers because they might find it difficult to dismiss them in view of the growing union control over hiring and firing practices. Nor would they increase their payrolls in an atmosphere of insecurity.

Thus neither labor nor industry did anything to prevent the law from interfering with production. "A double selfishness," Joseph Paul-Boncour noted in his memoirs, "of management and of labor, turned it into a simple reduction of working hours . . . to the benefit of those already taken care of—labor pleased to accept the advantages, and management not interested in seeing their labor costs increased." Only the government, placing the public interest first, he added, might have insisted on a forty-hour week with a succession of shifts to increase production. "But what government," asked the former Socialist and friend of Blum's, "Right or Left, would have been powerful enough?"[5]

Blum's later defense of the law during the long discussion that took place at the Riom trial in connection with the effect of the forty-hour

[3] Royan party congress, June 1938, p. 430.
[4] *Mouvement économique en France*, Table 62, p. 224, and cf. p. 136.
[5] *Entre deux guerres*, II, 332.

week on production was totally unrealistic. When the prosecution attacked Blum's "sincerity" in having stated, at the time of the law's adoption, that production could be maintained, and even increased, with a reduced work week, Blum responded indignantly. To support his position, he pointed to the record of factory legislation in England and elsewhere. Secondly, he demonstrated that production depended on the state of mechanization, the use made of the machinery, and the productivity per worker. In theory, a forty-hour week need not have interfered with production, he maintained, and he even argued that the forty-hour five-day week might have represented the optimum work week, making it possible to work the machinery of any given plant twenty-four hours a day, with three eight-hour shifts, on a five-day basis.[6] But the argument was highly hypothetical. Without multiple shifts, the forty-hour week could hardly maximize production. There was no ground for impugning Blum's "sincerity" at the time the law was adopted, but the administration of the law vitiated its objective.

Blum's position that the Popular Front reforms raised the morale of labor and hence increased efficiency and productivity was also true in theory only. "Do you not believe," he asked the court at Riom, "that all our social legislation was of such a nature as to improve the psychological and physical condition of the worker: a shorter work day, leisure, paid vacations, the sense of a newly acquired dignity and equality?"[7] Again the argument was hypothetical. There is even some evidence that average productivity declined in some branches of industry, notably in coal mining, despite the improved "morale" of the worker.[8] Neither the government nor the C.G.T. reminded the workers that a rise in output was the necessary complement to the shorter work week. As unemployment still persisted, the C.G.T. was not in a position to appeal for intensified work. Moreover, the Communist wing of the labor movement indulged in agitation, slowdown, and strikes for political reasons. Blum himself, in his memoirs, admitted what he could not say at the Riom trial: that "agitation had persisted in many plants; hourly production had declined."[9]

At the time of the parliamentary debate on the bill, the opponents of the measure—Reynaud and Flandin in the Chamber, Abel Gardy and

[6] Testimony at Riom trial, *Oeuvre*, V, 265–75.

[7] Ibid., p. 273.

[8] Ehrmann: *French Labor*, p. 92, and "The Blum Experiment," p. 161; but cf. Danos and Gibelin: *Juin 36*, p. 221, and *Mouvement économique en France*, p. 137.

[9] *À l'échelle humaine*, *Oeuvre*, V, 463.

Caillaux in the Senate—stressed the increased labor costs that would be imposed on industry and the inevitable strain on the economy. Blum had met these objections with his "increased production" argument: that once the economy recovered and production expanded, costs would be spread over a larger number of production units and readily absorbed.[1] But a five-day week, without additional shifts, added to labor costs, curtailed production, and failed to absorb the unemployed. It cannot be said that Blum, although aware of the shortcomings of the law, did very much to overcome them. On the contrary, on many occasions he praised the long weekend as a form of spiritual and physical benefit for the workers, glossing lightly over the production difficulties which had arisen.[2]

The truth was that he had a deep sentimental attachment to the reform; it symbolized the future society in which workingmen would receive their just share in the technological progress of civilization:

> . . . a state of affairs will arrive [he told the Riom court in 1942] when the common heritage of all men will benefit and profit all, when each man will receive his share, his small dividend, either in the form of additional compensation and comfort for the same work or in the form of additional leisure for the same wage. The forty-hour law possessed, and still possesses in my eyes, the tremendous significance that it represented payment to the workers of their dividend in the progress of civilization. It represented a deposit, a prior compensation that the workers might receive, that they might recognize as their legitimate share in the advance of civilization and progress which belongs to all men.[3]

The sad fact was that the reform, desirable in itself and part of the social legislation which French workers had long been denied in the Third Republic, came at the wrong time and under the wrong circumstances. Not only was the economy still trying to climb out of the depression, but many sectors of French industry were insufficiently modernized in machinery and in production methods to absorb the reform, and the lack of rationalization often necessitated the use of a disproportionately large number of scarce skilled workers. Moreover,

[1] See debates in Chamber and Senate, sessions of June 12, 16, 1936, respectively; Blum's replies are reprinted in *Oeuvre*, IV, pt. 1, 292–307.

[2] See, e.g., interview with the London *Daily Herald*, published also in *Le Populaire*, June 4, 1937.

[3] Testimony at Riom trial, *Oeuvre*, V, 285.

as we have seen, trade unions and employers, out of self-interest and mutual suspicion, prevented the greater flexibility that might have been possible and that was written into the law itself.

Yet it is one thing to assess and distribute the blame for France's economic difficulties (and national weakness in 1940) on a host of factors and quite another to place the blame, as the Vichy government later did, on the Popular Front legislation and especially on the forty-hour law. The retardation of the economy and the obsolescence of machinery and methods cannot be blamed on the Popular Front. They were present long before the Blum reforms, indeed long before the depression. Therein lay the true defense of the Popular Front against the accusations of Vichy.

There was another tragic aspect. It was Blum's fate that a social reform designed to cope with the ravages of the depression and to fulfill the long-postponed promise of a better life for labor had to be introduced at a time when the country's defense needs were increasingly urgent. A law intended to lighten the work load of labor, the prosecution at Riom could charge, had "as its most important effect" the idling of the country's industrial machinery and the curtailment of production—all this at a most critical time in history when, across the Rhine, German factories were working long hours and manufacturing armaments.[4] But here too, many other factors—wholly apart from the social reforms of the Popular Front—were responsible for France's military defeat. The obsolescence of the French General Staff was no less marked than that of French industry.

So far as defense production was concerned, exceptions to the forty-hour law were always permitted on a much broader scale and with greater flexibility. Neither the December 1937 inquiry into production nor the prosecution at Riom produced evidence that there was any overwhelming demand by defense industries to have their personnel work overtime.[5] Moreover, during Blum's ministry, the rearmament program was still in its planning and preparatory stage—models being drawn up, bids let out, contracts signed. There was no need for overtime in the plants themselves. When he returned briefly to office in March–April 1938 the situation had changed. He was able to get the metallurgical workers to accept forty-five hours as the normal work week without additional compensation in all establishments involved in national de-

[4] *Réquisitoire*, October 16, 1941, *Oeuvre*, V, 189.
[5] See discussion in Ehrmann: "The Blum Experiment," pp. 152–64.

fense work, and this later became the general pattern.[6] But the relationship of the Popular Front reforms to the fall of France in 1940 and Blum's defense at Riom is a story in itself, to which we shall return.

On balance, even if the labor reforms of the Popular Front were not as spectacular as Blum insisted, and even if with these reforms France was merely "catching up" with other industrial countries, they were not lightly to be dismissed. Given the relative backwardness of French social legislation under the Third Republic, the collective-bargaining and paid-vacation reforms were long overdue. Nor can it be overlooked that these labor gains were made at a time when the advances of totalitarianism were threatening to destroy the rights of labor in many parts of the world. Blum had reason to be proud of the social reforms of the Popular Front, inconclusive and incomplete though they were. It was unfortunate only that they were introduced so late in the life of the Third Republic, that they had to be put into effect all at once, and that their impact was felt at a time when the economy, the public finances, and international relations were all severely strained.

Despite the note of triumphant self-confidence and the pledges of continued advance, the initial pace of legislative action during the ten weeks from June to August 1936 was not maintained. The story of the Popular Front government was one of buoyant expectations, spectacular initial accomplishment, and then slowdown and standstill. Not a single important new reform was adopted after the first exciting weeks. Instead the government found itself on the defensive, facing insoluble currency and Treasury problems, a counteroffensive launched against the labor laws by industry, the hostility of financial circles, an economy that refused to revive, renewed labor unrest, and, above all, rising international tension that affected the decisions of the government in every area. In July 1936, the Spanish Civil War broke out; in August, Hitler announced the extension of German military service to two years. The government had no choice but to assume a heavy rearmament program. Blum with justification could say, toward the end of his premiership: "We are not running an ordinary race, but an obstacle race."[7] By some malicious conspiracy of fate," he noted, "all kinds of

[6] See his testimony at Riom trial, *Oeuvre*, V, 281–3. For the subsequent modifications of the forty-hour law, see Danos and Gibelin: *Juin 36*, pp. 248–50, and Ehrmann: *French Labor*, pp. 88–9.

[7] Speech to Socialist Federation of the Seine, *Le Populaire*, June 7, 1937.

trials and difficulties, foreseeable and unforeseeable, accumulated—and all at the same moment."[8]

Even the *élan* of the Popular Front was broken when the Communists (and many in his own party) opposed the government's non-intervention policy in Spain. Restlessness developed among the Radical Socialists because of continued outbreaks of sitdown strikes. The cold economic realities of rising prices awakened labor from the illusion of profound victory. The inflationary consequences of many of the Blum reforms and the very speed with which they had been introduced placed new strains on the economy and on the public finances. The Popular Front *mystique* foundered on the shoals of politics, economics, and international affairs.

Given time, the economy might have revived and all of the new social reforms might have been absorbed. But time was something that Blum did not have. The Popular Front government lasted less than thirteen months. If Spain broke the heart of the Popular Front, the burden of its financial and currency problems broke its back. Although Blum was aware of the financial and currency difficulties that lay ahead, he dismissed them as "less serious" than many other problems.[9] Yet they proved to be the Achilles' heel of the government; they cut short its life and made impossible the continuation of the Blum experiment.

Affirming that "a nation cannot get along without healthy and honest finances," Blum, like most of his contemporaries, did not question the desirability of a balanced budget. He refused, however, to seek a balanced budget as an end in itself and he repudiated the retrenchment policies of his predecessors. In his view, economic recovery and the resultant increased tax returns would restore a sound equilibrium to public finances. Prosperity would "resolve the budgetary problem by itself, since the deficit is not one of the causes of the depression but one of its side effects or symptoms." The country could temporarily accept deficits in order to combat the depression just as it had once fought the war—the "only true analogy," he called it.[1] He cited the success of the American New Deal in reinvigorating the economy by government spending, though he conceded that it was "an infinitely more ample and more vast experiment."[2] An editorialist in

[8] Speech to Marseilles congress, July 1937, p. 454.

[9] Speech to national council, May 10, 1936, *Exercice du pouvoir*, p. 36.

[1] Radio speech, April 21, 1936, speech of May 10, 1936, and speech to Senate, June 16, 1936; *Exercice du pouvoir*, pp. 23, 42, 94, and *Oeuvre*, IV, pt. 1, 240, 302–4.

[2] Speech to Senate, June 16, 1936, *Oeuvre*, IV, pt. 1, 303; cf. his editorial in *Le Populaire*, January 9, 1936.

Le Populaire wrote: "The Roosevelt experiment permits us to say that it is by means of a budgetary deficit that one can effectively struggle against the depression."[3]

Yet the Keynesian revolution never did reach Paris. Blum always remained fearful that large budgetary deficits would lead to increased flights of capital. He felt himself obliged to take into account the psychological reactions of investing groups within the country which were convinced that government expenditures could lead only to inflation and currency instability. Only in France could an announcement of government defense expenditures lead to a panic in investment circles, such as occurred in September 1936.[4] The Popular Front vacillated between the desire to stimulate the economy by government spending and the desire to keep the budgetary deficit down in order to inspire confidence in private investors. In neither tactic was it successful.[5]

Moreover, Blum faced the special problem of "an enormous internal hoarding of capital" and the continued flight of French capital abroad. With typical optimism, he believed that by creating an atmosphere of confidence it would be possible to induce individuals to return their capital to circulation and in that way help satisfy the government's financial needs as well as those of the economy.[6] It turned out that the Blum government's most difficult task was to create this confidence.

The emigration of capital—the "flight from the franc"—had been a continuing problem since 1934. Political unrest, economic stagnation, international tension, and anxiety over an inevitable devaluation had driven the holders of liquid capital to seek more attractive financial outlets in the United States, Switzerland, and elsewhere. French investors converted their francs to gold and purchased foreign currency. In June 1936, in his financial report to Parliament, Minister of Finance Vincent Auriol estimated the volume of capital "missing" from the French economy at about 60 billion francs, of which about 26 billion, he said, had fled abroad. He asked "capital" to consider carefully "the

---

[3] Marc Joubert, *Le Populaire*, August 21, 1936.

[4] Pierre Cot: *Le Procès de la république* (New York, 1944), I, 284.

[5] See, on larger deficit planning by the Popular Front government, M. Kalecki: "The Lesson of the Blum Experiment," *Economic Journal*, XLVIII (March 1938), 37–9; and Mossé: *L'Expérience Blum*, pp. 136–42; for arguments against, Marjolin: "Reflections on the Blum Experiment," pp. 186–91. See Blum's statements, *Le Populaire*, June 30, 1939, and January 3, 1940. Georges Boris has noted that he communicated some of Keynes's ideas to Blum but not until the summer of 1937, after the fall of the government; cited by Lefranc: *Mouvement socialiste*, p. 352, n. 3.

[6] Speech to Senate, June 16, 1936, *Oeuvre*, IV, pt. 1, 303.

historic fate of social classes or social regimes which did not foresee or consent in time to the sacrifices needed for the safety of their country."[7]

The flight of capital meanwhile caused a continuous drain on the nation's gold reserves, which had sharply declined in successive "hemorrhages" (the latest in May 1936, at the time of the election).[8] The drain on the gold reserves weakened confidence in the franc still further and promoted the widespread feeling that devaluation was inevitable. At the same time, the Treasury found it increasingly difficult to borrow on the private money market on a short-term basis, and was compelled to borrow at high rates of interest from the Bank of France, an added strain on the budget, which already groaned under the weight of burdens inherited from the past. Shortly after taking office, Blum's Minister of Finance described himself as a "receiver in bankruptcy rather than the executor of an estate. . . . I found myself facing an empty treasury."[9] The needs of the Treasury, the equilibrium of the budget, the stability of the currency, and the security of the nation's gold reserves were all dependent upon the return to circulation of the private capital that was being hoarded or had fled abroad. But try as he might, Blum could not create the confidence needed to bring back this capital.

His attempt to inspire confidence seemed doomed from the beginning. A Leftist coalition, with the Communists as a major component, campaigning on a platform denouncing "the 200 families" and "the financial bastilles of reaction," was not calculated to create an atmosphere of benevolence and good will. Yet Blum was convinced that he could personally allay the anxiety of the financial community. At first he had some reason for optimism. Before taking office, as we have seen, his words of assurance that his government would respect property rights and safeguard the franc had cut short the financial disturbances that accompanied the Popular Front election victory. His conciliatory efforts to end the sitdown strikes and his repeated pledges in the fall of 1936 to prevent new strikes and attacks on private property were also directed to that goal. But by autumn Blum was admitting the failure of his efforts to attract hoarded capital back into circulation.[1] Three

[7] *Chambre, Débats,* June 19, 1936; and cf. Auriol: *Hier . . . demain,* I, 39.

[8] For statistics and discussion, Mossé: *L'Expérience Blum,* pp. 123–4; René Théry: *Un An d'audaces et de contradictions: juin 1936–juin 1937* (Paris, 1937), pp. 205–6, and table, p. 208; Danos and Gibelin: *Juin 36,* p. 224; and Martin Wolfe: *The French Franc Between the Wars, 1919–1939* (New York, 1951), pp. 128–9, 144.

[9] Auriol: *Hier . . . demain,* I, 36.

[1] Speech to Chamber, September 28, 1936, *Oeuvre,* IV, pt. 1, 426.

months later, in a New Year's Eve radio broadcast, he appealed for the cooperation of all classes. After pleading with labor not to subject the convalescent economy to the strain of renewed industrial unrest, he appealed to "the mass of investors" and "the possessors of capital" to end the "mortal danger" caused by withholding needed capital from the country. He and his government had given every proof of moderation. There could be no grounds for fear:

> I know very well that six months ago the coming to power of the Popular Front government under Socialist direction threw fright into certain circles of the French bourgeoisie. . . . But how can these panic-spreading rumors reasonably persist? Is the evidence not clear? Is it not true that we have followed policies of economic liberalism more than any other government has in the past, more perhaps than any other government would have done in present conditions?
>
> Do I have to repeat once again that we are not a Socialist government; that we do not seek, either directly or insidiously, to put into effect our Socialist program; that we are working with complete loyalty within the framework of present institutions, present society, the present system of private property . . . ?[2]

Willing to accept their antagonism toward himself and the Popular Front coalition, he was unwilling to believe that Frenchmen would in their own selfish interests hurt the interests of their country. But the repeated protestations of moderation and the appeals to civic duty—embarrassing as they were for a Socialist leader who on other occasions had to account to his own party and to Popular Front mass rallies—fell on deaf ears. The sitdown strike of capital, which outlasted the sitdown strikes of labor, in the long run proved decisive in the failure of the Blum experiment.

When Blum spoke of economic liberalism and Auriol of "liberty," they meant, above all, the refusal to impose controls on foreign exchange. The government might have tried to retard the outflow of gold by restricting or forbidding the purchase of foreign currency. But Blum was unwilling to face the inevitable opposition of the Radicals in the cabinet and of the financial community; he feared that such a step would jeopardize the very confidence he sought to create. Moreover, he knew that the British and American governments were opposed; it would hurt his cherished ideal of political cooperation between the

[2] Radio address, December 31, 1936, ibid., pp. 470–4.

three democracies as well as his hope for wider economic cooperation. Measures of constraint, he said in April 1937, would have "broken the Popular Front, and broken indispensable friendships on the international plane."[3] To the very end Blum sought to avoid such measures, convinced that they were in the nature of totalitarian controls and implied a policy of autarchy and dictatorship. In his wartime memoirs he explained: "The dictatorial assumption of power over a closed economy was forbidden in advance to a government which had as one of its objectives to revive in France, in contrast to fascist-type procedures, the traditions, passions, and practices of democracy. . . ."[4] In his memoirs Auriol similarly insisted that exchange controls would have served only "to isolate ourselves in autarchy, separate ourselves from the great democratic nations at a time when, in the face of the Hitler danger, our diplomacy was successfully attempting to re-establish and strengthen the bonds of our foreign friendships broken by Laval." Moreover, with exchange controls, he noted, the government would have had to abandon all hope of attracting back the capital that had already fled the country; exchange controls, difficult enough to enforce, would have amounted to "setting the mousetrap after the mice had gone."[5] Thus in the interests of conciliating the financial community, strengthening ties with the Anglo-Saxon democracies, and avoiding any semblance of totalitarianism, exchange controls were never instituted. The refusal to impose them was another decisive factor in the ineffectiveness of the Blum experiment.[6]

Another fatal weakness of the Blum government was its failure to overhaul the Bank of France and the banking and credit structure of the nation. This failure to reorganize the French credit system, a system characterized by one observer as "unworthy of a civilized people,"[7] intensified the financial difficulties of the government and the economy. Even though some of the Left-wing criticisms of the Bank were overdrawn—the Bank had long been denounced as "a Bastille still to be

[3] Speech to Socialist Federation of the Seine, April 9, 1937, *Le Populaire*, April 14, 1937. For British and American attitudes see references in the Morgenthau diaries confirming Blum's grounds for anxiety, *Morgenthau Diaries*, pp. 143, 178.

[4] *À l'échelle humaine, Oeuvre*, V, 473–4.

[5] Auriol: *Hier . . . demain*, I, 38–9.

[6] Cf. Kalecki: "The Lesson of the Blum Experiment," p. 39; Louis R. Franck: *Démocraties en crise: Roosevelt, Van Zeeland, Léon Blum* (Paris, 1937), p. 62; and Mossé: *L'Expérience Blum*, p. 175.

[7] Mossé: *L'Expérience Blum*, p. 24.

taken"—it held enormous powers over the financial system of the country. Although privately owned and privately controlled, it had performed extensive public functions as a central bank ever since Napoleon's time. Guardian of the currency, it championed financial orthodoxy and frowned upon easy credit policies. By fixing the discount rate, it could severely limit the government's ability to raise short-term funds. Charges had long been heard that the Bank indulged in "credit blackmail" and could raise or cast down governments at will; the fall of Herriot's *cartel des gauches* government in April 1925 was vividly remembered. It was also asserted that the extension of private credit was influenced by the ties between big business and the "200 families" (the two hundred largest shareholders who chose the Bank's governing regents) and that credit was made available only to the larger industrial firms.[8]

When the Popular Front program was being hammered out, the C.G.T. Plan to nationalize the Bank and to transform it into a publicly controlled central credit agency had been scrapped because of the apprehension of both Radicals and Communists that nationalization would antagonize middle-class voters. Even so, the Popular Front program was pledged to "remove credit and investment from the domination of an economic dynasty" and to democratize control over the Bank. It would have been possible to move energetically.

Soon after taking office, Minister of Finance Auriol appointed an advisory committee to draft a reform bill. The committee, which, according to one of its members, was treated with suspicion and hostility by the permanent officials of the Finance Ministry,[9] unanimously recommended the more extreme measures advocated in the C.G.T. Plan— nationalization of the Bank (the shareholders to be compensated with government bonds), an internal reorganization, and an extensive revamping of the Bank's credit powers. But Blum, his personal wishes aside, feared that the proposal would antagonize the banking community, alienate the Radicals, and irritate the Communists, who had made clear that they opposed anything resembling expropriation. Blum refused to alter the Popular Front program as it had been adopted. The committee's original proposal was "discarded at the request of the

[8] For details see A. Dauphin-Meunier: *La Banque de France* (Paris, 1937), Francis Delaisi: *La Banque de France aux mains des 200 familles* (Paris, 1936), and Mossé: *L'Expérience Blum*, pp. 110–19.

[9] Dauphin-Meunier: *Banque de France*, p. 199; cf. Mossé: *L'Expérience Blum*, p. 151.

Premier's office"; an emasculated bill was drawn up instead and adopted by Parliament on July 25, 1936.[1]

The new law did little more than democratize control over the Bank: it reorganized its internal structure and arranged for the government and consumers of credit to have a voice in controlling the affairs of the Bank. To be sure, the reform abolished an anachronism in French public life; the narrow base of control by high finance was ended and some of the more patent abuses removed. Yet it did little to alter the unsatisfactory credit structure of the country. The hope expressed by the Socialist reporter of the bill in the Chamber remained unfulfilled. The reform, he predicted, would lead to "a complete revision of our public and semi-public sectors of credit distribution, and to a substantial control of the bank of issue over the entire banking system."[2] Except for a limited series of modest loans at low interest rates to small and medium-sized industrial establishments (to help absorb the initial impact of increased wage costs), credit remained unobtainable except at prohibitive interest rates ranging from 9 to 12 per cent. With private investment capital unavailable and with the government's needs ever pressing, the banks provided credit for the Treasury and little else— and that too at high rates.[3]

Like other reforms of the Popular Front, the reform of the Bank of France was more token than real, more symbolic than substantial. Ironically, the government, for all its effort to satisfy the financial community, received little gratitude.[4] The reform served only to irritate the financial community without effectively making the Bank a servant of the national interest. Because private capital failed to return to circulation and because credit facilities for both government and private enterprise remained inadequate, the revival of the economy, which alone could have made possible the absorption of the Popular Front social reforms, could not be achieved. The Blum experiment was caught in a vicious circle.

If the primary economic objective of the Blum experiment was to lift the country out of the depression, can it be said that he succeeded? In

[1] Dauphin-Meunier: *Banque de France*, pp. 199–200.

[2] René Brunet: *rapport*, cited by Dauphin-Meunier: *Banque de France*, pp. 216–17.

[3] Ehrmann: "The Blum Experiment," p. 157; Théry: *Un An d'audaces*, p. 212.

[4] See the episodes recounted in Dauphin-Meunier: *Banque de France*, pp. 221–226.

the first four months, from June to October 1936, every effort was made to avoid the devaluation of the franc. There was hope that prosperity would return because of an increase in the purchasing power of the population stemming from the social and economic reforms. However, industrial activity actually declined, the index of production (1928 = 100) dropping from 87.4 in May to 81.1 in September. Unemployment increased. There were good reasons for the failure of the economy to revive. International tension in the wake of Hitler's Rhineland coup and the outbreak of the Spanish Civil War in July, the uncertainty accompanying the Popular Front election victory, the sitdown strikes, and the shutdown of many plants in August because of the new paid-vacation law all played a part. Investment capital failed to return despite Blum's reassurances and entreaties; instead, additional capital and gold left the country. After June the currency problem became more serious. Labor costs rose markedly as a result of wage increases and other reforms—even apart from the forty-hour week, which had not yet been applied. The gap between French prices and world prices increased, making it even more difficult for French exports to compete abroad. The attempt to revive the economy in this first phase without devaluing the franc was not successful.[5]

For four months Blum delayed in devaluing the franc, although he had long been aware that devaluation might be necessary for the sake of the economy and France's position in international trade. He was reminded by Reynaud and others that the American government had devalued the dollar before undertaking social reforms. As early as September 1934, he had demonstrated in a series of articles in *Le Populaire* that devaluation was undoubtedly inevitable and represented a more satisfactory alternative than the retrenchment and deflationary policies currently being followed. He had called upon his own party to face up to the possibility of devaluation and not merely reject it "with indignation and horror."[6] As Premier, however, he announced his opposition to devaluation, for he was aware that, after the inflationary experiences of the mid-1920's, there was widespread anxiety in labor circles and in the country at large at the prospect of any tampering with

---

[5] *Mouvement économique en France*, pp. 129–31; Marjolin: "Reflections on the Blum Experiment," pp. 177–9; Wolfe: *The French Franc*, pp. 139–45.

[6] These articles in *Le Populaire*, September 15–30, 1934, are cited at length in Marcelle Pommera et al.: *Grandeur et déclin de la France à l'époque contemporaine* (Paris, 1946), pp. 372–4. Paul Reynaud was the persistent champion of devaluation in those years.

the currency.[7] After the elections he pledged that the government had no intention of devaluing the franc—a measure "to which we have always been and remain resolutely hostile." On June 6, he told the Chamber: "We do not intend to cover the expenses of our program by a currency manipulation . . . the country need not expect or fear that we will one fine day be posting on the walls the official proclamation of a devaluation, the official proclamation of a monetary *coup d'état*."[8] Auriol repeated the pledge.[9]

Yet, as Blum later admitted, he was aware that devaluation was "almost inevitable. . . . We knew it, Auriol and I. We are not children."[1] He understood, too, that if he devalued immediately, when he first took office, he could enjoy the psychological advantage of presenting the act as the direct consequence of the situation bequeathed to him by his predecessors.[2] Even some of his own cabinet ministers urged it. One member of his cabinet told Alexander Werth a few days before the government took office: "If we devalue at once, we'll be able to carry on for four years; without that we're finished."[3] But Blum delayed, hoping that an atmosphere of confidence, a recovery of the economy, and a flow of capital back into circulation might avert it. "As slight as the chance was of avoiding it [devaluation], we wished to take that chance to the very end," he later said.[4]

Despite his pledge that there would be no "monetary *coup d'état*," he had carefully hedged when he told the Senate on June 16 that there would be no devaluation "outside of international arrangements and a general and contractual alignment."[5] And in the meantime he had authorized confidential conversations with the United States and Britain. As early as June the American government, eager to support the Popular

---

[7] Is Reynaud not unfair when he ascribes Blum's delay solely to party considerations (*Mémoires*, I, 483–4)? Cf. my review of this volume in the *American Historical Review*, LXVII (1962), 481.

[8] Speech of May 10, 1936, *Exercice du pouvoir*, p. 37; and statements in Chamber, June 6, 1936, *Oeuvre*, IV, pt. 1, 279.

[9] *Chambre, Débats*, June 19, 1936.

[1] Royan party congress, June 1938, p. 498.

[2] He told this to the Chamber, session of September 28, 1936, *Oeuvre*, IV, pt. 1, 423–4.

[3] See Werth: *Destiny of France*, p. 330; and cf. Blum's remarks to the Chamber, September 28, 1936, *Oeuvre*, IV, pt. 1, 423–4.

[4] Royan party congress, June 1938, p. 498.

[5] Speech to Senate, June 16, 1936, *Oeuvre*, IV, pt. 1, 305.

Front, let it be known that the French might devalue without fear of retaliation.[6]

Finally, at the end of September 1936, his hand was forced. He was compelled to devalue by a renewed outburst of speculative activity and a new attack on the gold reserves. Blum explained that the economic recovery that might have made devaluation unnecessary had not materialized, that his government had been unable to make "a sufficient puncture" in the hoarded capital, that a renewal of industrial unrest and, above all, of international tension had interfered with recovery. The establishment of two-year military service in Germany in August had made imperative the immediate adoption of "a very vast and very costly program of armaments" involving additional expenditures within the next four years of at least 20 billion francs, half of which was to be budgeted for immediately. It was the cabinet decision on September 19 to propose these rearmament expenditures that had precipitated a new flight of capital and a further drain on the gold reserves. In the week ending September 25, the Bank lost so much gold that its reserves dwindled to almost 50 billion francs, the figure regarded as the minimum necessary for national defense.[7]

When Blum outlined the reasons for this policy reversal, he pointed to the example of the United States. "What has been most remarkable about the Roosevelt experiment," he said, "has been the courage of President Roosevelt to try one method after another, to refuse to take a stubborn stand against experience, to try something else until at last he found the method that succeeded." The Popular Front, too, was ready, he said, to tackle the problem of economic recovery "by new means." He conceded that the government had not proceeded in the "most logical way": social reforms had been introduced quickly, before devaluation, but he recalled the pressure of circumstances that had prompted them.[8]

The special form by which devaluation was accomplished not only permitted Blum to save face but synchronized with his foreign policy as well. A tripartite currency agreement between France, Britain, and the United States was announced simultaneously in Paris, London, and

[6] *Morgenthau Diaries*, pp. 145, 158; on the mission of Monick, the government's emissary, ibid., pp. 156–8.

[7] See his speech to the Chamber, September 28, 1936, *Oeuvre*, IV, pt.1, 422–435; cf. Auriol: *Hier . . . demain*, I, 38, and Mossé: *L'Expérience Blum*, pp. 119–29.

[8] Speech to Chamber, September 28, 1936, *Oeuvre*, IV, pt. 1, 425–6.

New York on September 25, 1936, pledging cooperation to insure the stability of the three great currencies. The United States and Great Britain announced their acceptance of the necessary "adjustment" of the franc and agreed that all three countries would work "to safeguard peace, promote the establishment of order in international relations and pursue policies that would develop world prosperity and improve standards of living." The three countries further promised steps to prevent exchange difficulties as a result of the devaluation.[9] Blum could speak euphemistically of a "currency realignment" and not of devaluation. "In my eyes," Blum told the Chamber, referring to the tripartite agreement, "its great merit resides precisely in the significance it holds for world opinion; it is an element in the total action to which we are most resolutely and most passionately attached: our action for peace, for the peaceful rapprochement and collaboration of peoples."[1] The United States Secretary of the Treasury, Henry Morgenthau, Jr., was equally enthusiastic. During the negotiations he had informed the British: "If this goes through I think it is the greatest move for peace taken in the world since the World War. . . . It may be the turning point for again resuming rational thinking in Europe."[2] The British Chancellor of the Exchequer, Neville Chamberlain, less friendly to the Popular Front, was convinced that devaluation had been "hastened by Blum's expensive social program." Yet, recognizing the need for concerted action, he agreed to the declaration.[3] The London *Times* greeted the accord, hoping that it might "prove to be a step, the first of several towards an ultimate stabilization of world currencies."[4]

Technically, the currency realignment permitted the gold value of the franc to fluctuate between an upper and lower limit, allowing a 25 to 35 per cent devaluation. (The dollar, formerly worth 15.19 francs, was worth 21.47 francs the next day, approximately a 30 per cent devaluation of the franc.)[5] As agreed during the negotiations with the United

[9] See Blum's press conference, *Le Populaire*, September 27, 1936. There are interesting sidelights on the original wording of the declaration; the American representative had to tell Auriol that in the United States one did not speak of "social classes"! *Morgenthau Diaries*, pp. 163, 168–9.

[1] Speech to Chamber, September 28, 1936, *Oeuvre*, IV, pt. 1, 430; and cf. press conference, ibid., pp. 419–22.

[2] *Morgenthau Diaries*, p. 171.

[3] Keith Feiling: *The Life of Neville Chamberlain* (London, 1942), p. 284.

[4] Cited in *Morgenthau Diaries*, p. 173. See also H. V. Hodson: "End of the Gold Bloc," in Arnold J. Toynbee (ed.): *Survey of International Affairs, 1936* (London, 1937), pp. 161–203.

[5] The franc subsequently declined to 22.46 to the dollar in June 1937, to 29.92 in January 1938, and to 32.23 in April 1938.

States and Great Britain, an Exchange Stabilization Fund was established similar to the American and the British. Operated by the Bank of France in behalf of the Treasury, it aimed to control the relationship of the franc to other currencies within the new legal limits and to support the franc in the exchange market. The sum of 10 billion francs accruing from the revalorization of the Bank's gold reserves was allocated to the fund, the United States insisting during the negotiations that most of the revalorization profit be used for this purpose and not to ease budgetary deficits and Treasury difficulties.[6]

Unfortunately, the Treasury derived little financial benefit from the revalorization of its gold holdings. Because its reserves were low, the revalorization produced only some 17 billion francs in "windfall profit." Of this sum, 10 billion, as we have seen, was placed with the new Exchange Stabilization Fund. But the government then surprisingly used the remainder to reimburse the Bank of France for "provisional advances," which had been made not only to it but also to preceding governments. Even a friendly and well-disposed economist characterized this action as "the height of naïve generosity."[7] No one was grateful for Blum's excessive scruples. The government failed to derive the kind of legitimate "profit" for the Treasury that the United States and other countries had enjoyed when they devalued.

The devaluation misfired in another way. It failed to produce an influx of gold into the Treasury as had occurred elsewhere after similar measures. Out of a desire to prevent speculative profits, the law and the accompanying decrees stipulated that holders of gold had to exchange it for currency at the old price, or declare it and pay a penalty equal to its increased value. These penalty provisions merely deterred the repatriation of gold. In addition, without exchange controls, nothing prevented continued speculation against the franc. A few months later the government, recognizing the futility of the penalty provisions, dropped them. They had represented "a highly 'moral' measure, but not an effective one," wrote an observer.[8]

The devaluation of September 1936 met with widespread indignation. The hostile press and the opposition in Parliament attacked the about-face executed by a government which had promised to avoid devaluation. The Popular Front parties, too, had little enthusiasm for the measure.

[6] *Morgenthau Diaries*, pp. 158, 161; but cf. Morgenthau's later remarks to Bonnet, ibid., p. 461.

[7] Mossé: *L'Expérience Blum*, pp. 130–2.

[8] Werth: *Destiny of France*, p. 336, n. 1; and cf. Mossé: *L'Expérience Blum*, pp. 132–3.

Georges Bonnet, a leading Radical, embarrassed his Radical colleagues in the cabinet by attacking the measure in the Chamber as a violation of the government's pledge and called the tripartite declaration merely an "alibi" and a "cover." (He was shortly after named Ambassador to the United States, undoubtedly to remove him from the political scene.) The Communists, already estranged as a result of the government's non-intervention policy in Spain, complained that they had learned of the step only at the time of the public announcement. They voted for it, but only reluctantly, and insisted on safeguards against inflationary consequences.[9] (There was a strange related episode on the international money market when the U.S.S.R., hostile to Blum because of the non-intervention agreement on Spain, suddenly dumped a large amount of sterling, possibly to sabotage the new agreement and perhaps embarrass Blum. Secretary Morgenthau in Washington had some strong words for this.[1])

The major debate in Parliament, which was called back at the end of September in special session to ratify the devaluation, focused on the protective measures to be provided against anticipated price rises. Acutely sensitive to the problem, Blum had included in the original government bill a sliding wage scale that would have permitted wages to rise in proportion to future price increases. Compelled to admit, however, that such a provision might encourage an inflationary wage-price spiral, Blum accepted a substitute proposal empowering the government to take "necessary measures" to safeguard purchasing power, among them compulsory conciliation and arbitration machinery to handle labor disputes that might arise out of increases in the cost of living. One of the indirect results of devaluation thus was the introduction of compulsory labor arbitration. The debate on devaluation also provided a forum for the opposition to attack the government for the recurrence of sitdown strikes that had broken out in September. Blum pledged firm action; the government, he said, was experimenting with a policy of "neutralization"; the plants were being evacuated but management was not permitted to operate them. In a few cases shops were evacuated by force.[2]

In the next phase of the Blum experiment, from the devaluation of the franc late in September to the "pause" of February 1937, un-

[9] *Chambre, Débats,* September 28, 1936.

[1] *Morgenthau Diaries,* pp. 174–6.

[2] See *Chambre, Débats,* September 28, December 1, 1936; *Sénat, Débats,* September 30, December 17, 27, 1936; for Blum's speeches, *Oeuvre,* IV, pt. 1, 322–4, 422–42.

mistakable signs of recovery appeared. There is no doubt that the "realignment of the franc" on September 25, 1936, favorably altered the relationship between French prices and world prices and for a time had an invigorating effect on the economy. Almost all indices showed improvement and pointed to an economic upswing.[3]

But the improvement was not a deep or lasting one; many sectors of the economy hardly showed signs of recovery. From January 1937 on, the government faced new troubles. Rising costs and rising prices destroyed the price advantage in the world market; the balance of payments grew more unfavorable. The forty-hour law was having a harmful effect on the economy. Most disheartening of all, private capital and gold failed to return to circulation despite the cheaper franc. Because of the scarcity of capital, the government had to borrow at increasingly high rates of interest. Moreover, it was now competing in a scarce money market with the private economy, which in a recuperative stage was beginning to seek capital.[4] The prospect of growing budgetary deficits, augmented now by rearmament expenditures, and the state of the hard-pressed Treasury contributed to a new round of currency instability. With renewed speculation against the franc and a continued assault on the gold reserves, the Exchange Stabilization Fund exhausted its entire ten-billion-franc gold allotment by the end of January. The Treasury obtained some additional credit from private British banks to subsidize the railway deficit, but these funds also were being exhausted. "No government," charged Flandin in the Chamber, "has ever been authorized by Parliament to borrow as much money as you, but you can find no lenders."[5]

The United States government, despite its good wishes for Blum's success, was of little help. "It is very important to keep Blum in," Morgenthau quotes Roosevelt as saying in January. The Secretary of the Treasury also believed Blum to be the only French leader "truly committed to social reform and opposition to fascism."[6] Yet the United

---

[3] *Mouvement économique en France*, pp. 131–3; Marjolin: "Reflections on the Blum Experiment," pp. 179–80; Wolfe: *The French Franc*, pp. 145–51. The index of industrial production rose from 81.2 in September 1936 to 93.6 in March 1937, a 15 per cent increase.

[4] See Blum's speech at Lyons, January 24, 1937, and at Saint-Nazaire, February 22, 1937, *Oeuvre*, IV, pt. 1, 474–8, 478–85.

[5] *Chambre, Débats*, February 26, 1937.

[6] *Morgenthau Diaries*, p. 456. What is to be thought of Chastenet's allegation (with no supporting evidence) that Blum "frequently telephoned President Franklin Roosevelt to obtain moral encouragement"?; see Chastenet: *Histoire*, VI, 285, n. 9, and cf. Lefranc: *Mouvement socialiste*, p. 390, n. 1.

States gave no aid. With the Johnson Act barring an outright loan to a nation that had defaulted on its war-debt payments, Morgenthau also vetoed what might have been possible, an advance from the American Stabilization Fund. Impatiently, he remarked that this would be "just flowing money into the Atlantic Ocean." Of French finances he said: "We patch up the French situation every so often, but with the constant increased percentage of their budget going for war purposes we really cannot help them." "The cost of arming," he added, "is what is breaking down the Treasuries of the world."[7] Ironically the American government was refusing Blum funds because of his military expenditures.

Blum continued to insist that economic recovery would solve the country's financial difficulties and spoke cheerfully of the economic upswing.[8] Yet, despite his optimistic words, in February he was compelled to embark on a new course which he announced in a radio speech to government workers who were demanding salary increases to keep pace with advancing living costs. Expressing his deepest sympathies with their demands, as only "a former government worker" could, and insisting that he was not abandoning his objective of increasing purchasing power, he explained the impossibility of granting their request. "It is the overriding duty of a government," he told the civil service workers, long one of the mainstays of the Socialist party, "to establish priorities in problems and to adopt measures in accordance with them." It would be impossible to increase government expenses and the budgetary deficit "without compromising the public credit." Elaborating on the financial problems of the government, he warned that a financial crisis would jeopardize the entire experiment. "That is why," he stated, "a 'pause' (*un temps de pause*) is necessary. That is why the state must today ask its civil service workers for moderation and patience." New reforms and additional expenditures would have to be postponed. After eight months of accomplishments, it was natural to "catch our breath a little." He promised that the "pause" would not be a "retreat" but "a phase of prudent consolidation."[9]

Early in March, the "pause" announced by Blum was reflected in a number of measures. Still hoping to attract liquid capital and gold, the government dropped the restrictions on gold conversion introduced at

[7] Ibid., pp. 458, 460.
[8] Speech, January 24, 1937, *Oeuvre*, IV, pt. 1, 476–7.
[9] Speech of February 13, 1937, *Le Populaire*, February 14, 1937.

the time of devaluation and restored a "free market" on gold trans-actions. The metal could henceforth be turned in freely to the Bank of France at the current price—with the very profit that the government had intended to prevent at the time of devaluation five months earlier. As proof of the government's new orientation—and to the consternation of the Communists and the Left-wing Socialists—Blum took a strange step. He named a committee of three conservative financial experts closely associated with banking circles, Charles Rist, Paul Baudouin, and Jacques Rueff, to serve along with Émile Labeyrie, the governor of the Bank of France, as advisers in directing the operations of the Exchange Stabilization Fund. The presence of these men was intended to inspire confidence in financial circles, but Blum, with singular lack of foresight, seemed utterly unaware that if they were to desert him, his government would be lost. Blum also took steps now to reduce expenditures, mainly by canceling public works projects that had been authorized but not yet begun. The mild flirtation with deficit financing and pump priming ended.[1]

After the "pause" went into effect, the government, making a patriotic appeal to the country, successfully launched a long-term national defense loan of ten and a half billion francs. The good news that the first portion of the loan had been oversubscribed was marred the very day that the announcement was made, March 16, by a political tragedy in the Paris suburb of Clichy. A Rightist meeting of the Parti Social Français, the political organization into which the disbanded Croix de Feu had been surreptitiously transformed, clashed with a counter-demonstration by Popular Front followers. The latter were aroused by the failure of the government to ban the meeting of the fascist group (the government had argued that it was awaiting a court decision on the organization). In the melee the Leftist demonstrators were un-accountably fired upon by the police; six persons were killed; André Blumel, Blum's *chef de cabinet*, sent there to assist in restoring order, was wounded.

Blum, who had been attending the opera that evening, rushed to the scene in his dress suit and top hat, something which Thorez and the Communists never let him forget.[2] The Clichy incident stunned Blum

---

[1] *Le Populaire*, March 6–7, 1937; cf. Mossé: *L'Expérience Blum*, p. 171.

[2] See Thorez's wartime article: "Léon Blum, tel qu'il est," first published in *L'Internationale Communiste*, February 1940, and reprinted in pamphlet form under that title by a Socialist editor, Charles Pot (Paris, 1956); see pp. 13–14.

and made him seriously consider resigning. To be compared with "bloody Noske" and other Socialists who over the years had used repressive measures against workers was more than he could take. Demands were raised for Marx Dormoy's resignation as Minister of the Interior and for a purge of the police. A half-day demonstration strike was called by the C.G.T. on March 18; it served to channelize the indignation and wrath in labor circles that might otherwise have turned against the government. Blum insisted that the calling of the meeting by the Rightist organization in an area known to be hostile to it had been a provocation. But he told his own party that his government could not ban "all but Popular Front meetings," and that he had to await the court ruling on the organization in question. After all his efforts at preventing bloodshed earlier in his government, blood had now flowed— and workers' blood at that.[3] Clichy added to the disenchantment of labor and to unsettled domestic conditions in general.

Clichy was the second of two tragedies during Blum's premiership that affected him deeply, dramatized the deep cleavages in French public life, and made impossible the development of an atmosphere in which the economy might have revived. A few months before Clichy, in November, the reactionary press of the extreme Right, led by *Gringoire,* had launched a slanderous campaign against Roger Salengro, Blum's first Minister of the Interior, and mayor of Lille, charging him with desertion in wartime. A special investigating committee headed by General Gamelin confirmed that he had long ago been completely cleared and acquitted of that charge. Blum relayed these findings to the Chamber on November 13. But four days later, the overworked minister, who had carried much of the burden in helping to settle the sitdown strikes in June, committed suicide. *Gringoire* had done its work well. At the funeral ceremonies at Lille, Blum appealed to the workers to refrain from acts of vengeance. He pledged legislation that would curb such irresponsible slanders in the future.[4]

[3] Blum spoke at length on the episode to the party national council, March 15, 1937, *Le Populaire*, March 16, 1937; to the Chamber, *Chambre, Débats*, March 23, 1937, reproduced in *Oeuvre*, IV, pt. 1, 485–500; and to the Federation of the Seine, April 9, 1937, *Le Populaire*, April 14, 1937. See also Danos and Gibelin: *Juin 36*, pp. 257–8.

[4] On the episode, see Blum's speech to the Chamber, November 13, 1936, and speech at Lille, November 22, 1936; the speeches and other documents are reproduced in *Oeuvre*, IV, pt. 1, 335–55. Gamelin explains his role in *Servir*, II: *Le Prologue du drame, 1930–août 1939* (Paris, 1946–7), 255–7. See also, with citations from *Gringoire* at the time, Bodin and Touchard: *Front Populaire*, pp. 210–20; Armand Coquart: "Roger Salengro ou l'exercice du pouvoir," *La Revue*

Political hatreds grew more impassioned as the months went by. A whole literature of calumny was directed against Blum; the hatreds evoked by Franklin D. Roosevelt fade to nothingness in comparison. Charles Maurras led the pack; Henri Massis and Henri Béraud followed. *L'Action Française, Gringoire, Je Suis Partout* were filled with vitriolic attacks. "It is as a Jew that one must see, conceive, hear, fight and destroy this Blum," wrote Maurras. "This man is anything but French."[5] His private correspondence was filled with similar attacks. Even fellow Jews wrote him: "Alas, three times alas, you furnish irrefutable arguments to the all too many antisemites who hold the Jews responsible for the disorder and disintegration that is going on in France and elsewhere. . . . You are a bad Frenchman and a traitor to your race."[6] Blum, who could weep over the bloodshed at Clichy or over the events in Spain, remained impervious to such personal attacks and criticisms.

The "pause," announced in February 1937, was clearly an about-face despite Blum's denials. The concessions were widely interpreted as a sign of weakness, as Blum's "trip to Canossa."[7] The words of *Le Temps* were widely quoted: "It is not only a pause, it is a conversion."[8] The opposition in the Chamber and the Senate began to take the offensive. Reynaud and Flandin pointed to Blum's financial difficulties as proof that he ought to have re-established financial stability before undertaking programs of social reform, which provoked Blum to reply: "Very well, M. Paul Reynaud, if you had decided last June to apply to the country a combination of devaluation and retrenchment while postponing to a far-off future the hope of social reforms, I can only ask where you would have ended up despite your fine intelligence!"[9]

Socialiste, June 1956, 57–74; and Le Parti Socialiste (S.F.I.O.): *En souvenir de Roger Salengro mort au service du socialisme* (Paris, 1936). A press bill introduced by the government and adopted by the Chamber was later so emasculated in a Senate committee that Blum decided to abandon it.

[5] *L'Action Française*, May 15, October 16, 1936, cited, with other examples, by Bodin and Touchard: *Front Populaire*, pp. 84–5. The worst of the pamphlets was *La Vie de Monsieur Léon Blum*, by Gustave Téry; it even dredged up charges of homosexuality at the time of Blum's leaving the École Normale Supérieure.

[6] Unpublished letter, November 15, 1938, Blumel files; courtesy of M. Blumel.

[7] Mossé: *L'Expérience Blum*, p. 148.

[8] *Le Temps*, March 5, 1937.

[9] *Chambre, Débats*, February 26, 1937.

The "pause" and the presence of the three orthodox financial advisers temporarily inspired confidence. The defense loan was successful. The outflow of capital and the decline in the gold reserves were checked for a short time. At the beginning of April the Exchange Stabilization Fund allowed the franc to decline to its lower legal limit in an orderly way. But the clash at Clichy, the recurrence of strikes, the pressure from the Communists for an end to the non-intervention policy in Spain, and the mounting self-assurance of the opposition in the Chamber and in the Senate conspired to undermine the government's position. Moreover, in the final phase of the experiment, from March to June 1937, economic recovery ended abruptly, in sharp contrast to the world-wide economic upsurge that was taking place at the very same time. The index dropped from 93.6 in March to 88.7 in June. The economic decline that then set in merged with the world recession of the winter of 1938. France, noted a French economist, was "the only country to have passed from one period of depression to another without enjoying an interval of prosperity in the meantime."[1]

In May and June 1937, the last act was played out. The Treasury once again found itself in a critical situation. With the economy failing to revive, the balance of trade declining, and tax receipts lower than anticipated, there was a wide gap between the Treasury's needs and its receipts. Unable to sell sufficient short-term government securities to replace bonds falling due, the Treasury was hard pressed to meet its June obligations. Even the banks were purchasing foreign exchange instead of Treasury bonds.[2] Amid persistent rumors of a new devaluation and in the face of the Treasury's difficulties, the emigration of "hot money," which had been temporarily checked by the "pause," took a serious turn. The gold reserves of the Exchange Stabilization Fund were consumed in a vain effort to maintain the exchange rate of the franc. From June 1 to June 22 the reserves declined by 5.2 billion francs; in the next week, by another 2.5 billion. The panic reduced the reserves to about 50.2 billion Auriol francs (about 37 billion of the 1928 francs), a level considered dangerous for the nation's security.[3]

Confidence in the franc was being destroyed. A "psychological depreciation of the currency," Blum later called it.[4] The speculative offensive, Auriol noted on June 16, was assuming "the proportions of

[1] Marjolin: "Reflections on the Blum Experiment," p. 177.

[2] Auriol: *Hier . . . demain*, II, 127, n. 1, and 88, n. 1.

[3] Théry: *Un An d'audaces*, p. 208 and tables; Wolfe: *The French Franc*, p. 156; Bonnet: *Défense de la paix*, I, 30.

[4] Speech at Bordeaux, *Le Populaire*, July 5, 1937.

1925, 1926, and May 1936."[5] On June 14 two of the three government-appointed financial experts, MM. Rist and Baudouin, resigned, saying that they could not defend the franc unless the government accepted immediately their suggestions for raising taxes and for government retrenchment. Baudouin privately told Auriol that what was needed was "a different majority."[6] Their resignation added to the sense of panic. The Blum experiment was all but over.

But before turning to the final scene, the fall of the government, and to an appraisal of the experiment as a whole, we must go back to examine the foreign policy of the Popular Front government. For the Blum experiment was undertaken in the troubled world of 1936–7; the quest for peace and security in an age of aggression and dictatorship was also part of the experiment.

[5] Statement to press, *Le Populaire*, June 16, 1937; cf. *Hier . . . demain*, II, 88, 127.

[6] Auriol, *Hier . . . demain*, II, 127, n. 1. For the Rist-Baudouin recommendations, see also Bonnet: *Défense de la paix*, I, 25.

VII

THE QUEST FOR PEACE:
Foreign Affairs and National Defense

Dictatorship and war, democracy and peace, can you dare deny the inescapable connection?[1]

BLUM and his Popular Front government took office scarcely three months after the most serious blow dealt to France's diplomatic position since the end of the First World War--Hitler's successful gamble in reoccupying the Rhineland on March 7, 1936. That event, along with the failure of the League of Nations to prevent Mussolini's conquest of Ethiopia, revealed to all Europe the impotence of the League and the weakness of its two champions, Britain and France. The smaller powers of Europe, such as Belgium, Poland, and the Little Entente countries, Czechoslovakia, Rumania, and Yugoslavia, were rapidly losing confidence in the Western democracies and the League, and in the treaties of alliance contracted with France after Versailles. To make matters worse, mutual recriminations and rancor after the Rhineland and Ethiopian setbacks had strained relations between England and France whereas the two military dictators had moved closer together. As to the U.S.S.R., its strength and policies in 1936 were still uncertain factors. The Franco-Soviet pact of mutual assistance, signed in May 1935 and ratified by the Chamber in February 1936, had remained without effect because the promised military conversations had never materialized; the treaty merely deepened existing divisions in French public opinion.

Internal unrest in France also undermined the confidence of France's

[1] Blum: *À l'échelle humaine, Oeuvre*, V, 416. Blum's wartime essay was completed at the end of 1941 and published in 1945.

allies in the ability of the French to play a strong role in foreign affairs. The *émeute* of February 6, 1934, the agitation attending the formation of the Popular Front, the physical assault on Blum in February 1936, the heated elections that spring, and the giant wave of sitdown strikes that followed the Popular Front victory at the polls contributed to an image of disunity and even of imminent civil war. General Gamelin experienced marked discomfort at the clenched fist greetings with which he and the Polish military leader General Śmigły-Rydz were received during the latter's visit to Paris in August 1936.[2]

The disfavor with which many *bien-pensants* elements viewed the Popular Front coalition of Socialists, Communists, and Radical Socialists was mirrored in matters of foreign policy. Equating the Popular Front with communism, many Frenchmen of the extreme Right envied the discipline, unity, and strength created by the German and Italian fascist dictators in their countries—no trade unions, no strikes, no Communists, no parliamentary scandals. To be "saved" from communism was their paramount concern. "Better Hitler than Stalin" was a sentiment which, if seldom on anybody's lips or pen, was in many people's hearts and could easily be transformed in June 1936 into "Better Hitler than Léon Blum."[3] General Gamelin, who was a loyal republican and not ill disposed toward the Popular Front, sadly recorded his observation: "The crisis of May—June 1936 terrorized a great segment of the French bourgeoisie. It made many of us lose sight of the dangers of Hitlerism and fascism at our doorstep because behind the 'Popular Front' one saw the specter of Bolshevism. Therein lies the origin of the slogans that disfigured the soul of the nation: 'Better Hitler than Stalin' and 'Why die for Danzig?' "[4] Paul Reynaud noted with alarm the "conditional patriotism" developing in France: one would fight for one's country provided it were not under a Leftist government.[5]

Largely as a result of ideological sympathies, attitudes on foreign policy had undergone a strange metamorphosis in France. The traditionally nationalist and even chauvinist Right had tended to become conciliatory and accommodating toward the fascist dictators, especially Mussolini. And the Left had increasingly adopted a position of firmness and resistance, demanding collective action to deter future

[2] *Servir*, II, 238.
[3] Like others, I have been unable to find the slogan in print. But *se non è vero, è bene trovato!*
[4] *Servir*, II, 219.
[5] *Au coeur de la mêlée, 1930–1945* (Paris, 1951), p. 70.

aggression. Blum commented in April 1936 on the "paradox." "We Socialists, who never ceased to preach peace, who were customarily treated as bleating pacifists (*pacifistes bêlants*), . . . today are denounced by the nationalists of yesterday as warmongers (*bellicistes*) . . ." They had first been designated as "warmongers," he noted, when they had supported sanctions against Mussolini "to frustrate the monstrous designs of a fascist dictator."[6] In actuality, Blum and the Socialists were less belligerent than the Right made them out to be. The pacifism of the French Socialists died hard; within the party, Paul Faure was beginning to head an important wing that opposed armaments, alliances, and any action, international or national, that might raise the threat of war. Blum himself, though increasingly committed to collective security and a strengthening of alliances, was bent also on exploring avenues of reconciliation, accommodation, and general arms control.

It was indeed a troubled scene that Blum inherited. His Minister of Foreign Affairs, Yvon Delbos, was no less a receiver in bankruptcy than Vincent Auriol, his Minister of Finance. To cope with the situation would have been difficult enough; the task was rendered vastly more complex by the outbreak of the Spanish Civil War in July. Blum's response to that episode, and its international ramifications, will be treated in the next chapter; it need only be said here that the nonintervention policy was conditioned, at least in part, by the Popular Front government's troubled diplomatic legacy.

Blum, naturally, was closely preoccupied with foreign affairs. For years he had been one of the chief spokesmen of his party in Parliament on foreign policy and had devoted countless daily columns in *Le Populaire* to the international scene, stressing the theme that peace could be preserved through collective security, a strengthened League, and progressive disarmament. Before and after taking office he repeatedly referred to the questions of war and peace as the major source of anxiety for the peoples of the world, more important than the anxieties stemming from the economic woes of the depression. "The problem of human life overshadows the problem of daily bread," he said in a campaign speech in April 1936. A few months later he told a Socialist meeting: "We shall not forget that in the slogan of the Popular Front ["Peace, Bread, Liberty"], 'peace' is the word that overshadows the other two, since without peace a people has no bread and in losing the peace it also risks losing its liberty." In a major speech before the

[6] Speech, April 21, 1936, *Oeuvre*, IV, pt. 1, 236, 237.

League of Nations Assembly on July 1, he pleaded for the governments of the world to end what he described, in Victor Hugo's haunting phrase, as "the great insomnia of the world."[7]

As might have been expected, Blum took a direct personal interest in foreign affairs during his year in office. He took it upon himself to read all of the important diplomatic correspondence from day to day. He and Foreign Minister Delbos occupied apartments in the same Paris building, and could confer at any hour.[8] During his premiership he arranged meetings with many of the foreign ministers and other leading representatives of the major powers. At one time or another during the year he saw and conferred with Baldwin, Eden, and Chamberlain; Spaak, Śmigły-Rydz, Litvinov, and Schacht; the German, Italian, and Russian ambassadors—Welczeck, Cerutti, and Potemkin; and William Bullitt, whom he counted as a special friend (Bullitt succeeded Jesse I. Straus as American Ambassador in September 1936).

Delbos, who had been chosen from the Radical Socialist ranks to serve as Foreign Minister, was not a colorful figure; he had distinguished himself principally by speeches in Parliament denouncing Laval's conduct in the Ethiopian affair. He seems to have been a loyal and sincere minister, sharing most of Blum's views, but certainly not a man of breadth or daring. Pierre Cot characterized him as "timid but honest."[9] Blum spoke of his relations with Delbos as always cordial and friendly: "A fine feeling of mutual confidence existed between the two of us."[1] Blum also enjoyed good working relations with the most important permanent official at the Quai d'Orsay, the poet-diplomat Alexis Saint-Léger Léger (Saint-John Perse), Secretary-General at the Ministry of Foreign Affairs since 1933. The collaborator and heir of Aristide Briand, Léger was held "in confidence and respect" by Blum and Delbos. He was a "good republican" who wished, however, to keep his judgment clear of politics or ideology. The cornerstone of France's policy in the 1930's, he believed, lay in the closest possible relations with Great Britain, a view which Blum shared completely. In later years, it was Léger's complaint that none of the ministers under whom he served had "the will and the vision" to pursue policies that would yield both a just peace and security for France. Without passing judg-

[7] Ibid., p. 235; speech of January 24, 1937, ibid., p. 383; and speech of July 1, 1936, ibid., p. 370.

[8] Testimony before parliamentary comn.ission, 1947, *Événements*, I, 126.

[9] *Le Procès de la république*, II, 338. Cot, the Air Minister, was, of course, one of the more militant Radicals in the cabinet.

[1] Testimony, 1947, *Événements*, I, 126.

ment on Blum, he described Delbos as "a man of narrow vision and distrustful of himself."[2]

Blum clearly recognized the critical state of European affairs in the summer of 1936. "For the first time in eighteen years," he told the League on July 1, "a European war is again envisaged as a possibility." Even worse, war was considered by some to be "nearly inevitable." Seeking first to dispel the impression that France, because of its recent internal troubles, had to be written off as a major power, he described his country as having emerged from its difficulties with a renewed faith in itself and its future. The Popular Front, by protecting republican liberties and by advancing social justice, had enhanced internal unity and patriotism: "A people is all the more attached to its independence and has all the more reason for defending it, the more it lives in freedom and in a just society."[3]

On a second note of reassurance, he sought to allay suspicion at home and abroad that his Popular Front government would embark on an ideological crusade against the fascist powers, insisting that it desired peace "for and with all peoples whatever their regime or principles of government."[4] He dismissed as "an absurd hypothesis" the speculation that his government might seek war or act belligerently in order "to revenge persecuted comrades or . . . destroy such and such a regime . . . We exclude completely the idea of a war of ideology or reprisals."[5]

Blum dismissed also any argument in favor of the "emancipating" virtues of war. "We do not believe, as our ancestors of 1792 and 1848 did," he told the American Club in Paris, "that war can have a liberating and revolutionary quality"; that "illusion" had been dispelled by the events following the First World War; moreover, even behind the revolutionary armies of 1792 there had lurked the shadow of Napoleon.[6] Blum's theme was peace, not antifascism. His words were reassuring to his Radical Socialist allies in the Popular Front coalition and to the pacifists in his own party. Others were reassured too. General Gamelin

[2] Cited by Elizabeth Cameron: "Alexis Saint-Léger Léger," in Gordon Craig and Felix Gilbert (eds.): *The Diplomats, 1919–1939* (Princeton, 1953), pp. 382, 392.

[3] *Oeuvre*, IV, pt. 1, 365.

[4] Ibid., p. 366.

[5] Speech of May 15, 1936, to American Club in Paris, *Exercice du pouvoir*, p. 127; cf. speech of September 17, 1936, *Oeuvre*, IV, pt. 1, 372.

[6] Speech of May 15, 1936, *Exercice du pouvoir*, p. 127; cf. speech of November 16, 1936, *Oeuvre*, IV, pt. 1, 373–9.

left Blum after a conference on June 10 completely won over by his "charm and intelligence," reassured that "ideologies" (*mystiques*) would play no part in the conduct of foreign affairs nor involve the country in unnecessary risks. And he added the testimonial that Blum "knows how to place the permanent interests of France above party struggles."[7]

Not only did Blum refuse to undertake an ideological crusade, he also refused to question the good faith of the dictators with whom he had to deal. In the case of Italy, which had so recently engaged in naked aggression against a helpless country, his attitude, as we shall see, was reserved. So far as Germany was concerned, he proposed to leave no stone unturned in working toward a rapprochement and toward a solution of existing differences. No one who had lived through the holocaust of the First World War, he maintained, would willingly cause such suffering again. "Chancellor Hitler," Blum told the Senate on June 23, "has on several occasions proclaimed his desire for an agreement with France. We do not intend to doubt the word of a former soldier who for four years knew the misery of the trenches."[8] Meanwhile the wrongs of recent months would be forgotten. "France sees only one sure means of liquidating the past," he said at Geneva; "that is to create a new future."[9]

Yet a note of firmness accompanied the proffered olive branch. Disturbed lest the failure of France to act more vigorously in the Rhineland episode be misconstrued as a sign of weakness, he asked: "Who would dare suppose that our reaction would have been the same if someone had actually violated our frontiers or the frontiers of those guaranteed by our treaties?" A durable peace presupposed a respect for international law and international agreements. The members of the League had to be resolutely determined to enforce treaties and obligations—no matter what the risks:

> International agreements will be defied or nullified if the powers who have subscribed to them are not resolved to go the whole way (*jusqu'au bout*). To go the whole way is . . . to accept the eventuality of war to save the peace. . . . I declare without hesitation that in the present state of the world, that risk must be envisaged in full conscience and in full courage.

[7] *Servir*, II, 222–5.

[8] Cabinet statement on foreign policy, *Sénat, Débats*, June 23, 1936, reprinted in *Oeuvre*, IV, pt. 1, 357–64.

[9] Speech of July 1, 1936, *Oeuvre*, IV, pt. 1, 369.

His bold words at Geneva, as strong as any he had uttered to that time, were somewhat tempered by the observation that the more clearly the risk of war was envisaged, the less its actual risk. He was still repeating his old theme that if "collective security" were combined with "general disarmament," the danger of war would be minimized. If nations accepted disarmament, the international community would be able to impose its decisions peacefully.[1]

Although he de-emphasized the importance of ideologies in foreign affairs, he spoke openly of France's "special affinity" and "special friendship" for countries which, like his own, were "passionately attached to liberty and the same ideal of social justice."[2] With the United States still remote from European affairs, it was on Britain that Blum pinned his hopes for a revival of the League and for collective security against renewed aggression. Above all, he was bent on rebuilding the ties with Britain that had been undermined in the Ethiopian and Rhineland episodes. Anthony Eden was greatly encouraged. He later recalled in his memoirs: ". . . a new and much happier era of relations with France now opened up. From this moment until my resignation in February 1938 French Ministers and I worked together without even a momentary breach of an understanding which grew increasingly confident." On Blum he found himself "reflecting ruefully how much it must have advantaged our two countries if he had been our partner in the last two years of missed opportunities." He and Blum were "at one," he said, "in their antipathy to dictatorships wherever they might be" and in their desire for "Anglo-French cooperation." And he added a personal note:

> As I grew to know Blum better, I several times met him in his own beautiful house on the Ile St. Louis in Paris, where he had a rare library in which it was a delight to browse. Many of his books had been presented to him by their authors. I was in those days, and still am, an admirer of the writings of Anatole France. On one occasion Blum gave me a copy of *La Rôtisserie de la Reine Pédauque*, inscribed to him by the author and re-inscribed to me. On another, I gave Blum an early edition of one of Fielding's novels. These were the pleasant by-paths of politics. I respected Blum's intelligence, integrity, and courage and our friendship was never marred by a serious difference or even a misunderstanding.[3]

[1] Ibid., pp. 365, 368–9.

[2] Speech of May 15, 1936, *Exercice du pouvoir*, pp. 126, 127; and cf. speech of July 1, 1936, *Oeuvre*, IV, pt. 1, 365.

[3] Anthony Eden: *Facing the Dictators* (Boston, 1962), pp. 418–19, 429.

The French Socialist and the British Conservative shared in common the determination to check the dictatorships and at the same time, if humanly possible, to preserve peace.

The foreign policy of Blum's government was summed up officially in the declaration read to the Senate by Blum and to the Chamber by Delbos on June 23. The government committed itself to work for peace and to cooperate in all efforts at general disarmament. The sanctions imposed on Italy had to be lifted since they now served no useful purpose. The government pledged itself, however, to work for collective security and a strengthened League of Nations, and looked to "the unreserved support of Great Britain, the cordial sympathy of the United States . . . and the powerful cooperation of the U.S.S.R." With these countries and with its old allies, Belgium, Poland, and the countries of the Little Entente, France would maintain the closest ties. The country hoped for collaboration and friendly relations with Germany too. Although Germany's rapidly progressing rearmament and recent repudiation of treaty obligations could not be ignored, the government announced its readiness to examine with sincerity any German suggestions that would contribute to peace.[4]

The first item of business went off well. A conference of the British, French, and Belgian prime ministers and foreign ministers had been arranged to discuss the status of the Locarno Pact in the wake of Germany's remilitarization of the Rhineland and to draw up plans for a future meeting to which Germany and Italy would be invited as well. Blum, Delbos, and their foreign-policy advisers flew to London on July 23. They seemed to convince the British Conservatives that the worst of the internal unrest in France was at an end. The French ministers, and especially Blum, made a favorable impression. "The success of the meeting was widely attributed to M. Blum's personal qualities," was one British observation.[5] The official communiqué stressed that the main purpose of the European nations was "to consolidate peace by means of a general settlement" and that such a settlement was to be "achieved by the free cooperation of all the powers concerned." "Nothing," it stated, "would be more fatal to the hopes of such a settlement

---

[4] *Oeuvre*, IV, pt. 1, 357–64.
[5] Toynbee (ed.): *Survey of International Affairs, 1936*, p. 350; for the conference, ibid., pp. 344–50.

than the division of Europe, apparent or real, into opposing blocs."[6] Germany and Italy would be asked to cooperate in negotiating a new arrangement as a substitute for the Locarno Rhineland pact.

Yet only a few days earlier an event had occurred that deepened the division in Europe and made it impossible to achieve the desired cooperation—the outbreak of the Spanish Civil War. From the moment Blum arrived back in Paris, the Spanish Civil War crowded everything else from the agenda, troubling relations with Britain and creating insuperable obstacles to the possibility of "a general settlement" involving Germany and Italy. But the Spanish Civil War was only one of many complications and setbacks. There was also Belgium's decision to reorient its foreign policy and to draw away from the side of France and Britain despite the cordiality of the three-power talks in London that July.

In the fall of 1936, the Belgian government took the momentous step of requesting release from its obligations under the Locarno Pact and announced its intention to end existing arrangements with France for mutual military assistance and joint defense preparations. The Belgians wished to revert to a policy of non-alignment lest their alliance with France be used as a pretext by Hitler for an attack on their country. With a remilitarized Rhineland, and under the new conditions of armored warfare, a Nazi attack, they believed, could only be disastrous. Ever since the signing of the Franco-Soviet pact of 1935, some Belgians had also feared that the country might be led into a war through France's connection with the Soviets. An independent policy, "exclusively and completely Belgian," in the phrase used by Foreign Minister Spaak and King Leopold III, was laid down as the answer to Belgian security. Ironically, the country was thereby regaining its pre-1914 status as a guaranteed neutral, with France and Britain committed to come to its aid in the event of an unprovoked military attack. Belgium could thus count on French and British assistance but, in turn, was relieved of any obligation to aid France or to permit the French to enter Belgian territory before an attack materialized.[7] The Belgians had all the advantages but none of the disadvantages of ties with the democracies.

[6] Communiqué, July 23, 1936, cited in Toynbee (ed.): *Survey of International Affairs, 1936*, pp. 348–9. Eden touches briefly on the conference in *Facing the Dictators*, p. 439.

[7] On the Belgian action, Toynbee (ed.): *Survey of International Affairs, 1936*, pp. 351–60; Blum's analysis in *Mémoires*, written in 1940, *Oeuvre*, V, 7–11; and testimony, 1947, *Événements*, I, 130–2.

The defection of Belgium, symbolizing the breakdown of confidence in collective security and in French military strength and diplomatic leadership, filled Blum with grave apprehension. "I sensed with cruel anguish," he recalled, "that here was a new sign, a new symptom of the progressive dismantling of all our European positions." Toward the end of 1936, a series of secret meetings was held between himself, Delbos, Chautemps, and the Belgian premier, Van Zeeland, in Paris and in Brussels to discuss questions of cooperation in the event of emergency—"several hours of painful conversation." Recognizing the impossibility of winning the Belgians back to the alliance—"one does not keep a people in an alliance against its wishes"—he warned that the help the Belgians could count on in the event of an attack would depend on Belgian military preparations and frontier defenses, and on continued cooperation between the French and Belgian General Staffs.[8] Little was ever accomplished along those lines.[9]

The new relationship with Belgium precipitated a major French decision. The Maginot Line had never been extended to the sea along the French-Belgian frontier, expressly so that Belgium might not consider itself cut off from the French defense system. Fortification works were now belatedly begun, but only a skeletal framework was ready by the time the war came. In September 1939, France had neither a Maginot Line built to the sea nor concerted plans between the French and Belgian General Staffs for mutual defense. Not until the moment of the German invasion in May 1940 were French troops permitted to enter Belgian soil—under the worst possible circumstances.

The defection of Belgium was the first setback to Blum's plans to rebuild alliances and strengthen the unity of the democratic powers. "After the Ethiopian affair, after the military reoccupation of the Rhineland, a new blow," as he described the event, "was administered to our idea of collective security . . ." As if by a fateful omen, on the way home from the secret talks in Brussels that winter of 1936–7, the automobile carrying Blum, Delbos, and Chautemps skidded on the icy road and almost went over the railing of a railway bridge; the scene of the near-accident was Compiègne.[1]

In the months that followed, another failure could be recorded. An effort was made to strengthen the Little Entente, the somewhat loose

[8] Testimony, 1947, *Événements*, I, 130–1.

[9] Gamelin: *Servir*, I: *Les Armées françaises de 1940* (Paris, 1946–7), 81–9; II, 239; and testimony, 1947, *Événements*, II, 444–5.

[1] *Mémoires, Oeuvre*, V, 9–10; and testimony, 1947, *Événements*, I, 131.

alliance of Czechoslovakia, Yugoslavia, and Rumania sponsored by France that dated back to 1920. The objective was to make it now into a more effective defensive alliance and to cement its ties with France as well. But again the lack of confidence in France after the Rhineland episode proved decisive. Rumania and Yugoslavia rejected French over- tures and moved toward closer relations with Italy and Germany; even Czechoslovakia, France's surest ally, found it necessary to think of sounding out Germany on possibilities of a *rapprochement*.[2]

Blum also encountered diplomatic difficulties with Poland, which had been linked to France as an ally virtually since Versailles. The treaty of February 19, 1921, had stipulated close military relations and the exchange of General Staff plans. Under Colonel Józef Beck's steward- ship of foreign affairs, and notably after the signing of the Polish- German treaty of non-aggression and friendship in January 1934, Poland had embarked on an ambivalent policy that was threatening to cut the ties with France. Yet after the boldness shown by Hitler in the Rhineland move, the Poles had reason to be concerned; they were well aware of Germany's interest in Danzig and the Corridor. The Poles, therefore, turned to France to obtain funds for a rearmament program as well as for French military and technical advice. Their desire to "warm up" the French-Polish friendship posed grave problems to Blum and his government. Could France trust the Poles with arms and mili- tary information so long as Colonel Beck entertained Göring on hunt- ing parties? Also, what were the Polish attitudes and intentions toward France's other allies, in particular Czechoslovakia, with whom Polish relations had long been strained over the Teschen border dispute? What of Polish relations with the U.S.S.R., Poland's traditional and perennial foe and France's ally? To Blum the solution was direct and simple. His government would have to force the Poles to make up their minds. After his colleagues had repeatedly raised questions about the security of French military information that might be transmitted to Beck, Blum described his patience as coming to an end. He told Minister of Defense Daladier and General Gamelin: "We cannot live this way. We are bound by an alliance with a state and a people, yet we have so little confidence in them that we hesitate to deliver them arms, designs, plans —for fear that they will betray us and deliver them to the enemy. . . . We must know whether the Poles are our allies or not." The existing relationship, he added, was "no more tolerable on the plane of inter-

[2] Testimony, 1947, *Événements*, I, 127.

national relations than it would be on the plane of personal relations."[3]

But international relations are not so simple as personal relations. Even Blum knew that he would not get a "categorical explanation" from Colonel Beck. The one strong step he might have taken was to demand Beck's ouster as a price for the desired French aid, as the French Ambassador in Warsaw, Léon Noël, was recommending.[4] Yet such a step would have alienated Hitler at a time when Blum was working toward improved relations with Germany. Blum tried another tack. Avoiding regular diplomatic channels, he sent General Gamelin, Chief of the French General Staff, to treat directly, as "man to man, soldier to soldier," with General (soon Marshal) Śmigły-Rydz, the top military leader in Poland and, as heir to Piłsudski's mantle, virtual head of the Polish military republic.[5] Gamelin visited Warsaw from August 12 to August 16 and Śmigły-Rydz returned the visit with a stay of almost two weeks in France at the beginning of September. The utmost cordiality prevailed. Śmigły-Rydz assured Blum that his country and France would "never be in opposite camps." He also insisted that the Czechs need have no fears regarding Polish intentions.[6]

Yet the cordiality was superficial and no more meaningful than the Polish assurances to the Czechs turned out to be. On the critical question of Colonel Beck's foreign policy, the Blum government hit a stone wall and rapidly retreated. When the question of Beck's dismissal was gingerly broached during Śmigły-Rydz's visit to Paris, it was discovered that although the General had no unswerving confidence in Beck, he approved Beck's qualities as a diplomat and, by implication, his foreign policy. To oust Beck, he made clear, would be to hazard a break with Germany.[7] Blum's reluctance to risk an anti-German gesture was the compelling factor in ending the pressure for Beck's removal. The Premier accepted the General's vague assurance that he would personally "exercise decisive and sovereign control over Poland's

[3] Testimony, 1947, *Événements*, I, 129–30. For details on the relationship with Poland, see Toynbee (ed.): *Survey of International Affairs, 1936*, pp. 393–401, and Henry Roberts: "The Diplomacy of Colonel Beck," in Craig and Gilbert (eds.): *The Diplomats*, pp. 579–614.

[4] Léon Noël: testimony, 1947, *Événements*, IV, 853; and his *L'Agression allemande contre la Pologne: une ambassade à Varsovie, 1935–1939* (Paris, 1946), pp. 140–5.

[5] Testimony, 1947, *Événements*, I, 130.

[6] Gamelin: *Servir*, II, 225–38, which includes documents relating to the visit.

[7] Ibid., p. 232.

foreign policy."[8] Blum had halfheartedly attempted to check Beck's ambivalent policy but had displayed no real firmness.[9] The Poles got the credits they sought and yet were free to pursue their Janus-faced policy. In the end, thanks only to Hitler, they and the French did not find themselves "in opposite camps." Beck's policy, like Belgian neutrality, proved to be little protection against the Nazi onslaught.

Another of the major problems inherited by Blum was the question of the French alliance with Russia, which Blum was resolved to strengthen. His old hostility toward the Communist movement, which had wrecked his party in 1920 and which year after year, at least until the formation of the Popular Front, had denounced him personally as a "social traitor," had to be subordinated to more important considerations. Ever since the German-Polish rapprochement of 1934, he had felt the need for closer ties with the U.S.S.R. Cautiously and somewhat reluctantly, he had come around to endorsing the Franco-Soviet pact of mutual assistance, overcoming his scruples concerning the military implications of the alliance. Russia played a key role in the "grand design" which he envisaged in order to counterbalance the weight of Germany and Italy. The ties of France with Britain would be strengthened first; closer relations between France and Russia would follow; and then a rapprochement between Britain and Russia. The end result he contemplated was a triple partnership—"a combination reproducing the Triple Entente of the years before 1914."[1] Many things conspired to interfere with that plan. In later years he noted ruefully: "The close rapprochement of the Anglo-Saxon and French democracies with Soviet Russia, that is to say, an international 'Popular Front,' would have been the salvation of the peace."[2]

Blum's attitude toward the U.S.S.R. was presented with a crucial test on the question of converting the Franco-Soviet pact into a meaningful military alliance. Since its signing and ratification, the pact had been allowed slowly to decay. Nothing had been done, despite overtures by the Russians, to arrange military conversations between the French and Soviet high command. Needless to say, there was strong opposition in France to such a step. Some argued that it would antagonize Germany and Italy, alienate Poland and the other Eastern nations, as well as strengthen domestic Communism in France. Many believed that

[8] Blum admitted this in his postwar testimony, 1947, *Événements*, I, 130.

[9] Cf. Roberts, in Craig and Gilbert (eds.): *The Diplomats*, p. 597.

[1] Testimony, 1947, *Événements*, I, 128; and see, e.g., editorial, *Le Populaire*, August 20, 1935. Cf. Cot: *Le Procès de la république*, II, 343.

[2] *À l'échelle humaine*, *Oeuvre*, V, 456.

the game was not worth the candle, that the Russian army was incapable of a sustained fight against a major power. Ambassador Bullitt, who had recently arrived in Paris from Moscow, was one of those who were skeptical of Soviet armed strength. Others, like Alexis Léger at the Quai d'Orsay, never enthusiastic about the Franco-Soviet pact, saw closer ties as endangering the all-important relations with Britain.

Blum's policies reflected his "Triple Entente" design. As Pierre Cot, Blum's Minister of Air and the firmest advocate in the Popular Front cabinet of strengthening the alliance with Russia, formulated it: "Blum intended to turn toward Moscow after having made a stopover in London." He accurately characterized Blum's attitude toward the Franco-Soviet pact as "*nuancé*."[3] Blum would do his utmost first to cement cordial relations with Britain: without an *entente cordiale* nothing would be possible. He would take into account British sensitivities and suspicions with respect to the U.S.S.R., but he would not neglect the bond with Moscow and would work toward a strengthening of the pact. In November 1936, he ordered that conversations be undertaken in the greatest secrecy with the Soviet military attaché in Paris to determine whether there existed a real basis for General Staff talks. Repeatedly, he pressed Minister of Defense Daladier and General Gamelin with inquiries on the status of the military talks; Gamelin later testified to Blum's active interest.[4] From the outset Blum encountered, if not an open resistance, at least a "reticence" on the part of the military. When he was shown the French military reports on the Russian maneuvers of that autumn, which were not of a nature to inspire confidence, he noted suspiciously that they seemed to contradict the reports of the previous year, 1935, which the same authorities had shown extreme reluctance to transmit to him.[5]

In February 1937, Soviet Ambassador Potemkin communicated to Blum a request for specific information on the kind of military cooperation that would be possible between the two countries. The memorandum drawn up by Daladier and General Gamelin in April clarified the attitude of the French General Staff, which balked at moving on to staff

[3] Cot: *Le Procès de la république*, II, 341, 343. For opinions in various circles on the question of strengthening the pact, see Reynaud: *Mémoires*, II, 153–67.

[4] *Servir*, II, 285.

[5] Testimony, 1947, *Événements*, I, 128. There was a vast difference between the report of General Loiseau in September 1935 and that of General Schweisguth in October 1936; the former praised the "high moral and material potential of the Soviets"; see Reynaud: *Mémoires*, II, 156–7, Bonnet: *Défense de la Paix*, I, 166, and General Loiseau's own account: "Une Mission militaire en U.R.S.S.," *Revue des Deux Mondes*, September 15, 1955, pp. 252–76.

talks before the preliminary conversations were exhausted.[6] The military argued that if the Soviets were to be of aid to France or to Czechoslovakia, the cooperation of Poland, Rumania, and the Baltic states would have to be obtained, which everyone knew was not likely. General Gamelin admitted that Soviet insistence on the right of passage through these states was "militarily logical," although he tried to convince the Soviets that they ought not to exaggerate its importance, because Poland and Rumania "would need the railways for their own troops."[7] The memorandum implied that the dubious value of Soviet military aid was not worth sacrificing the possible good will of the Eastern European countries. "Confidentially," Blum in retrospect commented on the French military attitude, "the General Staff regarded the military strength of Poland as superior, or in any event as more important for us, than the military strength of the U.S.S.R., except perhaps in air power."[8]

For a time Blum continued to exert pressure for military conversations with the Soviets. But then he too ceased his efforts. He later explained the reason. A private communication from President Beneš of Czechoslovakia informed him of Czech intelligence reports that various members of the Soviet General Staff were involved in "suspicious" relations with Germany and warned Blum to observe great caution in military dealings with the Soviets.[9] The political purges and trials of Soviet civilian leaders had already been launched and had yielded startling revelations; there was reason to believe that the military might also be involved. And, in June 1937, to be sure, in substantiation of the Czech reports, Marshal Tukhachevsky, Chief of the Soviet General Staff, and eight of the highest-ranking military officers were arrested, tried by court-martial, and executed. Blum could not have known at the time that there was little basis for the charge against the generals of treacherous relations with Germany, but the trials and purges were admittedly not of a nature to inspire the continuation of secret military talks. The information from the Czechs, Blum claimed, "in a way paralyzed me in the stubborn effort I had been making for several months to lend to the alliance a full military character and significance."[1]

Undoubtedly the information was just enough to deter Blum from

[6] See documents in Gamelin: *Servir*, II, 285–7; also testimony of General Villelume, 1951, *Événements*, IX, 2743–4.

[7] *Servir*, II, 287.

[8] Testimony, 1947, *Événements*, I, 128.

[9] Ibid., p. 129; cf. Reynaud: *Au coeur de la mêlée*, p. 97.

[1] Testimony, 1947, *Événements*, I, 128.

exerting further pressure, about which he probably was uneasy anyway. Blum's Ambassador to the Soviet Union, Robert Coulondre, described him in the autumn of 1936 as having a "more positive" attitude toward the pact than Delbos, Herriot, Gamelin, or President Lebrun, all of whom the Ambassador saw before leaving for Moscow, but the Premier gave him no specific instructions on the military agreement.[2] Even without the Czech disclosures, Blum probably would not have gone any further in ending the quiet sabotage of the pact by the French General Staff. He too desired not to offend Poland and the smaller countries of Eastern Europe if that were possible. Certainly he did not wish to disturb his friendship with the Conservatives in Britain by prematurely establishing an intimate relationship with the Soviets. Not least, he was sensitive to pacifist elements in his own party, men like Paul Faure, who believed that military ties with Russia would lead inevitably to war.[3] Perhaps what stayed his hand above all was his conviction that the ideological divisions existing in Europe could be bridged and that peaceful relations with Nazi Germany itself could be established. Such was the essence of the confidential talks he held in 1936 and 1937 with Hjalmar Schacht.

Blum's willingness to "examine sincerely" any German suggestions—as his government's foreign-policy declaration had stated—emerged in the private talks he held with Schacht in Paris on August 25, 1936, and in a second conversation nine months later. It was Schacht who took the initiative. Ostensibly, the German Minister of National Economy and Governor of the Reichsbank was returning a courtesy visit recently paid to him by Émile Labeyrie, Governor of the Bank of France. He had communicated, however, through André François-Poncet, the French Ambassador in Berlin, his desire to speak to Blum confidentially. Although too cynical to be a National Socialist himself, Schacht was intensely eager to make his way in the Third Reich. He sought means of gaining German objectives without actual war, and believed it quite possible to satisfy Germany's need for raw materials and foodstuffs and ease her foreign-exchange difficulties by regaining economic rights in former German colonial territories even without a formal

[2] Robert Coulondre: *De Staline à Hitler: souvenirs de deux ambassades, 1936–1939* (Paris, 1950), pp. 14, 13–20.

[3] See the assessment of Blum's attitude by Cot: *Le Procès de la république*, II, 338–43, and cf. Reynaud: *Au coeur de la mêlée*, p. 95, who stresses party considerations.

transfer of sovereignty. In the summer of 1936 he obtained Hitler's consent to broach this suggestion to the French although Hitler warned him that it would be rejected.[4]

The nature of the Schacht mission was obscured from the general public by the storm of disapproval and polemics that surrounded the visit itself. It was bad enough that Blum had permitted French athletes to participate in the 1936 Olympic Games in Berlin. It was intolerable that the Popular Front government should welcome an emissary of the Nazi state and an accomplice of Hitler. The rumor spread also that only non-Jewish ministers (except for Blum) would attend the state dinner to be tendered Schacht; the government took pains to note that only ministers involved in financial, economic, and commercial affairs (Auriol, Spinasse, and Paul Bastid, in addition to Delbos) were to be present, and none, it so happened, was Jewish.[5] Blum ignored the protests and accorded Schacht a cordial welcome. "My stay in Paris and my conversations with Léon Blum and his ministers . . . belong to some of my pleasantest recollections," Schacht later recalled.[6] Actually, both Blum and Schacht recognized the awkwardness and the drama of the situation. Their first private remarks touched upon the paradox of the visit: Hitler's emissary had come to deal with a Socialist and a Jew. Schacht flatteringly remarked that it did Blum credit to receive him in this way and insisted that the mission also demonstrated Hitler's sincerity in seeking to preserve peace.[7] In talking to Schacht—and on other occasions to the German Ambassador, Count Johannes von Welczeck—Blum could believe that he was dealing with rational, civilized Europeans. Yet Blum would have dealt with Hitler himself had the opportunity arisen.

Schacht presented his case convincingly and found Blum receptive. He dangled before Blum the prospects of opening up an entirely new phase in international life. Germany's cardinal need, as he outlined it, was the restoration of German economic prosperity, which was vital to

[4] On the genesis of the mission and other details, see Hjalmar Schacht: *My First Seventy-six Years: The Autobiography of Hjalmar Schacht*, tr. by D. Pyke (London, 1955), pp. 378–81; André François-Poncet: *Souvenirs d'une ambassade à Berlin, septembre 1931–octobre 1938* (Paris, 1946), pp. 281–2; and Blum's testimony, 1947, *Événements*, I, 221–2.

[5] For the rumors and protests, see exchange of letters between Blum and Thorez, and news story, *Le Populaire*, August 27, 1936; also *Le Populaire*, August 28, 29, 1936.

[6] *Autobiography*, p. 380.

[7] Ibid.; Blum: testimony at Riom trial, 1942, *Oeuvre*, V, 307, and before parliamentary commission, 1947, *Événements*, I, 221.

European stability and peace. This could be accomplished in part by the return to Germany of former colonies like the Cameroons; it was not necessary that they be transferred to German sovereignty from their present mandated status so long as they could be made available for German economic development and the acquisition of needed raw materials. Such a step, Schacht asserted, would be a source of satisfaction to the German people. It would make possible their return to the Disarmament Conference, and even to the League itself (provided that the League were divorced from the Versailles Treaty); peace, security, and a general European settlement would once again be a possibility. Blum, sympathetic, announced his readiness under the circumstances to "explore" the possibility, but he made it plain that he had to consult the British. Schacht, convinced that the proposal would be rebuffed by Eden, suggested that Blum circumvent Eden and the British Foreign Office, and first sound out other influential circles in Britain; he himself, shortly afterward, acquainted Montagu Norman, Governor of the Bank of England, with the proposition. But Blum would not hear of this. Schacht shrugged off Blum's self-righteousness and they parted, both hoping that the conversations might still have some chance of fruition.[8]

When Blum informed Eden of the German proposal early in October, when the British Foreign Minister was passing through Paris, he was thoroughly astounded (*"Il tomba des nues"*); he could not believe his ears. He rejected the proposition as utterly impossible; it would encounter the unreserved opposition of Britain and the Commonwealth. (Actually this was Eden's personal belief; many in Britain might have been willing to entertain a colonial "bargain.") He thought Blum had been "a little unguarded in his reaction" and that the German Foreign Office might make political capital of the episode. To Eden's satisfaction, Blum agreed to drop the matter.[9] In December, Blum let Schacht know through Count von Welczeck that negotiations on a European settlement could not be opened with a discussion of colonies, but that a settlement of political matters would have to come first; such a discussion would be warmly welcomed.[1] Publicly, in a speech at

[8] Blum summarized the conversations in his testimony before the parliamentary commission, 1947, *Événements*, 221–2; it is corroborated by Schacht: *Autobiography*, p. 380.

[9] Blum: testimony, 1947, *Événements*, I, 222; and cf. Eden: *Facing the Dictators*, p. 568.

[1] See communication, Ambassador in France (Welczeck) to the German Foreign Ministry, December 24, 1936, *Documents on German Foreign Policy*,

Lyons, Blum stated a few weeks later that if there were genuine efforts at stabilizing the peace and at ending the armaments race, economic cooperation would be a real possibility.[2] Eden also stressed this view.[3]

Meanwhile, Delbos, through Count von Welczeck, pressed for a reply from Berlin, summing up the French proposal that Germany "should have raw materials, colonies, and loans in return for which the only compensation required . . . was peace."[4] Conversations could begin at once. But only a "glacial silence" was forthcoming from Berlin to these overtures to continue general conversations; the complications of the Spanish Civil War, even if there had been a willingness to enter into negotiations, would have made a political settlement all the more difficult. The Schacht-Blum negotiations which had appeared "so promising" to the German Foreign Office could be considered at an end. The Wilhelmstrasse even regarded as "astonishing" the French belief that the discussions could still be pursued; other French proposals on political and economic cooperation were dismissed as "vague."[5]

Blum discussed the matter of Franco-German relations with Schacht a second time on May 28, 1937, on the occasion of Schacht's trip to Paris to open the German pavilion at the Exposition. Over teacups at the Matignon Palace, Blum spoke of having executed "a difficult and ticklish mission."[6] "I believe you will realize that I have done everything I could in order that we might reach an agreement." Setting aside entirely the proposition that he had been willing to entertain in August 1936, he now noted with firmness that a political *détente* had to precede

---

Series D (1937–1945), III: *Germany and the Spanish Civil War, 1936–1939* (Washington, D.C., 1950), Doc. No. 164, pp. 180–1; see also Blum's memorandum of second conversation, referred to below, note 6.

[2] Speech at Lyons, January 24, 1937, *Oeuvre*, IV, pt. 1, 379–83.

[3] Speech at Bradford, December 14, 1936, cited in Toynbee (ed.): *Survey of International Affairs, 1936*, p. 368.

[4] Ambassador in France to German Foreign Ministry, December 24, 1936, *Docs. on Ger. For. Pol.*, Series D, III, Doc. No. 164, pp. 180–1.

[5] Memorandum, Director of the Legal Department (Gans), December 26, 1936, *Docs. on Ger. For. Pol.*, Series D, III, Doc. No. 167, pp. 186–9; and communication, Foreign Minister (Neurath) to the Embassy in France, December 30, 1936, ibid., Doc. No. 174, p. 194.

[6] Both Blum and Schacht drew up memoranda of this second visit. For Blum's memorandum, "Conversation of Dr. Schacht with M. Léon Blum on May 28, 1937," see *Docs. on Ger. For. Pol.*, Series D, I, Doc. No. 83, "Enclosure," pp. 136–40. It was submitted for Neurath's attention by the French Ambassador, François-Poncet. For Schacht's memorandum, ibid., Doc. No. 72, pp. 119–21. Blum seems to have telescoped these two interviews in his testimony before the parliamentary commission in 1947, *Événements*, I, 221–2.

economic concessions. "How," he inquired, "can a country be expected to contemplate economic agreements capable of increasing the strength of another country which it fears may be an aggressor?" His other remarks also reflected his hardening attitude: "There are two illusions that Berlin must give up: the first is that one can succeed in separating Great Britain and France; the second is that through a latent revolutionary crisis, France is being destroyed as a factor in European affairs." If the political discussions materialized, Germany must not expect concessions from France "that disregard the rest of Europe, and that would paralyze us in any European conflicts in which our vital interests or our signatures might be at stake." Finally he would not give up the thought of a strengthened League even if Schacht thought him "sentimental" on that subject.[7] Schacht, who said very little during this second interview, petulantly blamed the "lost opportunity" on Blum's failure to act more promptly. The complications in Spain, particularly incidents directly involving Germany that spring, he knew, were diminishing the chances of peaceful negotiations.[8]

The German Foreign Office noted of this second interview that Blum had withdrawn "the compensation that he was still ready to offer us in August 1936." Rejecting "the rather old and familiar French arguments that a German-French settlement could be made only if all the allies of France were included," the Wilhelmstrasse considered it "not quite clear how Blum and the French Ambassador could believe that we would be prepared to regard this repetition of time-worn French demands, accompanied only by quite vague promises to make concessions to us, as a serious effort to negotiate."[9] By the end of 1937, the question was closed forever when Schacht was dismissed as Minister of National Economy although permitted to remain as Governor of the Reichsbank until January 1939. Not until April 1945 did he and Blum meet again—as fellow prisoners at Dachau.[1]

---

[7] Memorandum, "Conversation . . . May 28, 1937," *Docs. on Ger. For. Pol.*, Series D, I, 136–40.

[8] Schacht: "Report on my visit to Paris, May 25–29, 1937," ibid., Doc. No. 72, pp. 119–21; cf. *Autobiography*, pp. 380–1.

[9] German Foreign Ministry to German Embassy in France, December 24, 1937, *Docs. on Ger. For. Pol.*, Series D, I, Doc. No. 91, pp. 158–60. See also, on the end of these negotiations, ibid., Doc. No. 56, December 4, 1937, pp. 95–6; No. 70, December 13, 1937, pp. 117–18; and No. 71, December 13, 1937, p. 118.

[1] Blum: *Le Dernier Mois* (1946), *Oeuvre*, V, 534. See also below, Chapter XVI.

Relations with Italy were quite a different matter. In the spring of 1936, even before Blum took office, Mussolini was smarting under the sanctions imposed by the League after he had invaded Ethiopia in October 1935. Although he blamed the British government and British public opinion for taking the lead at Geneva, he reproached France equally for following the British. What made matters worse in the case of France was that the two countries had been cooperating closely under Pierre Laval's conduct of foreign affairs. For some time, the French Ambassador, Charles de Chambrun, had been a welcome figure at the Quirinal. Moreover, a large segment of French public opinion on the Right was eager to cement good relations between the two "Latin" nations, some out of ideological sympathy with fascism, others out of the belief that such a policy would keep Mussolini from embracing Hitler. In January 1935, Laval and Mussolini had signed the Rome accords, which aimed at continued friendship and provided for a settlement of old territorial differences in Africa. Suddenly, with the invasion of Ethiopia and the imposition of sanctions, the climate changed. The measures taken, to be sure, were not effective enough to prevent the conquest of Haile Selassie's hapless country, but they were sufficient to infuriate the Duce.

By the time Blum was about to take office in the spring of 1936, neither the British nor the French government knew quite what to do about the sanctions that were in effect. They could, of course, make a last-minute effort to tighten and enforce the system. In that case, Blum told Eden when they conferred in May 1936, Britain would have to assume the leadership because of the state of French public opinion. On the other hand, if they removed the sanctions, there was some hope that they could extract a promise from Mussolini to return to the League security system. By June, with the collapse of the Ethiopian government, Eden said he was "growing less confident that any good purpose was being served by continuing sanctions."[2]

By then Mussolini too was fully confident that the League sanctions were going to be lifted. Smug in his military victory and in his triumph over the effort to thwart him, he offered France "another chance." Through a French intermediary, Senator Jean-Louis Malvy, he let it be known that if France were willing to take the lead at Geneva in

---

[2] For Eden's discussions with Blum in Paris, May 15, 1936, and subsequent developments, see Eden: *Facing the Dictators*, pp. 430–7. See also Paul-Boncour: *Entre deux guerres*, III: *Sur les chemins de la défaite, 1935–1940* (Paris, 1945–6), 51–4.

proposing the removal of the moral condemnation by the League Council, he would find it "especially agreeable"; the two countries might then be able to resume their friendship and close relations.[3] He also let General Gamelin know that if France did not cooperate, the military conversations taking place with the French General Staff would be broken off.[4]

Blum was resolved to do nothing about Mussolini's gesture. In July, the League's sanctions were removed, but no effort was made to improve relations with Italy. Was Blum permitting ideological differences to block a rapprochement with Italy? To be sure, long before he had become Premier, Blum, with ill-concealed irritation, had written in *Le Populaire* of Laval's visit to Mussolini in January 1935: "For the first time a French minister is a guest of the assassin of Matteotti."[5] Yet his hostility toward fascism did not prevent him from supporting earlier efforts at a peaceful settlement with Italy. He had endorsed the Four-Power Pact of 1933, negotiated by Paul-Boncour, and had supported even the Rome accords of 1935 when they were announced.[6] With the invasion of Ethiopia, however, his opposition to Mussolini's overt aggression and obvious expansionist ambitions grew firmer. He was convinced that Mussolini was abandoning his older ambitions in Central Europe, particularly in Austria, where he had once clashed with Hitler, and was turning toward Africa and the Mediterranean, where he could obtain the close cooperation of Germany. Eden recalled Blum's conviction in May 1936 that "it would not be possible to keep these two dictators apart. Sooner or later their policies would converge."[7] Both men excluded the possibility of playing one dictator against the other as many influential men in Britain and France wished to do, the British Right favoring Hitler, the French Right, Mussolini. In July 1936, Mussolini's acquiescence in the signing of a treaty of friendship between Germany and Austria, was to Blum proof of the Duce's new orientation. As Blum saw it, Mussolini was surrendering his

[3] Malvy's dispatch to the Ministry of Foreign Affairs after an interview with Mussolini in June 1936 is quoted in Bonnet: *Défense de la Paix*, I, 177.

[4] Gamelin: *Servir*, II, 224.

[5] *Le Populaire*, January 5, 1935. Giacomo Matteotti, the Italian Socialist leader, was murdered by the fascists in 1924.

[6] Paul-Boncour: *Entre deux guerres*, II, 345, III, 52; and Blum's editorials, *Le Populaire*, June 14, 1933, and August 27, 1935. The Four-Power Pact was a scheme initiated in 1933 by Mussolini whereby France, Germany, Italy, and Great Britain were to act in concert on international affairs; it aroused considerable protest from the smaller European powers and quickly lost all significance.

[7] *Facing the Dictators*, p. 431.

dream of succeeding to the old Hapsburg monarchy in Central Europe and was turning to areas where his interests would inevitably clash with those of Britain and France; he wished to succeed not to the Hapsburgs but to the Caesars. "I was fully convinced," Blum later said, "ever since the German-Austrian agreement of July 1936, that a real rapprochement between Italy and France was no longer possible."[8] Italy's brazen intervention in the Spanish Civil War that summer afforded final proof of Mussolini's Mediterranean ambitions and cemented the Italian leader's friendship with Hitler.

Nonetheless, the idea persisted in the minds not only of Pierre Laval and many other Frenchmen but of Chamberlain and many others in Britain that to obtain a rapprochement with Italy was only a matter of diplomatic skill or opportune concessions. (To some, like Laval, the illusion persisted until the very moment that Italy entered the war at Hitler's side against an already defeated France.) Blum saw this illusion as one of the failures of French and British diplomacy: "An entire, and substantial, segment of European opinion, of English and French opinion, never wished to admit, acknowledge, or take into account this alliance, this complicity of Hitler and Mussolini."[9] Blum was substantially right, yet Mussolini had been opposed to Hitler at one point, and it was not completely out of the question that he might have been wooed away from the German dictator. There was a strange contrast between Blum's willingness to negotiate in every possible way with Hitler and his adamant attitude toward Mussolini; yet it must not be forgotten that it was Mussolini who to that time had been more guilty of overt aggression and breach of the peace.

Two episodes led to the charge in Rightist circles that Blum, as Premier, permitted his ideological hatred of fascism to block a reconciliation with Italy. In January 1937, Blum received a visit from Vittorio Cerutti, the Italian Ambassador, who brought a personal message from Mussolini. The Ambassador tried to convince Blum that Mussolini "detested" Hitler and sincerely desired a rapprochement with France and the creation of a Latin bloc. The principal issue that separated the two countries at the moment was Spain. If France would cease to involve herself on the side of the Spanish Republic, Mussolini could guarantee that he would obtain for France the friendship and good will of General Franco. Blum rejected the proposition out of hand

---

[8] Testimony, 1947, *Événements*, I, 220. For his views, in addition to many editorials, see his speech to the Chamber, *Chambre, Débats*, December 27, 1935.

[9] Testimony, 1947, *Événements*, I, 125.

and told the Ambassador that he too desired to improve relations with Italy, but that Italy would have to honor the international non-intervention agreement which she had signed.[1] The Ambassador had to report the failure of his *démarche*.

Three and a half years later, in the wake of France's military defeat, there was a sequel to this episode, played out in the Grand Casino at Vichy on July 10, 1940. The French Parliament had been convened to vote full powers to Marshal Pétain and to bury the Third Republic. Laval was Vice-Premier in Pétain's cabinet and his spokesman in Parliament. In his long, bullying harangue on the decadence of politics and diplomacy under the Third Republic, Laval singled out the Cerutti interview to embarrass Blum, who could only listen in silence and frustration. The Italian Ambassador had reported to him the tenor of the fruitless conversation with Blum. Mussolini was intervening in Spain, Cerutti had told Blum, only because he could not permit the establishment in Spain of "a Bolshevik or quasi-Bolshevik government (*gouvernement bolchévique ou bolchévisant*). Laval sarcastically quoted Blum's alleged reply to illustrate the naïveté and credulity of the men who were directing the affairs of France in the 1930's. "What do you mean by a '*quasi-Bolshevik*' government?" Blum had reprovingly asked, and had sent the Ambassador away. Blum and the men of the Left, Laval charged, had prevented the rapprochement which Mussolini had sincerely desired.[2] It was an opinion widely held in France.

The second episode dealt with the embarrassing question of the vacancy in the French embassy in Rome. In October 1936, Blum's government decided to remove Count Charles de Chambrun as Ambassador ostensibly on the grounds that he had reached retirement age; there was little doubt in anyone's mind that he was being replaced because of his Italophile sentiments. Blum did not anticipate what followed. Mussolini, in an outburst of petulance, announced that Chambrun's successor would have to be accredited to Victor Emmanuel III as King of Italy *and* Emperor of Ethiopia; France would thereby have to give official recognition to the conquest. If Chambrun had been permitted to remain, Mussolini generously told the Count, he would not have made this demand.[3] Blum and Delbos did not take Mussolini seriously and requested accreditation for René de St. Quentin as the new ambas-

[1] Blum described the interview in his postwar testimony, *Événements*, I, 220.

[2] See "Compte-rendu sténographique de la séance privée des membres de la Chambre des Députés et du Sénat tenue à Vichy le 10 juillet 1940," *Événements: Rapport (Documents sur la période 1936–1945)*, II, 489.

[3] Chambrun: *Traditions et souvenirs* (Paris, 1952), p. 227.

sador, but not in the form which Mussolini had insisted upon. The Duce refused to accept the new ambassador, and a *chargé d'affaires* had to take over. For two critical years, from October 1936 to October 1938—the years of the Spanish Civil War, the Austrian crisis, and the Munich crisis—France had no ambassador in the Farnese Palace. In October 1937, on the anniversary of Chambrun's departure from Rome, Mussolini dramatized the situation by withdrawing his own ambassador, Vittorio Cerruti, from Paris. Not until after Munich did the two countries exchange ambassadors again. During Blum's second government, in March–April 1938, Blum and Paul-Boncour made plans to name an ambassador. "We were both eager to end the long vacancy," wrote Paul-Boncour, Blum's Foreign Minister at the time.[4] But the government fell before anything could be done. When André François-Poncet finally took up residence in Rome in October 1938, he found a very hostile atmosphere[5]—proof, some charged, that a great opportunity had been lost.

The Right never forgave Blum. Years later, Chambrun, who was bitter and vindictive, claimed that when he protested the unfriendly turn in Franco-Italian relations, Blum told him: "You forget that I was the friend of Matteotti."[6] If Blum made the statement, it is out of character with every other act of his premiership and his conduct of foreign affairs. On the vacancy in the Rome embassy, however, Blum found no better explanation than that he had had no way of predicting whether Mussolini would insist on the new credentials and thus make it impossible to accredit a new ambassador.[7] Yet it is difficult to believe that Blum allowed an "antifascist ideology" to interfere with his government's relations with Italy. He seemed determined to "take Europe as it was," not to reshape it ideologically. The "exercise of power" within the existing framework of society applied to foreign affairs as well.[8]

Not ideology but resentment at Mussolini's overt aggression and the

---

[4] *Entre deux guerres*, III, 102.

[5] See François-Poncet: *Au Palais Farnèse: souvenirs d'une ambassade à Rome, 1938–1940* (Paris, 1961).

[6] Chambrun: *Traditions et souvenirs*, p. 228. The statement, as it makes its way into the history books, becomes stronger. Bonnet (*Défense de la Paix*, I, 177) writes that the following words are "attributed" to Blum: "I shall not treat with the assassin of Matteotti." This is then quoted, without qualification, in Chastenet: *Histoire*, VI, 159.

[7] Editorial, *Le Populaire*, April 27, 1940; see also editorials, April 28, 29, 30, 1940.

[8] *Le Populaire*, April 27, 1940.

conviction that it was impossible by the summer of 1936 to win Mussolini back to the structure of the League and away from Hitler was probably what motivated Blum's attitude toward Mussolini. He cannot be absolved for permitting a situation to develop in which France had no ambassador in Rome, but it would be fatuous to conclude that cordial relations with Italy would have resulted from a different attitude on Blum's part. As both the Conservative Eden and the Socialist Blum interpreted the situation at the time, Mussolini was "a tough and clever opportunist. . . . He would incline to whichever side seemed to offer him the greater advantages. We could not, for moral and practical reasons, enter such a competition or offer him the plunder he sought; therefore Hitler and Mussolini would inevitably be drawn closer together."[9] Nothing that Blum could have done in 1936 and 1937 would have stayed Mussolini's dagger in June 1940.

Against the treacherous course of foreign affairs, problems of national defense and rearmament loomed large. Ironically, the anti-militarist Popular Front government, with a pacifist-minded Socialist as Premier, voted larger sums for rearmament than any previous ministry of the interwar years and launched the country on an extensive, although fatally belated, national-defense program.

Never a doctrinaire pacifist, and at heart an ardent patriot, Blum had nonetheless been a persistent champion of disarmament over the years, and had stated his convictions in innumerable speeches and articles. Eden reports that in a private conversation as late as May 1936 Blum still clung to the hope for a European disarmament agreement and that he "somewhat reluctantly assented" to Eden's argument that disarmament, though a laudable ideal, seemed "hardly attainable" in the world of the dictators.[1] The Popular Front program itself pledged "a ceaseless effort to pass from an armed peace to peace and disarmament" (*paix désarmée*). The "nationalization of war industries," one of the planks in the platform, quickly introduced by the new government, was regarded as an initial step toward universal arms control; each nation must first curb its own munitions makers and war profiteers.[2]

On July 1, Blum had reaffirmed in his speech before the League

[9] Eden: *Facing the Dictators*, p. 474.
[1] Ibid., p. 429.
[2] Cabinet statement on foreign policy, June 23, 1936, *Oeuvre*, IV, pt. 1, 362.

that "collective security, to be complete, must be combined with general disarmament." Self-consciously conceding that one might appear "almost ridiculous" in proposing disarmament "to a Europe which is today resounding with the clash of arms," he insisted on its importance. "Without a doubt collective security is a precondition for disarmament . . . but the converse is also true. Disarmament is the precondition for complete collective security, for it is necessary that all states disarm substantially for arbitration judgments to count, for peaceful sanctions to be compelling." He appealed to all nations, including those who had left the Disarmament Conference and the League, to heed his plea.[3] In later years he admitted that he had expected no positive results from his appeal yet he felt impelled to issue a moral challenge. It was important to exert every possible effort "even if, in one's heart, one did not believe in the possibility of success."[4]

Yet we have seen that General Gamelin, despite his apprehension concerning Blum's ideas on disarmament, came away from his conversation on June 10, 1936, reassured on the Premier's "attitude toward the army and his concern for national defense." Blum had convinced him that his party and his government understood "the gravity of the situation that confronted Europe."[5] One specific development pleased the General: the establishment of a Ministry of National Defense to coordinate the War, Navy, and Air ministries. Though far from complete or effective, the administrative reform was nevertheless a step in the right direction.[6]

The real test of Blum's words to Gamelin came when Hitler on August 24 announced the re-establishment of two-year military service in Germany, thereby doubling the number of troops he had available. Daladier, Blum's Minister of National Defense, and the military authorities agreed that raising French military service to three years would lead only to retaliation by Hitler; the alternative was a four-year rearmament program involving a minimum expenditure of 14 billion francs (1928 value). The military authorities, Daladier later testified, viewed "the prospects of having it accepted by the government with a rather skeptical smile." But Daladier won Blum over without difficulty.[7]

---

[3] Speech of July 1, 1936, *Oeuvre*, IV, pt. 1, 369.

[4] Testimony at Riom trial, *Oeuvre*, V, 304–5.

[5] *Servir*, II, 224.

[6] Ibid., pp. 368, 251–2, and I, 200. See also Cot: *Le Procès de la république*, II, 249, and Reynaud: *Mémoires*, II, 141–2.

[7] Daladier: testimony, 1947, *Événements*, I, 16–17; cf. Blum: ibid., p. 222, and testimony at Riom trial, *Oeuvre*, V, 251–3.

Blum's only hesitation was on financial grounds: he and Auriol feared that the additional strain on the budget might have repercussions on the franc, apprehension that was well grounded.[8]

Despite the budgetary and currency difficulties of the government, the program was approved and adopted by the cabinet on September 7. Other large sums were later voted for aviation and for naval construction. From January 1, 1937, to the outbreak of the war in September 1939, the sum of 67 billion francs was expended on the modernization and expansion of the nation's armed forces.[9] The initial credits represented the starting point of the rearmament effort. No ideological considerations deterred the Blum government from meeting the defense obligations that had been imposed upon it.

However, after securing a favorable vote in Parliament for substantial rearmament credits, Blum and Daladier made two significant mistakes. First, they left to the military the sole responsibility for choosing the types and quantities of material to be ordered, and secondly, they abandoned to the military the formulation of over-all defense strategy. On these matters Blum deferred to Daladier, his Minister of National Defense, who in turn was convinced that civilian authority had to yield to the military. The mistakes were fatal. Although armaments were produced in quantity, they conformed for the most part to the defensive strategy and Maginot Line psychology, which, for all General Gamelin's unconvincing later protestations, remained the basis of French military thought. The French High Command prepared to refight the Battle of Verdun while the enemy was preparing a war of movement and of lightning offensive with Panzer divisions and dive bombers. The French High Command recognized the importance of tanks, but they were conceived as support weapons for the infantry and not as the components of independent armored divisions. The tactical use of air power was insufficiently appreciated as well. The defeat of 1940 arose from the failure of the French military to emancipate itself from a fatal defensive strategy and psychology.[1]

---

[8] Auriol: *Hier . . . demain*, I, 38, and Cot: *Le Procès de la république*, I, 284.

[9] Daladier: testimony, 1947, *Événements*, I, 17. The most complete statistics were given to the parliamentary commission by Robert Jacomet, secretary-general of the Ministry of National Defense from October 1936 to May 1940, ibid., pp. 187–213. See also Auriol: *Hier . . . demain*, II, appendix, pp. 343–6; Gamelin: *Servir*, I, 220–1, II, 246.

[1] There is now a large literature on the military aspects of the "fall of France"; a good starting point is Richard D. Challener: "The Military Defeat of 1940 in Retrospect," in Edward Mead Earle: *Modern France* (Princeton, 1951), pp.

Blum and the other civilian leaders of the nation were no more far-sighted and no more audacious than the military. On the question of armored divisions, Daladier later frankly admitted: "When I arrived at the War Ministry I was, for my part, much preoccupied not with the *idea* of armored divisions, for I was personally in favor of the plan, but with my right to impose it."[2] Almost alone, Paul Reynaud, spokesman in the Chamber for the independent armored divisions of Colonel de Gaulle, upheld another point of view. "Let us not misplace responsibilities," he told Parliament. "The General Staff is only an organ under the orders of the men in the government and that is how it must be. The responsibility—not for detail but for the general orientation of our military policy—we do not have the right to pass on to other shoulders. It must rest on ours."[3] It was not a responsibility that either Blum or Daladier was willing to assume. De Gaulle, who knew the military mind, was aware that the High Command would never shake itself out of its inertia or abandon its outmoded ideas; he believed that the "public authorities" had to take the initiative: he sought in vain "a Louvois, a Carnot."[4]

Even before taking office Blum had been brought into the "great quarrel" that de Gaulle was conducting with the support of Reynaud. The Socialist leader had read de Gaulle's *Vers l'armée de métier* when it appeared in 1934 and had studied the Colonel's proposals to meet the military and technological challenge of the new era with a mechanized corps of motorized and armored divisions manned by specially trained career men and officers and assisted by tactical air support. De Gaulle had found a sympathetic audience in a few Socialists who saw the merits of his recommendations;[5] after all, Jaurès, in his day, had recognized the need for revolutionary innovations in warfare. But Blum, it will be recalled, had entered the lists against de Gaulle in a

---

405–20, and Adolphe Goutard: *1940: la guerre des occasions perdues* (Paris, 1956). More will be said on this subject in a later chapter.

[2] Testimony, 1947, *Événements*, I, 23, Perhaps, as Paul-Boncour has said, to overcome the routine and inertia of the General Staff one needed a better record of past devotion to the military than Blum and the men of the Left could claim. And he adds: "After having been too long mistrustful of the military, one was too timid to control it when in power." See *Entre deux guerres*, II, 267.

[3] *Chambre, Débats*, March 15, 1935; and also session of January 26, 1937; cf. *Mémoires*, II, 142.

[4] *Mémoires de guerre*, I, 10; cf. his letter to Reynaud, January 28, 1937, Reynaud: *Mémoires*, II, 142–3.

[5] De Gaulle: *Mémoires de guerre*, I, 13–14.

series of editorials in *Le Populaire* in the autumn of 1934 and in the Chamber in March 1935, criticizing less the military aspects of the proposals than the political danger of a separate professional army, de Gaulle's *armée de métier*. That army, he feared, would have its own life, traditions, personal code, and undoubtedly, when the day came, its own politics. It would be of the kind, he had warned, "that issues pronunciamentos and makes *coups d'état*." Haunted by the memory of the antirepublican *émeute* of February 6, 1934, Blum found it impossible to shake off the fear of what such an army might mean.[6] For entirely different reasons, de Gaulle's ideas aroused also the implacable opposition of the High Command. Blum's most curious error was his insistence in his 1934 editorials that de Gaulle's theories had become "the vogue in the highest and most influential circles of our army."[7]

In his editorials he had also condemned de Gaulle's armored divisions as a threat to peace, warning that the very speed of the shock troops moving on the offensive would render impossible last-minute efforts at "international mediation, requests for arbitration, determination of the aggressor." Against these objections the argument could be made that only such an army could protect the smaller nations of Europe and effectively preserve the peace. In the Chamber debates in March 1935, Reynaud, directing his remarks to the Socialists—and even to Blum personally—pleaded that de Gaulle's armored divisions could be par excellence the instrument for collective security and mutual assistance which the Socialists had been championing. His argument that the armored spearhead could serve as an international police guard, of the kind advocated by Léon Bourgeois in 1919 and Paul-Boncour in 1932, came close to convincing Blum. Blum admitted to himself at the time: "On that point he is right."[8] Yet he had kept silent.

On the other hand, it is obvious that any support that Blum might have given to de Gaulle's proposal in those early days, either in Parliament or in his newspaper, would not have meant much. Yet in after years he regretted his silence as an error that "weighed on his conscience." If de Gaulle's ideas had prevailed in 1934, he wrote in 1940,

[6] The editorials appeared as "Soldats de métier et armée de métier," and with other slightly different titles, in *Le Populaire*, November 28, 30, and December 1, 1934. See also Blum's references in his speech to the Chamber, *Chambre, Débats*, March 15, 1935.

[7] *Le Populaire*, November 30, 1934; see, e.g., Gamelin: *Servir*, I, 254–7.

[8] *Chambre, Débats*, March 15, 1935; Blum: *Mémoires, Oeuvre*, V, 111.

France might have begun at once the preparation of the new armored units instead of launching the program belatedly, with meager results, once the war was under way.[9]

Blum's decisive chance to heed de Gaulle came during his Popular Front ministry. De Gaulle hoped for a new firmness after the German remilitarization of the Rhineland and even thought he saw in the emergence of the Popular Front and its promise of innovation a "psychological element that might permit a break with inertia." "It was not inconceivable," he later wrote, "that in the face of national socialism triumphant in Berlin, fascism reigning in Rome, falangism approaching in Madrid, the French Republic might wish to transform its social structure and refashion its military forces at the same time." He was gratified at many of the military measures adopted by the government, he wrote to Reynaud in September 1936, yet the program was still far from what he sought.[1]

In October, de Gaulle's hopes rose. Blum, at the urging of an old personal friend, Colonel Émile Mayer, who believed that de Gaulle's views deserved a hearing, invited de Gaulle for an interview. The accounts of the interview by the two men differ in detail but not in essence.[2] To Blum's profession of a warm interest in de Gaulle's views, the Colonel retorted that Blum had for a long time combated them. "One changes one's focus (*on change d'optique*)," the Premier remarked, "when one becomes the head of the government."[3] Although hostile to a "professional army," Blum was genuinely interested in the tactical use of armored units. On the other hand, Blum let de Gaulle know that he shared the prevailing military views on the invulnerability of French defenses. He pressed de Gaulle: "You will agree that our system, badly suited for attack, is excellent for defense." De Gaulle denied this, replying that with armor and air power no fronts were inviolable. Blum argued that the credits being opened up for the

---

[9] *Mémoires, Oeuvre*, V, 112.

[1] *Mémoires de guerre*, I, 18; for his letter, September 23, 1936, Reynaud: *Mémoires*, II, 133–4. De Gaulle, incidentally, indicates in this letter that Chautemps expressed interest in the political usefulness of a mechanized army in the event of public disorder.

[2] De Gaulle: *Mémoires de guerre*, I, 18–20, and Blum: *Mémoires, Oeuvre*, V, 113–15. De Gaulle places the interview in October 1936, the very day that the Belgian government had announced its new neutrality policy; Blum speaks of it as "either August or the beginning of September." See also Blum: testimony, 1947, *Événements*, I, 222.

[3] Cited by de Gaulle: *Mémoires de guerre*, I, 18.

acquisition of new material, and specifically for the purchase of "thousands of tanks and planes," would provide the kind of military strength that de Gaulle championed. When de Gaulle pointed out that the heavy tanks under order were not to be employed as independent mechanized units but were to be merged with the infantry, and that the planes were for interception and not for attack, Blum cut him short: "The use of the credits assigned to the War Ministry is the affair of M. Daladier and of General Gamelin."[4] The interview ended cordially but without results.[5]

Only in later years did Blum admit that "the use of the credits" ought to have been his affair too. At the time he ignored de Gaulle's protests and believed that the credits would be properly used—even that the armor scheduled to be purchased "would lead to the formation of Panzer, de Gaulle-type divisions." "I have many times reproached myself bitterly for not having checked that impression immediately with Daladier and General Gamelin," he testified after the war.[6] "I ought to have proceeded with more skepticism to an investigation, a closer verification," he wrote shortly after the defeat of 1940.[7] Blum, no less than Daladier, failed to see the fallacies in the defensive theories of the military and in the policies that flowed from them.

The pleas of Reynaud and de Gaulle remained without fruit. Reynaud constantly warned that the government was powerless from a military point of view to uphold the strong pledges to the smaller countries of Europe which Blum was making.[8] The Polish campaign in 1939 and the catastrophic events of the spring of 1940 were tragic proof that de Gaulle had been right. On June 7, 1940, at the height of the Battle of France, Blum hailed the belated appointment of de Gaulle to Reynaud's cabinet (an appointment delayed for sheer reasons of politics by Reynaud himself). Blum called it "in its way an almost revolutionary act. Here is a man who understands the meaning of the new warfare and will find the proper remedies to resist it."[9] But the midnight hour was already striking. Blum, like many other

[4] Ibid.

[5] Blum spoke of a possible assignment to the War Ministry, which de Gaulle declined; Blum: *Mémoires, Oeuvre*, V, 115; and testimony, 1947, *Événements*, I, 223.

[6] *Événements*, I, 223.

[7] *Mémoires, Oeuvre*, V, 115.

[8] See, e.g., Reynaud's speech, *Chambre, Débats*, January 26, 1937; and cf. *Mémoires*, II, 140–6.

[9] *Le Populaire*, June 7, 1940.

French leaders, accorded to the General in later years, in a stately phrase of de Gaulle, "the sad homage of their remorse."[1]

Although responsibility for the defeat of 1940 must be placed at the doorstep of the military, it is a truism that a nation gets the kind of army it deserves. Responsibility is an elusive thing, especially in an event like the defeat of a great nation; and responsibility in the case of France's defeat in 1940 becomes diffused in a complex of factors— psychological, political, geographical, technological, demographic, and historical. France was in the vanguard of the battle against Attila; she was much inferior to her foe in industrial strength and manpower; and the human losses of the last war haunted Frenchmen. The most blatant distortion of the facts was the shameful attempt by Vichy at the Riom trial in 1942 to place *all* blame on the civilian leaders of the republic, on the republic itself, and, in particular, on the Popular Front legislation and atmosphere of 1936—the sitdown strikes, the paid vacations, the forty-hour week, the nationalization of the armaments industries. (In the case of nationalization, a reform which grew out of the disarmament movement was actually transformed into an instrument for national rearmament.[2]) By any definition, Blum and the Popular Front government fulfilled the duties of their office. Yet in matters of national defense, as in the case of public finances, the economy, and foreign affairs, Blum's inheritance was too troubled to allow of any profound improvement in so short a time. Rearmament, to which he faithfully contributed so much, began too late. His predecessors and the country as a whole must share the blame for French weakness in 1940.

Despite the contributions of the Popular Front government to the rearming of France, Blum, to be sure, never abandoned the hope of reviving the Disarmament Conference. Yet he no longer spoke of unilateral disarmament. When the question of renewing the disarmament talks came up secretly before the "permanent committee of national defense" in May 1937, Blum strongly approved of cooperating but insisted that no steps be taken without complete agreement by all the powers and that "at the base of any limitation must be placed the fulfillment of the programs already under way." When Delbos reported the British government's concern that the Labour party would oppose British rearmament if they believed disarmament to be a possibility,

[1] *Mémoires de guerre*, I, 17.

[2] See, e.g., Paul Reuter: "La Nationalisation des usines de guerre," *Revue d'Économie Politique*, LIII (1939), 740–56.

Blum, who faced the same problem in his own party, argued that it was "easier" to rally labor and other segments of public opinion to rearmament if one showed one's good faith by working toward general disarmament.[3] This was the burden of the argument he presented also at the Riom trial when he was charged with weakening the "moral preparation" of the country at a critical time by supporting "dreams" like progressive disarmament. In his defense, he contended that the position of France had been strengthened by his persevering efforts toward the goal of disarmament:

> It was strengthened internationally because it gave to world opinion the proof of its profound will for peace . . . and it was also strengthened internally. It is easier and, above all, more legitimate to arouse a country to the supreme sacrifice needed in order to insure its armed defense, the more ardently and the more sincerely one has attempted to bar the road to war.[4]

It was typical of Blum that he overemphasized the efficacy of "world opinion" and "world conscience" in treating with the dictators of the 1930's. It was undoubtedly quixotic to cling to thoughts of disarmament in 1936–1937 and to dream of bringing Hitler and Mussolini to accept an arms-control agreement. On the other hand, Blum did not permit his long-range goal of disarmament, his pacifist ideals, and the pacifism of his own party to interfere with the rearming of the country. His contention that, so far from weakening the moral fiber of the nation, he helped to strengthen its political and moral position by working for disarmament should not be dismissed lightly. In all times and places the hope that the world can progress from armed peace to peace and disarmament provides men with the fortitude needed to accept the risks and costs of armed defense.

Ironically Blum had to face constant hostility and criticism in his own party for his government's acceptance of rearmament. Many in the party still clung to their ancient antimilitarism and never forgave Blum for his role in rearming France. "*À bas la guerre! À bas la guerre!*" was flung at him at party meetings whenever he mentioned rearmament. "To think you say that to me!" was his injured reply to an interruption on one occasion.[5] In many ways Blum, when he was in office, had to

[3] *Procès-verbaux, comité permanent de la défense nationale*, May 19, 1937, cited in Gamelin: *Servir*, II, 267–75.

[4] Testimony at Riom trial, *Oeuvre*, V, 303.

[5] See his speech to Federation of the Seine, April 9, 1937, *Le Populaire*, April 14, 1937.

draw upon the credit and prestige which he had accumulated in the party over the years. He felt the pain and anguish of the statesman doing what he believed to be right yet disappointing his followers. Rearmament, no less than Spain, was a poignant experience for Blum.

———————

"Ah, if it had been possible for the example of France, as in the great days of 1789, to spread its inspiration far and wide! If it had only been given to us to rekindle in all Europe that contagious enthusiasm which Michelet has described with a religious lyricism. But . . . Europe was skeptical or rebellious." In his Vichy prison in 1941, Blum lamented the failure of France in the 1930's to inspire Europe with the example of democracy, social progress, peace, disarmament, and internationalism, and he related the disasters that had followed.[6]

He never abandoned the belief that democracy was associated with peace, and dictatorship with war. "Try to determine," he asked in his wartime essay *A l'échelle humaine*, "at what moment and under what inspiration the possibility of war was reintroduced in Europe. Is it not evident that it was at the moment when Hitler took possession of power . . . ? It could not be otherwise: tyrannies are by nature bent on conquest, just as democracy is peaceful."[7] Parallel with this conviction ran the corollary that the essential principles of political democracy—liberty, equality, and fraternity—could be the cornerstone of international relations as well—the liberty of nations to dispose of their own destinies, the equality that must be guaranteed to all peoples, great or small, and the fraternity that would bring about international cooperation for peace. Such were Blum's articles of faith.[8]

Blum's reflections led him in the light of later events—the war and the defeat of France, personal trial and imprisonment—to one very different and startling conclusion. "In my opinion," he said in 1947, "there existed perhaps only one means of preventing the war of 1939 . . . to have undertaken at the very moment of Hitler's rise to power, a 'preventive action' (*une opération préventive*). I believe today, in my soul and conscience, that England and France, with Poland joining them, would have been able to undertake, and ought to have undertaken, an action of that kind back in 1933. . . . If we had proposed to

———————

[6] *À l'échelle humaine, Oeuvre*, V, 474.

[7] Ibid., p. 416.

[8] See especially his radio speech of September 17, 1936, shortly after one of Hitler's diatribes at Nuremberg, *Oeuvre*, IV, pt. 1, 370–3.

prevent by force the installation in Germany of the Nazi government, I believe that we would have been able to carry with us public opinion and a majority in Parliament."[9]

Blum made no claim that he or his party had believed in or advocated this proposal at the time. He admitted "with a kind of remorse" that they had never taken the initiative in such a step—for many reasons. As Socialists, they suffered from a self-consciousness that their motives might be misinterpreted as a desire to avenge their fellow Socialists in Germany who had fallen victim to Hitler. As pacifists they had "a religious horror of war." As political realists, they knew that so brutal an intrusion into internal German affairs would have fed German nationalism in other ways. No one urged it, and it would have enraged public opinion in all quarters, yet "it would have saved Germany and preserved Europe."[1] Admittedly, this was the wisdom and counsel of hindsight. A man who believed in the right of people to govern themselves and make their own mistakes, who believed in an international community of nations and in peace, could not have accepted the notion of a preventive war, let alone taken the initiative in promoting it.

Instead, he and others had done their utmost to prevent war and to work for "a peaceful coexistence between the democracies of Europe and the warlike autocracy that had established itself there." The result, he admitted, was a series of "increasingly costly sacrifices." Ethiopia, the Rhineland, Austria, Czechoslovakia, and the sacrifice that must be laid at his own doorstep, the Spanish Republic—the list was long. These "errors," he insisted, were of a "noble" species—"illusions testifying only to a premature faith in the future of peace."[2] Dedicated to peace, Blum had nonetheless striven to build the strength of France and the unity of the nations willing to check the dictators. With the heritage he had received, the task proved impossible; a Socialist Premier, moreover, was not the man to overcome the internal divisions in France or to lead the nation in a strong foreign policy. And the Spanish Civil War, to which we must now turn, enormously intensified the divisions within France and within the community of nations as well.

---

[9] Testimony, 1947, *Événements*, I, 121–2; and cf. *À l'échelle humaine, Oeuvre*, V, 424.

[1] *Événements*, I, 122.

[2] *À l'échelle humaine, Oeuvre*, V, 424.

VIII

DRAMA OF CONSCIENCE:
The Non-Intervention Policy
and the Spanish Civil War

Ma torture.[1]

T HE FRENCH POLICY of non-intervention in the Spanish Civil
War not only "broke the heart of the Blum government,"[2] it
baffled and exasperated sympathizers with the Spanish Republic
everywhere in the world. "History is still curious," Claude Bowers, the
ardently pro-Republican American Ambassador to Spain at the time,
wrote in the 1950's, "about the genesis of the plan through which the
European democracies aligned themselves stubbornly, if ignorantly,
on the side of the Fascists against the Spanish democracy."[3]

Blum himself was sensitive to the criticisms of the policy. "I know
very well," he wrote in a letter from his Vichy prison cell in 1942,
"that our liberal friends in the United States (the Foreign Affairs
group in particular and university circles) have always judged the
non-intervention policy with severity."[4] He bore, too, a haunting personal sorrow over the tragic fate of the Spanish Republic. Mary Tudor
had once said, he recalled privately to a friend, that the word "Calais"

---

[1] The haunting phrase appears in the rough notes which Blum prepared for
a speech to a national council of the party in the autumn of 1936; the notes are
in the files of André Blumel, Blum's *chef de cabinet* in his two Popular Front
governments. M. Blumel has kindly permitted me to use these Blum files.

[2] D. W. Brogan: *The French Nation: From Napoleon to Pétain, 1814–1940*
(New York, 1957), p. 288.

[3] *My Mission to Spain* (New York, 1954), p. 281.

[4] Letter to Suzanne Blum written from the prison at Bourassol, July 9, 1942.
I am grateful to Mme Suzanne Blum for this letter and other materials; portions
of the letter are cited in Audry: *Léon Blum*, pp. 123–4, 126–7. Suzanne Blum, a
French lawyer, was a longtime friend of Blum's (but not related to him). During

was engraved on her heart; on his, he said, was the word "Spain."[5]
Yet he always maintained that he had been right to initiate the policy
at the time. After the war, in 1945, he defended it before a Socialist
conference as "an attempt to save the Spanish Republic while at the
same time preserving peace. When one speaks of non-intervention,
as of Munich, our comrades can reply with their heads held high."[6]
Accepting full responsibility for having initiated the policy, he asked
only that it be examined in its political and diplomatic context, and
that the world know "certain of the events by which we were led to
conceive and apply it."[7] The historian can attempt to do no less.

The outbreak of the Spanish Civil War created another in the series
of emergencies that Blum had to face in his turbulent twelve and a
half months in office. The giant wave of sitdown strikes that accom-

---

the war, while living in New York, she published a selective anthology of Blum's
speeches and editorials on foreign affairs from 1932 to 1940: *L'Histoire jugera*
(Montreal, 1943), with a preface by William R. Bullitt. To clear up a minor
mystery about the book's introduction, signed S.-R.B.: Mme Blum informs me
that it was her way of paying tribute to Robert Blum, then a German prisoner
of war, who usually edited and anthologized his father's political writings. The
initials stand for Suzanne-Robert Blum.

[5] Typed memorandum in private files of André Blumel, not dated. M. Blumel
cited this in his unpublished lecture on Blum delivered to the Société de
l'Histoire de la III⁰ République, December 10, 1953. He has since published a
memorandum, dated September 22, 1964, summarizing his recollections of the
genesis of the non-intervention policy, in Lefranc: *Histoire du Front Populaire*,
Annexes, pp. 460–6.

[6] Informal speech to international Socialist conference in Paris, August 27–28,
1946, published by Robert Verdier as "La Vérité sur la non-intervention française
en Espagne: une déclaration inédite de Léon Blum," *Le Populaire*, July 19, 1950.
Blum's major explanations of his Spanish policy are to be found in this speech,
in his testimony before the parliamentary commission, July 23, 30, 1947, *Événements*, I, 215–20, 251–4; in his article "La Vérité sur la non-intervention en
Espagne," *Le Populaire*, October 15, 1945 (republished with confirming details by Oreste Rosenfeld in *Le Populaire-Dimanche*, March 25, 1951); and in a
series of articles in 1938: "Petite Histoire de la non-intervention," *Le Populaire*,
June 24, 25, 29, 1938. A selection of his writings and statements on Spain are
reprinted in *Oeuvre*, IV, pt. 1, 387–418.

A paper by Pierre Renouvin on the Blum government's foreign policy, prepared for the March 1965 colloquium described earlier, was made available to
me after my own manuscript was completed. Professor Renouvin, who has had
privileged access to the diplomatic archives (some of which is to be published
shortly in the series *Documents Diplomatiques Français, 1932–1939*), seems to
have found no documents that would change the main outlines of this or the
preceding chapter.

[7] Testimony, 1947, *Événements*, I, 220.

panied the Popular Front election victory and his entry into office had scarcely subsided when news arrived of the military rebellion against the Spanish Republic on July 18, 1936. "There are new complications ahead," Blum told a delegation of trade-union leaders who were visiting him at the Matignon Palace that day. "If we succeed in what we are undertaking, no one will be able to say that *events* made our task any easier."[8]

The anticipated complications soon appeared. On Monday, July 20, Blum received from the Spanish Premier, José Giral, a telegram requesting French assistance and permission to obtain arms and planes needed to put down the revolt of the Spanish generals. Blum's immediate reaction was to respond favorably to the perfectly legitimate appeal of the Spanish government. There was no question under international law of the right of the French government or of French private firms to supply war materials to a legal government coping with a rebellion; in this case the government involved was a friendly one, and even similar in ideology and orientation to the French Popular Front. Blum acted at once. At a conference attended by Foreign Minister Delbos, Minister of National Defense Daladier, and Air Minister Pierre Cot, it was decided that the planes, weapons, and ammunition requested would be assembled and prepared for shipment. The Spanish Ambassador, Juan F. de Cárdenas, was informed. Blum and his ministers knew, however, that the German and Italian press—and the Rightist press in France—had already hailed the military rebellion as a crusade to save Spain from communism; his political opponents would be sure to denounce any aid given to the Spanish Republic. They agreed, accordingly, to act with the least possible publicity.[9] To the French Right the specter of a "communist" triumph in Spain was more to be dreaded than the prospects of a fascist-type dictatorship, even if installed with German and Italian support.[1]

To keep the projected arms shipment quiet would have been difficult in any circumstances; in this case it was impossible, for the Spanish

---

[8] Delmas: *À gauche de la barricade*, p. 110.

[9] Testimony, 1947, *Événements*, I, 215–16; Cot: *Le Procès de la république*, II, 307.

[1] On reactions of the French public, see J. Bowyer Bell: "French Reaction to the Spanish Civil War, July–September 1936," in Lillian Parker Wallace and William C. Askew (eds.): *Power, Public Opinion, and Diplomacy* (Durham, N.C., 1959), pp. 267–96. Mr. Bell has permitted me to use an unpublished letter written to him by Pierre Cot on May 4, 1957. On the general framework of events, see Toynbee (ed.): *Survey of International Affairs, 1937*, II: *The International Repercussions of the War in Spain, 1936–7* (London, 1938); P. A. M.

Embassy was honeycombed with officials sympathetic to the military rebels. At once every detail of the French government's projected shipment was leaked from the Spanish Embassy in Paris to the Rightist press, which immediately launched a determined campaign to prevent the sending of aid to the Spanish Republic. On July 23, *L'Écho de Paris*, disclosing in full detail the government's plans, asked: "Will the French Popular Front dare to arm the Spanish Popular Front?" *L'Action Française* denounced the "treason of Léon Blum and Pierre Cot."[2] On that same day, the German Ambassador to France, Count von Welczek, reported to Berlin that he had learned "in strict confidence" of French plans to "supply the Spanish government with considerable amounts of war matériel during the next few days"; he provided exact details, adding that the government's intentions had been "expressly confirmed [by] a member of the cabinet."[3] The cabinet member remains unidentified; the estimates of the promised shipment were not far wrong.

Blum missed the initial outbursts in the press, for on Wednesday, July 22, he had flown to London accompanied by Delbos and top permanent officials of the Foreign Affairs Ministry, and did not return to Paris until forty-eight hours later. The trip was destined to be an important link in the chain of events that led to non-intervention. As we have seen, Blum and Delbos went to London to attend a conference of the prime ministers and foreign ministers of France, Britain, and Belgium arranged to consider the status of the Locarno agreement in the wake of the German military occupation of the Rhineland. The conference was designed to prepare the way for a later meeting which would include Germany and Italy so that a "new Locarno" might be drawn up and a renewed effort made to "consolidate the peace of Europe by means of a general settlement."[4]

---

van der Esch: *Prelude to War: The International Repercussions of the Spanish Civil War, 1936–1939* (The Hague, 1951); Pierre Broué and Émile Témime: *La Révolution et la guerre d'Espagne* (Paris, 1961); and Hugh Thomas: *The Spanish Civil War* (New York, 1961). The bibliography in Thomas is invaluable.

[2] Cited by Cot: *Le Procès de la république*, II, 307.

[3] *Docs. Ger. For. Pol.*, D, III, No. 3, July 23, 1936, p. 4.

[4] On this conference, see the preceding chapter. The interpretation that Blum was urged to attend by the British and by the French Ambassador to London, Charles Corbin, with the backing of Foreign Minister Delbos and Secretary-General Léger, seems unlikely. Cordell Hull states that Blum was invited to London "to discuss Spain" (*Memoirs*, New York, 1948, I, 476), and there is a dispatch from U.S. Ambassador Straus in Paris (but based only on "a reliable

Blum welcomed the trip to London as an opportunity to establish personal contacts with the British leaders and to strengthen the Anglo-French ties on which he pinned his hopes for reviving the prestige of the League and for preserving peace in Europe. In Anthony Eden, the British Foreign Minister, he saw a man who shared his views on close Anglo-French cooperation, collective security, and the need to rebuild the shattered League.

It did not trouble Blum that the Conservatives were at the helm of British affairs at the time. Blum was the kind of Socialist who took satisfaction in warm personal relations with British Conservatives just as he did with conservatives like Paul Reynaud or Louis Marin in his own country. A lifelong admirer of British parliamentary institutions and British political life, he had always envied Britain its Conservative party. Nor were the Conservatives ignorant of Blum's moderate political views and his cultivated background, even if the cabinet had been somewhat alarmed by the sitdown strikes that had just subsided. Was it necessary for Alexis Léger (as Léger reports) to hold Blum ostentatiously in conversation near a statue of Disraeli—"a Jew but obviously a gentleman and a statesman"—so that the British ministers might perceive the comparison?[5] The closest allusion to Blum's radicalism was some good-natured jesting about his book on marriage, written thirty years earlier and recently reissued, in which he had expressed somewhat advanced views on love and sex.[6] Blum seems to have made a favorable impression even on Neville Chamberlain, then Chancellor of the Exchequer, even though Chamberlain regarded Blum's social and economic policies as disastrous; he commented at the time that the Socialist leader was "more of an idealist than a realist" but seemed

---

press contact") that Corbin telephoned Blum personally on July 22 urging him to come over and discuss the situation with Baldwin and Eden (*Foreign Relations of the United States, 1936*, II: *Europe*, Washington, D.C., 1954, No. 668, p. 447). Hugh Thomas accepts this interpretation (*The Spanish Civil War*, p. 219), as does Dante A. Puzzo: *Spain and the Great Powers, 1936–41* (New York, 1962), p. 87. Neither Cot nor Blum ever mentioned it. Cot speaks of it as a trip planned well in advance (*Le Procès de la république*, II, 308); and Blum implies as much too (*Événements*, I, 216). Eden notes that Spain was not on the agenda and that it was only touched upon indirectly at the meeting (*Facing the Dictators*, p. 456). Esch also questions whether Hull's memoirs are accurate on this point (*Prelude to War*, p. 52, n. 1).

[5] As reported to Elizabeth R. Cameron: "Léger" (based on interviews with Léger), p. 391, n. 36. Pertinax refers to the currency gained by this legend: *Les Fossoyeurs*, I, 297.

[6] Reported by Blum to André Blumel, typed memorandum. See also above, Chapter I.

"straightforward and sincere."[7] There was a similarity of temperament between Blum and the British Conservatives that ran deeper than differences of political orientation; and it manifested itself clearly in their response to foreign affairs. Neither would take any course of action that might involve a risk of immediate war; both subscribed to the policy once described by Eden in the heat of a Commons debate as "peace at almost any price."[8] More than any other factor, this attitude would determine their policy on Spain.

In London the implications of the Spanish question for future Anglo-French relations began to emerge. One of the early callers at Blum's hotel was the journalist Pertinax (André Géraud), who asked Blum to confirm the reports being published in Paris of the government's plans to supply arms to the Spanish Republic, and warned him of the harmful effects such a step would have on Anglo-French relations. Blum shrugged off the warning and told Pertinax that he was firmly resolved to aid the Spanish Republic as best he could. "I can still hear Léon Blum replying to a French journalist who told him of the fears of the British Conservatives," the London correspondent of *Le Populaire*, Louis Lévy, wrote in 1940. " 'Never mind all that,' he said impatiently, 'the Government of Spain is a legitimate Government; what is more, it is a friendly Government.' "[9]

Pertinax's assessment of the British cabinet's attitude on Spain turned out to be quite accurate. From the outset the Conservative government had decided on a policy of neutrality in the Spanish Civil War. The Spanish Popular Front was viewed less as a citadel of democracy than as a potential bastion of communism and social revolution. There was no deep sympathy for General Franco, but at least his government could be counted on to respect British economic interests. The British Conservatives were convinced also that even if the war in Spain were won by Franco with the aid of Italy and Germany, the xenophobia of the Spanish would prevent concessions that would threaten British interests in the Mediterranean. As in the case of the French Right, there was a willingness to play down the potential threat to national interests if Franco were to triumph with the aid of Mussolini and Hitler. Only the Left—the Labour party in Britain and the Popular Front in France—could self-righteously pride themselves on

[7] Cited by Feiling: *Life of Neville Chamberlain*, p. 286.

[8] June 25, 1937, cited in Toynbee (ed.): *Survey of International Affairs, 1937*, II, 152, n. 2.

[9] Blum: testimony, 1947, *Événements*, I, 216; Lévy: *The Truth about France* (New York, 1941), pp. 113–14.

serving both the national interest and their own ideological sympathies by aiding the Spanish Republic; and they could boast that they wished to aid a "legal" government to boot.

In any event, so far as the Conservatives were concerned—and even some Labourites—non-involvement was the most prudent course to pursue; Britain wanted no new Peninsular War. Eden, no less than his colleagues, was bent on preventing the Spanish conflict from turning into a war of rival ideologies and a European cockpit. "If we take the long view . . . ," Eden a few months later told the House of Commons, "intervention in Spain is not only bad humanity, it is bad politics." And he added that it was not a British concern which form of government Spain should have: "For us to enter into a championship of that kind would be to enter into the war of rival ideologies which we have condemned."[1]

Winston Churchill shared the views of his fellow Conservatives. As he later recalled: "In the [Spanish] quarrel I was neutral. Naturally, I was not in favor of the Communists [*sic*]. How could I be when if I had been a Spaniard they would have murdered me and my family and my friends?" He firmly believed that "with all the rest they had on their hands the British Government were right to keep out of Spain."[2] In a private note written on July 30, he warned the French Ambassador, Charles Corbin, that if France helped Republican Spain, "the dominant forces here . . . would be estranged from France."[3] There were Labourites too who were afraid that involvement might lead to war. Hugh Dalton was disturbed to see the vast majority of his fellow Labourites "swept with emotion." "They had no clue in their minds to the risks, and the realities, for Britain, of a general war," he observed. "Nor did they even dimly comprehend how unrepresentative they were, on this issue, of the great mass of their fellow countrymen." It could not be ignored, he added, that "the Catholics, both in Britain and in France, were on Franco's side."[4]

[1] Speech of January 19, 1937, cited in Toynbee (ed.): *Survey of International Affairs, 1937*, II, 164, 159. See in this volume the excellent analysis of "the interests and motives of the British," pp. 151–77. Eden confirms his views at the time in his memoirs. The Spanish Civil War, he was convinced, was "not a war of liberty and democracy against tyranny"; *Facing the Dictators*, p. 455.

[2] *The Gathering Storm* (New York, 1948), p. 214, and pp. 212–15. To be sure, Churchill later modified his views; cf. Thomas: *The Spanish Civil War*, p. 220, n. 1.

[3] *The Gathering Storm*, p. 215.

[4] *The Fateful Years: Memoirs, 1931–1945* (London, 1957), pp. 100, 103; and see pp. 95–100 for his retrospective justification of his attitudes in the light of Franco's later neutrality.

Jean Jaurès, 1859–1914. The great French Socialist leader in the years before World War I and Blum's Socialist mentor.

Blum in a striking though unusual speaking pose in May 1936 just after the Popular Front election victories. The sitdown strikes were at their peak at the time. BELOW: A photograph taken on June 3, 1936, in the Paris suburbs during the sitdown strikes, showing workers occupying a factory, some playing cards, others sleeping.

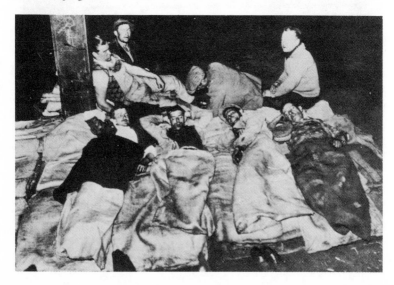

Blum at the first meeting of his Popular Front cabinet in June 1936. Left to right: Vincent Auriol, Minister of Finance; Charles Spinasse, Minister of National Economy; Camille Chautemps, Minister of State without portfolio; Léon Blum; and Paul Faure, Minister of State without portfolio. BELOW: Blum arriving in London in May 1939 to plead with the British Labour leaders to abandon their opposition to conscription.

Léon Blum returning from German concentration camps in May 1945, being greeted by his daughter-in-law Renée and granddaughter Catherine. BELOW: Blum before the French National Assembly in December 1946 presenting his cabinet and program. Vincent Auriol, President of the Assembly, is leaning forward at the table below M. Blum.

The subject of Spain was not on the agenda for the official talks and luncheons at London and came up only indirectly. Various members of the cabinet expressed what Blum later described as "great apprehension" over a policy of aiding Republican Spain. "It would be exaggerated," he said later in recalling the talks, "to speak of opposition. But counsels of prudence were dispensed and sharp fears expressed."[5] In a luncheon conversation some Conservatives spoke in favor of a war between fascists and Bolsheviks in which the extremists would exterminate themselves: Spain, it was implied, could be the scene of such a felicitous Armageddon.[6] Blum, Delbos, and Léger were clearly made to understand the negative attitude of the British Conservatives, who did not wish to take sides in the "faction fight" in Spain; they hoped that the Spanish Civil War could be prevented from turning into a European conflagration.

Yet, by Blum's own testimony, no direct pressure was exerted upon him during his stay in London to adopt a policy of non-intervention. When he was preparing to depart, Anthony Eden, who came to his hotel room to bid him good-bye, questioned him about French intentions to aid the Spanish Republic. When Blum confirmed the French plans, Eden said no more than: "That is your affair, but I ask only one thing of you, I beg of you, be cautious (*soyez prudent*)."[7] Any counsel of caution from Eden, whom Blum trusted fully, would weigh heavily on the Socialist leader.

In all Blum's references to his policy on Spain, he never once, at the time or later, blamed the British for initiating the policy or forcing him into it. Claude Bowers has asserted that the non-intervention plan "was hatched in London" and that Blum "was practically blackmailed into acceptance."[8] There is no convincing evidence for this claim. The thesis rests also on an unproved allegation that the British presented a virtual ultimatum that unless such a policy were adopted they would terminate all existing guarantees under the Locarno Pact and would not stand by France in the event of a war.[9] Eden, in the House of Commons

[5] Speech to Socialist conference, 1946, *Le Populaire*, July 19, 1950.

[6] Blum, private remarks at a dinner, March 27, 1939, at which Blumel was present: typed memorandum, Blumel files. For a slightly different version, see Blumel memorandum, Lefranc: *Histoire du Front Populaire*, p. 462.

[7] Cited by Blum: testimony, 1947, *Événements*, I, 216.

[8] *My Mission to Spain*, p. 281.

[9] See, e.g., J. Alvarez del Vayo: *Freedom's Battle*, tr. by Eileen E. Brooke, (New York, 1940), p. 68; cf. Esch: *Prelude to War*, pp. 54, 61. Hugh Thomas accepts the thesis of the ultimatum but bases his conclusion only on Spanish

(and in his memoirs), forcefully denied these charges. "It is suggested," he said on October 29, 1936, "that the French government took their initiative under strong British pressure . . . that we threatened the French government with all sorts of pains and penalties if they did not do this thing. Of course there is not a word of truth in that story. It is pure fabrication. The French government took this initiative on their own account."[1] Blum never denied this. He spoke of "*his* policy of non-intervention" to Hugh Dalton and a small group of Labour party leaders who visited him in September 1936. "It was he and not Eden . . . who had first proposed it," Hugh Dalton records him as saying.[2] On the other hand, the disapproval with which the British cabinet viewed the French plans to aid Spain, and Eden's words of admonition at a time when the closest Anglo-French cooperation was desirable, played a significant part in the ultimate decision. The British pressure was strong even if indirect. It was typical of Blum that he would not admit to such pressure and that he would later insist on assuming the entire blame himself. There is no doubt that he left London much disturbed over the official British climate of opinion and shaken in his determination to aid Spain even if he was not yet prepared to abandon his original intention.

It was in Paris that he encountered the decisive opposition. Upon returning to Paris the evening of July 24, he found awaiting him at the airport Camille Chautemps, one of the leaders of the Radical Socialist party and a minister of state in the Popular Front cabinet. Chautemps was there to inform him of the veritable "insurrection" brewing in Paris. He recounted the Rightist press campaign against aid to Spain, informing Blum that *L'Écho de Paris* and *Le Jour* had published full details of the military shipment being prepared. Strong feelings had been stirred up in Parliament not only on the Right but, even more important, among the Radical Socialists.[3]

When Blum set out to verify for himself the attitudes of the Radical

---

sources (*The Spanish Civil War*, p. 259). Blumel speaks of "two *démarches*" by the British Ambassador but makes no attempt to describe or date them. Professor Renouvin has found no direct evidence of any such *démarche*.

[1] Cited in Toynbee (ed.): *Survey of International Affairs, 1937*, II, 147; cf. *Facing the Dictators*, pp. 445–70.

[2] *The Fateful Years*, p. 95. Cot informed an American scholar in 1957 that he knew nothing of any such *démarche* (one may be sure that Cot would have made much of it in his memoirs); see Bell: "French Reaction," p. 281, n. 21.

[3] Blum described the details of his return from London in his testimony, 1947, *Événements*, I, 216–17.

Socialist leaders, every conversation confirmed Chautemps's report. Jules Jeanneney, the President of the Senate, reminded Blum that a few months earlier, in March, when the direct, immediate security of France was threatened in the Rhineland episode, the country had hesitated and in the end yielded; it would be inconceivable, therefore, at this time to embark on a policy that might lead to "war over the affairs of Spain." And Jeanneney added: "We are all certain here that if there were European complications provoked by intervention in the affairs of Spain, England would not follow us." With Eden's words still ringing in his ears, Blum could not contradict him. He found Édouard Herriot, the President of the Chamber, also filled with grave reservations. "I beg you," he implored Blum, "do not meddle in that business." (*"Ah, je t'en prie, mon petit, ne vas pas te fourrer là-dedans."*)[4] Despite any ideological sympathies the Radical Socialists, as good republicans, might have had for the Popular Front government in Spain, they desired to steer clear of involvement in war, especially a war in which the country would be divided and in which the support of England could not be counted on.

Blum had always maintained that Socialists must not take office unless they were in a position to exercise command. He was now Premier of a Socialist-directed cabinet, but it was a coalition cabinet responsible to a coalition majority in Parliament; Blum was not one to take lightly his obligations to the Radicals in foreign affairs. Although increasingly apprehensive, he was still resolved to go ahead with the planned shipments. The evening of his return from London, Blum, Auriol, Delbos, Daladier and Cot met privately at Blum's home from about 10 p.m. to midnight to discuss the situation; Fernando de los Ríos, the special emissary sent by the Spanish Republic, was also present. The ministers agreed to take precautions in order not to arouse hostile public opinion unnecessarily but arranged to proceed with an immediate shipment of materials. Delbos interposed more serious objections than anyone else and even placed various barriers in the way of the shipment.[5]

The next day, July 25, was crucial. The press campaign of the Right had grown more intense. "Will the French planes being handed over by Pierre Cot leave for Madrid?" *L'Écho de Paris* asked. Henri de Kérillis denounced the "abominable" and "criminal" action of the government and called attention to what he considered the legitimate anxiety and anger of the German and Italian press: any future com-

[4] As related by Blum: ibid., p. 216.
[5] Cot: *Le Procès de la république*, II, 308–9.

plications involving German and Italian intervention, he insisted, could be blamed squarely on the initiative taken by the French government.[6] On the other side of the picture, the Communists, the Socialists, and the C.G.T. were organizing mass demonstrations urging aid to the Spanish Republic. Public opinion was aroused on all sides. That morning, Blum found President Lebrun also extremely agitated and upset. He warned Blum that the proposed shipment of arms and planes could lead to war or to revolution in France, and he insisted that no action be taken until after a full cabinet discussion.[7]

It was becoming increasingly difficult for Blum to proceed as he had wished. Opposition was mounting not only among the Rightists but also among the Radical Socialists in Parliament and in the cabinet. With the Communists not represented in the cabinet, the Radicals carried far greater weight in the formulation of the government's policy than their strength in the Popular Front throughout the country warranted; thus the mass rallies organized by the Communists and other militant elements of the Popular Front could more easily be ignored. Jean Zay, one of the young Radical ministers, reports that Chautemps assumed the lead within the cabinet in opposing involvement in Spain. A few minutes before the first cabinet meeting on the subject, he wrote, Chautemps "took to one side the young ministers, and walking up and down with them on the Rue de la Varenne and the Boulevard des Italiens, lectured them vigorously, pointing out that the military insurrection would be victorious in a few weeks and that the republican government would crumble like a house of cards."[8]

Yet the question of aid to Spain was far from settled. The Socialists in the Cabinet, as well as the "Young Turk" Radicals, such as Pierre Cot and Jean Zay, and the independent Maurice Viollette, could be counted on in the cabinet debates to support a policy of aid to the Spanish Republic despite the risks involved. They could reinforce their ideological arguments by maintaining that French national security required a friendly republic across the Pyrenees and that everything must be done to thwart the establishment of a military dictatorship with German and Italian backing. Daladier, too, seemed sympathetic to that argument but was concerned over the possible military

---

[6] Cited by Cot: ibid., II, 309.

[7] *Témoignage*, p. 244; and see also statement attributed to him in letter, de los Ríos to Giral, cited below.

[8] *Souvenirs et solitude*, p. 114.

complications.[9] Cot also saw in the Spanish military rebellion a potential inspiration for French fascism: the success of the Spanish military
coup "might go to the heads of certain French generals."[1]

On the other hand, Blum was overwhelmed by the opposition he was
encountering in the country at large and from his own political allies
as well. In the afternoon, just before the cabinet meeting, Blum sadly
informed Fernando de los Ríos of this opposition. He was approaching
the cabinet meeting in a discouraged and disconsolate mood. "I am
heartbroken (*Mon âme est déchirée*)," he told the Spanish representative, who wrote that night that he had never seen Blum "so moved."
Nonetheless, Blum stressed his determination to maintain his original
position "at all costs and despite all risks."[2]

On July 25, the cabinet held the first of three meetings which, step
by step, within three weeks' time, led to the non-intervention policy.
It seems indisputable that, despite his sympathies, Blum did not assume firm leadership in the cabinet's deliberations on the subject. He
would not offend Chautemps or Delbos, or any of his other Radical
political allies who were urging caution, or indeed any of his pacifist-
minded Socialist colleagues. He would not risk the breakup of the
hard-won Popular Front coalition in the cabinet or in Parliament. In
the back of his mind were his apprehensions concerning the disapproval
of the British, the fierce opposition within the country, and the possibility of military involvement under the worst possible domestic and
international circumstances. His approach was one of caution and compromise. It was in his character to serve as a conciliator: he would
work out some compromise whereby unity would be maintained in the
cabinet and in the country at large and, at the same time, aid would be
given to Spain.

As he sized up the situation, time was needed to work out a solution.

[9] Ibid., pp. 114–15, and Cot: *Le Procès de la république*, II, 310–11; and
letter by Cot, May 4, 1957, cited by Bell: "French Reaction," p. 280, n. 18.

[1] Cot: *Le Procès de la république*, II, 310.

[2] See letter written by Fernando de los Ríos, July 25, 1936, to Premier José
Giral; the letter seems authentic, although it was first published in anti-
Republican books, e.g., Robert Brasillach and Maurice Bardèche: *Histoire de la
guerre d'Espagne* (Paris, 1939), pp. 216–18, and Léon de Poncius: *Histoire
secrète de la révolution* (Paris, 1938), pp. 109–15. As Thomas notes, its genuine-
ness is admitted by Republicans and is borne out by other evidence (*The Spanish
Civil War*, p. 224, n. 2).

The question could be debated in the French Parliament and then, the whole world, especially England, would learn the true state of French public opinion on the matter. With his inveterate optimism and supreme confidence in public opinion, Blum convinced himself that delay would work to the advantage of those who wished to aid Spain.

In this meeting the cabinet took the first step in appeasing the opposition, the beginning of a three weeks' policy of hesitation and vacillation that ended in disaster. The cabinet announced that in view of "possible international complications," the French government would suspend the shipment of war materials to Spain by the French government as well as by private French firms; it exempted only unarmed commercial aircraft ordered before the insurrection had broken out. The shipment of planes and munitions already assembled was for the moment suspended, pending further developments. Arrangements were quietly made, meanwhile, to transfer to the Mexican government some of the materials ready for shipment so that they might be delivered to the Spanish Republic.[3] But the retreat had begun. The Rightist journals exulted; the Leftist press began to protest.

On July 30, two days before the second cabinet meeting, the suspicion that the Italian government was supplying war materials to the Nationalist rebels received striking confirmation when three Italian military planes destined for the Franco forces in Spanish Morocco went off course and landed by mistake on French territory in North Africa. An official investigation confirmed that the planes had until recently been part of the Italian air force.[4] The episode exploded the Rightist argument that French assistance to the Spanish government would risk provoking intervention by Italy and Germany: Italy had already intervened.

The Italian incident gave Blum a measure of renewed self-confidence. When he appeared before the Senate Foreign Affairs Committee on July 30, and when Delbos spoke to the Chamber as a whole the next day, they confirmed the government's decision to suspend shipments to the Spanish Republic but implied that if shipments to Franco were made by other powers, the government would consider itself released

[3] Blum: testimony, 1947, *Événements*, I, 217; Cot: *Le Proces de la république*, II, 310–11; and see communiqué, August 8, 1936, summarizing action taken at cabinet meetings of July 25, August 1, and August 8, 1936, *Le Populaire*, August 9, 1936. Cf. Toynbee (ed.): *Survey of International Affairs, 1937*, II, 141, 232.

[4] Toynbee (ed.): *Survey of International Affairs, 1937*, II, 232; Cot: *Le Procès de la république*, II, 312–13.

from the restrictions it had imposed upon itself and would resume its freedom of action.[5] The episode, however, proved to have the opposite effect. With definite proof of foreign intervention now at hand, the danger of a general ideological war loomed on the horizon and made a policy of caution even more imperative. The debate in the country and in the cabinet was shaping up between those who saw the flagrant evidence of Italian intervention as justification for full aid to the Republic and those who saw intervention by any outside powers as increasing the danger of a general European war. Léger in the French Foreign Office, convinced of the peril, believed that a pledge of non-intervention by all the European powers was, as he later described it, "the best available insurance against the spread of the conflagration."[6] His office, accordingly, drew up a plan: the French government would propose an international agreement not to furnish arms to either side or interfere in any way with events in Spain. The idea of an international agreement on non-intervention seems to have originated with Léger and the permanent officials at the Quai d'Orsay.

But Blum accepted the plan quickly. For one thing, he was not one to turn his back on any appeal for international cooperation or on any plan aimed at the preservation of peace. Once again he convinced himself of the role to be played by public opinion. If Italy refused to accept the proposal, that country would stand condemned by world opinion, the British would adopt a more sympathetic attitude, and the French government could then proceed freely with its original intention to aid the Spanish Republic. If all the powers were to accept it, the conflict could remain localized and the dangerous competition in supplying arms to both sides could be prevented from developing into a general war.

At the second cabinet meeting, held the morning of August 1, after Delbos called attention to the delicacy of the international situation and stressed that the British were advising the government "semi-officially" (*officieusement*) not to become involved and to observe a strict neutrality, the cabinet endorsed the plan drawn up by the Quai d'Orsay. It would be proposed first to England and Italy as the principal Mediterranean powers, and then more widely. As a concession to the proponents of aid in the cabinet and in the country at large, an official communiqué

[5] Blum: testimony, 1947, *Événements*, I, 217; Toynbee (ed.): *Survey of International Affairs, 1937*, II, 141, 232; Delbos: statement in Chamber, *Chambre, Débats*, July 31, 1936.
[6] As related to Cameron: "Léger," p. 391.

stated that pending the signing of the proposed agreement and in view of the aid being furnished the rebels from other sources, the French government would "reserve its freedom of action" for the moment.[7] This stipulation allowed planes and munitions to be shipped until other countries ceased *their* shipments. A shipment of planes was quietly released at this time.[8] On the other hand, neither Blum nor anyone else foresaw the next logical step: that France had a moral obligation to lead in a policy of non-intervention if it wished others to follow.

The British response to the French *démarche*, as was to be expected, was prompt and favorable. They asked that the proposal be extended at once to Germany, Portugal, and the U.S.S.R., the three other European powers directly interested besides themselves and Italy. By August 5 the French government was circulating the draft text of a non-intervention agreement to all five of the powers directly involved.[9]

During this time the Rightist press in France and the Italian and German press were busily denouncing the assembling of materials for shipment to the Spanish Republic, which the Popular Front government had stipulated as its right so long as aid to the rebels continued. On the other hand, Leftist pressure for aid to the Republic mounted, despite the launching of the non-intervention appeal. On August 4, Jouhaux spoke up sharply: "In the face of the Spanish situation there can be no neutrality for the conscientious worker. . . . The defeat of the Spanish worker may well prove a setback for us not only to our social progress but even to the security of our country."[1] In Moscow, despite a favorable reception by the Soviet government of the non-intervention proposal, there were organized demonstrations and systematic collections were launched in behalf of the Spanish Popular Front. Maurice Thorez, speaking for the French Communists, demanded that Blum send aid to the beleaguered Spanish Republic and insisted that the Rome-Berlin Axis be prevented from installing a military dictatorship on France's border.[2]

In the meantime, one of Blum's last hopes for converting the British to a policy of aiding the Spanish Republic had vanished. At the suggestion of his Labour party friend Philip Noel Baker, Blum had dis-

---

[7] Cot: *Le Procès de la république*, II, 313–15; Toynbee (ed.): *Survey of International Affairs, 1937*, II, 233.

[8] Cot: *Le Procès de la république*, II, 315; cf. Blum: testimony, 1947, *Événements*, I, 219; the shipment was probably completed by August 8.

[9] Toynbee (ed.): *Survey of International Affairs, 1937*, II, 233–4.

[1] Cited by Cot: *Le Procès de la république*, II, 316.

[2] Toynbee (ed.): *Survey of International Affairs, 1937*, II, 142, 234.

patched Admiral Darlan to try to impress the strategic and military dangers of a Franco victory upon the British Admiralty, which in turn might be expected to exert its influence on the cabinet. The mission foundered. Darlan reported that Admiral Lord Chatfield and his colleagues were convinced that Franco, as a Spanish patriot, would defend himself against the encroachments of Mussolini and Hitler; the British authorities wished to do nothing to antagonize him. Blum later insisted that the failure of the Darlan mission had "a considerable influence" on his own stand and on the final cabinet decision at the next meeting. Time had not worked for him. The Soviet and Czech governments would have supported a policy of aid to the Spanish Republic, but no other countries would. "We felt ourselves almost isolated in Europe on the question of support for the Republican government."[3]

Blum was sensitive to the increasing pressure from the Socialists, the Communists, and the C.G.T. As the third cabinet meeting approached, however, his hands were tied. The Darlan mission had failed. Even more important, the very negotiations that had been initiated for the non-intervention agreement had destroyed his freedom of action; his government had launched an international appeal which it could not itself violate. "Once you put your finger in certain machinery," he later remarked of another political maneuver (the appeal for armistice terms in June 1940), "you are caught up completely."[4] This political *mot* now applied to him. He could no longer choose between direct help to Spain and non-intervention; he could only back the non-intervention proposal which in his heart he did not favor.

Reduced to despair, Blum was "strongly tempted" to resign so that he and his party would not be identified with a policy of which he did not approve. His resignation might mean the end of his "experiment," but he reassured himself that the major reforms of the Popular Front election program had already been enacted. Shortly before the cabinet meeting of August 8, he talked of resigning. He mentioned it to a number of close friends as well as to the Spanish Republican emissaries in Paris, Fernando de los Ríos and Ximenes de Asua. His attitude was now completely defeatist. The cabinet, he knew, would not support him if he insisted on reopening the question of direct aid to Spain; and even if it did, a cabinet that adopted such a policy would probably be overthrown in Parliament. The "popular masses," which always figured

---

[3] For the Darlan mission and the quotation, Blum: testimony, 1947, *Événements*, I, 217–18.

[4] Testimony, 1947, *Événements*, I, 261.

prominently in his Socialist theorizing, were conspicuously absent in his political calculations; he would not provoke discord and disunity, perhaps even civil war, at a time when the enemies of France were watching closely for every sign of weakness.

Fernando de los Ríos and Ximenes de Asua refused to have the fall of the French Popular Front on *their* conscience. After debating the matter and consulting Madrid, they resolved to dissuade Blum from resigning. The Spanish government could not see anything but a worse alternative in any cabinet that would follow, probably a Radical cabinet under Chautemps. Pointing out that the overthrow of the Blum government would be a catastrophic moral blow to the cause of the Spanish Republic, they pressed Blum not to resign. Louis de Brouckère, the Belgian president of the Second International, informed of Blum's intentions, added his entreaties.[5]

Wrestling with his conscience, Blum convinced himself that too much was at stake to resign and that more would be lost than gained. He set aside all thought of resignation. Ought he to have resigned and thereby dissociated himself from the non-intervention policy? The Socialist journalist Louis Lévy later argued that, had he done so, "popular pressure" would have returned him to office within a few weeks with a mandate to aid the Spanish Republic.[6] But such a turn of events was extremely unlikely. The Radicals would undoubtedly have formed a new cabinet and blocked any change in policy. Had he resigned, his name and that of his party would not have been forever tarnished with the betrayal of a democratic Popular Front government doing battle with the fascist dictators. Blum himself might have been spared a great deal of personal agony and humiliation. But resignation in order to evade responsibility would have been a cowardly solution.

In any event, after his threat to resign, Blum's conscience was clearer. He could believe that he had yielded to the entreaties of his Spanish Republican friends. As soon as he abandoned the thought of resigning and accepted non-intervention as a policy, a change came over him. He now began to defend the non-intervention policy as though it were his

[5] Blum discusses the "resignation" episode in various places: testimony, 1947, *Événements*, I, 218–19; speech to Socialist international conference, 1946, *Le Populaire*, July 19, 1950; and article of October 15, 1945, republished with comments by Oreste Rosenfeld, *Le Populaire*, March 25, 1951. Rosenfeld corroborates Blum's statements. Louis de Brouckère and the Spanish Socialists, including Negrín, verified the episode at the Socialist conference in 1946, *Le Populaire*, July 19, 1950. Cf. also Thomas: *The Spanish Civil War*, pp. 258–9.

[6] *Truth about France*, p. 115.

from the very beginning—as the proper course of action both to aid the Spanish Republic and to prevent a general war. It would be possible for Jean Zay, his Minister of National Education, to say: "Léon Blum did not accept it as something forced on him; he personally believed it to be sound."[7]

In open competition, Blum's argument now ran, the fascist states would be able to intervene freely with men and munitions in a way that the democratic countries were unable to do. "Ask yourselves," he soon was interrogating Popular Front rallies, "who would be able to furnish more—through secret operations, through the concentration of power in a single hand, through the intensity of arms production, through industrial potential—ask yourselves who would be able to assure themselves the advantage in such a competition?"[8] (In Britain, Arthur Greenwood was echoing this sentiment at a Labour party congress. The rebels, he said, "would get 50 aircraft and 50 guns from Germany and Italy for every one that the Republic would get from other countries."[9]) There was the possibility also that the fascist powers would give *de facto* recognition to the Nationalist rebels. The competition, Blum's argument continued, would not be limited to supplies and materials only; technicians and military intervention would follow; the Spanish Republic and all Europe would be engulfed in war. Only an international agreement on non-intervention, solemnly drawn up and rigidly observed, would aid the Spanish Republic and save the peace of Europe at one and the same time. The logic of Blum's argument rested on one major premise: that the signatories to a non-intervention agreement would observe it, that in the world of the 1930's such promises would be honored. If Germany and Italy could have been trusted to honor the obligations they assumed, the policy of non-intervention might have successfully kept all nations out of the Spanish Civil War. This was a very shaky conjecture. But Blum refused to permit himself doubts or suspicions about the honest intentions even of the dictators.

At the third cabinet meeting, on August 8, Pierre Cot continued to insist that aid be sent to the Spanish Republic regardless of the obstacles and risks involved. But by now the new policy had been launched. Delbos informed the cabinet of the success of the international negotiations which they were now jointly conducting with the British. The

[7] *Souvenirs et solitude*, p. 114.
[8] Speech at Luna Park, September 6, 1936, *Oeuvre*, IV, pt. 1, 391.
[9] Cited by Dalton: *The Fateful Years*, pp. 98–9.

responses thus far, including those from Italy, Germany, and the U.S.S.R., were all "favorable in principle." One further step remained. France had to set an example, to live up to the obligations of non-intervention which it was asking the other powers to accept. No longer could the French embargo be hedged with the provision that France might send aid pending the signing of the agreement by all the powers. The embargo, extended to cover commercial as well as military aircraft, was therefore now announced as complete, to take effect the following day, August 9.[1] By that act, the Blum government, suspending all exports to Spain, committed itself unilaterally to non-intervention— before the powers which were openly aiding Franco had done so. The government took the step, Blum explained a short time later, "hoping by this example to challenge the honor (*piquer d'honneur*) of the other powers and thus prepare the rapid conclusion of the general agreement . . ."[2] (Challenge the honor of Mussolini and Hitler!) The French government allowed itself only one last act of boldness. The last planes of the shipment that had been assembled were permitted to leave at once, before the embargo went into effect; a total of "40 to 50 planes" had been sent.[3] Its most significant effect was the uproar of the Rightist deputies in the Chamber on August 13.

Neither Blum nor Delbos had foreseen what soon occurred. On August 15 the initial French proposal became a joint Anglo-French proposal to all the states of Europe calling for a formal renunciation of intervention, direct or indirect, in the Spanish Civil War. But for close to three weeks, a crucial period in the initial stages of the fighting, Italy, Germany, and Portugal protracted the negotiations and utilized

---

[1] Cot: *Le Procès de la république*, II, 317–18; Toynbee (ed.): *Survey of International Affairs, 1937*, II, 234; communiqué of August 8, 1936, *Le Populaire*, August 9, 1936. Blum hoped that minutes of the preliminary unofficial cabinet meeting (*conseil de cabinet*) might have been preserved (testimony, 1947; *Événements*, I, 219), but all copies seem to have disappeared during the war. Of course, official minutes of regular cabinet meetings, which met with the President of the Republic presiding (*conseil des ministres*), were never kept, nor, strictly speaking, were even unofficial minutes permitted. For Blum's later comments on the Radical ministers, see *Le Populaire*, March 7, 9, 1939.

[2] Speech of September 6, 1936, *Oeuvre*, IV, pt. 1, 392.

[3] Blum: testimony, 1947, *Événements*, I, 219; Cot: *Le Procès de la république*, II, 315, 332; Jules Moch: typescript of remarks (p. 65) at *assemblée d'information*, February 8, 1951, organized by the Société des Amis de Léon Blum. I am grateful to Mme Cletta Mayer for this typescript. The discussion had been prolonged, Moch said, until there had left France "the last airplane of a series in process of delivery, my wife keeping me posted on the departure of the planes from Bordeaux."

the delay to send substantial aid to the rebels. To the chagrin and indignation of the friends of the Spanish Republic, French aid to the Republic was cut off at a most critical juncture. Italy deliberately delayed signing and interposed various obstacles in order to be able to continue arms deliveries to Franco as long as possible.[4] Germany eventually signed, partly because Hitler had resolved to announce the extension of military service at that very moment. He hoped that by signing the non-intervention agreement he might soften international reaction to his other decision.[5] The German government also frankly feared that with further delay Blum and Delbos might be unable to resist the "growing domestic political pressure" and might turn to giving unlimited support to the Spanish government.[6] Ironically, the top German advisers were convinced that German and Italian aid would *not* be able to compete with the flow of supplies from France if it were to materialize, let alone with aid that might be given by Russia and England as well. The German military had little confidence in a Franco victory in the early stages of the fighting and were not prepared for the moment to intervene militarily to aid him. On the other hand, the Germans, like Blum, recognized that a flood of arms could result in "the danger of very rapidly spreading complications in Europe."[7]

While the negotiations were still under way, an episode occurred to confirm Blum's belief in the danger of war. On August 18, the German merchant ship *Kamerun* was halted, by a shot across her bow, by Spanish government warships, searched, and forbidden to put in at any Spanish port on the grounds that she carried oil and other war materials. The German government responded with a stern warning that its navy would "oppose with force every unjustified act of force."[8] After some anxious hours—Blum expressed his deep concern to the American *chargé d'affaires* in Paris[9]—there was a sense of relief when the German government did not take any action. Blum later argued,

[4] See, e.g., the communications of the German *chargé d'affaires* in Rome, *Docs. Ger. For. Pol.*, D, III, No. 40, p. 38, and No. 60, p. 60.

[5] See Foreign Minister to Acting State Secretary, August 24, 1936, *Docs. Ger. For. Pol.*, D, III, No. 55, p. 56.

[6] See communication of German Ambassador, Count von Welczeck, August 21, 1936, *Docs. Ger. For. Pol.*, D, III, No. 49, p. 49.

[7] See memorandum by Acting State Secretary, August 22, 1936, and annex, opinion prepared under Admiral Raeder's supervision, ibid., No. 50, pp. 50–2.

[8] Foreign Minister to Acting State Secretary, August 24, 1936, ibid., No. 55, p. 56.

[9] Telegram, American *chargé*, August 25, 1936, *For. Rel. U.S.*, 1936, II, No. 788, p. 511.

with Eden's backing, that the non-intervention negotiations then going on helped avert hostilities over the *Kamerun* episode.[1] It cannot be denied that the Spanish situation was and remained explosive whether Hitler was prepared to risk war or not.

Meanwhile, reinforced by the aid they had been receiving from Italy and Germany during the extended negotiations, the Nationalist troops entered Irún, the Basque town not far from the French border, on September 6. The French initiative in unilaterally imposing an embargo without waiting for the other powers to accept the agreement had been a grievous mistake, for which the Spanish Republicans were paying the cost. Despite Blum's claims that the Spanish conflict was being localized and the threat of a European war averted, a large segment of the Popular Front was now aroused against the non-intervention policy—and not only the Communists and Communist sympathizers either.

Blum was painfully aware of the rising tide of criticism directed against him in his own party and elsewhere: the Spanish question was shattering the unity and *élan* of the Popular Front. Jeers, taunts, heckling, choruses of *"Des avions pour l'Espagne!" "Blum à l'action!"* were commonplace at Popular Front gatherings. Yet once embarked upon the non-intervention policy, Blum defended it despite the crescendo of impassioned opposition. On September 5, he warned a Communist-led delegation of metalworkers that their plans for a one-hour strike demonstration against the government's "blockade" of Republican Spain would be useless. "It cannot make me change my feelings on the policy that I judge to be necessary for the government under present circumstances."[2] The following day, September 6, the very day of the fall of Irún, at his own request he spoke to a giant mass meeting at Luna Park organized by the most militant group in his party, the Socialist Federation of the Seine Department. Though it was a hostile audience, much of the hostility dwindled as he portrayed in emotion-laden tones his personal agony. Had he suffered any less than they with the brave defenders of Irún? Did he sympathize any less than they with the fervent pleas for aid made by La Pasionara and other Spanish delegates?

---

[1] Speech of September 6, 1936, *Oeuvre*, IV, pt. 1, 392; cf. testimony, 1947, *Événements*, I, 219. Blum at this point in his testimony spoke of the *Deutschland* when he meant the *Kamerun;* the *Deutschland* episode occurred later, in June 1937. See also Eden's speech at Bradford, November 1, 1936, cited by Campbell-Johnson: *Eden*, p. 142.

[2] *Le Populaire*, September 6, 1936; and Delmas: *À gauche de la barricade*, p. 118.

It was a crucifixion for him to have accepted the policy: "I have known, I can assure you, some very cruel stations." If he had adopted the policy—and he assumed "full responsibility without exception of person or party"—they had to take his word that it was to prevent a competition in the sending of arms that could lead to the "gravest complications." They had to "take the word of a man who has never deceived you." The government's policy, despite their understandable chagrin and resentment at the course of events in Spain, "has in one or two perhaps particularly crucial hours saved Europe from the danger of a general conflagration." He knew that France's security required a friendly republic on its Pyrenees frontier; he knew that the Spanish government was a legal government with every right under international law to purchase arms and munitions to suppress the rebellion. But free competition would only give an advantage to the fascist supporters of Franco and would increase the grave danger of a war that would engulf the Spanish Republic as well. His words might seem "cruel or bitter" to his friends in Spain, but an international pledge of non-intervention was better for Spain than to "open the way to an armed struggle and a necessarily unequal competition." He conceded the error of having imposed an embargo on arms before the other powers. "For too long a time, much longer than we had foreseen, much longer than we would have desired, by reason of this offer, perhaps too trustingly made, we found ourselves with our hands tied while the other powers legally and politically retained . . . the freedom of action that we had forbidden ourselves." In the next breath he insisted that in the new phase, since the acceptance of the embargo by all, there was no evidence of violations. "There does not exist, to my knowledge, a single proof nor even a single solid presumption that, since the promulgation of the enforcement measures by the respective governments, any of them has violated the engagements to which it has subscribed." It was out of the question for France to go back on its decision and call for an end to the agreement that had been signed; even more unthinkable that it should betray its signature. He reminded the Communists that the agreement bore the signature of the U.S.S.R. as well.[3]

It required courage to face this angry audience which considered the non-intervention policy a shameful betrayal of the Spanish Republic. Unlike Blum, the masses of the Popular Front supporters had little faith in the value of "fascist" signatures. Yet they listened to him. His portrait of personal torment and of self-torture in the interests of peace

[3] For the speech of September 6, 1936, *Oeuvre*, IV, pt. 1, 387–96.

won them over. He repeated what he had told them on assuming office, six weeks earlier, that he did not know whether he had the qualities of a leader. Perhaps, he told them, "another might have done better than I."[4] This they shouted down and refused to accept.

It was anxiety over peace and war that kept the party from rebelling against him then and in the months that followed when the violations of the non-intervention agreement became patent. The non-intervention policy hurt the cause of the Spanish Republicans, ran counter to the wishes of his own party, alienated the Communists and other large segments of the Popular Front, and troubled his own conscience deeply. Yet it was designed to save the peace, to avert a war that everyone dreaded. His party wanted to hear him say: "I do not believe, I will never admit, that war is inevitable and fated . . . I shall refuse to the end to despair of peace and of the efforts of the French nation to work for peace."[5] In December 1936, when he faced the hostile Communist Deputies in the Chamber, his argument was the same: "With what can we be reproached? Having gone beyond our goal? Having feared war too much? Having done too much for peace? If there was an error on our part, gentlemen, it would be that. Such a reproach we can manage to accept. If we had to choose, we prefer to have exaggerated the risks of war than to have ignored it. Error for error, we prefer to have done too much for peace than too little."[6] The non-intervention agreement, as he saw it, could still save the Spanish Republic and save the peace of Europe at the same time.

The next stage, after the signing of the non-intervention agreement, is a story in itself—and again a painful one. "It caused us," Blum confessed in later years, "many disappointments, many vexations."[7] The proofs of violations by Italy and Germany were soon overwhelming. Only a few weeks after Blum's assurances on September 6 that there was no evidence of violation, the Spanish government was formally protesting to the newly formed Non-Intervention Committee in London, and to the League in Geneva, over the continuing flow of arms from Italy, Germany, and Portugal to the military rebels, a flow of arms that had never ceased. The protests of the Spanish government continued for

[4] Ibid., p. 396.
[5] Ibid., p. 395.
[6] Speech of December 5, 1936, *Oeuvre*, IV, pt. 1, 400.
[7] Testimony, 1947, *Événements*, I, 219.

the next two and a half years. The pleas of its Foreign Minister, Alvarez del Vayo, were part of Blum's torment. "It would be unjust," Alvarez del Vayo has written, "not to point out that later realization of the mistakes committed in those early weeks . . . was to cause the Socialist Premier much anguish. Every time I went through Paris it was my duty to go to him and tell him frankly how things were going; at such meetings I saw his grief and something like despair."[8]

Before long Mussolini boasted openly of the military aid and even of the troops he was contributing to Franco. German military and technical aid, although less obtrusive and less flamboyantly advertised, was no less significant. In October, the U.S.S.R. began to send tanks, artillery, planes, and technicians to the Spanish Republic as a riposte and threatened to abandon the agreement in view of the egregious violations by Germany and Italy. Volunteers from the democracies and antifascist émigrés meanwhile went to Spain to fight on the side of the Republic. The French and British governments responded to the new turn of events by pleading for observance of the agreement that had been solemnly signed by all and by urging the tightening of frontier controls. In December 1936 and January 1937 the two governments even secured an agreement from the major powers, including Germany and Italy, to prohibit the enlistment and dispatch of "volunteers." Again it troubled Blum, he confessed in the Chamber, to place on the same plane "two very different forms of enlistment or enrollment: the free gift of one's person to an ideal and faith, after the model of those legendary examples . . . Lafayette, Byron, Garibaldi, Villebois-Mareuil, as against service under compulsion." But he insisted that they had no choice. The ever-present danger of war could be avoided only by including "without distinction" the two types of "volunteers."[9] The new agreement also proved ineffectual; and the long discussion that ensued on the withdrawal of troops already in Spain proved fruitless as well.

As the months went by, the C.G.T., the Communists, and the Left-wing groups in his own party seethed with impatience and resentment. The agreement which the Blum government had initiated was being shamelessly violated, to the cruel disadvantage of the Spanish Republic. For "a period of months," Blum later explained, the French government remained "scrupulously faithful" to the agreement despite the overwhelming evidence of violations, but toward the middle of 1937 it could

[8] *Freedom's Battle*, p. 70.
[9] Speech of January 15, 1937, *Oeuvre*, IV, pt. 1, 406–7.

no longer tolerate the situation.[1] The government considered its alternatives: to denounce the agreement officially as null and void, or to preserve the agreement in form but refuse to exercise vigilance in enforcing it. Although there was pressure in the cabinet for open denunciation, the same reasons militated against such a step as had prompted the French government to initiate the policy: the desire to avoid a disagreement with Britain, the need to take into account the continued division in French public opinion, and the ever-present concern for the risks of war. Blum still clung to the agreement as a means of preserving peace. "In its tenacious desire for peace," Blum later explained his government's policy, "it feared to deliver the *coup de grâce* to an international agreement that possessed, in spite of everything, if only by its existence, a certain quality that made for peace."[2]

Such was the British position also. Baldwin, seconded by Eden and Chamberlain, stated firmly: "We might just as well say that a dam is not effective because there are some leaks in it . . . you can stop up the leaks. It is a very different thing from sweeping away the dam altogether." Eden used the very same figure: "A leaky dam may yet serve its purpose."[3] The British unqualifiedly defended the policy long after Blum recognized its unjustness. Even had he desired to scrap the agreement, he would have had to overcome stronger British resistance than at the outset.

The continued pressure from the Right in France, the British opposition to abandoning the policy, the difficulty of reversing a policy already in effect, all played a part in staying Blum's hand. Unable and unwilling to do away with the agreement altogether, the Blum government resolved from the spring of 1937 on to "disinterest" itself in the active enforcement of the agreement and to follow a policy of "indifferent neutrality."[4] Blum called it "a system of relaxed non-intervention" (*non-intervention relâchée*). "We voluntarily and systematically closed our eyes," said Blum, "to the contraband of arms." From about May 1937 on, in the closing days of his government, he testified in later years, the government "practically organized it." He described an official attached to the staff of Vincent Auriol, his Finance Minister, as "organizer-in-chief."[5] "I could not do very much," Auriol explained, "but

[1] Testimony, 1947, *Événements*, I, 219; and "Petite Histoire de la non-intervention," *Le Populaire*, June 24, 1938.

[2] "Petite Histoire," ibid.; also *Le Populaire*, June 25, 26, 29, 1938.

[3] Toynbee (ed.): *Survey of International Affairs, 1937*, II, 158, 357.

[4] "Petite Histoire," *Le Populaire*, June 25, 1938.

[5] Testimony, 1947, *Événements*, I, 219.

as head of the customs service, in agreement with Léon Blum, I aided the Spain of Negrín by facilitating the transit of arms that were being sent him from Mexico, Russia, and other countries."[6] Blum's Air Minister, Pierre Cot, who has provided the fullest details of the aid given in this way, also testified: "I did what I could to utilize the feeble rights which we had reserved to ourselves to aid those who were fighting our common enemies. . . . If it was a crime to have aided the Spanish Republicans, then I am guilty, and I have only one regret, that is not to have been even guiltier."[7]

The policy of surreptitious aid to the Spanish Republic continued during the two Chautemps governments that followed Blum's, that is, from June 1937 to January 1938 and from January 1938 to March 1938; Blum claimed that he demanded it as a precondition for Socialist participation in the first and for Socialist parliamentary support of the second.[8] The same policy continued and reached a high point under Blum's short-lived second Popular Front government (March 13 to April 8, 1938); it was carried on and then finally abandoned in June 1938 by the Daladier government. After the war, with a hint of boastfulness, Blum stated that this "contraband traffic . . . extremely active for nearly a year and a half . . . together with shipments arriving by sea from the Soviet Union, permitted the Spanish Republic on several occasions to be able to struggle against the Franco army without too substantial an inferiority of matériel."[9]

Yet, on balance, the amount of aid sent, and the timid and underhanded manner in which it was given, could not fill anyone with pride. Blum admitted candidly that the policy "lacked stature and grandeur (*carrure et grandeur*)"; he even used the word "hypocritical" to describe it.[1] The policy of "relaxed non-intervention" was only a *pis aller*, and certainly did not create equality for both sides in Spain. Moreover, the

---

[6] *Hier . . . Demain*, I, 48.

[7] Cot: testimony, 1947, *Événements*, I, 274; and *Le Procès de la république*, II, 330–4.

[8] Testimony, *Événements*, I, 219.

[9] Ibid. Although there was a tendency to exaggerate the amount of aid, there is no doubt that under Blum's second government, March–April 1938, substantial shipments reached the Spanish Republic via France. See memorandum, April 22, 1938, *Docs. Ger. For. Pol.*, D, III, No. 573, pp. 644–6; and dispatch, Ambassador in Spain to German Foreign Ministry, May 4, 1938, ibid., No. 580, p. 653. For the second Blum government and the Spanish question, see also Chapter X below.

[1] "Petite Histoire," *Le Populaire*, June 25, 1938; testimony, 1947, *Événements*, I, 219, 254.

aid, inadequate though it was, served to inflame Rightist public opinion. Blum had to confront angry charges in Parliament, documented by lists of French material that had allegedly passed the frontier as contraband; some of it had been purchased in France long before the rebellion.[2] Jean Zay, in his memoirs, criticized the clandestine aid as "a half-way policy." "One could intervene or not intervene," he wrote. "One intervened enough to see oneself reproached for it in the enemy camp, not enough to give the Republicans effective support." Zay recalled: "Our shipments were always ridiculous (*dérisoires*). The Spanish Ambassador would invite the French ministers to dine and would say to them in a low voice . . . 'Give us planes . . . Give us wheat.' "[3] Perhaps the best indication that the direct aid given was insubstantial was the willingness of the Vichy prosecution at the Riom trial to drop the charge that the Popular Front governments from 1936 to 1938 had furnished important material to the Spanish Republic. In effect, whatever boldness there was consisted not so much in the shipping of material as in the willingness of the authorities to close their eyes and permit material to pass through France, most of which came from the U.S.S.R.

Among the most embarrassing aspects of the affair for Blum were the taunts of the Communists, who repeatedly contrasted the aid given by the Soviet Union with the action followed by France. Blum did not belittle the importance of the Soviet aid. "This aid was considerable," he said in 1938. "No one can ignore the fact that in the most critical hours of the war it assumed a life-and-death character for the Republican army."[4] He argued, however, that his non-intervention agreement had made Soviet aid possible without war resulting. Soviet shipments had not led to war, he told the Chamber in December 1936, directing his remarks principally to the Communist Deputies, "precisely because of the reduced psychological tension, the lowering of the European temperature that the non-intervention pact had permitted."[5] The Communists, who were unconvinced, almost brought down the government by abstaining from the vote of confidence that followed the debate.

Months later, after the fall of the second Blum government, the policy of "relaxed non-intervention" itself came under attack. In the late spring of 1938 the Daladier-Bonnet government, after talks with

---

[2] See Gamelin: *Servir*, II, 331.

[3] *Souvenirs et solitude*, p. 115.

[4] "Petite Histoire," *Le Populaire*, June 29, 1938.

[5] Speech of December 5, 1936, *Oeuvre*, IV, pt. 1, 399.

Chamberlain and Halifax, prepared to re-establish a vigilant control at the frontiers to prevent the shipment of contraband and thus end all forms of French aid. Blum protested. He could not accept the "abominable sophism" that permitted intervention for the one side and proscribed it for the other. If it were still possible to enforce the policy for all the powers, he would still favor it, but since it had worked as it had, the only alternative was either to continue the procedure of "relaxed" enforcement or make plans to denounce the agreements completely.[6] He wrote disparagingly in *Le Populaire* of the latest agreement, signed in April 1938, which he said would be as frustrating as previous ones. "For it is not enough to place signatures at the bottom of an agreement or of a pact . . . Excessive confidence in the form of unilateral initiative or action taken in advance is the greatest of imprudences."[7] It was easier to lecture others now that he was no longer in the government.

In January 1939, a few months after the Munich agreement, he tried to persuade the Daladier government to resume French freedom of action in Spain. He spoke up now against excessive dependence on the British despite the urgent need for the closest Anglo-French relations. Although he accepted the need for joint action by the two democracies, he demanded: "Is it forbidden us, is it impossible for us to influence England in the determination of that common action? Is it always impossible to attract her to us, to orient her toward us"?[8] Had he asked such questions in 1936, the course of events might have been different.

Despite his disappointment at the many violations of the agreement and his grief for the tribulations of the Spanish government, Blum always remained convinced that the non-intervention policy had helped to avert a general European war in 1936–7 and, on that ground alone, was justified. He cited four critical episodes. The first was the halting by Spanish government warships of the *Kamerun* on August 18, 1936, while the negotiations for the agreement were still under way. "I believe that in the month of August," he said, referring to the episode, "Europe

---

[6] "Petite Histoire," *Le Populaire*, June 25, 1938. It was the plan to re-establish vigilant controls, supported in the Chamber by Flandin, that provoked this article and the series "Petite Histoire de la non-intervention." Blum used the phrase "abominable sophism" in his speech to the party congress at Royan in June 1938, referred to below.

[7] "Une Erreur funeste," *Le Populaire*, June 23, 1938.

[8] Speech in Chamber, January 26, 1939, reproduced as pamphlet, *La Question d'Espagne* (Paris, 1939), pp. 13–14.

was on the edge of war and I believe that it was saved from war by the French initiative."[9]

In January 1937, rumors of German landings in Morocco promised to develop into another menacing episode. The French Foreign Office, headed by Alexis Léger while Blum and Delbos were absent from Paris for the New Year's holidays, took a strong stand and the incident passed. "I am still convinced," Blum said years later, "that the risks of war were real . . ."[1]

In the spring of 1937, Spanish Republican planes bombed the *Deutschland*, a German battleship patrolling the coast of Spain under the international patrol scheme; thirty-one of the crew were killed and many wounded. Two days later, on May 31, German warships, in retaliation, mercilessly bombarded the civilian port of Almería. International tension ran high but nothing further developed. Finally, a few weeks later, on June 19, the fourth episode occurred. Hitler announced that Spanish government submarines had attempted to torpedo the cruiser *Leipzig*. There were vigorous protests and blustering threats, and Germany and Italy withdrew from the naval patrol agreement.[2] In the midst of this crisis, Blum's first government fell from office. It was the international tension as much as anything else, Blum maintained, that deterred him from an all-out fight with the Senate.

On all these occasions, Blum asserted, "the risks of war were real" and war had been averted "in large measure because of the lowering of the international temperature produced by our non-intervention initiative."[3] "In spite of everything," he told the uneasy Socialist party congress in July 1937, "the consideration that must in your minds prevail over all others is that in this last year Europe has not known war, by which I mean a generalized war." The non-intervention policy had admittedly become a "farce, a lie, a fiction," but nonetheless it had served a noble purpose. "A lie? A fiction? Call it what you will! These are lies and fictions by the help of which peace in some measure has been preserved."[4]

---

[9] Speech in Chamber, December 5, 1936, *Oeuvre*, IV, pt. 1, 399, and see speech of September 6, 1936, ibid., p. 392; cf. Eden's speech at Bradford referred to earlier, cited by Campbell-Johnson: *Eden*, p. 142.

[1] Testimony, 1947, *Événements*, I, 219; and see on this episode Cameron: "Léger," p. 391.

[2] On these episodes, Toynbee (ed.): *Survey of International Affairs, 1937*, II, 312–19.

[3] Testimony, 1947, *Événements*, I, 219.

[4] Speech to Marseilles congress, July 1937, pp. 461–2.

He clung to the notion that he had been right to initiate the non-intervention agreement. If it had been obeyed by all, it would have saved the peace and saved the Spanish Republic. "Even today," he told the Socialist congress the following year, in June 1938, amidst many hoots and jeers, "if it were possible for non-intervention to become a reality . . . if the withdrawal of volunteers were possible . . . I would be a resolute partisan of it . . . today as yesterday it would be the only means of re-establishing justice and equity among the men fighting in Spain . . . the only means of leaving to Spain the free disposition of its destinies."[5]

Chamberlain and the British Conservatives reinforced Blum's statements about the positive role played by the non-intervention agreement in preserving peace. "I have read," Chamberlain told the House of Commons on June 25, 1937, "that in the high mountains there are sometimes conditions to be found where an incautious move, or even a sudden loud exclamation may start an avalanche. That is just the condition in which we are finding ourselves today." The non-intervention agreement, he was pleased to say, had prevented the Spanish conflict from spreading and was "achieving the object which has been at the back of our policy the whole time. . . . If we can all exercise caution, patience, and self-restraint we may yet be able to save the peace of Europe."[6] Churchill too was saying: "I expect that the Non-Intervention Committee is full of swindles and cheats . . . but it is a precious thing in these times of peril that five great nations should be sitting around the table instead of blasting or bombing each other in a horrible war . . ."[7] "Tattered and full of holes no doubt," wrote Eden in his memoirs, "but better than total war in Spain and a European war out of that."[8] British Conservatives, like Blum, saw the non-intervention agreement, discredited though it was, as a means of preserving peace. The difference was that for them it was not a personal and political tragedy that peace had to be preserved at the expense of the Spanish Republic.

Cordell Hull has written that critics of the non-intervention policy may readily say, with hindsight, that it was a failure. The fascist forces in Spain triumphed, Hitler and Mussolini were strengthened, and Britain and France were humbled. "Yet," he notes, "the argument would be valid only if the peace-loving nations, including the United States,

[5] Speech at Royan congress, June 1938, p. 505.
[6] Cited by Toynbee (ed.): *Survey of International Affairs, 1937*, II, 160–1.
[7] Speech of April 14, 1937, cited by Hull: *Memoirs*, p. 482.
[8] *Facing the Dictators*, p. 463.

had been prepared militarily and psychologically to abandon their efforts toward maintaining peace and embark on a general preventive war. Such was not the case."[9]

Such was not the case, most certainly not for Blum. He was not the man ever to abandon efforts toward the preservation of peace. Nor would he embark on a policy of leading a divided country, without dependable allies, into an unpopular war. Blum's freedom of action was restricted by his obsession with peace, his sense of obligation to his Radical Socialist allies, his concern for national unity, and his dependence on Britain. All these considerations, Pierre Cot later wrote, "weighed like a coat of lead on the Blum cabinet, taking away its freedom of judgment, binding it to decisions which did not correspond to the true feelings of its leader, nor to the desires of the majority of its members, nor to the will of the French people." Of Blum himself he added: "I know what a drama of conscience acceptance [of the policy] was for him."[1]

Looking back upon the non-intervention policy while he was a Vichy prisoner during the Second World War, Blum tended to discount the dependence upon Britain as a decisive element. If war had come as a result of involvement in Spain, he wrote in 1942 to a French friend in the United States, it "would not have been undertaken then (even without England) under conditions more unfavorable than at the time of Munich or than in 1939." German rearmament was not yet advanced and "Czechoslovakia and undoubtedly the U.S.S.R. would have followed us." Yet the risk could not be taken for another reason. It was the internal situation that was decisive:

> What our American friends perhaps do not perceive and what the events in France in the past two years [1940–2] illuminate—and with a very bright light—is that, in the hypothesis that I am evoking, civil war would have broken out in France before foreign war. The affair of Spain took place between the 6th of February and the armistice [of 1940]. It was embedded deeply in the social crisis. . . . As soon as the situation would have been stretched to the danger point, we would have had in France a counterpart to the Franco *coup de force.*

There would have followed "civil war with slight chance of victory for the republic."[2] He repeated this contention after the war. "I have

[9] *Memoirs*, I, 484–5.
[1] *Le Procès de la république*, II, 306, 320.
[2] Letter to Suzanne Blum, July 9, 1942, cited previously.

realized since that time that we in France were also on the eve of a military *coup d'état*. Industry, and reactionary circles, infuriated by the passage of the social laws, would have utilized this as a pretext. I had a presentiment of it at the time. Since then I know it."[3]

It is not entirely fair to dismiss these reflections as afterthoughts, the product of the years following the military defeat, the collapse of the Third Republic, and the establishment of the Vichy dictatorship, although those events naturally confirmed his judgment. His concern over internal disunity and his fear of civil war troubled him deeply at the time. He told the Chamber in December 1936 that it was his "supreme duty" to avoid a war under circumstances in which "France would risk being isolated, or in which we would find Europe uncertain, or more than uncertain, and France itself divided."[4] He spoke of the potentially dangerous internal situation both to Carlo Sforza and to Hugh Dalton. When Sforza challenged Blum in 1936 to check the fascist tide in Spain, Blum said: "Yes, you are right, but put yourself in my place. I am a Socialist; if I do anything that risks leading France into a war it will be said that I did it for no other reason than to defend the Reds [*sic*] in Spain and I fear that half of France would not follow me."[5]

In September 1936 he told Hugh Dalton he was confident that if France were threatened with direct attack every Frenchman would rally to its defense, but not if it were a matter of "complications arising out of a confused quarrel on the other side of the Pyrenees." Moreover, if a general mobilization were necessary, the fascist leagues, which had been dissolved, would have to be rearmed.[6] In July 1937, he told the Socialist party congress that in a European conflict brought about by involvement in the Spanish struggle, they would run the risk of "threats within the country, divisions, schisms, dissension, going perhaps to the point of attempts at civil war."[7] The internal disunity in France cannot be discounted.

Blum recalled in later years, before the postwar parliamentary investigating committee, that the French military attaché in Madrid, deploring the weakness of the French government on the Spanish question, had said to him at one point: "*M. le Président du Conseil*, I have only these words to say to you—a king of France would make

---

[3] Speech to international Socialist conference, 1946, *Le Populaire*, July 19, 1950; and article, *Le Populaire*, October 15, 1945.

[4] Speech of December 5, 1936, *Oeuvre*, IV, pt. 1, 401.

[5] Count Carlo Sforza: *Contemporary Italy* (New York, 1944), p. 355.

[6] Dalton: *The Fateful Years*, p. 95.

[7] Marseilles congress, July 1937, p. 462.

war." Blum told the committee: "I was not a king of France. It was impossible for me to envisage war without the consent of Parliament and without the backing of public opinion."[8] Even though he was a democratic leader carried into office on a great wave of popular enthusiasm, he was not the man to ignore or overcome the deep divisions in public opinion and embark on a bold positive policy.

When Blum convinced himself that he could not have led a united country into a war that might have resulted from involvement in Spain, he was undoubtedly right. It would have been difficult for any political leader of the Third Republic to have done so. For Blum it was even more difficult, not only because of the opposition of the reactionary, Italophile, fascist-minded Right, the opposition of many of his own Radical Socialist political allies and of the peace wing in his own party, and the opposition of Britain, but also because there were special elements at work to restrain him from exerting a stronger leadership. As the first Socialist Premier in the history of France, he could not bring himself to jeopardize the social reform program to which his government was committed. When Sforza warned him that "social reform" would not save France from the fascist danger in Europe, he replied: "Yes, you may be right, but I am thinking of the many Socialists who, after attaining power, have completely forgotten their promises to the working classes. The world must see one Socialist who, after attaining power, does the very things he promised he would do."[9] As the first Socialist Premier of France, he also had to demonstrate that Socialists in France could govern the country not only without jeopardizing its fundamental social and economic structure but also without involving France in war—especially a war with ideological overtones. Perhaps in some ways he had to demonstrate, more than any other leader, that he sought reconciliation with all nations no matter how much he disagreed with their regimes or grieved at their brutal persecution of fellow Socialists and fellow Jews. He could not allow firmness to be misinterpreted as an ideological or religious vendetta.

There is no question that the Socialist leader did not enjoy full latitude of action. In the case of Spain, he was not able to take the risks that another ardently republican statesman might have taken. And these limitations were reinforced by his personal qualities: his desire not to offend political allies or even political opponents, his role as conciliator and advocate of compromise, his strong sense of moral

[8] Testimony, 1947, *Événements*, I, 253–4.
[9] Sforza: *Contemporary Italy*, p. 355.

integrity, his faith in the integrity of others. He launched France on the non-intervention policy without waiting for the other powers to do so, and he saw to it that France observed the agreement scrupulously for a crucial period of time when others did not. He clung to it long after the violations of the agreement by Germany and Italy had turned the policy into a sham and a farce. He was forced to accept the humiliating and hypocritical technique of surreptitious aid to the Spanish Republic without denouncing the agreement; only very belatedly, long after he was out of office, did he call for a restoration of free commerce.

No one, to be sure, could have foreseen the violations or the way in which the non-intervention agreement would work to the advantage of Franco. Honestly observed by all, it might have been a sound policy. Blum's sustained belief that the dictators would honor their signatures revealed one of his major weaknesses, the trust he put in all men. To one whose own good faith and integrity was above reproach it was inconceivable that governments should sign agreements and not abide by them. He believed, too, in the efficacy of public opinion in preventing wrongdoing. He learned belatedly that the world he lived in was not one in which signatures, or the sanction of world opinion, counted for much; the lesson was learned at the expense of the Spanish Republic. His most blameworthy error was that he lent his moral weight and prestige to the policy for so long, not only at the beginning, when there was a chance that it might work, but even later, after its failure had been revealed. It was possible for Cordell Hull to tell Fernando de los Ríos on October 10, 1936, that the United States could not be expected to aid the Spanish Republic when France and the other nations of Europe were following a policy of non-intervention. "The French government, the neighbor and special friend of the Spanish government," he could say, "has taken the lead in the movement."[1] Alvarez del Vayo noted its effect on the entire Second International. "The various sections of the Second International thought it incumbent on them to support a policy that, ostensibly at least, had been fathered by the distinguished head of the French Socialist party." What European Socialists would have rejected coming from a British Tory government, he remarked, they accepted from a French Socialist Premier.[2] Blum himself recognized that his own identification with the policy made it difficult to oppose it later on. In May 1939, he told Labour party friends that he "fully realized how embarrassing it was to have thrown across

[1] *Memoirs*, I, 484.
[2] *Freedom's Battle*, p. 66.

the floor of the House of Commons the taunt: 'But it was your friend Blum who first proposed non-intervention!' "[3]

That Blum suffered deeply because of the turn of events in Spain does not excuse him. Alvarez del Vayo's judgment deserves to stand: "That he felt this despair attested to his deep sensitivity but does not absolve Léon Blum from the political responsibility he incurred when he gave his name and that of the French Socialist party to the farce of non-intervention."[4] Though it is an exaggeration for Alvarez del Vayo to say that at the time of the Spanish Civil War "Léon Blum held the fate of two proletariats in his hand," he did have it within his power to alter the course of events. Instead he permitted events to follow the course desired by his opponents and by his country's enemies.

The tragedy lay in his lofty ambitions for France. He had hoped that France might lead Europe toward a peace with dignity and honor; the non-intervention policy in Spain and the sacrifice of the Spanish Republic meant abject surrender and humiliation on his country's own doorstep. He had hoped to create a sense of national unity and cohesion in France; the Spanish Civil War divided the nation still more deeply and destroyed the unity of the Popular Front as well.

He could only console himself that the policy had preserved the peace. Haunted by the memory of Lamartine and the Second Republic, and the failures of 1848, he recalled once asking Jaurès whether there were not moments when war was necessary, whether Lamartine had not been wrong in 1848, when all Europe was in revolt against the old autocracies, in proclaiming "a policy of non-intervention." Had not French workers only a few months later died on the June barricades in Paris? How more noble a death in battle against tyranny! "No," he claimed that Jaurès had replied, "it would not have been better. Every time that we can avoid war we must avoid it. War is evil. War cannot engender anything noble and good. It is not war that is revolutionary, it is peace that is revolutionary."[5]

Blum knew, on the other hand, the argument which he had often heard in his own party, and from the Communists and others, that "by a soft policy of concessions to the aggressor powers one creates in Europe a true danger of war." But the answer he gave was that strength consisted in the "will to peace," a refusal to accept war as "fated and

[3] Dalton: *The Fateful Years*, p. 253.
[4] *Freedom's Battle*, p. 70.
[5] Speech at Soissons, November 15, 1936, *Oeuvre*, IV, pt. 1, 375–6; and cf. speech at Royan congress, June 1938, p. 501.

inevitable."[6] In Blum's troubled dreams the chant of the Communists, Socialists, and militant sympathizers of the Spanish Republic—"*Des avions pour l'Espagne!*" "*Blum à l'action!*"—was drowned out by the counter-chant of those who loved peace—"*Blum c'est la paix!*" The cruel dilemma he had faced was that he could not save the Spanish Republic and the peace of Europe at the same time; and, tragically, the peace that he had helped to preserve was only a fragile one.

[6] Speech of September 6, 1936, and cf. speech of December 5, 1936, *Oeuvre*, IV, pt. 1, 394–5, 400–1.

IX

END OF THE
"EXERCISE OF POWER,"
JUNE 1937

As well as anyone, I knew the limitations.[1]

W ITH THE DEEPENING of the financial crisis in the spring of 1937, the opposition in the Senate attacked the government's budget plans and launched an assault on the forty-hour law. In the midst of these financial and political problems, as we have seen, a tempest was also brewing in international affairs—the bombardment of Almería by the Germans and their charges that the Spanish government had attempted to torpedo the *Leipzig*. There was reason for anxiety that war might break out while France was beset with serious domestic difficulties.

The run on the gold reserves and the drain on the Treasury became acute. The financial experts whom Blum had ill-advisedly called in as consultants resigned on June 14, adding to the general uneasiness. To meet the immediate financial crisis and to assist the Treasury in fulfilling its obligations, the government drafted a series of proposals for increased taxation, a rise in railroad fares and postal rates, a tightening up on tax evasion, and a new loan. On June 15 an emergency cabinet meeting decided to ask Parliament for temporary powers to enact by decree "all measures necessary" to meet the financial crisis. Drastic, though unspecified, steps were pledged against speculators and "deserters of the franc."[2]

Le Populaire, denouncing the "plot of high finance against the sovereign independence of the country," compared the crisis confront-

[1] Blum, speech to Royan congress, June 1938, p. 232.
[2] *Le Populaire*, June 15, 16, 17, 1937.

ing the Popular Front with the defeat of the *cartel des gauches* by the "wall of money" in the 1920's, but proclaimed: "The France of 1937 is not the France of 1925."[3] Blum and Auriol pledged resistance to the speculators, Auriol announcing with determination: "If they wish to strangle us, let them be sure that it will not be without a fight."[4]

But despite protestations of confidence and bold pronouncements, Blum went forward to the debates in Parliament not even certain whether he could count on the backing of the Communists. Although they had denounced the "financial blackmail" directed against the Popular Front, they were publicly attacking the government's plans to raise taxes in ways which, they charged, would increase the cost of living. In the Chamber, Blum had to plead for their support, which in the end they reluctantly gave him.[5]

Both Blum and Auriol singled out as the key element in the nation's economic and financial difficulties the absence of the capital vitally needed for the Treasury and the economy. They had "spared nothing" in trying to attract this capital, Blum lamented, but "a section of French capital" had gone on "strike."[6] Auriol likened the desertion of capital to desertion in wartime. "If every Frenchman had done his duty," he said, "we would not have anything to fear."[7] Opposition speakers, such as Flandin and Reynaud in the Chamber and Radicals such as Joseph Caillaux in the Senate, insisted that the migration of capital was not desertion but merely the reflection of a normal anxiety on the part of investors as a result of the government's social and economic program. They attacked the vagueness of the government's request for full powers, which, they intimated, might lead to exchange controls, expropriation, and nationalization measures; they insisted also that the right to levy new taxes could not be delegated to the executive.[8]

Making every effort to appease the opposition in the Chamber and Senate, Blum pledged that the decree powers, if granted, would not be used for a new devaluation of the franc or to impose exchange controls. He spoke with deliberate vagueness of measures that lay somewhere

[3] *Le Populaire*, June 13, 16, 1937.

[4] Press statement, *Le Populaire*, June 16, 1937.

[5] See resolution read by Duclos, *Chambre, Débats*, June 15, 1937; and *Le Populaire*, June 16, 17, 1937.

[6] *Chambre, Débats*, June 15, 1937; and *Sénat, Débats*, June 19, 1937.

[7] Auriol: press statement, *Le Populaire*, June 16, 1937; and to Senate, *Sénat, Débats*, June 19, 1937.

[8] *Chambre, Débats*, June 15, 1937; *Sénat, Débats*, June 19, 1937.

"between exchange control and absolute, total, unregulated [exchange] freedom." He agreed also to use the powers he was requesting only while Parliament was in session.[9]

In the Chamber, he overcame the objections of the opposition and received an affirmative vote of 346 to 247, a comfortable majority. The Senate, which, as he well knew, had never reconciled itself to the Popular Front social and economic program, saw its opportunity for revenge. Rejecting the government proposal despite Blum's concessions, the Senate imposed a long list of restrictions that would have severely curtailed the government's freedom of action. The Chamber, in response to Blum's appeal, promptly readopted its bill. Feeling ran high that the will of the electorate was being flouted by the upper house. A political, even a constitutional, crisis was at hand. Militant elements in the Federation of the Seine pressed Blum to call for a gigantic demonstration of popular support and to revive "the spirit of February 12."[1] In vain Blum tried to dissuade the Senate from persisting in its course. He reminded the Senators quite correctly that a year earlier, during the great sitdown strikes, they would have granted him the powers he now sought. He also warned of the need for preserving the stability of the government in the midst of grave international tension.[2] But the Senate was adamant; on the night of June 20 it readopted its bill by a vote of 198 to 82.

Blum consulted his cabinet. He could return to the Chamber a third time, seek a new vote of confidence, and bring the conflict between the two houses to a head. The Senate might yield; if it did not, he might demand its consent to a dissolution of the Chamber and the holding of new elections in the hope that the Popular Front majority would be returned triumphant. Vincent Auriol even argued that if the Senate (or the President of the Republic) refused to agree to a dissolution, the Deputies of the Popular Front majority might resign *en masse* and thereby force new elections. But no such plans materialized. The Radical ministers, deliberating separately, reported their unwillingness to prolong the crisis. They argued that to continue the conflict between the two houses would only aggravate the financial and international situation, that one could not expect to receive the Senate's consent to a dissolution, and that they would not consider

[9] *Sénat, Débats*, June 19, 1937.

[1] *Le Populaire*, June 21, 22, 1937; cf. Blum's statement at Marseilles party congress, July 1937, p. 468.

[2] Blum: *Sénat, Débats*, June 19, 20, 1937.

a more drastic step. Without the backing of his Radical associates, Blum refused to press the fight.[3] He was determined to end the crisis by resigning and to facilitate a peaceful transition to a new government. About three o'clock in the morning of June 21, 1937, Blum read to the press an official statement of his resignation and an "urgent appeal" to the supporters of the Popular Front to abide by his decision and to "preserve full calm and coolness."[4]

After 380 days of troubled existence, the Popular Front government came to an end. Privately, Blum told Ambassador Bullitt shortly after, with a gesture of weariness and disgust: "I have had enough! Everything that I have attempted to do has been blocked."[5]

The following day, June 22, at a hastily summoned national council of the party, Blum asked the party to ratify his decision and to accept participation in a new Popular Front cabinet under Radical Socialist leadership, with Camille Chautemps as Premier and himself as Vice-Premier. "We cannot refuse to participate in a Popular Front government under Radical leadership, for we must keep intact the Popular Front majority. We must safeguard the social legislation we have enacted. We must preserve the past and prepare the future." Reluctantly, the party yielded to his plea.[6]

Angry and indignant, many in the party, however, resented the fact that Blum had made no effort to arouse the country. The Left elements in the party, in particular, were infuriated with Blum for failing to appeal to the masses. Zyromski denounced the "myopia of June 20."[7] Pivert protested: "Several hundred thousand demonstrators in the Luxembourg Gardens the evening of June 19 would have helped certain stubborn Senators understand a great many things." And he charged: "That the freedom of decision of the national council was full and complete is not correct, for the prestige, pathetic appeal, and poignant anguish of Léon Blum changed the vote of numerous delegates."[8]

[3] On this cabinet meeting see Vincent Auriol's letter to *L'Express*, September 21, 1961, his further statement to Lefranc, and the discussion in Lefranc: *Histoire du Front Populaire*, pp. 250–4.

[4] *Le Populaire*, June 22, 1937.

[5] Cited by Morgenthau in *From the Morgenthau Diaries*, p. 474.

[6] For Blum's speech, discussion, and resolutions adopted, *Le Populaire*, June 23, 1937.

[7] See meeting of national council, *Le Populaire*, June 23, 1937, and Zyromski resolution, *Le Populaire*, July 1, 1937.

[8] *Le Populaire*, July 6, 1937; cf. *Le Populaire*, July 2, 1937.

The overthrow of the Popular Front government by the Senate, like the sitdown strikes of May–June 1936 and the Spanish Civil War, had again put Blum to the test. He knew that he had it within his power to unleash mass action. Why did he capitulate without a struggle and reject the possibility of fighting back by arousing the country?

Two years after the event, in June 1939, the journalist Wladimir d'Ormesson sarcastically remarked in *Le Figaro*: "It had so often been repeated that if the Senate took it upon itself to overthrow the Popular Front government, the paving stones would rise up and form barricades. I walked that day in the *banlieue*, I never saw them so peaceful." The remarks stung Blum to a reply. He conceded that the fall of his government had not led to mass demonstrations and protest. "But why? That is what M. d'Ormesson has forgotten and what others like him have undoubtedly forgotten. Because I did everything in the world so that it would be that way. If I had stood stubbornly against the Senate, if I had decided on resistance, if I had issued an appeal to the masses to support such resistance, if I had only given free rein to their instinctive reaction, perhaps M. d'Ormesson and his friends would have felt shivers running up and down their spine of the same kind as in May and June 1936."[9]

There is no doubt that Blum alone was responsible for the decision to capitulate to the Senate without a fight. He arrived at it after much soul searching. It was "a harsh ordeal," "a dramatic debate of conscience," he told the party. As usual, he understood all the arguments for the alternative course of action. He knew the latent strength of the masses and their probable reaction if they had been given a signal to act (or even if they merely had not been restrained). Morally he could have regarded his office as "a trust placed in him by the people itself, to be protected at all costs against anyone."[1] He had the legal means of pursuing the fight. "There is no doubt," he later said at Riom, "that the Chamber of Deputies, if I had asked it to, would have persevered in its vote [and provoked] a conflict between the two houses."[2] Since the constitutional power of the Senate to overthrow a ministry had never been settled with finality, he might have picked up the challenge issued years before, first by Léon Gambetta and then by Léon

---

[9] See quotation by Blum and editorial appropriately entitled "Frissons oubliés," *Le Populaire*, June 8, 1939.

[1] Statements to national council, June 22, *Le Populaire*, June 23, 1937; speech at Bordeaux, July 4, *Le Populaire*, July 5, 1937, and statements to Marseilles party congress, July 1937, pp. 451–82.

[2] Testimony at Riom trial, *Oeuvre*, V, 238.

Bourgeois, and challenged again the Senate's right to "the last word." He had the legal right to demand a dissolution of the Chamber and a new consultation of the electorate.[3]

Yet he did none of these things. He was convinced that a fight against the Senate could not have remained within political and constitutional bounds. It would have had to be a "revolutionary struggle." There was "no middle ground between yielding and fighting." Without the support of the Radicals, he would have had to turn to the uncertain backing of the Communists and the C.G.T. The Popular Front coalition of the middle classes and proletariat would have been destroyed.[4]

Finally, the political crisis coincided with the *Leipzig* episode. "The curve of internal tension ran parallel to the curve of international events," Blum noted. This, he claimed, was the overriding reason for his unwillingness to prolong the cabinet crisis. In so volatile a situation he refused to plunge France into a "long political conflict perhaps prolonged by a social conflict."[5] Once he had convinced himself that it would have been impossible to resist the Senate in a legal and constitutional way and make use of moderate mass pressure, once he saw the break-up of the Popular Front coalition which he believed essential for the defense of republican institutions, once he saw resistance turning into internal conflict and even civil war at a time of grave foreign danger, his capitulation inevitably followed.

It is difficult to escape the conclusion that his reasoning was the product of compartmentalized thinking: "resist or yield," resign or wage a revolutionary struggle. It could be argued that he owed it to the very republic that he cherished to have displayed greater firmness against the Senate's determination to thwart a government which had so recently issued from the will of the electorate. He might have displayed a greater flexibility, greater political maneuverability, and less timidity about the consequences of a political fight. Lloyd George tamed the House of Lords, and Franklin D. Roosevelt tangled with the Supreme Court, without bringing on a revolution. He himself later referred to Lloyd George's example—but after the event.[6]

[3] Even though the required consent of the President of the Republic and of the Senate would have been difficult to obtain, the effort might have been made. On the conflict see Lindsay Rogers: "M. Blum and the French Senate," *Political Science Quarterly*, LII (1937), 321–39; and Georges Dupeux: "L'Échec du premier gouvernement Léon Blum," *Revue d'histoire moderne et contemporaine*, X (1963), 35–44.

[4] Speech at Marseilles party congress, July 1937, pp. 465–72.

[5] Speech at Bordeaux, July 4, *Le Populaire*, July 5, 1937.

[6] Marseilles party congress, July 1937, p. 477.

Of course, a more extreme step, an appeal to the masses, as demanded by Zyromski and Pivert, was also possible. But to Blum "the spirit of February 12" meant an appeal to the masses to *defend* republican legality against subversion; the mass action that the Left Socialists sought would have been *against* legality; the difference, as he himself said, was "capital."[7] Here lay the key to Blum's attitude toward mass action—acceptable if it were in defense of republican institutions, intolerable if it were revolutionary or quasi-revolutionary and a threat to civil peace or the nation's security. Pierre Cot later suggested that the government might have declared "the republic in danger," ignored the Senate, and formed a crisis government. "To govern more boldly we would have had to imitate not Roosevelt but Robespierre," he said, but he conceded that this was a retrospective judgment.[8] As for Blum, such a course would have opened him to the charge of having assumed extra-legal powers; it would have defaced the portrait of a man who was determined to demonstrate that the Socialists could exercise power within the legal and constitutional framework of the republic. He was determined to leave office as he had entered it, legally and constitutionally. Words that he had written many years earlier were now put to the test. "For a Socialist party the way in which it quits office is more important than the way in which it occupies it."[9]

After the capitulation, Blum told the party: "The most difficult thing is not to fulfill one's duty, but to know what it is. The statement is true of parties as well as of individuals." In the interests of the country and of peace, he and the party had performed "an act of political abnegation."[1] No fair-minded person would pretend that the dilemma of June 1937 was a simple one, yet among the phrases culled from the memoirs of Cardinal Retz which Blum liked to read and quote on occasion was an allusion to "that heroic judgment that knows how to distinguish the extraordinary from the impossible." The crisis of June 1937 might have been the occasion for such "heroic judgment."[2]

---

[7] Ibid., p. 468.

[8] Cot: *Le Procès de la république*, I, 172–3.

[9] *Le Populaire*, May 25, 1930.

[1] Speech at Bordeaux, July 4, *Le Populaire*, July 5, 1937.

[2] For Blum's citation of Retz, *Mémoires*, 1940, *Oeuvre*, V, 38–9. Cf. the much harsher verdict of Audry, who criticizes him for not mobilizing the masses, *Léon Blum*, p. 151.

The Blum experiment was over—if one can call a political experience that lasted less than thirteen months an "experiment." Within the party, criticisms which had mounted during the Popular Front's year in office were sharply voiced at the annual congresses held in July 1937 and June 1938. Although the delegates paid tribute to the accomplishments of the government, they did not spare its shortcomings —the failure to curb the power of the banks and financial trusts, the failure to protect wages against rising living costs, the unhappy non-intervention policy in Spain, the capitulation to the Senate. The deep disquiet was expressed by one speaker: "Our faith," he said, ". . . derived, above all, from the fact that we believed that the party was not a party like all the others, that its leader was not a man like all the others . . ." They had not anticipated that the Popular Front government would fall from office—and accept its fall—in the traditional pattern.[3]

Blum was sensitive to the profound dissatisfaction within the party. He characterized the meeting of July 1937 as "one of the most difficult and in many respects most painful moments in its whole history." For himself, he confessed that he believed at times that he was living on credit within the party, "drawing checks" on the confidence he had stored up by his long years of service. He portrayed his own disappointment: "Something to which we were attached with every fiber of our body has just broken. There floats over this congress the sadness not of failure or humiliation, but of seeing interrupted something to which we were attached with all our being."[4]

Yet he refused to admit to failure or defeat. He catalogued the reforms ushered in by his government, whose vast scope, he asserted, was conceded by everyone. "We have brought to the country a profound transformation in the life of the nation . . . A change has been made in the human condition, in the material and spiritual condition of the working class and the rural masses. There has been a transformation of social relations . . . Life has taken on a new look . . . a new meaning."[5] That the "revolutionary" changes were not immediately perceptible was understandable, he pointed out at the 1938 congress of the party. "Every revolutionary change . . . is followed by a period,

[3] Pierre Brosollette: Marseilles party congress, July 1937, p. 327.
[4] Ibid., pp. 451, 452, 480.
[5] Ibid., pp. 456–7; cf. his statement and resolution at Royan party congress, June 1938, pp. 493 and 577.

short or long, of flux and reflux whose direction cannot always be discerned exactly, any more than when approaching the seashore one can discern at first sight whether the tide is rising or receding."[6]

To those who in June 1937, as in June 1936, had advocated mass revolutionary action, he recalled the party's obligations to the political coalition of which it was a part and the legal and constitutional conditions under which it had taken office. Behind the sense of frustration that more radical steps had not been taken in these crises, he found "the eternal, formidable, fatal confusion between the exercise of power and the revolutionary conquest of power." Of their "exercise of power," he reminded them: "We wanted it to be a government . . . not exactly like all the others but all the same a legal and constitutional one." Their primary duty, he insisted, was to remain faithful to the commitments they had accepted, to carry out the common program of all the parties of the coalition, and to govern within the framework of the existing legal and economic order. "Those," said Blum, throwing back the challenge to his critics, "were the rules of the game! (*C'était cela, la règle du jeu!*)"[7] To those who believed that they ought to have broken their pledges and acted otherwise, he said simply: "It is a question of revolutionary morality that separates us."[8] The brief words, spoken in the heat of debate, formed the heart of his political ethos.

Above all, Blum had demonstrated that the country was safe in Socialist hands. His deepest pride was that the party had not violated the trust that had been placed in it. He told the 1937 congress: "[The country] has come to understand that it could place its destiny in our hands without fear . . . It no longer fears us; it trusts us."[9] He had fulfilled his personal mission.

Blum never forgot a conversation he had had with Ramsay MacDonald in 1924, when the then British Socialist formed his first Labour coalition government. MacDonald had told Blum that regardless of what was accomplished he was determined to break down existing prejudices and demonstrate that Labour could form a government like any other party "without the earth opening up or the sky falling."[1]

[6] Royan party congress, June 1938, pp. 493–4.

[7] Marseilles party congress, July 1937, pp. 455, 463–7.

[8] Royan congress, June 1938, p. 132.

[9] Marseilles congress, July 1937, p. 482.

[1] See Blum's speech to the Federation of the Seine, *Le Populaire*, June 7, 1937; and cf. his lecture in later years, "Exercice et conquête du pouvoir," May 30, 1947, *Oeuvre*, VI, 431–2.

Blum was determined in his way to do the same thing. He was fulfilling also the ambition of Jean Jaurès, who over a quarter of a century earlier had been prevented, in the aftermath of the Millerand affair, from demonstrating his statesmanship and the republican loyalty of his party.[2] It was not until 1936–7 that the Socialists finally underwent the test of office, and they passed it; a decade later Blum's Socialist Minister of Finance would be President of the Fourth Republic.

Blum was satisfied, too, that his government had "watched over the preservation of peace" and had tightened the bonds of friendship with the democracies. It was worth the "days without respite and the nights without sleep" to hear a speaker at the congress praise his "heroic pacifism" and to hear the cheer *"Blum la paix!"*[3] To be identified with the preservation of peace was a supreme accolade despite his torment over the course of events in Spain.

Blum, who had to face the criticism of reactionaries that his government had stirred up class antagonisms and sown disunity in the country, had to face the criticisms of the Left that he had worked toward class collaboration, patriotism, and a new kind of *"union sacrée."* "I have never seen so many tricolor flags at a party congress," sneered one critic.[4] The criticisms of the Left were more valid than those of the Right. Although he had worked for social reform and for the rights of labor, he had also worked for social peace, to create a sense of national unity within the country, to bridge the gap between the classes. Victor Hugo's phrase *"O patrie, o concorde entre les citoyens"* was often on his lips—and in his heart. Quixotic though it may have been for a Socialist leader to hope to achieve this sense of national unity, it nonetheless dominated his thoughts and his deeds.

All these pressures, operating both consciously and subconsciously— the need to respect scrupulously the conditions of "exercising power" within the existing economic and legal framework, to keep faith with the Popular Front program and with his middle-class Radical allies, to retain the closest ties with the democratic countries for the preservation of peace, to work for national unity in the face of foreign danger, to demonstrate that the country would be safe under its first Socialist (and first Jewish) Premier—all these pressures limited Blum's freedom of action. Given also his temperament, his character, and his legalistic and political scruples, they made it impossible for him to apply the

---

[2] For Blum's statement on Jaurès, *Le Populaire*, August 1, 1937.

[3] Marseilles congress, July 1937, pp. 399, 454, 455.

[4] Pivert: Marseilles congress, July 1937, p. 437.

bolder measures that were required, to take the risks that were necessary, and to exercise the political flexibility that the exigencies of economic life and international affairs demanded. His sense of political morality made him the prisoner and not the master of the coalition which he headed. The Popular Front experiment was limited by its program, by circumstances, and by the personality of the man who presided over it.

For everyone today would agree that the Popular Front's year in office, the Blum experiment, was only a qualified success. Labor won important gains. The pattern of industrial relations was changed by the collective bargaining legislation and by the consequent growth in the strength of the trade unions. The notion of a "living wage" took permanent hold. The first steps toward the nationalization of the armaments industry were taken. The agricultural program benefited farmers and consumers. Yet no significant economic recovery took place, unemployment was not absorbed, inflation canceled out labor's wage increases. The forty-hour week, because of the mutual suspicions of labor and industry, was administered so inflexibly as to interfere with production and economic recovery. The promised public works program was postponed indefinitely. Little was accomplished to democratize the higher administrative echelons. The fascist-type organizations remained a lurking source of danger. A government minister could be hounded to suicide by the calumny of the reactionary press. The nonintervention policy in Spain turned into a fiasco. No attempt was made to transform the credit structure of the country or to breathe a new spirit into the economy that would foster economic growth and production. In the end, budgetary, currency, and Treasury difficulties, inherited from previous administrations but aggravated by the hostility of financial circles to the Popular Front, overwhelmed the government and brought it down. And it went down without a fight. Frustration and disillusionment followed the buoyant days of June 1936.

When Blum stressed the burden imposed on the economy by the rapidity with which the social reforms had to be introduced, or the strain on the Treasury of rearmament expenditures or the failure of capital to return to circulation, he only partially explained the shortcomings of the experiment.[5] Some of his associates were more forthright. The experiment had demonstrated, according to Jules Moch, "the difficulty or even the impossibility of trying to make coexist a bold

[5] See, e.g., his interview with the *Daily Herald*, published also in *Le Populaire*, June 4, 1937.

[280]

social policy and a classical financial and economic policy."[6] The experiment had demonstrated, said André Philip, the impossibility of raising purchasing power and improving the lot of the working class through "reforms of distribution" "except within very narrow limits" and with only "ephemeral" results. The attempt to woo the confidence of capital as an alternative to more stringent financial controls was also doomed in advance. "We ought to have known that we could never obtain the confidence of capital and that if a 'pause' was necessary it was for others to undertake and not for us."[7] Blum's Minister of National Production, Charles Spinasse, emphasized the difficulties under which they had operated. He did not conceal the harm done by the rigid application of the "five-day factory week" and he admitted the difficulty of applying uniform social reforms to a widely diversified economic structure, which varied from "the most highly developed, best equipped, best mechanized industries" to "industries organized and equipped as they were in the Middle Ages or in the seventeenth century." Given the economic problems and the "profound illness of the public economy," the limitations imposed on the experiment were impossible to overcome. The only alternative was to persuade government, industry, and labor to recognize the need for a vast program of modernization of the French economy with a large measure of government assistance, financial and technical, and a thorough revamping of the country's "superannuated credit system."[8] André Philip summed up the attitude of the disheartened majority: "The lesson that must be drawn from the events is not the weakness or errors of such and such a man, of such and such an organization, it is the weaknesses or errors that were inscribed in the inadequacies of the Popular Front program itself." The solution on which there was wide agreement was to work for a program of "structural reforms," especially in credit and banking, and including the nationalization of key industries.[9] That program would have to await another day.

Blum was less willing than his associates to concede the shortcomings of the experiment. Not only did he maintain that the country had been launched on the road to recovery but he insisted that this progress had been accomplished as planned—"by the exact means that we had anticipated, that is, by increasing purchasing power"; and he denied

---

[6] Royan congress, June 1938, pp. 309–12.
[7] Marseilles congress, July 1937, pp. 369–75.
[8] Royan congress, June 1938, pp. 430–1.
[9] Marseilles congress, July 1937, p. 372.

that price rises had nullified the increase in purchasing power. Here he refused to face the evidence that by the end of his government price rises had virtually canceled out for many groups the wage increases won during the year and that labor's real income was not substantially higher than in the worst period of the depression. He admitted only that the expected improvement in public finances had not followed economic recovery as rapidly as had been hoped; at this point their adversaries had moved in and cut the experiment short.[1] In that he was correct; time itself had been an enemy of the experiment.

Although he accepted the need to press for the extension of the original economic and financial reforms called for in the Popular Front program, he stubbornly opposed what he called "the arbitrary distinction between reforms of distribution and reforms of structure." Insisting that the nationalization of the great monopolies had an importance "more political than economic"—that is, that they involved more the "sovereignty of the democratic state than the transformation of the social order,"—he refused to accede to the demands of some members of the party that he press for extensive nationalization.[2] Persistent in thinking only in the categories of capitalism and socialism, he could not readily envisage a mixed economy with extensive nationalization. Blum was correct in believing that nationalization in itself could not expand production or equalize distribution of the national income, but by his own emphasis on "reforms of distribution" he failed to perceive that only some kind of broad program of industrial renovation could have inspired true economic recovery and expansion.

Twenty years later a Socialist writer scored the Popular Front government for its failure to recognize the extent to which French industry lagged behind the times. "Insufficiently aware of this defect, one overestimated in 1936 the ability of the national economy to increase its productive output and to compensate for the additional burden that was added to costs by the raising of wages and by the forty-hour week." Of Blum he wrote: "Believing, like all his contemporaries, that the French economic machine was healthy, that France's production had simply slowed down because of the unsatisfactory and unjust distribu-

[1] Ibid., p. 457, and see also his speech to the Federation of the Seine, April 9, 1937, *Le Populaire*, April 14, 1937. For observations on economic recovery, wage gains, etc., under the Popular Front, see especially the studies, listed in the Bibliography, by Albertini, Caunes, Ehrmann, Mossé, Sauvy and Depoid, and Théry, and the relevant tables in *Mouvement économique en France de 1929 à 1939*.

[2] Marseilles congress, July 1937, p. 479.

tion of income, he thought that a better distribution . . . would revive production at the same time that it would satisfy justice."[3]

Blum himself, in his wartime essay, scathingly indicted the failure of the bourgeoisie to modernize the productive apparatus of the country. It had displayed "no reserves of energy, no imaginative resources, no capacity for renovation and reconstruction in order to overcome the economic depression." He spoke of "the shabbiness of the installations, the inadequacy or ancient quality of its equipment. . . . On every plane of productive activity—industry, agriculture, commerce, banking—it dragged along in its routine traditions. . . . Denying all its classical principles, it knew how to do nothing but implore as a suppliant the aid of the state; whenever that aid was not forthcoming it dropped its arms to its sides in despair without even attempting an effort."[4] The indictment was justified, yet it underscored the failure of his own government to recognize these inadequacies and launch a determined assault upon them.

In a way Blum's attitude toward his experiment did not help. He insisted that the limitations of the experiment were known in advance. "As well as anyone," he said in 1938, "I knew the limitations within the framework of society as it is." The mission that he accepted contained, he said, "nothing unknown or unanticipated by its leaders."[5] The mission had fallen to them because of the despair growing out of the depression and because of the attacks upon the republic; it was a defensive mission. "If I dare say so," he wrote, "they (the Socialists) sacrificed themselves in order to preserve the country from a bloody crisis."[6]

Most important, they had accepted the mission without possessing full control of the apparatus of government. They had to contend with such hostile institutions as the Senate and the permanent bureaucracy (whether in the Finance Ministry or on the Quai d'Orsay), the Bank of France, and the General Staff. The "exercise of power" was "a kind of political falsehood (*une sorte de mensonge politique*)," he wrote.[7] The exercise of power had been the exercise of responsibility without power. Not least, he had had to depend every step of the way on the

[3] Weill-Raynal: "Les Obstacles économiques à l'expérience Blum," *La Revue Socialiste*, June 1956, p. 54. Cf. Sauvy's similar remarks in *L'Express*, April 7, 28, 1960; and Reynaud: *Mémoires*, II, 483.

[4] *À l'échelle humaine, Oeuvre*, V, 440–1.

[5] Royan congress, June 1938, p. 232; *À l'échelle humaine, Oeuvre*, V, 474.

[6] *À l'échelle humaine*, ibid., p. 474.

[7] Ibid., pp. 474 and 439.

good will of the Radicals and the Communists for the preservation of his Left majority.

Yet in some ways Blum was the captive of his own formulas. Having accepted the "exercise of power within the framework of capitalism," he could not press for bolder measures that his opponents or his middle-class allies might have labeled "socialist." From the beginning he had spoken of the possibility of failure, of learning whether it was "possible" to amend present society from within. Had he not told his party: "If I fail, I shall be the first to come and tell you"?[8] And two weeks before the fall of his government he said: "If we were to fail, we would then be obliged to ask ourselves . . . if there is not a more profound defect, a congenital defect—if what we thought possible was not possible."[9] Blum's habit of thinking in the rigid categories of capitalism and socialism made it impossible for him to do what the less doctrinaire Roosevelt could—that is, introduce such extensive government controls over capitalism that a virtual transformation of the old system might have resulted. On the other hand, the country possessed neither the elastic credit facilities of the United States, nor its self-sufficiency in natural resources, nor its technology. Nor did its industrial classes display a resiliency that might have made possible the absorption of great labor reforms. The French New Deal was tried under circumstances vastly different from the American. And an American President had four years—at least—in which to try out his program.

Everyone recalled Blum's statement, before becoming Premier, that because he was taking office "a new man" had to emerge in him. Did he possess the qualities of leadership? he had wondered. In June 1938 he confessed to his party: "I asked in June 1936: am I a leader? I did not know the answer and, to tell the truth, I do not know the answer any better today. But, perhaps, if I committed errors it was because of not having been enough of a leader and not because of having been too much of one."[1] Neither to his party nor to the country at large did he present the image of the strong leader, but only that of the humble servant, the conciliator of differences. Humility was a noble quality, but his party and his country needed strength.

He admitted that he had made mistakes, but he was not ashamed

[8] Speech, May 31, 1936, *Oeuvre*, IV, pt. 1, 263.
[9] Speech to Federation of the Seine, June 6, 1937, *Le Populaire*, June 7, 1937.
[1] Royan congress, June 1938, p. 133.

of them.[2] "It is a great weakness to be human: ruthless indifference to human life is a great source of power," he said in 1938.[3] A sense of humanity, like humility, was becoming rare in the management of public affairs in many countries in the 1930's. Blum was obsessed with such qualities. Although they were his strength, they were also his weakness. He once wrote that the great political virtues were "boldness, generosity of heart, rectitude of conscience and mind, sacrifice of the individual person to the collective welfare."[4] Of those he possessed all—save the boldness.

Yet it is not Blum's courage that is in question. What Blum himself said in later years of the failure of Lamartine and the men of 1848 could be said of him: They had refused to be identified with the idea of revolution for "fear of spreading fear, of frightening some sector of French society, of frightening Europe." They forbade themselves "any step that could be held as a usurpation." The result had been failure. The year 1848, he noted, was remembered not for its accomplishments, but for its promise—"the immense hope that it raised."[5] That conclusion could serve as an epitaph for his own Popular Front government.

[2] *À l'échelle humaine*, *Oeuvre*, V, 424; and cf. his remarks at Royan congress, June 1938, p. 500.

[3] Royan congress, June 1938, p. 498.

[4] *À l'échelle humaine*, *Oeuvre*, V, 489.

[5] Blum: speech on the centennial of the Revolution of 1848, February 24, 1948, *Oeuvre*, VII, 427, 430; see also his earlier editorial, *Le Populaire*, February 24, 1935.

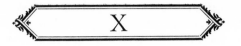

X

DECLINE OF THE POPULAR FRONT, JUNE 1937–APRIL 1938:
Vice-Premier, "National Unity," Second Government

*I loyally defended in my party, and even
at mass meetings, this program of which
I did not approve.*[1]

I N JUNE 1937, Camille Chautemps succeeded Blum as Premier. The Radical leader formed a new Popular Front coalition cabinet, in which the Socialists participated and Blum served as Vice-Premier. The "instinctive reaction" of the party, as Blum admitted, had been to reject participation, and only his plea to save the Popular Front coalition had persuaded the party to give its reluctant consent. Although the ministerial posts were almost equally divided between Radicals and Socialists, the orientation of the new government was very different from that of the Blum cabinet. The presence of such Radicals as Georges Bonnet as Minister of Finance and Henri Queuille as Minister of Public Works, both known for their hostility to the Popular Front, seemed to some Socialists a studied insult.[2] On the other hand, Blum was second in command, many Socialists, such as Minister of the Interior Marx Dormoy, continued in their old posts, and Chautemps himself pledged fidelity to the Popular Front program.

At the very outset the clash with the Senate was renewed when the upper house voted to censure Jean Lebas, Blum's former Minister of

[1] Blum, of his Vice-Premiership in the Chautemps cabinet: testimony at Riom trial, *Oeuvre*, V, 239.

[2] Discussion and resolutions, party national council, *Le Populaire*, June 23, 1937.

Labor, for a speech in which Lebas had demanded a curtailment of the Senate's powers. It further voted to print and post throughout the country the speech of Abel Gardey, reporter for its Finance Committee, attacking the financial policies of the Blum government. In pique, Blum refused to read the cabinet's ministerial declaration to the Senate as he would ordinarily have done as Vice-Premier, and the Socialist ministers were on the point of resigning. Chautemps intervened to smooth things over, describing to the hostile Senators his experiences in the Blum government: "Every time a serious question arose, such as the war in Spain or the labor troubles, I found in Léon Blum a clearsightedness and a sense of national duty to which I must pay homage."[3] Blum had well earned the tribute from the Radical Socialist leader; it filled him with satisfaction even though some Socialists believed that there were more important things than praise from a Radical politician.

Very quickly Chautemps and Bonnet were able to obtain from the Chamber and Senate the urgently needed grant of emergency financial powers which Blum and Auriol had been denied.[4] In a series of decrees, the government devalued the franc once again, establishing a "floating franc," its value to be controlled by the Stabilization Fund. To raise additional revenue the government increased taxes and announced a drastic reduction in expenditures for the coming year. Further devaluation, increased taxation, and retrenchment symbolized everything that the Popular Front had said it opposed. More than Blum's "pause," it was a retreat to the retrenchment program of Flandin and Laval, and a repudiation of Blum's purchasing power policy. As a concession to the Left, a plan for the immediate nationalization of the country's ailing railroad system was announced and soon put into effect. Ironically, the most important nationalization measure of the Popular Front years was adopted not under Blum but under the Chautemps government.

Three weeks after the formation of the new cabinet, at the Marseilles Socialist party congress in July 1937, of which we have already spoken, Blum and Auriol defended the financial measures of the new government as dictated by economic circumstances. They praised the steps taken against fraud and speculation, as well as the nationalization of the railroads. Blum was willing to admit only that the fiscal program

[3] *Sénat, Débats*, June 30, 1937. For the events, *Sénat, Débats*, June 29, 30, 1937; and *Le Populaire*, June 30, July 1, 3, 1937.
[4] There is much useful material on the two Chautemps governments in Bonnet's memoirs: *Défense de la paix*, I, 29–85. Bonnet was Minister of Finance in the two governments.

was "somewhat heavy for a convalescent economy."[5] The Left wing of the party, in contrast, was highly critical. Zyromski confessed himself "stupefied" to see the Bonnet decrees defended before the congress, and denounced the Chautemps cabinet as "an ersatz Popular Front government."[6] But on the whole, the delegates were willing to make sacrifices to preserve the Popular Front. As one delegate remarked: "Zyromski said we were in a tunnel. Better that than to go off the rails!"[7]

The congress adjourned as it had opened, with profound feelings of disappointment over the fall of the Blum government and uncertainty about the Chautemps government and the future in general. Little remained of the Popular Front *élan*. The Popular Front procession of July 14 a few days later was described by Alexander Werth as "a sad spectacle. The enthusiasm and vigor of 1935 and 1936 were gone."[8] The Communists, meanwhile, concentrated their attack on "the evil policy of non-intervention" and denounced Blum as its "initiator." In November, the unity negotiations that had been going on sporadically for some time between the two parties were suspended.

In the seven months of the Chautemps government, which lasted from June 1937 to January 1938, Blum consistently defended its policies before the party and before the country as a whole. He told a Socialist national council in November 1937 that the presence of the Socialist ministers in the cabinet was a guarantee that the Popular Front social reforms, such as the forty-hour week, would not be touched; moreover, they were able to press for such new reforms as the "modern statute of labor," a code of labor relations being prepared in cooperation with the C.G.T. and the C.G.P.F.—a "new Matignon agreement." His travels through the country had convinced him, he claimed, that the Popular Front "had not lost its vivacity or its strength."[9]

Yet these brave words could scarcely conceal Blum's chagrin. He and the other Socialists were a minority in a coalition cabinet, powerless to exercise initiative in policy making and compelled to support unsatisfactory policies over which they had no control. In later years Blum admitted the extent to which this had been the situation. One of

[5] Speech to Marseilles party congress, July 1937, pp. 471–80; Auriol: ibid., p. 274, and Auriol: *Hier . . . demain*, I, 42.

[6] Marseilles party congress, July 1937, pp. 338–9.

[7] Ibid., p. 402.

[8] *France and Munich* (London, 1939), p. 109.

[9] Speech to party national council, *Le Populaire*, November 8, 1937.

the examining magistrates accusingly said to him in the pre-trial questioning at Riom in 1941: "When a man like you is in the government everyone knows that he is the true chief!" Blum replied indignantly:

> It was not the case at all. M. Chautemps was very much the chief of the government over which he presided. During that whole period, because of the delicate relations involved, I made every effort to efface myself and to keep my attitude to myself as far as that was possible.
>
> M. Chautemps and M. Georges Bonnet, his Finance Minister, undertook from the beginning an economic and political program contrary to that which I had practiced and which alarmed me. I had myself at one point, in March, proclaimed the need for a "pause." But the "pause" was not a reversal. I feared the effect of a return to the policy of budget balancing and increased taxation on an economic expansion which was already beginning to manifest itself in a very substantial way. But I loyally defended in my party, and even at mass meetings, this program of which I did not approve.[1]

The old warnings against Socialist participation in a cabinet directed by another party had come home to roost. Blum was convinced that the party had no alternative if it wished to save the Popular Front, protect the labor reforms of 1936, defend republican institutions, and help build a strong foreign policy against the dictators. The stakes were too high to risk a break with the Radicals.

Although the international scene was relatively quiet in the latter half of 1937, internal developments reinforced the anxiety in Popular Front circles over the continuing threat from the extreme Right. Bomb explosions in the Étoile area in September were traced to two new fascist-type organizations, the Cagoulards, or "hooded men," and the C.S.A.R. (*Comité Secret d'Action Révolutionnaire*). Dormoy launched a sweeping investigation into their activities and intimated that their connections with men in high places would be revealed.[2] (His energetic efforts would cost him his life four years later in the Vichy era.) In addition, Colonel de la Rocque's Croix de Feu, although dissolved by decree, continued to grow as a respectable political "party." The

---

[1] *Oeuvre*, V, 239.

[2] *Le Populaire*, September 11, 1937; and statement by Dormoy: *Le Populaire*, January 11, 1938. On the involvement of some high-ranking army officers, see Gamelin: *Servir*, II, 303–4.

threat that had evoked the spirit of February 12, 1934, had not disappeared; the republic still had to be defended.

In the autumn and winter of 1937, the Chautemps government faced renewed labor unrest and a new rash of sitdown strikes—a sitdown strike at the Goodrich tire plant at Colombes, a truck drivers' strike, and, at the very end of the year, a twenty-four-hour work stoppage by the bus drivers and *métro* workers in Paris. Chautemps's efforts at arbitration were unsuccessful. He and Bonnet were convinced that the strikes were politically inspired, directed principally against the non-intervention policy in Spain.[3] In January 1938, the discussions between the C.G.T. and the C.G.P.F. on the code of labor relations were abruptly terminated. The employers' association broke off negotiations and announced that the government would have to bring about the enactment of the labor measures on its own. Among its reasons it specified the failure of the government to protect employers' rights adequately in the recent strikes.[4] To cap the situation, a new financial crisis developed with a renewed flight of gold and a weakening of the franc.

When Chautemps claimed that labor agitation was responsible for the financial unrest and was less critical of the employers who had just wrecked the industrial relations conference, Blum and the Socialists were annoyed. Yet they still tried to prevent a cabinet crisis. What finally precipitated the fall of the government was Chautemps's open break with the Communists in the Chamber on January 14. In response to Communist criticism and Fernand Ramette's statement that his party would abstain in a vote of confidence, Chautemps petulantly informed the Communists that he did not desire their votes and implied he could get the support of other groups in the Chamber. His statement embarrassed Blum and the Socialists, for it meant excluding the Communists from the Popular Front parliamentary coalition and indeed destroying the coalition. Even though Blum regretted the actions of both the Communists and Chautemps, he and his colleagues saw no alternative but to resign from the cabinet.[5] The cabinet fell in the early hours of January 15.

[3] Bonnet: *Défense de la paix*, II, 40.

[4] For the breakdown of these negotiations, Colton: *Compulsory Labor Arbitration*, pp. 58–9.

[5] Statement by Blum to party national council, *Le Populaire*, January 18, 1938, and letter of resignation, *Le Populaire*, January 14, 1938.

When President Lebrun asked Georges Bonnet to form a cabinet, the Radical leader talked at length with Blum, who told him: "I do not believe that our party will accept participation in any cabinet from now on, no matter who directs it. The general opinion of the party is that if we assume governmental responsibilities it can only be by directing the government ourselves."[6] After the disillusioning experience of serving under Chautemps, Blum was returning to his older formulation of the "exercise of power."

On the third day of the crisis, after Bonnet and others had failed, President Lebrun called upon Blum to try to form a cabinet. To end the crisis, Blum now proposed, not a cabinet based on the Popular Front parties alone, but one more broadly representative of the country as a whole— "a national unity combination rallied around the Popular Front (*rassemblement national autour du Front Populaire*)"—"from Thorez to Reynaud." The cabinet would range from the Communists on the Left to non-Popular-Front political leaders in the Center, that is, men who, like Paul Reynaud, opposed the Popular Front social and economic program but were known for their devotion to democratic liberties and for their strong stand on foreign affairs. He had in mind "a kind of political Matignon agreement." A national unity government, he sought to demonstrate, need not be oriented to the Right, as had always been the case in the past.[7]

The effort came to naught. The Radicals were unwilling to accept the Communists in the cabinet. Of the Center leaders, Reynaud insisted that to balance the presence of the Communists the cabinet would have to include conservatives farther to the Right as well. On January 18, Blum abandoned the attempt. To his annoyance the Communists implied that he had given up too easily. The government crisis was resolved when Chautemps succeeded himself, forming an all-Radical cabinet with a narrow and uncertain political base. The Socialists reluctantly agreed to back the cabinet without participating in it. The Communists were hostile.[8]

In the midst of this political turmoil Blum was beset with personal troubles. His wife Thérèse had undergone surgery in December; on January 19, she underwent a second operation and three days later she died. It was a cruel blow to Blum; Lise had died in 1931, and now, in

[6] Bonnet: *Défense de la paix*, I, 71.

[7] See his statements, *Le Populaire*, January 16, 18, 1938.

[8] See press accounts and Blum's speech to national council, *Le Populaire*, January 18, 1938; also his later references in speech of March 12, 1938, described below, and in testimony at Riom trial, *Oeuvre*, V, 241.

1938, his second wife was gone. Thérèse, a militant Socialist on her own, had been more politically active than Lise. Always at his side, accompanying him to public meetings and on his travels, she had given him sympathy and encouragement of every kind. For over a month Blum withdrew from all political activity and remained away from Paris.

He returned late in February. For the first time in over twenty months he was no longer in the cabinet and could resume his post as political director of *Le Populaire*. In one of his first editorials, he turned to the Moscow trials of the former Bolshevik leaders accused of treason and complicity with fascism. Expressing his distress at the trials when the need for unity on the international scene was more pressing than ever, he also confessed that he was confused by the evidence: "We can believe only what we can understand."[9]

Scarcely two weeks had elapsed since Blum's return to Paris when a new ministerial crisis broke. The second great opportunity to form a national unity cabinet presented itself, this time under such serious international circumstances, the *Anschluss*, that it did not seem possible that it could fail.

Again the question of finances precipitated the new cabinet crisis. The Chautemps government, contemplating a defense loan, had sought a renewed grant of full powers to cope with the situation. Although the Socialists did not explicitly oppose the plenary powers, they expressed anxiety over the projected financial program. Suddenly, on March 10, Chautemps announced his resignation without even waiting for a vote of confidence. To be sure, the Radical leader knew the narrow limits of his political support, but there may have been another factor. At that very moment trouble was brewing in Austria. Nazi agitation had been stepped up when Chancellor Schuschnigg showed his determination to hold a plebiscite which Hitler had forbidden. On March 11, when German troops crossed the Austrian border, and on March 12, when Hitler rode into Vienna, the French Republic was without a government. In later years Blum remained one of the few who charitably insisted that Chautemps did not resign because he suspected that something serious was about to happen in Austria.[1]

Immediately after Chautemps's resignation, and before the actual

[9] *Le Populaire*, March 8, 1938.
[1] Testimony, 1947, *Événements*, I, 252; see Bonnet *Défense de la paix*, I, 64.

invasion of Austria, President Lebrun had turned to Blum. Because Lebrun had shown no such haste in January, Blum suspected that his true intention was to see him fail quickly so that the Socialists would be removed from the political scene and the way prepared for a Right-oriented "national union" cabinet despite the Left majority in the Chamber. Nonetheless, Blum ignored this possibility and made an effort to form a government.[2] In the midst of his negotiations came word of Hitler's move into Austria. At once Blum announced that the Socialists would form a government "appropriate to the circumstances." He planned now to renew the effort he had made in January, convincing himself that this time he could rally all parties to a national unity government. He now envisaged a cabinet extending from the Communists on the Left to diehard conservatives and nationalists on the Right—"from Thorez to Louis Marin," a "combination of all republicans in the country rallied around the Popular Front (*rassemblement du pays républicain autour du Front Populaire*)."[3]

Since he expected to invite the parties of the Right into the cabinet, making it more than just an "enlarged Popular Front," he first had to obtain the consent of his party. Paul Faure and other party leaders informed him that he could not hope to win a majority in the national council for so extreme a step and tried to dissuade him from convening one. Despite their misgivings, Blum persisted and the delegates were summoned by telegram.[4]

March 12 was a day of feverish activity. In the morning, Blum went before the delegates of the national council and made an impassioned plea for support in his unprecedented enterprise. He emphasized that they now had an opportunity to form a cabinet of national unity that for the first time in history would be created under the auspices of the Left, not by parties of the Right. This was no "sacred union" as in 1914, which was formed for the purpose of waging war, but "a 'sacred union' to save the peace and defend the democratic institutions of the country." Zyromski, following the Communist line in favor of a strong foreign policy and national unity against aggression, supported the plan. Pivert and his group fought it, insisting that revolutionary Socialists must have nothing to do with national defense in a capitalist system. With very little debate, and by a vote of 6,575

[2] Statement to party national council, *Le Populaire*, April 10, 1938; and cf. *Mémoires, Oeuvre*, V, 125.

[3] *Le Populaire*, March 13, 15, 1938.

[4] Blum: statement to national council, *Le Populaire*, March 13, 1938; to Royan party congress, June 1938, p. 516; and in *Le Populaire*, July 9, 1938.

to 1,684, Blum received the party's authorization.[5] His confidence that he would win the support of the party for his endeavor was vindicated.

At twelve-thirty that afternoon, Blum announced his party's decision over the radio. The Radicals, the Communists, and the C.G.T. also agreed to back him. To his dismay, however, the parties of the Center and the Right opposed participation in the proposed cabinet. Undaunted, he insisted on consulting with the presidents of the Center and Right parties; some, like Louis Marin, he found sympathetic. In an unprecedented move, Blum prevailed upon them to convene a meeting of the Deputies of their parties, convinced that he could overcome all their objections in the light of the circumstances in which the country found itself. He let it be known that he would make many concessions; the opposition parties could, for example, name the Finance Minister.[6] Blum did not anticipate, however, a "memorandum" of specific questions on domestic and foreign policy which was submitted to him in advance of the meeting. Many of the questions were deliberately designed to cause him embarrassment and difficulty; others could not be answered explicitly without binding the hands of a future government. The list of queries formed a catalogue of all the problems facing the country. What would be the policy with respect to the annexation of Austria? Will the pledge of the non-intervention policy be maintained? Will the conquest of Ethiopia be recognized? An ambassador sent to Rome? Will controls be placed on the exchange market? Will the government have recourse to a forced loan? Will it go ahead with the labor relations bill on employment and dismissal practices? Will it prevent sitdown strikes in the plants? Will it increase production by an adjustment of the forty-hour law, especially for factories working for national defense?[7] Blum decided to sidestep these "imprudent" questions as best he could. He would seek support on a few broad principles.

That Saturday evening at six, in the Salle Colbert, one of the large meeting halls of the Palais Bourbon, Blum addressed the opposition Deputies. His carefully constructed appeal was at once eloquent, urgent,

[5] For Blum's statements and the debates, *Le Populaire*, March 13, 1938; a more complete version of Blum's speech appeared in *Le Populaire*, March 15, 1938 and again May 3, 1938.

[6] For Blum's description of these efforts, speech to Royan party congress, June 1938, pp. 516–19; testimony at Riom trial, *Oeuvre*, V, 241–2; and testimony, 1947, *Événements*, I, 252–3. See also the details provided by André Blumel in the article cited below.

[7] The questions are reproduced by Pierre-Étienne Flandin in his *Politique française, 1919–1940* (Paris, 1947), p. 240, n. 1.

insistent, and at some moments pathetic. He was tactful and vigorous, conciliatory and firm, at the same time. He insisted on their "common duty" to create national unity at so critical a moment. It was inconceivable to him that after the parties of the Left had rallied to his proposal, the traditionally patriotic parties would refuse. Should they let the moment pass, he warned, there was no guarantee that the opportunity would return.[8]

To their chief objection, the inclusion of the Communists, he pleaded the need to forge complete national unity. The country needed the cooperation of the entire working class, including the Communists, for the intensive increase in defense production that the times required. "You cannot conceive of national unanimity," he said, "if a part of the French nation is arbitrarily excluded from it. You cannot at this moment undertake a task of national salvation without the collaboration of all." In the event of war, the Communists could not possibly be excluded from a new "sacred union." His own record was proof that the Communists would not sway the foreign policy of the proposed government. "When I was head of a Popular Front government, not of a government including all segments of the republican camp [as this one would be], I believe that I preserved the independence of that government, as well as my personal independence, against certain demands and even against certain pressures." He dismissed as "abominable" and unworthy of consideration the argument that the inclusion of the Communists would antagonize certain foreign powers and thereby increase the risk of war; to accept "a kind of veto emanating from foreign powers" was inconceivable. The record of his government afforded proof also that there would be no socialization or "structural reforms." If his earlier government had remained scrupulously faithful to all partners in the coalition, how much more so would that be true in a broader coalition? Above all, his own record was proof that everything would be done to save the peace. "Did I conduct a policy of peace or a policy of war?" he inquired. Blum spoke with conscience and record equally clear; his scrupulous regard for constitutionalism, his loyalty to his non-Socialist colleagues in the first Popular Front government, his resistance to pressure from the more militant elements of the Popular Front, and his untiring efforts for peace, made it possible

[8] The full text of Blum's speech, along with details of the Salle Colbert meeting, was first made available after the war; see André Blumel: "Déclaration de Léon Blum aux groupes de la minorité, 12 mars 1938," *Les Temps Modernes*, VII (September 1951), 483–94. For Reynaud's description of the meeting, *Au coeur de la mêlée*, p. 201, and *Mémoires*, II, 196.

for him to come forward now as a man who could be trusted by the nation as a whole at so perilous a time. It was as if he had been living for such a moment.

He recalled also his earlier offer, in January, to President Lebrun to step down in favor of another political figure who might more easily rally the parties behind a national unity effort. He would make every sacrifice to enlist their support for a true national unity government. The hall rang with applause when he spoke of serving "what appears to me to be the common interest of all the parties of the republic because that represents the common interest of the nation itself." Many of the Deputies, some of his most stalwart opponents in the past, came up to shake his hand. Henri de Kérillis said to him: "M. Blum, you are a great Frenchman," and the next day he paid tribute in his newspaper to the exalted quality of Blum's language and thought.[9]

Blum left the hall, he later said, convinced that he had persuaded the Deputies.[1] But they continued their discussion after he left. Paul Reynaud, Georges Mandel, Henri de Kérillis, and Louis Marin were favorable to the proposal. Reynaud tried to answer the objections of those who were worried about the Communists: "It is not Stalin who is entering Vienna today and threatens Prague tomorrow; it is Hitler!"[2] The small group of Popular Democrats, aroused by what had happened to the Christian Democrats in Austria, supported Blum. But other speakers, Flandin and Fabry among them, nullified the effect of Blum's speech and defeated the proposal.[3] Flandin's speech was decisive. They had received no reply to the specific questions they had raised; they would be agreeing to participate in a government whose acts they would quickly have to disavow. "The problem," he later said, "was not to vote confidence in individuals but to formulate a program capable of winning general agreement." Such a program had to be on Flandin's own terms. The vote of the opposition Deputies rejecting Blum's proposal was 152 to 5; the resolution recorded that "M. Léon Blum has not furnished any precise clarification on the questions of foreign and domestic policy that legitimately concern the minority."[4]

[9] These reactions were reported in *Le Populaire*, March 13, 1938; see also Werth: *France and Munich*, pp. 126–7. Blum recalled much of this at his Riom trial, *Oeuvre*, V, 241.

[1] Testimony, 1947, *Événements*, I, 252.

[2] Press statement, *Le Populaire*, March 15, 1938; and Reynaud: *Mémoires*, II, 196.

[3] See Blumel: "Déclaration de Léon Blum," p. 492, n. 1.

[4] Flandin: *Politique française*, p. 240, n. 1; and testimony, *Événements*, IX, 2595.

Blum's failure was a watershed in the history of the Third Republic. Never again did the opportunity for a true "national unity" cabinet arise, one that had a place in it for the working-class political parties. The Communists, to be sure, excluded themselves from the body politic after the Nazi-Soviet pact of August 1939, but the process of excluding the working class began earlier, under Daladier and under Reynaud. From the summer of 1938 on, the working-class political parties and trade-union organizations no longer had a voice in the national political community or in the national defense effort. A "national unity" cabinet, "from Thorez to Louis Marin," would not have prevented any war that Hitler might have unleashed, but it would have guaranteed that a united France would have faced Hitler's challenges in 1938. It might have prevented Munich and much that followed. This may be extravagant speculation. What remains true is the tribute in later years by Vincent Auriol, then President of the Fourth Republic, to Blum's effort of March 12, 1938: "In the face of Hitler's expansion, in the face of the peril of war . . . he addressed the most pathetic, the most heart-rending appeal that a man ever addressed to opponents, that they unite and join with him so that a unified government might protect a threatened country and its liberty."[5]

———

Sadly, Blum accepted the refusal of the opposition. "I am conscious of having gone to the limit of any possible effort to fulfill the formula for a government which I judged the interests of the country dictated . . . I cannot conceal my surprise or my sadness . . . If I thought that the creation of 'republican unity around the Popular Front' had more chance of succeeding on the initiative of another political leader, I would at once resign my commission."[6] But no one came forward to make the effort. As a *pis aller*, Blum formed a new Popular Front cabinet on March 13; it would last hardly a month. "Everybody knew that it would be brief when it took office, and I assure you, I knew it as well as anyone," he later said.[7]

The second Blum government (March 13–April 8, 1938) was similar to the one he had formed in June 1936. It was a Socialist-directed coalition cabinet consisting of sixteen Socialists, fifteen Radicals, and a few Republican Socialist Unionists. Blum became his own Minister

[5] Speech at Blum's funeral, April 2, 1950, *Le Populaire*, April 3, 1950.
[6] *Le Populaire*, March 13, 1938.
[7] At Riom trial, *Oeuvre*, V, 241.

of the Treasury (as the Finance Ministry was now designated), thereby reversing his earlier recommendation against placing a ministerial department in the Premier's hands. Under the circumstances, he believed it necessary for the head of the cabinet to occupy "the most exposed position," and also make it possible "to link financial and currency problems to over-all national policy."[8] To assist him he asked Charles Spinasse to assume responsibility for the budget, and appointed as undersecretary of the Treasury a young, energetic Radical destined to become better known to a later generation, Pierre Mendès-France. The various ministerial posts were again grouped together, as in the earlier cabinet, so as to improve coordination and control. Joseph Paul-Boncour, a champion of collective security and long France's permanent representative at the League, replaced Delbos as Minister of Foreign Affairs. Marx Dormoy returned as Minister of the Interior. Vincent Auriol assumed responsibility for coordinating staff work in the Premier's office. Daladier continued as Minister of National Defense.[9]

In form almost a replica of the first Popular Front government, the new government was, in reality, "an anachronism."[1] It was too narrowly representative for the tasks that faced the nation or for obtaining the cooperation of the opposition either in the Chamber or in the Senate. Blum did not help matters by reiterating that it was not the kind of government that public opinion had hoped for and that circumstances dictated; he once again offered to step down in favor of a broader national government if that were possible.[2] On the other hand, he was resolved to make the government count. To the opposition in the Chamber he announced: "The tasks which we would have wished to accomplish with you, we shall accomplish without you."[3]

It was a crucial time. Eden had resigned in February in protest against Chamberlain's equivocal policies toward the dictators. The ill fated non-intervention policy in Spain was still in effect and the Spanish Republic was hard pressed. After the annexation of Austria, Hitler's well-advertised ambitions in the Czech Sudetenland assumed serious proportions. France needed military and economic strength, and unity. Despite its brevity, the second Blum government acted energetically

---

[8] Statement by Blum, *Le Populaire*, March 15, 1938.

[9] *Le Populaire*, March 14, 21, 1938.

[1] The phrase is Alexander Werth's: *France and Munich*, p. 127; cf. Reynaud: *Mémoires*, II, 195.

[2] See radio speech, *Le Populaire*, March 14, 1938.

[3] *Chambre, Débats*, March 17, 1938.

on many fronts. Blum's ministerial declaration pledged the government to increase production, provide a bold new approach in financial matters, and build collective security while working for peace. "We shall increase France's armaments . . . and endeavor to strengthen our friendships and alliances. Our slogan is peace with honor and liberty."[4]

Shortly after taking office, Blum and Paul-Boncour reaffirmed France's determination to honor its commitments to Czechoslovakia, and held a reception in honor of Ambassador Osusky at the Matignon Palace for that very purpose.[5] A special meeting of the *comité permanent de la défense nationale* was called to discuss the military implications of the French alliance system; and the important French ambassadors to the Central and East European countries were summoned home for a conference.

The non-intervention policy in Spain continued but its enforcement was "relaxed," as we have already noted. Because of the British attitude, it was now impossible to abandon it entirely. Chamberlain and Halifax were more attached than ever to the policy, and British support was indispensable after the *Anschluss* and with the Nazi threat to Czechoslovakia. Blum's government continued to relax controls at the frontiers and permitted large quantities of armaments and munitions to make their way across the Pyrenees. The surreptitious aid given to the Spanish Republic reached its peak during this period. The halfway measures, to be sure, did not satisfy his own party, or the Communists, who kept demanding an end to the embargo and continued to make things difficult for the government.[6] A projected bolder step did not materialize; the committee on national defense, at its meeting on March 15, discussed the possibility of a military thrust into Catalonia as well as naval action to protect the Balearics. The proposal was ruled out; to take the initiative, it was agreed, without some act of extreme provocation by the other side would mean the certain loss of British support and would increase the risk of a war under the worst possible circumstances.[7] If some new incident had

---

[4] Ibid., and *Le Populaire*, March 18, 1938.

[5] *Le Populaire*, March 15, 1938; testimony, 1947, *Événements*, I, 255.

[6] On Spain, see Chapter VIII.

[7] For the minutes of the meeting of the *comité permanent*, Gamelin: *Servir*, II, 321–8; also Blum's testimony, 1947, *Événements*, I, 254; and Paul-Boncour: testimony, 1948, *Événements*, III, 802–3.

presented itself at the time, Blum later consoled himself, France might have acted.[8] But independent action, which might have been possible in the summer of 1936, was hardly conceivable in March 1938.

The secret discussion of March 15, which leaked out to the press, was distorted in the next day's headlines into a government plan to intervene in Spain with three divisions. Paul-Boncour had to reassure the British Ambassador, Sir Eric Phipps, that there was no basis to the rumor.[9] And a high-ranking official of the German Foreign Office commented in a memorandum at the time: "It would really be ironical if Léon Blum . . . the father of non-intervention should decide to take such a step."[1] The Supreme Command of the Wehrmacht, assessing French capabilities, seemed quite convinced that French military intervention at that late date was out of the question. "The lack of internal unity" and the "weak position of the present French government" were cited as factors.[2] The assessment was accurate.

On the labor scene, the new government was beset with troubles almost from the beginning. For the first time since the spring of 1936, sitdown strikes broke out on a large scale among the Paris metalworkers in the automobile and aviation industries. Blum, Auriol, and the Minister of Labor, Albert Sérol, worked feverishly to settle the strikes but with little success. The immediate occasion for the labor dispute was the renegotiation of the collective-bargaining contracts in the metallurgical industry. Originally signed in June 1936, the contracts had been twice extended by government decrees with the consent of both parties; further extension in the same way was impossible. The employers showed themselves intransigent and unwilling to cooperate with the new government and its mediators. At the same time some C.G.T. leaders were undoubtedly emboldened by the advent of a new Popular Front government. The Communists, meanwhile, who were strong among the Paris metalworkers, were applying pressure in every possible way to end the embargo on shipments to Spain and fanned the strike movement. Other Leftist extremists, led by the Pivertists, were also stirring up trouble.[3] The strikes

[8] Testimony, 1947, *Événements*, I, 254.

[9] Paul-Boncour: testimony, 1948, *Événements*, III, 802–3; cf. Blum: speech to 1938 party congress, p. 505.

[1] Memorandum, March 16, 1938, *Docs. Ger. For. Pol.*, D, III, No. 545, p. 620; also Ambassador in France to Foreign Ministry, ibid., No. 546, p. 621.

[2] Supreme Command of the Wehrmacht (signed Keitel) to Foreign Ministry, March 22, 1938, ibid., No. 549, p. 623.

[3] See Ehrmann: *French Labor*, pp. 74–5, and Werth: *France and Munich*, p. 127.

came and went with the Blum government. As Auriol wrote shortly after the fall of the cabinet: "One certainly cannot impute to chance alone that extraordinary coincidence."[4]

As in June 1937, finances led to the fall of the Blum government once again. This time it was Blum's attempt to secure the adoption of a far-reaching financial and economic plan to cope with the Sisyphean problems of Treasury credit, the gold reserves, and the currency. (As Blum said, any of the mythological figures would apply—"the rock of Sisyphus, the bottomless vessels of the Danaïdes, the heads of the hydra."[5]) The trouble began when he requested authorization for supplementary credits to meet the government's current obligations. The Chamber acceded, but the Senate granted no more than 5 of the 9 billion francs requested; Joseph Caillaux and Abel Gardey, convinced that the Blum government could not inspire confidence in the financial community, refused to authorize additional inflation. *Le Populaire* published a series of front-page articles criticizing the Senate's continued usurpation of political power and remonstrated that the upper house for the second time was about to frustrate a Popular Front government. Blum let this first crisis pass, requesting the Chamber to accept the Senate's reduced grant. In about a week he expected to have his financial and economic plan ready.[6]

Blum's preoccupation with the sitdown strikes had delayed the preparation of the plan, but on April 4 it was presented to the Chamber Finance Committee, a comprehensive financial, economic, and social program designed to make rearmament the focus of an expanded economy.[7] To guarantee government control over foreign exchange and to check the depletion of the country's gold reserves, it

[4] *Le Populaire*, April 22, 1938; see Auriol's articles on the strikes, *Le Populaire*, April 17–22, 1938; and the unsigned article hinting at Communist trouble-making, *Le Populaire*, April 4, 1938.

[5] *Chambre, Débats*, April 5, 1938.

[6] See *Le Populaire*, March 23–26, 31, 1938.

[7] The long *exposé des motifs*, or preface, of the bill set forth the government's program; it was drawn up by Blum with the aid of Mendès-France and Georges Boris, who was *chef de cabinet* in the Ministry of the Treasury; for the text, *Le Populaire*, April 5, 1938. For Blum's comments on the program, speech to the Chamber, *Chambre, Débats*, April 5, 1938, and statements at Riom trial, *Oeuvre*, V, 243. It was through Georges Boris that Blum came to know of Keynes's work, which undoubtedly influenced the 1938 program; see statements cited by Lefranc: *Mouvement socialiste*, p. 352, n. 3, and Lefranc: *Histoire du Front Populaire*, pp. 275–6.

even provided for some control over the exchange market. Behind the scenes Blum had confidentially received word from Secretary of the Treasury Morgenthau that the United States and Britain would not interpose objections to the "temporary imposition of exchange restrictions."[8] Blum assured the American Secretary that he intended to make every effort to avoid exchange controls. On the other hand, if war broke out, as was a distinct possibility, the internal value of the franc would not be as important as gold and credit. In some way he had to prevent the depletion of the gold reserves in the Bank of France now being used endlessly and hopelessly to maintain the exchange value of the franc, but as yet he did not want an official approach made to him or to the British about exchange control. If circumstances later warranted it, he would inform the Secretary. For the present he would not even tell his own colleagues about Morgenthau's message.[9] It was this interchange that lay behind Blum's willingness to consider exchange controls at all. For the moment, his plan provided for minimum controls and for surveillance by the Bank of France.

Based on the paramount need of national defense, Blum's bill projected a major rearmament effort as a point of departure for industrial growth, an expanded economy, and continued social progress. He later described his proposal as "something that went far beyond an armaments program and took on the character of a plan analogous to the Russian Five-Year Plans or the Göring Plan." He spoke also of a "closed economy" and the "guaranteeing of credits to war industries by means analogous to those which Dr. Schacht had initiated in Germany."[1] That it was so far-reaching a plan may be questioned, yet in its way it was an impressive proposal. It was closer to a Keynesian-inspired program than anything in his first government had been. The conclusion rang with a stirring exhortation:

> Such, gentlemen, are the measures proposed. . . . They are dominated by the immense obligation . . . on all Frenchmen to assure the defense of the country. Certainly it is a kind of tragic irony that a nation devoted to peace and human progress is compelled to strain and concentrate all its resources for a gigantic military effort. We have not wanted this; our thoughts have

[8] *From the Morgenthau Diaries*, pp. 499–500.

[9] Ibid., p. 500; cf. Blum's reference to the changing attitude of "the Anglo-Saxon democracies" on exchange controls in his speech to the Royan party congress, June 1938, p. 500.

[1] Testimony, 1947, *Événements*, I, 255.

turned away from it with aversion and with horror. . . . But we shall prove that free peoples can rise to . . . their duties, that democracies are capable, through a voluntarily accepted discipline, to deploy strength that is not obtained elsewhere except through blind obedience. . . . We shall proceed in such a way that around the manufacture of armaments there will be coordinated an economy which will be the basis for a more abundant production in all domains, so that in the very midst of this painful task, undertaken and carried out in common, the work of social solidarity and human fraternity shall be continued and amplified.[2]

In the grim world of 1938, he demonstrated his understanding and acceptance of the needs of the nation, even if there was stark irony in the spectacle of Blum holding forth the vision of armaments as the avenue to economic and social progress. Concern for the defense of the republic had overcome all other considerations. Gone were the doctrinaire commitments to disarmament and internationalism. Far in advance of his party, he had reconciled in his own mind all possible contradictions between his patriotism and his socialism.

Even conservative commentators expressed their admiration for Blum's project. "One has to admit that the *exposé des motifs* is a masterpiece of writing," stated the financial editor of the London *Times*. "For the first time since M. Poincaré an effort has been made to face the economic problem not by improvised expedients but in its totality and to resolve it by means of a bold plan studied in its details."[3] But there was little hope that it would succeed in the legislature.

It was a bad omen when Blum received support for his bill in the Chamber by only a narrow margin; a number of Radicals and Socialist-Republican Unionists in the Popular Front majority voted against it. Many of the Radicals, along with the conservative opposition, were convinced that, although the program was necessary, only another kind of government could carry it out. They believed, too, that a profound political change could alone provide the psychological atmosphere for a return of investment capital, and that rearmament by itself would not suffice to revive the economy. When it became obvious that the Senate would reject the bill, the political temperature in the country began to rise; mass demonstrations were held. The Left-wing Socialists

[2] *Exposé des motifs*, Le Populaire, April 5, 1938.
[3] T. G. Barman: *The Times*, April 6, 1938; cited by Blum in speech to the Senate, April 8, 1938.

in the Federation of the Seine, led by Pivert, staged street demonstrations in the approaches to the Luxembourg Gardens where the Senate was deliberating. But the party executive denounced the demonstrations as unauthorized; shortly thereafter it took disciplinary action against the Federation of the Seine, dissolving and reorganizing it.[4] The "Revolution" would not be permitted to interfere with national unity.

As anticipated, the Senate rejected the bill; of 94 Radical Senators, only 24 voted for it. "I know what is in your minds," Blum told the Senate, "the return of confidence, a change in political climate, the repatriation of capital." He refused to put a vote of confidence to the Senate but also declined to press the issue. He saw no course but to resign again, and, as in June 1937, he rebuked the Senate for its usurpation of political authority.[5]

Blum once again excluded the possibility of an appeal to mass popular action, despite boastful hints about the power of the Popular Front masses that could be unleashed. He knew that this time there was far less enthusiasm for a show of resistance than in June 1937. The Communists had been unfriendly to his government and had remained strangely silent during the clash with the Senate. But most important, in the tense atmosphere of Europe only a few weeks after the *Anschluss*, political and social turbulence had to be avoided at all costs. He explained to the national council of the party: "We did not believe it possible, given the present state of France and Europe, and the gravity of the international situation, to encourage developments which would have spread in such a way as to provoke or initiate dangerous events in the world. It would have meant launching France on an adventure which we would not have been able to master, manage, or lead."[6] A few years later, William Bullitt recalled Blum's confiding to him that it would have been "easy" to break the opposition of the Senate "without even making an appeal to the people but only by giving free rein to their physical strength." But, according to Bullitt, Blum refused to take the responsibility, "for fear of weakening

[4] *Le Populaire*, April 7–8, 1938; and, for action by the party's executive committee, *Le Populaire*, April 13–14, 1938. See Blum's remarks upholding the disciplinary action, speech at Royan congress, June 1938, pp. 125–37; cf. Lefranc: *Mouvement socialiste*, pp. 355–8, and Ligou: *Socialisme*, pp. 442–3.

[5] Blum's speech to the Senate and general debate, *Sénat, Débats*, April 8, 1938.

[6] Speech to national council, *Le Populaire*, April 10, 1938; and later statement, *Le Populaire*, May 29, 1938. See also the anonymous front-page articles explaining the resignation, *Le Populaire*, April 9, 10, 1938.

his country in face of the growing threat of Germany . . ."[7] To be sure, it was part of Blum's temperament to recoil from strong measures, and it could be charged that he used the foreign danger as a rationalization of his political timidity. Yet in the critical state of affairs in the spring of 1938 his efforts at preserving national unity were statesmanlike even if they had little chance of success. In reality, his surrender to the reactionary elements in the country served mainly to spread disillusionment and demoralization in his own party and in Popular Front circles, which saw him as betraying his Socialist ideals in the name of "national unity."

The fall of the second Blum government deepened the rift with the Communists. At the last minute the Communist leaders, Jacques Duclos and Marcel Gitton, belatedly pressed Blum to resist the Senate. He inquired where their "full support" had been during the past weeks, and pointed out the grave international complications that might ensue.[8] Their increasing pressure against the Spanish non-intervention policy, their uncooperative role in the metallurgical strikes, their silence (until the last moment) on the obstructionism of the Senate, caused bitter resentment. "As in June 1937," an unsigned front-page article in *Le Populaire* charged, "the Communists kept shooting the Léon Blum government in the back at the very moment when all the forces of reaction were combining to bring it down."[9] The statement was stronger than any heretofore. A short time later, a second article further spelled out the Socialists' feelings: "To a certain extent, the Communist party's attitude—often incomprehensible—toward the two Socialist-led Popular Front governments helps to explain the progressive weakening of the Popular Front."[1] The Socialist-Communist foundation of the Popular Front was rapidly breaking up. And the Popular Front itself was in its last stages.

Édouard Daladier's predominantly Radical government succeeded Blum's on April 8, 1938; it would last on into the war. When it assumed office, the Daladier government was still technically a Popular Front government, dependent on a Left majority for support. The Socialists refused to participate, adopting a sympathetic but watchful

[7] Bullitt: preface to *L'Histoire jugera*, p. xi.

[8] Blum recalled the conversation in his speech to the national council, *Le Populaire*, April 10, 1938.

[9] *Le Populaire*, April 10, 1938.

[1] *Le Populaire*, April 23, 1938.

attitude. Blum announced himself satisfied that the new cabinet was not a *bloc national* government oriented to the Right even though it included ministers who had been in the opposition.[2] There was a genuine feeling of relief that the party itself had emerged from the crisis without worse results. Blum said of his government: "No one was unaware in advance of the obstacles it faced. . . . We escaped as we did, safe and sound, only by a kind of miracle."[3] It was a matter of chagrin to Blum, however, that the Daladier government, by a vote of 508 to 12, quickly received a temporary grant of full powers to cope with finances (in the Senate, all 290 votes) and that almost at once the big employers agreed to settle the sitdown strikes on the basis of the very terms that had been earlier proposed by his government.[4]

The day after the fall of his government, Blum celebrated his sixty-sixth birthday. He seems to have thought seriously of giving up political life.[5] The crushing pace of events that had followed so soon after the loss of his wife overwhelmed him. For a short time he lay sick in bed.[6] For about two months, while Parliament itself adjourned, he took a long rest and absented himself from party activities. He had time to ponder a heart-warming letter from Winston Churchill:

> I have thought much about you in these anxious and trying days, and I feel bound to express to you the gratitude which so many English people cherish towards you for the very great and real advance in the understanding between our two countries which marked your memorable Premiership. It is not for a foreigner, however friendly, to meddle in French politics. But I have never seen the good feeling between Britain and France so strong as during your terms of power.
>
> I am sure that in a private station for a while you will have immense opportunities of carrying forward this great work, so necessary for the rights of the common people in every land, and for the Peace and Freedom of the world.
>
> As a very old minister now in retirement (!) [Churchill's

---

[2] Speech to national council, *Le Populaire*, April 10, 1938, and speech to Royan party congress, June 1938, pp. 522–5.

[3] Speech to Royan party congress, June 1938, p. 133.

[4] See *Le Populaire*, March 31, April 15, 1938, and Blum's remarks at Riom trial, *Oeuvre*, V, 244.

[5] Statement to Nantes party congress, May 1939, *Le Populaire*, May 31, 1939.

[6] Reynaud recalled visiting him at the time; *Mémoires*, II, 201.

exclamation mark!] I thought I might without presumption send these few lines to you, and Believe me, etc., etc.[7]

Blum, as another "very old minister now in retirement," could no more turn his back on events than Churchill could. He could not reject what he considered to be his imperative duty. He knew that his own party was showing signs of serious division. He had led the party to accept a program of rearmament and a policy of national unity because of the threat of aggression. But many in the party did not believe that he had chosen the correct path; they could only remember that armaments and alliances had brought on the holocaust of 1914. The second-ranking Socialist in the party, Paul Faure, was among this number. To prevent war, many within the party and many in the country as a whole were prepared to make any sacrifice; Munich was not many months off.

[7] A facsimile of the letter, dated April 14, 1938, written from Chartwell in Churchill's own handwriting, is reproduced by Suzanne Blum in *L'Histoire jugera*, pp. 125–8.

The Years of Anguish

XI

PLOWSHARES INTO SWORDS:
Munich and War, April 1938–March 1940

*Vous dites, Paul, c'est subir l'idée de la
guerre. Qu'est-ce que vous voulez? C'est
affreux, mais c'est ainsi parce que l'Europe
dans laquelle nous vivons n'est pas la
nôtre; elle n'est pas celle que nous aurions
voulue.*[1]

F OR SEVERAL MONTHS after the formation of the Daladier cabinet in April 1938, Blum and the Socialists, as well as the Communists, supported Daladier, though guardedly. Daladier, one
of the earliest champions of the Popular Front and Minister of National Defense in Blum's two cabinets (and in fact in every cabinet
since June 1936), had generally accepted the Popular Front labor
reforms. On the other hand, the new cabinet included several outspoken opponents of the Popular Front labor legislation and had been
able to muster the backing of the Center and Right parties at the time it
was formed. Although Daladier's first financial decrees did not please
Blum, he warned the party's annual congress at Royan early in June that
the party had no practical alternative except to support the government
even though it might not be "overjoyed" with Daladier's actions. It was
of the utmost importance to keep the government dependent on the
Popular Front majority and away from the Center and Right parties
which were eager to embrace it. At the congress he defended the non-
Popular Front members of the cabinet, men like Paul Reynaud and
Georges Mandel, against loose charges that they were "fascists" because
they opposed the Popular Front social and economic program. They
were staunch republican patriots, he argued, despite their conservative

---

[1] Blum, before party national council, *Le Populaire*, November 8, 1938. His
remarks were addressed to Paul Faure.

economic views; nor was there any fear that the Daladier government would "betray the republic."[2]

The Royan congress, meeting in June 1938, witnessed the first serious party debate on foreign policy in which the "pacifist" (or "peace at any price") wing of the party, led by Paul Faure, Charles Spinasse, and Louis L'Hévéder, attacked Blum for taking them down the path to war. They opposed his program of rearmament and mutual assistance pacts designed to check the dictators. Insisting that the party must never slacken in its pursuit of negotiations and that concessions must be made in order to preserve peace, they asserted that Blum's program represented a flat repudiation of everything the party and he himself had long championed. Blum, repeating what he had said as Premier in 1936, did not try to conceal the dangers involved. "I know that to carry collective security to its logical end is to accept a risk of war. But I must say that to avoid war one must at certain moments agree to run the risk of war."[3] Only a vaguely worded compromise resolution to which Blum and Faure could both subscribe succeeded in temporarily glossing over some fundamental differences: "French socialism desires peace even with the totalitarian imperialist powers, but it is not disposed to yield to all of their enterprises."[4] It was one of the party's typical "*nègre-blanc*" resolutions, trying to be both black and white at the same time, and aimed solely at preserving unity.

So far as the Daladier government's foreign policy was concerned, Blum expressed his satisfaction with the show of firmness toward Germany in the first Czech crisis in May. "To this point you have nothing serious with which to reproach the foreign policy of M. Daladier," he told the congress. He warned Georges Bonnet, the Foreign Minister, however, that any thought he and others had of detaching Mussolini from Hitler by means of concessions and friendly gestures was "fanciful."[5] He also lectured the government on the special role that France could play: "The most important diplomatic task for France is, as in 1914, to mediate between London and Moscow, and to create

[2] Speech to Royan congress, June 1938, pp. 489–532, esp. pp. 522–7. See also Blum's editorials on the eve of the congress, *Le Populaire*, May 26–29, June 4, 1938.

[3] Royan congress, p. 511. Here and in the pages that follow, by "pacifist" I do not mean anything like traditional doctrinaire pacifism but rather the willingness to accept all possible concessions in order to avoid war.

[4] Ibid., p. 578.

[5] Ibid., pp. 509, 527.

between the English government and the government of the Soviet Union more harmonious and more confident relations than exist at the present moment."[6] It was not a task that either Daladier or Bonnet was prepared to assume with enthusiasm.

Shortly after the congress there were indications that the Daladier government, in response to British pressure, was reimposing strict controls over shipments across the Pyrenees frontier and thus abandoning the policy of "relaxed" controls inaugurated by Blum. As we have seen, Blum indignantly called on Daladier to refrain from this step. Such a policy, in the face of the egregious violations by the fascist powers, would be "not a homage rendered to virtue but a hypocritical affront to justice," he charged.[7] But Daladier and Bonnet were sealing the frontiers even as Blum was writing his editorials.

Despite his misgivings about Daladier's foreign and domestic policies, Blum still publicly supported the government in July 1938. The Radical leader, he said, "has not renounced anything of the principles or acts of the Popular Front."[8] Significantly, however, at the Popular Front celebration on July 14, by agreement of all the participating parties, no speeches were made.

The first open rift with the government developed after Daladier's shattering radio speech of August 2. The Premier spoke of the need "to put France back to work," indicating his intention to revise the forty-hour law drastically and to reduce overtime rates of pay. Two members of the cabinet resigned at once in protest. Blum reacted sharply to Daladier's "surprising and disturbing speech." The Socialist leader insisted that labor stood ready to accept adjustments in the forty-hour law but would not tolerate a one-sided censure of labor for all the problems and difficulties of French production. If Daladier were seeking to win the "confidence of capital" by leading an assault on the forty-hour law, he must learn that the confidence of labor was as important for the welfare of the nation as that of the financial community.[9] It was a message which he never successfully communicated to Daladier then or in the months to come.

On the other hand, Daladier's speech was delivered when the Sudeten crisis was already appearing on the horizon. Despite his anger

[6] Ibid., p. 511.
[7] *Le Populaire*, June 29, 1938; also his editorials, June 23–26, August 1, 1938. Cf. Werth: *France and Munich*, pp. 173–4.
[8] *Le Populaire*, July 26, 1938.
[9] See his editorials, *Le Populaire*, August 22, 25, 27, 1938.

at the Radical leader's open provocation, Blum restrained the party from deserting the government and from causing a cabinet crisis. "In the present state of Europe," he admonished, "when the balance oscillates between peace and war and when the slightest additional weight can make it shift one way or the other, . . . a political crisis in France would be a formidable event." Legitimate resentment at the government's attack on the Popular Front labor laws had to be subordinated to the need for internal unity. Blum would give Daladier every possible chance to make amends. He was still hopeful of "saving" Daladier from the "irredeemable" error of breaking with the Popular Front majority.[1]

Actually, the changes in the forty-hour week, which were announced in September, were not as drastic as had been expected, but they made it possible for employers to request permission for overtime work without consulting the trade unions. Daladier had left no ambiguity about the orientation of his government. From the summer of 1938 on, Blum was torn between his desire to support the government because of the grave international situation and his indignation at its anti-labor policies.

In September the Sudeten crisis approached its climax. The policy of firmness toward the dictators was put to the test. Blum himself was deeply involved. (It was symptomatic of the extent of rift among the Socialists that Blum's strong editorial pronouncement of September 2 on foreign affairs was crowded from its customary first-page position by party protests against the modification of the forty-hour law.) Blum unequivocally demanded that the government honor its obligations under the country's mutual assistance pact with Czechoslovakia. He felt himself personally engaged; only six months earlier, as Premier, he had reaffirmed France's commitments.[2] Convinced that the willingness of the Czechs to grant a large measure of administrative autonomy to the Sudeten Germans already "went beyond" the limit of "justice" and "prudence," he protested against further concessions under pressure from England and France. "We cannot allow the sovereignty and independence of Prague to be snatched from it bit by bit," he wrote in the second week of September. He called upon the French and British governments to "remove all room for misunderstanding or

[1] *Le Populaire*, August 28, 29, 1938.
[2] *Le Populaire*, September 2, 1938. He repeated his sense of personal commitment during the crisis, *Le Populaire*, September 21, 1938.

doubt still lingering in the minds of the leaders of the Reich. . . .
What is at stake is the fate of Europe, the fate of the freedom of Europe,
Great Britain and France included."[3] Yet strong words were one thing,
acts another. Blum, too, wanted to avoid war. He applauded the government for avoiding any steps that might make it appear that France
was mobilizing her forces and repeatedly called for calm and self-
control.[4] And on September 15 he paid "unreserved homage" to Neville
Chamberlain for his willingness to go to Berchtesgaden. "M. Chamberlain's decision stirs our minds and our imagination. . . . It marks a
noble and bold step in the will for peace."[5]

Events moved rapidly in the days immediately following Chamberlain's return from Berchtesgaden. Having convinced his own cabinet
that territorial concessions alone could prevent Hitler from unleashing
war, the British Prime Minister next had to win over Daladier. It was
at this point that Blum indirectly played a part in the events that
culminated in Munich.

Daladier and Bonnet planned to fly to London on Sunday, September 18, at Chamberlain's pressing invitation. On September 17, Blum
received a visit from a Socialist member of the Czech cabinet. Dr.
Jaromír Nečas. Blum later recounted: "Nečas came to tell me on behalf of Beneš: 'Things are now developing in such a way that England
and France are going to demand concessions of us. I am sending you
a map on which Daladier will be able to see, from the clear marking of
our military works and fortifications, the furthest boundary beyond
which we would consider Czechoslovakia to be abandoned and lost.' "[6]
The next morning Blum had the map delivered to Daladier before the
Premier embarked on his flight. Blum later insisted that he acted out
of the conviction that he was communicating the *final limits* of the
territorial concessions that Beneš was prepared to make, not communicating the *willingness* of the Czechs to make territorial concessions.
Yet Daladier was able to go to the meeting (Bonnet providing other
reassurances of the Czechs' willingness to make concessions) convinced that Beneš was prepared to cede certain mountain salients in
the Sudeten territory with a population of almost one million. Daladier

[3] *Le Populaire*, September 8, 1938; also editorials, *Le Populaire*, September 7,
9, 1938.

[4] *Le Populaire*, September 6, 12, 13, 1938.

[5] *"Une noble audace dans la volonté de paix,"* *Le Populaire*, September 15,
1938.

[6] For this and the details that follow, see Blum's testimony before the postwar
parliamentary commission, 1947, *Événements*, I, 256.

later claimed that he was "singularly embarrassed by [Blum's] communication. . . . It would perhaps have been better if I hadn't received [it]."[7] After some hesitation, he decided he had to communicate it to Chamberlain even though it was "an additional argument in favor of the London thesis."[8] From the meeting that Sunday emerged the Anglo-French Plan demanding of the Czechs the "transfer to the Reich of all territories with over 50 per cent Sudeten inhabitants," a cession which Beneš never accepted and which, of course, went far beyond the territorial limits that Blum had transmitted.[9]

Blum's unfortunate role in the Sudeten crisis is inescapably clear. He had acted in good faith, trying to prevent too extreme a betrayal, yet he had contributed to the appeasement atmosphere that reached its climax at Munich two weeks later. Unwittingly, he helped to undermine whatever determination Daladier may have had to reject the territorial concessions demanded by Hitler; at the very least he made it easier for Daladier in later years to rationalize his acquiescence in the British proposal.

Once the general nature of the British and French proposals were known and it was apparent that the territorial dismemberment of Czechoslovakia was imminent, Blum was repelled not only by the settlement but by the intention to impose it upon Czechoslovakia without her consent.[1] He felt himself overwhelmed with shame. On September 20, he openly described his troubled conscience: "War has probably been avoided. But under such conditions that I who have never ceased to struggle for peace, I who for many years have dedicated my life to it, cannot feel joy. I feel myself torn between a sense of cowardly relief and shame."[2] He refused to add "to the humiliation and indignation of the Czech people by tendering hypocritical sympathies."[3]

At that point the crisis was still in its initial stages. Tense and anguished days followed, filled with fear that war still might not be

---

[7] Daladier: testimony, 1947, *Événements*, I, 33. Daladier mistakenly believed the Czech emissary to be Professor Dominois, of the French Institute of Czech Studies. Blum identified him as Dr. Nečas, Minister of Social Security in the Czech cabinet; Blum: testimony, ibid., p. 256.

[8] Daladier: testimony, 1947, *Événements*, I, 33.

[9] For these events and many of the relevant documents, John W. Wheeler-Bennett: *Munich: Prologue to Tragedy* (London, 1948, 1963), esp. pp. 94–199 and appendix.

[1] See *Le Populaire*, September 19, 1938.

[2] *Le Populaire*, September 20, 1938.

[3] *Le Populaire*, September 22, 1938; see also resolution of Socialist parliamentary group, ibid.

averted. When Chamberlain returned to see Hitler at Godesberg, the Führer raised his demands and the British and French governments rejected them. Hungary and Poland entered their bids for territory. Roosevelt's appeal for a conference between all the important nations, to be held on neutral soil, went unheeded. The war clouds grew darker; in France reservists were called up. Suddenly came the announcement of a meeting to be held at Munich of the four powers, Germany, Italy, Britain, and France. Even though the Czechs and the Russians were to be excluded, it raised in Blum "an immense response of joy and hope." "The Munich meeting," Blum wrote on September 29, "is an armful of tinder thrown on the sacred flame at the very moment the flame was flickering and threatening to go out."[4]

When Hitler had his way at the four-power meeting at Munich, and the peace was saved for the moment, Blum again experienced the same sense of relief and shame as earlier—shame that peace had been bought at the expense of the Czech nation, relief that war had been averted. On the morrow of Munich he admitted:

> There is not a woman and not a man to refuse MM. Neville Chamberlain and Édouard Daladier their rightful tribute of gratitude. War is avoided. The scourge recedes. Life can become natural once again. One can resume one's work and sleep again. One can enjoy the beauty of an autumn sun. How would it be possible for me not to understand this sense of deliverance when I feel it myself?[5]

Nor could Blum bring himself to condemn the enthusiastic reception for Daladier upon his return to Paris, a reception that embarrassed Daladier himself. The nightmare had passed. The Socialist group called the Munich conference a "barrier in the race toward war."[6] Heartsick nonetheless, Blum perceived immediately two urgent tasks now imposing themselves: to protect the Czech state and its democratic regime from further disintegration and to repair the damage done to the Franco-Soviet pact.[7]

A few days later, Daladier sought a "vote of adjournment" in the Chamber, the equivalent of a vote to approve the government's action at Munich. Every party shared in the sense of humiliation, but the

[4] *Le Populaire*, September 29, 1938.
[5] *Le Populaire*, October 1, 1938.
[6] See resolution, *Le Populaire*, October 1, 1938.
[7] *Le Populaire*, October 1, 1938.

motion upholding the government received the votes of all the Deputies
except the seventy-two Communists and three other intransigent Deputies. It was Blum's onerous duty to read the Socialist declaration of
support, voted after a bitter debate by the party's parliamentary
group. The minority, the pacifist wing of the party, rejoiced that peace
had been preserved and was convinced that sacrifices were necessary
to avoid the irrevocable disaster of war. To them Munich was less a
defeat than a victory. They wanted no pledge of firmness for the
future, no rearmament, no renewed commitments to the other smaller
nations of Europe. Blum, and others like him, was saddened that
peace had been bought by the sacrifice wrung from the Czechs and
was convinced that any new concessions could only strengthen the will
of the dictators to embark upon further conquest and war. Blum took
the floor in the name of the entire group to present the majority resolution but also to try to unite the "two factions within the party which had
just fiercely confronted each other." He made no attempt to conceal
the conflicting emotions of relief and sorrow within the party and within
himself at the recent events. But he concluded on a note of warning to
those who might interpret the will for peace to mean further surrender
and concessions. "This deeply felt and impassioned will for peace
cannot lead a people to accept everything; on the contrary, it strengthens
the resolve to struggle, to sacrifice itself, if necessary, for its independence and freedom; it does not abolish the distinction between what is
just and what is unjust." Demanding that there be no repetition of
Munich, he called for unity within the nation so that the country might
face the future resolutely.[8] More than that he could not say. "But it
was not very difficult to read between the lines, and indeed one did
not even have to read between the lines at all," he later explained.[9]

The drama of Munich laid bare the division in the party and
its deep-seated pacifism. Paul Faure could think only of 1914 and
described the crisis as "the mad result of the armaments race . . .
Our conclusion is that civilization has everything to lose and nothing
to gain from a military solution." Munich was hailed as "the victory
of peace."[1] Ludovic Zoretti, a leader of the pacifist wing in the party
and in the C.G.T., injected an overtone of antisemitism into the
debate, insinuating that Blum's initial firmness had been prompted by
sympathy for his fellow Jews. "The French people do not want to see

---

[8] For Blum's speech, *Chambre, Débats*, October 4, 1938.

[9] Testimony, 1947, *Événements*, I, 258.

[1] See *Le Populaire*, September 7, 10, 11, 30, October 2, 1938.

millions of human beings killed and a civilization destroyed in order to make life more agreeable to the 100,000 Jews of the Sudetenland. They know that the high motives presented as reasons for fighting are mere hypocrisy."[2] Blum refused comment on such wild charges.

Blum never denied the spontaneous feeling of relief that swept the country and his own party too at the time of Munich. "I can understand the relaxation in nervous tension of a people that came to the brink of war and then suddenly, in a few minutes, by a kind of enchanted magic, saw itself delivered and freed," he remarked a few weeks later. He refused to dismiss the danger of war; he understood the "drama of conscience" of the men in office. Yet of the surrender itself it remained his conviction that he "would not have allowed himself to be carried by circumstances to that point."[3] Hitler, he believed, was fortified by the certainty that France would not stand by its obligations. The impotence and weakness of the French cabinet he blamed on the pressure for peace within the country as well as on the pressure from Britain. He criticized Daladier less than he did Georges Bonnet and the British ministers. But he knew deep in his heart that the pacifism in the whole country, and in his own party too, had made the betrayal possible.[4] With a touch of irony, he proposed on October 6 that the Nobel Peace Prize that year be awarded to Eduard Beneš.[5]

Desperately attempting to override the pacifist wing in his own party, Blum now directed his energies toward rallying the country to a strong stand against the dictators. In editorial after editorial, he called for a solid front of all nations that desired to preserve peace, and urged the building up of French armed strength. (Sadly, he recognized that inferiority in air power had played a role in French and British diplomatic weakness even if it had been exaggerated for political ends.[6]) The fatuous notion that Munich would lead to a general European settlement was quickly dispelled. No one, he pointed out,

[2] *La Lumière*, September 30, 1938, cited by Ehrmann: *French Labor*, p. 106. See testimony of Delmas on the pacifism of the Left at the time of Munich, *À gauche de la barricade*, pp. 132–3.

[3] Speech to party national council, *Le Populaire*, November 8, 1938.

[4] Ibid., and testimony, 1947, *Événements*, I, 255.

[5] *Le Populaire*, October 6, 1938.

[6] See *Le Populaire*, October 17, 1938, and series of editorials, October 17–25, 1938.

would object to a general conference to discuss political and economic questions, but cooperation did not depend on the good will of the democracies.[7]

Conditions had indeed worsened after Munich. The territorial settlement was aggravated by the international commission charged with enforcing the Munich agreements. The Bonnet-Ribbentrop declaration of friendship on December 6, the clear intention of Hitler to exclude France entirely from Central and Eastern Europe, Mussolini's demands for French territory—all were unhappy sequels to Munich. At the end of January 1939, after an inflammatory speech by Hitler, Blum wrote with despair: "In sensing the world hanging on his decisions, in thinking that one man, one single man, holds peace or war in his hands, and the lives of millions of men, I feel an insurmountable sense of oppression."[8] His words mirrored the anguish and anxiety of a generation.

In February, Blum was further disheartened when France and Britain recognized the Franco government; it was the final act of the Spanish drama. The headline in *Le Populaire* on February 25 exposed his own deep chagrin: "The Chamber of May 1936, the Chamber of the Popular Front, has recognized General Franco." "I left the meeting," Blum wrote of the session in which the recognition was ratified, "overwhelmed by an almost intolerable disgust and anxiety."[9] It was the denouement to his own personal Munich.

On March 15, 1939, came still another shattering blow when Hitler, in flagrant violation of the Munich agreements, overran Prague and destroyed Czechoslovakia as an independent state. Blum, speaking in the Chamber, called Hitler's act "the clearest, most brutal sign of the regression of civilization." All the arguments heard at the time of Munich were now vitiated. Blum questioned whether the Daladier government could any longer be trusted to defend the country's security and peace. It was still possible, he believed, to check the race toward catastrophe, but only by united resistance to the dictators. The democracies must reaffirm their commitments to the smaller nations and strengthen their ties with each other. "In the first rank" was the need

[7] See especially his series of editorials in *Le Populaire*, October 27–November 6, 1938; speeech to party national council, *Le Populaire*, November 8, 1938; and many other editorials after October 1938.

[8] *Le Populaire*, January 31, 1939.

[9] *Le Populaire*, February 26, 1939; also speeeches of January 16, 26, 1939, in the Chamber.

to renew contacts with the U.S.S.R. and repair the damage done by the exclusion of the Soviets at Munich.[1]

When the British in March and April stiffened, and affirmed their determination to defend Poland, Rumania, and Greece, pledges which the French government endorsed, Blum applauded, but noted sadly that the French government seemed incapable of taking the initiative; it did not even summon Parliament so that added weight might be given to these commitments. (Parliament had been virtually adjourned indefinitely after repeated grants of "full powers" to Daladier.) The new firmness and determination shown by the British and French governments, the pledge to defend the integrity of the smaller nations, and the rearmament effort under way in both countries filled him with satisfaction[2]—even if it hurt the remnants of his pacifist conscience. "This is the state to which the dictators have led Europe," he lamented. "For us Socialists, for us pacifists, the appeal to force is today the appeal for peace."[3] He supported one peace effort only, that made by President Roosevelt in April, because he saw it as a complement to the new unity being forged.[4]

Out of his growing belief that armed strength alone could halt the fascist dictators, he appealed to the members of the Labour party in Britain to give up their fight against conscription. While sympathizing with their opposition to the Chamberlain government and with their reluctance to believe that the "men of Munich" had undergone a complete transformation, he urged them not to oppose conscription on those grounds. "I do not hesitate to state to my Labour comrades my deepest conviction that at the very moment at which I write, conscription in England is one of the capital acts upon which the peace of the world hangs."[5]

At the same time, he also managed to convey to Neville Chamberlain, in the course of a visit to London, his belief that peace rested on demonstrating to the dictators that a profound change had taken place. "I had the opportunity yesterday," said Chamberlain in a speech on May 11, "of exchanging a few words with M. Blum, the French Socialist leader and former Prime Minister, and he said to me that

[1] *Chambre, Débats,* March 17, 1939; and editorial, *Le Populaire,* March 21, 1939.

[2] See, among others, editorials in *Le Populaire,* April 1, 10, 14, 15, 1939.

[3] *Le Populaire,* April 16, 1939.

[4] Ibid.

[5] *Le Populaire,* April 27, 1939.

in his view, and in the view of all the Socialist friends with whom he had talked, there was only one danger of war in Europe, and that was a very real one: It was that the impression should get about that Great Britain and France were not in earnest and that they could not be relied upon to carry out their promises. If that were so, no greater, no more deadly mistake could be made—and it would be a frightful thing if Europe were to be plunged into war on account of a misunderstanding. In many minds the danger spot in Europe today is Danzig . . . if an attempt were made to change the situation by force in such a way as to threaten Polish independence, that would inevitably start a general conflagration in which this country would be involved."[6] The experiment in appeasement was ending. And Chamberlain was using Blum to needle the Labour party opposition as well. A few days later, Blum reiterated in the Chamber the views he had expressed to Chamberlain and called upon his own country "to fulfill without equivocation and without fail its pledges of mutual assurance and guarantee."[7]

That spring and summer he awaited with impatience the outcome of the French-British negotiations with the U.S.S.R., clinging to the hope that war was not inevitable because the dictators now recognized the determination of the "peace front" to resist any new enterprises of violence. There was no reason, he wrote, for the "cloud of pessimism" which he observed in many quarters; the date was August 22, 1939.[8]

Meanwhile the rift in his own party deepened in the post-Munich period. It was impossible to reconcile the two camps. At a meeting of a national council in November 1938 and at congresses in December 1938 and May 1939, the party came close to open schism over the foreign policy that Blum was advocating. Perhaps, Blum reflected in later years, it would have been wiser to have permitted an open break.[9]

The question of doctrinaire pacifism or "integral pacifism," as Blum termed it, was not at stake; there were few Tolstoyans in the party. Nor, with the expulsion of Pivert's group in April 1938, was the question of "revolutionary defeatism" at issue. Moreover, everyone could

[6] *The Times* (London), May 12, 1939.

[7] *Chambre, Débats*, May 12, 1939; and editorials, *Le Populaire*, May 23, 24, 1939.

[8] *Le Populaire*, August 22, 1939.

[9] *À l'échelle humaine*, Oeuvre, V, 455.

agree on the deep desire for peace. "There is," Blum said, "no Socialist who is not a pacifist deep inside him."[1] Everyone agreed further that a war imposed from without would have to be accepted and fought; even war was preferable to capitulation under threats and pressure. The pivotal disagreement came on the question of taking supreme measures in behalf of the smaller nations of Central and Eastern Europe to which France was bound by its alliances and pacts, and on rearmament. The group led by Paul Faure objected to pacts which the party had had no voice in approving, and to rearmament. Unless there were a *direct* threat of enslavement, they insisted, war could not be accepted. They must continue their work for peace, demand an international conference to discuss political and economic problems, prevent the creation of a war psychosis in the country, and continue to work for disarmament and a strengthening of the League. They must persevere in their search for the "conditions for a possible coexistence between the democratic countries and the totalitarian countries."[2] There persisted also some traces of the old pre-1914 proletarian internationalism and a refusal to accept the realities of fascism. They spoke of the will for peace of "the German people and the Italian people" as if those peoples still retained some independence.[3]

Blum, once the party's most eloquent champion of internationalism, disarmament, and pacifism, countered with the impossibility of closing one's eyes to the world that had come into existence—a world threatened by "an international fascism animated by fanaticism and a spirit of conquest and domination." The emergence of fascism had rendered obsolete the old formulas and traditions.[4] Reiterating the thesis that only diplomatic and military strength would impress the dictators and save peace, he warned that there could be no further capitulation as at Munich. "There are moments when one must say no," he told the national council in November 1938 on the morrow of Munich, and addressing himself directly to Paul Faure: "You say, Paul, that that is to accept the idea of war. What else is there to do? It is frightful, but that is the way it is. And it is that way because the

---

[1] *Le Populaire*, October 27, 1938; see also editorials in preparation for the national council, *Le Populaire*, October 27–November 6, 1938, and speech to national council, *Le Populaire*, November 8, 1938.

[2] See resolution introduced by the Paul Faure group, *Le Populaire*, November 29, 1938, and Félix Gouin's speech at the Montrouge congress, *Le Populaire*, December 27, 1938.

[3] Gouin: speech at Montrouge congress, *Le Populaire*, December 27, 1938.

[4] *Le Populaire*, October 29, 1938.

Europe in which we live is not ours, it is not the Europe which we would have wanted."[5]

In preparation for the special congress to be held in December 1938 at Montrouge, an *ad hoc* committee was chosen to work out a compromise on the party's foreign policy stand. Blum threw all of his personal prestige into the debate. For the first time in the party's history he prepared a resolution in his own name defending his views. At so grave a time he refused to play the "more agreeable role of conciliator and arbitrator." He even let it be known through friends that if he could not win over the congress to his views he might resign as president of the Socialist group in Parliament and as political director of *Le Populaire*, perhaps even abandon public life entirely.[6]

At the congress, despite protestations of personal affection and fraternal solidarity, the two leaders of the party confronted each other in open conflict. Blum defended a policy of firmness and resistance even at the risk of war. Paul Faure contended that, except in the case of direct aggression against France, war could not be accepted. Paul Faure's resolution summed up the position of the pacifist wing, calling for the rapprochement of the "peoples of Europe" and the search for "conditions for possible coexistence." Blum's resolution called for the strengthening of existing alliances, effective rearmament, and a firm stand against the dictators. It stated unequivocally: "If the nation were forced to choose between enslavement and war [the party] would not counsel enslavement." Only as an attempted gesture of conciliation did he add: "But its clearly determined will is to extricate the French people from this terrible alternative, standing ready to accept all efforts and initiatives aimed at that goal." He accepted the call for an international conference "to discuss all political and economic differences" although he realized how hollow such hopes were.[7]

Emphasizing again the hostile forces that made it necessary to break with the party's traditions, he pointed out to the congress that it was not he who had changed, and ridiculed the whispered allegations that his new position was in any way influenced by the antisemitism of the Nazis. The world had changed. He was still the man who had fought the unfair provisions of Versailles, opposed the occupation of the Ruhr, fought steadfastly for peace and general disarmament as

[5] Speech to national council, *Le Populaire*, November 8, 1938.

[6] "Appel au parti," *Le Populaire*, December 17, 1938.

[7] For the Blum and Paul Faure resolutions, *Le Populaire*, November 29, 1938; for Blum's motion as amended, *Le Populaire*, December 27, 1938.

the prerequisites for peace and security. The pre-1914 Socialist idea of international proletarian action to prevent war was no longer valid; the working class had already been destroyed as an independent force in the fascist countries. For many years the Socialists had counted on the League and on disarmament for security, but the League no longer had "the authority or the power necessary to impose peace" on a rearmed Germany. Against the coalition of forces extending from Rome to Berlin to Tokyo, only a policy of strength based on rearmament and a firm binding together of all the nations prepared to resist the dictators, could save them from the "atrocious choice between submission and war." He again pleaded with the party to set aside all preconceptions, prejudices, and outworn formulas.[8]

Blum's appeal carried the Montrouge congress of December 1938 with 4,332 votes against Paul Faure's 2,837 votes, but with a large number of abstentions (1,014).[9] Everyone knew, as Blum later confessed, that the appeal for a firm foreign policy embodied in the triumphant resolution did not reflect the united will of the party.[1] In the months that followed, as the policies advocated by Blum became a reality, Paul Faure and his associates sulked in resentment.

What made it even more difficult for Blum to carry the party with him on a foreign policy that called for national unity was the open break that developed between the Daladier government and the working-class parties, for in the months after Munich the Popular Front was completely liquidated. The first signs of rift had appeared in August 1938 with Daladier's radio speech attacking the forty-hour week and in other ways indicating the orientation of his government. Open conflict then developed between Daladier and the Communists. In the Munich crisis the Communists had agitated to prevent the appeasement of Hitler and the exclusion of the Soviet Union from the settlement. After the Munich agreement, the Communists alone, as a party, refused to grant Daladier the vote of support he requested, and also voted against his request for renewed plenary powers. On October 14, an official Radical party statement declared that the Communist party had "deliberately withdrawn" from the Popular Front, a euphemism for demanding their expulsion. Later that month, at a Radical congress

[8] *Le Populaire*, December 27, 1938; also *L'Histoire jugera*, pp. 199–203.
[9] *Le Populaire*, December 28, 1938.
[1] *À l'échelle humaine*, *Oeuvre*, V, 455.

Daladier not only denounced the Communist crusade against his government at the time of Munich and after, but also renewed his attack on some of the social legislation of 1936.

Blum refused to accept the exclusion of the Communists from the Popular Front. To be sure, he had his own grievances against the Communists, who had never ceased denouncing him for his policy toward Spain and now attacked him for supporting the Munich agreement as well. But a vote against the Munich agreement and opposition to the anti-labor orientation of the Daladier government were hardly evidence of infidelity to the Popular Front. "We will not accept the exclusion of the Communists and allow ourselves to be enlisted in an anti-Communist campaign, for we know where that will lead," he told a national council of the party on November 5, 1938.[2] At the same time he still restrained the party from an open break with the Daladier government, insisting that the country expected them to rise above party quarrels and polemics.[3] A week later, however, on November 11, 1938, the Radicals formally withdrew from all coordinating agencies of the Popular Front in order to dissociate themselves from the Communists.

The Popular Front majority in the Chamber broke up too. Early in November, the Finance post was assumed by Paul Reynaud, who had again and again attacked the forty-hour law for interfering with production, increasing labor costs, and destroying the confidence of the business community. He soon announced a three-year plan designed to increase production by liberalizing controls, to rearm the country, and to insure financial stability. Despite its merits—the plan resulted in a significant increase in production in the months before the war and in a remarkable return of investment capital—Blum saw it primarily as an attempt to woo the confidence of business by destroying the labor reforms of the Popular Front governments. The very phraseology used by Reynaud in attacking "the week of two Sundays" confirmed that view. Decrees soon abolished the five-day forty-hour week, cut down drastically on overtime pay rates, and established penalties for refusing overtime work.[4]

The offensive against the labor laws of June 1936 disquieted Blum. In other respects he admired Reynaud as a firm opponent of appeasement, as "the most intelligent and the most courageous of the conserva-

---

[2] *Le Populaire*, November 6, 1938; and also *Le Populaire*, October 15, 28, 1938.

[3] *Le Populaire*, November 7, 1938.

[4] On the decrees and the Reynaud Plan, Ehrmann: *French Labor*, pp. 88–9, and Wolfe: *French Franc*, pp. 183–6.

tives," and he wished to support his rearmament program. Yet when national unity was most needed, the government was driving a wedge between itself and labor. Blum had always insisted that labor would accept adjustments in the forty-hour law provided these adjustments were accompanied by steps to increase productive efficiency in other ways. At the moment, he regarded the assault on the forty-hour law (despite its admitted deficiencies) as a political concession to industry rather than as an economic measure to raise production.[5] The sad truth was that the forty-hour law had become as much a sacred cow of the Left as it was the *bête noire* of the Right.

The C.G.T., the Communists, and the Socialists took up arms against the Daladier-Reynaud decree laws. Prompted by its Communist elements, the C.G.T. voted overwhelmingly to oppose the decrees and authorized its executive committee to make plans for a protest strike. Resentment over the Munich agreement was also clearly involved in the labor protests in November 1938. Daladier had not yet embarked on his "new" foreign policy; he was still the "man of Munich." When Chamberlain and Halifax visited Paris in the last week of November, the metalworkers at the Renault plant staged a sitdown strike and Daladier ordered the use of tear gas to evacuate the plants. Blum at once demanded the resignation of the government. Was Daladier seeking to win the confidence of the Bourse, he inquired, at the price of repeating the June days of 1848? He accused the government of trying to restore its prestige, shattered at Munich, by fighting labor.[6] *Le Populaire* denounced the Radicals as "traitors to the oath of July 14, 1935."[7] Events were throwing the Communists and Socialists together.

Matters reached a climax when the C.G.T. called a general protest strike on November 30, 1938. Resolved to crush the strike, the government requisitioned the railroads and public services and threatened dismissal of government workers. The strike itself was a failure. Severe reprisals by the government and by private industry followed.[8] Blum himself had no heart for the general strike. When it was crushed, but at the expense of further undermining national unity, he commented sadly. "It is not a victory for the working class, but is it a victory for the government?"[9] The C.G.T. itself soon rapidly dwindled in strength

[5] Speech at Lille, *Le Populaire*, November 14, 1938.
[6] *Le Populaire*, November 25, 26, 1938.
[7] *Le Populaire*, November 29, 1938.
[8] Ehrmann: *French Labor*, pp. 93–6.
[9] *Le Populaire*, December 1, 1938.

and was ousted from the position of importance it had occupied in national life since 1936. France would enter the war with labor deprived of a voice in public affairs.

When the Chamber reconvened on December 9, the breakup of the Popular Front parliamentary majority was complete; the Daladier-Reynaud government now looked for its majority to the Radicals and to those parties of the Center and Right that had formed the opposition at the opening of the 1936 legislature. The old law of French parliamentary life had once again become operative: a Left election victory (as in 1924 and 1932) had been followed in two years by a Rightist combination in Parliament. Daladier had broken with the Popular Front, Blum charged, in order to insure himself a stable, conservative majority; for the first time, the Radicals headed a "national bloc" cabinet.[1]

Blum's relationship with Daladier became more complex, however, when the government after March 1939 abandoned its policy of appeasement and turned to a strengthening of alliances. The exigencies of the foreign situation, Blum wrote, posed "a heavy trial of conscience."[2] When, in May, he had to serve as spokesman for the party in opposing the government on a vote of confidence, he did so with reluctance. Were it possible, he would have separated the vote on foreign policy from the vote on the government's economic and social policy.[3] He resented the repeated requests for plenary powers and the subordination of Parliament—the "anesthetization of the republican spirit."[4] When a decree in August postponed the general elections scheduled for 1940, Blum summed up his troubled position: "It is our duty as Socialists and republicans to inform the country of the seriousness of the action just taken against its liberties, to awaken its democratic feelings, to draw it out of its skepticism, indifference, and torpor. We shall fulfill this duty without failing in another duty, the full importance of which we feel, and that is, not to weaken either in reality or in appearance our national cohesion and strength."[5] As so many times before in his lifetime, Blum was once again walking a tightrope. He was attacking Daladier's domestic policies and at the same time valiantly trying

[1] Speech to Chamber, *Chambre, Débats*, December 9, 1939; editorials, *Le Populaire*, January 1, March 7, 8, April 21, August 5, 13–16, 1939.

[2] *Le Populaire*, August 16, 1939.

[3] See his speech in the Chamber, *Chambre, Débats*, May 12, 1939, and editorial, *Le Populaire*, May 16, 1939.

[4] *Le Populaire*, June 7, 1939.

[5] *Le Populaire*, August 5, 1939.

to support his foreign policy. Most difficult of all, he was even trying to pretend that national unity was still a reality.

But no one could conceal the steady weakening of national cohesion.
The intransigence of Daladier and Reynaud matching the intransigence
of labor, the profound anti-Popular Front sentiment sweeping the
country as it sought a scapegoat for its economic and military weakness,
the ignoring of Parliament, the estrangement of labor and the working-
class parties from the national community, the deep pacifism dividing
the country as well as Blum's own party—all were ill omens for the
future. And soon the German-Soviet pact of August 23, 1939, would
strain the fabric of national unity still further.

Blum had been very much disturbed by the setback to Franco-Soviet
relations after the exclusion of the Soviet Union from the Munich conference and had placed "in the first rank of importance" the need to
repair the damage done.[6] Shortly after the Munich agreement, he inquired of Daladier and the Soviet Ambassador, Jacob Souritz, whether
he might go to Moscow on a private basis to explore ways of improving
relations. Daladier did not respond "with any great enthusiasm."
Souritz, on the other hand, expressed interest and promised to forward
the suggestion to his government. But no word was ever forthcoming
from his superiors; a Blum "mission to Moscow" never materialized.[7]

In the weeks after Hitler's seizure of Prague, Blum followed closely
the British and French efforts to work out a diplomatic and military
agreement with the Soviets, confident that a strong alliance between the
Western democracies and the Soviet Union might still be created and
a "peace bloc" formed.[8] Early in May, when Blum saw Chamberlain
and Halifax in London, he tried to impress upon them, he later claimed,
the need to send a mission of high standing and prestige to satisfy
Soviet sensitivities—something which was never satisfactorily arranged.[9]

Yet in the spring of 1939 Blum felt certain that matters were pro-
ceeding well. He dismissed rumors that Litvinov's replacement by
Molotov presaged the detachment and isolation of the Soviets from

----

[6] Speech to Chamber, *Chambre, Débats*, October 4, 1938.
[7] Blum first disclosed this after the war; testimony, 1947, *Événements*, I,
258–9.
[8] "Le 'bloc idéologique de la paix,'" *Le Populaire*, March 21, 1939.
[9] Testimony, 1947, *Événements*, I, 259.

European problems.[1] Like many others, he considered it inconceivable that Stalin and Hitler might bury their deep ideological differences or that Stalin would underestimate the threat posed to Soviet national security by Hitler's openly expressed expansionist designs. "I have never attached the slightest credence to rumors predicting a reversal of position of Soviet Russia. I consider such a reversal impossible."[2] He was aware, however, that in the negotiations going on in Moscow, Poland and the Baltic states were interposing various objections. Although he agreed (as he had once said of Belgium) that "one cannot guarantee a state in spite of itself,"[3] he had little sympathy with the position of Poland and the Baltic states at so critical a time. Like Churchill, he refused to give much weight to their anxiety over Soviet designs; the "peace front" against Hitler was at stake. Repeatedly, he expressed his impatience at the delays and blamed all three major powers. Was the barrier still "the eternal dispute over the Baltic states"? he asked that summer. As Hitler's demands on Poland were raised, he kept warning that there was "not a day, not an hour to lose."[4]

Suddenly, on August 23, 1939, the astonished world learned that a Soviet reversal was possible and that the Soviets and Germany had negotiated a treaty of non-aggression even while the diplomatic and military talks with the Western democracies had been going on. Blum reacted with amazement and anger that day. "I would try in vain to conceal my stupefaction."[5] It was "a truly extraordinary event, almost incredible; one is dumfounded by this blow." He recognized immediately that this was no innocuous pact of non-aggression. At a time when the Polish crisis was reaching its peak, with troop movements and feverish diplomatic maneuvers under way, and with the signing of an Anglo-French-Soviet agreement expected momentarily, it signified that Stalin was throwing his weight "to Hitler's side," assuring him he had nothing to fear from the Soviets. "One would hardly be able to demonstrate greater audacity, scorn for world opinion, and defiance of public morality." He could not find words of opprobrium strong enough to denounce Stalin's breach of faith. Although he rejected any argument that there were legitimate grounds for so extreme a step, he tried to fathom the Soviet motives in their "double game." Their incurable suspicion of England and France (the result of Munich intensified by

[1] *Le Populaire,* May 5, 1939.
[2] *Le Populaire,* May 17, 1939.
[3] *Le Populaire,* June 7, 1939.
[4] *Le Populaire,* June 25 and July 1, 2, 5, 1939.
[5] *Le Populaire,* August 23, 1939.

the delay in the negotiations that spring) was not a satisfactory explanation. He could only warn the Soviets, in prophetic terms, that disinvolvement from the threat posed by Hitler was impossible. "If [the Soviet Union] removes itself from Europe, one day Hitler Germany will come to it."[6]

In view of the new situation created by the pact, the only deterrent to Hitler and the only guarantee of peace lay in a renewed pledge by Britain and France to maintain unity/and firmness. In the tense days that followed, Blum hailed the reaffirmation of British and French pledges to Poland and applauded President Roosevelt's peace appeal. But the march to war proceeded inexorably. Mobilization began and censorship was imposed. Hitler's reply to all overtures was the bombing of Warsaw on September 1. "Only one man wanted war" was Blum's terse comment.[7] On September 2, he took part in the unanimous vote in the Chamber (the Communists included) granting the government war credits. "The session was simple, grave, and grand," he wrote. The speeches of Herriot, president of the Chamber, and of Daladier were "worthy of the circumstances, worthy of the country." It was difficult, Daladier said in his speech, for men who had dedicated their lives to the defense of peace to respond with war, even to acts of aggression and violence. Blum's conscience was clear too: "Never was the violence more flagrant on the one hand, and never the will for peace more certain and more tenacious on the other."[8]

In the months between Munich and the outbreak of hostilities, and in the quiet months of the "phony war" in the autumn of 1939 and the spring of 1940, the deep antagonisms in France rose increasingly to the surface. The moral tone decayed as the divided nation faced an uncertain future. Now began the attacks that later came to full fruition under Vichy. Widespread grumbling and resentment in Rightist circles erupted against the "warmongers," who were accused of having led France into war when further efforts at accommodation with the dictators would have been possible. There was resentment at the Popular Front for having weakened France by introducing the forty-hour week and other labor reforms instead of concentrating on the nation's armed strength. Blum was one of those who bore the brunt of

[6] Ibid.
[7] *Le Populaire*, September 2, 1939.
[8] *Le Populaire*, September 3, 1939.

the charges both as a "warmonger" and as symbol of the Popular Front. At the time of Munich, *L'Action Française* had published "a little nursery rhyme" about the bullets that had to be prepared for the "cannibals" who were leading the country to war:

> *S'ils s'obstinent ces cannibales*
> *A faire de nous des héros*
> *Il faut que nos premières balles*
> *Soient pour Mandel, Blum, et Reynaud.*[9]

The fact that Blum and Mandel (the vigorous, patriotic Minister of Colonies, once a protégé of Clemenceau) were Jewish was suggested as the prime reason for their anti-Nazism. A privately printed brochure alleged that Blum, born Karfunkelstein, traitor to his adopted country, had been born in "Vidin, Bulgaria." There was not a shred of truth in the accusation but Blum felt himself impelled to protest the vicious pamphlet in an editorial.[1]

He received letters filled with invective and abuse from people in all walks of life. Many were outright calls for his assassination. "The hour for the settlement of accounts is approaching, Léon Blum," said one. Another, addressed to *"Président du conseil, Monsieur le Juif,"* stated: "Personally I hold you responsible for all the present misfortunes of which our country is victim," and concluded: "One ought to do away with individuals as dangerous as you are." He was told to "go back to Vidin." He received a formal calling card on which a gentleman and his wife "wish [ed] to express to Monsieur their profound revulsion and scorn toward his odious attitude with respect to the government charged with repairing the stupidities and misdeeds of the Popular Front." There were letters in the same vein from workers as well. Referring to the assassin of Jaurès, one correspondent impatiently asked: "Are there no Villains left in France?"[2]

One of the vivid recollections which Sumner Welles carried back from his European mission in the spring of 1940 concerned his visit to Blum on March 9. Although Blum occupied no official position in the government, Welles wished to consult him as a former Premier and as leader of what was still the largest party in Parliament. The following day Welles left for London and the press published a report of the visit.

---

[9] Cited in Werth: *France and Munich*, p. 347.

[1] Blum refuted the charges in *Le Populaire*, November 19, 1938; see also *Le Populaire*, October 9, 1938.

[2] I am indebted to M. André Blumel for permitting me to examine these unpublished letters.

"When I returned to Paris four days later," he recalled, "my secretaries estimated that while I was in England almost three thousand letters had been received, addressed to me by Frenchmen, and in no stereotyped form, protesting against my visit. The vast majority of these letters were written in the most violent and insulting terms. A few of them were couched in moderate words of reproach. They were all written, however, solely because, as a representative of the President of the United States, I had dared to call upon a Jew." The diplomat who had known France since his earliest childhood was shocked into realizing "for the first time how far the penetration of Nazi ideas had already proceeded in perverting the mentality of at least a portion of the French people . . . how widely the poison engendered by the Nazis had already seeped into Western Europe."[3]

The campaign of abuse continued. In March 1940, Blum protested against a special issue of *Gringoire*, which was devoted to vicious caricatures and attacks on him.[4] In May, *Le Populaire* protested the personal attacks on Blum. "We shall not allow a repetition of the monstrous campaigns which ended in the assassination of Jaurès and which over the bodies of new victims could end tomorrow in the assassination of the republic."[5] At that date, the assassination of the republic was only six weeks distant.

The differences in Blum's party also persisted. They had been submerged but not resolved by the majority resolutions adopted in December 1938 and May 1939. The pacifist wing sulked in deep resentment once the war broke out. They had accepted France's entry into the war and Germany's responsibility for it but insisted on the need to examine seriously all peace proposals that might be made. Paul Faure for a time refused to collaborate with Blum on *Le Populaire* and even created a new periodical, *Le Pays Socialiste*. When eventually he returned, he and J. B. Séverac filled their columns with appeals for a return to peace and disarmament, demands for the protection of labor's rights, and pleas "to spare the blood of our soldiers."[6] Letters poured in to the newspaper denouncing the Blum leadership for having created a "sacred union" before the war and for having destroyed the independence of socialism. All the trouble, wrote one contributor,

[3] *The Time for Decision* (New York, 1944), pp. 129–30.
[4] *Le Populaire*, March 18, 1940.
[5] *Le Populaire*, May 30, 1940.
[6] Faure returned to the newspaper on January 31, 1940; see his editorials and those of Séverac from February 6, 1940, on, especially those of March 8, 29, 1940.

stemmed from the "harmful idiolatry of a leader" who, when he had his opportunity, refused to transform the "exercise of power" into the "conquest of power."[7] The secretary of the Haute-Vienne Federation wrote to Blum privately, denouncing *Le Populaire*, "in which I no longer find anything of Socialist thought. . . . The censorship which you make an affectation of protesting against cannot take from *Le Populaire* what it had already lost in the year preceding the war—courage and intellectual probity. You are in my eyes the principal artisan of this failure and you have accumulated too many grave errors to permit me to continue, even if only with my subscription, to be in the slightest way associated with your action." Some letters were harsher. "I adored you, I defended you," wrote a former young Socialist official of Brest in the first week of the war, "and yet for the last eighteen months I regret that you are not dead. Now I no longer have anger or scorn for you. I have only pity; I wish you different nights from those of Lady Macbeth."[8]

In the fall of 1939 the Zoretti episode highlighted the embitterment of the pacifist group. On September 13, Ludovic Zoretti, a leader of the pacifist wing in the party and in the teachers' federation, wrote a letter to a Swiss Socialist, appealing for a joint effort by the various neutral Socialist parties to bring about an early peace after the fall of Poland. "It is not only on behalf of myself personally that I am writing to you, it is in part in the name of our comrades of the Socialist party grouped around our position, and also of Paul Faure and his friends who share exactly the same feeling. . . . In practical terms, it is extremely difficult for us to act in France; all we can do is to prevent stupidities that are too excessive, for example, the formation of a cabinet in which Blum and Herriot would outdo one another in incitement to collective murder."

Zoretti never denied authorship of the letter. He claimed, however, to have written it the day after a conversation with Paul Faure in which in the presence of others, Faure had boasted of his efforts to prevent the formation of a war cabinet with Socialist participation. He quoted Faure: "Do you know the two men whom I consider the most dangerous at the present moment? Blum and Herriot." He also quoted Faure as remarking that he could find support for a negotiated peace in various quarters, mentioning Pierre Laval. Paul Faure disavowed the conversa-

[7] Berthe Fouchère: "Penser et agir en socialistes," in "Tribune du parti," *Le Populaire*, February 9, 1940.

[8] The letters are from M. Blumel's private files.

tion as partly invented and partly distorted. In January 1940 the executive committee expelled Zoretti from the party.[9] At a party meeting in February, Charles Spinasse, himself in the pacifist camp, made a special point of insisting that differences of opinion did not alter the party's profound affection for Blum.[1] But this was not entirely true. Anti-war sentiment and antisemitism combined to make Blum a special target of abuse and attack in the party as well as in the country as a whole. Paul Faure had already embarked on the road that would lead to a post on Vichy's national council.

Blum was sadly conscious of the profound division within the party ever since Munich. It was this internal split that vitiated any influence it might have brought to bear on the government. In later years he wrote frankly:

> In truth, since Munich, French socialism was divided into two factions profoundly opposed on the key problem of political life. . . . it was this internal division that condemned it to impotence and nearly to silence. It wished at all costs to preserve its formal unity; and any clear-cut action or even any categorical statement would have made the latent division appear openly, and undoubtedly would have provoked a schism. . . . It dragged on thus, for nearly two years, leading a humiliating shadowy existence, in such a way that in the end one did not even seem aware of its presence.

It would have been better, Blum declared, "if a frank break would have separated the irreconcilable elements." But he, like others, could not bring himself to accept schism; "the religion of unity" was too strong.[2]

The once proud leader of a powerful Socialist party now headed a rapidly disintegrating party, a house divided against itself, a large segment of which repudiated him as a false leader, a warmonger, and a traitor to Socialist ideals. With his party deserting him, with the government failing to inspire confidence and even threatening dictatorship, with the country turning on itself in savage attacks, these

---

[9] Copies of the documents are in M. Blumel's private files, including Zoretti's letter to Dr. Oprecht in Zurich and Zoretti's statement to the party executive committee attesting to Paul Faure's remarks; cf. Lefranc: *Mouvement socialiste*, p. 377, n. 1.

[1] *Le Populaire*, February 12, 1940.

[2] *À l'échelle humaine, Oeuvre*, V, 455–6.

early war months were a time of deep distress for Blum. His spirits were buoyed only by the burning conviction that the cause of the war was just and that the war itself would be followed by the triumph of democratic ideals and a durable peace.[3]

Despite their differences, all factions of the Socialists united in condemning Stalin's actions in 1939 and 1940. In the confusion that accompanied the pact with Hitler, the partitioning of Poland, and the war on Finland, Blum saw an opportunity to win back to the fold of democratic socialism many French workers bewildered by the Communist defense of the Soviet acts. Blaming the outbreak of the war itself on the German-Soviet pact, he impatiently dismissed the Communist argument—once the party leaders had caught their breath—that the pact was a "service to the cause of peace." "Cease your game," he exhorted them on August 27, "you cannot believe what you are saying. Some other time we will enjoy the agility of your dialectics."[4] He pleaded that here at last was the opportunity to throw off their subservience to Moscow. "I know the discipline and solidarity of the party. But it is inconceivable that the existence of a proletarian party should rest in the final analysis on the dogma of one man's infallibility. Find in yourselves the courage to emancipate yourselves. You have been released from your vows. Let yourselves become free men once again."[5]

After the Soviet invasion of Poland, Blum's indignation redoubled when the Communists defended that "atrocious event" as well. "The curtain has been lifted," he noted, "the Soviets are accomplices of Hitler. The Soviets, the only proletarian state of the world, the one that had boasted of having 'constructed socialism,' has become the bloody accomplice of the most monstrous iniquity." His old warnings ever since 1920 about Communist subservience to Russia were being vindicated by events. Repeatedly he appealed to the Communist leaders to break the "alliance with Moscow."[6]

After Poland was crushed, Blum had new grounds for exasperation. Two Communist Deputies wrote to Édouard Herriot, president of the Chamber, requesting that Parliament be convened to examine publicly the peace offer made by Hitler. Neither "the fomenters of imperialist war" (i.e., Britain and France) nor "Hitler Germany," but the Soviet

[3] See, e. g., editorial, *Le Populaire*, October 31, 1939.
[4] *Le Populaire*, August 27, 1939, and also September 9, 1939.
[5] *Le Populaire*, August 27, 1939.
[6] *Le Populaire*, September 18, 1939.

Union alone, they announced, stood ready to arrange a just and durable peace. When Blum learned of the letter's contents, a "wave of nausea," he said, came over him.[7] Even the pacifist wing of the Socialist parliamentary group joined in a resolution denouncing "the impudent lie by which the totalitarian governments of Russia and Germany pretend to place on France and Britain responsibility for the prolongation of the war."[8]

In December came the Soviet attack on Finland. "What shade of excuse can they give?" demanded Blum, who dismissed the argument that they had acted to strengthen the security of their borders. To him this new "crime" was proof that Stalin was motivated solely by the interests of the Russian state, not the cause of international proletarian revolution: Stalin was the successor to Peter the Great, not to Lenin.[9] Praising the "sublime resistance" of the Finns, he questioned whether the aid promised to the Finns by Britain and France would arrive in time.[1] There were moments when he seemed unconcerned even about Western involvement in open belligerency with the Soviets.[2] Yet at the same time he was concerned lest the war against Hitler be converted into an anti-Soviet war. "It is possible that for a number of years the Hitler danger concealed from Europe the Russian danger. Let us be on guard that the Russian peril not divert our eyes from the Hitler danger!"[3] In March 1940, he shared in the general indignation at the failure of the Western Allies to save the Finns from defeat; it was added evidence, he believed, of the ineptitude of Daladier's leadership.[4]

However, despite his own criticism of the Communists, Blum's conscience was troubled by the Daladier government's repressive measures against them. Two days after the announcement of the German-Soviet pact, Daladier had banned the two Communist dailies, *L'Humanité* and *Ce Soir*, and prohibited all Communist-sponsored meetings. Despite the enthusiasm with which many in his party greeted these and later anti-Communist measures, Blum demurred. Although he shared the government's anxiety over possible Communist subversion

[7] *Le Populaire*, October 4, 1939. On the letter and the episode, Walter: *Parti communiste français*, p. 351; and cf. for the Communist position during these months, ibid., pp. 341–59.

[8] *Le Populaire*, October 6, 1939.

[9] *Le Populaire*, December 4, 1939.

[1] *Le Populaire*, January 14, 19, 1940.

[2] *Le Populaire*, February 13, 1940, and after the fall of Finland, *Le Populaire*, March 26, 1940.

[3] *Le Populaire*, December 6, 1939.

[4] *Le Populaire*, March 21, 1940.

at so critical a moment, he considered these steps morally wrong and politically ill-advised. For one thing, the Communists, in their attempt to defend the pact, were floundering helplessly in a sea of contradictory arguments; he would let them drown in their own arguments and would avoid creating sympathy for them as martyrs. Secondly, in the name of national defense and unity, the government must not "allow all France, and the whole outside world, to believe that the hundreds of thousands of workers in Communist organizations are bad Frenchmen and bad patriots." Drawing a distinction between the party leaders and their misguided followers, he pleaded that the latter not be cut off from the body politic.[5]

In the weeks that followed, the government dissolved the Communist party itself and banned the publication and distribution of all Communist materials. The penalties for violations included prison terms and heavy fines. Blum again, speaking for himself personally and not for his party, argued against the measures and protested that repression would only win sympathy for the Communist party when its fortunes were in decline. But another consideration colored his outlook, and his conscience forced him to speak out: "I remain incorrigibly a republican and a democrat. There are authoritarian measures with which I cannot find myself in agreement." The only proper remedy, he believed, lay in legal and judicial processes. "If the Communists are individually accused of treason, let them be prosecuted and executed like all traitors. But the Communist party in itself is not actionable in my opinion except before the bar of public opinion and the only penalty which ought to be administered is universal reprobation."[6] Blum's scorn for the Communists was strong but not overpowering enough to make him break faith with his lifelong devotion to working-class liberties.

After the Soviet attack on Finland the Chamber voted in December 1939 to suspend parliamentary immunity and the government proceeded to arrest several of the leading "ex-Communist" Deputies. Shortly thereafter, the Communists themselves deliberately provoked the Chamber. Four "ex-Communists" attending the session of January 9, 1940, remained seated, refusing to join in the tribute paid by the presiding officer to the soldiers of the republic. After the uproar subsided, a vote of censure was passed and the four were expelled from the Chamber. Two days later, the government introduced a bill to disqualify all Deputies

[5] *Le Populaire*, August 27, 1939; see also *Le Populaire*, November 14, 1939.
[6] *Le Populaire*, September 27, 1939.

who by January 9, 1940, had not publicly disavowed their connection with the Communist party.

The government's bill posed a new dilemma for Blum. Although appalled by the behavior of the Communists, he maintained that Parliament had no right to disqualify any of its members since they had been elected by universal manhood suffrage and were not removable save for grave personal misconduct as provided by law. If Parliament alone, without the courts, were permitted to disqualify them, he asked, "who could consider themselves safe?"[7] The alternative, again, was recourse to legal and judicial procedures. When the question was discussed in the Socialist group, Blum voted to propose such procedures, but a majority supported the sterner government measure by a vote of 69 to 38. After all, it was argued, the Convention had considered itself justified in voting the execution of Louis XVI![8] In the end, it was a Socialist, Georges Barthélemy, who reported the bill to the Chamber as spokesman for the appropriate parliamentary committee. The date of "renunciation" was even pushed back to October 1, 1939, and the bill passed by a vote of 521 to 2, Blum voting for the measure out of respect for party discipline. A spokesman for the Socialist group, François Chasseigne, commented that in Russia the traitors would have received " a bullet in the back of their heads";[9] Paul Faure echoed that statement a few weeks later.[1]

In April 1940, forty-four of the ex-Communist Deputies were tried before a military tribunal and condemned to prison sentences of two to five years; nine, including Thorez and Duclos, were condemned *in absentia*. Shortly thereafter, the death penalty was decreed for those guilty of treasonous activities; a Socialist, Albert Sérol, was at the time Minister of Justice. The two proletarian parties had traveled in very different directions. The Communists, obeying the dictates of Moscow, had forfeited the right to speak in the name of the French working class. Yet their persecution by a government hostile to the working class earned them sympathy. The Socialists, on the other hand, had identified themselves with the government's measures of repression, dismaying many of their supporters.

[7] *Le Populaire*, January 13, 1940.

[8] Ibid.; see also *Le Populaire*, January 12, 1940.

[9] *Le Populaire*, January 17, 1940. See also Walter: *Parti communiste français*, pp. 352–5.

[1] Speech of February 22, 1940, reprinted in *Le Populaire*, April 23, 1940.

For Blum these events were but another part of those anguished days. Against the majority in his own party, he had opposed the extreme measures taken by the government as undemocratic and even "totalitarian." His conscience had compelled him to speak out, and years later he continued to "regret" the repression which had been imposed.[2] He had, at least as an individual, tried to protect those legal rights of the Communists which he believed to be most egregiously outraged.

Ironically, Blum's defense of Communist rights earned him no gratitude from the Communist leaders. In February 1940, Thorez singled Blum out for special excoriation, summing up in wondrously distorted fashion the record of Blum's anti-Communist activities:

> The hyena Blum placed himself at the head of the mob barking furiously at the heels of communism and the Soviet Union. After the Soviet-German non-aggression pact was signed, Blum . . . addressed insulting and shameless invitations to the members of the party. He pressed them to deny their party and their International, to disavow the Soviet Union, to betray the interests of the working class if they did not wish to be haled before a court-martial. . . . He fell into the most profound abyss of infamy; he proposed to the government that it bring the Communist leaders to justice, to judge them, and to execute them. . . . Blum demanded and obtained the arrest of the Communist Deputies; he demanded and obtained the annulment of the mandate entrusted to them by universal suffrage. . . . With cynical irony he expressed his joy at knowing that thousands of Communist workers were sleeping on the wet straw of prison cells.

There is no evidence that Blum ever read Thorez's wild charges. They appeared simultaneously in *L'Internationale Communiste* and in the German newspaper *Die Welt*.[3]

The events he had lived through convinced him, Blum wrote in 1941 in his wartime memoirs, that the Communist party was "not an internationalist party but a foreign national party," "a sect foreign to the nation" serving solely "the particular interests of a single state, the

[2] Editorial, *Le Populaire*, July 10, 1945, *Oeuvre*, VI, 37.

[3] "Léon Blum, tel qu'il est," *L'Internationale Communiste*, February 1940, reproduced, along with other Communist articles on Blum, in Maurice Thorez: *Léon Blum tel qu'il est*, edited by Charles Pot. The quotation is on p. 16. The article in *Die Welt*, February 16, 1940, was entitled "Léon Blum, wie er leibt and lebt."

Soviet Union."[4] After Hitler's attack on the Soviet Union in June 1941, the French Communists could once again be French patriots, and their heroism and sacrifices during the occupation years compelled his admiration. Even so, he discerned that after the war the nation would still face an "unbearable anomaly"—the existence in political life of "a foreign national party." That problem he bequeathed to the future.[5] But in the spring of 1940 the future held many other uncertainties as well.

[4] *À l'échelle humaine, Oeuvre*, V, 458.
[5] Ibid., pp. 458–9.

XII

WITNESS TO COLLAPSE:
Paris and Bordeaux, May–June 1940

*Why, from hour to hour, should one not
have awaited the dawn of a new Marne?*[1]

BLUM always denied that he had been part of a political maneuver to overthrow Édouard Daladier and replace him with
Paul Reynaud, as eventually happened in March 1940 in
the wake of the Finnish debacle. At the outbreak of the war Blum
had pledged that he would have no part in any intrigue against Daladier.
"Circumstances," he wrote on September 15, 1939, "have made him the
only leader possible at the present moment."[2] Yet relations between
Blum and the Radical leader were strained, and Blum directed a heavy
barrage of criticism against the government during the months of
hostilities. It was difficult to forget Daladier's anti-labor orientation ever
since the summer of 1938 and his failure to enlist labor in the war effort
once the war broke out. When, in September 1939, Daladier, in a
gesture of conciliation, offered two cabinet seats to the Socialists, the
party rejected the offer. Blum said nothing about the opposition within
his own party but protested that such a government would not be "one
that the situation demanded." He called instead for a true national unity
cabinet in which the Socialists, the largest party in the Chamber, would

---

[1] Blum: *Mémoires*, 1940, *Oeuvre*, V, 19. Blum's memoirs on the events of
1940, written shortly after his arrest in September 1940, were not published until
after his death (and then with some deletions); see Robert Blum's editorial
note, *Oeuvre*, V, 3–4, for explanation of the "rare passages suppressed." Such
passages, he asserts (and has assured me personally), have to do only with
judgments on events of which his father did not have firsthand knowledge.

[2] *Le Populaire*, September 15, 1939; cf. speech in Chamber, *Chambre*, *Débats*,
March 22, 1940; and testimony, 1947, *Événements*, I, 259.

assume their fair share of authority and responsibility.[3] He pressed also for the formation of a small, compact "war government" on the British model, capable of coordinating and directing the war effort efficiently and energetically.[4] His own candidate to head such a cabinet was the president of the Senate, Jules Jeanneney.[5]

Throughout the early months of the war Blum protested, in editorial after editorial, against the ineptitude of the censorship, the inadequacy of the government's information and morale services, and the infringements on civil liberties. He repeatedly demanded that Daladier convene Parliament so that the nation's representatives, like their counterparts in Britain, might share in the war effort.[6]

In part because of Daladier's unwillingness to keep Parliament in session, the Socialists refused to vote him the exceptional powers he sought at the end of November 1939. "In defending the power of the republican Parliament," said Blum, "we are convinced that we are fortifying the strength of the French nation at war."[7] The government received its grant of powers, nevertheless, without difficulty. In February 1940, Blum was chiefly responsible for persuading Daladier to permit the Chamber to meet in secret session to examine the military situation.[8] Blum also sat as a member of the parliamentary committee on the army and heard disheartening testimony on the unpreparedness of the nation's armed services. The four-year rearmament program launched at the end of 1936 could not be accelerated and would not be completed before the end of 1940.[9]

In the tense autumn and winter of 1939–40 the French armies decayed behind the Maginot Line; there was no attempt to apply the lessons of the German blitz in Poland. Late that autumn Blum met with Paul Reynaud and Colonel de Gaulle, and found himself in accord with both men on the need for a more vigorous prosecution of the war. Reynaud, although in the cabinet as Minister of Finance, had little influence either on Daladier in military matters or on General Gamelin.

[3] *Le Populaire*, September 14, 1939, and *Le Populaire*, February 2, 1940.

[4] *Le Populaire*, September 10, 11, 1939.

[5] Testimony, 1947, *Événements*, I, 259. The choice, when it was revealed in later years, surprised many; yet see also Paul-Boncour's tribute, *Entre deux guerres*, III, 185.

[6] See, e. g., editorials in *Le Populaire*, September 24–26, 1939, and various dates thereafter until March 1940.

[7] Speech in Chamber, *Chambre, Débats*, November 30, 1939.

[8] See *Le Populaire*, February 5, 10, 12, 1940; see also Bonnet: *Quai d'Orsay*, p. 316.

[9] Testimony, 1947, *Événements*, I, 229, 259.

De Gaulle lamented that the army did not have a single armored division: it had only light tanks thinly distributed throughout the infantry units like "dust." In the hope that Blum, along with Reynaud, might exert some influence, de Gaulle prepared a memorandum which the Socialist leader tried to communicate to the authorities. Little was accomplished, however. Not until the first weeks of 1940 were three armored divisions belatedly formed; and the deficiencies in air-power were never overcome.[1]

On March 21, 1940, Reynaud replaced Daladier as Premier. The immediate reason was Daladier's failure to prevent the collapse of Finnish resistance, but there was widespread dissatisfaction with the general conduct of the war. Blum viewed the defeat in Finland as the first striking evidence of the inability of the Daladier government to coordinate and direct the war effort effectively.[2]

Reynaud, for his part, deliberately moved to make his cabinet more representative than Daladier's had been. Technically, he himself was a member of the Alliance Démocratique, a Center party, but he had broken with the party's leader, Flandin, and others who had supported the Munich agreement. Although opposed to the Popular Front economic policies, he had never flagged in his campaign to rally the country to a strong military and diplomatic policy. In his new cabinet he included three Socialist ministers, Georges Monnet as Blockade Minister, Albert Sérol as Minister of Justice, and Albert Rivière as Minister of Pensions; three Socialist undersecretaries were appointed as well. He appointed the six Socialists out of the conviction that "so important a party could not be excluded when it was a question of waging a total war." Although he seems genuinely to have desired to include Blum in the cabinet, he was sensitive to his own precarious margin of support in the Chamber. If he invited Blum, he convinced himself, he would assuredly lose the support of the Right. By mutual consent, any thought of naming Blum was dropped. "By reason of the state of public opinion," Reynaud later wrote, "I had to give up the idea of inviting M. Léon Blum." At the same time he paid tribute to Blum's "complete personal disinterestedness."[3] Blum put the best

---

[1] For the episode, Blum: *Mémoires*, 1940, *Oeuvre*, V, 115–17; Reynaud: *Mémoires*, II, 293.

[2] *Le Populaire*, March 21, 1940.

[3] *Au coeur de la mêlée*, pp. 376–7; *Mémoires*, II, 304–5. Note also Churchill's tribute to Blum's "voluntary withdrawal," cited by Reynaud: *Au coeur de la mêlée*, p. 378. André Février, Fabien Albertin, and François Blancho were the undersecretaries.

countenance on the situation, informing some of his disappointed colleagues that he had declined to press for the invitation. "I replied no, for I think that for many reasons I shall be more useful to my party outside the government."[4] Conscious of the animosity aroused by his name, he did not wish to endanger Reynaud's support either in Parliament or in the country at large. His refusal to press for a seat in the cabinet deprived him of the opportunity to play a more direct role in the momentous events to come, to say nothing of the kind of role that the British Labour leaders played in Churchill's cabinet.

The delicate balance of political forces was clearly apparent when Reynaud received the support of the Chamber for his new cabinet on March 23 by only a bare majority, with a large number of abstentions. The parties of the Center and Right opposed him because of the presence of Socialists in the cabinet. The Radicals bitterly resented the replacement of Daladier as Premier, even though Daladier stayed on as Minister of National Defense and Chautemps was Vice-Premier. Several speakers at the session spoke of an "intrigue" between Reynaud and Blum. Blum vehemently protested and, undeterred by the recriminations and accusations, sounded a moving appeal for national unity, calling for "the largest possible union of all the vital energies, of all the republican forces of the country."[5] Charles de Gaulle, who had been summoned to Paris by Reynaud, was present at the session:

> It was frightful. After the Government's declaration, read by its chief to a skeptical and gloomy Chamber, one heard in the debate that followed nothing but the spokesmen for groups or for men who believed their interests hurt in the ministerial combination. The danger faced by the country, the need for a national effort, the cooperation of the free world, were evoked only as a façade for personal claims and grudges. Only Léon Blum, even though no post had been offered to him, spoke with elevation. Thanks to him, M. Paul Reynaud won his victory, although an extremely narrow one.[6]

Blum remarked of the demoralizing session of March 23: "The best that one can do is to chase the memory of it from one's mind like that of a bad dream."[7]

[4] *Le Populaire*, March 22, 1940.
[5] *Chambre, Débats*, March 23, 1940.
[6] *Mémoires de guerre*, I, 25.
[7] *Le Populaire*, March 24, 1940.

In the weeks that followed, Blum lauded Reynaud's appeals for an energetic and vigorous pursuit of the war, even though he was well aware that public opinion classed him, along with Reynaud, as one of the "bloodthirsty."[8] Still not satisfied that a true war cabinet had been created, he nonetheless accepted Reynaud's cabinet reorganization as a step in the right direction.[9] His Socialist colleague and protégé, Georges Monnet, as Blockade Minister, was now a member of the small "inner cabinet." He was, as Chautemps later described him, "Blum's spokesman in the cabinet."[1]

Suddenly, in the spring of 1940, the "phony war" came to an end with Hitler's onslaught in April against Denmark and Norway, and then on May 10 with his attack on Holland, Belgium, and Luxembourg. The Battle of France was not far off. Blum applauded Reynaud's call for the defense of the nation in its time of peril. He "reserved judgment" when Reynaud took into his cabinet on May 10 two Rightist Deputies, Louis Marin and Jean Ybarnegaray, at the same time that he dropped two of the three Socialist undersecretaries.[2] More favorably impressed by events across the Channel, Blum hailed the replacement of Chamberlain by Churchill, the inclusion of Attlee as Deputy Prime Minister in the Churchill cabinet, and the creation of what he considered to be a true "war cabinet."[3]

Three days after the invasion of the Low Countries, just before he was scheduled to fly to Bournemouth to represent the French Socialists at a British Labour party congress, Blum dined with Reynaud, whom he found "grave and even somber." The Premier implored him to convey to the British the seriousness of the situation, and to urge the dispatch of all possible help. "It is on the Meuse," Blum recalled Reynaud's intense words, "that we must at this moment with all our strength together defend our common safety."[4]

In England, the difference of mood was instantly apparent. Blum found an atmosphere of vibrant self-confidence at the Labour party meeting. Churchill was in the midst of forming his coalition government with broad representation for Labour and had included Attlee and

[8] *Le Populaire*, April 7, 1940.

[9] *Le Populaire*, March 25, 27, 1940.

[1] Interview, *Journal de Montréal*, September 22, 1940, cited by Reynaud: *Au coeur de la mêlée*, p. 936.

[2] Blum confined himself to paying tribute to Albertin and Blancho, the two Socialist undersecretaries who were dropped, *Le Populaire*, May 11, 12, 1940.

[3] *Le Populaire*, May 15, 1940.

[4] Blum: *Mémoires*, 1940, *Oeuvre*, V, 6–7; Reynaud: *Mémoires*, II, 347.

Greenwood in his five-man war cabinet. (Since even under Chamberlain there had been close consultation with Labour, Blum could not help but contrast the situation in France.) Welcomed with a standing ovation and a rousing "Marseillaise," Blum delivered a short address in French. At the request of a number of the delegates, he analyzed the reasons for the stringent anti-Communist measures adopted in France. They had been considered necessary for reasons of national security; with the Communists present, it would have been impossible, he pointed out, to convene Parliament in secret session to discuss the conduct of the war. Conceding the harshness of the measures taken and personally regretting their rigor, he denied that freedom of criticism had otherwise been abridged or that France had become "fascist" or a military tyranny. He urged wholehearted support by European labor for the war effort, vehemently repudiating the Communist charge, heard ever since the Moscow pact, that the war was being fought by capitalists in the interests of capitalism. "The war that we are waging against Germany is not a capitalist war. I do not know what would become of capitalism if Hitler were to win the war, but I know very well what would become of socialism if Germany were victorious. Wherever the motorized Attila has passed, every movement and every institution created by the workers has been destroyed."[5]

In London, on May 15, the day after his speech, Blum received the distressing report from Clement Attlee that German mechanized elements had broken through the French lines and were advancing rapidly. Attlee desired to impress upon Blum the gravity of the situation without causing him excessive apprehension, but his communication of the news in halting French only added to the confusion. Blum, in his "naïve confidence," as he later described his feelings, could only ask himself whether the news was so terrible and whether Attlee's mournful expression was justified. "What if German tanks had broken through the lines? Were there not tens and hundreds of thousands of French soldiers behind those front lines?" Shortly after this talk with Attlee, two telegrams arrived from Paris, one from Georges Monnet and another from Marx Dormoy, urging him to return at once; these communications shook his confidence and quickened his anxiety.[6]

While he was in London, panic had spread in the French capital. On

---

[5] Speech at Bournemouth, *Le Populaire*, May 16, 1940, and cf. *Mémoires*, 1940, *Oeuvre*, V, 11–12. The speech was also published in an English translation, *France at War* (London, 1940).

[6] *Mémoires*, 1940, *Oeuvre*, V, 13–14.

the night of May 15–16, German armored units had broken through the line of the Meuse at several points in French and Belgian territory. The point of the thrust had reached Laon, less than eighty miles from Paris. The High Command, fearing that the German advance might be pushed at full speed toward Paris, had warned that measures for the evacuation of the government must be taken at once. Spreading outward from official circles, consternation and fear enveloped the city. Automobiles filled to capacity stretched out all along the roads from Paris. Documents of the Quai d'Orsay were burned in the courtyard. Then suddenly, toward the end of the morning, when the German columns had not advanced further in the direction of Paris but had turned west, the military command and the government regained their composure. Reynaud took to the radio, denied that the government was leaving Paris, and reaffirmed the government's will to defend the city. To the Chamber, which convened that afternoon, he delivered a sober but ardent address. The Chamber responded with a show of unity and patriotic determination—an upsurge of the "old Jacobinism," as *Le Populaire* reported. Blum learned of these events from his friends when he returned to France on May 17.[7] The panic had been real but it had subsided; it was a dress rehearsal for the drama that would take place three weeks later.

Although the immediate danger to Paris had passed, the emergency continued. When Blum talked with Reynaud upon his return, he learned that German armored units had crossed the bridges of the Meuse, penetrating and dislocating the French divisions below Sedan. Psychologically and technically, the French army was unprepared for the massed German tank units; the onslaught had come as "a terrible surprise. . . . The same stupefaction seemed to have seized it as once had seized the Roman legions before Hannibal's elephants."[8] The lessons of the German blitz in Poland eight months earlier had not been heeded. That same evening Reynaud informed Blum of two major changes he was planning: the replacement of General Gamelin as commanding general and his own assumption of the National Defense and War ministries. Ever since Reynaud had formed his cabinet, he had been anxious to take the direction of the war into his own hands, but, dependent on Radical Socialist support in the Chamber, he feared to replace Daladier, who refused to surrender the post. The new cir-

---

[7] *Le Populaire*, May 17, 1940; *Mémoires*, 1940, *Oeuvre*, V, 15–16. Cf., on these and related events, Reynaud: *Au coeur de la mêlée*, pp. 413–84.

[8] *Mémoires*, 1940, *Oeuvre*, V, 16.

cumstances permitted no further hesitation. "I have called for General Weygand," Blum quoted Reynaud as telling him. "He will be in Paris tomorrow, Saturday. I am waiting for him to fix my choice definitely." "I had the feeling," Blum wrote in his memoirs, "that Paul Reynaud's plan was not to give General Weygand the command of the French armies but to create for him in the government a post of technical adviser, or chief of staff, analogous to that which Marshal Foch had filled during a part of the other war." Blum had the distinct impression that the Premier intended to entrust the command to a younger man.[9] (Weygand was then seventy-three, though he was vigorous and spry.) Whether Reynaud had this in mind has never been clarified, but Blum's impression was substantiated by Paul Baudouin's journal entry to the same effect.[1] In any event, the plan was not carried out. Weygand was named commanding general on May 18, to preside over the final stages of the defeat. That Gamelin, despite many sterling virtues, lacked resilience and other qualities of leadership was undoubtedly true; whether Weygand was superior to him or possessed the extraordinary qualities that the situation demanded, as well as confidence in his own ability to snatch victory out of defeat at that late hour, was another matter.[2]

There were other changes on May 18. To soften the blow to Daladier and the Radical party, Reynaud gave him the Foreign Affairs Ministry. To demonstrate the government's will to resist, he shifted to the Ministry of the Interior Georges Mandel, the "Tiger's cub," who had helped Clemenceau stamp out defeatism in the First World War and who enjoyed an almost legendary reputation for Jacobin energy and determination. To dramatize the danger facing the country and the need for national unity—and to mollify the Right—he asked Marshal Pétain to enter the cabinet as Vice-Premier.

With misgivings Blum observed the cabinet's increasing orientation to the Right, first on May 10 and now on May 18. He was disturbed, too, at the continuing failure to create a British-style war cabinet. But whatever apprehension he felt about some of Reynaud's appointments, he would do no more than hint at them in the midst of the military crisis. "I shall do as the public at large," he wrote in *Le Populaire*. "I

[9] Ibid., pp. 17–18.

[1] *Neuf Mois au gouvernement, avril–décembre 1940* (Paris, 1948), journal entry, May 19, 1940, p. 60.

[2] See Philip C. F. Bankwitz: "Maxime Weygand and the Fall of France: A Study in Civil-Military Relations," *Journal of Modern History*, XXXI (1959), 225–42.

shall postpone to some other occasion comments called for by the cabinet reorganization: its composition, the balance of political forces represented in it, and its internal organization." What counted was the "will to win." He expressed confidence that the changes "would raise the war-making potential of the country to the highest point."[3]

Blum had no more prescience than anyone else on the outcome of the Pétain and Weygand appointments. No suggestion was made that the appointment of either Marshal Pétain or General Weygand might introduce an atmosphere of defeatism and pessimism into the cabinet. What his Socialist colleague Georges Monnet said after the war summed up Blum's attitude also: "The responsibilities entrusted to Marshal Pétain and General Weygand did not appear to any of us . . . as signs of weakness."[4] Pétain had always enjoyed the respect of the Left for the defense of Verdun and for his humane conduct after the mutinies of 1917. When a few months earlier Pétain had been appointed Ambassador to Spain, Blum himself had written that Franco did not deserve the honor of having so fine a soldier as ambassador— "the noblest, the most human of our military chiefs"[5] Blum could only admit later: "I lived . . . in the same illusion as all France."[6]

During the next few weeks, from May 18 to the evacuation at Dunkirk, Blum alternated "between the cruelest anguish and the most ardent hopes," between "exaltation and distress."[7] The military situation was grim but not hopeless. The German armored divisions which had forced the Meuse had opened the way for a massive invasion. The German maneuver, aimed not at Paris but at the Channel ports, threatened to cut off the elite of the French and British armies that had gone to the aid of Belgium—Belgium which had abandoned its alliance with France in 1936 for a futile "neutralism." Yet in Blum's mind these events were not reason enough for despair; the German armies could themselves be trapped. In his opinion, the situation seemed infinitely more favorable than that at the beginning of September 1914. "Why," he later asked, "should one not have awaited the dawn of a new Marne from hour to hour?" A counterattack by the armies in Flanders and Belgium and by the troops assembled behind the Somme and the Aisne

---

[3] "La Volonté de vaincre," *Le Populaire*, May 20, 1940; and *Le Populaire*, May 19, 1940.

[4] Testimony, 1949, *Événements*, V, 1435.

[5] *Le Populaire*, March 3, 1939.

[6] Testimony at Pétain trial, 1945, *Le Procès du maréchal Pétain, compte-rendu sténographique*, I, 246.

[7] *Mémoires*, 1940, *Oeuvre*, V, 18–20.

seemed "written into destiny."[8] Actually General Weygand had hopes, as late as May 24, of pinching off the Nazi thrust and opening up a passage for the Allied divisions caught in Belgium, but it was already too late.[9] The battle of Flanders ended in disaster; the Allies salvaged what they could of men and equipment at Dunkirk.

On June 5, while the German radio was still boasting of the successful completion of operations in Belgium and Flanders, the front on the Aisne and the Somme was under attack. The Battle of Paris had begun. Within forty-eight hours the line was yielding and German motorized elements were advancing along the routes from Rouen and Dieppe.

In the midst of the new crisis, on June 5, Reynaud reorganized his cabinet for the third, and last, time. On the surface, the changes appeared to strengthen the will to resist. Reynaud eliminated Anatole de Monzie, whose sympathies with Italy were well known. (The disgruntled de Monzie promptly complained: "Our elimination from the cabinet delights Léon Blum's followers."[1]) As his Undersecretary of War, he appointed Charles de Gaulle, whose Cassandra-like warnings about the importance of armored warfare had gone unheeded in the pre-war years. With men like Georges Mandel, Louis Marin, César Campinchi, Georges Monnet, and de Gaulle, the cabinet gave an appearance of resolute determination. Monnet remained Blum's link with the cabinet. It was less noticeable that Reynaud had either promoted or introduced into the cabinet other men, such as Paul Baudouin, who were far less determined to fight on. By now, unknown to the public, Marshal Pétain and General Weygand were frankly resigned to military defeat, a defeat for which they were already blaming the republic's politicians.[2]

For fear of disturbing the unity of the nation, Blum's public pronouncements on these new cabinet changes were once again restrained. He disapproved of Reynaud's concentration in his own hands of so many portfolios: Reynand was not only Premier but Minister of National Defense and of War, and had replaced Daladier as Minister of Foreign Affairs too. Again, the reshuffling had failed to produce a true war cabinet.[3] Only one change filled Blum with enthusiasm, the

[8] Ibid., pp. 19–20.

[9] Reynaud: *Au coeur de la mêlée*, pp. 896–906 and cf. William L. Langer: *Our Vichy Gamble* (New York, 1947), p. 11.

[1] *Ci-devant* (Paris 1942), journal entry, June 5, 1940, p. 245; and cf. p. 220.

[2] On the changes, Reynaud: *Au coeur de la mêlée*, pp. 701–8.

[3] *Le Populaire*, June 7, 1940.

appointment of de Gaulle—"in its way an almost revolutionary act." Events had given "a brilliant and cruel confirmation of his heretical theories." Here, he said, was the man best qualified to check the armored thrust of the enemy: "The doctor can choose the remedy because he knows the disease."[4] But in the second week of June the patient was beyond saving.

Blum's confidence in the firmness of the Reynaud government first seems to have been shaken by its decision to leave Paris. In the beginning he discounted the various rumors to that effect, for the move seemed incompatible with the government's announced resolution to defend the capital. He first learned of the decision from the Socialists in the cabinet, who informed him on June 8 that the ministers had been ordered to prepare the evacuation of their records and personnel to the countryside surrounding Tours.[5]

The following day, as the German motorized columns drew closer and the civilian population began to crowd the roads leading from the metropolis, Blum's Socialist colleagues pressed him to leave, insisting that they could not depart and leave him behind, and that he did not have the right to let himself fall into the hands of the Germans. But even after he had dispatched his daughter-in-law and granddaughter to Marx Dormoy's home in Montluçon (his son, Robert, was with the army), he still resisted the thought of leaving. He had the deep conviction that the government should have remained in Paris in order to demonstrate its determination to fight to the bitter end; to leave was a symbol of resignation and defeat.[6]

He now grew increasingly uneasy over the possibility that the government did not even intend to defend the city. He had anxiously questioned the Socialist ministers about the government's intentions. "Our leaving," they had replied, "will not change anything. Paris will be defended *à fond*."[7] But speaking with Roger Langeron, the Paris Prefect of Police, on June 8, he received a different impression. The government had not altered its original decision to defend the city, but M. Langeron "had the feeling that no one was paying any attention to carrying it out."[8] What Blum considered unthinkable was precisely

[4] *Le Populaire*, June 8, 1940.
[5] *Mémoires*, 1940, *Oeuvre*, V, 21–3.
[6] Ibid., p. 23.
[7] Ibid., p. 22.
[8] Ibid., p. 21; and testimony, 1947, *Événements*, I, 260.

what happened. The last members of the government left the capital on June 10. Paris was declared an open city on June 12 and no defenses were set up in the surrounding belt of fortifications.

Blum remained indignant over the decision to declare Paris an open city. After the war he told the parliamentary investigating committee: "It had always been understood that Paris would be defended to the bitter end no matter what the cost, even if it meant fighting in the streets."[9] He was supported by Louis Marin, a member of the cabinet, who at the same postwar hearings and in the presence of President Lebrun said: "The declaration of Paris as an open city astonished me profoundly, given the fact that we were not very far removed in time from May 16, when Reynaud had given Gamelin the order to defend Paris at all costs."[1] Blum was convinced that from a military point of view it had been "absurd, senseless, criminal, to give up the defense of Paris." A few months later, in the midst of the Battle of Britain, he could not refrain from speculating upon what would have happened if the city had been defended "as Gallieni in 1914 had been determined to defend it, in the spirit in which . . . London is being defended while I write."[2]

The defense of Paris undoubtedly would have resulted in a terrible destruction of the brilliant treasures of the capital and a massacre of the population. Yet the mass exodus and the panic that followed the decision to abandon Paris heightened the people's feeling of desperation. The move strengthened the defeatist attitude of Marshal Pétain and other ministers in the cabinet. In the chain of events that led to capitulation, the decision to abandon Paris was an important link; Blum's indignation was not ill-founded.[3]

Meanwhile, yielding finally to the last-minute telephone entreaties of Georges Monnet, who had just attended a cabinet meeting, Blum left for Montluçon, a hundred and eighty miles south of Paris, arriving there early in the morning of June 10. That evening he heard the dramatic news of Mussolini's entry into the war after ten months of hesitation. His persistent belief that the Italian dictator would join his German ally was vindicated. Restless and ill at ease, and eager for further information, Blum persuaded Marx Dormoy the next day to return with

[9] Testimony, 1947, *Événements*, I, 260.

[1] *Événements*, IV, 1009; see also *Mémoires*, 1940, *Oeuvre*, V, 26–9. Cf. Albert Kammerer: *La Vérité sur l'armistice* (Paris, 1944), pp. 71, 77.

[2] *Mémoires*, 1940, *Oeuvre*, V, 28–30.

[3] Cf. Lebrun: *Témoignage*, p. 73.

him to Paris. He had no idea that every member of the government had already left the city. On the trip north, he and Dormoy ran straight into the mass exodus, which was then reaching its peak. They caught sight of the long lines of vehicles loaded with passengers and baggage, crawling along bumper to bumper. Reaching Paris by various side roads, Blum and Dormoy entered from Vincennes and found the streets empty, the shops closed, their shutters drawn. Blum tried in vain to reach any members of the government who might still be in the city. He succeeded only in talking with M. Langeron, the Prefect of Police, and General Héring, the military governor, and learned of the ambiguous instructions which the government had left them.[4]

Blum also saw his good friend the American Ambassador, William Bullitt, who had resolved to stay behind and do what he could when the Germans entered the city. Bullitt, no less than Blum, was confident at the time that Reynaud would stand firm and that his own presence near the new seat of the government was unnecessary. It turned out to be unfortunate that he would be separated from the French government and unable to use his considerable influence with Reynaud in the days to come.[5] Blum, sympathizing with the Ambassador's motives, gave his silent approval to Bullitt's decision to remain in Paris.[6]

Blum and Dormoy left the "necropolis" late that afternoon and set off on the return journey south to Montluçon. At one point, unable to avoid one of the main highways, they again ran into the great exodus: "We were fully prepared for a crowd, for congestion, for confusion," he later wrote, "but my imagination would not have been able to conceive anything like the spectacle that met our eyes as soon as we reached it. . . . The great highway, including its shoulders and its bicycle paths, was completely covered to the very edge of the houses and the fields." He could think only of a river about to overflow its banks. Here and there, people on foot, with packs on their backs, threaded their way in and out among the densely packed vehicles. He estimated that the traffic was inching along at no more than a kilometer an hour. He had never seen, he said, " a spectacle so poignant as this immense human migration." With dread, he pictured the catastrophe that would occur if enemy aircraft suddenly appeared to strafe the refugees, as had happened elsewhere.[7]

[4] *Mémoires*, 1940, *Oeuvre*, V, 25–31.

[5] A point made by Langer: *Our Vichy Gamble*, p. 22.

[6] *Mémoires*, 1940, *Oeuvre*, V, 27–8.

[7] Ibid., pp. 27–32. For details on the great exodus see Jean Vidalenc: *L'Exode de mai–juin 1940* (Paris, 1957), with a preface by Daniel Mayer.

When Blum and Dormoy finally made their way back to Montluçon, they learned that the government was moving from Tours south to Bordeaux, further from the enemy line of advance. The Germans had entered Paris on June 14 without a shot being fired. An urgent phone call from Georges Mandel in Bordeaux informed him that important political developments were afoot and that Blum's presence might be useful.[8] Unwilling to remain on the sidelines, Blum resolved to go to the new seat of government. He soon found himself in an atmosphere of political tension and crisis that far exceeded anything he had anticipated.

Blum arrived at Bordeaux in the early-morning hours of Saturday, June 15. The bustling city, already overcrowded with refugees, its hotels almost all requisitioned by the government, reminded him of the last war. Here, a quarter of a century earlier, in the autumn of 1914, he had spent several months as aide to Marcel Sembat, one of the Socialist ministers in the 1914 cabinet. That cabinet, although staggering under the initial German successes, began at Bordeaux the task of reorganizing the resistance that eventually had led to victory. Could history not repeat itself?

In the morning, from Georges Mandel and other ministers gathered in Mandel's office, Blum learned for the first time of the momentous cabinet meetings that had been held earlier in the week at the Château de Cangé near Tours. Marshal Pétain and General Weygand, convinced that the military situation was hopeless, were demanding an immediate suspension of hostilities and an armistice to prevent further bloody and useless struggle. A number of cabinet ministers had rallied to them immediately; others were being won over if only because they believed they had no right to question the judgment of the two soldiers on military matters.

Blum was completely overwhelmed by this amazing news, stunned, unable to think, he later wrote.[9] It was only a few short weeks since March, when Paul Reynaud had gone to London to sign a mutual pledge with Britain never to conclude a separate peace. In all his public speeches, Reynaud had reiterated the government's inflexible will to resist and to continue the war—from the provinces or, if necessary, from overseas France.

---

[8] *Mémoires*, 1940, *Oeuvre*, V, 33; testimony at Pétain trial, 1945, *Le Procès de Pétain*, I, 234; and testimony, 1947, *Événements*, I, 260.

[9] *Mémoires*, 1940, *Oeuvre*, V, 36.

The men in Mandel's office that morning, representing a variety of political parties, and including a number of cabinet ministers as well as Jules Jeanneney, the president of the Senate, and Édouard Herriot, the president of the Chamber, were unanimously opposed to an armistice. On the other hand, Blum has related, all those present, even Monnet, had accepted Weygand's analysis that the army was incapable of further resistance in France itself. They were resolved, however, that the country had to fight on, that the government had to leave metropolitan France and continue the struggle from North Africa. Under such a plan, the President of the Republic, the cabinet, the presidents of the two assemblies, and, insofar as possible, the members of Parliament, too, would proceed there at once.[1]

Concern was voiced, however, over the reaction of the country: the move to North Africa might be too great a shock for public opinion to absorb without some kind of preliminary preparation. Would not the people feel that the government was deserting them and abandoning the country to the will of the conqueror? Blum again encountered this anxiety regarding the public state of mind when he spoke with Albert Sérol, one of the three Socialist ministers in the cabinet. Blum found Sérol "visibly concerned" over the possible repercussions of the move on the already confused and distressed population.[2] Nonetheless, Mandel and others adjourned that morning confident that they could win over the cabinet to their proposition.

This is not the place to unravel the complex and disputed events that led to Paul Reynaud's resignation the evening of Sunday, June 16, yet a few observations must be made to clarify Blum's role, indirect though it was, in those events.[3] That weekend the cabinet was deadlocked over two courses of action: to sue for an armistice or to leave for North Africa and fight on from there. It was the solution proposed to break the impasse that led to the undoing of the cabinet. The trouble began when on June 15, Vice-Premier Camille Chautemps, supported

[1] For the meeting in Mandel's office that morning, ibid., pp. 35–8; and cf. Blum, testimony, 1945. *Le Procès de Pétain*, I, 234.

[2] *Mémoires*, 1940, *Oeuvre*, V, 38.

[3] On the cabinet crisis of that weekend, see Robert Aron: *Histoire de Vichy, 1940–1944* (Paris, 1954), pp. 11–50; Langer: *Our Vichy Gamble*, pp. 3–41; and Kammerer: *La Vérité sur l'armistice*, pp. 126–60. For Paul Reynaud's own account, *Au coeur de la mêlée*, pp. 830–53, and *Mémoires*, II, 418–37. There are many pages of testimony on the episode in the published record of the Pétain trial, and in the volumes of the postwar parliamentary investigation (*Événements*). Camille Chautemps: *Cahiers secrets de l'armistice, 1939–1940* (Paris, 1963) throws little new light on the events.

by L. O. Frossard, then Minister of Information, introduced a compromise resolution which rejected the proposal to seek an armistice but called instead for negotiations with the enemy to determine what the terms of an armistice would be: "to ask of the Reich the conditions that it would set for the cessation of hostilities." As Chautemps and Frossard persuasively explained, the German armistice terms would surely be so odious and unacceptable that everyone would unite in opposing them. The government could then successfully rally public opinion to support the move to North Africa and the war could be continued from there.

Whatever the motives of Chautemps and Frossard, their proposition had a devastating effect on those who might have remained partisans of resistance. The cabinet discussion on Saturday and Sunday, June 15 and 16, focused on the ambiguous Chautemps-Frossard formula, not on any clear-cut issue of armistice versus continued struggle from abroad. The Chautemps resolution (which was opposed by Mandel, Monnet, Marin, and other ministers, as well as Reynaud himself, as not very different from an outright armistice proposal) found substantial support. Of the three Socialist ministers, Monnet alone firmly opposed it. Sérol spoke against it at first but then seems to have wavered. Albert Rivière favored an outright armistice.[4] Yet almost everyone left on Sunday with the understanding that the issue was far from settled and that they would meet again that evening. Mandel even asked Blum after the meeting to use his influence to stiffen the vacillating Socialist ministers, notably Sérol.[5] But, to the consternation

---

[4] The evidence would indicate that Rivière favored the armistice in principle and that Sérol, though opposed at first, was swayed by the Chautemps-Frossard resolution. Monnet seems to have remained firm; Ligou: *Socialisme*, p. 465, seems incorrect about him. See various testimony in the postwar parliamentary investigation, *Événements*, especially Monnet, V, 1428–31; Louis Marin, V, 1428; Alphonse Rio, V, 1321; Laurent Eynac, V, 1454; Albert Lebrun, IV, 1080. See also Baudouin: *Neuf Mois*, pp. 149, 163, and testimony, VII, 2068. Blum's judgment on the Socialist ministers is in *Mémoires*, 1940, *Oeuvre*, V, 42. Reynaud includes in his most recent memoirs a list he drew up after the June 15 cabinet discussion, showing thirteen ministers favoring the proposal and only six opposing (including Monnet and Sérol); see *Mémoires*, II, 367. Yet the six were only those ministers who spoke up against it, not all who were opposed. Moreover, this was not the final meeting. Reynaud, in his postwar writings, has tended to exaggerate the number in his cabinet unwilling to support him in resisting the armistice initiative. And he fails to answer the question whether such a matter could ever be decided by a majority vote.

[5] Blum: testimony, 1945, *Le Procès de Pétain*, I, 236; and testimony, 1947, *Événements*, I, 261; cf. Blum: *Mémoires*, 1940, *Oeuvre*, V, 41–2.

of many of the ministers, Reynaud, deciding that he no longer had a majority with him and that the cabinet could not continue in office, submitted his resignation to President Lebrun shortly after the meeting adjourned. As his successor President Lebrun named Marshal Pétain.

Neither at the time nor later did Blum cast doubts on Reynaud's integrity. Vincent Auriol, recalling a conversation with Blum the very next day, reported: "Léon Blum cannot explain Paul Reynaud's decision; he does not know the motives behind it."[6] In later years Blum preferred to remain silent on Reynaud's failure of nerve at this crucial moment. He never disputed Auriol's judgment that Reynaud gave way because he was overcome by strain and fatigue and found himself surrounded by defeatist ministers and military commanders whom he had himself appointed.[7]

Blum chose to stress the Chautemps-Frossard proposition as the "decisive turning point," claiming that it "threw the discussion out of focus," sowing confusion in the cabinet and weakening the partisans of continued resistance, such as his own Socialist colleague Sérol.[8] Drawing upon his own intimate knowledge of the game of French politics, he interpreted the incident as a "maneuver of a familiar parliamentary type." Chautemps and Frossard, in the midst of a divided cabinet, and aware of the division in public opinion, resolved to take a gamble by initiating negotiations with the Germans. "The terrible fatal error that they committed was to have supposed that one could play with the idea of an armistice at such a moment, as one played in the Chamber with a motion to refer to a committee. . . . The mistake was not to have understood that from the moment that one put one's finger into the machinery one was caught." The maneuver misfired also because it upset those wavering members of the cabinet opposed to an armistice who were "tempted and seduced" by the Chautemps-Frossard proposition.[9]

---

[6] Auriol: *Hier . . . demain*, I, 66.

[7] Ibid., pp. 67–8. There is a passage omitted from Blum's published memoirs on this episode: *Mémoires*, 1940, *Oeuvre*, V, 42. Blum restricted himself to stressing that no definite decision had been reached by the cabinet before Reynaud resigned; see testimony, 1945, *Le Procès de Pétain*, I, 236, and testimony, 1947, *Événements*, I, 262. Reynaud's plucky determination up to that point and Vichy's later persecution of him undoubtedly explains Blum's refusal to add his criticisms.

[8] *Mémoires*, 1940, *Oeuvre*, V, 40–1; and testimony, 1945, *Le Procès de Pétain*, I, 236.

[9] Testimony, 1947, *Événements*, I, 261; and *Mémoires*, 1940, *Oeuvre*, V, 41.

At the time, however, Blum saw no more clearly than anyone else that once the machinery of negotiations had been put into motion, it would move on to its "logical" end. He innocently believed that the new Pétain cabinet, with Chautemps as Vice-Premier, was also committed to fighting on and to transferring the seat of government to North Africa. He too believed that the request for armistice terms was a maneuver, designed merely to win wider public support for the move to North Africa.[1] This attitude partly explains his acquiescence in the inclusion of Socialists in the Pétain cabinet.

When President Lebrun asked Marshal Pétain to form a new government on the night of June 16, the Marshal was ready with a list of ministers. To the amazement of President Lebrun and Chautemps, Pétain (or whoever had prepared the list) had designated Paul Faure as Minister of Labor—Faure, leader of the pro-appeasement and pacifist faction in the Socialist party, and Blum's hostile rival since before Munich and even on into the war period. We have it on good authority that, when it was pointed out that the appointment of a man with such well-known defeatist tendencies would have a harmful effect on public opinion, the Marshal accepted the objection but remarked to President Lebrun: "I had been told that that would irritate Léon Blum" (*"Ah, on m'avait dit que cela embêterait Léon Blum"*).[2] That the men close to Pétain were occupied, at this desperate time, in finding means to "irritate" Léon Blum bespeaks the low ebb of political morality.

Yet Pétain and his advisers wished to have Socialists in the cabinet— only those, of course, who had given signs of favoring an armistice. Georges Monnet was ruled out; Albert Sérol was asked to stay on as Minister of Justice, but he refused. When Albert Rivière was invited to remain in the cabinet and serve as Minister of Colonies, he replied favorably but requested permission to consult his Socialist colleagues; he also informed the Marshal that he did not wish to be the only member of his party in the cabinet.

Rivière sought out Monnet and together they consulted Blum. There was no time in the hurried consultation for recalling Blum's admonitions over the years on Socialist participation in the government. It was decided that Rivière should enter the cabinet and, to satisfy Rivière's

---

[1] *Mémoires*, 1940, *Oeuvre*, V, 42.
[2] The incident is attested to by Reynaud and Lebrun. See Reynaud: testimony, 1945, *Le Procès de Pétain*, I, 68, and *Au coeur de la mêlée*, p. 854; Lebrun: testimony, 1948, *Événements*, IV, 1020, and *Témoignage*, p. 85; cf. Monnet, citing Chautemps, who also would have been present, testimony, 1949, *Événements*, V, 1430.

personal objection to serving alone, that André Février should join as well.[3] It was believed that the presence of the two Socialists might forestall any attacks that might be launched against the party and against Blum personally.[4] Monnet, in later years, added that the decision was taken "to prevent the acceptance of any unconditional armistice conditions" and at the same time to try to avert the establishment of "a government with a totalitarian spirit."[5]

The Pétain cabinet's first act was to request the Spanish Ambassador to determine from the enemy what the armistice conditions would be. The very next day, Pétain, making a "gift of his person" to France in her hour of misfortune, announced to the country in a radio broadcast that armistice negotiations were under way. Did Pétain at any time seriously entertain the thought that they were merely sounding out the enemy on its armistice terms prior to moving the seat of government to North Africa? It seems unlikely, yet Blum was not alone in the view that the Pétain-Chautemps government would remain faithful to the Chautemps "plan" and fight on from North Africa. President Lebrun, Herriot, Jeanneney, and other important personages shared this view, and they all participated in the arrangements for the government's departure. When Lebrun, Jeanneney, and Herriot met with Pétain to discuss the arrangements, the Marshal made plain that he personally would not leave France but raised no objections to the government's official departure. He was even willing to hand over to Chautemps, his Vice-Premier, a delegation of powers. Blum did not criticize Pétain. He accepted the "nobility" of Pétain's motives for remaining in France, seeing his name, his reputation, and his venerable age as protection for the French nation in the hands of a cruel enemy.[6]

While the armistice negotiations were under way and departure plans were being arranged, the Deputies and Senators were gathering in Bordeaux. Ever since the government's arrival in that city, several members of Parliament led by Pierre Laval and Adrien Marquet, the mayor and Deputy of Bordeaux, had been holding informal meetings, first at the town hall and then in larger quarters. The group had attracted many of the prewar pro-appeasement leaders and some Social-

---

[3] Monnet: testimony, 1949, *Événements*, V, 1430–1; cf. Baudouin: *Neuf Mois*, p. 176.

[4] Blum: *Mémoires*, 1940, *Oeuvre*, V, 60.

[5] Monnet: testimony, 1949, *Événements*, V, 1431. See also the testimony on the episode gathered by André Février and published as *Expliquons-vous* (Paris, 1946).

[6] *Mémoires*, 1940, *Oeuvre*, V, 42–3.

ists too, among them Charles Spinasse, who had been Blum's Minister of National Economy in the 1936 cabinet. Marquet himself had been an important Socialist until he broke with the party in 1933 to found with Marcel Déat the authoritarian, nationalist, neo-socialist movement. Laval and these men not only accepted France's military defeat as final and repudiated any thought of leaving the country, but also were bent on exploiting the crisis as an opportunity to sweep away the "system" that had brought the country to defeat.[7]

On Tuesday, June 18, at a meeting of some fifty or sixty Deputies in a Bordeaux schoolroom, Blum heard for the first time with his own ears the refrain of this Bordeaux group: that England's downfall was imminent, that France had to make the best possible peace immediately (abandoning, of course, all thought of fighting on from North Africa), and that the regime responsible for the defeat had to be buried.[8] He heard Charles Spinasse, carefully averting his gaze from Blum and Auriol, say: "We ought not to have waged this war. We have lost it. Let us bow to that. And let us tear out the pages of the past. Let us construct a regime with authority, a new world. Let God grant that we have the strength for it." Gaston Bergery, one of the earliest Radical supporters of the Popular Front but who had long broken with it, turned directly to Blum and called for his support in reforming the country's "institutions."[9]

To reform the country's institutions at such a time, and in the design of these men, was an appalling thought. Blum spoke up but refused to engage in a full-dress debate. This group, for whom Bergery, Spinasse, and Marquet were spokesmen, was vocal and powerful but, he believed, still a minority. Replying to Bergery, he agreed that the country's institutions and practices were in need of reform, but he emphasized that nothing of that kind was possible until France had assured its independence and security; the first order of business was to fight on.[1]

---

[7] Jean Montigny conveys the attitude of this group of which he was a part in his *Toute la vérité sur un mois dramatique de notre histoire* (Clermont-Ferrand, 1940), 5–32. See also Auriol's comments on the "Bordeaux club" in *Hier . . . demain*, I, 79–80.

[8] Blum: *Mémoires*, 1940, *Oeuvre*, V, 43.

[9] See Auriol: *Hier . . . demain*, I, 70–1. See, on the prevailing attitude toward Blum, Marcel Héraud's testimony, 1949, *Événements*, VI, 1517; he recalled Bergery's saying of Blum: *"Moi, aussi je vais lui serrer la main. Peut-être qu'il n'a pas beaucoup de temps à vivre."*

[1] Auriol: *Hier . . . demain*, I, 71; Blum: *Mémoires*, 1940, *Oeuvre*, V, 43.

Blum still had no suspicion that any obstacle would develop in the government's plan to leave France. In the afternoon of June 19, he even received confirmation of the government's intentions from Chautemps. At that time Blum told Chautemps that, as the head of the Socialist party, he intended to follow the government, along with the other leading members of Parliament, and received Chautemps's comment: "Think it over carefully. Not everybody has the greatest affection for you. They will not all be delighted at having you there as a companion." Blum retorted that he knew all about such feelings, but that the government to be established in North Africa had to represent France and he was part of France. He still "meant something" for many Frenchmen as well as for France's allies. Chautemps shrugged his shoulders and the conversation ended.[2]

Pure chance saved Blum in the next few days from being caught up in the confused and painful *Massilia* episode, in which thirty Deputies and one Senator sailed June 21 on the cruiser *Massilia*, only to learn too late that the Pétain government had canceled its plans to leave France.[3] Under the initial plan, the President of the Republic, the cabinet, and the presidents of the two houses were to make the trip to Casablanca by seaplane from Bordeaux. Since the members of Parliament were too numerous to be transported in the same way, the government, through Admiral Darlan, agreed to place at their disposal a cruiser, which they were to board on June 19 at Le Verdon, the port close to Bordeaux. The following day, after many frustrating hours, the group received new instructions that they were to embark from southern France. A special train would transport them to Port-Vendres, near Perpignan, at the Spanish border. Blum decided to travel by automobile instead so that he might stop at Toulouse and pay a last visit to his daughter-in-law and his granddaughter, who were now living with the Vincent Auriol family in that area. Georges Monnet accompanied him. Not until Blum and Monnet arrived at Toulouse did a message reach them that they were to leave from Bordeaux after all, not from Perpignan! Blum then returned to Bordeaux only to discover that the *Massilia* had sailed without him. At that moment he suddenly learned that the government itself was *not* going to leave—not from

---

[2] Blum: *Mémoires*, 1940, *Oeuvre*, V. 44–5.

[3] On the *Massilia* episode and related events, Aron: *Histoire de Vichy*, pp. 68–73; Kammerer: *La Vérité sur l'armistice*, pp. 198–203; Langer: *Our Vichy Gamble*, pp. 51–3.

Perpignan, not from Bordeaux, not from anywhere. Yet the boatload of political passengers had been permitted to sail.[4]

Blum was angered and saddened. The Deputies had sailed in completely good faith in a ship provided for them by Admiral Darlan so that they might be at the government's side when it moved to North Africa. Now they were steaming toward Casablanca as isolated individuals, among them some of the most ardent opponents of capitulation.

No one can fully explain what lay behind the decision to let the ship sail at a time when the government's plans had been canceled. No one knows whether it was negligence, oversight, slowness in communication, or—a trap. Blum later judged that it was "something of a trap," not completely drawn up and plotted in every detail but including some elements of chance: "Let them go, we shall see what happens; anyway, so much the worse for them!"[5] In any event, the *Massilia* sailed from France with men whose presence was not desired for the next few weeks; they would not be on hand to oppose the armistice or to fight Laval's interment of the Third Republic at Vichy. Almost at once, the government-inspired press took the lead in condemning the men as deserters; eventually, some were even arrested and imprisoned for military desertion or tried on other charges. An observer at Vichy noted in his diary on July 9: "More and more those who left are treated as traitors. . . . Laval's friends are denouncing this 'band of Jews.' "[6] Mandel, Grumbach, Mendès-France, and a few other Jews were in the group, to be sure, as if that mattered, but men of all persuasions— Daladier, Delbos, Campinchi, and others—were also in it.[7] Laval and his associates would have been delighted if Blum had been caught. Chance alone, or his star, preserved him from that fate.

[4] For Blum's description of the episode, *Mémoires*, 1940, *Oeuvre*, V, 43–54; testimony, 1945, *Le Procès de Pétain*, I, 238–9; testimony, 1947, *Événements*, I, 262. For corroboration see Monnet: testimony, 1949, *Événements*, V, 1431; Herriot: *Épisodes, 1940–1944* (Paris, 1950), p. 97; Lebrun: *Témoignage*, pp. 91–3; and Louis Noguères: testimony, 1950, and journal, *Événements*, VII, 2233.

[5] *Mémoires*, 1940, *Oeuvre*, V, 53.

[6] Louis Noguères: journal entered in testimony, 1950, *Événements*, VII, 2246. Cf., on Laval's attitude toward the men, Blum: *Mémoires*, 1940, *Oeuvre*, V, 68. Noguères's journal is an invaluable source for the atmosphere at the time. M. Noguères, a Socialist Deputy and after the war president of the Haute Cour de Justice, entered the journal into his testimony before the postwar parliamentary committee, *Événements*, VII, 2227–63.

[7] For the list, Montigny: *Toute la vérité*, p. 24.

As word of the armistice negotiations at Rethondes was awaited, the already tense atmosphere in Bordeaux grew more charged and dangerous. Upon Blum's return from his Toulouse trip, his friends informed him that the streets of the city were in ferment: extremist bands were actively whipping up public feeling against those held responsible for France's entry into the war and the subsequent defeat, and he was one of the special targets of abuse. The police warned that they could not guarantee his safety. Yielding to the pleas of those close to him, Blum agreed to remain out of sight in the small apartment of friends.[8] There he spent Saturday, June 22, the day of the armistice.

Inactive and alone, he became moody and introspective. The bitter thought assailed him that he was a source of embarrassment to his friends and that his extreme unpopularity rendered impossible any further political activities on his part. His own Socialist colleagues, even without being conscious of it, were instinctively trying to dissociate themselves from the hatred and passion that his very name evoked. He decided to leave Bordeaux and its lynch atmosphere, and to go to Toulouse. To his Socialist colleague in the Pétain cabinet, Albert Rivière, he sent a message informing him where he could be reached should the government revise its plans for leaving.[9]

Not until Blum arrived at Toulouse at dawn the following day did he learn the news of the armistice from the bold headlines in the *Dépêche de Toulouse*. It was one of the black hours of his life. "There are figures of speech weakened by excessive everyday use, but sometimes a special experience restores their force: I read, literally, without believing my eyes."[1] To his mind the document was not a negotiated armistice but a *Diktat* imposed by the enemy. He dismissed the various concessions as unimportant, or not to be relied upon, among them the German assurance that the demobilized French fleet would not be used for war purposes against France's allies and the provision that one third of France would be left unoccupied under a French government with its capital at Vichy. The latter arrangement he saw as a thinly disguised subterfuge by which Hitler would more easily rule a France broken in two. He was outraged by one "abominable" clause under which France

[8] *Mémoires*, 1940, *Oeuvre*, V, 55. On the atmosphere at Bordeaux, see Héraud: testimony, 1949, *Événements*, VI, 1517.

[9] *Mémoires*, 1940, *Oeuvre*, V, 55–6.

[1] Ibid., pp. 56–7.

agreed to hand over to the German government those political exiles who had found asylum on French soil in the 1930's, a stipulation that eventually cost the lives of such German Socialists as Rudolf Hilferding and Rudolf Breitscheid.

Blum was unable, either at the time or later, to formulate a balanced judgment of the armistice, to admit that the terms accorded France, though harsh, were more generous than those meted out to Poland or other conquered states.[2] Actually, without exaggerating Hitler's generosity, the Führer was in a position to exact a more onerous armistice than he did. Given his immediate objective, to lay England low, he apparently acted on the assumption that lenient terms to France would better serve his purpose. An outright demand for surrender of the French fleet might have been rejected even by the Pétain government; hence the more limited provision for its demobilization. No German or Italian troops, moreover, were to be stationed in North Africa; one day Allied troops would use that area as a gateway to Hitler's Europe. It would be difficult to contend that the armistice accepted by the Pétain government was completely dishonorable—once it was decided that France would not fight on. Whether the Pétain government properly defended France's rights and honor after the armistice is a different matter.[3]

Blum spent the ten days following the news of the armistice secluded in the country home of friends at L'Armurier, near Toulouse. His friends, especially Vincent Auriol and Mme Auriol, and his daughter-in-law, Renée, pleaded with him to leave the country while it was still possible. Herriot had also warned him at Bordeaux: "Do not fall into the hands of the men in power today. I know too well what hatred they bear you." But his mind was made up. He had earlier been resolved to leave the country to accompany a government determined to continue the war from abroad, but that plan had collapsed. The idea of leaving now as an isolated individual, he rejected. If he left France at this point, his enemies, and others as well, would charge that he had left to save his skin; he would be denounced as a coward who had fled because of a guilty conscience and fear of punishment. To his friends he repeated what he had told Herriot, that men in the Pétain cabinet like Chau-

[2] Testimony, 1945, *Le Procès de Pétain*, I, 239.
[3] See Langer's judgments on the armistice, which of course are far from universally shared, *Our Vichy Gamble*, pp. 53–65, and cf. Aron: *Histoire de Vichy*, pp. 74–80.

temps, Pomaret, Frossard, Baudouin, Alibert, were weak creatures who did not have it in them to turn vicious. The two Socialists in the cabinet would provide some measure of protection as well.[4]

His friends argued, more realistically, that the men then in the cabinet would give way to others, that the only true sovereign in France henceforth was Hitler, that French governments would be compelled to adopt the principles and methods of the Nazi regime. "They will have their Gestapo and their assault squadrons, they will move from individual executions to collective persecution; they will track down the Socialists, vilify the Jews, and to their delight lay their hands on Léon Blum in the bargain."[5] A few months later, writing in a Vichy prison, Blum realized the accuracy of his friends' prophecies; events had borne out their judgment. They had been correct, too, in attacking his optimism, his inability to accept in his mind the baseness to which human beings could descend.[6] In any event, he ignored the entreaties of his friends, resolved to stay behind and await with serenity the dangers of the future.

What can one say of his decision? Would a "true revolutionary" have let himself be hindered by thoughts of what his enemies would say about him? Would a Lenin or a Trotsky have hesitated to flee in such a situation?[7] Only a few months earlier Thorez had fled to Moscow. But Blum was constitutionally unable to sacrifice personal honor even for the most sacred of causes; he could not separate the two. Flight would have sullied his personal honor; he convinced himself that it would also have hurt the cause he wished to serve. His obsession with "conscience" and "honor," his constant self-examination and introspection, made it impossible for him to be a "true revolutionary" or even a strong political leader, even if they bespoke an integrity and nobility of character rare in the world in which he lived. A "true revolutionary" would have had to travel lighter.

From a practical point of view, Blum, if he could have accepted the taunt of "desertion," might have joined the Gaullist cause and perhaps made an important contribution in some capacity. One of its weaknesses in the eyes of British and American official circles—especially American—was its lack of leading political figures. In some cases, those who served the Free French group lacked the diplomatic skill that

---

4 *Mémoires*, 1940, *Oeuvre*, V, 57–62.

5 Ibid., p. 61.

6 Ibid. His phrase was *"certaines aberrations humaines."*

7 These are questions Audry asks: *Léon Blum*, p. 174.

Blum might have brought.[8] That Vichy would have had an additional weapon with which to belabor the Gaullists is hardly significant, as its diatribes could scarcely have been more violent. As it was, in the months ahead, Blum served the cause of resistance in France, but in his own fashion. At Vichy he was able to cast a ballot against the death of the republic. He lent his support to de Gaulle and the Resistance movement in France. And for a moment—at the Riom trial—he symbolized in a dramatic and moving way the spirit of liberty and courage in the face of oppression. Blum never regretted his decision to stay on in France in June 1940, even though in the end it meant French prisons and German concentration camps for almost five long years.

[8] See, e.g., Arthur Layton Funk: *Charles de Gaulle: The Crucial Years, 1943–1944* (Norman, Okla., 1959), p. 46; and British Embassy to Department of State, *aide-mémoire*, May 14, 1942, *For. Rel. U.S.*, 1942, II, *Europe*, 520.

XIII

VICHY, JULY 1940

At the hour when the nation awaited a clarion call, a rallying cry, no great voice could come from our ranks.[1]

WHILE BLUM rested at L'Armurier, from June 23 to the first week in July, recovering his strength after the exhausting tension of the past two weeks, events moved rapidly toward the dramatic end of the Third Republic at Vichy on July 10. Shortly after the signing of the armistice, Laval had entered Marshal Pétain's cabinet and become Vice-Premier. Obsessed with the need to transform France through a national revolution, he persuaded the cabinet to convene Parliament in order that it might grant the government the authority to prepare a new constitution. Even in the Pétain cabinet some ministers were astonished at Laval's boldness; they underestimated the death wish of Parliament.[2]

Early in July, in response to the official convocation, over six hundred and fifty Deputies and Senators converged on Vichy, where the government, after its departure from Bordeaux, was now located. Laval had six days, from July 4 to July 10, in which to win over Parliament; his success deserves to rank among the most astonishing feats in the history of politics. We cannot relate those events in any detail here, but, it may be noted, nowhere are they more masterfully described and the atmosphere of fear and moral disintegration more artfully conveyed than in the superb pages of Blum's memoirs written only a few

[1] Blum: *À l'échelle humaine, Oeuvre,* V, 460.
[2] On these events, see especially Aron: *Histoire de Vichy,* pp. 95–155; on the Socialists, Lefranc: *Mouvement socialiste,* pp. 382–9, and Ligou: *Socialisme,* pp. 464–70.

months after the events themselves.[3] Here we must concentrate on Blum himself at Vichy.

Convinced that his political usefulness had ended and that his presence would only hurt the cause of his friends, Blum seems to have thought first that he would not go to Vichy. Those in his immediate circle were also concerned over his safety. Yet, despite misgivings and his "repugnance" at the machinations in Vichy, he resolved to go. There is no doubt that one of his motives was to refute by his physical presence the widespread rumors then circulating that he had fled the country. He wished also to inquire into the future status of *Le Populaire*.[4]

Accompanied by Marx Dormoy, who hardly left his side that entire week, Blum arrived at the famous resort city the afternoon of Thursday, July 4. He proceeded at once to the Petit Casino, where an informal session of the Deputies was being held under government auspices —Laval called them "informational sessions." All at once he found himself plunged into the same kind of atmosphere as at Bordeaux prior to the armistice. But the men who had even then talked of a "new regime" were now more active and vocal. They denounced the political leaders of the republic who had led France into a "mad, criminal" war which they knew they could not win. They denounced those who had left on the *Massilia* as cowardly deserters. As the debate went on, Blum realized at one point that Laval had left the hall. Blum found him in the lobby continuing the animated discussion. He and Dormoy joined the group. "The Marshal," Laval insisted to the small group, "never agreed to leave France." When pressed by Blum, he could not deny that Pétain had approved the plan for the others to leave, but his face hardened, and Blum later recalled his words: "So much the worse. They are all men who wanted the war—this mad, criminal war." "But," protested Blum, "was it France that wanted the war?" "There were Frenchmen—fools, criminals—who wanted it," Laval replied. "Those over there are among them . . ." He stopped, looked at Blum as if he were going to add: "And you too," but checked himself.[5] In his acid remarks was the kernel of the later charges at Riom that the political leaders of the republic had led France into war, a war for which the country was woefully unprepared.

The stormy interchange with Laval was not propitious for the business Blum had to negotiate; he was informed in no uncertain terms that

[3] *Mémoires*, 1940, *Oeuvre*, V, esp. 63–97.
[4] Ibid., pp. 64–5.
[5] For the episode, ibid., p. 68.

Le Populaire would cease to appear. Later, Blum recalled that he had never in their twenty-five years of acquaintance seen Laval as he appeared during that ten-minute conversation: "bloated with an incredible pride . . . handing out orders without appeal . . . visibly trying himself out in the role of a despot."[6]

Blum did not return to any of the "informational sessions" on subsequent days but decided to await developments at the home of his Socialist friend Isidore Thivrier, mayor and Deputy of Commentry, whose home in the suburbs was about an hour's drive from Vichy.[7] He had made up his mind, however, that he would attend the official meetings. If there was going to be a public debate on the causes of the disaster and an attack launched on the Popular Front government, he wanted to be present. Also, he could not accept without protest the subversion of the constitution. He would be present, he resolved, "to fulfill his duty as a Socialist, as a republican, as a Frenchman."[8]

The afternoon of July 8, the day before the official session of the Chamber, an informal caucus of the Socialist Senators and Deputies met; it was understood, however, that under the circumstances the traditional rule of party discipline was not to apply. Blum proceeded to the meeting conscious of the division in the party's ranks but fully confident that some common program might be agreed upon to protect the democratic institutions of the republic.

While at Commentry, he had formulated a plan of action. On Tuesday, July 9, the Chamber and the Senate were to convene separately to consider, according to the prescribed formula, whether there were sufficient grounds for a joint meeting of both houses as a National Assembly in order to revise the constitution. If the two houses agreed, the National Assembly would meet the following day to consider Laval's proposal that Marshal Pétain be given a blanket delegation of constitution-making powers. Blum had resolved that the Socialists must begin the fight in the separate meetings of the Chamber and Senate, and refuse to agree that there were grounds for meeting jointly as a National Assembly to revise the constitution. They would argue that neither the times nor the circumstances were appropriate for

[6] Ibid., p. 69.

[7] The English translation of Aron: *Histoire de Vichy* (tr. Humphrey Hare, London, 1958), p. 88, incorrectly asserts that Laval won the backing of "Léon Blum" at the informational session of July 6. Blum's name has been substituted for that of the Rightist Senator and former minister Léon Bérard; the French edition, p. 120, correctly names the latter.

[8] *Mémoires*, 1940, *Oeuvre*, V, 70.

changing the fundamental laws of the nation. Blum conceded that the constitution would one day have to be rewritten; he had always believed that the parliamentary republic and the machinery of the Third Republic had egregious faults. Moreover, he agreed that in order to meet the chaotic situation after the armistice the executive arm needed extensive powers; but it already possessed them, he maintained. The Pétain government had not hesitated to sign the armistice without consulting Parliament. Revising the constitution had to wait until the enemy was gone.[9]

He received his first jolt shortly before the meeting of the Socialist group when he outlined his views to his friends Vincent Auriol, Georges Monnet, Marx Dormoy, and Jules Moch. To his shock and distress he discovered that they did not agree with him on the need to combat the proposal to revise the constitution. To him this was a matter of principle as well as of tactics. To them it was a foregone conclusion that the motion to revise the constitution would carry overwhelmingly. They considered it useless to resist as an isolated opposition; moreover, since the party had always declared itself in favor of revising the constitution of 1875, they could not now defend it. They were determined instead to fight for the right of Parliament to supervise the framing of a new constitution and for democratic safeguards. Their hope rested on a counterproposal introduced by Senator Jean Taurines and supported by various Senators and Deputies of the Center and Left, which stipulated that the new constitution be prepared with the cooperation and under the supervision of Parliament and then be submitted to a referendum of the people as soon as circumstances would permit. In the brief discussion, Blum's alienation even from his intimate circle of friends was forcefully brought home to him. His colleagues were supporting the proposal that the regime be buried and a new constitution be written. So deep was his sense of isolation that he abandoned all thought of presenting his view at the Socialist caucus.[1]

Of the approximately 175 Socialist representatives in both houses, about 60 were present at the caucus. More would arrive that night and the following morning; some, like Paul Faure, could not manage to get out of occupied areas; some, although in Vichy, deliberately absented themselves. From the first words spoken, Blum's spirits were

[9] Ibid., pp. 77–8.

[1] Ibid., p. 77; and Auriol: *Hier . . . demain*, I, 111, 115. Auriol incorrectly gives the date of this Socialist meeting as July 9, after the Chamber session, which would have made it quite pointless. See also Aron: *Histoire de Vichy*, pp. 122–3.

raised. He perceived with a feeling of relief and joy that there was "a strong current of agreement." There were many, from the pacifist wing of the party, who had favored the armistice, but now "their Socialist and republican conscience had risen." Only a few present, like Fernand Roucayrol and Armand Chouffet, expressed themselves in favor of the Laval bill. They were answered effectively by Georges Monnet, Marius Moutet, Charles Hussel, Marx Dormoy, Auriol, and others. Blum rejoiced in the avowed determination of his comrades to defend republican principles. When his advice was sought, he spoke briefly to encourage their efforts to struggle for democratic safeguards.[2]

The confidence of the group was bolstered when Albert Rivière, who was Minister of Colonies in the cabinet, pledged that he would fight inside the cabinet to have the Taurines counterproposal substituted for Laval's bill. The meeting voted to send delegations to request that Jeanneney and Herriot, the presidents of the Senate and Chamber, use their influence to gain Marshal Pétain's support for the Taurines proposal. In an informal vote the group agreed that if that proposal were rejected by the government, the Socialists would reject the Laval bill; the vote was 56 to 4.[3]

By the end of the meeting, Blum's hopes had soared. He was satisfied that a pattern of Socialist resistance was emerging and he had confidence in the ability of the presidents of the two houses, Jeanneney and Herriot, to coordinate the fight against Laval. "I was proud. I was almost happy; for the first time in three weeks I felt myself alive again." Although there had been a number of absences and reservations, and some reticence on the part of several of those present, he believed that the "great majority had declared themselves firmly . . . in favor of defending the republic."[4]

His optimism was completely unfounded. Despite the show of agreement he had witnessed, the Socialists were thoroughly confused and divided. Some of the Deputies who had swung over to Laval did not, of course, attend the caucus. They had taken their stand at the various "informational sessions." At the session of July 5, for example, François Chasseigne, a Socialist Deputy from L'Indre, had announced that the time had come to liquidate all parties, that Parliament's duty was to

[2] *Mémoires*, 1940, *Oeuvre*, V, 79–80; cf. Paul Faure's remarks, *De Munich à la Ve République* (Paris, 1947)), pp. 91, 95.
[3] Auriol: *Hier . . . demain*, I, 79–80.
[4] *Mémoires*, 1940, *Oeuvre*, V, 79–82.

place itself at the disposition of Marshal Pétain to allow him to remake France by giving the country the constitution he deemed best. Laval, delighted, applauded his remarks: "Henceforth . . . there will be only one party, that of all Frenchmen, a national party that will provide the leadership for our national action."[5] The next day Charles Spinasse, Blum's former minister, made a stirring speech which, according to one observer, "literally gripped the audience." It had mystical, religious overtones. "Parliament," he said, "must take upon itself the burden of all our wrongs. A crucifixion is necessary to prevent the country from sinking into violence and anarchy. Our duty is to permit the government to make a revolution without the spilling of blood. . . . We must break with the past without thought of return. That past was full of illusions. . . . A new faith must be born, based on new values."[6] Spinasse's remarks were publicly endorsed by an old foe of the Socialists, the extreme Rightist Deputy Xavier Vallat, who at the time of Blum's premiership had publicly deplored in the Chamber the sad state of affairs under which a "Gallo-Roman nation" was being ruled by a Jew; he would soon serve the Pétain government as Commissioner for Jewish Affairs. Laval, a few days later, said that he "wept" when he thought of the speeches in which Spinasse and Vallat had made common cause. He added that Spinasse "had spoken, I believe, for his party."[7] At these meetings other Socialists spoke in a similar vein. Twenty-two Socialists joined with others in a "Declaration" drafted by Gaston Bergery, which denounced in scathing terms all republican parties that had existed since 1919, both Right and Left. The Blum ministry, "behind which maneuvered men like Duclos and Marty," was said to have "betrayed" the people and helped fill them "with disillusionment after disillusionment." The manifesto called for a grant of full powers to Marshal Pétain so that he might establish a new regime that would be "authoritarian," "national," and "social" and would create a "France integrated into the new Europe." It called also for an investigation and punishment of those political figures responsible for France's "unconstitutional" entry into the war and for the lack of preparedness

[5] Cited by Noguères: journal, entry for July 5, 1940, *Événements*, VII, 2231.

[6] Noguères: journal, entry for July 6, 1940, *Événements*, VII, 2234; see also Auriol's acid sketch of Spinasse in *Hier . . . demain*, I, 95–7. For Spinasse's later explanation of his speech, see his personal note to Lefranc, in *Mouvement socialiste*, pp. 385–6.

[7] Stenographic record of joint private session, Chamber and Senate, July 10, 1940, *Événements, Rapport*, II, 490.

that had led to its defeat. The twenty-two Socialist signatures, out of a total of sixty-eight, outnumbered those of any other party.[8] Seven Socialists also signed a resolution drawn up by Vincent Badie, a conservative Radical Socialist; it stated that the signers would "refuse to vote a measure that would inevitably lead to the disappearance of the republican regime," but conceded that for the "moral and economic recovery of the country and an honorable peace" it was "indispensable to accord to Marshal Pétain . . . all powers to accomplish this work of public welfare and peace."[9]

Blum was aware of differences and disagreements in the party. On the fight against the revision of the constitution he realized that he was cut off from the thinking of the party, and even from that of his closest friends. But he did not yet comprehend how advanced the disintegration of the party was and how complete it soon would be. A Socialist Deputy captured in his journal the prevalent mood of bitterness, confusion, and division. "Laval was right in declaring that there were no parties any more. For the Socialist party this was more and more exact. One could even add that there were no more Socialists— or very few."[1]

At the formal parliamentary sessions the disintegration of the party was finally brought home to Blum. Writing a few months later, he recalled with anguish the two days of official sessions on July 9 and 10. "The spectacle that I must now describe is frightful. Months have gone by, and yet even today, when I evoke it, shame rushes to my face and a bitterness seizes my throat. What a scene! How I wish that the memory of it could be erased; how I wish, above all, that I could forget it myself." Years later he still could not remember it "without a certain shudder."[2]

What he found most frightful was the pervasive mood of fear and corruption in the meeting hall and corridors. The Senators and Deputies seemed to have been "plunged . . . into a poisonous bath of

[8] For the declaration and the signers, Montigny: *Toute la vérité*, pp. 139–54, and Noguères: journal, entry for July 8, 1940, *Événements*, VII, 2242–3.

[9] Nogueres: journal, entry for July 8, 1940, *Événements*, VII, 2240. Noguères himself signed it.

[1] Noguères: journal, entry for July 7, 1940, *Événements*, VII, 2238; cf. p. 2236.

[2] *Mémoires*, 1940, *Oeuvre*, V, 83; testimony, 1945, *Le Procès de Pétain*, I, 240.

such strength that whatever touched it even for an instant emerged poisoned. The venom operated before one's very eyes—one could observe its progress." In a matter of hours the "thoughts, the speech, the faces" of many became "almost unrecognizable." It appeared to him as though some motion-picture director had wished to depict in an animated cartoon the "spread of fear." Socialist friends who had shaken hands with him when he arrived shunned him at the end of an hour. Men of all parties avoided contact with former friends.

Fear, bordering on panic, permeated the atmosphere. Word spread that the Germans, then only thirty miles away, might advance; or that General Weygand, who had already used strong language about the need to preserve civil order, might impose a military dictatorship; or that Laval would treat obstructionists in his own fashion. Outside the Grand Casino, the gangs of Jacques Doriot, the ex-communist turned fascist, whipped up a lynch spirit. The rumor went around that those who voted "no" to the government's bill "would not sleep in their beds" that night.

Laval, exploiting the nervousness of those present and utilizing the prestige of Marshal Pétain, convinced many that only Pétain could save the country from brutality at the hands of the conqueror. With some, Laval held out the promise of spoils and patronage; with others, he employed veiled threats; with still others, he played upon the existing anti-British sentiment rampant after the firing on the French fleet at Mers-el-Kébir. Persuasion, corruption, intimidation, and deception combined with fear to create the poisonous atmosphere that Blum painted.[3]

The extent to which Blum was deserted by his Socialist comrades has been described by Vincent Auriol in harsher words than any that Blum ever permitted himelf to use. "This exhibition of miserable humanity," Auriol reconstructed the scene, "Léon Blum certainly sees it. He is too sensitive not to suffer from it. He protects himself against it. He smiles." He and Blum saw former comrades pass them by "with an air of indifference" or "with an arrogant affectation of independence." Of one Deputy "who cordially holds Laval by the arm," Auriol wrote: "I know him well. He is the Socialist Deputy of a district in my department. He has not pardoned Léon Blum for not having named him Colonial Undersecretary in 1936 and me for not having presented his candidacy; he lets us see it very well today." By all but a handful of friends Blum was deserted and shunned. "Where," Auriol asked,

[3] *Mémoires*, 1940, *Oeuvre*, V, 83–7; Auriol: *Hier ... demain*, I, 130.

[375]

"are the 175 Socialist members of Parliament? . . . Some, of course, could not come . . . but the others? Where are they, those Deputies who in former times acclaimed him in a standing ovation in the party caucus, in the Chamber, in our congresses, at mass meetings? Where are those who, seeking election or re-election, called him to their district so that he might give them his backing with his eloquence, his authority, his prestige? Where are those who crowded the antechambers of the Matignon Palace to solicit favors, those who owed him everything . . . ?[4] There was double grief for Blum at Vichy: he witnessed the collapse of the republic and the desertion of his own party. No longer Moses, he was now Lear.

His followers had melted away. Some had deserted because they believed that he was not revolutionary enough and had succeeded only in diluting the original Marxist creed of the party into a simple reformism. But mainly, the parliamentary Deputies identified him with the war and the parliamentary regime responsible for the disastrous defeat. They recalled how he had rallied them to the war effort and how he had asked them to make repeated sacrifices in the name of national unity. Under the cruel impact of the military collapse, the hollowness of the regime stood exposed and at the same time the bankruptcy of the party's policies which had offered no constructive alternative. For all his subtlety and caution, Blum had allowed himself, in his zeal as a good republican, to be identified with the Third Republic. The Socialists who were deserting the regime were deserting him at the same time. Demoralized by the armistice, obsessed with a sense of collective guilt, anxious over the country's fate at the hands of the German conqueror, yielding to the blandishments and threats of the new ruling group who promised that they could better integrate a New France into Hitler's Europe, the Socialist Deputies in large numbers abandoned their party and its leader and rushed to join the "national revolution."

Tuesday, July 9, was devoted to the two preliminary meetings of the assemblies, the Chamber in the morning, the Senate in the afternoon. They met simply to decide whether there were grounds for the two houses to convene jointly as a National Assembly to revise the constitution. At these preliminary meetings no one spoke up, not even those who the following day voted against Laval's bill. Herriot, presiding at the Chamber meeting, was perhaps the only man who might have sounded a trumpet call of resistance. Instead, he urged the

---

[4] *Hier . . . demain*, I, 129–30.

Deputies to unite in supporting Marshal Pétain. ("I had no suspicion," he later wrote apologetically, "of the abuse of confidence that the Marshal was going to commit and of the *coup d'état* that he intended."[5]) With no spokesman for resistance, the vote was a mere formality. Of the 396 votes in the Chamber, only three were opposed; in the Senate there was only one dissenting voice. One of the three stubborn Deputies, the Socialist Jean Biondi, agreed with a colleague that the party had always demanded revision of the constitution, but added: "I, too, have said it and repeated it, but today the *salauds* wish not to democratize the republic but to suppress it. . . . I will not go along."[6]

Blum himself abstained from voting, resolved, he later explained, "not to separate himself publicly" from his friends. "Few sacrifices," he sadly remarked, "have been more cruel."[7] He remained convinced, at the time and even years later, that the tactic adopted by his friends had been wrong; the delay in opposing Laval merely afforded the contagion a chance to spread.[8] Auriol has agreed that Blum was right.[9] Even an "outsider" like President Lebrun expressed surprise that the opposition had not voted "no" at the opening meetings.[1] With no opponents, the first round went to Laval, virtually by default. The drama moved on to its inexorable conclusion the next day.

It was agreed that before the formal meeting of the National Assembly, scheduled for the afternoon of July 10, a closed session would be held in the morning, from which the public and press would be barred. Here the government bill was, in theory, to be discussed openly and freely before the final vote took place.[2] At the morning session, Laval again succeeded in having everything his way, although Flandin made a stirring twenty-minute speech that received almost unanimous acclaim. He demanded that France remain faithful to its own traditions and reject any servile imitation of other regimes. But

[5] Herriot: *Épisodes, 1940–1944*, p. 136; and cf. Auriol: *Hier . . . demain*, I, 130.

[6] Biondi to Noguères, in Noguères: journal, entry for July 9, 1940, *Evénements*, VII, 2244.

[7] *Mémoires*, 1940, *Oeuvre*, V, 79.

[8] Ibid., pp. 79, 94; and editorial, *Le Populaire*, July 20, 1949.

[9] *Hier . . . demain*, I, 115, 130.

[1] Testimony, 1945, *Le Procès de Pétain*, I, 164.

[2] A stenographic record was kept but was not published until 1950. It appears as "Compte-rendu sténographique de la séance privée des membres de la Chambre des Députés et du Sénat, 10 juillet 1940," in *Événements, Rapport*, II, 479–97. In his memoirs, Blum seems to have telescoped the private morning session and the public afternoon session and writes that the galleries that morning were filled with Laval's henchmen; *Mémoires*, 1940, *Oeuvre*, V, 88.

he, too, ended by giving his full support to Laval's bill; the government would need as much authority as possible, he contended, in order to negotiate with the conqueror.

The Taurines counterproposal had already been slyly sidetracked by Laval at a cabinet meeting on July 8; Rivière, in Auriol's words, had been successfully "hoodwinked."[3] When the proposal was once again brought up from the floor, Laval disarmed its proponents by accepting an amendment to his own bill and agreeing that the new constitution should be "ratified by the nation." The second major point—that the constitution be prepared in collaboration with Parliament—he skillfully evaded by reading at the appropriate moment a letter from Marshal Pétain. The letter threw all the Marshal's prestige behind the government's bill as "necessary in order to ensure the salvation of our country." The argument was overwhelming. The Taurines counterproposal, on which many of the Socialists had placed their hopes, was destined never to reach the floor.[4]

It was at this morning session that Laval singled out Blum for his invective and sarcasm. He inveighed against the dying regime and against those who had "declared war without having prepared for it in either the diplomatic . . . or the military sphere."[5] He attacked the Popular Front for having thwarted his own efforts at building up friendship with Italy. "Do you remember? You could call someone a thief, a scoundrel, a bully. But there was one insult that was more serious and surpassed all others: that was when you called someone a fascist." After the laughter, he continued: "Yes, it is a fact that antifascism was the foundation of all our domestic policy and of all our foreign policy."

It was now that he recounted the incident to which we have already referred in an earlier chapter, how in January 1937, in the midst of the Spanish Civil War, the Italian Ambassador, under instructions from Mussolini, had informed Blum that Mussolini would be pleased to use his influence with General Franco to bring about a friendlier relationship between Franco and the French. "And do you know—I say it without emotion—I am only trying to demonstrate how our political practices were out of harmony with the interests of the country—do you know what the reply was? The reply to M. Cerutti was that the *démarche* was friendly, but that a Popular Front government could

---

[3] *"On vous a roulés"* were his words; *Hier . . . demain,* I, 125–6.

[4] See Aron: *Histoire de Vichy,* pp. 131–54, for various details and documents.

[5] "Séance privée," July 10, 1940, *Événements, Rapport,* II, 485.

not accept the offer! And nothing more!" Blum, he recalled, to the amusement of the audience, had even pretended not to know what the Italian Ambassador meant when he called the Spanish Loyalist government "a Bolshevik or quasi-Bolshevik government (*gouvernement bolchévique ou bolchévisant*)"![6] An eyewitness watched Blum as Laval spoke: "He had the appearance which he usually assumes when his attention is fixed on a speaker: his body erect, his head high, a light, persistent movement of his lips; under his mustache, two fingers of his right hand raised to his mouth." When Laval finished his anecdote, a hubbub of indignant exclamations filled the hall. The observer continued: "For one brief moment I thought that Léon Blum was going to reply. All looks were directed toward him. . . ."[7] But he said nothing and allowed the incident to pass.

In his memoirs Blum denied that fear had prompted his silence. He had never shrunk from speaking out to hostile audiences, but at Vichy, as he himself explained, there was a tragic difference. In the past, he had had at his side his party comrades and friends. That was no longer true. In the turmoil that would have broken out if he had risen to speak, the great majority of his comrades, he was convinced, would have abandoned him and many would have chimed in with the chorus of those insulting him. "I refused to make a public spectacle of this renunciation. That alone paralyzed me, sealed my lips."[8]

His explanation is not to be dismissed. The work of a lifetime was crumbling before his eyes. Everything precious was collapsing. He had witnessed the defeat of his country; now he saw the end of the republic, the disintegration of his party, the desertion of his comrades, the estrangement of his closest friends. To understand the situation he found himself in is to understand his silence. If he had chosen to speak, what could he have said in that atmosphere? Could he have explained the foreign policy he had sought to follow—his attempt to prevent ideologies from interfering with foreign affairs, as in the case of Spain or even in the case of Nazi Germany? Could he have defended the Popular Front or explained the meaning of "antifascism"? Could he have convinced anyone that the Popular Front had begun to rearm France after the Right had failed to do so? Any speech he might have made would have been used against him more than his silence.

[6] Ibid., p. 489.

[7] Noguères: journal, entry for July 10, 1940, *Événements*, VII, 2250. Auriol reports that during the session Blum said to him, referring to Laval: "What a mountebank!" (*"Quel bateleur!"*); *Hier . . . demain*, I, 123.

[8] *Mémoires*, 1940, *Oeuvre*, V, 89.

He would have been shouted down and subjected to ridicule; Laval would have twisted his statements to serve his own purposes. Perhaps, an observer at the session has suggested, Laval hoped to provoke Blum to reply in order to add to the confusion.[9]

The morning session was the last opportunity for anyone to speak out, for in the formal public session that afternoon all opposition was outmaneuvered by Laval and his associates, or silenced by jeers and hooting from the public galleries. When an attempt was made to re-introduce the Taurines counterproposal, the speaker could not even make himself heard. The government bill was steamrollered through with only a brief adjournment for a committee meeting to clarify the intent of the bill. Marx Dormoy was present at the committee meeting as a member of the standing Senate committee on legislation. Laval was scornful of opposition, self-confident, and evasive. When questioned about the government's intentions with respect to personal liberties, he flared up: "If you mean by personal liberties rights for all immigrants and all foreigners . . . I will make it clear that no one will be eligible to be a Deputy if he has not been a Frenchman for many generations. That is our kind . . . of a race policy." Of the forty-eight members of the joint committee, only four refused to accept the bill; Marx Dormoy was the sole Socialist dissenter.[1]

When the committee returned with its favorable report, nothing remained but the formality of voting. As soon as Blum placed his negative ballot in the voting urn, he left, not even waiting for the final tally. He was spared the remark of a Socialist colleague: "Blum is finished."[2]

The results on Laval's bill were even more overwhelming than might have been expected: 569 for, 80 against, 17 formal abstentions. The 80 opposing votes included 35 Socialists (7 Senators and 28 Deputies). The fifty-six who had pledged their determined opposition at the informal party caucus on July 8 had dwindled by a third. Of the 569

[9] Noguères: journal, entry for July 10, 1940, *Événements*, VII, 2250. Aron has written: "*Sans doute son intervention eût-elle provoqué contre lui les clameurs des auxiliaires de Pierre Laval, et n'eût-il pu, en aucun cas, se faire entendre*"; *Histoire de Vichy*, p. 133. Audry, on the other hand, reproaches him his silence; *Léon Blum*, pp. 165–6.

[1] "Compte-rendu de la séance tenue par la commission constitutionnelle de l'Assemblée Nationale, le 10 juillet 1940," *Événements, Rapport*, II, 498–502; for the Laval statement, p. 501.

[2] Reported by de Monzie, journal entry, July 10, 1940, *Ci-devant*, p. 261.

who voted for the Laval bill, 90 were Socialists. Of the 17 who abstained—that is, formally declared their intention not to cast a vote—6 were Socialists.[3] The abstention most cruel to Blum was that of Georges Monnet, his friend and protégé. He had stood firmly against capitulation in the Reynaud cabinet and had been at Blum's side when the government was still thinking of leaving the country to continue the war. Now he, too, had yielded or at least abstained.[4]

Avoiding the excited crowds pressing outside the building, Blum left by a side exit and returned to Commentry. The next day he departed for Toulouse, stopping first at the headquarters of his son's regiment at Maurs. He learned that his son was alive although a prisoner of war. The heaviest of his private worries was somewhat relieved.[5]

Blum's decision to be present at Vichy and his vote of opposition symbolized his personal sense of duty and his courage. Nothing deterred him from fulfilling the obligations imposed by his conscience—neither his age (he was now past sixty-eight), his exhaustion after the Bordeaux days, his despair over the division within his own party, his anxiety over the fate of his son, nor any concern for his own safety. A Socialist observer commented: "One must understand that Blum was the object of constant threats on the part of all the antisemitic madmen who controlled the streets. One must understand also that the Cagoulard chiefs . . . were at their command posts. When I speak of guts [*cran*] I know whereof I speak."[6] His journalist-friend Louis Lévy, in London at the time, wrote: "His attitude gave comfort and courage to many a heartbroken party member."[7] And Paul-Boncour paid tribute to him:

[3] For a breakdown of the Socialist vote, see Noguères: journal, entry for July 10, 1940, *Événements*, VII, 2254–5; Lefranc: *Mouvement socialiste*, p. 389; and Ligou: *Socialisme*, p. 469; see also the recapitulation at the postwar Socialist party congress, *Le Populaire*, November 14, 15, 1944. Twenty-seven Socialists were absent or excused for reasons beyond their control. For a convenient list of "the eighty" (57 Deputies and 23 Senators), see Aron: *Histoire de Vichy*, p. 153, n. 1.

[4] See, on Monnet and his reasons for abstaining, remarks of Auriol: *Hier . . . demain*, I, 136 and n. 1; Noguères: journal, entry for July 10, 1940, *Événements*, VII, 2253; and Lévy: *The Truth about France*, p. 175.

[5] *Mémoires*, 1940, *Oeuvre*, V, 96–7. He also saw Ambassador Bullitt briefly before leaving Vichy; ibid., pp. 94–6.

[6] Noguères: journal, entry for July 10, 1940, *Événements*, VII, 2250.

[7] Lévy: *The Truth about France*, p. 176.

"In the Chamber, where Blum necessarily kept silent, [his] mere presence was an act of courage."[8]

Could he have spoken out with any effect when not one of the republican leaders of the Left or Center spoke up? Paul Reynaud had been seriously hurt in an automobile accident, in which his mistress had been killed; he appeared briefly, swathed in bandages, and left before the vote. Daladier, Mandel, Campinchi, Delbos, Jean Zay, and others had not returned from their ill-fated voyage on the *Massilia*. Jules Jeanneney, president of the Senate and ex-officio presiding officer of the National Assembly, proved ineffectual against Laval's maneuvers. Herriot displayed courage in openly defending the men of the *Massilia*, but that discussion was peripheral to the main issue; in the end, he abstained from voting. President Lebrun, who always bent in whichever direction the stronger wind blew, was completely cowed by Laval and his associates. His resignation after the vote was simply a matter of form. Chautemps, who was still in the cabinet as Vice-Premier, only shrugged his shoulders disconsolately when Blum said to him just before the final vote: "*Alors*, Chautemps, it is the end of the republic?"[9] He went on to serve the new regime for a time and then lived out his days in exile in the United States.

What could Blum have accomplished when these men remained silent? He had not succeeded in 1938 in rallying the country to a union of all political forces. Now he had no great party behind him. Moreover, he was the very symbol of the despised Popular Front, a Socialist, and a Jew. Who would have heeded him now?

The speech Blum did not make in reply to Laval, he wrote into his memoirs three months later. He denounced Laval's accusations against the republic and his sinister designs for the future: "When he poured forth his admiration for the Nazi and Fascist dictatorships, when he retrospectively attacked the parliamentary regime—not for its faults or its excesses, but in its very principle—declaring it responsible at one and the same time for the war and for the defeat, when he treated as criminals and fools the men who had wished to honor France's commitments as well as those who had wished to persevere in the struggle imposed by the enemy, when he denounced as partisan politics the refusal to consent to the enslavement of the country, when he vituperated against the opposition of parties and against the 'fictitious' class strug-

8 *Entre deux guerres*, III, 273.

9 *Mémoires*, 1940, *Oeuvre*, V, 91. For Georges Bonnet's silence at the time, *Défense de la paix*, I, 369–71, and II, 390–1.

gle, against the complicity of the two Internationals, the one of capitalism, the other of Marxism—he did not yet speak of the Jews, the moment had not yet arrived but their place was already provided for—no one could be mistaken about the intentions he did not dare formulate. His obvious objective was to cut all the roots that bound France to its republican and revolutionary past. His 'national revolution' was to be a counterrevolution eliminating all the progress and human rights won in the last one hundred and fifty years."[1] Blum wrote these words as a prisoner of the new regime.

Although Blum condemned those who had yielded at Vichy, he did not forget the atmosphere in which the vote had taken place. "What will never be proclaimed loudly enough," he wrote, "is that rarely if ever was a more serious decision taken by a French assembly but that never was a decision less free."[2] He always maintained that the vote at Vichy was not a "free" one and that, as in the case of a private contract signed under coercion and duress, the result was invalid.[3] Yet his argument was more rhetorical than legal. Like some other twentieth-century events, the overthrow of the Third Republic took place legally, even if in the borderlands of political legality. The verdict at Vichy, as has been said, was a "free vote in an atmosphere of anguish."[4] That eighty men, including Blum, found the moral courage to demonstrate their resistance and to vindicate their conscience was no small matter.

A few years after the war, Blum was asked whether those who had voted for the Laval bill at Vichy had not merely committed a mistake in judgment such as he himself might often have made in his political life. "I have probably committed many errors," he replied, "but I do not believe I have ever committed an act of betrayal. The republican representatives who voted *for* at Vichy did not make a mistake. They betrayed their mandate, which is an entirely different thing."[5] The threat of personal danger was no excuse, he contended; danger was an "occupational hazard" for a Deputy or a Senator. "An elected representative of the people is chosen not only to place his vote in a ballot urn, to speak from a rostrum, to intervene for his constituents with the authorities, and to receive a salary at the end of the month. When

[1] *Mémoires*, 1940, *Oeuvre*, V, 92.

[2] Ibid., p. 93.

[3] Ibid., and testimony, 1945, *Le Procès de Pétain*, I, 244.

[4] Aron: *Histoire de Vichy*, p. 154.

[5] Editorial, *Le Populaire*, July 20, 1949, replying to André Bougenot, writing in *L'Époque*.

circumstances demand it, he must, like a mobilized soldier, pass from garrison life to life in the field. He must, like a soldier, risk his liberty or his life to fulfill the mandate that he himself has solicited."[6]

One conclusion Blum could not bring himself to admit was that in July 1940 the elected representatives of the people had lost confidence in themselves and in the parliamentary institutions of the Third Republic. For that reason no one raised a voice to defend the republic or even to deliver a decent funeral oration. He himself was too closely identified with the republic to make the admission; it would have meant the rejection of everything he had championed all his life. On the main point he was right. The vote at Vichy was not a vote for or against the Third Republic, whose faults everyone recognized; it was a vote for or against republican liberties.

[6] *Mémoires*, 1940, *Oeuvre*, V, 86.

XIV

THE PRISONER,

1940–1942

*Prison was missing from my experience in
life, and Providence has filled the gap.*[1]

AFTER THE EVENTS at Vichy, Blum took up residence in the
countryside near Toulouse in the home of friends, where he
rested, listened to the clandestine broadcasts from London,
and followed the course of the war.[2] At the end of July, he learned
that the Pétain-Laval government was undertaking an investigation
of persons responsible for France's entry into the war and for her disastrous defeat.[3] Constitutional Act No. 5, adopted on July 30, 1940,
established a high court, the Cour Suprême de Justice, empowered to
judge "ministers, former ministers, or their immediate subordinates,
civilian or military." The court was to institute proceedings against
those persons who had "betrayed the duties of their office by acts
which contributed to the passage from a state of peace to a state of
war before September 4, 1939," and by acts "which subsequently
aggravated the consequences of the situation thus created."[4]

[1] Blum: letter to Mme Grunebaum-Ballin (wife of the prominent jurist and
longtime friend of Blum), September 24, 1940, *Oeuvre*, V, 141.

[2] *Mémoires*, 1940, *Oeuvre*, V, 5–6, 98, 118, 130, and passim.

[3] Ibid., pp. 5, 100, 124–5.

[4] On the legislation, and for many other details on the Riom court and its
proceedings, see Paul Soupiron: *Bazaine contre Gambetta, ou le procès de Riom*
(Lyons, 1944), pp. 21–3; Maurice Ribet: *Le Procès de Riom*, pp. 299, 517, and
passim; and Pierre Cot: *Le Procès de la république*, I, 188–93. Soupiron, a
journalist present at the trial, has compiled the most detailed account of the
testimony and proceedings; Ribet was Daladier's attorney. On the sources for
the trial see John C. Cairns: "Along the Road Back to France 1940," *American
Historical Review*, LXIV (April 1959), 591, n. 20.

Although no individuals were mentioned, Blum conjectured that the investigation would be directed primarily against Édouard Daladier, Premier and Minister of National Defense at the outbreak of the war, Paul Reynaud, Premier at the time of the German blitz in the spring of 1940, and Georges Mandel and others in the Reynaud cabinet who might have "aggravated the consequences" of the military defeat by refusing to accept an armistice sooner. The phrase "acts which contributed to the passage from a state of peace to a state of war" and the reference in an official press release to the responsibilities of those who had "launched the country on a course of war" had an ominous ring. Would the Pétain government charge the French republican leaders with having initiated the war? Would it raise the charge of French "war guilt"? Also, if the question of inadequate preparation for the war was to be investigated, how far back would responsibility be sought?[5]

On August 8, the newly appointed members of the court met in the small town of Riom in central France, north of Clermont-Ferrand, and were sworn in by the Minister of Justice, Raphaël Alibert, who had played a key role in the adoption of the new legislation. The court consisted of ten members, who were appointed for life. Except for one general and one admiral, they were all drawn from the higher judiciary. Pierre Caous, the president of the criminal chamber of the country's regular supreme tribunal, the Cour de Cassation, was *ex officio* the presiding magistrate.[6]

At the beginning of September, Blum learned that proceedings had been instituted against Pierre Cot, who had been his Minister of Air from June 1936 to June 1937 and in the subsequent Chautemps cabinet until January 1938, and against Guy La Chambre, Cot's successor in that office from January 1938 to March 1940. Both men were in the United States at the time. Almost simultaneously, the government announced that Daladier, Reynaud, Mandel, and General Gamelin, the commanding officer of the army at the time of the German breakthrough, had been taken into protective custody by administrative order of the Minister of Interior as persons constituting a potential danger to the national defense and security. They had been imprisoned in an old castle, the Château de Chazeron, in the mountains not far from Clermont-Ferrand.

[5] *Mémoires*, 1940, *Oeuvre*, V, 124, 129–30; Soupiron: *Riom*, pp. 19–23.
[6] For the composition of the court and the opening session, Soupiron: *Riom*, pp. 27–30.

Although Blum was filled with indignation at these arrests, he did not realize that he would soon be the victim of the same fate. All of those arrested had held high office at the time of the country's entry into the war and at the time of the defeat in June 1940. Pierre Cot was an exception, but Cot undoubtedly had been included in the group because he had left for the United States and because the press was seeking a scapegoat for the airplane shortages at the time of the defeat. Blum himself had been out of office for a long time. In the year and a half preceding the outbreak of the war, and in the nine months of the war itself, he had held no cabinet office at all. With his usual optimism, he gave little heed to the dangers ahead.[7]

Yet there were sufficient grounds for apprehension. Ever since the military defeat, various segments of public opinion had been clamoring for a full investigation into responsibility for the disaster of June 1940. Some had in mind principally the military. But Laval and his associates, during the armistice negotiations at Bordeaux and during the parliamentary sessions of July 9 and 10 at Vichy, had made plain that they sought to fix responsibility on the political leaders of the prewar years. Marshal Pétain, in his earliest public addresses to the nation, had clearly indicated also that blame was to be placed on those political leaders who not only had failed to supply the armed forces with the weapons that were needed but had weakened the moral fiber of the country as well. "The disaster, in reality," in the Marshal's words, "was only the reflection on the military plane of the weaknesses and faults of the old political system." The Vichy and Paris press were openly condemning the Popular Front government for the country's unpreparedness at the time of the war. As might be expected, Blum's name figured prominently in the lists of those who must be punished.[8]

Nonetheless, when Vincent Auriol, at the beginning of September 1940, warned Blum of the possibility of his imminent arrest, he merely shrugged off the warning.[9] In the second week of September he was preparing to move to an unoccupied house belonging to old friends a few kilometers from Saint-Raphaël, and was awaiting the necessary police permit for a vehicle to transport his belongings. The permit did not arrive. Instead, on Sunday morning, September 15, the house was surrounded by police vehicles. On the ground that he was "dangerous to the security of the French state," the Vichy government had

[7] *Mémoires*, 1940, *Oeuvre*, V, 129.
[8] Soupiron: *Riom*, 19–24, 40; Auriol: *Hier ... demain*, I, 140.
[9] Auriol: *Hier ... demain*, I, 140.

ordered his administrative internment.[1] After driving all that day
north from Toulouse, he and his police escort arrived at the stately
Renaissance Château de Chazeron, before which a sentry marched
with rifle and fixed bayonet. Blum was led up a spiral staircase to a
prison room in the tower; he soon discovered that he was a fellow
prisoner of Daladier, Reynaud, Mandel, and General Gamelin.[2]

Blum spent the next two months at Chazeron. (It was one of the
less unpleasant of the French and German prisons in which he passed
the next five years of his life.) His room was spacious and well furnished. Through the barred window he could see a meadow, some
magnificent old trees, and a patch of sky. The accommodations were
rudimentary for there had been little time to prepare the castle for
its new function. The regulations permitted two brief walks alone in a
small enclosed courtyard. Visits were closely supervised, and correspondence and reading material censored. No communication with
the other prisoners was permitted.[3]

At the age of sixty-eight, he was a prisoner—a political prisoner in
France while his son was a prisoner of war in Germany. Here was an
experience he had missed in his crowded and varied life, and now,
he mused, "Providence has filled the gap." He could jest in a letter
to a friend that, as Premier, he had grown accustomed to being accompanied everywhere by armed guards. "The life of a Premier," he wrote,
"bears some resemblance to that of a political internee."[4] He also noted
that his search for a place to live had been conveniently settled for
him. In more serious vein, he admitted that his arrest had "profoundly
upset" him and that he could "not quite grasp it." But he quickly put
aside all self-pity. His immediate concern was whether, "after so
many fatiguing experiences, ordeals, and disappointments," he still
had enough mental energy left to arrange for himself a routine "of
profitable reflection and work."[5]

Such a routine, he soon discovered, was possible. He read a great
deal, corresponded with friends, and began to write. He turned first
to his recollections of the hectic events he had lived through in the

---

[1] *Mémoires*, 1940, *Oeuvre*, V, 130–1.

[2] Ibid., pp. 5–6.

[3] Ibid., p. 6; and letter to Mme Grunebaum-Ballin, September 24, 1940, ibid.,
p. 141. On the choice of letters published in the 1940–5 volume of the collected
works, see Robert Blum's note, *Oeuvre*, V, 140. The unpublished letters, principally to Jeanne-Léon Blum, are not of major political importance.

[4] *Mémoires*, 1940, *Oeuvre*, V, 6; and letter, September 24, 1940, ibid., p. 141.

[5] Letter, September 24, 1940, ibid.

spring and summer of 1940: the military defeat, the armistice, the parliamentary sessions at Vichy. His memoirs of those turbulent days, finished in the autumn of 1940, were secreted out of prison and subsequently published after the war.[6] After the memoirs, he began work on his long reflective essay on the political experience of his generation. Completed in December 1941, long after he had been moved from the Château de Chazeron, it was published after the war as *À l'échelle humaine* (*For All Mankind*, his English translator called it).[7] It was a brilliant distillation of his political thought, a searching analysis of a world that had come to disaster, and a testament to his abiding faith in democracy, democratic socialism, and internationalism.

The essay was, first, a dissection of the errors, illusions, and misfortunes of the 1930's. "The generation to which I belong," he openly confessed in the preface, "has not succeeded in its task."[8] This failure demanded a frank and probing analysis, not self-exculpation or a search for sacrificial victims. After the disasters of 1940, it was almost inevitable that the nation would blame everything on the republic and even on the principles of democracy itself. Had not the republicans of 1871 similarly turned against the imperial regime of Napoleon III? But the republic, he argued, symbolized the aspirations of men for a just society founded on the principles of liberty and equality; above all, it had labored for peace, without which there could be no civilized progress. The greatest error of the 1930's was the failure to recognize Hitler's designs "promptly enough and clearly enough."[9]

While acknowledging that some of the blame for the nation's troubles had to be placed on the form that parliamentary institutions had taken in France, he would not permit abuse of the principles of democracy and republicanism as such. As in his earlier articles on French governmental reform, he scored the weakness of executive leadership, the absence of sound executive-legislative relationships, the failure to create coherent, homogeneous, and disciplined political parties.[1] He was willing to admit that the parliamentary system of the Third Republic was not the "sole, exclusive, and necessary form of

[6] On these memoirs, see first footnote of Chapter XII above.

[7] The essay is reprinted in *Oeuvre*, V, 409–95, with the preface to the original edition (1945) by Bracke. It was subsequently translated into many languages. The excellent English translation (1946) is by William Pickles.

[8] "Avant-propos," *À l'échelle humaine*, *Oeuvre*, V, 409.

[9] *À l'échelle humaine*, *Oeuvre*, V, 424.

[1] Ibid., esp. pp. 429–38.

democracy" for France—a statement that would often be cited in the postwar years, often without the reservations he had added.[2]

For the decline and decay of the French economy, he blamed the "governing class," the bourgeoisie. It had failed to keep alive the spirit of innovation, risk, and technological creativity that had once been its hallmark. Once the old "vital sap" dried up, competition gave way to reliance on the state. The ruling class not only had failed to create an equitable society but had failed to provide an adequate industrial base for meeting the challenges of the twentieth century.[3] Yet he candidly admitted that the working class was not free of blame. What he would not concede to the masters of the Vichy regime or to the magistrates of the Riom court, he freely confessed in his essay. With searching honesty he measured himself, the Socialist party, and the working class, censuring the defects, limitations, and shortcomings that he found. There had been no possibility of a legitimate transfer of authority from the bourgeoisie to the working class. One could not shout "The King is dead! Long live the King!" The laboring class had failed to display a morality superior to that of the bourgeoisie, but had itself obeyed motives of calculated material self-interest.[4]

Nor did he spare his party. It, too, had failed to incarnate the old heroic spirit of struggle and sacrifice. Even its pacifism was often less an idealistic response than a desire to "save one's own skin." Hopelessly divided in the two years before the war because of its pacifism, it was impotent in the critical hours of the war and defeat. "At the hour when the nation awaited a summons, a rallying cry, there could come from our ranks no great voice." In part, the party had been "compromised" in the public eye by its close identification with the Communists. He had no regrets over the common front of the Socialists and Communists against the fascist threat to the republic after February 1934. But later, when the Communists accepted the German-Soviet pact of August 1939, and their actions in the early months of the war had seemed like "treason" to the nation, the Socialists had been tarred with the same brush.[5] (In the pages he wrote after June 1941, he had nothing but praise for the valor of the Soviets, then

[2] Ibid., pp. 429–30, 468–9; and see below, Chapter XVII.

[3] See *À l'échelle humaine*, *Oeuvre*, V, 439–49; and cf. John B. Christopher: "The Desiccation of the Bourgeois Spirit," in Edward Mead Earle (ed.): *Modern France: Problems of the Third and Fourth Republics* (Princeton, N.J.: 1951), pp. 44–57.

[4] *À l'échelle humaine*, *Oeuvre*, V, 450–1, 462–4.

[5] Ibid., pp. 453–8, 464–6.

locked in the struggle against Hitler, and for the self-sacrifice and courage of the French Communists, but that, he emphasized, did not change the past.[6])

In the manner natural to him, he looked with hope to the future. The new society after the war must rest on the three pillars of democracy, social democracy, and international federation. Even if France's institutions required change and purification, the task had to be accomplished through the strengthening, not the repudiation, of democracy. The new era would demand a broadening out of political democracy— "the great human ideals defined in 1789"—into social and economic democracy, but in the effort to reform the economic structure of society, vigilance must be maintained against any perversion of the democratic principle itself as had occurred in the dictatorships.[7] Blum always returned to his fundamental belief that political democracy and economic democracy must be fused without sacrificing the one to the other.

Finally, a federation of nations would have to be created after the war; only a federation of free democratic republics could provide peace for future generations of mankind.[8] The conclusion of his long essay conveyed, even in the dark days of 1940 and 1941, his faith in the future: "When a man grows troubled and discouraged, he has only to think of humanity."[9] It was a tribute to his courage and optimism that even in those troubled days he could look forward to a new era. His essay was one of the wellsprings of inspiration for the wartime Resistance movement and for postwar republican France.

———

But we must return to Blum at the Château de Chazeron. Three weeks after his arrest, he received, on October 8, 1940, the first indication that he, too, was to come under the jurisdiction of the Riom court and that preliminary hearings would soon begin. Sufficient evidence existed, the Prosecutor General's bill of charges stated, that under the recently adopted legislation "crimes and misdemeanors were committed by M. Léon Blum, former Premier and Vice-Premier, in the exercise . . . of his functions, and that he betrayed the duties of his office . . ." His case was to be associated with the proceedings already begun against

[6] Ibid., pp. 458–9; he was completing the essay in December 1941.
[7] Ibid., p. 472, and see pp. 468–73.
[8] Ibid., pp. 473–94.
[9] Ibid., p. 495.

Édouard Daladier, General Gamelin, Pierre Cot, and Guy La Chambre.[1] Reynaud and Mandel, facing charges which were complicated by various additional accusations, would be dealt with separately.[2] Like the others, Blum would remain a prisoner under the court's jurisdiction during the proceedings.

Blum set aside his writing and turned to the preparation of his defense. He was presented by the court with the testimony that had already been gathered, the depositions of hundreds of witnesses—government officials, army officers, industrialists, former political leaders, and others from all walks of life. He was flooded with documents and reports. He wrote to friends asking them to help gather the data he would need for his defense and he requested a young Socialist lawyer, Samuel Spanien, to do the necessary legwork and research for him in the parliamentary documents and newspaper files.[3] He himself undertook to absorb and correlate the mass of information. In some ways the materials held the fascination of history for him. He studied the documents with an "objective" interest, "the interest of the historian who studies the archives about events that stir his thoughts and emotions."[4] As a lawyer, too, he could find an "objective" challenge in the case. "I am doing what a lawyer would do," he wrote, "and I am doing it almost as if for somebody else."[5]

In the middle of November 1940, Blum's stay at Chazeron came to an abrupt end. He was transferred to a new prison, an old broken-down country estate at Bourassol, a small town only four kilometers south of Riom, and hence closer to the court, where he would remain for many months. Daladier, General Gamelin, and Guy La Chambre (who had returned from the United States) were transferred with him; Robert Jacomet, controller-general of the army from 1936 to 1940, also under charges, joined them later. Reynaud and Mandel were taken elsewhere.

His "new residence," Blum wrote, "makes no pretense at being anything more than a prison."[6] A Swiss correspondent described the place that winter: "a very old building, dilapidated, without the most elementary conveniences . . . of repulsive squalor . . . The rooms are not

[1] The *réquisitoire supplétif* is reprinted in *Oeuvre*, V, 144.
[2] See communiqué, Minister of Justice, reprinted in Soupiron: *Riom*, pp. 41–2.
[3] Letters to Vincent Auriol, October 25 and November 9, 1940, *Oeuvre*, V, 145–6, 152–3.
[4] Letter to Auriol, February 13, 1941, ibid., pp. 168–9.
[5] Letter to Marx Dormoy, November 16, 1940, ibid., p. 153.
[6] Ibid.

heated . . . Water freezes in the wash basin."[7] There was only one advantage in Blum's new location. His daughter-in-law, Renée, and Jeanne, his devoted "Janot," who would one day join him in a German concentration camp and become his third wife, had been faithful visitors at Chazeron despite its inaccessibility. Now they could live at a hotel in Riom and be closer to him. He could "feel their nearness," he wrote.[8] Each day Renée bicycled the four kilometers from Riom to carry a noonday meal to him. His health was beginning to cause him some trouble. He had begun to lose weight at Chazeron and continued to do so, but he remained cheerful and not lacking in energy. Toward the end of December his daughter-in-law wrote to friends in America: "My father-in-law is full of fight and in very good condition, but I am afraid that he could not survive if he were sent to some military prison." Her letter reflected the general apprehension about conditions in France. To the irritation of the Germans, Laval had been ousted on December 13 and replaced by Flandin. "At any moment," she wrote, "France can be occupied completely, and my only hope, you can well understand, is that my father-in-law not fall into the hands of the Germans." As to his trial, she was thoroughly reconciled to its outcome: "Everyone knows that he will be condemned. There is nothing to be done about that."[9]

But the trial was still a long way off. Only the pretrial interrogation had begun. After a brief preliminary interview, three extended sessions with an examining magistrate took place over the next few months. Blum was charged with having weakened and demoralized the country by failing to act decisively during the sitdown strikes of June 1936 and by introducing legislation providing for the forty-hour week, paid vacations, and the nationalization of the armaments industry. "At a time when the international situation imperatively demanded that everything be subordinated to the need of national defense," he was told, "you, as head of the government, allowed the productivity of our defense plants to be compromised and you thereby reduced France to a state of moral and physical inferiority with respect to neighboring peoples." Blum refused at these pretrial interrogations to discuss in any detail the testimony and documents gathered by the public prosecutor, insisting that such discussion had to take place in

[7] *Le Jour* (Montreal), May 3, 1941. I am indebted to Mme Suzanne Blum for this clipping.

[8] Letter to Dormoy, November 16, 1940, *Oeuvre*, V, 153.

[9] Renée Blum to Suzanne Blum, December 25, 1940, unpublished letter; courtesy of Mme Suzanne Blum.

open court with full opportunity to cross-examine witnesses. He firmly defended the record of his government, however, in strengthening the national defenses of the country and in launching a rearmament program when other governments had failed to do so. The true causes of the military defeat, he insisted, had to be sought not in the actions of his government but in the narrowness, lack of vision, and outright errors of the High Command. It was not inadequacy of equipment but the failure to use properly what the armed forces possessed that had led to defeat.[1]

He himself, he pointed out, was accused not of personal acts of wrongdoing but of actions taken as a political leader faithful to a political program approved overwhelmingly by the electorate. He had acted legally and constitutionally as the head of a coalition government supported by both houses of Parliament. The accusations, thus, were directed not against any individuals or political leaders, but against the republican regime itself—which he was determined to defend.[2]

Because he was accused of having followed "policies contrary to the interests of the country," he resolved not to diminish the political character of the trial. He chose as trial counsel André Le Troquer, a militant Socialist Deputy from Paris, well known in Parliament and in the Socialist party. He "would defend himself," he wrote, "with a political friend at his side."[3]

As the months went by and there was no indication of a trial date, Blum began to show signs of depression. The challenge and excitement of preparing his defense had worn off and he could no longer sustain his interest in the details. The material he needed for his defense and for the cross-examination of witnesses had been almost completely assembled. A slow stream of new documents trickled in, but they were repetitious or merely added minor details and held nothing to revive his interest. One of his complaints was that the tedious preparation for the trial had "distracted" him from his "personal work," his writing. He wistfully remarked that he was not the man he had formerly been. "Once, a double undertaking like that would have been child's play for me. But it has to be accepted that with age my mind has lost something of its agility."[4] In the winter and spring of

---

[1] The record of these interrogations, November 4, December 21, 1940, and February 4, 1941, is reprinted in *Oeuvre*, V, 148–51, 156–9, 165–7.

[2] Interrogation of February 4, 1941, ibid., p. 167.

[3] Letter to Auriol, November 19, 1940, ibid., p. 154.

[4] Letter to Auriol, February 13, 1941, ibid., pp. 168–9.

1941, periods of mental gloom recurred. There were stretches of time, he wrote, during which he "was not good for very much." He could do little more to prepare for the trial, yet he could not turn his mind to other things. The oppressive uncertainty was wearing him down.[5]

In May 1941, unable to contain himself any longer, Blum addressed a letter to the court. It had been three months since his final interrogation and he was still without word of the forthcoming trial. He understood that embarrassing diplomatic questions would inevitably arise in any public trial examining the events of the 1930's and the outbreak of the war. If the interests of the country required that there be no public trial, he would loyally "bow without a word." He would "accept without reservation the sacrifice of his own clear and most cherished interests to that of the country." On the other hand, he wrote with firmness, the government ought to have thought of such embarrassing possibilities earlier and never have initiated the trial. He resented most that judgment was being passed on him in the press and before the bar of public opinion while he was unable to defend himself publicly in open court. He protested especially against certain "invidious" newspaper articles based on information furnished by the investigating magistrates themselves. He demanded the right to appear before his judges with the least possible delay so that he might exonerate himself of the charges against him.[6]

He expressed these same opinions in private letters. Personally, he wished the trial to take place and to take place quickly. But there was another consideration. The Vichy government seemed bent on appeasing the conqueror by accepting French responsibility for the outbreak of the war. "In the interests of the country," wrote Blum, he would "see [such a trial] open only with pain and even humiliation," and he wished the country could be spared it. Apart from his own personal situation, he was at heart overwhelmed by a sense of grief and shame that the men governing the country should have so debased themselves as to have initiated these proceedings.[7]

By the summer of 1941, Blum had reconciled himself to an indefinite adjournment of the trial and to a prolonged detention in prison. "They will not hold the trial," he predicted, "but they will keep us in prison

[5] Ibid., and letter to André Blumel, June 14, 1941, ibid., pp. 177–8.
[6] Note for the Riom court, May 19, 1941, ibid., pp. 175–6.
[7] Letters to Dormoy, January 21, February 27, 1941, ibid., pp. 163–4, 169–70.

indefinitely. They will not dare either to judge us or to free us."[8] Although the tensions of these anxious months were "taking their toll" of his nerves, he wanted no one to feel sorry for him. "I am not to be an object of pity and I am not pitying myself." To Marx Dormoy, who praised his courage, he replied: "You are creating an image of me superior to what I am. I say this without false modesty. I know approximately my own worth, but your friendship makes me a bigger man."[9] That summer came the cruel news of Marx Dormoy's assassination. Under house arrest at Montélimar, Dormoy was killed on the night of July 25–26 by the explosion of a bomb placed in his hotel room—the vengeance of the fascist leagues on the man who as Minister of the Interior in 1937 and 1938 had spared no effort to track them down. "I lost much with him," Blum wrote, "and the blow has deeply wounded me. . . . Alas, this unfortunate friend will not see the day of victory and deliverance."[1]

The new events of the war in the spring and summer of 1941 gave Blum cause for satisfaction. He considered the German invasion of Russia in June 1941 evidence that Hitler "had lost confidence in his own victory." Meanwhile, Russian resistance was making impossible a quick German victory or "an armistice of a well-known type." Of the Russian army he wrote: "Do you recall with what scorn they used to speak to us of that army? Only the Polish army could be counted on for something. As to a comparison with tne French army, no one would have hazarded such an impious thought!"[2] His confidence in the final outcome of the war, which at the beginning had rested only on "faith," now had firm foundations—the British and Russian resistance, the Italian setbacks in the Balkans and Africa, and the flow of aid from the United States.[3]

From the United States, to cheer him in his prison cell on his sixty-ninth birthday on April 9, 1941, he received a telegram of good wishes and friendship signed by over a hundred distinguished American writers, artists, and educators, among them Mrs. Franklin D. Roosevelt. Deeply touched, he was able to express his pride and gratitude in a telegram forwarded through the American Embassy. He would be no

---

[8] Letter to Suzanne Blum, April 29, 1941, and to Blumel, July 14, 1941, both unpublished.

[9] For both statements, letter to Dormoy, February 27, 1941, *Oeuvre*, V, 170.

[1] Letters to Mme Grunebaum-Ballin and to André Blumel, July 30, August 17, 1941, ibid., pp. 182–3. On the assassins, Aron: *Histoire de Vichy*, p. 397.

[2] Letter to Marx Dormoy, July 16, 1941, *Oeuvre*, V, 179–80.

[3] Letter to Mme Grunebaum-Ballin, July 22, 1941, ibid., p. 182.

less moved by a similar telegram received on his seventieth birthday the following year.[4] That he "meant something" to these illustrious representatives of American culture buoyed his spirits and self-confidence.

In the winter of 1941, a new element of uncertainty was added to Blum's status with the promulgation of Constitutional Act No. 7. The measure empowered Marshal Pétain to investigate and punish appropriately, on his own *personal* authority, any "betrayal of the duties of office." Most astonishing was the stipulation that the Marshal's authority applied also to "former ministers, high dignitaries, and high functionaries who have held office within the last ten years." Pétain now had the power to investigate and punish even the men now facing trial before the Riom court. The punishment he was authorized to administer ranged from deprivation of political rights, house arrest, and administrative internment to detention for life in a military prison.[5]

Blum was understandably bewildered by the meaning of the new law and by its possible effect on him. For months, however, nothing further was heard of it. In February 1941, Flandin, who had succeeded Laval in December 1940, was replaced by Admiral Darlan as head of the government. For fourteen months, from February 1941 to April 1942, Admiral Darlan played a game of trying to placate the Nazis and at the same time trying to preserve the fleet and the colonies.[6] It was in the "Darlan period" that important changes in the status of the political prisoners took place.

In June 1941, Blum expressed the belief that the government had no intention of using its new authority under Constitutional Act. No. 7, although he prophetically added: "It could float to the surface any day."[7] On August 12, 1941, it did exactly that. Marshal Pétain announced in a radio speech to the nation that, under the powers conferred on him by Constitutional Act No. 7, he would proceed to judge those responsible for the military disaster. He was appointing a Council of Political Justice which would report its findings to him by October 15. In the same speech he announced his determination to strengthen

---

[4] The telegrams were initiated in the United States by Suzanne Blum and her husband, Paul Weill. See Blum: *Le Dernier Mois, Oeuvre,* V, 531, and *The New York Times,* April 9, 1942.

[5] For the legislation, Soupiron: *Riom,* pp. 48–9.

[6] See, e.g., Aron: *Histoire de Vichy,* pp. 371–89.

[7] Letter to André Blumel, June 14, 1941, *Oeuvre,* V, 177.

the "national revolution" and to "destroy" the "followers of the old system."[8]

Blum accepted the Marshal's announcement with resignation. No one knew yet whether the appointment of a Council of Political Justice would affect the public trial which Blum had now been awaiting for over a year or in other ways involve the men already under the jurisdiction of the Riom court.[9] These questions were answered when, on the evening of October 16, 1941, the Marshal broadcast a new speech to the nation.

The Council of Political Justice, Pétain stated, had submitted its recommendations to him. In the case of Édouard Daladier, Léon Blum, and General Gamelin, it had unanimously recommended the most severe penalty provided by Constitutional Act No. 7—detention in a military prison. He was consequently ordering their transfer to Le Portalet, a fortress in the Pyrenees, not far from the Spanish frontier. Next, Pétain went on to say, with incredible logic, the Supreme Court at Riom would continue its own judicial proceedings despite this judgment and would be asked to arrive at a verdict as quickly as possible. He, too, might have awaited the unfolding of the court's proceedings, but he believed that "the judicial process, with its prudence, its slowness, its cautious pace, was aggravating the uneasiness that oppressed the country." To relieve that uneasiness he had taken these "grave decisions," even though a public trial was still necessary. "A country which has seen itself betrayed has a right to the truth, the whole truth. The verdict that will close the Riom trial must be rendered in the full light of day. It will strike at individuals but also at the methods, the practices, the regime . . . It will mark the end of one of the most painful periods in the life of France." The accused thus were being given "a preliminary penalty" which could be transformed into "a graver penalty." In the same speech he announced that Reynaud and Mandel, on the basis of a majority opinion of the Council, were also being condemned to the fortress at Le Portalet; judicial proceedings against them would continue too. Guy La Chambre and Jacomet would remain confined at Bourassol. Pierre Cot, still in the United States, was condemned *in absentia.*[1]

The following day the press published the findings and recommendations that the Council of Political Justice had submitted to the

---

[8] Soupiron: *Riom*, pp. 47–8.
[9] Letters to Blumel, August 17, September 9, 1941, *Oeuvre*, V, 183–4.
[1] Pétain's speech is reproduced in *Oeuvre*, V, 195–6.

Marshal. Because of the misdeeds of the accused, the Council stated, the country had entered the war without adequate preparation. As to Blum, it charged: "Twice Premier, the first time for over a year, Vice-Premier for more than seven months, M. Blum was in power during the period preceding the war. The diplomatic and military situation, which had just grown more serious at the time of his entry into office, was known to him. He was informed of the deficiencies in the national defense. His office imposed on him the duty of giving France the necessary weapons to assure her security. He ignored this duty, neglecting to give to the manufacture of armaments the encouragement that the situation urgently demanded; on the contrary, he discouraged production by the nationalization of the arms factories. . . ." His labor reforms, it went on to say, were distorted by him into instruments of class struggle. The moral vigor of the country had been "dangerously weakened," and he had "put France in a state of peril."[2]

The Council consisted of eight members—"elite combat veterans and eminent public servants," as Marshal Pétain described them. The president and leading spirit was Emmanuel Peretti della Rocca, a diplomat and Marshal Pétain's predecessor as Ambassador to Spain in 1940.[3] Significantly, the Council had been named on September 29 and had rendered its verdict only two weeks later, on October 15. Even if it had so desired, it could not have examined the mountains of testimony that had been gathered by the Supreme Court at Riom, which by then amounted to some 100,000 pages of depositions and reports.[4] The Council had made no effort to question the accused or to give them an opportunity to testify, but had based its verdict on the bill of charges drawn up by the Prosecutor General at Riom, employing at times even the same phraseology.

The amazing procedure adopted by Pétain's government, of condemning the men to life imprisonment for their crimes and then announcing a public trial for the same offenses, seemed like sheer fantasy, an *Alice in Wonderland* episode. The incredible procedure cried out for an explanation. For all his speculation at the time, Blum had little idea how he and the other political prisoners were involved in the game being played by Vichy and Germany. Even now the story can be only

[2] The report is reproduced in Soupiron: *Riom*, p. 55, and Cot: *Le Procès de la république*, II, 322.

[3] For the composition of the Council, Soupiron: *Riom*, pp. 49–50; Cot: *Le Procès de la république*, I, 323–4; also Reynaud: *Au coeur de la mêlée*, p. 1023.

[4] Soupiron, *Riom*, pp. 13, 60; and official résumé of proceedings reproduced in *Oeuvre*, VI, 221.

partially reconstructed. There is no doubt that the German government, through Otto Abetz, the German Ambassador in Paris, had been exerting pressure on Pétain to punish the men "responsible" for the war. The Germans were well aware that the Riom court was not going to charge the accused with responsibility for the outbreak of the war, but only with lack of preparedness for the war, a charge in which the Germans could not be less interested. Abetz was willing even to strike a bargain. If these men were punished, he informed the French government in March 1941, it might be possible to set aside the death sentence against one hundred and twenty French home guards captured during the spring of 1940 and accused of guerrilla warfare.[5]

Neither Pétain nor Darlan, any more than the Riom court, could bring themselves to accuse France of "war guilt," but they resolved to take some action to placate the Germans. They would at least hasten the condemnation of the men responsible for the defeat. Hence the naming of the Council of Political Justice on August 12, and the quick political verdict and sentence on October 12. Thus, at least in part for the benefit of the Germans, the Marshal condemned the accused men, and at the same time he proceeded with the Riom trial as if nothing else had occurred. Also, early in 1941 Joseph Barthélemy, a distinguished professor of constitutional history and once French delegate to the League of Nations, had replaced the erratic and unbalanced Raphaël Alibert as Minister of Justice. Barthélemy had no love for the political leaders of the Third Republic but had something of a conscience with respect to the law.[6] Having satisfied the conqueror with the political verdict, he too wanted to proceed with the public trial in which the accused would be permitted to defend themselves.

Not just by coincidence but by design, on the very evening of Marshal Pétain's broadcast announcing the political verdict, Blum and the other defendants received their copy of the Riom Prosecutor General's formal indictment (the *réquisitoire*), dated October 9, 1941. A document of 184 pages, it examined in detail "the unpreparedness for war, the inadequacy of armaments and equipment, the lack of moral preparation, the unfavorable climate for the conduct of war." There was not a word about responsibility for the outbreak of the war. Blum and his Popular Front government were charged with responsibility for the nation's "material" and "moral" lack of preparedness.[7]

[5] Reynaud reproduces the correspondence between Abetz and Ribbentrop introduced at Abetz's postwar trial; *Au coeur de la mêlée*, pp. 982–92.

[6] See Aron: *Histoire de Vichy*, p. 379.

[7] Soupiron: *Riom*, p. 60; for the portion relevant to Blum, *Oeuvre*, V, 187–94.

The defendants were given five days in which to present a written defense and to offer reasons why they should not be arraigned. Blum lost no time. On October 20 he addressed a sharp letter to the court attacking the "cruel mockery" of the procedures. He had received a copy of the charges only "a matter of minutes" before his condemnation and sentencing by Marshal Pétain. "It is as a man already condemned— and condemned for exactly the same crimes—that you invite me to reply to the Prosecutor General's bill of charges." He informed the court in strong terms that despite the Marshal's words of tribute to the independence of the judiciary, the court's independence of judgment in the case had been destroyed. "The case," he informed the court, "has been decided for you as well as for me." How could the court go counter to a verdict already rendered by the supreme authority of the state? He recalled that throughout the pretrial hearings he had not called a single witness, produced a single document, or attempted to refute the contradictions and errors in the testimony of witnesses against him. All this he had explicitly reserved for the public trial. Now he had been condemned without any opportunity to defend himself. "A public figure, openly accused of having compromised the interests and security of my country by my official acts, I had the right to public justification and public satisfaction. I repeat with regret that I can no longer hope for redress under your jurisdiction, but I maintain and demand the right to justify myself before the country, before international opinion, and, I dare to say, before history."

He summed up again the position he had taken in his interrogations before the examining magistrate, insisting that the court seek the causes of military defeat in the errors made by the High Command in its conduct of operations and in its employment of the weapons and equipment at its disposal. Insisting, finally, that he was being tried for actions which he had legally and constitutionally taken as head of a government responsible to a democratically elected parliament, he repeated the charge he had made to the examining magistrate in his final interrogation. They were placing on trial "the republican regime and the republican principle itself." "Such a trial," he informed the court, "in the name of my lifelong convictions, I am proud to accept."[8]

In accordance with the government's instructions, the court now moved with greater celerity. Officially ignoring the Marshal's condemnation of the accused, it proceeded as though nothing had happened and as though there had been no prejudgment of guilt. It would solemnly

[8] For the letter of October 20, 1941, *Oeuvre*, V, 197–9.

honor the traditional separation of the judicial and executive branches of the government.

On October 28, 1941, the Riom court rendered its decree of arraignment and commitment to trial. "From the preliminary inquiry," the decree read, "it would appear that on September 3, 1939, the date of the opening of hostilities between France and Germany, the French armed forces, ground and air, were not ready to fulfill the mission that was incumbent upon them." The defendants were all accused of responsibility for failing to insure the country's armed strength in the years since June 1936. Blum was specifically charged "with having compromised the national defense by the manner in which he enforced labor legislation, especially by rendering practically impossible recourse to overtime hours, with having allowed the law on the nationalization of the armaments industry to be applied in a manner harmful to the interests of national defense, with having by his weakness in the face of revolutionary agitation—especially by tolerating the occupation of factories—been responsible for a considerable diminution of production."

The document stated flatly that it was not within the court's power to examine the conduct of military operations or the methods of employing available armaments and equipment. Its jurisdiction applied only to ministers or their "immediate subordinates"; hence, of the military commanders only General Gamelin could be tried, and even so, he was being charged exclusively with responsibility for the army's lack of preparedness for war, not for errors made during the campaign. If military or diplomatic matters came up "indirectly," the decree stipulated, the court would go into closed session.[9]

The court had dropped all charges of responsibility for the outbreak of war. The trial would focus not on responsibility for the war but on responsibility for the defeat. Yet since investigation into the role of the military was excluded or at least rigidly circumscribed, how could there be a full exploration of the causes of the defeat? And since responsibility for the lack of preparedness was to be sought only from June 1936 on—the beginning of the Popular Front government—how probing could the search for responsibility be? There was a special reason why one could not go back beyond June 1936. Marshal Pétain had been Minister of War in the Doumergue government of 1934.

[9] The *arrêt de mise en jugement*, October 28, 1941, is reproduced in Soupiron: *Riom*, pp. 63–6; and in Cot: *Le Procès de la république*, I, 296–9; for the *arrêt de renvoi*, same date, Cot: *Le Procès de la république*, p. 201.

Blum wrote in his letters of "our strange ambivalent condition of being both condemned men and men held for trial." "But you have to agree," he noted with wry humor in one letter, "that the situation the Supreme Court finds itself in—although more comfortable—is no less strange than ours."[1] He now awaited transfer to his fortress prison. From newspaper accounts he had learned about Le Portalet, especially about its rigorous climate and inaccessibility. "I do not say," he wrote, "that I am insensitive to the blow, but I am bearing it with firmness."[2]

On November 22, 1941, Blum was transferred to Le Portalet; fortunately he remained there only six weeks. The fortress, built in 1838, was lost in the Pyrenees, only ten miles from the Spanish border. Situated on the side of a valley, it was almost completely shut off from the sun. In some ways, however, the physical arrangements turned out to be less dreadful than Blum had expected. The narrow low-ceilinged room, he wrote, resembled a monastery cell more than a prison. From a curved window in the room he could see a majestic mountain peak. There was even modern plumbing and a washbasin with running water.[3] Yet the winter cold was intensely bitter; he could feel the bite of the mountain winds when he took the daily walks permitted him. A cold dampness permeated the place and chilled the marrow of his bones. The stone walls were always moist from the humidity. Another problem was the extreme difficulty of access for visitors who had to make the ascent on foot along a steep, twisting path, braving the snow and wind. It was hard on visitors like Renée and Janot as well as on the lawyers who came to consult with Blum, Daladier, and the others in preparation for the trial.

The lawyers for the accused pointed out the manifest inconsistency and injustice in the transfer of the prisoners. The court had been ordered to proceed with the trial as quickly as possible, yet at the same time the defendants were cut off in this nearly inaccessible place. How, they asked, could they properly prepare the defense of their clients?[4] With the public trial imminent, the government ordered the prisoners returned to Bourassol. On December 30, Blum, Daladier, and General Gamelin made the fourteen-hour return journey. Reynaud and Mandel stayed on until 1943, when they were taken to Germany. In after years,

[1] Letter to Blumel, October 21, 1941, *Oeuvre*, V, 200.
[2] Ibid.
[3] Letter to Mme Grunebaum-Ballin, November 25, 1941, *Oeuvre*, V, 201.
[4] Ribet: *Riom*, pp. 304–9.

Le Portalet was heard of once again. After his postwar condemnation, Marshal Pétain briefly occupied the cell in which Mandel had been incarcerated.

Despite his initial cheerfulness, Blum had fallen ill while at Le Portalet. Blood tests showed him suffering from uremia. Once he was back at Bourassol various medicines and a better diet helped him to recover gradually. He not only sensed the alarm and anxiety of Renée and Janot, he too had been depressed by his sickness. "I must confess," he wrote a few weeks after his recovery, "I had no heart for things. To go to trial under such conditions would certainly have been a rough ordeal." Once recovered, he jested about his appearance at the forthcoming trial. "I have grown much thinner . . . I shall swim in my fine Sunday clothes . . . but that will immediately create interest and sympathy!"[5] But a rare note of self-pity also crept into his letters. His son, Robert, was still a prisoner of war; his younger brother, René, to whom he had always been very devoted, had been arrested as a hostage. "Robert, René, myself, that makes too many prisoners for a single family," he lamented.[6]

At Le Portalet, Blum had prepared a detailed outline of the points to be raised at the trial by himself and his lawyers: the procedural and technical irregularities of the pretrial hearings, the unprecedented situation created by the Marshal's political sentence, the court's refusal to examine the faults and errors of the military during the hostilities, and the unwillingness to extend the inquiry back beyond June 1936. He stressed the attempt to place the blame for the defeat of 1940 on the legally elected Popular Front government and thereby on the republican regime itself. The outline fixed clearly the ideas and some of the very phrases that he would use in court.[7]

After one more postponement, the public trial was finally set for February 19. The court announced that about nine hundred persons had been heard in the pretrial inquiry and that two hundred and fifteen witnesses would be called to the stand once the defendants themselves had been heard.[8] Almost a year and a half after his arrest in September 1940—after two months in the Château de Chazeron, over a year at Bourassol, and six weeks at Le Portalet—Blum would now have his opportunity to defend himself, and the republic, in open court.

[5] Letter to Blumel, February 2, 1942, unpublished.
[6] Ibid.
[7] Reproduced in *Oeuvre*, V, 202–18.
[8] Soupiron: *Riom*, p. 60.

WITNESS FOR THE REPUBLIC:
The Riom Trial, 1942

*If the republic is the accused, we shall be
at our combat posts as its witnesses and its
defenders.*[1]

THE FIRST of the twenty-four public sessions of the Riom
trial opened on the afternoon of February 19, 1942, in the
completely renovated and refurbished courtroom of the Riom
Palais de Justice. The setting, the government stated, was to be
"worthy" of the important occasion. Seats were available for some
two hundred journalists, French and foreign, as well as for a scattering
of invited guests, mainly from the diplomatic corps. In contrast to
the icy streets and snow-covered city, the courtroom was stuffy and
overheated. Six small tables, three on each side of a narrow aisle, were
reserved for the accused and their counsel; they sat facing the bench
of the court, their backs to the spectators. The defendants and the
witnesses testified from a Louis XIV armchair facing the court. Blum
sat to the left of the central aisle, as did Robert Jacomet, controller-
general of the army from 1936 to 1940. To the right of the corridor
were Édouard Daladier, Premier at the outbreak of the war and
Minister of National Defense from 1936 to 1940; General Maurice
Gamelin, commanding general of the army from 1935 to 1940; and
Guy La Chambre, Minister of Air from 1938 to 1940. Blum's attorneys,
André Le Troquer, Samuel Spanien, and Félix Gouin were seated
directly behind him.[2]

[1] Blum: testimony, 1942, Riom trial, *Oeuvre*, V, 227.
[2] These details may be reconstructed from Ribet: *Riom*, pp. 30–3; Soupiron:
Riom, pp. 60–3; and the anonymous *Le Procès de Riom par un témoin* (Paris,

Promptly at one-thirty the ten magistrates of the Cour Suprême de Justice filed in, led by Pierre Caous, president of the court. Seven of the magistrates had been selected from the higher judiciary, including the Cour de Cassation and the Conseil d'État. One of the judges was from the University of Paris Faculty of Law; an admiral and a general also served. The Public Prosecutor was M. Cassagnau.[3] Immediately after the opening of the court and the reading by the clerk of the bill of charges, the president of the court felt it necessary to refer to Marshal Pétain's political condemnation of the accused four months earlier. Directing his remarks to the men before him, he said: "Gentlemen, the judgments that have been reached with respect to certain of you and the explanations that have been published for these judgments have no validity for this court."[4] The words of reassurance failed to dispel the skepticism of Blum and the other defendants.

In the opening minutes of the trial, the simple formality of having the accused identify themselves took a dramatic turn when General Gamelin announced that "after mature reflection" he had "resolved not to participate actively" in the public trial. He had already been condemned under a political verdict that had given him no opportunity to speak out in his defense. At the public trial he would be unable to defend himself "without the risk of pronouncing names, French and foreign, which the higher interests of the country must eliminate from these proceedings."[5] It was Blum who first recognized the implications of General Gamelin's statement. The withdrawal of the only military man among the accused, coupled with the court's earlier decision to exclude from the trial the military campaign itself, would turn the proceedings into a trial exclusively of political responsibility for the defeat. This he quickly pointed out when, following the General, he took

---

1945), pp. 21–3. For observations on the sources available for the Riom trial, see the preceding chapter, note 4, p. 385. Blum's major speeches at the trial were published in pamphlet form (1942) and circulated clandestinely during the war; the pamphlet appeared in expanded form after the war as *Léon Blum devant la cour de Riom, février–mars 1942* (Paris, 1945). His major speeches and testimony and other relevant documents were republished in *Oeuvre*, V, 221–348.

[3] Ribet: *Riom*, pp. 33–4; Soupiron: *Riom*, p. 27.

[4] Ribet: *Riom*, p. 35.

[5] For General Gamelin's statement, Ribet: *Riom*, pp. 35–6; Soupiron: *Riom*, pp. 68–9. Gamelin in his memoirs states also that he was unwilling to be "used" against his civilian superiors; moreover, he did not wish to bring into the open at such a time the various jealousies and rivalries in the army; see *Servir*, I, iv–xv, 44; and III: *La Guerre, septembre 1939–19 mai 1940* (Paris, 1946–7), p. 456 and passim.

the stand to identify himself. The identification was brief: "Born in Paris, April 9, 1872, Deputy, retired magistrate of the Conseil d'État." Receiving permission to present certain observations inspired by General Gamelin's announcement, he fired the initial salvo of the trial.

Here was an inconceivable "paradox," he charged, his voice at first contained and muffled and then rising to a passionate pitch. Although the court's mission was to establish and punish responsibility for a military defeat, it had ruled even before the trial that it did not have jurisdiction over the conduct of military operations. The participation of General Gamelin in the public proceedings would have compelled some consideration of such matters; now that possibility had been barred too. He himself did not blame General Gamelin for refusing to share in the examination of responsibility. General Gamelin had refused to turn against his chief, the Marshal—"the most important source of inspiration for our military doctrines"—and against those who had been the General's subordinates and companions in arms. But the result was shocking. "In a debate on responsibility for the defeat, the war itself will be absent. . . . You who have opened the door for so many things in this trial," he told the court, "have excluded the war." He affirmed that the court had the responsibility of inquiring into the High Command's erroneous and outmoded ideas on modern warfare and its conduct of operations. If the court rejected that task, the defendants would have to assume it in order to restore to the trial its true purpose.

He praised the patriotism of the court for its refusal to make the trial one of "war guilt"—of responsibility for the outbreak of the war— as originally envisaged. Such a trial would have been "a trial of France," which the court had properly rejected. The trial was now restricted to responsibility for the defeat. On the other hand, if military responsibility were excluded, the proceedings would be a "trial of the republic, a trial of the regime, of democratic practices and methods." His own duty was plain. "If the republic is the accused, we shall be at our combat posts as its witnesses and its defenders."

There was a second "revolting" paradox, a "legal monstrosity," he noted, in the fact that he and the others were appearing in court as men already condemned. Speaking as a man of the law himself, associated for nearly a quarter of a century with the Conseil d'État, one of the nation's highest courts, he lashed at the magistrates where they were most sensitive, pointing out that the Marshal's verdict had deprived *them* of all independence and freedom of judgment. "The case had been decided," he said, "against you as against us." And he refused to be satisfied when the presiding magistrate broke in to remind him of the court's opening statement.[6]

Blum's speech had a powerful impact on the courtroom. An eyewitness noted: "No matter how prejudiced they were—and especially against Léon Blum—the audience was moved by his initial passionate eloquence."[7] Another observed: "One listened first with surprise, then with growing interest to this legal discussion which little by little was transformed into an appeal for true justice and then reached the heights of a protest in defense of the French republican ideal."[8] Blum set the tone for the Riom trial in its very first hour.

Scarcely had Blum been seated when his defense counsel André Le Troquer embarrassed the court by reading to it the government's detailed censorship instructions to the press, instructions which made very clear the direction that the Vichy government intended the trial to take. The press was instructed to remember that the trial was "limited to France's lack of preparation for war in the period 1936 to 1940" and was not to be a trial of "the army which, troops and leaders, had to fight without having at its disposal the weapons that are indispensable in a modern war." The journalists were to concentrate on "the state of affairs from which the catastrophe emerged" so as to enable the French people "to pass judgment on the methods of government of which it became the victim." Strict censorship would be invoked "if the person and policies of the Marshal were called into question." Le Troquer's mischievous performance nonplused the court. M. Caous indignantly protested that the instructions to the press had nothing to do with the court. This was, of course, true, but the public would learn little of what transpired at Riom from the newspapers. Each day Vichy officials carefully censored the news stories and, in addition, provided reporters with "arguments and refutations" bearing on the proceedings, which they were instructed to use.[9] Le Troquer also moved to have the court declare itself illegal on the ground that the constitutional act establishing it had not been ratified by the nation. Finally, he launched a diatribe against the Vichy regime—its suppression of representative institutions, its curbing of free speech, its arbitrary arrest and imprisonment practices. He called on those in power to reread and meditate on the old Jacobin

[6] For this long opening statement by Blum, *Oeuvre*, V, 223–8.

[7] *Le Procès de Riom par un témoin*, p. 33.

[8] Soupiron: *Riom*, p. 76.

[9] For the censorship instructions, *Oeuvre*, V, 222; and on the episode, including the court's reaction, *Léon Blum devant la cour de Riom*, pp. 8–10; Soupiron: *Riom*, pp. 77–9; and Ribet: *Riom*, pp. 38–9.

declaration of June 1793. "When the government violates the rights of the people, insurrection is for the people the most sacred of rights and the most indispensable of duties."[1] Blum had deliberately chosen a militant Socialist as his defense counsel; if Vichy wished a political trial, it would have one.

In the succeeding preliminary sessions of the court, other legal arguments attacking the irregularities of the trial and motions for dismissal were presented. The proceedings, the lawyers argued, violated the "universally recognized principle" banning *ex post facto* laws: the accused were being tried for acts committed in earlier years under legislation adopted on July 30, 1940. Secondly, the legislation spoke of "acts that contributed to the passage from a state of peace to a state of war on September 4, 1939, and acts that subsequently (*ultérieurement*) aggravated the consequences thereof." What did the word "subsequently" mean? Did it not apply only to acts committed after the *entry* into the war? If so, how could the defendants be tried for failure to build up the country's defenses from 1936 on? How could Blum, who had not even held office in September 1939, or at any time thereafter, be tried under this legislation? The court had proceeded in its pretrial inquiry, however, as if the word "subsequently" did not exist and had even eliminated the word from its decree of arraignment, something which the lawyers denounced as a deliberate "manipulation" of the text. Finally, in examining the period before 1939, the court had refused to go back beyond June 1936, the date when the Popular Front government had taken office, even though under the law they had every right to investigate earlier responsibility. Was it to prevent the involvement of Rightist ministries like that of Doumergue from February to November 1934 when Marshal Pétain had been Minister of War, or that of Flandin from November 1934 to June 1935 when General Maurin had been Minister of War?[2]

Both Daladier and Blum spoke in support of the arguments of their lawyers. Daladier, in his first important speech, charged his predecessors, the Ministers of War in the years before June 1936, with failure

[1] Ribet: *Riom*, p. 40; Soupiron: *Riom*, pp. 79–82; *Léon Blum devant la cour de Riom*, pp. 10–19.

[2] Ribet: *Riom*, pp. 41–50, 57–71; statement by Spanien: *Léon Blum devant la cour de Riom*, pp. 20–31; Soupiron: *Riom*, pp. 82–6. The ambiguous phrase "acts that subsequently aggravated the consequences [of entering the war]" was originally aimed at Reynaud, Mandel, and others in the Reynaud cabinet who had refused to seek an armistice earlier in 1940. For echoes of these legal arguments at the Pétain trial in 1945, see testimony of Blum and M. Caous, *Le Procès de Pétain*, I, 242, 3003.

to modernize and equip the armed services. It was the government of 1936, he maintained, that had corrected their failures. He too denounced the refusal to examine the military leaders' responsibility for the defeat and the effort to make the political leaders the scapegoats. He charged that he was being tried also for refusing to accept an armistice earlier. Recalling that in 1870 Marshal Bazaine had capitulated while the republican leader, Léon Gambetta, had fought on, he inquired sarcastically "whether under present circumstances Gambetta would not be in prison and Bazaine in the government."[3] Courageous and spirited, the "bull of the Vaucluse" had regained the firmness that had often been absent in his political career. If in the past Blum had often disagreed with the Radical leader, at Riom they joined in a common defense of the republic that each in his own way had served.

Blum, in a second speech, denounced the court for "arbitrarily" choosing June 1936 and his Popular Front government as the opening date for their investigation. He and the others were prepared to demonstrate the breadth and significance of the rearmament program initiated in 1936. But, he needled the court: "Did the rearmament of France impose itself as a governmental duty only from June 1936 on?" The errors of the High Command included fallacious military doctrines that had their origin long before 1936: "doctrines of invulnerable fronts, absolute faith in fortifications and defensive strategy, scorn for armor and for the role of air power in combat." Unless the scope of the trial were extended in time and in subject matter, he informed the court, "you would be admitting that this trial is a political enterprise, that you are political judges . . ." He would refuse to let them place the blame for military defeat "on the Popular Front, on the labor and social program that it introduced and, thereby, on [the country's] democratic institutions."[4]

From the outset, the defendants were on the offensive, leveling charges at those who were prosecuting them and refusing to allow responsibility for the military defeat to be shifted from the military to the political leaders. Before this tribunal there could be no admission that responsibility had to be shared by political and military leaders alike. "In listening to M. Léon Blum," wrote one observer, "the older among us recognized certain accents that forty-four years earlier had

---

[3] Ribet: *Riom*, pp. 51–6; Soupiron: *Riom*, pp. 88–93. From this speech of Daladier, Soupiron derived the title of his book on the trial, *Gambetta contre Bazaine*.

[4] *Oeuvre*, V, 229–34.

struck our ears." The accents were those of Émile Zola's *J'Accuse*, he said.[5] There is no denying that the court allowed the defendants and their counsel to speak freely, more freely than might have been anticipated, perhaps out of self-consciousness over the Marshal's political sentence. M. Caous again and again interrupted to call the defendants to order, to bring them back to the "framework" of the trial, to prevent them from citing "foreign governments," to chide them for using words like "manipulation" of the legislative texts, and to defend the pretrial hearings, but by and large he allowed them wide latitude. The Prosecutor General was exasperated at what he termed speeches that at best belonged, as summations, at the conclusion of the trial.

The court, however, supported the Prosecutor General on every technical point and rejected the defense contentions. The legislation did not require, it ruled, that the acts in question be committed after September 4, 1939, because acts or dereliction of duty prior to that date "subsequently" affected the situation arising out of entry into the war. That ruling placed the social reforms of the Popular Front squarely on trial. Second, the court ruled that developments in the period before June 1936 did not alter the defendants' responsibility. Third, it refused to extend the scope of the investigation. Military responsibility was to be left untouched. Finally, on the matter of retroactivity, it ruled that a law such as that of July 30, 1940, set up specifically to investigate acts committed before its passage, did not violate the principle of non-retroactivity.[6] Daladier's attorney, who still insisted that the Declaration of the Rights of Man forbade *ex post facto* laws, acidly remarked: "Our children will read the jurisprudence of the year 1942 and will not understand it."[7]

After a three-day recess, the trial resumed on February 27 with the interrogation of Daladier. For three consecutive afternoons, and later in the cross-examination of witnesses, the former Premier and Minister of National Defense defended himself with forcefulness, precision, and detail. On some matters, such as the effects of the forty-hour law and the nationalization of armaments plants, his defense anticipated Blum's; in others it was quite distinct. The details of his defense are beyond our scope here, but, in general, he sought to demonstrate that in the three years preceding the war he had accomplished more for the national defense and assured the armed forces more credits and more

[5] Soupiron: *Riom*, p. 117.
[6] Soupiron: *Riom*, pp. 118–19; Ribet: *Riom*, pp. 71–4.
[7] Ribet: *Riom*, p. 50.

military equipment than had any preceding ministry, and especially
more than the Rightist ministers of 1934 and 1935, when Germany
had already revealed its aggressive intentions. The rearmament program
of 1936 "had assured the French armed forces of equipment equal in
quality and hardly inferior in quantity" to that of Germany, despite the
enemy's enormous industrial superiority. He attributed France's defeat
to those who could not or would not make effective use of the arms they
had. The defeat had followed from the strategic and tactical mistakes
of the military. It was Marshal Pétain, he recalled, who in 1934 had
uttered the famous words: "The Ardennes forests are impenetrable."
With eloquence and defiance, he held his own during the questioning
on all the charges against him in one of the most stirring performances
of his career.[8]

Obviously his defense could not exonerate him of a share of responsibility for the fact that France was not equipped to withstand the Nazi
onslaught in May 1940. On the other hand, no true assessment of
responsibility could take place at Riom, for the court had refused to
investigate the military. What Daladier and Blum accomplished was to
prevent Vichy from shifting to the political leaders of the republic the
complete blame for the inadequacy of France's preparation for war.
There seems to be no doubt that, save in air power, there was an
"honorable equality" between French and German arms, even including
tanks. The major reason for defeat lay less in the inadequacy of equipment than in the failure to use effectively what was available and the
failure of the High Command to develop "a theory of warfare adequate
to the twentieth century."[9] If the responsibility of the civilian leaders
could not be discounted, the responsibility of the military also loomed
large; Vichy was trying to foist the blame entirely onto the shoulders
of the political leaders of the republic, particularly those of the Left.

Blum's own interrogation took place on the two successive afternoons
of March 10 and March 11. For close to four hours each afternoon, in
an exhibition of energy, concentration, and endurance that would have
done credit to a man half his age, the seventy-year-old Socialist leader
explained, justified, and defended the policies associated with his name.
This was Blum's day in court, the tribunal he had awaited, the op-

[8] For Daladier's statements, Ribet: *Riom*, pp. 75–148; Soupiron: *Riom*, pp.
132–79.
[9] Challener: "The Military Defeat of 1940 in Retrospect," p. 407; and see A.
Goutard: *1940: La Guerre des occasions perdues.*

portunity to vindicate himself before public opinion and history. It mattered little what the court would decide, since he was already a man condemned; the judgment of his countrymen and of posterity alone counted.

Sounding the same note of defiance as in the earlier sessions, but now addressing himself to the specific charges in the indictment, he reconstructed the social atmosphere of the 1930's, explained the origins and nature of the Popular Front government, and revealed much of himself and his life as a public man. Never did he seem more sincere, more eloquent, more convincing. He relived the anguish and uncertainty of the "just" man in political life, of the intellectual who had struggled to reconcile his Socialist convictions with his duties as head of the government, of the political leader who had sought to serve as conciliator and champion of national unity in a troubled time. He never minimized the fact that he was a Socialist, but he believed that his socialism had enhanced his patriotism. Although Marx had once said that the proletariat had no country, with the birth of the republican ideal the working class had acquired a reason for loyalty and devotion to its country. The republic had made it possible to fight for labor's rights and a decent life, for employment and a living wage, for leisure and recreation, for equality and dignity. He counted himself among those who had participated in the struggle for those rights. Thus the social reforms of the Popular Front, he maintained, far from creating division and disunity, had given the workers a greater stake in the society in which they lived, created in them a love for the republic and a loyalty to France.

Charged with "weakness" in the face of "revolutionary" agitation in the crisis of June 1936, he sought to demonstrate that he had acted with one principal objective: to preserve national unity, to prevent bloodshed and civil war—civil war, he claimed, that would have brought foreign war in its wake. He recalled the tension of those spring days: the Popular Front election victory, the spontaneous outbreak and spread of the sitdown strikes, the exhilaration of the workers at the victory of the Left and their insistence on a rapid redress of the grievances accumulated in the depression years. Panic and terror had spread among the propertied classes. Was it the Revolution? they had asked. They had turned to him to use his influence to restore order; they had promised concessions, asking only that he and the new Parliament act quickly to end the fearful situation which was, "if not revolutionary, at least quasi-revolutionary." It was in those desperate circumstances that he had arranged the Matignon agreement between the representatives of industry and labor, that he had pledged to the strikers the rapid passage by Parliament of the social legislation they demanded, legislation that was promptly adopted and put into effect—the collective bargaining law, the paid vacations act, the forty-hour week. He had played, he repeated, "the role of a conciliator," and he had succeeded in ending the labor upheaval without bloodshed.[1]

When the presiding magistrate pressed Blum to explain why, with his sense of obligation to the duties of his office, to the national community and to its laws, he had not enforced court orders calling for evacuation of the plants and ended what he himself admitted was a violation of property rights, Blum countered with a lecture to the court on the dilemma of every government:

> A government does not have only one duty at a time . . . For governments as for individuals there are contradictions and sometimes incompatibilities between different duties. There are for the head of a government situations that resemble what in private life are called cases of conscience. One is torn between duties that are different and are—either in appearance or in reality—opposed; and one is obliged as head of a government or as a private individual to establish a hierarchy among duties that are undeniably clear, such as to enforce respect for property rights on the one hand and to preserve public peace on the other."[2]

He was convinced that in 1936 his choice had been the correct one. He defiantly told the court, moreover, that no judicial body had the right to judge the choices and decisions that a man in public office had to make. A court could not decide on the basis of any "code" what the duties of political office were at any given time and what constituted betrayal of such duties. Men in political life, he told them, have to act in accordance with their sense of responsibility and conscience, and are answerable only to parliamentary assemblies or to the people.

If he had persuaded the working class not to abuse its strength, he believed that he had also kept faith with those who had put their trust in him. He had refused to write a new chapter in the long history of betrayal of the working class by socialist leaders. He had refused to use force to expel the workers from the factories, although that would have delighted his political enemies. "What a bargain! A bloodbath

[1] *Oeuvre*, V, esp. 254–67, and 321.
[2] Ibid., p. 309.

instituted by a representative of the Socialist party in power!" Nor would he have stooped to the duplicity of failing to enact the legislation he had promised the workers. He spoke proudly of the labor legislation of his government, of the collective bargaining law which had ended the old "divine right" industrial order, of the provision for labor representation in the factories through elected workers' delegates, of the arbitration law that provided machinery for the settlement of industrial disputes, the paid vacations act, the shortened work week.

Still another reason lay behind his sponsorship of the social legislation of 1936. He had campaigned and taken office as head of a coalition government based on the program of the Popular Front. When that coalition won an overwhelming endorsement at the polls, he, as head of the leading party in the coalition, had a constitutional and political obligation to support its program. Repudiation of this program would have involved more than a violation of his pledge; it would have undermined the faith and confidence of the masses in parliamentary democracy itself. In that he would have no part.

There was much else that he rehearsed for the court. He recalled his refusal to appeal "to the streets" when the Senate overthrew his government in June 1937 and again in April 1938, and his efforts each time to assure a legal and peaceful transition to the new government. He recalled his efforts in January 1938 and in March 1938 to create a true government of national unity by appealing to the parties of the opposition, and almost, but not quite, succeeding. Finally, he recalled his program of economic and financial measures, during his second brief government from March to April 1938, which were designed to strengthen the country's economy, improve its control over foreign exchange, and permit rearmament on a sound financial basis, a program that was rejected by the Senate. All his acts as head of the government, he reiterated, had as their objectives the strengthening of the nation, the furthering of national unity, and the reinforcement of loyalty to the country. Whenever there was disagreement within his party—over military credits, Spain, the "pause," the attempt in 1938 to form a national unity cabinet—he had rallied the party to his views: "It was not I who bowed before the will of the party. It was I who won the party over to the political view that I judged necessary in the national interest, for which I was responsible. . . . I persuaded the party to submit to what I believed to be the collective interest, the interest of the nation."[3]

The same was true of his relations with the Communists. Not "on

[3] Ibid., pp. 324, 257; and for all of the foregoing, pp. 235–329.

a single occasion" had he yielded to pressure from them. They had objected to his negotiations with Schacht, they had opposed devaluation of the franc, they had fought his policy of non-intervention in Spain. Despite their opposition, he had not deviated from the course which he had judged best for the country.[4]

Hardly a word of Blum's could be contradicted by the record. From his testimony emerged his patriotism, his devotion to democracy, and his high personal sense of duty. For some, his testimony at Riom would confirm the view that he was the very epitome of the "social reformist" and "social patriot," advocating "sacred union" and class collaboration, abandoning and betraying revolutionary socialism.[5] Yet all his life his socialism and his republican patriotism were fused into a single mold; at Riom he attempted to demonstrate the harmony and consistency of the two ideals.

On the specific question of the rearmament effort, he, like Daladier, insisted that the Popular Front had been responsible for launching, in September 1936, the country's first major rearmament program of the prewar years. Despite the difficulties confronting the Treasury and his own personal commitment to the cause of disarmament, he had vigorously pressed for the program and had secured the support of his party as well—a party that had traditionally voted against military credits. Like Daladier, he maintained that the rearmament program reflected the country's military needs as judged by the General Staff.[6] Before this tribunal, he too would make no admission of civilian responsibility for overseeing the requests of the military and for sharing in responsibility for outmoded concepts of warfare.

Even if it were conceded that his government had launched a rearmament program which its predecessors had failed to initiate, the question remained whether, in his own phrase, he had "taken with one hand what he had given with the other."[7] Patiently and firmly, he sought to prove that neither the sitdown strikes, nor the arms nationalization law, nor the forty-hour week had seriously impaired production or interfered with the defense effort. Again he exposed the prosecution's effort to blame the military defeat of 1940 on the Popular Front reforms as a smoke screen to conceal the responsibility of the military.

As to his "weakness" in the face of the sitdown strikes, he had already

[4] Ibid., pp. 322–4.
[5] See Audry: *Léon Blum*, pp. 172–81.
[6] *Oeuvre*, V, esp. 251–3.
[7] Ibid., p. 249.

explained his refusal to use force in the tense atmosphere of June 1936. The strikes themselves, he demonstrated, had had little material effect on defense production. The prosecution's impressive figure of 19 million man-hours lost in the spring of 1936 amounted to no more than the loss of a "few days" at a time when the new rearmament program had not yet even been launched. For aircraft, the production loss represented "two or three dozen planes of the antiquated type being manufactured under the old Denain arms program." The armed forces had a super-abundance of these obsolete planes in 1939–40 and could not even use them in the fighting.[8] No reasonable person could regard the strike losses of the spring of 1936 as a serious factor in the military defeat four years later. (In the privacy of his memoirs General Gamelin supported that conclusion too.[9])

The forty-hour week, of course, was one of the major targets in the prosecution's bill of charges. Here indeed was the cardinal sin of the Popular Front—a measure which, according to official Vichy pronouncements, had betrayed the national interest, fostered a spirit of idleness and leisure in the country's working classes, and seriously interfered with defense production. Once again, this was not the tribunal before which Blum could candidly admit the shortcomings and defects in the administration of the law or concede the narrow selfishness of the labor unions, which he well knew; nor could he concede the tragic mistiming of a reform desirable in itself but unfortunate in the circumstances under which it was adopted. He could only point to matters of which the prosecution said nothing. Touched where he was most sensitive—the impugning of his intelligence and his sincerity—he first defended the proposition that a shorter work week did not necessarily mean reduced production, an argument, he noted, that was as ancient as the factory-law debates in nineteenth-century England. He attempted also to demonstrate that the law had been administered flexibly to permit overtime in defense industries and that only in non-defense industries were exemptions "doled out parsimoniously." It was true that in his first government the four-year rearmament program was in its preparatory stages, in which models and prototypes had to be agreed upon, contracts signed, materials and machinery ordered. But he could point to the record of his second government, which, once assembly-line production had begun in 1938 and overtime work had

[8] For the interchange on the effects of the sitdown strikes, see ibid., pp. 309–12; for Blum's postwar testimony, 1947, *Événements*, I, 228–9.

[9] *Servir*, I, 214–15, II, 461.

become necessary, had negotiated with labor and management the extension of the regular work week to forty-five hours.[1]

Blum was correct in insisting that the law had to be understood in the context of the conditions under which it had been adopted. It had been part of a body of measures designed to cope with the depression by absorbing unemployment and increasing purchasing power, not merely to provide greater leisure. It had been adopted and applied also in the midst of unrest that could have led to civil war. On the other hand, his own sentimental attachment to the law emerged clearly when he maintained (as we have seen in an earlier chapter) that it had an even more profound significance—that it was a symbol of the day when men would share more equally in the technological advances of society. The forty-hour law, he informed the court, represented for the workers a "share in the forward movement of civilization and progress that belongs to all men."[2] He could not resist transforming himself from defendant to missionary and delivering his socialist message to the Riom judges.

The second measure which was attacked for its adverse effect on defense production was the arms nationalization law. Denying that this reform was peculiar to the Popular Front, Blum pointed to the agitation for it after the First World War and the widespread resentment at profits derived from the private manufacture of armaments. To be sure, the removal of the manufacture and sale of arms from private hands was viewed as an essential preliminary to international arms control and to world disarmament. Yet the law had been voted with little opposition because it was expected to benefit the national defense as well by providing for more effective government control over war industries. His own personal part in drawing up the bill and in its application had been small. Mainly, his arguments coincided with those of Daladier, who had demonstrated that nationalization had not been widely applied, and that where it had, production had increased, the government having used its powers principally in backward industries. In airplane manufacturing, for example, some companies had been operating virtually under a primitive handicraft system of production, each making aircraft of its own design; the nationalization law had permitted concentration on a few standard models, a better division of labor between the plants, and more efficient production. The Morane pursuit plane was cited as

[1] For the discussion of the forty-hour law, see the Prosecutor General's bill of charges, *Oeuvre*, V, 189–90, and Blum's testimony, ibid., pp. 265–85.

[2] Ibid., p. 285.

one of the important fruits of the reform.[3] A reform which had grown out of the disarmament movement had been transformed into an instrument for national rearmament.

During the discussion of the arms nationalization law the presiding magistrate implied that Blum's entire attitude on international affairs and disarmament had weakened the country. The preamble to the nationalization act, M. Caous pointed out, stated that the law could make "a signal contribution to the international organization of peace, collective security, and progressive world disarmament." It echoed the Popular Front program: "Peace will never be secure in a world given over to the competition of armaments and the munitions merchants. There is no peace but a peace without arms." M. Caous asked: "Was there not on your part a certain imprudence, at a time when the international situation demanded that all efforts be concentrated on national defense, on the defense of the country, on preparing it for all possible danger . . . to speak to the country . . . of certain—what shall I say— *dreams*, like collective security and progressive disarmament?"[4] Blum flared up at the word "dreams." The preamble to the bill had been written deliberately, he stated, to encourage the work of the Permanent Commission on Disarmament, which had recommended government control of arms as a preliminary step to international control. He admitted freely his championship over the years of the thesis that peace and disarmament were inextricably linked. But he rejected out of hand any contradiction or duplicity in working to arm France and in simultaneously working toward world disarmament, that is, in maintaining the "hope"—not the "dream," as the presiding magistrate had contemptuously termed it—of possible disarmament.

What had mattered most was not tangible results. It was a foregone conclusion that Germany and Italy had turned their backs on disarmament. He had sought, however, to define a foreign affairs position that was both politically and ethically sound, that offered world opinion proof of a "profound will for peace" and that could arraign the dictatorships "before the conscience of the world." It was this approach that had enabled him to rearm France, for rearmament was necessary so long as security was not certain, and had permitted him at the same time to pursue relentlessly efforts at universal disarmament, no matter

---

[3] See prosecution's bill of charges, ibid., 190–1, and Blum's statements, pp. 289–97; for Daladier's testimony, Ribet: *Riom*, pp. 126–32; Soupiron: *Riom*, pp. 282–91; for Gamelin's acceptance of the reform in 1936, see *Servir*, I, 210–13.

[4] *Oeuvre*, V, 298–9.

how slight the chance of success. He recalled his willingness in September to hold personal conversations even with Hitler's emissary, Dr. Schacht, on possible arms limitations and other matters. Where the country's interests and the slightest hope of international peace were at stake, nothing had deterred him.

He admitted the change in his ideas over the years. Once an advocate of disarmament as the only road to peace, he had undergone a metamorphosis when he had seen the independence of nations threatened, agreements violated, and the world delivered over to designs of conquest and domination. He had supported the effort to check aggression and had backed the war effort itself despite his own party's opposition. Blum's voice quivered with the intensity of his emotions as he described the forced reconciliation of his desire for disarmament and peace with the cruel necessities of rearmament and war in the 1930's.[5]

Throughout his long testimony he rejected what he termed the "venom argument," the accusation that he had "injected into French society and especially into the working class a venom, a poison, a toxic element." To have given the workers a feeling that they had a stake in society, and that the old system of divine-right rule in the factories had ended, was not subversion but the highest patriotism, he maintained. He had helped to teach the workers of France to sing the "Marseillaise" once again: "perhaps not the official 'Marseillaise,' perhaps not the 'Marseillaise' of the official processions and railroad station ceremonies, but the 'Marseillaise' of Rude's statuary, the 'Marseillaise' of Hugo. . . ."[6] He had striven to renew the sense of national unity that the country had once known in the "sacred union" of 1914. He had shared in the "silent and grave determination which took our sons, mine with the others, to their regiments." And he told the court in his concluding remarks:

> You will naturally be able to condemn us. I believe that, even with your decisions, you will not be able to erase our work. I believe that you will not be able—the word will appear perhaps presumptuous—to expel us from the history of the country. We do not mean to be presumptuous, but we have a certain pride. In a very perilous time, we personified and incarnated the authentic tradition of our country, which is the democratic and republican tradition. Of that tradition, in the perspective of history, we

[5] Ibid., pp. 299–307.
[6] Ibid., pp. 322, 324.

have, in spite of everything, been a stage. We were not, I am convinced, some monstrous excrescence in the history of this country because we were a people's government: we were in the tradition of this country, in the tradition of the French Revolution. We have not destroyed the chain, we have not broken it, we have fortified and strengthened it.[7]

Sincere, impassioned, eloquent, his words had a telling effect. Before this tribunal he spoke with a clear, untroubled conscience. For he *had* accepted his obligations to the national community and his very reforms had been designed to give the workers a stake in French society. His own personal patriotism and integrity were unimpeachable. His record was that of a man faithful to the parliamentary republic and to democracy. If there were questions that might be raised concerning his record as a political leader of the Left, or as a Socialist, they were not for this tribunal to judge. It was one of the supreme ironies of Blum's life that he who had sacrificed so much to serve the national interest and who had won his party over to policies that ran counter to its traditional pacifism, revolutionary ideals, and internationalism, should stand accused of betraying the duties of his office. Here was the true drama of Blum at the Riom trial.

Blum's peroration was a political speech but it could hardly have been otherwise. Daladier's lawyer, Maurice Ribet, later recalled the rapt attention with which the judges listened to Blum. Neither he nor the judges had ever heard Blum speak before and they were immensely impressed with his skill as an "astonishing dialectician." "His speech, precise, arranged to the minutest detail," he noted, "was ornamented with all the attractions of a luminous mind . . . His arguments had the multi-faceted sparkle of a skillfully shaped diamond. His eloquence evoked a purely intellectual satisfaction and not the irresistible emotion that carries one away in verbal arguments. The thought was set and molded in precise formulas. M. Léon Blum, with his tall supple figure, his voice filled with nuances that held one's attention, seemed to be the pacifier of souls and of peoples. He seemed toward M. Caous and his assessors to be carrying the gospel to the Roman procurators."[8] Another eyewitness observed, not without accuracy, that Blum had found in this courtroom the perfect audience for his dialectical talents

[7] Ibid., pp. 328–9.
[8] Ribet: *Riom*, p. 170.

and for his own legal tastes, far more suited to his style of eloquence than working-class meeting halls.[9]

The representatives of the press were deeply impressed. The New York *Herald Tribune* correspondent described Blum: "He spoke with his old fire, shaking his head so that his drooping gray mustaches waved."[1] The *New York Times* correspondent, referring to his peroration, wrote: "During the last fifteen minutes he held spellbound an audience not by any means prejudiced in his favor."[2] There were "two big events in 1942 that gave hope to Europe," noted Janet Flanner in *The New Yorker*, "the Russian entry into the war and the Riom trial. There was more European interest in the Riom trial than in any other in modern times except that of Dreyfus. Once again a government was being tried, for the second time an intelligent Jew was involved, and, as usual, France, though captive now, was a testing ground for Continental values."[3] The *Neue Zürcher Zeitung* observed that instead of replying to the precise questions of the presiding magistrate Blum persisted in retracing the history of the Popular Front and his ministry "with a detail and a warmth that glorified it." It went on to note that the court never succeeded in checking the oratorical flow of the speaker. "Without using his notes, holding his white handkerchief in his left hand and making broad gestures, he would turn toward his fellow accused on the right and toward the public as he once did in the Chamber and at the congresses of the party."[4] The *Pariser Zeitung* commented: "Place in the service of his apologia an undeniable speaking talent, a quick and subtle mind, and a culture that one could never deny him and you have the impression of that session in which he spoke for almost four hours without being interrupted. . . . His inflamed peroration . . . left everybody breathless."[5] In another vein Jean Luchaire's *Nouveaux Temps* wrote: "We will never regret enough that today's accused were not, a year and a half ago, tried in twenty-four hours, sent before a firing squad, and buried deep in some forest."[6]

The Vichy government had made the mistake of providing a rostrum for the Socialist leader. In a remarkable performance, he had held the court under his sway for hours on end. The censorship, to be sure,

[9] James de Coquet: *Le Procès de Riom* (Paris, 1945), p. 126.

[1] John Elliott: New York *Herald Tribune*, February 20, 1942.

[2] Lansing Warren: *The New York Times*, March 12, 1942.

[3] "A Reporter at Large," *The New Yorker*, August 1, 1942, pp. 24–32.

[4] *Neue Zürcher Zeitung*, March 31, 1942. For this and the following two items I am grateful to M. Maximilien Rubel and the Société des Amis de Léon Blum.

[5] *Pariser Zeitung*, March 13, 1942.

[6] *Nouveaux Temps*, February 2, 1942.

eliminated from the press accounts the more damaging charges that Blum had made in his speech, including his criticisms of the Pétain regime, the reference to the conversation with Dr. Schacht, the allusion to pre-1933 Germany as "a country then free," the reference to Germany's "policy of revenge and desire for hegemony," and all reference to the execution of Communist hostages.[7] But none of this was of any avail. The trial was backfiring badly.

The sessions that followed the appearance of Daladier and Blum on the witness stand seemed anticlimactic, although Jacomet presented important economic and financial data on the rearmament program to support the position taken by Daladier and Blum.[8] After the first thirteen sessions the trial entered a second phase, a parade of witnesses, mostly of high military rank, who repeated the testimony they had presented in the pretrial hearings about the country's unpreparedness and the reasons for it. The forty-hour week and the social legislation of the Popular Front were blamed for the lack of tanks, airplanes, antiaircraft guns, etc.[9] As one observer sarcastically noted, the answer to the question of why the war had been lost was "so consistent that one might have been listening to a phonograph record—it was the fault of the vacations with pay."[1] Daladier and Blum occasionally intervened, requesting the presiding magistrate to put questions to the witnesses. Blum countered one general's complaint that military units were not fully equipped, as prescribed, with the reminder that the theoretical quotas were the goal of the *completed* rearmament plan, and could not have been fulfilled by September 1939.[2] When another general remarked how unfortunate it was that among those who had led the country in the prewar years "there were some who did not even think like Frenchmen," Blum exploded in anger. He challenged him to spell out what he meant and the general retreated, claiming that he had not aimed the charge at Blum personally.[3] Otherwise, the testimony droned on, repetitious, monotonous.

Meanwhile, in the spring of 1942, important changes were taking place in the inner councils of the Vichy government. The fourteen months of Darlan's uneasy tenure as Vice-Premier were coming to an

[7] Ribet: *Riom*, p. 171, reproduces the censorship instructions on Blum's testimony.

[8] Soupiron: *Riom*, pp. 194–208; Ribet: *Riom*, pp. 172–3.

[9] See testimony, Ribet: *Riom*, pp. 179–275; Soupiron: *Riom*, pp. 209–64.

[1] Soupiron: *Riom*, p. 16.

[2] *Oeuvre*, V, 330–3.

[3] Ribet: *Riom*, pp. 254–5; Blum: *Oeuvre*, V, 343–4.

end. Abetz was increasing his pressure for the return of Laval, with open threats that otherwise a *Gauleiter* would be named. Laval himself was convincing Pétain of the grave dangers the country faced if he were not reinstated.[4]

The decision to reinstate Laval and to collaborate more closely with Germany had an important bearing on the Riom trial. The Germans, of course, had been extremely dissatisfied with the course of the proceedings. The German press had expressed open annoyance that the trial had concentrated on preparedness for the war rather than on political responsibility for the war itself. On March 15, the Führer, speaking in Berlin, attacked the Riom trial, which "has not devoted a single word to the responsibility of the accused in the unleashing of this war and has limited itself to demanding an accounting for the inadequate military preparations . . . We observe with astonishment this spectacle in which the charges are directed not against the mad decision that caused the new war but only against negligence involved in preparation for the war."[5] Pressure mounted from Abetz and from Hitler's personal envoy, Dr. Friedrich Grimm, for the suspension of the trial.[6]

The trial had gone "off the rails"[7] from the Vichy point of view also. The freedom of defense allowed the defendants and their counsel by the court had created a forum for both Blum and Daladier. From the trial had emerged evidence that the civilian leaders of the republic had not failed the country, but that the High Command—even the Marshal himself—had been responsible for the lack of military preparedness and the failure to reorient the army to new strategic concepts of war. Vichy had wanted a trial of the French Republic, not of the High Command. Admiral Leahy wrote home to Washington that the Vichy government "appears very definitely to have in Riom 'a bear by the tail'!"[8]

On April 14, four days before Laval's return to office, a cabinet decree announced the suspension of the public proceedings at Riom. The decree stipulated, however, that the court was to continue its inquiry, and on an even broader scale. It was to investigate and judge all responsibilities, whatever they might be, involved in the country's entry into the war on September 4, 1939; it would also investigate

[4] See especially Aron: *Histoire de Vichy*, pp. 466–88.

[5] Hitler's *Heldentag* speech of March 15, 1942, was read into the record by the prosecution at the Pétain trial in 1945; *Le Procès de Pétain*, II, 932.

[6] Aron: *Vichy*, pp. 413–14, 480; cf. Louis Noguères: *Le Véritable Procès du maréchal Pétain* (Paris, 1955), pp. 328–31.

[7] Werth's phrase, *Twilight of France, 1933–1940* (London, 1942), p. 385, n. 1.

[8] Letter to Undersecretary of State, March 4, 1942, *For. Rel. U.S.*, 1942, II, *Europe*, 146.

all acts "committed before or after that date [which] aggravated the consequences of the situation thus created." The phrase "before or after that date" replaced the ambiguous word "subsequently."

The significance of the decree was apparent in the accompanying report of M. Barthélemy, the Minister of Justice, who, in paying tribute to the court, noted that the tribunal had in its proceedings limited itself to responsibility for the country's lack of preparedness. It was necessary, he said, to extend the scope of investigation in order to search out "all responsibility incurred in acts that contributed to the passage from the state of peace to the state of war." Here was the concession desired by Hitler and Abetz—to fix responsibility for the outbreak of the war on France. At the same time, to satisfy public opinion, the government pledged a continued investigation of the "political errors" that had led to the disaster as well as a supplementary investigation into "the conduct of military operations." There emerged from M. Barthélemy's report clear evidence of the government's uneasiness at the turn taken by the Riom trial and its impact on events at home and on relations with Germany.[9]

The decree suspending the trial seems to have taken the court itself by surprise, for when the news reached it on the morning of April 14 preparations were under way to reopen proceedings that afternoon after the Easter recess. M. Caous accepted the suspension with relief. He and the other magistrates, despite their brave words, had been placed in an extremely awkward position by Marshal Pétain's political condemnation of the accused before the opening of the trial. M. Caous had tried to conduct the proceedings with dignity and a sense of professional pride. The court had refused to consider France's responsibility for the outbreak of the war. Yet in many ways it had served the Vichy government faithfully. It had helped focus responsibility for the defeat on the Popular Front government; it had shielded Marshal Pétain by not pushing the date of inquiry back to 1934; it had protected the General Staff by excluding the conduct of military operations from the investigation. Yet, on the other hand, it had permitted the defendants full freedom of expression even to the point where the republican leaders had successfully turned the spotlight of accusation on the military and on the Vichy regime itself.

The question of the Riom judges came up after the war in the summer of 1945 at the Pétain trial. Daladier paid tribute to the Riom

[9] For the decree and accompanying *rapport*, April 11, 1942, Ribet: *Riom*, pp. 281–3, and Blum: *Oeuvre*, V, 347–8.

court and to the Prosecutor General for refusing to pursue the charges of French responsibility for the outbreak of war. The Prosecutor General at the Pétain trial, M. André Mornet, associated himself with the tribute paid by Daladier to the French magistracy. All of the criticisms of the Riom court, he said, "disappear before the refusal of the court to declare France guilty."[1]

Blum, however, was less charitable. He refused to associate himself with the homage paid by Daladier to the Riom judges and spoke out sharply against the notion that they deserved commendation. Certainly, if they had handed down any decision that France was responsible for the war, they would have deserved to be called traitors. "But I cannot all the same praise them for not having been traitors!" And he insisted that they had debased themselves by agreeing to hold a trial of men already condemned by the Marshal. Blum's further remarks that the bench as a whole had not shown much courage or independence under Vichy brought down on him a storm of protest.[2] M. Caous's testimony the very next day that the court had maintained its full independence of the Vichy government did not satisfy Blum; he refused to believe that the Riom court would have gone counter to the Marshal's political condemnation of the accused.[3]

On the other hand, the Marshal's political condemnation of Blum and the others, through the Council of Political Justice, was not defended by anyone, not even by Pétain's defense attorney.[4] And in 1947, the Marshal himself, in his fortress prison on the Île de Yeu, tried in despair to explain to a parliamentary investigation commission: "It was through a misunderstanding of the duties of the office that I was then engaged in. I thought that I had the authority to do it. I was mistaken." When the commission asked him whether he thought that Reynaud, Gamelin, Daladier, Blum, Jacomet, and Mandel deserved to be condemned to life imprisonment without a trial, he burst out in pained surprise. "But he was a friend of mine. Not Paul Reynaud, nor Mandel, but Blum. . . . You take me by surprise. . . . Under what circumstances could I have committed such a stupid blunder?" The reference to "friendship" with Blum was an exaggeration, but the two men had always had correct and cordial relations. The Marshal protested that he could not remember any of the details about the arrest of the men,

---

[1] For Daladier's statement, *Le Procès de Pétain*, I, 123, 127, 130; for Mornet's statement, ibid., p. 132, and II, 932.

[2] Blum: testimony, ibid., I, 241–2, 244–5.

[3] Caous: testimony, and statements by others, ibid., pp. 298–304.

[4] See statements by M. Jacques Isorni, ibid., II, 1052–3.

the ordering of the Riom trial, his speech of August 1941 announcing the Council of Political Justice, his condemnation of the men in October 1941, their confinement to Le Portalet fortress.[5] But at ninety-one human memories fade, and men have more than human tribunals to face.

———————

Blum, Daladier, and the other defendants could have only mixed reactions to the new turn of events. They derived immense satisfaction, of course, from the suspension of the trial and from the government's admission that the investigation of responsibility had to be widened to include military responsibility. "Bring on the bouquets and laurel wreaths," cried out Blum's lawyer, André Le Troquer. Maurice Ribet, Daladier's lawyer, called it a striking victory. "The Marshal," he boasted, "is now asking *us* for an armistice!"[6] But the gloomy fact remained that the defendants were still condemned men under Marshal Pétain's political sentence.

Thus the victory was no more than a hollow one. The government's official report to Marshal Pétain was an ominous reminder: "The situation of the accused men will remain fixed by the decision you have taken in application of Constitutional Act No. 7."[7] They faced a return to the fortress at Le Portalet for life imprisonment. Or they might remain at Bourassol if the trial were to be resumed. Blum wrote on May 13: "The suspension of the trial put us in a very great state of uncertainty, especially at first. We were completely ignorant—and we still are—of what the consequences will be so far as we are concerned. Will private hearings be resumed or not? Will we remain at Bourassol? Will we return to Le Portalet? Will we go elsewhere? All sorts of rumors have been floating in the air and I stopped my letter writing until the day—it then seemed soon—when I would have some more precise information to furnish. That day has not yet come. The status quo is continued and it seems likely that it will continue."[8]

By "status quo" he meant his incarceration at Bourassol. Destiny would not return him to the fortress at Le Portalet. He would remain for another year at Bourassol, until the end of March 1943, when he would be transferred to Germany.

[5] *Événements*, I, 181.

[6] Ribet: *Riom*, pp. 283–4.

[7] *Rapport*, April 11, 1942, Ribet: *Riom*, p. 282.

[8] Unpublished letter to André Blumel, May 13, 1942.

XVI

BOURASSOL, BUCHENWALD, LIBERATION,

1943–1945

Liberated France will be a free France.[1]

I N THE WEEKS immediately following the trial, Blum looked back with a sense of elation. To André Blumel, who had written to congratulate him, he replied: "I can well believe that you have been satisfied. To tell the truth I am not too displeased with myself."[2] In another letter he called attention to what he considered the "most important result" of the trial: the failure of the prosecution to prove its case on the lack of armaments. "Capital fact: the carrying out of the program recommended by the General Staff was not behind schedule but clearly ahead of schedule at the moment of entry into the war." He expressed satisfaction also that the Vichy government had been unable to prevent the trial from reverberating throughout the country. Instead it had caused the "old republican spirit to vibrate through all of France . . . If the nation awakens and finds its true self once again . . . our trial will have counted for something: everything is therefore for the best."[3]

With his personal mission fulfilled, Blum could ponder the future. His decision to remain in France rather than to seek refuge abroad had been made in part because of his conscious identification with the nation in its suffering and defeat. His imprisonment and trial had helped to transform the national humiliation into new stirrings of republican solidarity. But there are limits to what one can accomplish as a symbol, especially behind bars. There is some indication that Blum at this point

[1] Letter, Blum to de Gaulle, March 15, 1943, *Oeuvre*, V, 400.
[2] Unpublished letter to André Blumel, March 25, 1942; and cf. letter to Suzanne Lacore, May 15, 1942, *Oeuvre*, V, 356.
[3] Unpublished letter to Suzanne Blum, July 9, 1942.

would not have been averse to outside intervention to secure his release. He intimated this cautiously in a letter written April 30, 1942, to President Roosevelt, whom he knew to be sympathetic to his plight. "Since the suspension of the proceedings at Riom—most significant in itself— I have, however, wondered whether I have not reached the limit of the results which it was possible for me to attain from the depths of a prison, and I have come to the belief, on my part, that henceforth my tasks would be better carried on in freedom."[4] Admiral Leahy transmitted the letter to Roosevelt, but nothing came of it; Blum stayed on, a prisoner of Vichy.

Blum's health had held up well during the trial, but at the very moment of the decree in April suspending the proceedings, he fell victim to an excruciating attack of sciatica. "It has nailed me to my bed," he wrote, "like someone paralyzed, unable to move my back and legs." A month passed before he could sit at a table and write for brief intervals, and at least four months before the attack subsided. That summer an enervating enteritis added to his miseries.[5] Life in prison was beginning to tell.

On his seventieth birthday, April 9, 1942, he was again cheered by a telegram from the United States signed by some two hundred prominent persons who wished to express "their sympathetic greetings and their admiration" for his "courageous stand in the cause of freedom and democracy." Again, among the signers, to his special satisfaction, was Eleanor Roosevelt. Several thousand trade-unionists, under the auspices of New York labor unions, also marked his birthday with a mass meeting in Carnegie Hall. *The New York Times* editorialized on the occasion: "When M. Blum was Prime Minister of the French Republic, he may have made errors of judgment. What man in public life hasn't done that? At Riom he spoke for the clear-eyed heroic France that every free man on earth loves and respects."[6] Blum's stature was never so high as in the months after his eloquent stand at Riom and during these months of imprisonment and martyrdom.

His own concern for family and friends mounted, especially after

---

[4] "President's Secretary's File, France, B-5," Franklin D. Roosevelt Library, Hyde Park, New York. I am grateful to Professor Richard Lowitt for this item.

[5] Unpublished letter to André Blumel, May 13, 1942; and letters to Suzanne Lacore, May 15, 1942, and to Marcel Blum, August 21, 1942, *Oeuvre*, V, 356, 362.

[6] *The New York Times*, April 9, 1942, news story, and editorial, "To Léon Blum." As previously indicated, Mme Suzanne Blum and her husband, Paul Weill, initiated the telegram. "Susan Pohl," one of the signatures, was intended to convey this to Blum.

the arrests and executions of hostages in the summer of 1942. His son, Robert, was still a prisoner of war in Germany. His brother René, who in June 1940 had insisted on returning to France from the United States, where he had been touring with his Ballets Russes company, had been arrested in December 1941 and was interned at Drancy; another brother, Georges, who was in his sixties, was rounded up in April but released because of his age. Blum despaired because other members of his family would not leave the Paris area. "They imagine that the atrocities of last month will be the last," he wrote in August 1942, "or at least that the universal horror that they have provoked will lead to a long respite. They do not realize, I fear, that the gears move faster and faster and that one can always go further in atrocities; the limit is never reached."[7] It was a prophetic warning. Conditions grew worse for those who were close to him. That summer Robert was transferred from his prisoner-of-war camp to a special *Oflag* at Lübeck, where he was kept in isolation; Stalin's son, captured on the Russian front, was a fellow prisoner.[8] In September, his brother René was deported and sent to Poland. The S. S. *Obersturmführer* in charge of the convoy of a thousand Jews noted in his report the presence of "the brother of Léon Blum, former French Premier." René Blum never returned from Auschwitz.[9]

André Blumel, his friend and former *chef de cabinet*, was arrested and interned, with no reason given. Blum wrote to him: "At the moment I can see only one conceivable explanation—our friendship and your faithful attachment to me. If anyone wished to hurt me, they have succeeded. The blows that my friends receive because of me—or rather those that I receive because of their suffering—are those which I feel the most."[1]

In September 1942, back at Bourassol, he began his third year in prison. His daughter-in-law, Renée, and Janot, were faithful visitors. That autumn the pace of the war quickened. A few days after the Allied landings in North Africa on November 8, the Germans entered and took over control of unoccupied France. Blum was now a prisoner not only of Pétain but of Hitler. He was, he described himself, "under double escort." The new status of the Vichy government recalled to him Ros-

---

[7] Letter to Marcel Blum, August 21, 1942, *Oeuvre*, V, 362.

[8] Letter to Félix Gouin, October 21, 1942, *Oeuvre*, V, 376.

[9] See George Wellers: *De Drancy à Auschwitz* (Paris, 1946), pp. 125–48 (a photostat of the German report, September 23, 1942, is included); and see also the memorial volume *René Blum, 1878–1942* (Paris, 1950).

[1] Unpublished letters to Blumel, September 1, 17, 1942.

tand's verses in *Cyrano*—his captors themselves had been made captive!

> *Nous assiégeons Arras. Nous-mêmes pris au piège,*
> *Le Cardinal Infant d'Espagne nous assiège.*[2]

Although exhilarated by the accelerated march of events in North Africa and on the Russian front, he soon saw his own personal situation worsen. Under the authority of the occupying power, a sterner prison regime was introduced; for a time, even visits were forbidden. He refused to contemplate his own future. "As to the world, that is different," he wrote, "and that is what counts."[3]

Ever since his imprisonment, Blum from his prison cell had maintained contact with Socialist groups that were working to rebuild the shattered party and to fuse it into the wider Resistance movement. In July 1940, he had urged Daniel Mayer not to go to London but to remain behind and work in the southern zone to help organize an underground Socialist organization.[4] Mayer was one of the "new, young men" who could be counted on to replace the older leaders of the party in the tasks ahead.[5] His work in organizing a Committee of Socialist Action (C.S.A.) was so effective that a small "congress" could be held in the spring of 1941; it agreed to exclude from the party all those who had voted full powers to Pétain in July 1940 and it launched an underground *Le Populaire*. In the northern zone similar steps were taken.[6] Through visitors such as Renée, Janot, André Le Troquer, and others, Blum was able to communicate his ideas on the program of the clandestine Socialist organization in both zones and on its relation to the Resistance movement. "The prison at Bourassol," Daniel Mayer later wrote, "was the crucible in which the most powerful arms were forged. . . . It was not the least of the paradoxes of those days that a prison became a command post in the battle against the government of the time."[7]

Never having accepted the defeat of 1940 as final, Blum could reinforce in his fellow Socialists the will to resist the Pétain government and the German conquerors. His speeches before the Riom court, typed by students at night under cover of darkness in Riom itself, made their

---

[2] Letter to Camille Soula, December 3, 1942, *Oeuvre*, V, 385.

[3] Unpublished letters to Blumel, December 17, 1942, and January 3, 1943.

[4] Daniel Mayer: "Chez Léon Blum à Bourassol," *Le Populaire*, March 29, 1953.

[5] Blum: *Mémoires*, 1940, *Oeuvre*, V, 98.

[6] Ligou: *Socialisme*, pp. 483–91; Henri Michel: *Histoire de la Résistance, 1940–1944* (Paris, 1950), pp. 36–7.

[7] Introductory note, *Oeuvre*, V, 138.

way via underground channels throughout France; they appeared in brochure form in July 1942 under the aegis of the Committee of Socialist Action. One of the younger Socialist leaders described "the powerful effect of his vehement replies and his exalted hymns to justice and liberty. . . . From the Riom trial, from village to village, from individual to individual, from cell to cell, there was repeated the good news of a France that was lost and that had found itself again."[8]

With respect to the outstanding symbol of French resistance in London, Blum, unlike some Socialists, lent unstinting support to General de Gaulle from the very beginning. As he reminded the General in March 1943: "We have never wavered in our absolute opposition to collaboration. . . . Because you first incarnated the spirit of resistance, communicated it to the country, and continue to personify it, we have from the very first hour recognized you as chief in the present battle, and we have neglected nothing that could validate and consolidate your authority."[9] Blum did not share the fears of some French Socialists in London and official circles in London and Washington that de Gaulle had dictatorial propensities. From his prison cell, Blum did all he could to support the General in his long stubborn fight to secure recognition by Britain and the United States for the Committee of National Liberation. With Blum's endorsement the Socialist André Philip was delegated by the Resistance movement in France in the summer of 1942 to accept appointment as Commissioner of Interior and Labor in the Free French organization.[1] Aware of the friction within the Free French movement, Blum wrote in October 1942 to Félix Gouin, who was then in London: "Rather than occupy myself with the difficulties and quarrels of London I would rather make an effort to picture the General and the French in London as they will be back in Paris when they are restored by victory to their normal political atmosphere. . . . I retain my earliest feelings expressed to André Philip and you. . . . I believe firmly and completely in the rectitude and loyalty of the General. I trust him. My personal instinct is corroborated by the unreserved judgment that men like Georges Boris and Maurice Schumann have drawn from a long acquaintance with him."[2]

[8] Samuel Spanien: speech at memorial meeting, Société des Amis de Léon Blum, December 11, 1951, *Oeuvre*, V, xi–xv.

[9] Letter to de Gaulle, March 15, 1943, *Oeuvre*, V, 399; and cf. *Mémoires*, 1940, ibid., 117–24.

[1] See letters to friends in London, May 5, August 15, October 21, 1942. *Oeuvre*, V, 349–55, 357–61, 369–77; and see Michel: *Histoire de la Résistance*, 12, 36–7.

[2] Letter to Gouin, October 21, 1942, *Oeuvre*, V, 369–77.

Convinced that de Gaulle would allow the people to decide freely on the permanent institutions of France, Blum even pledged his own word as bond for the General to President Roosevelt and Prime Minister Churchill. At the end of 1942, at the suggestion of friends in London, Blum wrote a note for the attention of the Allied leaders: "I have been, like millions of Frenchmen, the daily witness of his great accomplishments. In a France overwhelmed and struck down by an incomprehensible disaster, suffocated by a double oppression, it is he who revived little by little, day by day, the nation's honor, its love of liberty, its patriotic and civic conscience. . . . One serves democratic France by helping General de Gaulle to assume at once the position of a leader." (Blum did not fail in the same letter to inform the Allied leaders of the "stupefaction and revulsion" in France at the recent cooperation with Admiral Darlan despite the "need for military success.")[3]

De Gaulle used Blum's support to bolster his authority in his dealings with Washington. "It is worth noting," the General wrote to President Roosevelt in the autumn of 1942, "that no one in France has accused us of aspiring to dictatorship. Léon Jouhaux, Édouard Herriot, Léon Blum, even the leaders of the Communist party, have placed themselves at our disposition and have informed us that we can count on them in our work . . ." Roosevelt and the State Department remained unimpressed.[4]

One of the critical questions on which the Socialist leaders sought Blum's advice was whether to resurrect the party as such or to keep the new Socialist Action committees subordinated to the broader Resistance movement. Many former Socialists believed it unwise and even impossible to revive any of the discredited prewar political parties, including the S.F.I.O. They feared that such a step would only arouse political dissension, reawaken old rivalries, and harm the unity necessary for the Resistance.

Blum, however, uncompromisingly advocated the revival of the party once necessary reforms and renovations had been made, and insisted, furthermore, on the need to revive the other republican parties as well, under the same conditions. In an important "scheme of instructions" drawn up on August 28, 1942, for the Socialist leaders in both London

[3] "Note addressée au Général de Gaulle pour le président Roosevelt et M. W. Churchill," and covering note, November [*sic*] 1942, *Oeuvre*, V, 379–84.

[4] *For. Rel. U.S.*, 1942, II, *Europe*, 542; and see State Department memorandum, *ibid.*, p. 544. For de Gaulle's relations with London and Washington, see Funk: *Charles de Gaulle: The Crucial Years, 1943–1944*, passim, and Milton Viorst: *Hostile Allies: FDR and Charles de Gaulle* (New York, 1965).

and France, he specified: "A liberated France, an independent France, will be a democracy. . . . And no matter what may be the future constitution of the French democracy, it will be impossible to conceive of any kind of a democratic state without organized political parties."[5] It was a lesson that he sought to communicate to General de Gaulle as well.[6]

Adamant on the relationship between democracy and free political parties, Blum maintained, however, that the parties must purge themselves of the vices of the prewar years, and that the prewar parliamentary system itself had to be strengthened and reformed. His own party should set the example. "It must, from this moment on," he wrote in August 1942, "give the clear impression that in reconstructing itself it does not intend purely and simply to continue as in the past in the same form or in the same condition." He stressed the party's obligation to revamp its leadership, its recruitment, its organizational structure, its propaganda.[7] Nonetheless, he refused to join with those who would change the name of the party so as to symbolize a broader labor and middle-class orientation. "It is a Socialist party," he wrote, "because socialism exists. The Socialist party must continue with its name, as the French republic must continue with its name." Nor would any revision in the party's doctrine be necessary; it would have only to be reaffirmed as "the doctrine which combines personal and civil liberties with economic order and social equality."[8] The program of the reconstructed Socialist party drawn up by Daniel Mayer early in 1943 bore a striking resemblance in spirit and wording to Blum's *À l'échelle humaine*.[9]

Blum envisaged a reconstructed Socialist party as playing a large role in aiding the provisional government immediately after liberation and in shaping the nation's future. For the moment, however, its special task was to formulate a common program of action for a united Resistance movement under de Gaulle's leadership, stressing the postwar restoration of democratic liberties, basic economic reforms, and joint international action. ("I am thinking naturally—it is impossible for the

[5] "Schéma d'une sorte d'instruction pour mes amis, Paris-Londres," August 28, 1942, *Oeuvre*, V, 363–8.

[6] See, e.g., letter to Gouin in London, October 21, 1942, *Oeuvre*, V, 369–77.

[7] "Schéma," August 28, 1942, *Oeuvre*, V, 363–8.

[8] Note for the party, March 1, 1943, *Oeuvre*, V, 392–3, and "Schéma," August 28, 1942, ibid., pp. 364–5.

[9] For the program, Henri Michel and Boris Mirkine-Guetzévitch (eds.): *Les Idées politiques et sociales de la Résistance* (Paris, 1954), pp. 202–8; also Henri Michel: *Les Courants de pensée de la Résistance française* (Paris, 1963).

memory not to return to my mind—of the program of the Popular Front, and it is a democracy of the same nature that I envisage."[1])

Although Blum prodded the party to work toward the "revival of political life," he cautioned it against any step that might endanger the unity and discipline of the Resistance movement. Again and again, he warned against the selfish competition of parties and reiterated that the paramount need was a tight federation of the Resistance movement under de Gaulle's leadership and the subordination of all interests to the common task that lay ahead.[2]

At the very time that Blum was helping to orient the Socialists toward this role, a special problem arose in connection with the Communists. After June 1941 they had emerged from their year of ambiguous collaboration to throw themselves into the forefront of the Resistance movement. Their party grew rapidly, creating a number of militant Resistance organizations and even its own combat units. For a time, as the one political party proclaiming itself as such, it enjoyed a monopoly of prestige which General de Gaulle in London did nothing to check, despite various protests. On February 5, 1943, an agreement was even signed between the various metropolitan Resistance organizations and the Communist party which openly recognized the party and gave it a voice in the coordination of the metropolitan Resistance movement.[3] The Socialist leaders, infuriated, threatened to withdraw from the Resistance organizations of which they were a part. They pointed to the anomaly of their members serving in organizations which were now under orders of a central authority in which the Communists had a voice and they none. When Blum was consulted, his daughter-in-law Renée acting as intermediary, he restrained them from any divisive action, specifically urging them not to withdraw from the Resistance organizations or to think of forming combat units on their own.[4] Yet he too resented the recognition accorded the Communists and regarded the slight to the Socialists as a "moral and political breach." Convinced that so important a step could not have been taken without de Gaulle's approval, he wrote a strong letter of protest to the General, his last political communication before his deportation to Germany.[5] A short time later, the Socialists received satisfaction when the

[1] "Schéma," August 28, 1942, *Oeuvre*, V, 368.

[2] Ibid., and communications to the party, February 5, March 7, 1943, *Oeuvre*, V, 387–91, 394–5.

[3] Michel: *Histoire de la Résistance*, pp. 37–9.

[4] " 'Consultation au pied levé' pour le parti," March 7, 1943, *Oeuvre*, V, 394–5.

[5] Letter to de Gaulle, March 15, 1943, *Oeuvre*, V, 397–405.

London Committee, through Colonel Passy, conceded that an error had been made and abrogated the agreement of February 1943.[6]

Throughout this period, Blum seized every opportunity to "educate" de Gaulle on the meaning of democracy. He accompanied his unswerving support with reminders to the General of the necessary role to be played in a future French democracy by revived and "purified" political parties. Aware of the onus placed on the prewar parties for the disasters that had befallen France and sensitive to the problems involved in reconstructing his own party, he agreed on the need for re-examining the role of the parties and their relationship to the general political structure of the nation. Always, however, he returned to the basic premise that a democratic state required organized, free political parties. "The negation . . . of political parties," he wrote, "is equivalent to the negation of democracy."[7]

Many questions were left unsettled when Blum was taken from his prison cell in Bourassol in March 1943 and removed to Germany, among them the organization and program of the Resistance movement. Eventually, the objectives that Blum had sought were fulfilled. Political parties received representation alongside other organizations in the National Resistance Council formed in May 1943. Moreover, the program adopted in March 1944 was thoroughly socialist in inspiration, with Daniel Mayer and the Socialists playing a large part in its formulation. It would have a profound effect on the shaping of the new republic in its early years;[8] the Fourth Republic would be closer to Blum's ideas than de Gaulle's. But all that lay in a dim, uncertain future in March 1943.

On the morning of March 31, 1943, Blum penned a brief note at his Bourassol prison for Janot: "At this very moment German officers are entering. We leave at noon. The die is cast. I promise you I shall return safely."[9] These might well have been his last words to the outside world; he was en route to Germany.

The alleged reason for his deportation, along with that of Daladier, General Gamelin, Reynaud, and Mandel, was soon officially announced

[6] Ligou: *Socialisme*, p. 503.

[7] Letter to de Gaulle, March 15, 1943, *Oeuvre*, V, 397–8; cf. earlier letter to Gouin, ibid., pp. 369–77.

[8] Ligou: *Socialisme*, pp. 500–10; and René Hostache: *Le Conseil National de la Résistance: les institutions de la clandestinité* (Paris, 1958), esp. pp. 48–139, 457–63.

[9] Personal note, Jeanne-Léon Blum.

by Berlin. The German government had received "proof based on the most reliable information that the British and American governments intended to gain physical custody of various persons in France in order to establish a rival government." When Laval protested the deportation, the German government assured him that the men were being moved for "military reasons," that they would receive favored treatment as important political prisoners, and that they would be returned to French jurisdiction as soon as circumstances permitted.[1]

In April 1943, the night of the German concentration camp closed in on Blum. Yet the promise of protected treatment was honored. At Buchenwald he was confined, with other special prisoners, in a house close to the officers' and soldiers' quarters. Georges Mandel was a fellow prisoner. Two and a half months later, Janot, after successfully cajoling and bribing the authorities, was permitted to join him at the camp; it was an act of the highest courage and devotion. At Buchenwald she became his wife. Blum was overjoyed by her presence; his life, he wrote, was "entirely transformed."[2] Janot found him in good condition, although somewhat troubled by periodic attacks of his sciatica. "You know him well enough," she was able to inform Blumel, "for me not to have to tell you about his morale."[3]

Blum spent two years, almost to the day, at Buchenwald, from April 1943 to April 1945. Fortunately, the privileged treatment continued; the special prisoners were being spared for their possible hostage value. They read, pooled and exchanged books, and talked.[4] Blum discussed with Mandel the prospects of the postwar world. He began to sketch his thoughts for a philosophical essay on "liberty and equality." ("My point of departure is that the idea of liberty, in the political sense, is in reality as complex as the conception of liberty in the philosophical sense. . . . What is the notion of political liberty that would enter into symmetry with the metaphysical liberty of Kant, Schopenhauer, Bergson?"[5])

The prisoners received French newspapers published in Paris and

[1] *Le Matin*, April 6, 1943; Laval: testimony, *Le Procès de Pétain*, I, 603.

[2] Unpublished letter, Jeanne-Léon Blum to Blumel, August 20, 1943. Like Blum, she had been married twice before: to Senator Henry Torrès, whom she had divorced, and to a department-store magnate, M. Reichenbach, who had recently died.

[3] Jeanne-Léon Blum, unpublished letter to Blumel, same date.

[4] *Le Dernier Mois*, 1945, *Oeuvre*, V, 517–18; unpublished letters, Jeanne-Léon Blum to Blumel, August 20, 1943, and September 25, 1943.

[5] "Notes d'Allemagne," *Oeuvre*, V, 500, 510, and see other notes and comments, ibid., 499–514.

followed events on the radio. And in 1944 the events of the war moved rapidly—D-Day, the liberation of Paris, the Allied advance, the recognition of the French Provisional Government. But what the future held for the internees no one could predict. Cut off completely from the rest of the camp, they saw only the S. S. guards and the orderly assigned to them. Blum described his hut as "less a prison than a burial vault or grave." One could only wonder what was happening in the other parts of the camp. The "peculiar odor" that reached them in the evening through the open windows was a puzzle: who could have guessed that it was the crematory ovens? Only on one occasion did they have contact with the prisoners in the other areas. After an aerial bombardment, a number of prisoners were brought to their area for emergency fire fighting and repairs. "Like draft animals, they were hitched to wagons heavily loaded with stones and sand, or else they dragged along, supporting on their bent backs a long tree trunk like prisoners in certain Egyptian or Assyrian friezes. It was enough to see the drawn and hollow faces, their bodies swimming in the striped concentration camp garb, their bare feet in wooden shoes, to understand the slow torture to which they were being subjected." Through a window Blum was able to exchange a few words and learn something of their lodgings and food, and of the brutality and cruelty of their guards. But he remained ignorant of the more awesome mysteries and demented horrors of Buchenwald.[6]

Special treatment or not, death constantly hovered near. Not for a single moment did he or Janot suppose that they would ever live to see France again. He was aware that he represented to the Nazis "something more than just a French political figure," that he was "the incarnation, in addition, of what they hated most in the world," for he was "a democratic Socialist and a Jew." He could feel the approach of doom in July 1944 when the Gestapo came to take Georges Mandel from the house in which they had all lived together for about fifteen months. Blum and Janot bade him farewell as he embarked on his fateful journey.[7]

Not until later did Blum learn of Mandel's tragic end—and of how close he himself had come to meeting the same fate. Once in Paris and transferred to French jurisdiction, Mandel was shot by his French guards, members of Joseph Darnand's Militia, in the forest of Fontainebleau on July 7, 1944, while being transported from one prison to an-

[6] *Le Dernier Mois, Oeuvre*, V, 518–19.
[7] Ibid., pp. 517–18.

other—a victim of a war of reprisals of which he knew nothing. Otto Abetz, the German Ambassador in Paris, had earlier convinced the German government that only the choicest hostages and the threat of reprisals might save from execution the French soldiers who had been captured fighting at the side of the Germans in North Africa and who were awaiting court-martial by the Provisional French Government in Algiers. The only effective reprisals, he insisted, would be the execution of important Resistance leaders and of "certain French personalities who hold a real interest for the Jews, the Gaullists, and the Communists of North Africa." Among such personalities—"responsible for the war," as he described them—he nominated "Léon Blum, Paul Reynaud, and Georges Mandel." On May 30, 1944, he received the Führer's "consent" to his proposal. The execution of the former African Phalangists in Algiers and the assassination in Paris on June 28 of the arch-collaborationist Philippe Henriot precipitated action. Mandel was returned to Paris; the others were to follow.[8] It remained one of Pierre Laval's most substantial later claims in vindication of his wartime record that he protested the move; his intercession was too late to save Mandel, but, to be sure, neither Blum nor Reynaud followed. There seems to be no reason to doubt that Laval's intercession was the deciding factor in saving the lives of the republican leaders. On the other hand, that act was hardly enough to redeem his other deeds. Few were moved to censure Blum or Reynaud for their silence when Laval wrote to them in October 1945 while he was facing execution after his postwar trial and condemnation. "I addressed a final supreme appeal to two political leaders whose lives I saved: Léon Blum and Paul Reynaud," read his last note. "It was all in vain."[9]

Although Blum was spared Mandel's fate, there were those who believed him already dead. In August 1944, *The New York Times* noted with sadness a report from a Soviet war correspondent that Blum had probably perished in a concentration camp near Lublin. "If ever he made errors of judgment," the editorial read, "he wiped out the memory of them when with Daladier he faced the infamous court at Riom two

---

[8] The documents produced at the Nuremberg trial were first published in *Le Monde*, January 15, 1948, and then in the official record. See also Reynaud: *Au coeur de la mêlée*, pp. 993–8; Aron: *Histoire de Vichy*, pp. 681–4; and Laval's testimony, 1945, *Le Procès de Pétain*, I, 600–2, 604.

[9] Josée Laval (ed.): *The Diary of Pierre Laval* (New York, 1948), photostat of "last note," pp. 236–7; see also *ibid.*, pp. 105–6, 227–8. Not really a "diary" but an English translation of *Laval parle . . . notes et mémoires rédigés à Fresnes d'août à octobre 1945* (Paris, 1948).

years ago and answered the cooked-up charges against him by accusing
his Vichy jailers of treason and complicity with the enemy. . . . If he
died, his valor went unwavering to the grave, the body broken, but the
spirit a heritage forever to France and to mankind."[1] It was a noble,
though premature, obituary.

Yet it was only by a miracle, or combination of miracles, that Blum
escaped death in that last nightmarish month between April 3, 1945,
when he and his wife were evacuated from Buchenwald, and May 4,
when they were found in the Italian Tyrol by American troops. Death
was a "constant companion" during that hectic odyssey. Almost every
line of the rough journal he kept was written with the feeling that it
would be his last.[2] The end could have come at any moment—every
time they put up at a new camp, every time they left a car or passed
through a doorway.

At the beginning of April 1945, the American Third Army had
reached the Weser; its advance armored units were only seventy kilometers from Erfurt—and Buchenwald. Blum and the others feverishly
awaited developments. Would the American tanks come rumbling in
before the S. S. guards had the chance to evacuate them? If they were
evacuated, what then? The great danger was that they would be taken
south to the mountain redoubt where Hitler had promised to stage his
supreme resistance effort and that they too would be crushed in the
final crumbling of the Nazi edifice. "Hitler would perish, but like the
despots of the East—like Sardanapalus in the Delacroix painting, piling
up on his funeral pyre his companions, his slaves, his hostages."[3]

Blum shuddered at the holocaust of the last days of the war. He
sorrowfully noted the triumph of the Nazis even in their defeat:

> You are already conquerors in this sense: you have succeeded
> in communicating to the entire world your cruelty and hatred.
> At this very moment your resistance without hope . . . appears
> only as the extreme mark of a sadistic ferocity. . . . And we re-
> spond, waging the war like you, in exasperated rage; everywhere
> it takes on the face of Biblical extermination.
>
> I tremble at the thought that you are already conquerors in
> this sense: you have breathed such terror all about that to master

[1] *The New York Times*, August 12, 1944.
[2] *Le Dernier Mois* is based on these notes, *Oeuvre*, V, 517–44.
[3] Ibid., pp. 519–20.

you, to prevent the return of your fury, we shall see no other way of fashioning the world save in your image, your laws, the law of Force.[4]

The only true victory, he reflected, would spring from forgiveness and a casting aside of vindictiveness. He rejected punitive sanctions, massive reprisals, dismemberment of a defeated Germany[5] "A wretched Germany would be a cause of misery for all Europe, for the whole world. There is not a single people whose liberty and prosperity are not important in a future community."[6] Despite the cruelty and barbarity he witnessed, he never condemned the German people as a nation. Even in his concentration camp he could write: "I do not believe in fallen and condemned races. I do not believe in that any more for the Germans than for the Jews. . . . Truly the slightest change in circumstances is enough to revive the beast in man—in all men."[7] He accepted, however, the need for a trial of war criminals by an international tribunal—if only to end "the centuries-old notion that in war all is permissible."[8]

On April 1, Blum and his wife were informed that they were to be evacuated from Buchenwald immediately. An onset of the crippling sciatica that had been periodically troubling him ever since Riom and for which he had been treated at the camp delayed their departure briefly. On the evening of April 3 he was carried from his bed into a waiting car. He and his wife sat in the rear; an S. S. chauffeur and an S. S. officer in front. In excruciating pain, he hardly moved for the next twenty-four hours. Their car was the lead vehicle in a convoy of several large trucks in which a number of other prisoners were also being transported. Although they were evidently headed south, they first traveled east in the direction of Regensburg and the Czech border. At Neustadt, they climbed a steep mountain road and arrived at a camp located in a desolate mountain area; it was Flossenburg. The prisoners, he noted, looked "even more lamentable and haggard than at Buchenwald." They had stopped, it turned out, to take into the convoy in a large, sealed, armored truck other special prisoners. At Regensburg, he was taken to a prison, carried up a flight of stairs, and placed in a cell; a momentary fear seized him that he was to be separated from his

---

[4] "Notes d'Allemagne," February 21, 1945, *Oeuvre*, V, 514.

[5] Letters to friends in England, February 5, March 15, 1943, *Oeuvre*, V, 390, 396.

[6] "Notes d'Allemagne," December 1944, *Oeuvre*, V, 509.

[7] Ibid., p. 513.

[8] Ibid., p. 511.

wife, but she followed shortly. On the wall of their cell, scratched with a nail or a knife, were the last entries of those who had passed through earlier and had left for some dread fate. When an air-raid alert brought them together with the other prisoners, he learned the reason for their detour. The mysterious armored truck was transporting various surviving German military and civilian personages implicated in the July 20 plot against Hitler.[9]

After leaving Regensburg, the convoy moved into the Bohemian Forest and put up for twelve days at a pleasant village named Schönberg. The prisoners were housed in the hospital and school, Blum and his wife in the empty home of the Nazi district leader. In Schönberg, on April 12, he heard the news of President Roosevelt's death. The event evoked a flood of reminiscences. He had always hoped to meet the American President personally. In March 1939, he had completed all preparations for a trip to the United States and had received an invitation to the White House when Georges Mandel warned him that the international situation was too tense for him to leave; a few days later, Hitler had taken over Prague. In the spring of the following year, when Sumner Welles came to Europe as Roosevelt's emissary, Blum was the only French political figure outside the cabinet whom Welles visited. Through William Bullitt, Blum also knew of Roosevelt's personal interest in the Popular Front political and social experiment, the "French New Deal." But his sense of personal loss and bereavement was overshadowed by other considerations. Like so many others in the world that spring day of 1945, he underscored "the turn of fate worthy of the climax of an ancient tragedy that carried the President off on the eve of a victory to which he had contributed so much." He had been needed for the war, but how much more so for the postwar peace, and for the struggle for "law and justice conceived of as a universal rule for states as for individuals."[1] Blum, like the American President, believed that the consummation of those ideals would make the sacrifices of the war meaningful.

When they left Schönberg in mid-April, he realized with chill dread that they were headed for Munich, that is, Dachau, which even then, save for Auschwitz, was the camp that evoked the most sinister rumors in the world of prisoners and deportees. They arrived there on April 17 at dawn, Prisoners in hideous striped garb, with ravaged faces and emaciated bodies, passed them on their way to work details outside the

---

[9] *Le Dernier Mois*, *Oeuvre*, V, 519–30.
[1] Ibid., pp. 530–2.

camp. The group of special prisoners was taken to a separate walled area of the camp, and Blum and his wife were lodged in a narrow cell-like room. The place had a sinister look but the special prisoners were free to come and go between their rooms and the small courtyard. And what surprises in the roster of fellow prisoners! One of the first to introduce himself was Dr. Schacht, the former head of the Reichsbank and Minister of the National Economy, who had been a prisoner since the July 20 affair; Blum had last seen him in 1937, while still Premier, at the Matignon Palace. Another was Kurt Schuschnigg, the Austrian nationalist leader who had been the foe of the Austrian Socialists and who had looked in vain to Mussolini for his country's salvation. Now Blum could only nod agreement to his words: "We both wanted the welfare of our countries, we both wanted peace, and now we have only the same enemies." There were other political notables, too, as well as the German officers implicated in the July 20 plot. After the broadcasts of the official German communiqués, the German military men would spread out their maps and mark the battle lines. The German generals, Blum noted ironically, were following the course of the war from the Allied point of view.[2]

Anguish and hope mounted in those April days with indescribable tension. On April 20, the Russians entered Berlin; by April 25, the Americans had taken Augsburg and were only forty kilometers from Dachau.

On April 26, the evacuation of Dachau began. There were heart-rending scenes as thousands of prisoners were assembled in the hot noonday sun and left standing for hours without food—men, women, and children, a somber sea of humanity. When the special prisoners were led through the assemblage, a tremor surged through the throng as they recognized some of the famous men and called out their names. Blum's heart beat, he said, as though it would burst. In trucks they drove through Munich and arrived the next morning at a camp outside Innsbruck in the Austrian Tyrol. Here others joined the distinguished gathering: Frenchmen such as the bishop of Clermont-Ferrand and Prince François Xavier de Bourbon-Parme, both arrested for participation in the Resistance movement, Germans such as Prince Frederick of Prussia, Pastor Niemöller, General Falkenhausen, and others of various backgrounds.[3] The Prince de Bourbon-Parme later recalled the "twenty-seven nationalities represented there, of which a great number were

[2] Ibid., pp. 533–6.
[3] Ibid., pp. 537–40.

Germans. It was rather curious to see us dressed in prison garb mingling with the German officers in full uniform all being guarded as hostages by the S. S."[4]

The last days were lost in confusion. The convoy of about 150 special prisoners and their S. S. guards headed that evening for the Brenner Pass. Turned away at one mountain resort hotel by a German unit already in possession of it, they wandered, lost in the mountains "like the passengers of a shipwrecked vessel," until they put in at Niederdorf. The S. S. men themselves were bewildered. It was impossible to pursue their original plans. The rapidity of the American advance had precluded any thought of retreat toward the Tyrolean redoubt; the Americans were threatening Innsbruck and the Brenner Pass. Meanwhile the German army in Italy was crumbling, men throwing away their arms and hailing the end of the war. The S. S. contingent, more eager to save their own skins than to guard their hostages, were still unwilling either to release or to dispatch them. On April 30, a *coup de théâtre* occurred. One of the German generals succeeded in getting word of their presence to the commander of the retreating Wehrmacht troops, an old friend. A Wehrmacht company, sent from German army headquarters, entered Niederdorf, disarmed the S. S., and took over. Captain Count von Alvensleben, stiff and formal, elegant in an impeccable uniform, assured the prisoners that they were under the protection of the military honor of the German army. It was as though the world had moved back to the pre-1914 days in which Blum had grown up; there had been a Kaiser then, but no Hitler, no Buchenwald, no Dachau. Transported up a mountain path through the deep snow, the group was soon lodged in a summer hotel. "We were no longer prisoners but we were not yet free." It was intensely cold in the unheated hotel. On May 4, at the first streak of dawn, trucks of Italian partisans and American soldiers of the Fifth Army drove up. "My wife and I looked at each other in a sort of ecstasy. For some days we had known we were living; now we knew we were free." They were showered with generous gifts of food, medicine, and clothing. By car and by plane they were transported first to Verona and then to Naples. On May 14, an American airplane delivered them to Orly airport in Paris.[5] Another life was about to begin—for Blum, for France, and for the world.

[4] Testimony, 1945, *Le Procès de Pétain*, II, 635.
[5] *Le Dernier Mois, Oeuvre*, V, 541–4.

Epilogue: The Return

XVII

THE LAST YEARS, 1945-1950
Humanist Socialism, the Fourth Republic

"Perish our memory and let the republic be saved!"[1]

A FTER HIS MIRACULOUS RESCUE in the last weeks of the war in Europe, Blum returned to Paris on May 14, 1945. His courage at Riom and his fortitude during his long imprisonment and exile had made him a heroic figure. Although his health was never fully restored after his wartime ordeal, he still retained at seventy-three much of the mental and physical vigor he had possessed as a younger man. "He came to see me in London," Eden recalled, "frail but with all the natural dignity I had remembered, which no harsh treatment could impair."[2] Refusing to run for a parliamentary seat, he chose for the moment only to resume his old post as political editor of *Le Populaire*. Living in a modest country villa owned by his wife at Jouy-en-Josas in the quiet Seine countryside between Paris and Versailles, he was somewhat shielded from the tensions and excitement of Paris itself but he always remained in close touch with events. Before long, he was drawn back to the political scene.

Two days after his return, his first editorial appeared in *Le Populaire*. Eight months had elapsed since the liberation of Paris. The Resistance and Liberation had not only resurrected the old Popular Front spirit of innovation and reform but infused it with a sense of national unity that the Popular Front had never known. It had strengthened the two working-class parties, the Socialist and Communist, and had helped create the M.R.P., the new, progressive republican Catholic

---

[1] Blum to National Assembly, November 21, 1947, citing Vergniaud, *Oeuvre*, VII, 128. Pierre Vergniaud was the famous Girondist leader in the French Revolution.

[2] *Facing the Dictators*, p. 429.

party. At the moment of liberation the three major parties, and the Resistance movements allied with them, were filled with enthusiasm and ardor and envisaged a program of social and economic change heralding a rebirth of France. General de Gaulle, presiding over the Provisional Government, had encouraged this mood and put into effect the first nationalization measures. Although governing with a firm hand, the General had pledged that the country itself would decide as soon as practicable on its political and constitutional future.

Even so, in May 1945 the feeling was prevalent that the opportunity for a radical renovation of society was dwindling, that the Liberation had turned into a *révolution manquée*. The immediate and pressing needs—to provide relief for the hungry, to absorb the returning prisoners of war and deportees, to restore production, to combat the black market, to stabilize the currency—all of these, concurrent with de Gaulle's stress on reviving the country's importance in military and international affairs, were interfering with the cherished hope for a new France. Although grateful for the Liberator's services, the political parties, restricted to a consultative role, were growing restive.

Blum regarded the political scene with mixed emotions. He approved the spirit of social innovation and noted with pride that the program of all parties was deeply impregnated with "socialism." "Who is there," he asked, "who does not call himself socialist?" The war had rung the changes on the old capitalism, the unregulated capitalism of the "economic liberals." His phrase "Socialism is the master of the hour" was widely quoted. He rejoiced to find his own party "so powerful, so ardent, so alive."[3] Yet he recognized that for both the country and the party a great task of "moral regeneration" lay ahead. "In the week since I have regained the soil of France," he told a meeting of Socialist party federation secretaries on May 20, "I confess that I am filled with disappointment and anxiety. . . . I have not found what I was expecting. I was expecting something which would be filtered and purified, and in many respects I find myself in the midst of a country that is, shall I say, corrupted." He saw the country as fatigued, sluggish, unconcerned about the future—a convalescent running the danger of a renewed infection.[4]

[3] Speech to party conference, May 20, 1945, *Oeuvre*, VI, 8; editorial, *Le Populaire*, May 16, 1945, ibid., p. 3; and speech to party congress, August 1945, ibid., pp. 65–78.

[4] Speech, May 20, 1945, *Oeuvre*, VI, 10; and editorial, *Le Populaire*, May 17, 1945, ibid., p. 4.

As in his wartime writings, he paid full tribute to General de Gaulle as leader of the Resistance and Liberation, "the only man who could unite around his name the pure, honest forces of liberated France," a heroic figure assured of "a place in history close to that of George Washington." But when Blum spoke of de Gaulle and the political future, a note of caution asserted itself. "I for one do not believe that the Resistance created a right to power for anyone. No one has a prior right to power in a democracy. A sovereign people even has the right to be ungrateful." If services rendered were considered a reason for uncontested authority, nearly all dictatorships would find justification.[5]

It was indeed apparent that General de Gaulle had his own vision for the future, different from that of the political parties. He sought, above all, to prevent the country from returning to the unstable political regime that had led to the disaster of 1940. Recalling Blum's outspoken criticism in his wartime writings of the old prewar parliamentary system, with its party feuds, chronic instability, and weak executive, de Gaulle hoped to win his support and to enlist him in the effort to create a "presidential" system of government. Had Blum not even explicitly written: "I incline for my part toward systems of the American or Swiss type founded on a separation and balance of powers . . . which assure the executive power in its proper sphere of action an independent and continuing authority"?[6]

Shortly after Blum's return to France, de Gaulle offered him a post as Minister of State in the Provisional Government. Blum declined, citing as reasons his age and health, and his intention to spare his available strength for his work on *Le Populaire*. Irritated by the refusal, de Gaulle considered it proof of Blum's "resolve to devote himself entirely to his party." In the months that followed, as the debate on the proposed constitution went on, Blum repudiated his wartime advocacy of a presidential system, frankly fearing that with de Gaulle in command the power of the political parties would be throttled. The General's disappointment and resentment mounted, especially because he believed that Blum's editorials, "by the quality of their content and form, exercised a great influence in political circles." He could only conclude sadly: "Léon Blum was quickly recaptured by the old ideas of the Socialist clan. . . . He, too, had readopted the fundamental rule

---

[5] Speech, May 20, 1945, *Oeuvre*, VI, 9–11; and editorial, *Le Populaire*, June 19, 1945, ibid., pp. 22–4.
[6] *À l'échelle humaine*, *Oeuvre*, V, 469.

of the French parliamentary regime: Let no head be seen above the thickets of democracy!" Blum was no different from the other prewar republican leaders, who, he feared, had also learned nothing and were preoccupied only with reviving the old parties and the old parliamentary regime.[7]

Yet Blum too proclaimed the need for change. Like de Gaulle and almost all segments of public opinion (with the exception of a few Radicals), he strongly opposed restoring the old constitution of 1875. Convinced that events and the popular will had buried it for good, Blum did not even consider a referendum necessary. Principally, he opposed a revival of the Senate, which had served as a barrier to social progress in the prewar years, but he wished to remedy many other faults of the older system as well. In the referendum held in October 1945, an overwhelming vote (96.4 per cent) recorded the formal demise of the old constitution. All France agreed that a new order was needed.[8]

On a second question of the same referendum there was less agreement. De Gaulle proposed that the country begin at once to move in the direction of a stronger executive; he urged a limitation on the powers of the new Assembly and the investing of considerable initiative and power in the hands of the executive, even during the constitution-writing stage. The Communists vehemently opposed any such restrictions on the Assembly as an infringement on the rights of the people's representatives. The Socialists and the M.R.P. also opposed these restrictions, and through their efforts de Gaulle's proposal was watered down into a compromise whereby it was made difficult for the legislature to overthrow the cabinet but otherwise the legislature remained supreme. Blum had thrown his full support behind the compromise. He wanted the Assembly to retain full power to reverse the cabinet on any subject yet he was eager for safeguards against the "abuses and caprices of ministerial instability."[9] The compromise was far from satisfactory to de Gaulle. While Blum and the political parties were only elaborating techniques to prevent excessive ministerial instability,

[7] For the foregoing, de Gaulle: *Mémoires de guerre*, III: *Le Salut, 1944–1946* (Paris, 1959), pp. 258–9.

[8] For Blum's position, see editorials, *Le Populaire*, June 2–6, August 11, 1945, *Oeuvre*, VI, 12–21, 32–4; and radio speech, October 4, 1945, ibid., pp. 104–5. For the early years of the Fourth Republic, see the annual volumes edited by André Siegfried from 1944 on, *L'Année politique* (Paris, 1945–   ), and various works cited in the Bibliography, especially those by Goguel, Pickles, Williams, and Wright.

[9] *Le Populaire*, August 10, 29, 1945, *Oeuvre*, VI, 32, 92.

the General had more fundamental changes in mind.[1] The Socialists and the M.R.P., along with a dissatisfied de Gaulle, called for a "yes" vote on the modest restrictions on the new Assembly; the Communists persisted in opposing all limitations. The proposal was adopted by a 66.3 per cent vote.

The elections for the Constituent Assembly, held concurrently with the referendum, were something of a disappointment to the Socialists, as Blum frankly conceded. Despite the predictions of most observers that the Socialists would emerge as the leading party, the Communists came in first, the M.R.P. second, and the Socialists third. Not only had the Communists advertised their Resistance record more effectively than anyone else; they had also successfully exploited popular discontent with social and economic conditions since the Liberation. But because a Communist-M.R.P. coalition was out of the question, the Socialists would have to be the key party in any political combination.[2]

De Gaulle, elected Provisional President, immediately faced a Communist demand for a number of ministries in the cabinet commensurate with their strength in the Assembly, including at least one of the "key ministries," National Defense, Interior, or Foreign Affairs. When the General stubbornly refused to hand over to them one of the "essential command levers of the state," Blum and the Socialists concurred, even though they were reluctant to have their own party accept governmental responsibilities without the Communists. Confidentially, Blum and Vincent Auriol suggested that the Defense and Interior ministries, if they were given to the Communists, might be reorganized so that military and internal security functions would remain under de Gaulle's control. The proposal was unnecessary. The Communists agreed to accept four ministries devoted only to economic and social welfare matters.[3]

The Constituent Assembly had begun badly. De Gaulle's dissatisfaction with the course of events was no secret. Shortly before the elections, he had confidentially informed Blum that, since he could not count on the cooperation of the political parties in shaping the country's future, he was planning to retire from political life. "If that happens, I believe that it is you who will have to assume charge of the government, given your ability, your experience, and the fact

[1] De Gaulle: *Mémoires de guerre*, III, 262–5.

[2] For Blum's comments, *Le Populaire*, October 23–25, 1945, *Oeuvre*, VI, 116–121.

[3] De Gaulle: *Mémoires de guerre*, III, 274, and appendix, 625–6; Blum: editorials, *Le Populaire*, November 16–22, 1945, *Oeuvre*, VI, 132–8.

also that your party will be one of the most numerous in the next Assembly and, in addition, will be the axis of the dominant wing. You may be certain that under such circumstances I would facilitate things for you." Blum refused the offer. "I cannot accept it," de Gaulle records him as saying, "because I have for so long a time been so dishonored and reviled by a segment of public opinion that I find repugnant the very idea of exercising power." He added, also, that his physical strength was not equal to the task. Pressed by de Gaulle for an alternative, he referred to the recent replacement of Churchill by Clement Attlee and suggested his Socialist colleague Félix Gouin, then president of the Constitutent Assembly, as "someone who most resembles Attlee." To de Gaulle this was additional evidence that Blum was considering the problems facing the country "only in a Socialist focus."[4] As time went on, relations between the two men continued to deteriorate.[5]

Meanwhile, Blum followed closely the deliberations on the constitution; and, as de Gaulle had ruefully noted, his comments in *Le Populaire* helped shape public opinion. In the debate then under way, he threw his weight behind the proposal for a single sovereign Assembly which would hold the Premier and the cabinet strictly accountable to it. He adamantly opposed anything like the presidential system favored by de Gaulle. "Heavy historical precedents weigh against it. It wounds and alarms republican susceptibilities. It is suitable, moreover, only for nations, for epochs, for moments of history when the principles of democracy themselves are not exposed to debate or risk." He noted that in his past writings he had referred to its suitability only in countries with a federal system like the United States and Switzerland, where regional and local administrative powers were widely distributed. Centralization of power and the Bonapartist tradition, he warned, militated against it in France—especially with a powerful personality on the horizon.[6] Blum's apprehension over de Gaulle's intentions rigidly circumscribed his own flexibility in meeting the problem of constitutional reform.

On January 21, 1946, the General abruptly resigned without offering any specific reasons. He had already clashed with the Assembly that month; in addition, the commission drafting the new constitution

<hr>

[4] For the foregoing, de Gaulle: *Mémoires de guerre*, III, 259–60.

[5] See, e.g., his editorial, *Le Populaire*, November 17, 1945, one of a long series of criticisms, *Oeuvre*, VI, 133.

[6] *Le Populaire*, November 20, 1945, *Oeuvre*, VI, 151; *Le Populaire*, July 4, 1946, ibid., pp. 220–2; and see *À l'échelle humaine*, *Oeuvre*, V, 469.

was proposing a single sovereign Assembly with the executive branch subordinate and responsible to it. Convinced that the political parties were up to their "old tricks," he saw the undermining of executive authority as an ominous portent for the future.[7]

When de Gaulle's resignation was announced, Blum went through the motions of expressing the deep gratitude of the nation to the General for his services but denounced de Gaulle's attitude toward the new institutions and toward the political parties. "The parties at present are assuredly not perfect. No one feels that more keenly than I. How could there be anything perfect in an imperfect France? But with us, until a new order of things, there is no viable and stable democracy outside the parliamentary system, and there can be no viable and stable parliamentary system outside the existence of organized parties."[8] Blum was too much wedded to older political ways to accept the more fundamental innovations that de Gaulle had in mind, even if the threat of a personal dictatorship were not present.

The crisis produced by de Gaulle's brusque resignation was settled with the installation of Félix Gouin as head of a Socialist-directed tripartite cabinet. Blum and the party could see no alternative for the Socialists but to accept the heavy burdens and responsibilities of leadership even if there lay ahead giant problems of economic rehabilitation and reconstruction, currency weakness and inflation, food scarcities, black-marketeering, and mounting international tensions. It was for them to demonstrate that the new parliamentary institutions could function effectively; the success or failure of parliamentary and even of republican government in France would rest on their capacity for proving to the country that coherent majorities and stable cabinets were possible.[9] With Gouin as Premier and Vincent Auriol as the new president of the Constituent Assembly, the Socialists were in the most exposed positions.

Blum himself came to serve the Gouin government in an unexpected role—as special ambassador to the United States, charged with presenting the country's economic needs in Washington. Financial assistance was necessary if the imaginative and farsighted Monnet Plan for the modernization of French equipment and methods of production, which had been drafted under the Provisional Government, was to be launched. Accompanied by Jean Monnet, the commissioner-general of the Plan,

---

[7] De Gaulle: *Mémoires de guerre*, III, 276, 280, 285.

[8] Editorials, *Le Populaire*, January 21, 22, 24, 1946. *Oeuvre*, VI, 163–7.

[9] Blum: editorial, *Le Populaire*, February 3–4, 1946.

and Emmanuel Monick, governor of the Bank of France, Blum spent about two months in the United States. When he addressed the National Advisory Council in Washington, explaining his government's requests, he assured them that there was no contradiction between the evolution in his country toward a managed, or even a collective, economy and full international economic cooperation.[1]

The trip to the United States was a personal as well as a political success for Blum. President Truman received him with great cordiality. He was tendered a testimonial dinner, held on the first commemoration of President Roosevelt's death, at the Waldorf-Astoria Hotel in New York. The patrician Socialist paid his respect to the memory of the patrician democrat and to the American democracy: "What renders your people at this moment so great among all others, more than its wealth and its strength, is that it desired to create out of this war the first elements of a peaceful community of nations, that it has taken the first initiative in that effort, and has assumed the principal responsibility for it. . . . This common work of the free nations will forever remain under the inspiration of the great man whom the world lost a year ago. . . . He was truly one of those extraordinary men who at long intervals are beacons for the centuries, who bear witness for humanity and stand bond for the future."[2]

His negotiations culminated in the signature of the Blum-Byrnes agreement on May 28, 1946. French debts resulting from Lend-Lease arrangements were sharply reduced, arrangements were made for the purchase of American surplus items at discount rates, and credits were granted by the Export-Import Bank for the purchase of industrial equipment and raw materials. On his return to France, Blum assured everyone that the negotiations had involved no political or economic conditions of any kind or any "interference" by American economic experts in French planning.[3] The agreement was ratified enthusiastically by the Assembly.

Blum returned home in time for the election of the Second Constituent Assembly. Shortly before, a referendum in May 1946 had rejected the constitutional draft providing for a single all-powerful legislative chamber. Many voters feared the inadequate safeguards against the possible danger of a one-party dictatorship—that of the

[1] Speech to National Advisory Council, *Oeuvre*, VI, 188–96.
[2] Speech, April 12, 1946, *Oeuvre*, VI, 197–200.
[3] Statement to press, May 31, 1946, *Oeuvre*, VI, 201–3; and later editorial *Le Populaire*, November 6, 1947, *Oeuvre*, VII, 119–20.

Communists. The Socialists, discounting this danger, had argued that government by assembly would more faithfully reflect the "democratic will" than any other form. The Communists and Socialists had backed the draft; the M.R.P. had opposed it. The defeat of the proposed draft necessitated the election of a Second Constituent Assembly, which now had to provide for some kind of upper house, a proposition which Blum at that stage reluctantly accepted.[4]

To the dismay of the Socialists, the elections of June 2, 1946, for the new Constitutent Assembly resulted in a serious setback for the party; it lost almost one million votes and over twenty seats. Identification with the defeated constitution was partly responsible for the Socialist losses, but identification with the government in the six months since de Gaulle's resignation was also a factor. The electorate had manifestly blamed the Socialists for the difficulties confronting the nation. The party had assumed the obligations of government in order to insure the country's transition to republican institutions, but the electorate had shown little gratitude. All this Blum recognized, but he defended the party's assumption of responsibility as inevitable and laudable.[5] The story of the next few years was one long repetition of this situation.

Although the Socialists now relinquished the premiership to the M.R.P., Vincent Auriol was elected president of the Constituent Assembly, André Philip became chairman of the new constitutional commission, and the Socialists were again the mediating party in the new tripartite coalition government. They were still a government party par excellence.

During this immediate postwar period, in which the Socialists played an important governmental role, Blum held close control over the reins of party leadership, with his protégé, Daniel Mayer, serving as general secretary of the party. But an opposition group led by Guy Mollet and other "neo-Guesdists" who sought to revive the orthodox Marxian heritage of the party slowly gathered strength. For a time Blum successfully countered the various rumblings of discontent at his ideological leadership with a sweeping vision of a newly broadened

[4] Radio speech during the campaign, May 31, 1946, *Oeuvre*, VI, 209–10; and editorial, *Le Populaire*, November 9, 1946, ibid., pp. 144–6.
[5] See his analysis of the election results in *Le Populaire*, June 4, 5, 6, 9–10, 1946, *Oeuvre*, VI, 209–16.

party. His deepest ambition was to shape the party along the lines of the democratic, humanist socialism he had outlined in his wartime writings. Blum appealed to the Socialists not only to seek new ideas and new techniques but also to expand the party's appeal to all economic classes. They had to shed their timidity about appealing to the middle classes, and not fear an *"embourgeoisement"* or loss of the party's proletarian class character. "The greatest error you can commit, in my opinion," he told them, "is to believe that what we gain in one segment of the French population we necessarily lose in another."[6]

As he addressed various Socialist conferences in 1945, he expounded his thesis of the historic fusion of socialism and political democracy. He urged the party to remain faithful to the synthesis that Jaurès had helped to create between Marxism, and its promise of economic emancipation, and the French Revolution, which had brought self-government and freedom. He was convinced that socialism, more than ever, in view of the recent past, had to be linked to the defense of democracy and individual human rights. "Political democracy and social democracy are inseparable" was his constant theme. One had to abandon once and for all the pre-1914 thesis of August Bebel and the German Social Democrats that socialist parties could develop and grow regardless of their political environment. Recent history had taught "in letters of blood" the fallacy of that view.[7]

To charges at the congress of August 1945 that he was failing to accent sufficiently the revolutionary nature of the party, he replied that he had never considered reform as "an end in itself." The party sought reforms because reforms contained within themselves a revolutionary potential. "There is only one socialism and that socialism by itself and in its essence is revolutionary." On the other hand, it was crucial to understand that the substitution of one system of property relations for another was not "the final goal," (the mistake of the Bolshevik Revolution and of the Communists), but only "the means, the necessary prerequisite, for the transformation of the human condition."

> The revolutionary objective is not only to liberate man from economic and social exploitation . . . but to assure him within a collective society the fullness of his fundamental rights and his

[6] See especially speech of May 20, 1945, "Les Devoirs et les tâches du socialisme," *Oeuvre*, VI, 5–11; and speech to 37th party congress, August 13, 1945, "Le Socialisme maître de l'heure," ibid., pp. 65–78; the sentence quoted is on pp. 74–5.
[7] Speech of August 13, 1945, *Oeuvre*, VI, 66.

personal potential . . . Our true goal in the future society is to render the human person not only more useful but happier and better. . . . It is in that sense that we say of our socialism that it is human; and it is not the less revolutionary for that.[8]

Blum never liked the term "humanist socialism"; it savored too much of an "intellectual" socialism, a socialism divorced from the "masses."[9] Yet the term was widely used in the years after 1945 to describe his credo and it had a strong ring of accuracy. Although he claimed fidelity to many of the traditional tenets of Marxism, he actually retained little. Perhaps, like Jaurès, the only elements of Marxism that he did not abandon were the concepts of social and economic class arising out of existing property relationships and the central role of the working class in the necessary transformation of society. Even then, he sought to substitute the term "class action" as preferable to the more inflexible "class struggle."[1]

More than ever, Blum rejected "dialectical materialism" as an underpinning to his socialist thought. He accepted the "dialectic" only as a "logical" means of demonstrating that a socialist society would emerge from capitalist society. Yet he expected socialism to emerge not as a result of dialectical or historical inevitability, but because men would recognize it as desirable and just—"the terminal point, the culmination of all those great currents that have traversed humanity since human civilization began, currents of the mind and of the conscience, aspirations toward justice, toward humanity, toward human charity."[2] Blum, like Jaurès and Bernstein, owed as much to Kantian idealism as to Marx. For his repudiation of dialectical materialism he was excoriated, of course, both by the orthodox in his own party and by the Communists.[3]

While Blum was orienting the party along the lines of his humanist socialism, he was also restraining it from any rash unification with the Communists. In the wake of the close cooperation of the two parties in the Resistance and Liberation, the question of reunification

[8] Ibid., pp. 69–70.

[9] See his speech to the 38th party congress, September 1, 1946, *Oeuvre*, VI, 279.

[1] See especially "Notes sur la doctrine," *Oeuvre*, VI, 271–5.

[2] Speech of August 13, 1945, *Oeuvre*, VI, 66, 70; speech to 38th party congress, September 1, 1946, ibid., pp. 280–1; editorial, *Le Populaire*, June 29–30, 1947, *Oeuvre*, VII, 83–5.

[3] See, e.g., his editorial replying to these criticisms, "Les Excommunications de M. Thorez," June 29–30, 1947, *Oeuvre*, VII, 83–5. In this editorial Blum referred also to the false rumors of his conversion to Catholicism after his return from Germany.

had arisen. Even before Blum's return to France, a joint committee had been appointed to study the possibility. The Communists, filled with ebullience and self-confidence, had seized the initiative in June 1945 and, ignoring the negotiations under way, had published in *L'Humanité* a proposed "charter of unity" for a great new "French Workers' Party" (*Parti ouvrier français*). In every phrase the document made clear that the new party would mirror faithfully the ideological and organizational doctrines of the Communist party alone.[4] The lion and the lamb would lie down together and only the lion would get up.

In the summer of 1945, as in the mid-1930's, Blum once again took it upon himself to analyze the "problem of unity." He was not one to dismiss lightly the hope of working-class unity. Ever since the schism twenty-five years ago, he had never lost hope for a reconciliation, that the Communists would someday return to *"la vieille maison."* He was also convinced that, just as in the Popular Front days, "unity of action" by the two parties was essential for the protection of democratic liberties; with an eye cocked at de Gaulle, he foresaw that the two proletarian parties and the trade unions might once again be "the supreme guarantor of democracy." He rejected also the thought that the Socialist party could allow itself to be led into "anything resembling an anti-Communist coalition." But, all things considered, he concluded that "organic unity" was not possible. Personally, he had never wavered in the belief that there could be no viable international community without the U.S.S.R. and no true democracy in France without a Communist party. Yet he pointed out during the war years: "It will be necessary for a radical change to take place, either in the nature of the bond which unites French communism to Soviet Russia, or in the nature of the relationship which will unite Soviet Russia to the international community." Sadly, he reported that neither of these changes had taken place. French communism was still closely bound to the Soviet Union, and the Soviet Union under Stalin's leadership was seeking to consolidate and extend its military power with little heed to the international community. The Communist party itself he believed to be "an immense apparatus still enveloped in mystery" and its post-Liberation activities too devious and unscrupulous to inspire trust. The publication of the proposed charter of unity was a case in point.[5]

The congress that met in August 1945 accepted Blum's arguments

---

[4] *L'Humanité*, June 12, 1945; and see Blum: *Oeuvre*, VI, 34.

[5] See his editorials, July 5–August 7, 1945, *Oeuvre*, VI, 36–64.

and overwhemingly rejected the Communist offer of reunification.[6] Thus Blum held the line in the summer of 1945 against a fusion that, in view of the Communists' dynamism, surely would have resulted in a disappearance of the old Socialist party. De Gaulle, for his part, had blocked Communist postwar ambitions by disarming the Communist Resistance militia and by holding steadfast against granting the Communists any of the "key ministries" in his government. Blum and de Gaulle, each in his own way, and with little appreciation for each other's efforts, had kept France from being engulfed by communism.

The Communists never forgave Blum for his role in blocking unity; twenty-five years after the schism at Tours he had again barred the way to a Communist monopoly of working-class allegiance. His actions in the summer of 1945 were added to the long catalogue of sins that they imputed to him.[7]

In the party itself, Blum's humanist socialism had triumphed over the orthodox hard line in the early postwar period. But in the summer of 1946, at the 38th annual congress of the party, smoldering resentment at the continuing identification of the party with the government and at the Socialist setbacks at the polls flared into open revolt. Guy Mollet and the disgruntled orthodox wing of the party succeeded in persuading the congress to repudiate the postwar party leadership and to reject by a two-thirds majority the political report prepared by Daniel Mayer. The profound causes of the Socialist decline in strength were alleged to stem from a mistaken ideological orientation; the sponsors of the resolution singled out for attack several key principles unmistakably identified with Blum. They condemned "all attempts at revisionism, notably those which are inspired by a false humanism whose true significance is to mask fundamental realities—that is, the class struggle." The "weakening of Marxist thought in the party" had led it to neglect mass action and "to confine itself to parliamentary and governmental activity." In modifying its social base, the party had neglected the "most exploited segments of the population." Mollet called for a renewed emphasis on "scientific socialism" and reliance on working-class action. Socialists had to keep clearly in mind that "the

---

[6] For the resolution adopted, *Oeuvre*, VI, 100–1.

[7] For a sweeping summary of Communist charges against Blum, see article on Blum in the *Soviet Encyclopedia*, 1950 ed., trans. into French, *Preuves*, November 1951, pp. 19–21. For Blum's reply to various Communist charges, *Le Populaire*, August 22, 23, 1945, *Oeuvre*, VI, 84–8.

goal of our party is not the exercise of power within the framework of the regime but the suppression of that regime."[8]

One by one, Blum was forced to defend his policies and his doctrines. Not only his ideological leadership but his political philosophy was under attack. The assault on a "false humanism" and on the "exercise of power" were personally aimed at him. He explained the attitude in the party as a reaction to its setbacks at the polls and a reflection of uneasiness at the strength of its proletarian rival, the Communists. It was not "purity of doctrine" that was at issue, but a sense of insecurity and self-consciousness vis à vis the Communists. Speaking sharply, he told the congress that their resolution was "a kind of moral alibi" by means of which they sought to salve their "bad conscience." They looked with envy on the "dynamism" of others instead of blaming their own "lack of ardor, courage, and faith." Agreeing on the need for class action, he argued that class action meant political action, and political action automatically raised questions of governmental responsibilities. Better than anyone, he knew the difficulties involved when a Socialist party became "manager of the society it condemns." "I understand them so well that for fifteen years . . . I did all in my power to keep the party from the exercise of power in a capitalist system." But the true test lay in the counterbalancing compensations which they had obtained. Most recently, they had taken and retained office to insure the functioning of republican institutions at a perilous time. They had every reason to be proud of assuming that obligation.[9]

Blum's stand was an unqualified defense of his democratic, humanist, personalist socialism. Once again he had assigned to the party, as its supreme task, the defense of republican institutions and the protection of human rights. All his old warnings about Socialist participation in governments were subordinated to the higher imperative of serving the parliamentary republic. The congress, however, rejected Blum's appeal; Guy Mollet succeeded Daniel Mayer as general secretary. Ironically, in the years that followed, Blum's doctrines on the exercise of power came to prevail. Guy Mollet also accepted the responsibilities of national office and grew less intransigent; eventually other Socialists attacked *him* on much the same grounds. In the remaining years of the Fourth Republic (and in the Fifth too), the party was subjected

[8] For the resolutions, *Oeuvre*, VI, 289–93.

[9] For Blum's speech to the 38th party congress, September 1, 1946, *Oeuvre*, VI, 276–88.

to frequent secessions and expulsions; it never regained the strength and prestige it enjoyed at the time of the Liberation.

Actually, the party was in an impossible dilemma in the post-Liberation era. Although Blum had diluted the Marxian heritage of the party beyond recognition, he could not surrender it entirely, for to do so would have meant abandoning the revolutionary proletarian tradition in its entirety to the Communists. Thus the S.F.I.O. was neither a reformist nor a revolutionary party. The Mollet group self-consciously tried to revive all the old shibboleths of Marxian orthodoxy yet accepted the path that Blum had cut out for the Socialists as a responsible political party of the republic. The results were unhappy. Those who preferred orthodoxy turned to the Communists or to various splinter groups; others drifted away. The Socialists failed to attract a proletarian following and increasingly drew their clientele from such horny-handed sons of toil as schoolteachers, civil service functionaries, and white-collar workers. "The workers have walked out of the S.F.I.O. on tiptoes, as one leaves the chamber of a dying man," wrote one disillusioned Socialist. The party's membership declined markedly from its record high of 338,625 in 1945; subscriptions to *Le Populaire* dropped precipitously.[1]

While the Socialists wrangled in 1945 and 1946, de Gaulle returned to the political scene. The Second Constituent Assembly had adopted a new constitutional draft which provided for a second chamber with limited powers but which otherwise did not differ much from the first draft.[2] De Gaulle openly intervened to attack the proposed constitution, appealing for its rejection in the referendum to be held in October 1946. The referendum took shape as a choice between the constitutional draft proposed by the Second Constituent Assembly and the presidential form of government pressed by de Gaulle.

Blum threw himself directly into the contest. His theoretical and historical objections to a presidential system in France were reinforced

[1] The quotation is from Jean Rous, cited by Ehrmann: "The Decline of the Socialist Party," in Earle (ed.): *Modern France*, p. 187. This chapter by Ehrmann is a penetrating analysis; see also Colton: "The French Socialist Party: A Case Study of the Non-Communist Left," *The Yale Review*, XLIII (Spring 1954), 402–13, and the article in *The Journal of Politics*, XV (1953), already cited. The vicissitudes of the postwar party are discussed in some detail in Ligou: *Socialisme*, pp. 513–607.

[2] For Blum's reluctant acceptance of the second house, see editorials, *Le Populaire*, August 23, 24, 1946, *Oeuvre*, VI, 296–9.

by anxiety over de Gaulle himself. If the country had rejected the first constitutional proposal because it was tailored to the measure of a party, it must not accept a new one "tailored to the measure of a man."[3] No longer did Blum see a confrontation of two proposed systems of government but a contest between de Gaulle and the popularly elected Assembly. Although he conceded that de Gaulle was no "conspirator of the type of Louis Napoleon Bonaparte spinning out a shadowy adventure against the liberty of his country," nonetheless he feared the elevation of the General, with his immense prestige and popularity, and his known views on the nature of authority, to a presidential office designed to his specifications. In editorial after editorial he inveighed against de Gaulle. Democracy, he predicted, although it would retain its form under the General, would be "emptied entirely of its substance . . . nothing would serve as an obstacle—neither his ministers nor the chambers—to his deep personal conception of command." Blum had visions of "a non-hereditary monarchy," a "monocracy."[4]

Despite de Gaulle's intervention, the constitution proposed by the Second Constituent Assembly was approved in the referendum of October 1946, but by an extremely narrow plurality, 9,263,000 "yes" to 8,143,000 "no," with a large number of abstentions. No one could be pleased with the outcome. But the constitution of the Fourth Republic was now formally adopted, the country could proceed to the election of a National Assembly, a Council of the Republic (the new upper house), and a President of the Republic. De Gaulle, for the moment, retired to write his memoirs. The Socialists, and Blum personally, faced new responsibilities.

On November 10, 1946, elections were held for the National Assembly under the newly adopted constitution. Despite de Gaulle's condemnation of all three major parties for supporting the constitutional draft, the total strength of the parties emerged unaltered. The Socialists, however, suffered new losses (twenty-seven seats and almost 750,000 votes—a cumulative loss of 1,750,000 votes in the last two elections). The electorate had again blamed the Socialists for the government's continued difficulties. The large floating vote on which the Socialists

[3] See editorials, *Le Populaire*, June 21, July 4, 1946, *Oeuvre*, VI, 217–18, 220–2.

[4] See his editorials of September and October 1946 reprinted in *Oeuvre*, VI, 305–19. The reference to "monocracy" is in "Démocratie ou monocratie," October 9, 1946, ibid., pp. 315–16.

depended to maintain their parliamentary strength was melting away. Blum consoled himself with the thought that the actual loser in the election was de Gaulle.[5]

The political atmosphere at the end of 1946 was highly charged. For one thing, a campaign for revision of the constitution opened almost at once on the grounds that the large majority who had voted against it could not be ignored. Moreover, the M.R.P., smarting under de Gaulle's attack, was seeking to dissociate itself from the Communists and the tripartite coalition; the Communists retaliated, raising charges of "clerical" reaction. When the Bidault government submitted its resignation after the elections, as required, the Communists and the M.R.P. were hopelessly deadlocked on a successor. Various combinations were tried; all failed. Despite their reduced strength, it was the Socialists once again who had to find a way out of the impasse if the Fourth Republic was even to be launched.

On December 12, Vincent Auriol, now president of the National Assembly, asked Blum, his old friend and comrade in arms, to form a broad coalition government to serve on an interim basis. It was a tribute to the personal esteem that the seventy-four-year-old Blum enjoyed that he was "invested" by a vote of 575 votes of the 583 in the National Assembly. Yet for five days he tried without success to form a broad coalition government, and finally resolved on the unprecedented step of forming an all-Socialist government. On December 17 he received the backing of the Assembly by a nearly unanimous vote. It was understood that his cabinet would hold office for about five weeks until the election of the President of the Republic, which was scheduled for January 1947. It was a short but crucial period. Again Blum emphasized the danger to the republic. "We must at all costs put an end to a governmental crisis . . . which could run the risk of becoming perilous. It is necessary to give the country the impression that the parliamentary system has moved forward again, in a nearly normal manner."[6] It was anomalous that the Socialist party, with not much more than one sixth of the seats in the Assembly, should be forming a homogeneous Socialist government, the first time in republican history that a single party had formed the government. Yet there was wide satisfaction that Blum had stepped into the breach.

Despite its brief tenure, Blum's all-Socialist government of Decem-

[5] Editorial, *Le Populaire*, November 13, 1946, *Oeuvre*, VI, 335.
[6] Radio speech, December 16, 1946, *Oeuvre*, VI, 345.

ber 1946–January 1947 made an impressive showing and acted vigorously on many fronts. In his ministerial declaration Blum stressed the necessity to reverse the inflationary trend: " a psychological shock" was needed to protect the currency and to satisfy the demands of labor. Perviously, Blum had praised the Belgian effort to protect real wages by reducing prices rather than by yielding to labor pressure for wage increases. He now announced, in a radio speech on December 31, a 5 per cent general reduction in all prices, declaring that he had received the full support of labor and industry for the measure. It was envisaged that a second reduction would be announced in sixty days.[7] The price reduction was necessary and effective, even though its benefits were not enduring. The Communists, meanwhile, did not let Blum forget that an all-Socialist government had blocked wage increases.[8]

It was during Blum's government that the Monnet Plan received final approval and went into operation; his own mission to Washington earlier in the year had guaranteed American financial aid. The four-year plan for modernizing and expanding the productive base of French industry, first adopted under de Gaulle's Provisional Government, was now launched in six major sectors of the economy. France could move forward to build the industrial base "which," as Blum recalled in a radio speech inaugurating the Plan, "she lacked in so markedly a tragic manner in 1940."[9] The Monnet Plan made possible a transformation of the structure of French industry and French society far more extensive than the Popular Front distributive reforms of 1936. Blum, too, was learning the lessons of productivity and economic growth.

In international affairs the government also moved briskly. Retaining the post of Minister of Foreign Affairs for himself (again rejecting his own theoretical objections to this practice), Blum flew to London in mid-January, met with Attlee and Ernest Bevin, and laid the groundwork for the treaty of alliance and friendship signed at Dunkirk two months later on March 4, 1947. Some progress was made also in London in ironing out differences on the problem of Germany and the Ruhr, and Blum received concrete assurances that France would have

[7] Radio speech, December 31, 1946, *Oeuvre*, VI, 356–7; also ministerial declaration, December 17, 1946, ibid., p. 351, and editorials, *Le Populaire*, July 10, 11, 1946, ibid., pp. 252–5.

[8] For Blum's replies, *Le Populaire*, February 2–3, 4, 5, 1947, *Oeuvre*, VI, 360–5.

[9] Radio speech, January 7, 1947, *Oeuvre*, VI, 359.

priority on the coal of the Ruhr.[1] But neither such problems nor the larger problems of peace and security could be settled by France and Britain alone. Blum's Anglo-French pact, like de Gaulle's Franco-Soviet pact of 1944, was relatively unimportant in the larger alignments of the postwar world.

Once again, it was Blum's misfortune to be in office just as a serious foreign crisis broke out. In July 1936, it had been Spain; in December 1946, it was Indochina. Insurrection had been brewing for some time. Although an agreement had been reached during the year with the independence leader Ho Chi Minh to recognize the independence of Vietnam, a dispute had developed over interpretation of the agreement; sporadic fighting broke out anew about a month before Blum took office. Sympathetic to the colonial independence movement, Blum had published in *Le Populaire* Ho Chi Minh's appeal to the French people and had condemned any attempt to reconquer by force of arms all or part of Indochina. He rejected the argument that "firmness" was needed to guarantee the agreement already reached and called for a vigorous, enlightened direction of policy, "not by the military authorities or the civilian *colons* of Indochina, but by the government in Paris."[2] In his ministerial declaration on December 17 he emphasized with pride and confidence the nature of the French Union: "France has become today the center of a vast federation of peoples distributed over all parts of the world. . . . We shall make every effort to make it an intimate and durable union through confidence and reciprocal friendship."[3]

But on December 19, two days after he took office, large-scale fighting broke out. In the middle of the night, Marius Moutet, his Socialist Minister of Colonies, brought him news of bloody fighting in Hanoi. Upon Blum fell the painful task of restoring order. He pledged, however, that the need to suppress the insurrection would not alter the country's long-range policy. "The old colonial system . . . is today a thing of the past. . . . In our republican doctrine, colonial possession does not reach its final goal and its true justification until the day it comes to an end, that is to say, the day on which the colonial people has been rendered fully capable of living as an emancipated people and

[1] See *Oeuvre*, VI, 333–4, and Blum's comments, *Le Populaire*, February 12, 13, 1947, ibid., pp. 360–9. For critical comments on the treaty, Bonnet: *Quai d'Orsay*, pp. 396–7.

[2] Editorial, *Le Populaire*, December 10, 1946, *Oeuvre*, VI, 342–3.

[3] *Oeuvre*, VI, 348.

of governing itself."[4] They were noble, high-sounding words, but they did not avert bloodshed. The nation embarked in 1946 on the long and bloody road to the disaster of Dien Bien Phu eight tragic years later. French socialism, with the best intentions, was now identified with the "imperialist war" in Indochina, just as, a few years later, after Blum's day, it was identified with the war in Algeria.

With the election of Vincent Auriol as President of the Republic in January 1947, Blum's interim government came to an end, and he refused all requests to continue in office with his all-Socialist cabinet. In domestic affairs, it had been a successful government. In a poll of 1947 asking which of the several postwar governments, including that of de Gaulle, had done the best job, the one-month government of Blum was favored with 60 per cent of the answers. And the distinguished political analyst André Siegfried wrote in his annual review of French political events: "When France, on an exceptional and temporary basis, possessed under Léon Blum a homogeneous cabinet, it suddenly realized the value of unity of direction under a leader with broad views and a high-minded platform. . . . It underscored for us the conditions for effective government."[5] Blum facilitated the transition from the constitution-making era of the Liberation to the Fourth Republic and made possible a fair trial for parliamentary government in the next few years. But on the two counts of political instability and colonial policy, the troubles that would prove the nemesis of the Fourth Republic had already emerged.

In January 1947, Blum was back in his villa in Jouy-en-Josas, contributing his daily column to *Le Populaire* and watching over the fortunes of his party and of the young Fourth Republic. Aware of the trials that both faced, he was resolved to protect the new republican institutions against threats from the Left and the Right. The year 1947 was the year of Blum's "Third Force."

Over all strictly internal problems there loomed in the spring of 1947 the shadow of the Cold War, the now open division of the former wartime Allies into two opposing blocs. Dismayed by the effort of the Soviets to seek "security" through military power and satellite

[4] Statement to National Assembly, December 23, 1946, *Oeuvre*, VI, 353–5. That Blum did not show much forcefulness in dealing with the High Commissioner at Saigon, Admiral Thierry d'Argenlieu, is revealed in *Le Populaire*, June 18–19, 1949 (not reprinted in *Oeuvre*).

[5] *L'Année politique, 1946* (Paris, 1947), p. x; and see also Howard K. Smith: *The State of Europe* (New York, 1949), p. 163.

states instead of through international cooperation,[6] Blum nonetheless refused at first to commit himself unconditionally to the Western camp. Although he defended President Truman's strong words of March 18, 1947, on the Moscow Conference, he added the criticism: "I did not personally find to my taste either the argument or the language of the speech, and I would wish, in particular, that on the other side of the Atlantic one would break once and for all with the dangerous habit of designating by the same epithets the Hitler regime and the Soviet regime." While recognizing that the Americans sought results by plain talk and firmness, he felt compelled to note that "the firm manner easily becomes the strong manner."[7] Calling on the United States to take into account the suspiciousness and sensitivity of the Soviets, he also pleaded that American policy not assume the character of a "systematic anticommunism," compelling it, in order to check the Soviets, to take antidemocratic positions in various parts of the world.[8] He proposed to replace the American monopoly of leadership in the Western camp with a partnership of all states, large and small. "Peace will not and cannot be the act of power of a single state—even if it is the strongest, wealthiest, and most idealistically peaceful state in the world."[9] Like other Europeans, Blum could not refrain from lecturing the United States. Not a neutralist, he believed in the spring of 1947 that reconciliation was possible; he hoped not to win but to end the Cold War.

When the Marshall Plan was announced, Blum was pleased that it was not projected as a political weapon in the Cold War. That the Plan called for an effort at European economic organization and unification by the European nations themselves, and that it was open to the Soviet satellite states as well, satisfied him still further of its intent. For a time he even believed that the Soviets would cooperate.[1] But the French Communists, echoing the opposition of the Soviets, were soon denouncing the Plan as a weapon of American imperialism and heaping opprobrium on supporters of the Plan: to the "social-traitor" and "social-fascist" of earlier years was now added the epithet "social-American."

[6] See his comments, August 28, November 25–26, 1945, *Oeuvre*, VI, 175–9.

[7] Editorial, *Le Populaire*, March 19, 1947, *Oeuvre*, VI, 374–5.

[8] Editorial, *Le Populaire*, April 13, 1947, *Oeuvre*, VI, 389–91; also comments on Greece, *Le Populaire*, July 12, 25, 27–28, 1947, ibid., p. 391.

[9] Editorial, *Le Populaire*, April 13, 1947, *Oeuvre*, VI, 391.

[1] See editorials in *Le Populaire*, including those critical of Acheson's original pronouncements, in May, June, and July 1947, *Oeuvre*, VII, 12–39.

The rift between the Soviets and the Western bloc in 1947 generated serious domestic repercussions which Blum watched with anxiety.[2] In January 1947, Paul Ramadier, one of the Socialist reformist leaders, had formed a coalition cabinet which included the Communists. That spring, the Communists refused to cooperate with the Ramadier cabinet in which they were serving. There were differences over Indochina and other matters, but what finally brought the issue to a head was the change in the Communist line on labor. Since the Liberation the Communists had been supporting the "battle of production," calling for austerity and sacrifices on the part of labor, and generally cooperating with the price-and-wage-holding policy although at times critical of the efforts to block wage increases. In the last week of April, when a serious strike broke out in the nationalized Renault automobile plant, the Communist-controlled C.G.T. at first denounced the work stoppage as a wildcat strike and the work of extremists but then suddenly embraced the cause of the strikers. On April 30, the Communist ministers in the cabinet publicly denounced the deflation experiment and the government's labor policy. On May 2, the Communist Deputies, and the ministers as well, voted against the govenment on a vote of confidence.

The Socialists were in a quandary, with Guy Mollet and Ramadier in open disagreement. Mollet insisted that the Socialists must not remain in office unless the Communists continued to assume their share of responsibility for the unpopular policies that had to be carried out. Ramadier and Blum countered that the party could not open up a political crisis at this time. By a narrow margin, the party supported Ramadier, who remained in office but dismissed the Communist ministers in his cabinet. Blum defended the party's position as proof of its sense of national responsibility in so formidable a crisis. He rejected as less important the disadvantages of the new situation.[3] By May 1947, for the first time since the Liberation, the Communists were no longer in the government, nor would they enter any future cabinet of the Fourth Republic. The Communists had unloaded on the Socialists responsibility for colonial and economic policies that were increasingly unpopular. To safeguard political stability and republican institutions, some of the Socialists, with Blum's backing, willingly assumed the burden.

In the summer and fall of 1947 tension mounted. With the foreign

[2] See editorials, *Le Populaire*, March 21–24, 1947, *Oeuvre*, VI, 395–8.
[3] *Le Populaire*, May 8, 1947, *Oeuvre*, VI, 410–11.

ministers of the wartime Allies at an impasse and the world solidifying into two hostile blocs, the Communists embarked on a program of systematic opposition, attacking the Marshall Plan, criticizing the government's food distribution program, embracing labor grievances, utilizing their powerful hold on the C.G.T. to launch new strikes, and accusing the Socialist government of strikebreaking. Blum saw the Communists as ready to "deny and destroy" their entire contribution to political life since the Liberation.[4]

And suddenly a second threat appeared. At the very time that the Communist opposition grew, an attack from the Gaullist quarter was launched. From March 1947 on, General de Gaulle made a series of speeches denouncing the weak institutions of the Fourth Republic, urging the nation to end its "sterile games," and calling for a "rally of the French people." By April a new Gaullist organization, the R.P.F. (Rassemblement du Peuple Français), was formally founded and was soon growing rapidly.

De Gaulle's speeches, and, even more, the call for organization and action, filled Blum with a deep foreboding that a crisis of the republican regime was at hand. His earlier apprehension was intensified. He charged de Gaulle with flouting the constitution despite his professions of allegiance to legal procedures and republican institutions. In editorial after editorial he now placed Gaullism squarely in the lineage of the classical threats to the republic. Like the Boulangist movement, Gaullism represented a "syndicate of the discontented," calling for dissolution of Parliament and constitutional revision but with no true doctrine or program. The nation was asked to rally around a great man, but "the greatness of men is always as ephemeral as they are." He described the R.P.F. as "embracing all reactionary and ex-fascist elements preparing for personal power." He called on de Gaulle to carry his views to "their logical conclusion" and admit that his scorn for political parties and parliamentary democracy separated him ineluctably from the republic.[5]

Blum never could see that de Gaulle in his way believed in the republic too, although not in the parliamentary institutions of the Third, which had led to the disaster of 1940, nor those of the Fourth, which threatened fresh disaster. The truth was that Blum's whole life

---

[4] *Le Populaire*, June 5, 1947, *Oeuvre*, VII, 53; and November 5, 6, 8, 1947, ibid., pp. 117–23.

[5] See his comments in *Le Populaire* in April and May 1947 and later that same year: *Oeuvre*, VI, 399–406, VII, 87–9, 123–4, 136–8.

was tied up with the parliamentary sovereignty and the political parties that de Gaulle denounced as "sterile games." Given the traditions of France, Blum saw in de Gaulle only the latest in a long line of threats to the republic. And in 1947 the memory of dictators seizing power over the corpses of old-fashioned political parties and parliamentary institutions was still vivid.

The crisis of 1947 soon came to a head. The Gaullist R.P.F. made an impressive showing in the municipal elections in the fall. Many M.R.P. and Radical Deputies, now in the Gaullist camp, no longer supported the Ramadier Socialist coalition government. In November, when strikes broke out in the coal mines, Jules Moch, the Socialist Minister of Interior, used the army to suppress them. In the wake of the strikes, on November 20, the Ramadier government fell.

Blum and Auriol feared the opening of a great crisis in which the very life of the republic would be at stake, threatened by the Communists on the Left and the Gaullists on the Right. Auriol again turned to Blum, who agreed to seek the support of the National Assembly for a "Third Force" government, a rallying of all republican forces against the "double threat" and designed to demonstrate what a progressive coalition could accomplish. On November 21, 1947, Blum made his last speech in the Palais Bourbon. In stirring tones, he described the double threat to domestic peace, parliamentary government, and civil liberties—from the Communists, who had "openly declared war" on French democracy, and from the Gaullists, who sought to "rob the country's representative assembly of its fundamental rights." On the economic front, he appealed for sympathy and firmness in dealing with the great labor conflicts, for distinguishing between "aggression and destruction against the institutions and doctrines of the republic" and "the legitimate and natural product of anxiety and suffering." On colonial matters he pledged to act "by opposing at the very same time nationalist fanaticism and colonial exploitation." He entreated the Deputies to rally to the republic—"the republic which for us is identified with *la patrie*."[6]

But the situation demanded more than eloquence and a sounding of the alarm to rally the absolute majority required for investiture. The hostility of the Communists and of the confirmed Gaullists was a certainty. But many liberal republicans, especially among the Radicals, were not convinced that Gaullism was as serious a threat as communism;

[6] Statement read to National Assembly, November 21, 1947, *Oeuvre*, VII, 125–8.

many believed that de Gaulle intended not to subvert republican institutions but to strengthen them; they believed Blum's passion worthy of a nobler cause than denunciation of de Gaulle. There is no doubt that had he been a little more flexible he might have enlisted the support of some Radicals. But Blum's later explanation was that he had to keep himself uncontaminated. "We could not, thinking of the working class which we wish to free from the grip of the Communists, yield to any appearance of complicity, even tacit, with the Gaullist party."[7] Receiving 300 of the 309 votes required, he failed of investiture. The effort of November 1947, like the effort to rally support for a national unity cabinet in March 1938, was a brilliant failure. But it would be difficult to forget his moving peroration in the Assembly that autumn day: "The phrase which has been haunting me for some hours is the sublime phrase of Vergniaud: 'Perish our memory and let the republic be saved!' "[8] It was his valedictory in the Palais Bourbon; no better summary of his entire career could be written.

After November 1947, Blum was once again the elder statesman and journalist watching over and commenting on the country's affairs, and lending counsel and guidance to the party, which still listened respectfully even if it did not always heed his advice. He returned only for a brief moment to active political affairs when in July 1948, still championing the cause of the Third Force, he agreed to help strengthen the coalition cabinet of Radicals, Socialists, and M.R.P. formed by André Marie. He served as Vice-Premier in the inconsequential cabinet which lasted only a month.[9] Robert Schuman, André Marie, Henri Queuille, Georges Bidault—cabinet followed cabinet in the years 1947 to 1950 and filled even Blum with disillusionment. The Third Force, originally conceived of as a republican progressive coalition, perhaps paving the way for the creation of a great labor party, determined to demonstrate what republican institutions could accomplish, had turned into a lifeless and apathetic phenomenon. Yet circumstances made it impossible for the Socialists to abandon these cabinets for fear of creating a political vacuum from which the enemies of the republic could still profit.

[7] Statement to national council, *Le Populaire*, December 17, 1947.
[8] *Oeuvre*, VII, 128.
[9] See his comments, *Le Populaire*, September 7, November 3, 4, 5, 1948, *Oeuvre*, VII, 228–30, 239–44.

For the double threat to the republic continued. The reconstruction of the Cominform had crystallized the opposition of the Communists. Cold War on the international front led to "cold insurrection" on the domestic front. Blum denounced the violent strikes in the coal mines in the fall of 1948 as "strikes against the nation." The workers were being led "by fools or criminals in pernicious and senseless enterprises." He excoriated "the fanatical caste which had made itself master of the trade-union organization in France, which had openly placed its authority in the political interests of a foreign state."[1] As to the Gaullists, he saw their support as coming increasingly from the Right and charged them with abandoning all vestiges of a Christian-Democratic reform spirit. "Gaullism is nothing more," he wrote in November 1948, "than a reincarnation of the old Right, the historic Right, the classical Right."[2] By 1950 he was referring to de Gaulle as "the Pretender."[3]

The burden of Blum's labors in these last years of his life was to prevent political instability at almost any cost. Although the Third Force coalition of Socialists, M.R.P., and Radicals was an uneasy and uninspiring alliance, too much was at stake to allow it to founder. The Socialists alone could preserve the coalition even though participation in the cabinet meant supporting policies of which they did not approve —in church-state relations, budgetary economies, the war in Indochina, the repression of labor unrest, the creeping conservatism in economic matters. As Blum himself recognized, it was ironical that he who had labored in the years from 1924 to 1936 to keep the party from participating in the cabinet because of the dangers to its own program now championed continued participation. Always, in each crisis, the defense of republican institutions and responsibility to the nation as a whole were the compelling motives. The more faithfully the Socialists participated in each cabinet, the more their image as a militant party dwindled and the more restive and disgruntled grew the rank and file.

When the Queuille cabinet fell at the end of October 1949, Blum took cognizance of the strong pressure in the party to end Socialist participation in the government and took the occasion to look back on the party's recent experiences. He admitted that his own old injunctions against the disadvantages of Socialist association with the government

[1] *Le Populaire*, October 28, 1948, *Oeuvre*, VII, 234–6; for editorial welcoming the non-Communist *Force Ouvrière*, *Le Populaire*, December 26, 1947.

[2] *Le Populaire*, November 11, 1948, *Oeuvre*, VII, 247.

[3] *Le Populaire*, January 19, 1950.

had been ignored in the years since the Liberation. The party had first participated in the provisional cabinets of de Gaulle; then had directed the cabinet under Félix Gouin, under Blum himself, and under Ramadier; and finally had taken part in all Third Force coalition cabinets since November 1947. Yet what other policy was possible? In a revealing editorial, he described the dilemma:

> At the beginning, it was the extension on the governmental plane of the "sacred union" and the general fraternalism of the Resistance. From 1947 on, it was a response to the powerful conviction that democratic liberties . . . were placed in jeopardy on two fronts, by Stalinism and by Caesarism, and that the Socialist party had to subordinate everything to the imperative duty to defend them. . . . Thus we passed from government to government, in theory, free each time to make our decision but, in fact, compelled by the gravity of circumstances and dangers, prisoners of our duty, which was quite simply our republican duty.[4]

Here was the epitaph of Blum as a Socialist leader—and of French socialism. The party had become the "prisoner of its republican duty." To prevent the political instability which could lead to the destruction of free institutions, it had identified itself with unpopular policies and had subjected itself to a continued attrition of membership and voting strength. Blum had taught it to defend republican liberties as the precondition for democratic socialism. "One does not save socialism without the republic," he had said.[5] But what would be left of socialism to save? asked his critics.

In February 1950 the Socialists for the first time removed themselves from the cabinet when the Bidault government refused to grant a bonus to low-paid government workers. Blum reluctantly accepted the party's decision. In the last months of his life, his efforts were directed toward restraining the party from following a policy of "systematic opposition," warning the younger, more militant leaders against the misleading analogy of two-party Anglo-Saxon countries. He urged the party to remain faithful to the parliamentary majority, to exercise pressure but to help the government to avoid difficulties.[6] He was convinced that the danger to the republic was not over.

---

[4] *Le Populaire*, November 5–6, 1949, and February 11–12, 1950, *Oeuvre*, VII, 261, 267.

[5] Speech, August 8, 1948, *Le Populaire*, August 10, 1948.

[6] See his editorials, *Le Populaire*, February 10–16, 1950, *Oeuvre*, VII, 265–76.

END OF THE APOSTOLATE

As for me, I am old, and I shall not reach the Promised Land. I shall not see the perfect union of peoples in justice and peace . . . but what marks the nobility of man is to foresee, to hope, to anticipate, to labor at a work which he will not gaze on completed and from which he will not himself profit.[1]

I N THE FIRST HALF of 1949 Blum's activities, and even his writing, were interrupted by severe illness, which was in part the product of his wartime confinement; surgery and a long convalescence were necessary, incapacitating him for a full six months. In June 1949 he resumed his column in *Le Populaire*. "Illness teaches serenity, like prison or old age; and I have not missed any of these schools," he observed.[2]

Still buoyed by an unquenchable optimism, he predicted that the spiritual defeatism in his own party would pass. His proud allegiance to democratic socialism was indestructible; he had "complete faith in the cause that I have been serving ever since I possessed a man's reasoning power." "My dominating conviction . . . ," he wrote, "is that the Socialist position is being consolidated throughout the entire world, that the march toward socialism is being accentuated and accelerated before our eyes in France as in the rest of the world." The true conflict of the postwar years was not the power struggle between the Western and Soviet blocs, nor between capitalism and communism, but the struggle between socialism and communism: between "democratic socialism and a false dictatorial pseudo-socialism." Realistic enough **to**

[1] Speech in New York, April 12, 1946, *Oeuvre*, VI, 200.
[2] *Le Populaire*, June 11–12, 1949.

be aware of the waning strength of the Socialist party in his own country and of democratic socialism in Europe as a whole, he found it necessary to explain that socialism was making its gains "outside itself" —in the free trade unions, in Christian socialism, among democratic liberals, in the very idea of the welfare state.[3] If not democratic socialism, at least welfare democracy was triumphant. The old capitalism was dying; political democracy was broadening its social and economic frontiers.

The cause of internationalism was ascendant too. The East-West power conflict he confidently expected to diminish "like so many conflicts of the same order in the past." He persistently championed the cause of European political and economic unity—"to create Europe while thinking of the world"[4]—and along with Édouard Herriot and Paul Reynaud, served on the permanent committee for the study and promotion of European federation. The hesitancy and indecision of the British Labour party in supporting European unity disturbed him, and he was disappointed also with the first session of the Council of Europe at Strasbourg in August 1949.[5] He did not live to see the far more concrete results of European economic cooperation in the decade that followed.

Blum also played an active role in the launching of UNESCO, heading the French delegation at its first organizational meeting in London in November 1945.[6] Elected president of the UNESCO Assembly in August 1946, he helped define its goals of cultural and intellectual cooperation.[7] Here in many ways was an ideal channel for his talents. Jaime Torres-Bodet, the Mexican poet and general secretary of the organization, remarked of Blum that the Socialist leader was not "simply a connoisseur of belles-lettres" but a statesman determined to "serve all men by opening up before them the perspectives of knowledge and beauty at the same time as those of peace and justice."[8] In the final years of his life it was fitting for it to be recalled that Blum was a humanist who had strayed into politics.

[3] *Le Populaire*, June 11–12, 13, 14, 1949. On the "people's democracies," see also speech at Stresa, April 9, 1948, *Oeuvre*, VII, 170–90.

[4] *Le Populaire*, June 13, 1949; and see also *Le Populaire*, August 10, 1949, *Oeuvre*, VII, 281–2.

[5] *Le Populaire*, August 26, 1949, *Oeuvre*, VII, 285–7.

[6] See speech, November 1, 1945, *Le Populaire*, November 2, 1945.

[7] See speech, August 5, 1946, *Le Populaire*, August 6, 1946.

[8] Remarks at a public meeting of the Société des Amis de Léon Blum, December 11, 1951, typescript, pp. 44–5. See also remarks of Mrs. Roosevelt at the same meeting, typescript, pp. 57–62.

Epilogue: The Return

On the most important problem of postwar Europe, the future of Germany, Blum was not entirely satisfied with the trend of events, especially with the return of the Ruhr to private enterprise. Yet he believed that European political and economic unification, with British participation, would allay anxieties about the Germany of the future. "We must create Europe," he wrote. "We must do it with Germany and not *for* her. We must do it with Great Britain and not *against* her."[9] As to Germany, he preferred to forget the past: "Nothing fruitful, nothing lasting is built on hatred and enslavement." He rejected the idea of collective guilt and collective punishment and urged that his fellow Jews especially understand and accept this.[1]

In his last years he came to regard Zionism with more active sympathy than ever before. Although never actively identified with the Zionist cause, he had supported the Balfour declaration in the First World War and, at the time of the Paris Peace Conference, had encouraged his friend Philippe Berthelot to press for a British mandate over Palestine.[2] In 1929, along with such other European Jewish notables as Albert Einstein, he had been invited as one of three French delegates to attend a meeting at Zurich which inaugurated the activities of the Jewish Agency. In a brief speech at the time he expressed his sympathy and moral support for Zionist objectives.[3] Yet he always considered himself an assimilated French Jew attached to French soil, French problems, and French destinies—"a French Jew, of a long line of French ancestors, speaking only the language of his country, nurtured predominantly on its culture."[4]

In the 1920's, the antisemitism of the Dreyfus case had seemed far in the past. It was the age of Adolf Hitler that created in Blum a renewed consciousness of his birth and background. "One has often asked," he wrote in 1950, "whether there is a Jewish race. The scholars reply no. But Hitler gave an incontestable definition. The Jewish race includes the women, the children, the men whom Hitler had condemned to total

[9] *Le Populaire*, November 19–20, 1949, *Oeuvre*, VII, 302; and editorials, November 30, December 1, 1949, ibid., 303–7.

[1] *Le Populaire*, July 6–7, 1947, *Oeuvre*, VII, 35; and two articles in the *New York Jewish Daily Forward*, October 16, December 11, 1949, reprinted in the original French in *Oeuvre*, VII, 308–15.

[2] See Blumel: *Léon Blum: juif et sioniste*, p. 11; and Blum's message to a banquet in honor of Chaim Weizmann, February 1, 1950, *Oeuvre*, VII, 441–2.

[3] Blumel: *Léon Blum*, pp. 11–12; for summaries of the sessions and speeches, see *L'Univers Israelite*, August 1929, pp. 562–4, 595–6.

[4] Message of February 1, 1950, *Oeuvre*, VII, 442.

extermination."[5] In a sense this was Sartre's definition too: "The Jew is a man whom other men consider to be a Jew." Though accorded the favored treatment of a political dignitary, Blum knew how close he, too, had come to death at the hands of the Nazis.

After the war, finding it inconceivable that the civilized world would not make every effort to assist those who had survived the extermination centers, he protested the closing of the doors to Palestine. What grieved him most was the identification of Ernest Bevin and the British Labour party with this policy; and in August 1947, he added his voice to those who protested the cruel drama of the *Exodus*.[6] (The question of Palestine was one of the few issues that ever separated him from the British Labour party—and Britain. Among his most cherished honors was the honorary degree awarded him by Oxford in June 1948.) As to his own position on Zionism, he made clear that he sought a haven for the pitiful remnants of Hitler's victims, not for all Jews: "In the free democracies of Europe and the world, those who have acquired a country and who cherish it do not seek any other."[7] Once the new independent state of Israel was established, Blum lent it his full support. It would assure, he wrote, "a fatherland of dignity, equality and freedom for all Jews who have not had, like myself, the good fortune to find one in their native country."[8] His memory in Israel was perpetuated in the name of the communal village, Kfar Blum, dedicated to him in 1943 when he was still a prisoner in a German concentration camp.[9]

The end came in the last days of March 1950. On March 27, he wrote a moving obituary for Harold Laski, who had just died. The British Socialist had pursued his "spiritual apostolate in all ways, through his masterful teaching, public speeches, books, articles, persuasion, and personal influence . . . as an active fighter as well as a scholar and thinker."[1] The words might have been written of Blum himself.

On March 29 appeared his last editorial, a protest against the inadequate compensation of French labor in comparison to the wages in

[5] Message to French Zionist organization, cited by Blumel: *Léon Blum*, p. 5.
[6] See editorials, *Le Populaire*, August and September 1947, *Oeuvre*, VII, 385–92.
[7] *Le Populaire*, September 1, 1947, *Oeuvre*, VII, 392.
[8] Message of February 1, 1950, *Oeuvre*, VII, 442.
[9] In 1957 a square in Paris was named for him: Place Léon Blum.
[1] *Le Populaire*, March 27, 1950.

other capitalist countries, and an explanation of the reasons. It was his "belief and hope" that the country would understand and act on the problem of excessive production costs and inefficient operations. "*Je l'espère et je le crois. Je le crois parce que je l'espère.*"[2] His last editorial, like so many others over the years, was a blend, in the customary Blum style, of emotional protest, rational analysis, and optimism.

That evening he attended a party to celebrate the 100,000th subscription to the Sunday edition of *Le Populaire*, which was enjoying a far greater success than the daily edition. The following afternoon, on March 30, at about three-thirty, ten days before his seventy-eighth birthday, while he was at home writing, he suffered a heart attack and died in a few hours. Serenity was his companion even at the end. "It is nothing, do not be afraid for me," were his last words to his wife.[3]

When the news reached the Palais Bourbon, Édouard Herriot adjourned the National Assembly and in a moving eulogy spoke of the "loss to France, to the republic, and, I can well say without exaggeration, to all thinking humanity." Clement Attlee said of Blum: "He was the most remarkable Socialist of his generation and an admirable leader of free men." An Israeli political leader described him as "a perfect balance between the purest elements in French humanism and the noblest elements in the prophets of Israel."[4] On Sunday, April 2, national funeral services were held in the Place de la Concorde; thousands stood with bared heads in an icy-cold rain. His old comrade in arms, Vincent Auriol, President of the Republic, paid homage to his friend's selflessness and devotion.[5] A special radio broadcast transmitted the tributes of those who had known and worked with him in public life. Some spoke of the literary years before 1914, some remembered the Popular Front and the 1930's, some recalled his wartime imprisonment and trial at Riom. The announcer read from the concluding passage of *À l'échelle humaine*:

> The human race has created knowledge, science, and art; why should it be powerless to create justice, fraternity, and peace? It has given birth to a Plato and a Homer, a Shakespeare and a Hugo, a Michelangelo and a Beethoven, a Pascal and a Newton, human heroes whose genius consisted in making contact with the essential

[2] *Le Populaire*, March 29, 1950, *Oeuvre*, VII, 374–6.

[3] Jeanne-Léon Blum: *Léon Blum, 9 avril 1872–30 mars 1950*, p. 56.

[4] For these and other testimonials, *Le Populaire*, March 31, 1950; also the French (and world) press on this and subsequent days.

[5] *Le Populaire*, April 3, 1950.

verities, with the central reality of the universe. Why will the same human race not produce leaders capable of taking it toward the forms of collective life that most closely approach the laws and harmony of the universe? Social systems surely have their laws of attraction and gravity just as the stellar systems. Man does not have two different souls: one to sing and to discover, the other to act; one to sense beauty and understand truth, the other to sense fraternity and understand justice. Whoever envisages this prospect finds himself inspired by an invincible hope. Let man contemplate his goal, let him trust his destiny, let him not fear to use his strength. When a man grows troubled and discouraged, he has only to think of humanity.[6]

When Blum died, an apostle passed—an apostle of social justice, fraternity, and peace, a champion of a humanist religion, dedicated to the mission of improving the quality of the human condition. Even his socialism was not of a sectarian kind; it was rather a universal faith, an ethical creed like the great religions of mankind or the enduring humanistic ideals of thinkers over the ages. He was in the direct line of the eighteenth-century *philosophes*, firmly convinced that the natural laws of human society could be discovered by the genius of mankind just as the natural laws of the universe could be uncovered, that the Heavenly City could be built on this earth.

If he believed in "the Revolution," he meant by it continued progress toward a more equitable society—"the Revolution" which in European terms has been defined as "the extension of the liberal and humanist tradition."[7] Above all, he believed in the democratic republic, by which he meant civil liberties, democratically elected assemblies, and the right to compete in the marketplace of ideas with programs of reform. He subordinated everything, even his socialism, to the defense of his democratic political ideal—the republic. If it can be said that he consumed the prestige and strength of his party and its socialist program in that cause, that after 1934 the republic had become an end in itself, it must not be forgotten that he was the champion of democratic socialism in an age when democracy was threatened from many quarters. If he did not abjure doctrines of class action and Marxism—merely tempering them with his own humanist and humanitarian socialism—it must also

---

[6] *Le Populaire*, April 9, 1950; for the passage, *Oeuvre*, V. 495.
[7] Raymond Aron: *Le Grand Schisme* (Paris, 1948), p. 110.

be said that in the age of the Bolshevik Revolution he tried to prevent a powerful rival from annexing the revolutionary tradition of France.

He made no profound theoretical contributions to political philosophy or to socialist thought, although his writings, especially his wartime essay *À l'échelle humaine*, are filled with graceful and stirring expositions of the democratic socialist credo. His cardinal tenet was the interdependence of "political" and "social" democracy:

> Political democracy and social democracy are, at least in France, inseparable terms. Political democracy will not be viable if it does not develop into social democracy; social democracy would not be real or stable if not founded on political democracy. The French people will not wish to sacrifice either the great human ideals defined in '89 or the great "imperatives" which have emerged from material reality; it will wish to combine economic order and social equality with political, civil, and personal liberty.[8]

His theoretical writings were devoted primarily to the analysis of "revolution." There was a difference, he repeatedly noted, between a mere shift in political power, as had occurred frequently in nineteenth-century France, and a social revolution involving the transformation of society, especially its economic base. But there was a difference also between the mere economic transformation of society, as had happened in twentieth-century Russia, and a socialist transformation of society in which the essential goal of socialism would be preserved—the enhanced worth and dignity of the individual human being. Neither Soviet communism nor the postwar "people's democracies" satisfied that criterion. The "revolution" was yet to come. It would come ultimately without "forcing," without barricades or bloodshed, the result of the cumulative effect of imperceptible changes when conditions were fully ripe for it. Only at such a time would heroic actions succeed in effecting a "true" revolution. Blum belonged squarely in the camp of reformism despite his protestations otherwise. He helped "prepare the revolution," but could never make one.

He would best be remembered for his distinction between the "exercise of power" and the revolutionary "conquest of power." By the "exercise of power" he meant the agreement by a Socialist party to hold office within the constitutional, legal, and economic framework of existing society, never to take advantage of a constitutionally limited exercise of power to push forward to its own goals, never to commit the "swindle"

[8] *À l'échelle humaine, Oeuvre,* V, 472.

of transforming a tenure of office into an effort to introduce socialism. Because he understood the difficulties involved when a Socialist party agreed to act as manager of a society to which it was fundamentally opposed, he hedged with subtle reservations the various circumstances in which the party might fill that role. Eventually he taught the party to accept the responsibilities of political life in a parliamentary democracy and taught it only too well, asking it to make repeated sacrifices in the defense of that democracy. His legalism, his fidelity to the constitutional system, his insistence that one does not transform an "exercise of power" into a "conquest of power," were both his strength and his weakness.

In his own party he led by persuasion, not by imposition of his views. He sought always to serve as conciliator—to draft the compromise resolution, to calculate, as a mathematician or physicist might, the resultant of contending forces. Yet there were times when he was in a minority, even when he was almost alone, as in the case of Spain or rearmament in the late 1930's. On those occasions he steadfastly maintained his position and sought to win the party to his views.

In becoming the first Socialist Premier of France, Blum accomplished the unfulfilled dream which many had held for Jaurès. To be sure, the record of the Popular Front government of 1936–7 which he headed was a mixed one. It did not unite the country, but divided it. Blum himself became a household word of opprobrium for the Right. The high promise and subsequent disillusionment helped to create a feeling of apathy and disenchantment from which communism and Vichy alone profited. His government did not help rebuild the obsolescent economic structure of the country, but placed additional burdens on an inefficient economy. Labor reforms were introduced at a time when the Nazi menace made rearmament imperative. Yet these reforms were long overdue in France, and they staved off possible civil war and bloodshed at a critical time. Moreover, Blum's reforms laid the foundation for a new conception of the welfare republic in which the workers would not be alien sons: the spirit of the Resistance, the nationalization measures of the Liberation, and the mixed economy of the Fourth and Fifth Republics were tribute to the reforms of the Popular Front.

The most serious miscalculation of his government was the desertion of the Spanish Republic out of the misconceived notion that totalitarian dictatorships would honor agreements they had signed and that peace and the Spanish Republic could both be saved. But to have acted resolutely in that crisis would have meant flouting the will of the British,

France's only major ally at the time, overruling the opposition of the more conservative members of the Popular Front, and outraging the sensibilities of the political Right to the point of possible civil war. A bolder leader might have ignored these risks as well as the sensitivities of his allies and his domestic enemies; Blum could not. Perhaps, too, they were risks that were more difficult for the first Socialist (and Jewish) Premier of France to take. On the other hand, it cannot be forgotten that Blum, despite his lifelong antimilitarism and pacifist-mindedness, accepted, against the opposition of many in his party and the long Socialist tradition, the need for rearmament in the age of fascist aggression and inaugurated the country's first serious, though hopelessly belated, effort at rearmament. That the program came too late and that the country's military leaders were unprepared for the demands of twentieth-century warfare could not be blamed on him.

His personal courage cannot be questioned. He displayed it in leading the minority rear-guard action against the Communists at the congress of Tours in 1920. He remained unruffled when riots raged outside the Chamber in February 1934. He endured physical assault by fascist ruffians in the streets of Paris in February 1936. He appeared at the fateful July 1940 meeting in Vichy when Laval was using the Popular Front as the sacrificial goat for the defeat and capitulation and was whipping up a lynch spirit against its leaders. He faced up to his Vichy accusers at Riom and turned the tables against the prosecutors. He did not falter in the darkest moments of incarceration in his Vichy and German prisons. The intellectual could reveal an indomitable will and an iron courage. His character, like his mind, was of a fine, tempered steel.

He was an intensely moral man, and he insisted upon a politics of morality. Free from vulgar ambition, opposed to the abuse of power, faithful to his pledges and to his political allies, he could not conceive of some kind of revolutionary morality that dialectically can turn present evil into future good. For this he has been censured in some quarters. It is the chief indictment of Colette Audry's book-length essay which bears the imprimatur of Jean-Paul Sartre and is written from the point of view of a "Left revolutionary" socialist. Here Blum is attacked for perpetually seeking to reinforce in every act the image which he wished to project of himself as a "just man." He is depicted as unable to allow himself the necessary compromises of the true revolutionary leader, fearful that he might thereby lose the universal esteem to which he aspired. In the end he saved his own soul but deserted "the Revolution."[9] The thesis is provocative but not completely satisfying. Blum, without doubt, refrained at certain crucial moments from bold decisions as he eternally weighed alternatives and wrestled with his conscience. He searched himself at every stage, more like Hamlet than Lenin, wondering whether he was equal to the task ahead. There is little question also that he lacked political flexibility, the ability to interpret political obligations elastically, the skill to find varied means to serve the cause he led. He found it difficult, and in later years impossible, to separate the welfare of the party from the welfare of the republic. In all of this lay his weakness as a revolutionary leader, but it is unfair to portray him as seeking fulfillment of his image as a "just man." There is a deeper explanation. Blum was unwilling to isolate the cause he served from the mainstream of civilized progress, to isolate his party from the cause of republican democracy, to isolate "the Revolution" from considerations of human welfare. He refused to believe that there was a "revolutionary morality," that dishonorable means could lead to noble ends. If he was a just man, it was because he could not conceive that a just world could ever be created by any but just men. His record, therefore, was one of complete personal integrity and mixed political success, his most fitting epitaph the words of Machiavelli: "A man who wishes to make a profession of goodness in everything must necessarily come to grief among so many who are not good."[1] In the age of Hitler and lesser tyrants Blum's integrity shone like a beacon, yet he lacked the ruthlessness to cope with ruthless men.

He always considered himself an amateur in politics. Poet, writer, literary critic, jurist, humanist, it was chance that pushed him into political life in his mature years, and then into national leadership. "The leadership of a great modern nation demands so many qualities and talents," he wrote a few months before he died, "so many kinds of knowledge and skill, so much reasoning power and so much imagination, so much caution and so much energy, that no one would dare claim himself equal to such a task and one would require much presumption to assume it without a certain anxiety about oneself."[2] He possessed to an excess the soul searching and self-consciousness of the intellectual in politics. His diffidence and humility in the face of power, despite his unassailable courage and strength of conviction, were not the strongest equipment for statesmanship.

[9] Audry: *Léon Blum*, p. 193.
[1] *The Prince*, Ch. XV.
[2] *Le Populaire*, October 13, 1949, *Oeuvre*, VII, 259.

Thus Blum had his share of weaknesses and shortcomings as a political leader. His unbounded optimism, his passion for integrity, his faith in human beings, his desire for wide esteem, his eagerness to serve as conciliator, his sentimental attachment to the effectiveness of an enlightened public opinion, were not the best assets for leadership in any age; in his age, they were fatal flaws. He could not be lion and fox; he could be only a human being placing his high intellectual, humane, and moral qualities in the service of his ideals, his party, his country, and humanity.

APPENDIX I

Glossary

Action Française: Nationalist, Rightist organization in France founded by Charles Maurras in 1905.

Bataille Socialiste: Pro-communist faction of the French Socialist party in the interwar years led by Jean Zyromski.

bloc national: Coalition of Right and Center parties victorious in the November 1919 elections and dominant in the Chamber of Deputies, 1919–24.

cartel des gauches: Coalition of Left parties (Radical Socialists and Socialists) victorious in the elections of May 1924.

chef de cabinet: Personal administrative assistant of a Premier or a cabinet minister.

C.F.T.C. (Confédération Française des Travailleurs Chrétiens): Confederation of French Catholic trade unions, founded in 1919.

C.G.P.F. (Confédération Générale de la Production Française; after 1936, Confédération Générale du Patronat Français): Confederation of French employers' associations.

C.G.T. (Confédération Générale du Travail, General Confederation of Labor): Confederation of French labor unions; after the First World War, Communist unions seceded but rejoined in 1936; after the Second World War, became Communist-dominated.

C.G.T.U. (Confédération Générale du Travail Unitaire, General Confederation of Unified Labor): Designation for the Communist wing of the French labor movement in the interwar years.

commission administrative permanente: Executive committee of the Socialist party in the interwar years, consisting of 20 to 30 members; elected at the annual party congress on a proportional representation basis to represent various "tendencies" in the party.

Conseil d'État (Council of State): The highest appellate court of administrative law in France with jurisdiction over disputes involving individual citizens and the state; possesses also advisory functions in law-making processes.

conseil national (national council): Meeting of French Socialist party delegates convened periodically to give direction to the party between annual or special congresses.

Croix de Feu: Originally a combat veterans' organization; in the 1930's the best known of the paramilitary antiparliamentary "leagues."

C.S.A. (Comité de l'Action Socialiste, Socialist Action Committee): Underground Socialist organization associated with the Resistance movement during the Second World War.

École Normale Supérieure: Distinguished French institution of higher learning which prepared students for university teaching and research careers; many *normaliens*, as its students were known, became prominent in French republican politics.

Force Ouvrière: Non-communist branch of the French labor movement formed in 1948 after secession from the Communist-dominated C.G.T.

Front Populaire (Popular Front): Term popularly used for the coalition of Left parties and organizations formed on July 14, 1935; more accurately, the *Rassemblement Populaire.*

Gauche Révolutionnaire (Revolutionary Left): Extremist, revolutionist-minded faction of the French Socialist party in the 1930's led by Marceau Pivert; often close to Leon Trotsky in its outlook; expelled from the party in 1938.

L'Humanité: Newspaper founded in 1904 by Jean Jaurès; after the Communist secession of December 1920, it became the official organ of the French Communist party.

Le Populaire de Paris: Official French Socialist daily newspaper; Blum served for many years as its political director.

Matignon agreement: Agreement signed by representatives of French employer and labor organizations on June 8, 1936, guaranteeing collective bargaining and other rights of labor.

militants: French term for "rank and file" of labor unions and of working-class party organizations.

M.R.P. (Mouvement Républicain Populaire): Progressive Catholic party that played a prominent political role in the early years of the Fourth Republic.

neo-Guesdist: Term used to designate a disciple of the Socialist leader Jules Guesde, who in the pre-1914 Socialist party had advocated a more orthodox Marxist position than the more flexible Jean Jaurès.

neo-Socialists: A group of Socialists who seceded from the official Socialist party in 1933 because they favored a revision of the party's doctrines and practices.

Président du Conseil des Ministres (President of the Council of Ministers): Technical designation of the Premier, or Head of the Cabinet, under the Third and Fourth Republics.

Radicaux Socialistes (Radical Socialists or Radicals): A major party of the Left in the Third Republic, led in the interwar years by Édouard Herriot, Édouard Daladier, and Camille Chautemps; neither "Socialist" nor "Radical," and generally the political spokesman for the lower middle classes.

Rassemblement Populaire: Technically correct designation for the *Front Populaire*, or Popular Front, described above.

R.P.F. (Rassemblement du Peuple Français, Rally of the French People): Founded in 1947 by followers of General de Gaulle seeking drastic revision of the constitution of the Fourth Republic.

Appendix I

S.F.I.O. (Section Française de l'Internationale Ouvrière, French Section of the Labor [Second] International): Official designation of the French Socialist party after the unity congress of April 1905.

Third Force: As used in 1947, the designation for an attempt at a coalition of Socialists, the M.R.P. and other liberal democratic groups to protect the Fourth Republic from both communism and "Gaullism."

union sacrée ("sacred union"): National unity, patriotic cabinets of the First World War, in which all parties, including the Socialists, participated.

APPENDIX II

Heads of French Cabinets during Blum's Political Career, 1914–1950

[*Party affiliations are listed for Premiers affiliated with the major Left parties (Radical Socialist, Socialist, and M.R.P.)*]

THIRD REPUBLIC

First World War Cabinets

René Viviani	June 1914–August 1914
René Viviani	August 1914–October 1915
Aristide Briand	October 1915–December 1916
Aristide Briand	December 1916–March 1917
Alexandre Ribot	March 1917–September 1917
Paul Painlevé	September 1917–November 1917
Georges Clemenceau (Rad.)	November 1917–January 1920

Chamber of 1919–1924

Alexandre Millerand	January 1920–February 1920
Alexandre Millerand	February 1920–September 1920
Georges Leygues	September 1920–January 1921
Aristide Briand	January 1921–January 1922
Raymond Poincaré	January 1922–March 1924
Raymond Poincaré	March 1924–June 1924
Frédéric François-Marsal	June 9, 1924–June 13, 1924

Chamber of 1924–1928

Édouard Herriot (Rad.)	June 1924–April 1925
Paul Painlevé	April 1925–October 1925

Paul Painlevé	October 1925–November 1925
Aristide Briand	November 1925–March 1926
Aristide Briand	March 1926–June 1926
Aristide Briand	June 1926–July 1926
Édouard Herriot (Rad.)	July 19, 1926–July 21, 1926
Raymond Poincaré	July 1926–November 1928

Chamber of 1928–1932

Raymond Poincaré	November 1928–July 1929
Aristide Briand	July 1929–October 1929
André Tardieu	November 1929–February 1930
Camille Chautemps (Rad.)	February 1930–March 1930
André Tardieu	March 1930–December 1930
Théodore Steeg	December 1930–January 1931
Pierre Laval	January 1931–June 1931
Pierre Laval	June 1931–January 1932
Pierre Laval	January 1932–February 1932
André Tardieu	February 1932–June 1932

Chamber of 1932–1936

Édouard Herriot (Rad.)	June 1932–December 1932
Joseph Paul-Boncour	December 1932–January 1933
Édouard Daladier (Rad.)	January 1933–October 1933
Albert Sarraut (Rad.)	October 1933–November 1933
Camille Chautemps (Rad.)	November 1933–January 1934
Édouard Daladier (Rad.)	January 1934–February 1934
Gaston Doumergue	February 1934–November 1934
Pierre Flandin	November 1934–May 1935
Fernand Bouisson	June 1, 1935–June 4, 1935
Pierre Laval	June 1935–January 1936
Albert Sarraut (Rad.)	January 1936–June 1936

Chamber of 1936–1940

Léon Blum (Soc.)	June 4, 1936–June 21, 1937
Camille Chautemps (Rad.)	June 22, 1937–January 14, 1938
Camille Chautemps (Rad.)	January 18, 1938–March 10, 1938
Léon Blum (Soc.)	March 13, 1938–April 8, 1938
Édouard Daladier (Rad.)	April 10, 1938–March 10, 1940
Paul Reynaud	March 21, 1940–June 16, 1940
Marshal Philippe Pétain	June 16, 1940–July 10, 1940

Appendix II

VICHY REGIME

Marshal Philippe Pétain   July 1940–June 1944

HEADS OF THE PROVISIONAL GOVERNMENT

Charles de Gaulle	September 1944–January 1946
Félix Gouin (Soc.)	January 1946–June 1946
Georges Bidault (M.R.P.)	June 1946–November 1946
Léon Blum (Soc.)	December 16, 1946–January 17, 1947

FOURTH REPUBLIC

National Assembly of 1946–1951

Paul Ramadier (Soc.)	January 1947–April 1947
Robert Schuman (M.R.P.)	May 1947–November 1947
Robert Schuman (M.R.P.)	November 1947–July 1948
André Marie (Rad.)	July 1948–August 1948
Robert Schuman (M.R.P.)	August 1948–September 1948
Henri Queuille (Rad.)	September 1948–October 1949
Georges Bidault (M.R.P.)	October 1949–June 1950

APPENDIX III

A Note on Political Parties
and Elections in the Third Republic

Political Parties

The names of parties and party groupings in the Third Republic were confusing and often misleading. The parties of the Right, in particular, bore names which were often carry-overs from earlier periods and were politically meaningless. The diagram on the following page indicates the composition of the Chamber of Deputies after the Popular Front election victory of May 1936, and gives some idea of the party groupings.

Electoral Procedures

The Chamber of Deputies: General elections for the Chamber of Deputies were held every four years by direct universal manhood suffrage. In the interwar years elections were held in 1919, 1924, 1928, 1932, and 1936. Two systems of voting were in use. Under the small-district system (*scrutin uninominal* or *scrutin d'arrondissement*), which generally prevailed, a single Deputy was elected from a small geographical district (the *arrondissement*). A candidate receiving a clear majority was elected on the first ballot; otherwise a runoff election was held the following Sunday. This small-district system was criticized for putting a premium on the candidate's personal following in his district and for discouraging the growth of stable, disciplined parties.

Under the alternative system (*scrutin de liste*), which was employed only in 1919 and 1924, party lists were prepared for a larger district, the *département*, and the parties were awarded seats on the basis of the votes they received. It was combined with a system of proportional representation; runoff elections were also held. In 1919, the parties of the Right (*bloc national*) profited from this system; in 1924, the parties of the Left (*cartel des gauches*) benefited. Abandoned after 1924, the departmental lists, with proportional representation, were resumed under the Fourth Republic for elections to the National Assembly, as the Chamber was renamed.

The Senate: The upper house under the Third Republic, the Senate, was elected indirectly through electoral colleges in which each *commune*, regardless of its population, had equal representation; the result was to give the preponderant voice to rural areas. The Senate sat for nine years, one third of the Senators standing for election every three years. Under the Fourth Republic, the Senate was replaced by the Conseil de la République, and its role was somewhat reduced.

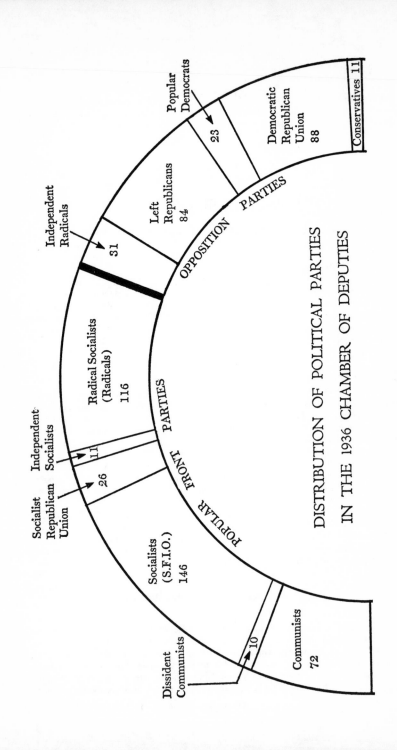

DISTRIBUTION OF POLITICAL PARTIES
IN THE 1936 CHAMBER OF DEPUTIES

Popular Democrats
23

Democratic Republican Union
88

Conservatives 11

Left Republicans
84

OPPOSITION PARTIES

Independent Radicals
31

Radical Socialists (Radicals)
116

PARTIES

Independent Socialists
11

Socialist Republican Union
26

POPULAR FRONT PARTIES

Socialists (S.F.I.O.)
146

Dissident Communists
10

Communists
72

It was elected for a six-year term, with half the terms expiring every three years; an effort was also made to curtail the electoral advantage of the rural areas.

Under the Fifth Republic the two houses are the National Assembly and the Senate; some of the electoral machinery (but not the practice of legislative predominance) has been carried over from the Third and the Fourth.

BIBLIOGRAPHY

The Bibliography is organized as follows:

Introductory Note

There are few unpublished sources available for a study of Léon Blum. His own private papers were removed from his residence in Paris during the German occupation and, despite various searches, no trace of them has been found. Those closest to Blum have assured me, however, that Blum was not ordinarily in the habit of writing long letters or of keeping a journal. Except for brief vacation trips, he was generally in Paris and in personal communication with friends and associates. My own research in Paris for unpublished materials proved fruitful in one respect. M. André Blumel, Blum's law partner, lifetime friend, and *chef de cabinet* during the two Popular Front governments, generously placed his private collection of Blum materials at my disposal, consisting of extensive newspaper clippings, some unpublished letters, particularly of the Second World War years, a large sampling of the "hate" literature of which Blum was a recipient, and miscellaneous documents. Both Robert Blum, the Socialist leader's son, and Jeanne-Léon Blum, his widow, have verified the absence of any substantial body of unpublished materials of political importance.

The Société des Amis de Léon Blum, organized shortly after Blum's death, has assembled some, but not very extensive, unpublished materials. The Société, which is in the process of preparing various analytical summaries and indexes of Blum's editorials and other articles, periodically publishes a *Bulletin*.

Blum's voluminous writings and speeches comprise the single most important source for the study of his career in all its varied aspects. For Blum's role as a political leader, the most valuable sources are: his signed daily editorials in the Socialist newspaper, *Le Populaire de Paris*, for which he wrote for some twenty years; his speeches and reports to the party's annual congresses, special congresses, and national council meetings; and his speeches in the Chamber of Deputies, in which he served from 1919 to 1940 (with a year interruption in 1928–9). His testimony as a defendant in the Vichy-sponsored Riom trial in 1942, as a witness at the Pétain trial in 1945, and as a witness before the postwar parliamentary investigating commission in 1947 are also of prime importance.

In the early 1950's Blum's friends undertook, as a memorial to him, the publication in several large volumes of his writings and speeches, beginning with his early literary years, under the general title *L'Oeuvre de Léon Blum*. Unfortunately, it did not prove feasible to publish all of his writings and speeches within the scope of the project as planned; only his major works and a large representative selection of his other writings are included. (See Robert Blum's preface to the first volume, pp. xv–xviii.) Although it is regrettable that Blum's complete collected works will not be available, the venture is a highly commendable one for which students of Blum are grateful. (See my review notice in *The American Historical Review*, LX (July 1955), 957.) The volume for the war years, 1940–1945, was especially welcome because it included unpublished correspondence and memoir materials (even if in edited form) on the events of 1940 and the Riom trial.

Of the projected volumes, all but one have appeared:

L'Oeuvre de Léon Blum (Paris, Éditions Albin Michel, 1954–   )

> Volume I, 1891–1905. *Critique littéraire, Nouvelles Conversations de Goethe avec Eckermann, Premiers Essais politiques*. Paris, 1954.

> Volume II, 1905–1914. *Du mariage, Critique, dramatique, Stendhal et le beylisme*. With a bibliographical index of the literary writings of Blum, 1891–1914, prepared by Louis Faucon. Paris, 1962.

> [Volume III, 1914–1934. Projected.]

> Volume IV, Part 1, 1934–1937. *Du 6 février 1934 au Front Populaire, Les Lois sociales de 1936, La Guerre d'Espagne*. Paris, 1964.

> Volume IV, Part 2, 1937–1940. *La Fin du Rassemblement Populaire, De Munich à la guerre, Souvenirs sur l'Affaire*. With a bibliographical index of writings and speeches, 1934–1940. Paris, 1965.

> Volume V, 1940–1945. *Mémoires, La Prison et le procès, À l'échelle humaine*. Paris, 1955.

> Volume VI, 1945–1947. *Naissance de la Quatrième République, La Vie du parti et la doctrine socialiste*. Paris, 1958.

Volume VII, 1947–1950. *La Fin des alliances, la Troisième Force, Politique européenne. Pour la justice.* With a bibliographical index of writings and speeches, 1945–1950. Paris, 1963.

I · Writings and Speeches of Léon Blum

1 · BOOKS AND COLLECTIONS OF ARTICLES AND SPEECHES
(in chronological order)

Nouvelles Conversations de Goethe avec Eckermann. Paris, 1901, 1909, 1937. Based on articles that appeared originally in *La Revue Blanche* from 1894 to 1901. The original edition appeared anonymously, the 1909 edition under Blum's name.

Les Congrès ouvriers et socialistes français. 2 vols.: *1876–1885* and *1886–1900*. Bibliothèque Socialiste, Nos. 6–7. Paris, 1901.

En lisant: réflexions critiques. Paris, 1906.

Au théâtre: réflexions critiques. 4 vols. Paris, 1906, 1909, 1910, 1911.

Du mariage. Paris, 1907, 1937. English translation, *Marriage*, tr. Warren Bradley Wells. Philadelphia, 1937.

Stendhal et le beylisme. Paris, 1914, 1930.

Lettres sur la réforme gouvernementale. Paris, 1918. Published first as articles in *Le Revue de Paris*, December 1917–January 1918; both the articles and the book originally appeared anonymously. Reissued in amended and expanded form as *Le Réforme gouvernementale* (Paris, 1936) with a foreword by Robert Blum.

Les Problèmes de la paix. Paris, 1931. A collection of articles that appeared in *Le Populaire*, November 1930–February 1931. English translation, *Peace and Disarmament*, tr. Alexander Werth. London, 1932.

Souvenirs sur l'Affaire. Paris, 1935. Appeared originally as articles in *Marianne*, July–September 1935.

L'Exercice du pouvoir: discours prononcés de mai 1936 à janvier 1937. Paris, 1937. A collection of speeches during the first half of Blum's first ministry, with a preface by Robert Blum.

L'histoire jugera. Montreal, 1943; Paris, 1945. A selection of Blum's editorials in *Le Populaire* and speeches, principally on foreign policy, from January 13, 1932–May 28, 1940, plus Blum's statements before the Riom court in 1942. Edited by Suzanne Blum with a preface by William R. Bullitt, and, in the later edition, with a foreword by Blum.

À l'échelle humaine. Paris, 1945. Completed in prison in December 1941. English translation, *For All Mankind*, tr. W. Pickles. London, 1946.

2 · MAJOR ARTICLES, PAMPHLETS, AND SPEECHES
PUBLISHED SEPARATELY
(in chronological order)

I am deliberately omitting here a listing of Blum's eight hundred-odd literary articles, book reviews, and drama criticisms which appeared from 1891 to 1914 in such periodicals and newspapers as *La Conque, Le Banquet, La Revue Blanche,*

Bibliography

Mercure de France, Notes Critiques, La Petite République, La Renaissance Latine, Gil Blas, L'Humanité, Les Lettres, La Grande Revue, Comoedia, La Revue de Paris, Le Matin, and *Excelsior;* about a fourth of these articles were later collected and published in *En lisant* and the four volumes of *Au théâtre.* For a detailed listing of these literary writings from 1891 to 1914, see the *"index bibliographique"* prepared by Louis Faucon in *L'Oeuvre de Léon Blum,* II, 601–39. I am also omitting the many prefaces Blum wrote; a number of these are reprinted in *L'Oeuvre.*

"Les [*sic*] Progrès de l'a-politique en France." *La Revue Blanche,* July 1, 1892, pp. 10–21. Omitted from Vol. I of *L'Oeuvre de Léon Blum,* the article was reprinted in *Preuves,* February 1956, pp. 38–44.

L'Article 7. Paris, 1900. Reprint of an article in *La Revue Blanche* in defense of anticlerical legislation.

Doctrines françaises contemporaines (École Socialiste): leçon de Léon Blum, May 18, 1901. Unpublished typescript of lecture, Bibliothèque de la Documentation Contemporaine Internationale, B 2912.

Conférence sur Jean Jaurès, July 31, 1917. *La Revue Socialiste,* May 1950, pp. 385–406.

Commentaires sur le programme d'action du parti socialiste. Speech to special party congress, April 21, 1919. Paris, 1919.

Pour être socialiste. With dedication *"à mon fils."* Paris, 1919. Many subsequent reprintings.

Pour la vieille maison. Paris, 1921, 1934. Reprint of speech, December 27, 1920, to Tours party congress.

Discours au congrès international de Hambourg, May 1923. Typescript, M. Blumel's collection.

"L'Idéal socialiste." *La Revue de Paris,* May 1924, pp. 92–111.

La Politique financière du parti socialiste: discours prononcé a la Chambre des Députés, le 26 juin 1925. Paris, 1925.

(With Paul Faure) *Le Parti socialiste et la participation ministérielle: discours prononcés au congrès national extraordinaire du 10 janvier 1926.* Paris, 1926.

Radicalisme et socialisme. Paris, 1927. Based on articles originally published in *Le Populaire,* January 31–February 20, 1927.

Bolchevisme et socialisme. Paris, 1927. Based on articles originally published in *Le Populaire,* March 13–25, 1927.

Notre Tactique électorale. Paris, 1928.

Le Devoir international vis à vis du foyer national juif. Paris, 1928. Blum's authorship of this pamphlet has been questioned.

Discours, conférence constituante de l'Agence Juive pour la Palestine. Zurich, August 11–14, 1929. Typescript. M. Blumel's collection.

La Méthode socialiste. Speech delivered November 10, 1931, at the École Socialiste, originally published in *Révolte,* December 1932; reprinted as pamphlet, Paris, 1945.

Notre Plate-forme: élections législatives de 1932. Speech at special party congress, January 30–31, 1932.

"L'Odieux Procès de Moscou." Chapter in Friedrich Adler et al.: *Le Procès de Moscou et l'Internationale ouvrière socialiste.* Paris and Brussels, 1932, pp. 40–50.

Le Socialisme devant la crise. Speech of December 9, 1932, at the Palais de la Mutualité. Paris, 1933.

Bibliography

Jean Jaurès. Lecture delivered February 16, 1933, at the Théâtre des Ambassadeurs. Paris, 1933, 1945.

La Jeunesse et le socialisme. Speech of June 30, 1934, at the Palais de la Mutualité. Paris, 1934.

Les Radicaux et nous, 1932–1934. Paris, 1934. Based on articles in *Le Populaire,* August 28–September 2, 1934.

"La Déclaration des droits de l'homme." In Anatole de Monzie et al. (eds.): *L'Encyclopédie Française.* Vol. X: *L'État moderne.* Paris, 1935.

Le Socialisme a vu clair. Speech of January 13, 1936, to Seine Federation. Paris, 1936.

Les Événements d'Espagne. Speech of September 6, 1936, at Luna Park. Paris, 1936.

Léon Blum en action pour la paix: une séance historique à la Chambre des Députés. Speech of December 5, 1936, in the Chamber. Paris, 1936.

"Déclaration de Léon Blum aux groupes de la minorité, le 12 mars 1938." With comments by André Blumel, *Les Temps Modernes,* September 1951, pp. 482–94.

Contre le racisme. Speech of November 26, 1938, to banquet of the 9th national congress of the Congrès de l'antiracisme. Paris, 1938.

La Question d'Espagne. Speech of January 26, 1939, in Chamber of Deputies. Paris, 1939.

Des Attaques auxquelles nous devons répondre. Speech of May 20, 1939, at Clermont-Ferrand. Paris, 1939.

France at War. Speech at Labour party conference in Bournemouth, May 1940. London, 1940.

Le Dernier Mois. Experiences of April 3–May 4, 1945. Paris, 1946.

Les Devoirs et les tâches du socialisme. Speech of May 20, 1945, to conference of Socialist party federation secretaries. Paris, 1945.

Le Problème de l'unité. Based on articles originally published in *Le Populaire,* July 5–August 7, 1945. Paris, 1945.

Le Socialisme maître de l'heure. Speech to 37th national congress, S.F.I.O., August 11–15, 1945. Paris, 1945.

"Notes sur la doctrine." *La Revue Socialiste,* July 1946, pp. 257–61.

"Révolution socialiste ou révolution directoriale." *La Revue Socialiste,* January 1947, pp. 1–10. Served also as preface to French translation of James Burnham's *Managerial Revolution.*

"Exercice et conquête du pouvoir." *La Revue Socialiste,* November 1947, pp. 383–95. Lecture delivered at École Normale Supérieure, May 30, 1947.

"Un Demi-siècle de destin français." *Évidences,* January 1950, pp. 1–9. A collection of obituaries on leading republican statesmen written by Blum for *Le Populaire* over the years.

3 · NEWSPAPER EDITORIALS

Contributions to *L'Humanité,* April 8, 1917–November 19, 1920.

Contributions to *Le Populaire de Paris,* April 1921–December 1925; January 22, 1927–March 29, 1950. After *Le Populaire* became established on a regular daily basis on January 22, 1927, with Blum as political director, he wrote a signed editorial almost daily. He was on leave during the Popular Front governments from June 1936 to April 1938; and his contributions were interrupted during the war from 1940 to 1945. He

returned to his post after the war and continued to write from May 16, 1945, to March 29, 1950. One would estimate that he wrote close to four thousand editorials during his association with *Le Populaire*.
Contributions to various French and foreign newspapers.

4 · MISCELLANEOUS: OTHER COLLECTIONS

Pages choisies de Léon Blum. *La Revue Socialiste*, June–July 1950. Special issue devoted to a well-chosen selection of his writings and speeches.
Léon Blum: *Des Nouvelles Conversations de Goethe avec Eckermann (1897– 1900) à l'échelle humaine (1942)*. Edited by Olga Raffalovich; parallel passages of earlier and later writings to demonstrate continuity of Blum's thought. Paris, 1957.
Bibliothèque Nationale: *Léon Blum*. Catalogue of exhibition devoted to Blum at the Bibliothèque Nationale in 1962. With a preface by Julien Cain. Paris, 1962.

II · Documents

1 · OFFICIAL

Journal Officiel, Chambre des Députés, Débats parlementaires, compte-rendu sténographique, 1919–40.
Journal Officiel, Sénat, Débats parlementaires, compte-rendu sténographique, 1919–40.
Journal Officiel, Assemblée Nationale, Débats parlementaires, compte-rendu sténographique, 1946–50.
Les Événements survenus en France de 1933 à 1945: Témoignages et documents recueillis par la Commission d'Enquête Parlementaire, 9 vols.; *Rapport*, 2 vols.; Paris, 1947–54. Blum's testimony, presented to the commission on June 18, July 23, and July 30, 1947, appears in *Témoignages et documents*, I, 121–32, 215–29, 251–62.
Statistique Générale et Institut de Conjoncture: *Mouvement économique en France de 1929 à 1939*. Paris, 1941.
Documents on German Foreign Policy, 1918–1945. From the Archives of the German Foreign Ministry. Series D (1937–1945). Vol. I: *From Neurath to Ribbentrop, September 1937–September 1938*. Vol. III: *Germany and the Spanish Civil War, 1936–1939*. Washington, D.C., 1949, 1950.
Foreign Relations of the United States, 1936. Vol. II: *Europe*. Washington, D.C., 1954.

2 · EXTRACTS FROM COURT TESTIMONY

Le Procès de l'assassin de Jaurès, 24–29 mars 1919. Paris, 1919. For Blum's testimony, pp. 72–9.
Léon Blum devant la cour de Riom. Blum's testimony before the Riom court, February 19 and March 10, 11, 1942. With other documents. Paris, 1942, 1945. An English translation appeared as *Léon Blum before His*

Bibliography

Judges at the Supreme Court of Riom. London, 1943. See also, for testimony and many other documents, *L'Oeuvre de Léon Blum*, V, 221–348,
and also the volumes on the Riom trial by Maurice Ribet and Paul
Soupiron listed in the last section of this Bibliography.

Le Procès du maréchal Pétain, compte- rendu sténographique. 2 vols. Edited by
Maurice Garçon. Blum's deposition, given on July 27, 1945, appears in I,
233–47.

3 · SOCIALIST PARTY CONGRESSES

*Parti socialiste (Section française de l'Internationale ouvrière). 17ᵉ congrès
national.* Strasbourg, February 25–29, 1920. *Compte-rendu sténographique*
and *rapports.* Paris, 1920.
——. *18ᵉ congrès national.* Tours, December 25–30, 1920. *Compte-rendu sténographique* and *rapports.* Paris, 1921.

For the 19th national congress (1921) to the 23rd national congress (1926), only
the reports are available. For the 24th national congress (1927) to the 35th national congress (1938), both the stenographic minutes and the reports are available.
Publication of the stenographic minutes was not resumed after 1944. Wherever
the official proceedings are not available for annual congresses, or for special
congresses, the summary of proceedings in the appropriate issues of *Le Populaire*
must be used. For the Popular Front years the stenographic minutes and reports
are available for the congresses held at Toulouse (May 1934), Mulhouse (June
1935), Paris (May 1936), Marseilles (July 1937), and Royan (June 1938).

III · Memoirs, Diaries, and Published Correspondence
of Contemporaries

Alvarez del Vayo, J.: *Freedom's Battle.* Tr. Eileen E. Brooke. New York, 1940.
Andler, Charles: *Vie de Lucien Herr.* Paris, 1932. Both a biography and a memoir.
Auriol, Vincent: *Hier . . . demain.* 2 vols. Paris, 1945.
Baudouin, Paul: *Neuf Mois au gouvernement, avril–décembre 1940.* Paris, 1948.
Benda, Julien: *La Jeunesse d'un clerc.* Paris, 1936.
Bloch, Marc: *L'étrange défaite: témoignage écrit en 1940.* Paris, 1946.
Blum, Jeanne-Léon: *Léon Blum, 9 avril 1872–30 mars 1950.* Paris, 1951. Origi-
nally published anonymously.
Blum, John Morton (ed.): *From the Morgenthau Diaries: Years of Crisis, 1928–
1938.* Boston, 1959.
Blum, René: "Mon Frère Léon." *Vu*, No. 430, June 10, 1936, p. 661.
Bonnet, Georges: *Défense de la paix.* 2 vols. Vol. I: *De Washington au Quai
d'Orsay.* Vol. II: *Fin d'une Europe (de Munich à la guerre).* Geneva,
1946, 1948.
Bourgin, Georges: "Léon Blum: de la rue Cujas à Jouy-en-Josas." *Revue Politique
et Parlementaire*, October 1950, pp. 142–4.
Bourgin, Hubert: *De Jaurès à Léon Blum: l'École normale et la politique.* Paris,
1938.
Bowers, Claude G.: *My Mission to Spain.* New York, 1954.
Caillaux, Joseph: *Mes Mémoires.* 3 vols. Paris, 1942–7.

Bibliography

Chambrun, Charles de: *Traditiòns et souvenirs.* Paris, 1952.

Chautemps, Camille: *Cahiers secrets de l'armistice, 1939–1940.* Paris, 1964.

Cot, Pierre: *Le Procès de la république.* 2 vols. New York, 1944.

Coulondre, Robert: *De Staline à Hitler: souvenirs de deux ambassades, 1936–1939.* Paris, 1950.

— Dalton, Hugh. *The Fateful Years: Memoirs, 1931–1945.* London, 1957.

de Gaulle, Charles: *Mémoires de guerre.* 3 vols. Vol. I: *L'Appel, 1940–1942.* Vol. II: *L'Unité, 1942–1944.* Vol. III: *Le Salut, 1944–1946.* Paris, 1954, 1956, 1959.

Delmas, André: *À gauche de la barricade: chronique syndicale de l'avant guerre.* Paris, 1950.

Diary of Pierre Laval. Edited and with a preface by Josée Laval, New York, 1948. Not a diary but the English translation of *Laval parle . . . notes et mémoires rédigés à Fresnes d'août à octobre 1945.* Paris, 1948.

Duchemin, René: "L'Accord Matignon: ce que j'ai vu et entendu." *Revue de Paris,* February 1937, pp. 584–94.

— Eden, Anthony: *Facing the Dictators.* Boston, 1962.

Faure, Paul: *De Munich à la Ve République.* Paris, 1947.

Février, André: *Expliquons-nous.* Paris, 1946.

Flandin, Pierre-Étienne: *Politique française, 1919–1940.* Paris, 1947.

François-Poncet, André: *Souvenirs d'une ambassade à Berlin, septembre 1931–octobre 1938.* Paris, 1946.

———: *Au Palais Farnèse: souvenirs d'une ambassade à Rome, 1938–1940.* Paris, 1961.

Frossard, L. -O.: *De Jaurès à Lénine: notes et souvenirs d'un militant.* Paris, 1930.

———: *Sous le signe de Jaurès: de Jaurès à Léon Blum, souvenirs d'un militant.* Paris, 1943.

Gamelin, Maurice (General): *Servir.* 3 vols. Vol. I: *Les Armées françaises de 1940.* Vol. II: *Le Prologue du drame, 1930–août 1939.* Vol. III: *La Guerre, septembre 1939–19 mai 1940.* Paris, 1946–7.

Gide, André: *Journal, 1889–1939.* Paris, 1948.

———: *Journal, 1939–1949.* Paris, 1954.

———: "Léon Blum." *Vendredi,* June 5, 1936.

Gregh, Fernand: *Souvenirs.* 3 vols. Vol. I: *L'Âge d'or: souvenirs d'enfance et de jeunesse.* Vol. II: *L'Âge d'airain: souvenirs, 1905–1925.* Vol. III: *L'Âge de fer: souvenirs, 1925–1955.* Paris, 1947, 1951, 1956.

Guéhenno, Jean: *Journal d'une "révolution" (1937–1938).* Paris, 1939.

— Guérin, Daniel: *Front Populaire: révolution manquée.* Paris, 1963.

Herriot, Édouard: *Jadis.* 2 vols. Vol. I: *Avant la première guerre mondiale.* Vol. II: *D'une guerre à l'autre, 1914–1936.* Paris, 1948.

———: *Épisodes, 1940–1944.* Paris, 1950.

Hull, Cordell: *Memoirs.* 2 vols. New York, 1948.

Jacomet, Robert: *L'Armement de la France, 1936–1939.* Paris, 1947.

Laval parle . . . notes et mémoires rédigés à Fresnes d'août à octobre 1945. Paris, 1948. In English translation as *Diary of Pierre Laval.* New York, 1948.

Lebrun, Albert François: *Témoignage.* Paris, 1946.

Leclercq, P.: "Memories of Léon Blum." *Nineteenth Century,* June 1950. pp. 378–80.

Lévy, Louis: *Comment ils sont devenus socialistes.* With a preface by Blum. Paris, 1932. Interviews with various Socialist leaders, including Blum.

Bibliography

Mayer, Daniel: "Souvenirs sur la Résistance: Léon Blum." *Évidences*, 1950, pp. 2–4, 13–16.

Moch, Jules: "Avec Léon Blum en juin 1936." *Le Populaire*, March 29, 1953.

Montigny, Jean: *Tout la vérité sur un mois dramatique de notre histoire.* Clermont-Ferrand, 1940.

Monzie, Anatole de: *Ci-devant.* Paris, 1942.

Naegelen, Marcel Edmond: "Quelques images de Léon Blum." *La Revue Socialiste*, May 1950, pp. 407–11.

Noël, Léon: *L'Agression allemande contre la Pologne: une ambassade à Varsovie, 1935–1939.* Paris, 1946.

Paul-Boncour, Joseph: *Entre deux guerres: souvenirs sur la IIIᵉ République.* 3 vols. Vol. I: *Les Luttes républicaines, 1877–1918.* Vol. II: *Les Lendemains de la victoire, 1919–1934.* Vol. III: *Sur les chemins de la défaite, 1935–1940.* Paris, 1945–6.

Péguy, Charles: *Notre jeunesse.* Paris, 1910. *Cahiers de la Quinzaine*, 2nd ser., LXVII, No. 12.

Le Procès de Riom par un témoin. Paris, 1945.

Renard, Jules: *Oeuvres complètes de Jules Renard: Correspondance inédite.* 2 vols. Paris, 1927.

———: *Journal inédit.* 5 vols. Paris, 1925–7.

René Blum, 1875–1942. A memorial volume with many contributors. Paris, 1950.

Reynaud, Paul: *Au coeur de la mêleé, 1930–1945.* Paris, 1951.

———: *Mémoires.* 2 vols. Vol. I: *Venu de ma montagne.* Vol. II: *Envers et contre tous, 7 mars 1936–16 juin 1940.* Paris, 1960, 1963.

Schacht, Hjalmar: *My First Seventy-six Years: The Autobiography of Hjalmar Schacht.* Tr. D. Pyke. London, 1955.

Sembat, Marcel: *La Victoire en déroute.* Paris, 1925. With a preface by Léon Blum. In English translation as *Defeated Victory.* London, 1925.

Sforza, Count Carlo: "Léon Blum vu par un étranger non socialiste." *La Dépêche de Toulouse*, July 3, 1936.

———: *Contemporary Italy.* Tr. Drake and Denise DeKay. New York, 1944.

Simone (Pauline Porché): "Souvenirs sur Léon Blum." *Les Nouvelles Littéraires*, April 6, 1950.

Thorez, Maurice: *Fils du peuple.* Paris, 1937, 1949, 1960.

———: *Oeuvres de Maurice Thorez.* Paris, 1950– .

Torrès, Henry: *De Clemenceau à de Gaulle: ce que je n'ai jamis dit, chronique du temps retrouvé.* Paris, 1958.

Trotsky, Leon: *Whither France?* Tr. John G. Wright and Harold R. Isaacs. New York, 1937.

Weill-Hallé, Dr. B.: *Léon Blum vu par un ami.* Lecture to Alliance Française, New York City, October 19, 1936. Privately printed.

Welles, Sumner: *The Time for Decision.* New York, 1944.

Zay, Jean: *Souvenirs et solitude.* Paris, 1946.

* * *

Assemblée d'information. Organized by the Société des amis de Léon Blum at the Sorbonne, February 8 and December 11, 1951. Speeches and reminiscences by Bracke (A. M. Desrousseaux), Jean Texcier, Pierre Juvigny, Marius Moutet, Ernest Labrousse, Jules Moch, Samuel Spanien, Robert Verdier, Jaime Torres-Bodet, Eleanor Roosevelt, and Édouard Herriot. Unpublished typescript, courtesy of Mme Cletta Mayer, Secretary, Société des amis de Léon Blum.

Bibliography

Colloquium: "Léon Blum, chef de gouvernement, 1936–1937." Organized by the Fondation Nationale des Sciences Politiques, March 26–27, 1965. Mimeographed papers by various scholars and discussion; entire proceedings to be published by the Fondation.

Among special issues of *Le Populaire* and *Le Populaire-Dimanche* devoted to Blum, with reminiscences: March 31, 1950; April 1–2, 1950; April 9, 1950; March 25, 1951; March 30, 1952; March 29, 1953.

IV · Selected List of Books and Articles on Blum

(Longer biographical studies are starred.)

*Audry, Colette: *Léon Blum ou la politique du Juste: essai. Collection Les Temps Modernes dirigée par Jean-Paul Sartre.* Paris, 1955. A tendentious though highly knowledgeable and perceptive biographical essay (written by a French novelist and Leftist Socialist) which scores Blum for failing to serve adequately the cause of revolution.

Baleine, Philippe de: "L'Homme le plus injurié de France." *France-Dimanche*, December 22, 1946.

Barjac, Claude: "M. Léon Blum, chroniqueur et moraliste à la Grande Revue." *La Grande Revue*, June 1936, pp. 575–90.

Blumel, André: *Léon Blum: juif et sioniste.* Paris, 1951. A reprint in pamphlet form of articles that appeared originally in *La Revue de la Pensée Juive*, No. 9, Autumn 1951.

Borne, Étienne: "Les Dernières Années de Léon Blum." *Études*, June 1950, pp. 346–53.

Cain, Julien: "Léon Blum." *Évidences*, May 1950, pp. 1–2.

Carat, Jacques: "Léon Blum, écrivain." *Paru*, May 1950. pp. 55–60.

*Dalby, Louise Elliott: *Léon Blum: Evolution of a Socialist.* New York, 1963. A topical and chronological analysis of Blum's thought and career; more useful for Blum's writings and ideas than for his career.

Dintzer, Lucien: *L'Oeuvre littéraire de Léon Blum, ou Blum inconnu.* Pamphlet. Lyons, 1937.

Drachkovitch, Milorad M.: *De Karl Marx à Léon Blum: la crise de la social démocratie.* Geneva, 1954.

Ferenzy, Oscar de: "La Généalogie de M. Léon Blum." *La Voix d'Alsace et de Lorraine*, July 5, 1936.

*Fraser, Geoffrey, and Thadée Natanson: *Léon Blum: Man and Statesman.* London and New York, 1938. Written by one of the Natanson brothers who edited *La Revue Blanche* and long a friend of Blum, its value lies principally in its memoir quality, and is very useful in this respect. Never published in French, although a Spanish translation appeared in Chile. The designation on the title page, "The Only Authorized Biography," is inaccurate. Mr. Victor Gollancz, publisher of the book, informs me that he asked reviewers to disregard this statement after Blum withdrew his tentative authorization for the book.

Genêt (Janet Flanner): "Letter from Paris." *The New Yorker*, XXVII (March 31, 1951), 74–82.

Bibliography

Giraud, Pierre: "Colette Audry ou l'injustice de la politique." *La Revue Socialiste*, January 1957, pp. 78–85.

Halperin, S. William: "Léon Blum and Contemporary French Socialism." *Journal of Modern History*, XVIII (1946), 241–50.

Harmel, Claude: *Lettre à Léon Blum sur le socialisme et la paix.* Paris, 1949.

Izard, Georges: "Le Testament socialiste de Léon Blum," *La Nef*, June–July 1950, pp. 117–25.

*Joll, James: *Intellectuals in Politics: Three Biographical Essays.* (Blum, Rathenau, Marinetti.) London, 1960. A critical though sympathetic analysis of Blum, penetrating and scholarly.

Juvigny, Pierre: "Un Grand Commissaire du gouvernement: Léon Blum." In *Le Conseil d'État: livre jubilaire publié pour commémorer son 150ᵉ anniversaire.* Paris, 1952. Pp. 337–40.

"Léon Blum: The 'Aristocrate' of the Left: An Appreciation by a Friend." *The Times* (London), June 13, 1936.

Lévy, Louis: "Léon Blum, tel qu'on ne le connaît pas." *Vu*, No. 426, 1936, pp. 542–43.

Luc-Verbon, Philippe: "Le Socialisme de Léon Blum." *La Revue Socialiste*, December 1951, pp. 577–9.

Mayer, Daniel: "La Jeunesse de Léon Blum." *Évidences*, May 1954, pp. 9–15.

Middleton, W. L.: "Léon Blum." *Contemporary Review*, May 1950, p. 262.

Mirkine-Guetzévitch, Boris: "La République parlementaire dans la pensée politique de Léon Blum." *La Revue Socialiste*, January 1951, pp. 10–24.

Natanson, Thadée: "Léon Blum au congrès de Tours," *La Nef*, June–July 1950, pp. 88–99.

Pagosse, Roger: "L'Oeuvre de Léon Blum." *La Revue Socialiste*, October 1954, pp. 310–13; October 1955, pp. 322–3.

Rabi: "Léon Blum . . . vu par André Gide: une amitié singulière." *La Terre Retrouvée*, April 15, 1950.

Ramadier, Paul: *Le Socialisme de Léon Blum.* Pamphlet. Paris, 1951.

*Stokes, Richard L.: *Léon Blum: Poet to Premier.* New York, 1937. Written in somewhat sensationalist and naïve fashion at the time of Blum's premiership by a *St. Louis Post-Dispatch* journalist.

Thiébaut, Marcel: *En lisant M. Léon Blum.* Paris, 1937.

*Vichniac, Marc: *Léon Blum.* Paris, 1937. A reliable reconstruction of Blum's life and career to 1937 based on investigation among family and friends but uncritical and adulatory.

Weill-Raynal, Étienne: "Léon Blum ou la politique du Juste." *La Revue Socialiste*, November 1955, pp. 408–12.

Zévaès, Alexandre: "Léon Blum écrivain." *Les Nouvelles Littéraires*, June 6, 1936.

*Ziebura, Gilbert: *Léon Blum: Theorie und Praxis einer sozialistischen Politik.* Vol. I: *1872 bis 1934.* Berlin, 1963. The first volume of this projected two-volume study by an extremely able German political scientist is a comprehensive, exhaustive investigation of Blum's thought, French socialism, and French politics. Less a biography than an analysis of the relationship between the theory and practice of French socialism as exemplified by Blum, it is enriched with many statistical tables, charts, and maps on the history of the Socialist party.

Bibliography

A SAMPLING OF HOSTILE ANTI-BLUM LITERATURE
(*excluding articles in extremist publications such as* L'Action Française,
Je Suis Partout, Gringoire, *etc.*)

Béraud, Henri: *Popu-Roi.* Paris, 1938.
D'où sort Karfunkelstein dit Blum. Broadside. No date.
Herbette, François: *L'Expérience marxiste en France, 1936–1938.* Paris, 1959.
Léon Blum: l'homme qui se trompe toujours et qui trompe les autres. Pamphlet.
    Paris, Imprimerie de la Nation, no date.
Lombard, Paul: *Front Populaire.* Paris, 1936.
————: *Quatorze Mois de démence: l'expérience Léon Blum.* Paris, 1937.
Maxence, Jean-Pierre: *Histoire de dix ans (1927–1937).* Paris, 1939.
Ploncard, Jacques: *La Vie de Léon Blum.* Pamphlet. Paris, 1938.
Suarez, Georges: *Nos Seigneurs et nos maîtres.* With illustrations by Sennep.
    Paris, 1937.
Téry, Gustave: *La Vie de Monsieur Léon Blum.* Pamphlet. Paris, 1936.
Viguier, Laurent: *Les Juifs à travers Léon Blum: leur incapacité historique de
    diriger un état, la marque juive dans le christianisme.* Paris, 1938.

*   *   *

Léon Blum vu par l'Encyclopédie Soviétique. (Vol. V. Moscow, 1950.) French
    translation, *Preuves,* November 1951, pp. 19–21.
Thorez, Maurice: "Léon Blum tel qu'il est." *L'Internationale Communiste,* Febru-
    ary 1940. Also in German as "Léon Blum, wie er leibt und lebt." *Die
    Welt,* February 16, 1940. Reprinted also in pamphlet form by a Socialist
    editor, Charles Pot. Paris, 1956.

V · Selected List of Writings on France, French Socialism, the Popular Front, and Related Subjects Cited or Used

Albertini, Rudolf von: "Zur Beurteilung der Volksfront in Frankreich (1934–
    1938)." *Vierteljahrshefte für Zeitgeschichte,* February 1959, pp. 130–62.
Aron, Raymond: *Le Grand Schisme.* Paris, 1948.
Aron, Robert: *Histoire de Vichy, 1940–1944.* Paris, 1954.
Aubery, Pierre: *Milieux juifs de la France contemporaine.* Paris, 1957.
Auclair, Marcelle: *La Vie de Jean Jaurès ou la France d'avant 1914.* Paris, 1954.
Bankwitz, Philip C. F.: "Maxime Weygand and the Fall of France: A Study
    in Civil-Military Relations." *Journal of Modern History,* XXXI (1959),
    225–42.
Baumont, Maurice: *La Faillite de la paix, 1918–1939.* Paris, 1945, 1950.
Bell, J. Bowyer: "French Reaction to the Spanish Civil War, July–September,
    1936." Chapter in Lillian Parker Wallace and William C. Askew (eds.):
    Power, Public Opinion, and Diplomacy. Durham, N.C., 1959. Pp. 267–96.
Beloff, Max: "The Sixth of February." Chapter in Joll (ed.): *The Decline of the
    Third Republic,* pp. 9–35.

Bibliography

Bettleheim, Charles: *Bilan de l'économie française, 1919–1946.* Paris, 1947.

Binion, Rudolph: *Defeated Leaders: The Political Fate of Caillaux, Jouvenel, and Tardieu.* New York, 1960.

Blumel, André: "Déclaration de Léon Blum aux groupes de la minorité, 12 mars 1938." *Les Temps Modernes,* VII (September 1951), 483–94.

Bodin, Louis, and Jean Touchard: *Front Populaire 1936.* Paris, 1961. With a useful bibliography.

Bonnefous, Édouard: *Histoire politique de la Troisième République.* Vol. III: *L'Après guerre, 1919–1924.* Vol. IV: *Cartel des gauches et union nationale, 1924–1929.* Vol. V: *La République en danger: Des Ligues au Front Populaire, 1930–1936.* Paris, 1959, 1960, 1962.

Bonnet, Georges: *Le Quai d'Orsay sous trois républiques.* Paris, 1961.

Bonnevay, Laurent: *Les Journées sanglantes de février: pages d'histoire.* Paris, 1935.

Bourgin, Georges: "Un Tournant de l'histoire de la France et du socialisme." *La Revue Socialiste,* March 1947, pp. 257–64.

Bourgin, Georges, J. Carrère, and A. Guérin: *Manuel des partis politiques en France.* Paris, 1928.

Bourgin, Georges, and Pierre Rimbert: *Le Socialisme.* Paris, 1950.

Brogan, D. W.: *France under the Republic: The Development of Modern France (1870–1939).* New York and London, 1942.

——: *The French Nation: From Napoleon to Pétain, 1814–1940.* New York and London, 1957.

Broué, Pierre, and Émile Témime: *La Révolution et la guerre d'Espagne.* Paris, 1961.

Burbank, L. B.: "The French Popular Front." *Current History,* October 1951, pp. 194–201.

Cairns, John: "Along the Road Back to France 1940." *American Historical Review,* LXIV (April 1959), 583–603.

Cameron, Elizabeth: "Alexis Saint-Léger Léger." Chapter in Craig and Gilbert (eds.): *The Diplomats,* pp. 378–405.

Caunes, Paul de: *La Théorie du pouvoir d'achat: ses applications en France durant "l'expérience Blum."* Thèse, Toulouse, 1939.

Challener, Richard D.: "The Military Defeat of 1940 in Retrospect." Chapter in Earle (ed.): *Modern France,* pp. 405–20.

——: *The French Theory of the Nation in Arms, 1866–1939.* New York, 1952.

Chapman, Guy: *The Dreyfus Case: A Reassessment.* London, 1955.

Chastenet, Jacques: *Histoire de la Troisième République.* Vol. V: *Les Années d'illusions, 1918–1931.* Vol. VI: *Déclin de la Troisième, 1931–1938.* Vol. VII: *Le Drame final, 1938–1940.* Paris, 1960, 1962, 1963.

Christopher, John B.: "The Desiccation of the Bourgeois Spirit." Chapter in Earle (ed.): *Modern France,* pp. 44–57.

Cole, G. D. H.: *A History of Socialist Thought.* Vol. V: *Socialism and Fascism, 1931–1939.* London, 1960.

Colton, Joel: *Compulsory Labor Arbitration in France, 1936–1939.* New York, 1951.

——: "Léon Blum and the French Socialists as a Government Party." *The Journal of Politics,* XV (1953), 517–43.

——: "The French Socialist Party: A Case Study of the Non-Communist Left." *The Yale Review,* XLIII (Spring 1954), 402–13.

Coquart, Armand: "Roger Salengro ou l'exercice du pouvoir." *La Revue Socialiste,* June 1956, pp. 57–74.

Bibliography

Coquet, James de: *Le Procès de Riom*. Paris, 1945.

Craig, Gordon, and Felix Gilbert (eds.): *The Diplomats, 1919–1939*. Princeton, 1953.

Danos, Jacques, and Marcel Gibelin: *Juin 36*. Paris, 1952.

Dauphin-Meunier, A.: *La Banque de France*. Paris, 1937.

Delay, Jean: *La Jeunesse d'André Gide*. 2 vols. Paris, 1956, 1957.

Delevsky, J.: *Les Antinomies socialistes et l'évolution du socialisme français*. Paris, 1930.

Derfler, Leslie: " 'Le Cas Millerand': une nouvelle interprétation." *Revue d'Histoire Moderne et Contemporaine*, X (1963), 81–104.

Dolléans, Édouard: *Histoire du mouvement ouvrier*. 3 vols. Paris, 1936–1953.

—— and Gérard Dehove: *Histoire du travail en France, mouvement ouvrier, et législation sociale*. Vol. II: *1919 à nos jours*. Paris, 1955.

Dournes, Pierre: "Le Socialisme de Péguy face au parti socialiste." *La Nef*, V (June–July 1950), 79–87.

Dupeux, Georges: *Le Front Populaire et les élections de 1936*. Cahiers de la Fondation Nationale des Sciences Politiques, No. 99. Paris, 1959.

——: "L'Échec du premier gouvernement Léon Blum." *Revue d'histoire moderne et contemporaine*, X (1963), 35–44.

Duverger, Maurice (ed.): *Partis politiques et classes sociales en France*. Cahiers de la Fondation Nationale des Sciences Politiques, No. 74. Paris, 1955.

Earle, Edward Mead (ed.): *Modern France: Problems of the Third and Fourth Republics*. Princeton, 1951.

Ehrmann, Henry W.: *The French Labor Movement from Popular Front to Liberation*. New York, 1947.

——: *Organized Business in France*. Princeton, 1957.

——: "The Blum Experiment and the Downfall of France." *Foreign Affairs*, XX (1941–2), pp. 152–65.

——: "The Decline of the Socialist Party." Chapter in Earle (ed.): *Modern France*, pp. 181–99.

Esch, P. A. M. van der: *Prelude to War: The International Repercussions of the Spanish Civil War, 1936–1939*. The Hague, 1951.

Fagen, Melvin M.: "The Lesson of France." *The New Republic*, CIII (1940), 296–9, 341–3.

Farmer, Paul: *Vichy: Political Dilemma*. New York, 1955.

Feiling, Keith: *The Life of Neville Chamberlain*. London, 1942.

Fourchy, P.: *Les Doctrines du parti socialiste français*. Thèse pour le doctorat. Nancy, 1929.

Franck, Louis R.: *Démocraties en crise: Roosevelt, Van Zeeland, Léon Blum*. Paris, 1937.

——: *French Price Control: From Blum to Pétain*. Washington, 1942.

Freedeman, Charles E.: *The Conseil d'État in Modern France*. New York, 1961.

Funk, Arthur Layton: *Charles de Gaulle: The Crucial Years, 1943–1944*. Norman, Okla., 1959.

Gaucher, François: *Contribution à l'histoire du socialisme français (1905–1933)*. Thèse. Paris, 1934.

Godfrey, E. Drexel: *The Fate of the French Non-Communist Left*. New York, 1955.

Goguel, François: *La Politique des partis sous la III' République*. Paris, 1946, 1958.

——: *France under the Fourth Republic*. Tr. Roy Pierce, Ithaca, N.Y., 1952.

Goldberg, Harvey: *The Life of Jean Juarès*. Madison, Wis., 1962.

Bibliography

Goutard, Adolphe: *1940: la guerre des occasions perdues.* Paris, 1956.

Hérard, Lucien: "La SFIO." *La Nef,* June–July 1950, pp. 135–44.

Hostache, René: *Le Conseil National de la Résistance: les institutions de la clandestinité.* Paris, 1958.

Hytier, Adrienne: *Two Years of French Foreign Policy: Vichy, 1940–1942.* Geneva, 1958.

Joll, James (ed.): *The Decline of the Third Republic.* St. Antony's Papers, No. 5. London, 1955.

———: "The Making of the Popular Front." Chapter in Joll (ed.): *The Decline of the Third Republic,* pp. 36–66.

Kalecki, M.: "The Lesson of the Blum Experiment." *Economic Journal,* XLVIII (March 1938), 26–41.

Kammerer, Albert: *La Vérité sur l'armistice.* Paris, 1944.

Knapp, W. F.: "The Rhineland Crisis of March 1936." Chapter in Joll (ed.): *The Decline of the Third Republic,* pp. 67–85.

Kolarz, Walter: *Das Regime Blum.* With a preface by Georges Monnet. Prague, 1937.

Kriegel, Annie: *Aux origines du communisme français.* 2 vols. Paris, 1964.

Lachapelle, Georges: *Les Élections législatives des 26 avril et 3 mai 1936.* Paris, 1936.

Landauer, Carl: *European Socialism.* 2 vols. Berkeley, Calif., 1960.

Langer, William L.: *Our Vichy Gamble.* New York, 1947.

Lapie, P. O.: "De Karl Marx à Jules Moch." *La Nef,* June–July 1950, pp. 160–6.

Larmour, Peter J.: *The French Radical Party in the 1930's.* Stanford, Calif., 1964.

Laroque, Pierre: *Les Rapports entre patrons et ouvriers.* Paris, 1938.

Laufenburger, Henry: "Expérience Roosevelt et Expérience Blum: la revalorisation du pouvoir d'achat." *Revue Économique Internationale,* XXIX (June 1937), 436–63.

Lefranc, Georges: *Le Mouvement socialiste sous la Troisième République, 1875–1940.* Paris, 1963.

———: *Histoire du Front Populaire, 1934–1938.* Paris, 1965.

Lévy, Louis: *The Truth about France.* New York, 1941.

Ligou, Daniel: *Histoire du socialisme en France, 1871–1961.* Paris, 1962.

Lorwin, Val R.: *The French Labor Movement,* Cambridge, Mass., 1954.

Louis, Paul: *La Crise du socialisme mondial.* Paris, 1921.

———: *Histoire du socialisme en France.* Paris, 1946, 1950.

Manevy, Raymond: *Histoire de la presse, 1914–1939.* Paris, 1945.

Marabuto, Paul: *Les Partis politiques et les mouvements sociaux sous la IVe République.* Paris, 1948.

Marcus, John T.: *French Socialism in the Crisis Years, 1933–1936: Fascism and the French Left.* New York, 1958.

Marjolin, Robert: "Reflections on the Blum Experiment." *Economica,* V (May 1938), 177–91.

Maurette, Fernand: "A Year of Experiment in France." *International Labour Review,* XXXVI (1937), 1–25, 149–66.

Mazé, P., and R. Génébrier: *Les Grandes Journées du procès de Riom.* Paris, 1945.

Micaud, Charles: *The French Right and Nazi Germany, 1933–1939.* Durham, N.C., 1943.

Michel, Henri: *Histoire de la Résistance, 1940–1944.* Paris, 1950.

———: *Les Courants de la pensée de la Résistance.* Paris, 1963.

Bibliography

——— and Boris Mirkine-Guetzévitch (eds.): *Les Idées politiques et sociales de la Résistance* (Paris, 1954).

Mitzman, Arthur: "The French Working Class and the Blum Government, 1936–37." *International Review of Social History*, IX (1964), 363–90.

Montagnon, Barthélemy, Adrien Marquet, and Marcel Déat: *Néo-socialisme? ordre, autorité, nation.* Paris, 1933.

Montreuil, Jean: *Histoire du mouvement ouvrier en France des origines à nos jours.* Paris, 1947.

Mossé, Robert: *L'Expérience Blum: un an de Front Populaire.* Paris, 1937.

Nef, La, special issue: "Le Socialisme français victime du marxisme?" June–July 1950.

Noguères, Louis: *Le Véritable Procès du maréchal Pétain.* Paris, 1955.

Noland, Aaron: *The Founding of the French Socialist Party, 1893–1905.* Cambridge, Mass., 1956.

Osgood, Samuel M.: "The Front Populaire: Views from the Right." *International Review of Social History*, IX (1964), 189–201.

Paz, Maurice: "Échec de 1936." *La Nef,* June–July 1950, pp. 100-16.

Pertinax (André Géraud): *Les Fossoyeurs: défaite militaire de la France, armistice, contre-révolution.* 2 vols. New York, 1943.

Pickersgill, J. W.: "The Front Populaire and the French Elections of 1936." *Political Science Quarterly*, March 1939, pp. 69–83.

Pickles, Dorothy M.: *The French Political Scene.* London, 1939.

———: *France Between the Republics.* London, 1946.

———: *French Politics: The First Years of the Fourth Republic.* London, 1953.

Piettre, André: *Politique du pouvoir d'achat devant les faits.* Paris, 1938.

Pivert, Marceau: "Juin 1936 et les défaillances du mouvement ouvrier." *La Revue Socialiste*, June 1956, pp. 2–33.

Pommera, Marcelle, et al.: *Grandeur et déclin de la France à l'époque contemporaine.* Paris, 1946.

Prélot, Marcel: *L'Evolution politique du socialisme français, 1789–1934.* Paris, 1939.

Priouret, Roger: *La République des partis.* Paris, 1947.

Rémond, René: *La Droite en France de 1815 à nos jours: continuité et diversité d'une tradition.* Paris, 1954.

Reuter, Paul: "La Nationalisation des usines de guerre," *Revue d'Économie Politique*, LIII (1939), 740–56.

Revue Socialiste, La, special issue: "Il y a vingt ans, le premier gouvernement à direction socialiste . . . ," No. 98, June 1956.

Ribet, Maurice: *Le Procès de Riom.* Paris, 1945. Reproduces most of the court testimony.

Rieber, Alfred J.: *Stalin and the French Communist Party, 1941–1947.* New York, 1962.

Rimbert, Pierre: "L'Avenir du parti socialiste," *La Revue Socialiste*, February 1952, pp. 123–32; March 1952, pp. 288–97.

Robert, Fernand: "Il était déjà trop tard: les travaux de la commission Jacquet sur les événements de 1933 à 1945 en France." *La Revue Socialiste*, June 1956, pp. 34–48.

Roberts, Henry: "The Diplomacy of Colonel Beck." Chapter in Craig and Gilbert (eds.): *The Diplomats*, pp. 579–614.

Rogers, Lindsay: "M. Blum and the French Senate." *Political Science Quarterly*, LII (1937), 321–39.

Bibliography

Rosmer, Alfred: *Le Mouvement ouvrier pendant la guerre*. 2 vols. Paris, 1936, 1939.

Rossi, A. (Angelo Tasca): *Physiologie du parti communiste français*. Paris, 1948.

——: *Les Communistes français pendant la drôle de guerre*. Paris, 1951.

Sauvy, Alfred: *Le Pouvoir et l'opinion: essai de physiologie politique et sociale*. Paris, 1949.

——: "Information clef de la démocratie." *Revue Française de Science Politique*, 1951, pp. 26–39.

——: Bien public et biens privés," and rejoinder to Robert Blum. *L'Express*, April 7, 28, 1960.

—— and Pierre Depoid: *Salaires et pouvoir d'achat des ouvriers et des fonctionnaires entre les deux guerres*. Paris, 1941.

Schaper, B. W.: *Albert Thomas: trente ans de réformisme social*. Assen, 1959.

Scott, William Evans: *Alliance Against Hitler: The Origins of the Franco-Soviet Pact*. Durham, N.C., 1962.

Sherwood, John: "The Tiger's Cub: The Last Years of Georges Mandel." Chapter in Joll (ed.): *The Decline of the Third Republic*, pp. 86–125.

Siegfried, André (ed.): *L'Année politique*, from 1944 on. Paris, 1945– .

Sokolova, Maria: *Les Congrès de l'internationale socialiste entre les deux guerres mondiales*. Paris, 1953.

Soulié, Michel: *La Vie politique d'Édouard Herriot*. Paris, 1962.

Soupiron, Paul: *Bazaine contre Gambetta, ou le procès de Riom*. Lyons, 1944. Reproduces much of the court testimony.

Sturmthal, Adolf: *The Tragedy of European Labor*. New York, rev. ed., 1951.

Tabouis, Geneviève: *Vingt Ans de suspense diplomatique*. Paris, 1958.

Tannenbaum, Edward R.: *The Action Française: Die-Hard Reactionaries in Twentieth-Century France*. New York, 1962.

Théry, René: *Un An d'audaces et de contradictions: juin 1936–juin 1937*. Paris, 1937.

Thomas, Hugh: *The Spanish Civil War*. London and New York, 1961.

Toynbee, Arnold J. (ed.): *Survey of International Affairs, 1936*. London, 1937.

——: *Survey of International Affairs, 1937*. Vol. II: *The International Repercussions of the War in Spain, 1936–7*. London, 1938.

Valiani, Leo: *Histoire du socialisme au XXᵉ siècle*. Paris, 1948.

Vaucher, Paul: "Social Experiments in France." *Politica*, III (1938), 97–117.

Verdier, Robert: *La Vie clandestine du parti socialiste, 1940–1944*. Paris, 1944.

Viorst, Milton: *Hostile Allies: FDR and Charles de Gaulle*. New York, 1965.

Walter, Gérard: *Histoire du parti communiste français*. Paris, 1948.

Warner, Geoffrey: "The Stavisky Affair and the Riots of February 6, 1934." *History Today*, June 1958, pp. 377–85.

Weber, Eugen: *Action Française: Royalism and Reaction in Twentieth-Century France*. Stanford, Calif., 1963.

Weill-Raynal, Étienne: "Les Obstacles économiques à l'expérience Léon Blum." *La Revue Socialiste*, June 1956, pp. 49–56.

——: "L'Expérience du gouvernement Léon Blum." *La Revue Socialiste*, March 1947, pp. 265–80.

——: "Les Classes sociales et les partis politiques en France." *La Revue Socialiste*, December 1950, pp. 545–61.

Wellers, George: *De Drancy à Auschwitz*. Paris, 1946.

Werth, Alexander: *France in Ferment*. London, 1934.

——: *The Destiny of France*. London, 1937.

Bibliography

————: *France and Munich*. London, 1939.

————: *The Last Days of Paris*, London, 1940.

————: *The Twilight of France, 1933–1940*. A condensation of earlier volumes. London, 1942.

————: *France, 1940–1955*. London, 1956.

Wheeler-Bennett, John W.: *Munich: Prologue to Tragedy*. London, 1948, 1963.

Williams, Phillip: *Politics in Post-War France*. London, 1954, 2nd ed., 1958.

Wolfe, Martin: *The French Franc Between the Wars, 1919–1939*. New York, 1951.

Wright, Gordon: *The Reshaping of French Democracy*. New York, 1948.

————: *France in Modern Times, 1760 to the present*. Chicago, 1960.

————: *Rural Revolution in France: The Peasantry in the Twentieth Century*. Stanford, Calif., 1964.

Zévaès, Alexandre: *Le Socialisme en France depuis 1904*. Paris, 1923, 1934.

————: *Histoire du socialisme et du communisme en France de 1871 à 1947*. Paris, 1947.

INDEX

Index

Index

Index